THE SHADOW OF ISANDLWANA

THE SHADOW OF ISANDLWANA

The Life and Times *of* General Lord Chelmsford *and his* Disaster in Zululand

JOHN LABAND

Foreword by
IAN KNIGHT

Greenhill Books

The Shadow of Isandlwana

First published in 2023 by
Greenhill Books,
c/o Pen & Sword Books Ltd,
George House, Unit 12 & 13,
Beevor Street, Off Pontefract Road,
Barnsley, South Yorkshire S71 1HN

www.greenhillbooks.com
contact@greenhillbooks.com

ISBN: 978–1–78438–770–9

CIP data records for this title are available from the British Library

Edited and designed by Donald Sommerville
Typeset in 11/14.2 pt Adobe Caslon Pro
Maps by Peter Wilkinson

Printed and bound by CPI Group (UK) Ltd, Croydon, CRO 4YY

FSC www.fsc.org MIX Paper | Supporting responsible forestry FSC® C013604

Contents

Abbreviations and Acronyms

AAG	Assistant Adjutant-General
ADC	aide-de-camp
AG	Adjutant-General
AMS	Assistant Military Secretary
AQMG	Assistant Quartermaster-General
BNI	Bombay Native Infantry
BPP	*British Parliamentary Papers*
CB	Companion of the Order of the Bath
CinC	Commander-in-Chief
CMG	Companion of the Order of St Michael and St George
CO	Colonial Office Confidential Print
CP	Chelmsford Papers, National Army Museum, Chelsea
DAA	Deputy Assistant Adjutant
DAAG	Deputy Assistant Adjutant-General
DAG	Deputy Adjutant-General
DAQMG	Deputy Assistant Quartermaster-General
DCL	Doctor of Civil Law
DCM	Distinguished Conduct Medal
DQMG	Deputy Quartermaster-General
DSO	Distinguished Service Order
FAMP	Frontier Armed and Mounted Police
FLH	Frontier Light Horse
FRS	Fellow of the Royal Society
GBE	Knight Grand Cross of the Order of the British Empire
GCB	Knight Grand Cross of the Order of the Bath
GCIE	Knight Grand Commander of the Order of the Indian Empire
GCMG	Knight Grand Cross of the Order of St Michael and St George
GCSI	Knight Grand Commander of the Order of the Star of India
GCVO	Knight Grand Cross of the Victorian Order

GH	Government House Natal, Papers, Pietermaritzburg Archives Repository
GOC	general officer commanding
HMS	Her Majesty's ship
HQ	headquarters
HRH	His or Her Royal Highness
KBE	Knight Commander of the Order of the British Empire
KCB	Knight Commander of the Order of the Bath
KCMG	Knight Commander of the Order of St Michael and St George
MBE	Member of the Order of the British Empire
MP	Member of Parliament
MS	Military Secretary
NCO	non-commissioned officer
NMP	Natal Mounted Police
NMV	Natal Mounted Volunteers
NNC	Natal Native Contingent
NNPC	Natal Native Pioneer Corps
OFS	Orange Free State
PC	Privy Councillor
PP	Chelmsford–Pearson correspondence, National Army Museum, Chelsea
psc	passed Staff College
QC	Queen's Counsel
QMG	Quartermaster-General
RA	Royal Artillery; Royal Archives, Windsor Castle
RBL	Rifled Breech Loader
RE	Royal Engineers
RMA	Royal Military Academy (Woolwich)
RMC	Royal Military College (Sandhurst)
RML	Rifled Muzzle Loader
RN	Royal Navy
SAR	South African Republic (Transvaal)
TS	Sir Theophilus Shepstone Papers, Pietermaritzburg Archives Repository
VC	Victoria Cross
WC	Wood Collection, Pietermaritzburg Archives Repository
WO	War Office; War Office Papers, National Archive, Kew
WP	Wood Papers, Campbell Collections of the University of KwaZulu-Natal, Durban

Maps

Genealogical Table

Plates

Colour Plates

Black and White Plates

PLATES

Foreword

LATE IN THE AFTERNOON of Wednesday 22 January 1879, Lieutenant-General Lord Chelmsford and his staff, an isolated group of horsemen casting long shadows across a sea of green grass in the southern African summer landscape, sat looking at a distinctive rocky outcrop, known as Isandlwana, a few miles away. Before dawn that same morning Chelmsford, commanding the British invasion of the independent Zulu kingdom, had set out from his camp there at the head of over a thousand men; now, after a day of exhausting marches and futile skirmishing, he was leading them back, and they were scattered across the veld behind him. As the sun sank steadily beyond the hill, it cast a shadow over the camp at its foot, obscuring, even through field glasses, the details of what was happening there, but a pall of gunsmoke hung around the mountain and here and there fires flickered in the shadows. Off to the right, dense masses of men could be seen retiring slowly over the crest of a ridge that overlooked the camp. Reports had reached Lord Chelmsford throughout the afternoon that something was happening at Isandlwana; now, it was only too clear that whatever that was had gone badly wrong for the British.

As the staff sat and waited for their men, a solitary horseman rode up to them from the direction of Isandlwana. He was Rupert Lonsdale, a Commandant in an auxiliary unit, the Natal Native Contingent, and he had returned unfit to Isandlwana earlier that afternoon. The tale he told was astonishing; not thinking clearly after a heavy fall from his horse, he had ridden almost into the camp before a sudden shot had alerted him to the fact that it was full, not of British troops, but of Zulus. As he looked around, images crowded in upon him of dead soldiers strewn through the grass, and Zulu warriors stripping them of their weapons and uniforms;

he had only just managed to turn his horse and ride back to Lord Chelmsford. The camp at Isandlwana had been over-run.

Lord Chelmsford was astonished. 'I can't understand it', one of his staff heard him say, 'I left a thousand men to guard the camp!'

In that moment lies not only the disbelief of an experienced professional soldier, beginning to grasp a shocking reality, but also the key to the fascination the Anglo-Zulu War has exerted ever since. Lord Chelmsford was a veteran of some of the greatest conflicts of the early Victorian era – he had witnessed the British attacks upon the Russian fortifications outside Sevastopol, had taken part in the brutal suppression of the 'Indian Mutiny', and played a crucial staff role in the expedition to Abyssinia – and he had only recently brought another messy war in southern Africa, against the Xhosa people on the Eastern Cape Frontier, to a successful conclusion; and yet now British troops under his command had suffered what would prove to be the bloodiest single defeat of the whole Victorian period. Over 1,300 British regulars and their African allies were killed at Isandlwana – a greater butcher's bill than would be paid for the Charge of the Light Brigade, the disaster at Maiwand in Afghanistan, or even at Spioenkop or Magersfontein in the Anglo-Boer War, and they were killed, moreover, by an African enemy still largely reliant on close-quarter traditional weapons.*

Like the men whose bones still lie there, Lord Chelmsford would never escape the field of Isandlwana, and the battle tarnished his reputation for the rest of his days, despite the fact that he had not been present when the Zulus attacked, and notwithstanding that he went on to win the Anglo-Zulu War, personally commanding, with phlegmatic bravery, in two subsequent victories. As John Laband's biography reveals in detail for the first time, Chelmsford was very much the product of his era and class, the ambitious son of a newly ennobled family on the make, who had passed through the right schools, had been dedicated to his career, but who knew well how to play the game of securing preferment through connections and patronage. Undeniably, he was no less competent than

* The British retreat from Kabul, during the 1st Anglo-Afghan War, was far more costly in lives, but was not a single battle, rather a series of attacks upon a demoralised army and their defenceless civilian camp-followers which took place over a number of days.

many of his contemporaries, and more so than some, and yet it is true that the disaster at Isandlwana was due to more than a single wrong decision made at 2 a.m. on the 22nd, in his candle-lit tent at Isandlwana, which led him to divide his force, fatally confirmed the extent to which he had been out-manoeuvred by the Zulu generals Ntshingwayo kaMahole and Mavumengwana kaNdlela, and which would leave his men exposed to a well-executed and courageous Zulu counter-attack.

John Laband's searching biography provides the context of the man who made that decision and reveals the flaws which shaped his command, none of them fatal in themselves, yet all of them deeply damaging in combination – his conservative approach to soldiering, the lack of substance behind much of his earlier experience, his failure to appreciate the capabilities of his enemies, and his tendency to micro-manage a war and carry the burden of command and organisation upon his own shoulders rather than delegate. It reveals, too, how the controversies which followed Isandlwana placed him at the centre of broader, and occasionally bitter, ideological wrangles within the British Army between conservative and progressive factions.

The shock of the defeat at Isandlwana almost paralysed Chelmsford's command, and only the support of the Victorian military establishment, and the Royal Family itself, allowed him the opportunity to regain his composure, regroup, and continue with the war. Yet, even after resigning his command in the aftermath of his final victory at Ulundi, and basking in the acclamation of his influential supporters, he was well aware of the mutterings behind his back which would dog him for the remainder of his career. Although his friend, the Commander-in-Chief The Duke of Cambridge, graced him with a succession of impressive sinecures, it escaped the attention of neither his supporters nor his detractors that he was never allowed to command an army in the field again.

But for one wrong decision Lord Chelmsford might have passed his career in the comfortable anonymity with which most Victorian generals are regarded today. Certainly few of his contemporaries in Zululand distinguished themselves either; and it might be appropriate to remember Napoleon's (probably apocryphal) remark that what he most required of his generals was 'that they be lucky'. Other Victorian generals made mistakes which were not caught out, and thereby not so costly as Lord Chelmsford's, and history remembers them more kindly; and yet, as John

Laband reveals, mistakes are not made in isolation, but are a product not only of the choices of the moment, but of the character and background of the men who made them.

Evan S. Connell, in his seminal study of George Armstrong Custer's disaster at Little Big Horn, *Son of the Morning Star*, has pointed out that Custer's image will never escape his 'last stand'; he is stuck for all eternity on that Montana hillside, frozen in the moment of his death, the moment that, for all his glittering career in life, has come to define him. Lord Chelmsford, it seems, has endured a similar fate, for even now he remains stuck on the veld near Isandlwana, on that summer evening, shocked and overwhelmed by the realisation of his defeat. This, then, is his story – of who he was, of how he got there, and how he came to make the catastrophic mistake of Isandlwana.

Ian Knight
Author of *Zulu Rising*

PREFACE

A Case of Incompetency?

J. EDWARD JENKINS, A LANKY, SPRUCE FIGURE with a pointed ginger beard and a thick ruff of hair that set off his bald, domed pate, rose on 14 March 1879 to address the House of Commons. The son of a Presbyterian minister, he had been largely raised and educated in Canada and the United States and now practised in England as a barrister. Best known as the author of several satirical novels, in the general election of 1874 that had brought Benjamin Disraeli's Conservatives to power, he had won the Dundee seat for the opposing Liberals.[1] The House was debating the government's handling of the Zulu War in South Africa, a colonial campaign that ought to have been a routine Victorian 'small war' against an unequally matched 'savage' adversary. Instead of the easy walk-over the invading British had confidently anticipated, at Isandlwana on 22 January 1879 they had suffered what Jenkins characterised as 'one of the most deplorable and disgraceful disasters that had ever happened to the British Army'. As Sir Robert Peel,[2] the son of a former prime minister and the politically free-floating but nominal Liberal MP for Tamworth who had been the public-spirited patron of the *Times* Crimean Fund for the Relief of the Sick and Wounded during the Crimean War, would remind the incredulous government benches on the third day of the debate: 'As many officers fell in that battle as fell in the great battle of Inkerman' in 1854 during the Crimean War.[3] In fact, even more officers – fifty-two of them – had died at Isandlwana than at Inkerman where forty-four had been left dead on the field.[4]

How such an almost unparalleled disaster could have befallen British arms was what the House wanted to know, and blame had to be apportioned. Jenkins, when he rose on the first day of the debate, was convinced he knew who was responsible. To repeated cries of 'Withdraw!'

and other interruptions from the government benches, Jenkins resolutely singled out two related figures. The first was Lieutenant-General Lord Chelmsford, the General Officer Commanding (GOC) in South Africa. With regard to him, Jenkins insisted in his lawyerly way that 'when any General suffers such a defeat as was suffered by General Lord Chelmsford at Isandula [*sic*], there is a *primâ facie* [*sic*] case of incompetency against him'. He followed up this accusation by insisting that 'some explanation is required from the Government to justify their continuing in command a man who seems to have exhibited a great want of discretion, if not of military misconduct and incapacity. ["Oh!"].' Pre-empting any reply, Jenkins immediately furnished his own explanation and declared over a rising barrage of indignant interjections: 'It is time someone rose in the House to point out that the Horse Guards is a centre of intrigue, where incompetence is shielded by Court influence or by favour with the Royal Person at the head of it. ["Order, order!"]'[5] The royal personage to whom Jenkins was unmistakably alluding was none other than Queen Victoria's cousin, HRH Prince George, Duke of Cambridge and Field Marshal Commanding-in-Chief, the fount of patronage and promotion in the British Army.

The interrelationship Jenkins emphatically posited between the disgraced General and the military establishment as personified by the Duke suggested the path I should take when attempting the first full life of Lord Chelmsford since Major the Hon. Gerald French's biography published in 1939 and titled *Lord Chelmsford and the Zulu War*. French had been stung into action by W. H. Clements's work of 1936 called *The Glamour and Tragedy of the Zulu War* in which the author based his criticism of Chelmsford's generalship primarily on the often ill-informed and prejudiced commentary of contemporary journalists. French, in his biography, made full use – as I do too – of Chelmsford's military correspondence (the Chelmsford Papers, housed today in the National Army Museum, Chelsea), a mass of private, semi-official and official papers the general had preserved, and which General Matthew Gossett, who had served as a major on Chelmsford's personal staff during the Zululand campaign, carefully classified and annotated. When Gossett wrote to Adria, Lady Chelmsford (the general's widow), in June 1906, fourteen months after her husband's death, reporting he had completed the task, he declared that although it had been 'a painful one,' it had served to raise his old chief in his estimation. Gossett commended Chelmsford's 'foresight, his consideration for everyone under his command & his zeal for the public service'. He could only admire 'the brave front he opposed to calumny & misrepresentation' and devoutly hoped that one day 'justice' would be done to the memory of that 'great & good man'.[6]

French, in the introduction to his biography, while admitting to the 'bitter controversy' Chelmsford's questionable conduct of the Zululand campaign had engendered, nevertheless firmly endorsed Gossett's sentiments and saw it as his mission to rehabilitate Chelmsford's reputation.[7] And certainly, many at the time of the Anglo-Zulu War perceived how they could manipulate the public censure of the general's defective performance to score political points against the government and the conservative Army establishment, and were not much interested in assessing Chelmsford's generalship dispassionately. But the problem with French's approach is not only that it is marred by what Donald Morris called its 'continual air of righteous indignation and triumphant vindication',[8] but that it was conducted as if by a counsel retained for the defence, one whose case relied on evidence that is open to reassessment, or is incomplete.

Central to French's brief as the Chelmsford Papers undoubtedly were, and as they have continued to be for me when attempting this biography, they are far from comprising the only primary sources now available to historians. Further vital correspondence is to be found, among other pertinent manuscript collections, in the papers of the Duke of Cambridge in the Royal Archives in Windsor Castle, in the papers of Sir Evelyn Wood in the Pietermaritzburg Archives Repository and in the Campbell Collections in Durban, and in the War Office Papers in The National Archive, Kew. The publication in 1984 of the Alison Collection by Sonia Clarke in *Zululand at War 1879* was of particular significance because it made available the letters (now in the Brenthurst Library, Johannesburg) solicited by Major-General Sir Archibald Alison from officers serving in the field with Chelmsford, reports that provided confidential information on the conduct of the war for the Intelligence Branch of the War Office. These semi-official, semi-private letters were of such a controversial and sensitive nature that they had been kept confidential. Crucial private diaries are also now available in printed, edited editions, notably Chris Hummel's *The Frontier War Journal of Major John Crealock 1878*, and

Adrian Preston's *The South African Journal of Sir Garnet Wolseley 1879–1880*. Much official correspondence relating to Chelmsford's campaigns in South Africa has long been in the public domain in printed form, primarily in the *British Parliamentary Papers*. These printed papers, along with various others, have been conveniently collected in the six volumes of the *Archives of Zululand: The Anglo-Zulu War 1879*, edited by Ian Knight and myself. Numerous other contemporary publications such as memoirs and histories are also ready to hand in reprinted editions; while there are a number of edited collections of soldiers' letters and newspaper reports available, with Frank Emery's pioneering *Red Soldier* of 1977 leading the way. This rich array of evidence, of which the foregoing is but a sampling of the choicest items, can be found laid out in full in the bibliography at the end of this book. Taken together, this great mass of evidence makes an informed reassessment of Chelmsford's career both possible and necessary.

It is now over eighty years since French wrote his biography of Chelmsford. Since then, very few works devoted exclusively to Chelmsford's life have been published. In 1994 I wrote a detailed introduction to a selection of documents I edited for the Army Records Society entitled *Lord Chelmsford's Zululand Campaign*. I followed this with an entry on Chelmsford in the *Oxford Dictionary of National Biography*, first published in 2004, and then in 2009 with an extensive chapter discussing his career in a collection of biographical essays edited by Steven Corvi and Ian Beckett and called *Victoria's Generals*. In 2022 Steven Manning brought out *Britain against the Xhosa and Zulu Peoples: Lord Chelmsford's South African Campaigns* that appeared while I was completing the first draft of this work. Despite its somewhat misleading title, Manning's book is very much a biography of Lord Chelmsford. A secure, accessible and relatively concise account, it nevertheless lacks the depth and insight that come with a more comprehensive reliance on the archival and other primary sources. And, to be fair, Manning specifically makes no claim to have written a ground-breaking new biography of Chelmsford.[9] To date, the best and most comprehensive study of Chelmsford's generalship in South Africa – it only touches lightly on other phases of his career – is Jeffrey Mathews's excellent doctoral dissertation of 1986, 'Lord Chelmsford: British General in Southern Africa', that makes full use of all the available sources. It has remained unpublished, so that it has shared the fate of many another dissertation and has languished unknown and unread except by a very few, of which number I am fortunately one.

What claim, then, can I make for my life of Chelmsford? I believe it can offer a fresh way of approaching Chelmsford's career by attempting two things. It can make use of the extensive evidence referred to above to situate him squarely in his specific context as an aristocratic officer of the Victorian age enmeshed in the pervasive system of patronage, and manipulated by the politics of command; and it can assess him as a commander in the field in terms of the prevailing military doctrine of the day. And in doing so, it can make extensive use of the primary sources to permit Chelmsford and the other *dramatis personae* to speak for themselves.

In the course of this enquiry I shall be endeavouring to explain why a general who had previously enjoyed what was conventionally recognised in the Victorian age as a successful military career should ultimately have been found so wanting in his conduct of the Zululand campaign. For, make no mistake, Chelmsford's record of service up to the Anglo-Zulu War was one that his partisans in the House of Commons had no difficulty in defending. On the third day of the Zulu War debate, Colonel the Hon. Frederick A. Stanley, the Secretary of State for War (he would succeed his elder brother as the sixteenth Earl of Derby in 1893 and would cap his political career as a highly successful Governor General of Canada) summed up what other MPs of similar military background – he had been commissioned, as had Chelmsford, in the Grenadier Guards – had been declaring over the previous days:

> I can refer to Lord Chelmsford's brilliant services in the Crimea, in India, in Abyssinia, in almost every part of the world where of late years active service was to be found . . . In all those duties which he has discharged he has earned the love, respect and esteem of those with whom he has been brought into contact . . . The representations of officers who have been his superiors have invariably been in his favour . . . If an officer were to be selected for the command in South Africa, Lord Chelmsford would still be the man to select.[10]

Of course, Stanley was defending his administration's military appointee, but he brought up a vital point in referring to Chelmsford's previous career. Chelmsford is only ever remembered or discussed in terms of the Anglo-Zulu War, and scarce a thought is given to considering the point he had reached in 1879 as a 51-year-old general officer who had served for thirty-five years in the British Army, an institution that, during that same period, had undergone significant changes in organisation, armaments, uniforms and tactics. The entire range of Chelmsford's military career and his varied experiences serving in various capacities in diverse parts of the world need to be taken into account to explain the mainsprings of his actions as GOC, South Africa. And these in turn have to be understood in the context of the existing situation in South Africa and the challenges it posed to any general undertaking a military campaign there.

Ultimately, it must be asked how well Chelmsford performed as a commander within the constraints of the military system in which he was embedded, and how successfully he adjusted its military doctrine to the specific conditions of the area of operations in which he found himself. For, when discussing the career of any general officer on campaign in Queen Victoria's empire, note should be taken of Philip Haythornthwaite's conclusion that it is generally less useful to blame the prevailing military system for any defeats that occurred than to censure those who interpreted it, for most disasters were the result of failure in command. The central principle of tactics in colonial campaigns was the necessity to adapt to the nature of the terrain and to the fighting methods of the enemy, and to accept that the prescribed, conventional system of warfare was not necessarily appropriate to the circumstances.[11]

The scale of the Isandlwana disaster indicates that this precept was not always followed in the Anglo-Zulu War, and it is inevitable that this notorious battle has formed the pivot for all contemporary and subsequent discussions concerning Chelmsford's questionable generalship. Nothing else he did, not even his subsequent victory at Ulundi that effectively ended the war, could wipe away that stain. Indeed, had it not been for Isandlwana, and if the Zulu campaign had played out in the same predictable fashion as did most colonial campaigns, Chelmsford would hardly be remembered today.[12] As it is, his name and that of Isandlwana are fatally intertwined, and it would be quixotic if I were to follow Gerald French in attempting to rehabilitate his irretrievably bruised reputation. Neither Mathews nor Manning set out to do so, and nor shall I. Rather, my task is to assess Chelmsford's degree of culpability for the many British failures in the Zulu campaign through an exploration of his limitations as a conservative professional general officer of the Victorian era. This investigation will be held in conjunction with a consideration of any personality traits and flaws that may have played their deleterious part in determining his decisions and actions. Whether such a reappraisal will serve to excuse, censure or even exonerate Chelmsford as a commander is not the real point. The objective is to understand why he acted as he did.

PART I

A Burgeoning Military Career, 1844–1877

CHAPTER 1

The Thesigers: A Family on the Rise

FREDERIC AUGUSTUS THESIGER WAS BORN on 31 May 1827, the third child and eldest son of Frederick Thesiger (1794–1878) and Anna Maria Tinling (1799–1875).[1] On 5 October 1878 he would succeed his father as the second Baron Chelmsford and was thereafter know by that title, rather than by his surname. (Father and son shared the same first name: Frederic(k). The father seems to have been uncertain which spelling he preferred, so to prevent confusion, he will be referred to as 'Frederick' and his son as 'Frederic'.) Frederic's parents had been married in 1822 and produced a typically Victorian, numerous brood of offspring. Their first-born, a daughter named Sidney Louisa, died at birth in 1823. Frederic had an older, surviving sister, Augusta (1824–1912), and seven younger siblings: Sidney Maria who lived and died in 1831; Charles Wemyss (1831–1903), Julia Selina (1833–1904), George Cochrane (1837–53), Alfred Henry (1838–80), Mary Lincoln (1840–1914), and Edward Peirson (1842–1928). (*See* Thesiger Family Tree, *overleaf.*)

Frederic grew up with his seven surviving siblings in a very comfortable, upper-class environment. But his family were not of the old established aristocracy, or even of the landed gentry. Rather, the Thesigers were a middle-class family determinedly ascending the social ladder, and at the time of Frederic's birth his father was a rising barrister, a member of the so-called higher professions that included the church, law and medicine. Frederic's great-grandfather, John-Andrew Thesiger (1722–83), was by repute a gentleman of Dresden, the capital of what was then the small kingdom of Saxony, a region of eastern Germany where the surname 'Thesiger' certainly originates. John-Andrew Thesiger settled in England in the mid-eighteenth century. Although of modest means, he was evidently an educated, competent and discreet person, attributes that led to his being

Thesiger Family Tree

John-Andrew Thesiger (1722–1783) *m.* Miss Gibson (d. 1814)

- Charles Thesiger (d. 1831) *m.* Mary-Anne Williams (d. 1796)
  - Sir Frederick, 1st Baron Chelmsford, PC, KB, DCL, FRS (1794–1878) *m.* Anna Maria Tinling (1799–1875)
    - Sidney Louisa (1823)
    - Hon. Augusta (1824–1912) *m.* William Higgins (d. 1891)
    - Gen. Sir Frederic Augustus, 2nd Baron Chelmsford (1827–1905) *m.* Adria Fanny Heath (1845–1926)
    - Sidney Maria (1831)
    - Lt.-Gen. Hon. Charles Wemyss (1831–1903) *m.* Charlotte Handcock (d. 1880)
    - Hon. Julia Selina (1833–1904) *m.* Maj.-Gen. Sir John Inglis, KCB (1814–62)
    - George Cochrane (1837–53)
    - Rt. Hon. Alfred Henry, QC (1838–80) *m.* Henrietta Handcock (d. 1921)
    - Hon. Mary Lincoln (1840–1914)
    - Hon. Sir Edward Peirson, KCB (1842–1928) *m.* Georgina Stopford-Sackville (d. 1906)
- Capt. Sir Frederick Thesiger, RN (d. 1805)

— *issue*

- Sir Frederic John Napier, PC, GCSI, GCMG, GCIE, GBE, 1st Viscount Chelmsford (1868–1933)
  m. Hon. Frances Guest (1869–1957)
  — Andrew Charles, 2nd Viscount Chelmsford (1903–70) — Frederic Jan, 3rd Viscount Chelmsford (1931–99) — Frederic Corin Piers, 4th Viscount Chelmsford (b. 1962) — Hon. Frederic (b. 2006)

- Capt. Hon. Percy Mansfield, MBE (1869–1959)
  m. Katharine Wallace (d. 1958)
  — *issue*

- Capt. Hon. Wilfred Gilbert, DSO (1871–1920)
  m. Kathleen Vigors (1880–1973)
  — Sir Wilfred Patrick, KBE (1910–2003)

- Hon. Harold Lumsden (1872)

- Lt.-Col. Hon. Sir Eric Richard, DSO (1874 –1961)
  m. Pearl Coupland (d. 1923)
  — *issue*

- Hon. Alfred Sullivan (1880–1889)

— *issue*

— *issue*

— *issue*

employed as amanuensis, or secretary, to the influential Whig statesman the second Marquess of Rockingham, who was briefly prime minister in 1765–6 and again in 1782. The eighteenth century was still very much an age when a successful career depended on patronage. Charles Thesiger (d. 1831), John-Andrew Thesiger's son and Frederic's grandfather, made effective use of the influential connections forged by his father to secure the lucrative post of Comptroller and Collector of Customs in the Island of St Vincent in the West Indies, a British possession since 1783. With the proceeds of office, he purchased a sugar estate, Esperanza, on the island of Trinidad, and another, Duvalle's, on St Vincent itself, thus joining the plantocracy whose estates were worked by slaves. It is not recorded how many slaves were on Duvalle's, but there were 109 on Esperanza.[2]

Frederick Thesiger, born on 15 July 1794, was Charles's third and youngest son. His mother, Mary-Anne Williams of London, died when he was only two years old. Frederick was early destined for a career in the Royal Navy, following in the footsteps of his father's elder brother, Frederick, after whom he was likely named.[3] His uncle was certainly an heroic figure to emulate. After serving with distinction with the Royal Navy in the West Indies, he had obtained permission in 1789 to enter the Russian naval service in the war between Russia and Sweden. Once again, he gave brave service of the highest order, and was decorated by the Empress Catherine the Great herself with the Order of St George, Russia's highest military honour. After the Empress's death in 1796 he re-joined the Royal Navy and served with his hallmark gallantry in the Napoleonic Wars as a volunteer expert on Baltic affairs with Vice-Admiral Lord Nelson at the first battle of Copenhagen in 1801. In recognition of his service, he was promoted post captain and received a knighthood. Sir Frederick died in 1805, two years before his thirteen-year-old nephew Frederick joined the frigate *Cambrian* as a midshipman. Frederick was on board when the *Cambrian* participated in the Royal Navy's bombardment of Copenhagen between 16 August and 5 September 1807 that destroyed Denmark as a naval power.

Frederick was not destined to make the Navy his career, however. On the death of his last surviving elder brother, he became the sole heir to his father Charles's West Indian estates on Trinidad and St Vincent. To prepare him for his inheritance, he was taken out of the Navy and sent back to school for a couple of years, and in 1811 he joined his father on

St Vincent. There he had little time to enjoy his patrimony. St Vincent is one of the Lesser Antilles, a chain of volcanic islands. On 30 April 1812 La Soufrière, the high, conical stratovolcano on the northern side of the island that had last been active in 1718, erupted again with a major explosion that comprehensively devastated the Duvalle's estate.[4]

It seems that at this time Charles decided to leave the surviving Esperanza estate on Trinidad to be divided among his three daughters. The government partially recompensed Charles for the loss of Duvalle's. Presumably, most of the stock, comprising the enslaved people as well as the steers and mules, would have been saved and subsequently sold, but the land itself was gone, along with buildings such as the factory, stables, workshops, slave quarters and overseer's house. The sum the government paid was £3,750 just less than half of the £7,800 Charles estimated he had lost. (To gain a sense of the current worth of pounds mentioned in this book, the simplest rule of thumb is to multiply them by one hundred.)[5] This sum – or what was left of it – would eventually be Frederick's on Charles's death in 1831. Meanwhile, with no future income from the obliterated estate on St Vincent's, the Thesiger family finances were straitened. Frederick had no choice but to abandon any expectations of an easy life as a West Indian planter and knuckle down to earning a living.

Frederick had been raised as a gentleman, and now that his inheritance was largely lost, that meant only a limited choice of occupations was open to him if he intended to maintain his caste. He had already thrown over his career in the Navy, and the established church required preferment. That left only the law, a profession that carried the requisite social prestige and had the advantage, if pursued successfully, of being very remunerative. And, as it turned out, Frederick possessed the cerebral focus (although he never pretended to be an intellectual with a deep knowledge of the law), along with the unremitting industry and peculiarly legal cast of mind, necessary to prosper prodigiously. He entered Gray's Inn in 1813 and in 1818 was called to the bar, joining the home circuit. His many successes in civil and criminal cases brought him to public attention as a painstaking and exceptionally effective cross-examiner, even if he lacked consummate oratorical skills, and he rapidly built up a large practice. In 1834 he took silk as King's Counsel. His distinguished legal career secured his entry into politics, and in 1840 he was returned to parliament as a Conservative MP, representing three different constituencies over the following eighteen years. By temperament and conviction, he was a die-hard Tory. As a bigoted Protestant, he deplored *Universalis Ecclesiae,* the papal bull of 29 September 1850 by which Pius IX re-created the Roman Catholic diocesan hierarchy in England and Wales that had been abolished in the reign of Queen Elizabeth I; and he determinedly spoke out against the passing of the Jews Relief Act of 1858 that removed the barriers which had prevented Jews from entering Parliament.

During the course of the Tory Sir Robert Peel's second administration, Frederick Thesiger was appointed Solicitor-General in April 1844 and knighted. In June 1845 Sir Frederick (as he now was) next became Attorney General, but retired on the fall of Peel's administration in July 1846. He became Attorney General again between February and December 1852 in the fifteenth Earl of Derby's first short-lived Tory administration. When Lord Derby formed his second administration between February 1858 and June 1859, Thesiger was appointed Lord High Chancellor of Great Britain and a Privy Councillor. His office required that he take a seat in the House of Lords, and on 1 March 1858 he was created Baron Chelmsford in the County of Essex in the Peerage of the United Kingdom.[6] He chose Chelmsford as his title, not because of any territorial connection with that circuit town in Essex, but as a gesture of commemoration. It was at the Chelmsford assizes that, in 1832, he had won the hard-fought civil action of ejectment to recover possession of disputed land that had established his legal reputation. Lord Chelmsford (as he now was) served again as Lord Chancellor in Derby's final administration formed in June 1866.

Derby resigned in February 1868, and his successor Benjamin Disraeli left Chelmsford out of his first Cabinet because he thought him an incompetent Lord Chancellor and wished to replace him with Lord Cairns. Chelmsford went with considerable ill-grace, afterwards complaining that he had not been given so much notice as a housemaid. When it came to surrendering the Great Seal to Queen Victoria, he literally clung to it. Only the sternest possible rebuke, recorded the Queen, followed by 'a very undignified tug-of-war, enabled Her Majesty to wrench the Seal from his grasp. It was really most disagreeable.'[7] Chelmsford never held political office again, for Disraeli, who was of Jewish descent, did not look kindly on the anti-Semitic and intransigently-minded Chelmsford or the 'bad taste' of his going in 1868, and did not appoint him to his second Cabinet in 1874 when Lord Cairns served once again as Lord Chancellor.

Although aggrieved, Chelmsford did not repine, continuing to be active in judicial work in the House of Lords and the Privy Council.

The first Baron Chelmsford outlived his wife by three years and died on 5 October 1878 at 7 Eaton Square, London, his plain yellow-brick house in a terrace on the south-eastern corner of the square with two elegant Ionic pillars supporting the white stucco entrance porch. Such a house, although not quite as fashionable as one in nearby Belgrave Square, nevertheless proclaimed that he was well-to-do and fully assimilated socially into the ruling establishment. His wealth at death was close to £60,000. This, while certainly a respectable fortune for a patrician professional, was not on anything like a truly aristocratic scale. Nor, unlike many a Lord Chancellor before him, had Chelmsford acquired a landed estate and a family seat to underpin his new standing as a peer. The Chelmsfords would remain that relative social anomaly peers without land until the cataclysm of the Second World War and its aftermath upended the old order.[8]

During his lifetime, Frederick's earnings were sufficient to ensure that his sons were expensively educated, and to settle the customary marriage portion on his daughter Augusta when in 1843 she wed William Higgins, Master of the Court of Bankruptcy, and likewise on Julia in 1851 when she married a soldier called John Inglis, a son of the Bishop of Nova Scotia. But his fortune was not so large that his surviving sons (George died aged only sixteen) were not obliged to pursue careers of their own within the circumscribed, socially acceptable parameters of their class, and in the short term this required a considerable further outlay of money to set them up in their chosen professions. Shepherded by his formidable father, Alfred followed him successfully into the law and his Tory political persuasion and, before his premature death aged forty-two, took silk in 1873 as a QC and in 1877 was appointed Lord Justice of Appeal and Privy Counsellor during Disraeli's second Conservative administration.[9] (Disraeli had been raised to the peerage in 1876 as the first Earl of Beaconsfield, and shall henceforth be referred to by that title.) Edward pursued a career in the civil service that culminated in his becoming Clerk-Assistant to Parliament from 1890 to 1917, and was made Knight Commander of the Bath (KCB). Their two elder brothers, Frederic and Charles, both joined the Army, Frederic serving in the infantry, and Charles in the cavalry. They did not enter the Navy despite their father's brief service as a midshipman and their great-uncle Captain Sir Frederick Thesiger, RN's stellar career. Likely, their socially ambitious father decided that while the Royal Navy offered a good, life-long career, the Army was more highly regarded in society. He would have calculated that a commission, especially in one of the more prestigious regiments, would confer social recognition and status on the sons of a prominent lawyer and MP who was still a newcomer to the ruling class and had yet to be raised to the peerage.[10]

Frederic's military career is the subject of this book, but it should be noted that his younger brother Charles did extremely well in the Army in his own right. At the time of his father's death in 1878, he was a lieutenant-colonel in command of the 6th (Inniskilling) Dragoons and Inspector of Yeomanry Cavalry. He was promoted major-general in 1885 and made Inspector General of Cavalry in Ireland. Promoted lieutenant-general in 1890, he was also Colonel of the 14th (King's) Hussars at the time of his death in 1903, the colonelcy of a regiment being an honour awarded to distinguished generals. The two brothers' father would have had every reason to be proud of their exemplary progress in the military. For their part, they held their formidable father, with his long sharp nose and searching gaze, in awed respect, and would have been very conscious of the ever-higher positions he held in the counsels of the land. It must have been one poor but real consolation for Frederic that his father did not live quite long enough to witness his heir's very public disgrace over the battle of Isandlwana and the ignominious end to his active military career.

CHAPTER 2

The Making of an Officer

THAT THE MILITARY CAREER HE HAD SET his heart on would end so ignominiously was naturally undreamed of by the young Frederic Thesiger when he left Eton College where, between 1840 and 1844, he had been exclusively and expensively educated among the sons of the elite. There he would have become accustomed to a shared and unquestioned upper-class outlook. His years at Eton would also have instilled attitudes desirable in an aspirant officer because the public school system was designed to meet the requirement of an imperial ruling caste. That entailed inculcating the ideals of a gentleman where perfect manners, signifying moral virtue, and a classical education, implying a well-tuned mind, were held to be better qualifications for leadership than any amount of expert practical training. With these gentlemanly qualities went physical aptitude, a love of healthy sports and exercises. School team sports were intended as the model for manliness and military discipline that taught boys to subordinate themselves to the needs of the group and to the code of fair play. In fine, at Eton Thesiger had received the sort of education that translated into the military qualities of leadership, courage and self-discipline.[1]

Ideally, the profession of officer requires men who have mastered the requisite technical skills in warfare and who possess the ability to inspire the soldiers under their command 'to perform deeds beyond their expectations, to endure hardship, toil and monotony, to subordinate their own interests to those of the team, to face and overcome fear and be committed to the death'.[2] In reality, in the early nineteenth century British officers were still divided from their men, as they always had been in the past, by class cleavages, indifference and even contempt, and kept them under control through draconian discipline and fear of punishment. During the course of Thesiger's service in the Army, however, officers' perception of their role and their responsibilities towards their men progressively widened and deepened until they came to regard themselves as members of a profession with its own special vocation of service. Even so, this growing professionalism blended with an enduring tradition of gentlemanly amateurism with its associated code of honourable conduct. Indeed, the essential quality expected of a mid-nineteenth-century officer (an expectation that persisted well into the next century) was that, above all, he must comport himself like a gentleman. Inherent in that expectation was the assumption that a gentleman's innate qualities of character, good breeding, self-confidence and physical prowess would always trump book-learning and the mechanics of military training as the necessary qualifications for an officer. Indeed, an officer's attempt to improve his professional knowledge through study might well be perceived by his peers as somewhat deviant, ungentlemanly behaviour. Above all, an officer's military service was legitimised and elevated though his holding the Queen's commission and through his personal oath of allegiance to his sovereign.[3]

When Thesiger joined the officer corps, he shared a common educational and cultural background with his fellows. All were further bonded together in their collective values and attitudes by regimental camaraderie and by shared leisure pursuits, primarily the field sports of hunting, shooting and fishing associated with the landed gentry and aristocracy. Officers zealously pursued these diversions while on leave and also as a means of relieving the monotony of garrison duty and campaigning.[4] An interest in the turf was another connection, as was membership of the London gentlemen's clubs where they could socialise and network, the military ones being the Guards Club (founded in 1810), the United Service Club (1819) known as 'The Senior' because membership was restricted to senior officers, the Army and Navy Club (1837) called 'the Rag', and the Naval and Military Club (1862) which was referred to as the 'In and Out'.[5] Inevitably, such an environment of gentlemanly exclusiveness confirmed and fostered a conservative outlook among officers and committed them to preserving the existing class structure and the Army's function in upholding it.[6]

The nineteenth-century officer corps gave the impression of being predominantly aristocratic, even if that was actually not quite so. In 1883 there were 137 peers serving in the British Army and 417 officers from the so-called 'greater gentry' with estates of between 3,000 and 10,000 acres yielding a prodigious annual income in excess of £3,000.[7] But when the social composition of the officer corps as a whole is considered – and it remained essentially constant during the entire Victorian period – we see that roughly only 13 per cent of colonels were from the peerage and baronetage while 26 per cent came from the landed gentry (if ownership of 2,000 acres is taken as the minimum requirement for that status). A further 23 per cent came of families with a long tradition of military service and were the sons of military and naval officers. Most of the remaining 38 per cent of officers (like the two Thesiger brothers) were drawn from families in the higher professions of the church, law and medicine who saw a commission as a path for upward social mobility. Many of these families had ties with the aristocracy and gentry through distant descent, or were forging them through marriage alliances. Exalted social connections did not necessarily ensure wealth, however. Even if in the mid-1870s close to 40 per cent of the officer class as a whole was directly of the aristocracy and gentry, many were younger sons who would not inherit estates. Without great expectations, such officers were materially no different from officers lower down the social scale who could expect little more than an allowance from their family to augment their pay, and had to make a living from their military profession.[8]

When Frederic Thesiger was gazetted as second lieutenant (or cornet) to the Rifle Brigade on 31 December 1844, it was by a very different process from that today. Certainly, it was possible then to be promoted from the ranks in recognition of ability and good service. In the 1830s nearly 30 per cent of all commissions were by that route, but thereafter this opportunity steadily closed so that by the end of the nineteenth century only 2 per cent of officers came up that avenue. In any case, most of those promoted from the ranks never rose beyond captain and suffered from the social prejudice, not only of their fellow officers, but of the rank-and-file who preferred to be led by 'gentlemen'.[9]

There was provision for the training of cadets to take up commissions once they had graduated. The Royal Military Academy had been founded in 1741 to train cadets as officers for the Royal Artillery and Royal Engineers. The RMA moved in 1806 to a large complex of buildings at Woolwich where the educational focus was on mathematics, mapping, fortification, gunnery, engineering, land-surveying and the like, and its cadets emerged with the practical, technological and professional skills they could receive from no other institution of higher learning at that time. The training of Royal Engineers was carried forward at the Royal School of Military Engineering established at Chatham in 1812, and by 1857 the Royal Engineers had their headquarters there, leaving Woolwich to the Royal Artillery. Successful cadets at these institutions went on to receive their commissions in the Royal Artillery and Royal Engineers.

While these technical arms of the service required officers proficient in skills based on mathematics and science, it was not the same for those in the infantry and cavalry for whom the Royal Military College, Sandhurst, had been established in 1801. Entrance was by interview and examination in mathematics, history, geography, drawing and Latin. The standard was not very demanding and applicants passed almost as a matter of course. After the Crimean War (1853–6) the majority of future line infantry officers and many cavalry officers would pass through Sandhurst, but it was only in the late 1870s that the decision was taken that all future officers – except those in the Royal Artillery and Royal Engineers at Woolwich and Chatham – should attend Sandhurst as cadets.

When Frederic Thesiger was first commissioned, it was not necessary for cavalry or infantry officers to have passed through Sandhurst, although to have done so carried one important benefit. Until 1859, when the system was abolished, a fortunate handful of applicants were nominated for Direct Commission into the army, and priority was given to those who had attended Sandhurst. The great draw of a Direct Commission was that it was not obtained by purchase, any more than was a commission in the Royal Artillery or Royal Engineers. But for a young man like Frederic Thesiger who wished to join the cavalry or infantry, a commission could only be had through the purchase system, which required of the purchaser no professional military training or knowledge.[10] In the thirty years prior to the abolition of purchase on 1 November 1871, two-thirds of commissions in the infantry of the line were purchased, and five-sixths of those in the Guards and cavalry. Nor was a purchased commission to be had at will. A first commission could only be taken up when a vacancy occurred, and permission to purchase one was not easy to come by. Much depended on the right social connections and on patronage.

In Frederic Thesiger's case, his father early placed his name on the list of candidates for the highly prestigious Grenadier Guards. On the strength of his position as a prominent QC and a Tory MP, he then followed up by approaching the influential Baron Lyndhurst, the Lord Chancellor in Sir Robert Peel's second administration, to lobby the Duke of Wellington (likewise a member of Peel's cabinet and Leader in the Lords) on behalf of his son.[11] Wellington, as the Commander-in-Chief of the Army from 1842 until his death in 1852, was the fount of all military patronage.[12] He was, moreover, since 1827 the Colonel of the Grenadier Guards, and in the Brigade of Guards first commissions were in the gift of the regimental colonels.[13] Wellington was not to be chivvied, however. In his characteristically courteous, laconic and unbending way he replied to Lyndhurst on 22 July 1843 concerning young Thesiger that 'there have been very few vacancies lately and there are still more names I am sorry to say before his'.[14] Even so, once appealed to, Wellington was reluctant to leave his Tory colleague empty-handed. Since 1820 he had been Colonel-in-Chief of the Rifle Brigade that, along with the King's Royal Rifle Corps, ranked socially only just behind the Household Cavalry and Guards regiments. He therefore used his influence to smooth the way for Frederic Thesiger to secure the consolation prize of a commission in the Rifle Brigade in December 1844.[15] Sir Frederick (who was by then Solicitor-General) still aimed higher for his son, but for the moment had to be content.

In purchasing a commission for his son in the Rifle Brigade, Sir Frederick was making a heavy financial commitment. The cost of a commission, as established by Royal Warrant in 1821, was very high.[16] A cornetcy in a line regiment of foot cost £450, one in the cavalry £840 and one in the Foot Guards even more at £1,200. Nor did the expense of a commission end there. Within a regiment, each step up in rank to lieutenant-colonel was purchased when the opportunity arose to fill a vacancy at the relevant rank. These steps were subject to qualifying periods: nine years for a lieutenant to reach the rank of captain; another ten years for a captain to reach the rank of major, and four and a half more years for a major to reach the rank of lieutenant-colonel. Regimental seniority was all but sacrosanct. An officer could not purchase a step ahead of another officer of the same rank who was his senior in years of service if the senior was willing, and able to afford, to purchase that step himself. The cost of each new step was partially defrayed by selling the one vacated to the purchaser next in line. But as each step was increasingly expensive, the difference in price meant that for an officer to rise from cornet to lieutenant-colonel would ultimately cost him in total, over and above his initial purchase price of a commission, an additional £4,050 in the infantry, £5,335 in the cavalry, and £7,800 in the Foot Guards. The cost of purchase meant that some officers could not afford the price of the next step and languished at their current rank. Often, too, there were no vacancies in the regiment at higher levels, so many officers advanced into middle age trapped in the junior ranks. Active service was welcomed, not only because it broke the monotony of peace-time soldiering and presented opportunities to perform distinguished service that brought an ambitious officer to his superiors' notice, but because casualties from disease and combat created vacancies in the regiment and broke up the logjam in promotions.

Prior to the abolition of purchase in 1871, officers could sell out (when they would hope to secure an inflated price from the eager buyer), retire on half-pay at their current rank after twenty-five years' service, or retire on full pay after thirty years' service. The capital value of a commission was forfeit to the state upon the death of a serving officer, thus introducing an element of unwelcome financial jeopardy into the system. It was also forfeit on an officer's promotion to general rank, so that the prestige was accompanied by negative financial consequences.[17] Later in his career, in 1881, Chelmsford would bemoan the large sum he had invested in purchase,[18] but it had been essential for advancement in his military career up to the rank of lieutenant-colonel.

These steep financial demands meant that only the comfortably well-to-do could afford to purchase a commission and become locked into buying further expensive steps of rank, always knowing that the capital they had invested might ultimately be forfeit. It is not surprising, therefore, that the rich landed classes were up to the game. But so too were the wealthy professional and commercial classes (such as the Thesigers) who looked on a commission as a social, rather than financial investment. There was a limit, though, to how many commissions a family could afford to purchase. Frederick Thesiger stumped up for his eldest son and heir, but not for his younger brother Charles. Purchase did not apply in the East India Company's armies where 80 per cent of the officers were middle class (a far higher proportion than in the British Army). True, promotion was normally glacially slow, but the frequent campaigns in India offered an enterprising young officer many an opportunity to shine. When

Charles was seventeen, his father exercised his influence to secure him a cadetship in the East India Company's service, and a year later, in 1849, he was commissioned as a cornet in the 5th Madras Light Cavalry. In 1853 Charles succeeded in transferring into the 14th (The King's) Regiment of Light Dragoons that had been posted to India in 1841 and was in need of promising young officers on the spot to fill vacancies that had arisen.[19] Henceforth, Charles's successful career would be with the regular British cavalry which he had succeeded in joining through the side door, as it were, after only four years with the less prestigious Company's cavalry.[20]

Once commissioned in the Army and committed to their career there, regular officers (unless they were totally lacking in ambition) were like self-serving men in every other profession seeking career advancement and the material rewards of success at the expense of their equally competitive fellows. They strove to improve their competence in the profession of arms, to impress their superiors with their martial skills and leadership abilities, and lobbied to secure patrons who would help advance their careers and secure them the honours, decorations and promotions they craved. The glamorous pageantry of military life and the affable camaraderie of the mess were consequently always shot through with unpleasant strands of competitiveness, jealously, soured disappointment and barely disguised self-satisfaction.[21]

CHAPTER 3

With the Rifle Brigade in Halifax, Nova Scotia, 1845

IMMEDIATELY AFTER BEING COMMISSIONED by purchase as second lieutenant in the Rifle Brigade with seniority from 31 December 1844, Frederic Thesiger sailed across the Atlantic in stormy winter weather to the British colony of Nova Scotia where the 2nd Battalion had been in garrison since 1842, guarding the headquarters of the Royal Navy's strategic North American Station.[1] Britain had emerged in 1815 from the Napoleonic Wars not only supreme at sea, but also as the world's greatest imperial power with forty-three colonies overseas. Although the Royal Navy was the prime, essential arm in defending this empire, its more than two dozen naval bases and dockyards scattered across the world had to be guarded by ground troops against possible attack. Numerous unstable frontier regions as in India, and porous and expanding frontiers of white settlement as in southern Africa and New Zealand, also had to be protected. For the rest of the nineteenth century, colonial defence of this sort constituted the major commitment of the British Army, which, in the ninety-nine years between its final victory over Napoleon at Waterloo and the outbreak of the First World War, waged only one major conventional campaign in Europe, in 1854–6 during the Crimean War. Throughout this period, colonial defence was chronically constrained by the taxpayers' reluctance to pay for large naval and military establishments when there was no military threat to the United Kingdom itself, and by a financially responsible Parliament's persistent insistence on economy and retrenchment. Consequently, to meet Britain's myriad imperial naval and military commitments abroad, the government scaled back on the defence of the British Isles themselves. In 1846, when Thesiger had only just embarked on his military career, of the 112 battalions that made up the Army's infantry, twenty-three were stationed in India, fifty-four elsewhere in the Empire, and only thirty-five at home.[2]

Throughout the Victorian period the standard infantry tactical unit was the battalion. The service element was employed in active campaigning while the depot element remained at home to raise the recruits who were sent out in drafts to top up service companies. When Thesiger joined the Rifle Brigade in 1844, the typical battalion consisted of six service companies and four depot companies. Each service battalion consisted of a headquarters with a lieutenant-colonel and a major, and six companies each under the command of a captain. There were eight lieutenants, four ensigns/cornets (increasingly known as second lieutenants), a surgeon and his assistant, four staff sergeants, thirty-six colour sergeants and sergeants, twenty-four corporals, twelve drummers and 546 privates. This gave an establishment of ninety-one privates per company. One corporal and ten privates were designated pioneers, and one sergeant and twenty privates were trained as bandsmen, whose duties in battle included stretcher-bearing. The depot companies were significantly smaller than their service counterparts. It should be noted that battalions were rarely up to strength on active service since disease and desertion thinned their ranks even before any combat casualties were incurred. Moreover, when battalions were committed to battle, they were often short of a number of their companies that had been detached for duties such as guarding the lines of communication and manning depots.[3]

Over-stretched and scattered across the globe, and often under-strength, garrisons such as the one in Halifax were a form of imperial bluff that masked real vulnerability, not least because in an emergency it took time to reinforce them over the great stretches of ocean. The burden of supplying soldiers for imperial garrisons fell largely on the infantry regiments of the line. The elite Guards regiments that had been established as the monarch's personal bodyguard were always based at home, and were only sent overseas as part of a specific expeditionary force, such as to the Crimea. Regular cavalry occasionally saw overseas service, but the belief was that, on the whole, locally raised or volunteer colonial troops, mounted on horses better acclimatised to local conditions than cavalry chargers, performed more successfully. Small detachments of Royal Engineers with their specialist skills were posted all around the Empire. Batteries of Royal Artillery served with garrisons everywhere except India. There the East India Company had its own locally recruited military establishment, the Presidency Armies of Bengal, Madras and Bombay, each with its own infantry, cavalry and artillery units.

Before the Enlistment Act of 1870, military service was long, normally for twenty-one years in the infantry and twenty-four in the cavalry. Any man enlisting could expect to spend much of his period of service overseas because regiments were stationed abroad for protracted periods of ten to twelve years, or nearly twenty if sent to India where they served alongside the Company's armies.[4]

British imperial garrisons across the globe served a variety of purposes. They might be the garrisons in Australia that had little strategic purpose but acted as jailers for settlements of transported convicts. There were garrisons strung in little forts along volatile open frontiers such as in New Zealand, the Eastern Cape and Natal, where the objective was to keep the peace between indigenous societies and white settlers and to protect colonists from attack. And then there were the major military stations such as those at Gibraltar, Halifax, Malta and Cape Town that safeguarded the strategic stations of the Royal Navy upon whose control of the seas the security of the Empire depended.

Halifax, where Thesiger landed in early 1845, was the capital of the British colony of Nova Scotia acquired from France by the treaty of Utrecht in 1713. Halifax itself was founded in 1749 and provided a secure base for the British between 1754 and 1763 in their ultimately successful struggle with the French for control of North America.[5] Four citadels in turn were built on the hill above the town, which had been laid out in a regular grid pattern, in order to command the harbour and the Royal Navy dockyards, to control entry to the St Lawrence River which was the main route into the interior, and to protect the settlers of Nova Scotia. The first citadel was only a small redoubt, and that was replaced in 1776 with a three-storied blockhouse during the crisis of the American Revolutionary War of 1775–83. The blockhouse slowly fell into a ruinous state, and with the fresh threat of the French Revolutionary Wars of 1792–1802, succeeded by the Napoleonic Wars of 1803–15, work began in 1796 to create a strong bastioned fortress surrounding barracks and a magazine. Known as Fort George, it was considered vital for the control of the St Lawrence River and the Great Lakes in the War of 1812 (1812–15) against the United States of America.[6] Undiminished fear of American aggression against British

Canada and its support for a number of troublesome rebellions against British rule led to the decision to replace Fort George with a stone-built, star-shaped fortress with bastions, ravelins and casements (vaulted bomb-proof chambers for cannon and barracks). Work on the Halifax Citadel began in 1828 and would not be completed until 1856, eleven years after Lieutenant Thesiger had returned to England.[7]

The rifle regiment Thesiger joined in Halifax was not a typical infantry one. In January 1800, during the Napoleonic Wars, the Experimental Corps of Riflemen had been formed from elements of fourteen different regiments to provide sharpshooters, scouts and skirmishers. On 25 August 1800 the unit was named the Rifle Corps. In December 1802 it became a regular line regiment titled the 95th Regiment of Foot (Rifles) and was armed with muzzle-loading Baker rifles. Its 2nd Battalion, the one Thesiger would join, was formed in 1805. All three of the regiment's battalions fought at Waterloo in 1815. When the Army was reduced after Napoleon's defeat in this climactic battle, the musketry skills of the 95th Regiment were considered too valuable to lose, so it was taken out of the line and on 23 February 1816 became the Rifle Brigade, popularly known simply as 'The Rifles'.[8]

The Army Thesiger joined was still dressed in the gaudy, multi-coloured uniforms that had come into full flower in the Napoleonic era, and which have inspired some modern commentators to note the homoeroticism implicit in the male exhibitionism and sexual allure of such garb.[9] Nevertheless, by Thesiger's day some of the excessiveness (especially in the flamboyant cavalry regiments) was beginning to be toned down for reasons of practicality and expense. The Rifles were distinguished by the wearing of ceremonial uniforms of very dark green in the place of the tight, scarlet coatees and white trousers of the regular line regiments, and were consequently sometimes called 'The Grasshoppers'. The men wore a double-breasted coatee with two rows of buttons in front, tails at the back, and facings to collar and cuffs in black, the regimental colour. Their trousers were also green and their boots black. Officers wore a Hussar-style jacket with heavy black braiding, a pelisse (a jacket trimmed with black fur hanging loose over the left shoulder) and a crimson sash. Until 1844 infantry headgear (except for the Guards who wore bearskins) was a large, black, bell-shaped shako. It was then replaced by the more practical, cylindrical 'Albert' shako with a somewhat lower crown that tapered slightly inwards at the top and was crowned by a ball tuft. It had a peak in the front and a second one at the back intended to protect the wearer's neck from the sun. The silver regimental badge of a bugle on a Maltese cross was attached to the front of the shako. We cannot be sure that Thesiger wore the new Albert shako because uniforms had to last for a year (two in India) and a new one was issued every 1 April. Consequently, changes in uniform design could only be reflected in the next issue of uniforms, and in India and the remoter garrisons obsolete items continued to be worn alongside the new patterns. It is likely, though, that Thesiger sported the new shako because officers, who purchased their own uniforms, often adopted the latest patterns ahead of their men.

Thesiger would have found that the Rifle Brigade in garrison in Halifax presented a motley effect because, alongside the ceremonial uniforms some would have been wearing on duty, others would have been in undress uniform. This consisted of a short green 'shell jacket' with black facings, no braid, and cut off at the waist with no tails behind. The officers' version had silver epaulettes on the shoulders. Undress headdress for the men was a plain, green 'pork-pie' forage cap. Officers' green caps had a black leather peak, a band of black oak-leaf lacing around the crown, and the regimental badge embroidered on the front. Because officers were permitted a degree of latitude in their dress, they would seldom have been identical in their turnout. When Thesiger arrived in Halifax it was the middle of the Canadian winter, and he would have found that the freezing climate had forced various practical modifications in dress on the garrison. To augment their inadequate grey greatcoats with a cape over the shoulders, the men had adopted heavy fur mittens, fur-lined boots and caps with fur earflaps.

While Thesiger was stationed in Halifax, the Rifle Brigade was not called out on active service, but it should be noted that until well into the 1860s no official differentiation was made between ceremonial and field dress – as is done today – and any modifications on campaign to climate or terrain were at the discretion of the commanding officer. Consequently, some fortunate units campaigned in comfortable undress uniforms, while others, when their commander was a stickler, marched through dense bush or desert dressed as if they were on parade. Shakos, which were expensive items, were always protected on campaign with black, waterproof 'oilskin' covers to shield them from the elements. In the field, the infantryman carried knapsack equipment that was introduced in 1808 and remained in service with only minor variations until the Valise pattern was introduced in 1871. The knapsack itself, which was worn between the shoulders, consisted of a large canvas box, painted black, with board reinforcements inside it to keep its shape and reinforced at the corners with leather. It was carried by two vertical straps around the shoulders held in place by a horizontal strap across the chest. The rolled greatcoat was carried in straps above the knapsack. The black leather cartouche bag hung on one hip and the bayonet and scabbard on the other supported by broad leather straps over each shoulder. The regimental device was placed where these straps crossed over each other in the centre of the chest. All this equipment was black for the Rifle Brigade, but white for line regiments. Full marching equipment could weigh as much as sixty pounds and the men hated it for its weight and discomfort.[10]

Officers, on the other hand, had their extensive *impedimenta*, including military chests, bedding, supplies of brandy, wine, cigars and other luxuries, transported on the baggage train, and were required to carry little more than a sword, and possibly their own pistols and spy-glasses. The sword Thesiger would have worn was likely of the 1822 pattern, as one of the slightly modified 1845 pattern probably would never have reached him in Halifax. This pattern of sword, which was not replaced until 1891, had a slightly curved steel blade thirty-two inches long. The hilt – made of steel for The Rifles and of brass for all other units – was a 'half-basket' lined with black patent leather and with bars which were shaped to form the Royal cypher across the knuckles. The Rifle Brigade carried it in a steel scabbard, although the Guards and regiments of the line had a black leather scabbard with brass mountings. As a weapon, the sword was weak and liable to break in combat, and was a cumbersome liability in the field, especially in thick bush and jungle. Its only real use was confined to flourishing it to spur on the men in an attack.[11]

The infantrymen themselves were equipped with the percussion lock smoothbore musket, introduced between 1838 and 1842 and issued to all units by the late 1840s. The percussion lock replaced the old flintlock mechanism that used gunpowder as the primer. With the new mechanism, a brass percussion cap, coated with fulminates of mercury that ignite when struck, is placed in a hollow metal 'nipple' on top of the touchhole. When hit by the hammer released by the trigger, it explodes and ignites the charge inside the barrel. This new system almost entirely did away with the misfires so common with flintlocks and remained usable in wet weather. Moreover, in its simplicity it greatly speeded up the possible rate of fire. Yet, without rifling – a system of grooves cut inside the barrel that imparts a spinning motion to the projectile in flight and improves both range and accuracy – it remained inaccurate and possessed an effective range of no more than 150 yards.

As Thesiger would have discovered, the Rifle Brigade did not carry the standard infantry musket. Instead, in 1839 it had adopted the percussion cap Brunswick rifle with an adjustable backsight that replaced the Baker rifle and was further modified in 1842. However, because the ball it fired had a raised belt around it that fitted down the barrel of the Brunswick rifle only when correctly aligned with its two grooves, loading was a slow, fiddly process. It was consequently considered one of the worst weapons ever issued to British troops. The bayonet pattern for the Brunswick rifle had a blade with a slightly leaf-shaped tip and a brass hilt shaped something like that of a Roman sword. The order in the regiment was therefore always to 'fix swords!' and not to 'fix bayonets!'[12]

The Army Thesiger joined in 1844 reflected and magnified the class structure of society. It was masculine, hierarchical, tightly knit and paternalistic.[13] The Army depended on voluntary service, not recruitment, and the 'other ranks' were drawn from the opposite extreme of society from officers, primarily from the rural and urban poor, the unskilled who were least likely to find stable, full-time employment. Rural recruits were preferred because of their physical strength, stamina and perceived docility. Until the mid-nineteenth century, areas of regional poverty such as rural Ireland and the highlands of Scotland were disproportionately over-represented with half the rank-and-file coming from the Celtic fringe rather than from England. But, as the century progressed, recruits came increasingly from the depressed industrial centres of the English Midlands. After the Irish Potato Famine (1845–52) the number of Irish in the ranks dropped significantly both because of mass emigration and because growing Irish nationalism made service in the British Army less acceptable. There was no denying, though, that at the time the Army provided the most effective form of social welfare in the United Kingdom, and about 90 per cent of those who signed up were unemployed when they did so. Nevertheless, 'going for a soldier' was not considered honourable by society at large and was resorted to by most recruits only as a very last resort. Certainly, among those who signed up there were habitual criminals escaping justice, drunkards without hope of employment and those avoiding marriage, child maintenance and other unwelcome domestic entanglements. Yet, also among recruits were some who were enticed by the prospect of travel and adventure, and others who wished to join friends or family in the regiment, especially lads who had grown up as children in the regiment and could envisage no other way of life.

That said, it was undeniable that liquor and deception were the recruiting sergeant's usual tools to entice men to join the Colours, and in these unpromising circumstances it was not possible to be over-selective. So, while in theory the Army wanted only men of good character and physical condition, respectability and sobriety were actually of no concern to the recruiters. All that was required of a prospective soldier was a minimal degree of physical fitness and a minimum height, that for the infantry being five feet six inches (the other arms of the service required a few additional inches, notably the Guards regiments where between 1788 and 1839 the minimum height remained five feet eleven inches).[14] Even the five feet six requirement (about average height at the time) was frequently lowered in practice to a puny five feet three inches. Until 1871 the minimum age for enlistment was seventeen (eighteen thereafter) and the maximum was twenty-five.

Army pay was fixed at a shilling a day. As much as half this pay could be 'stopped' to cover the cost of a soldier's food, barrack services such as tailoring, laundering, the barber and medical treatment, as well as repairs for any damage inflicted on the fabric of the barracks themselves. As we have seen, uniforms and equipment were regularly replaced, but any loss or damage to them was recovered out of the soldier's pay. Out of what was left of his daily shilling after these multifarious stoppages, a soldier had to pay for tobacco for his clay pipe, consoling alcohol from the regimental canteen, and groceries and vegetables to augment and vary his basic and unappetising rations. These were made up of a mug of coffee and a pound of bread for breakfast, and of three-quarters of a pound of meat for the midday meal crudely boiled in a pot. Quite understandably, stoppages were ever a matter of deep grievance for soldiers, not least because military pay was poor in the first place, less than factory wages and less even than minimal agricultural ones. Yet, on the plus side, a soldier's Army pay was regular throughout the year, something that could never be said of labourers' wages. And it was also possible to earn a little extra as an officer's servant (paid for by the officer), or by providing skilled services to the regiment (should he possess them) as a carpenter, tailor, cobbler or the like. Moreover, he was also fed, no matter how basically, and provided with a roof over his head. Certainly, barracks, whether those in the United Kingdom or in one of the garrisons dotted around the Empire, were overcrowded, squalid, insanitary and cheerless. The lack of ventilation intensified the reek of the urine tub, and outbreaks of contagious diseases were common. Still, bad as they were, living conditions in a barracks were probably better than in a rural hovel or a slum tenement.[15]

The life a soldier led in peacetime was one of crushing monotony, discipline and boredom, and desertion was a perennial problem, especially from remote garrisons where it was easier to disappear into frontier society. Until the practice was discontinued in 1871, recaptured deserters were tattooed under the arm with a capital D. The repetitive dullness was broken only when in transit from one station to another – and a long sea voyage stiflingly packed below decks in a troopship had its own dangers. On 26 February 1852, HMS *Birkenhead*, an iron-hulled troopship with steam-driven paddle-wheels, was carrying drafts for several regiments fighting in the Eighth Cape Frontier War. It was sailing too close to the shore between Cape Town and Algoa Bay, and in the dark hours after midnight it struck a rock off Danger Point. The troops were mustered on deck and remained calm while the few serviceable lifeboats were lowered and the seven women and thirteen children on board took their places in them first. The troops who could not find room in the boats stood in their ranks shaking hands until the ship broke up and sank. Of 638 passengers and crew, 445 were drowned or eaten by sharks.[16]

In many parts of the Empire garrisons were prey to fatal, endemic tropical diseases like malaria and gastrointestinal infections such as dysentery and the even more deadly cholera and typhoid. And when they went on campaign in these foreign parts, life in the field could be very harsh with lengthy marches through deserts or thick bush or over mountains, with scant shelter against all sorts of inclement weather, in temporary encampments and with inadequate supplies. And then there was the personal risk of operating in enemy territory, of being ambushed or fighting pitched battles against a bewildering variety of enemies, each with his own particular style of combat.

When in garrison, as Thesiger would have found in Halifax, reveille sounded at 6 a.m. At 7.30 a.m. the men paraded and then breakfasted. This was followed by 'fatigue duty' that included polishing kit, cleaning the barrack rooms and latrines and peeling potatoes. At 12.45 p.m. the men paraded before dinner. In the afternoon they were drilled again in the very old-fashioned and complex drill evolutions of the eighteenth century, tempered only slightly by subsequent experience in the Napoleonic Wars: wheeling a close column; deploying a marching column into line, forming square from column, and various even more complicated sequences. Tea followed at 4.30 p.m., and then the troops were allowed free time for the next five hours. Soldiers leaving camp had to be properly turned out and were checked by the armed sentry at the barrack gate. At 9.30 p.m. roll call was taken and guard duty assigned for the following twenty-four hours. 'Lights out' was sounded at 10.15 a.m.

With an almost complete lack in the 1840s of organised recreation for the troops, soldiers drowned out the soul-destroying routine of their lives in the cheap rum and brandy – and ale in hot, thirsty climes – bought in the military canteens run by licensed civilian contractors. Drunkenness was a severe, recurrent problem and a major factor in ill-discipline that would never be overcome while Thesiger was a serving officer, one (as we shall see) he nevertheless would attempt to curb. The unsavoury reputation of soldiers as hard-drinking brawlers was well-earned, and drink was inevitably bound up with prostitution. In the first half of the nineteenth century the Army expected soldiers to be drunk and depraved and to find sexual relief with prostitutes. Concern over prostitution was therefore not a moral one, but a practical one relating to the incidence of venereal disease and the number of soldiers it hospitalised.

Some soldiers had no pressing need to resort to prostitutes because they had wives. Certainly, the Army preferred unmarried men with no entanglements and regarded wives as a liability, but was prepared to permit a small number of them and their children to live in barracks 'on half-strength', that is, receiving half rations and using military transport and other facilities. In return, wives and children performed domestic chores and earned a few pence washing clothes and tending the sick. There were no married quarters and wives and their children lived in the barracks with their husbands alongside the other soldiers with only a blanket curtain for minimal privacy. Soldiers who married without the consent of their commanding officer were not permitted to have their wives in barracks and leave to visit them outside was restricted. Thesiger would have found few soldiers' wives in Halifax because when a regiment was ordered overseas, only six wives per hundred soldiers (excluding sergeants) were allowed to accompany it and were chosen to do so by ballot. The government took no responsibility for the desperate unfortunates left behind to destitution and likely prostitution. However, the regiment took better care of soldiers' children than their wives because boys at least could prove an asset. They were put into the regimental school run on military principles by a master-sergeant and were taught a useful trade. The idea was that, growing up in the regiment, they would be qualified to become the NCOs of the future and would strengthen the regimental 'family'.

An officer demanded implicit obedience from his men, not only because he was their officer, but because he was their social superior, their natural-born leader as a gentleman. Indeed, when Thesiger joined the Rifle Brigade, a wide, unbridgeable gap of social standing and human sympathy yawned between officers and the rank and file. Certainly, officers had nothing in common with the men they commanded. Not only were they moneyed and socially privileged, but they shared the values of their class and possessed their own code of honour as gentlemen. Their pastimes and field sports were not shared by the troops, and their educated accents and vocabulary differed markedly from those of the men they commanded. Officers and men worked more closely together in the field when on active service, but in a peace-time garrison such as Halifax, where officers had their own lodgings or quarters and messed together, they scarcely mixed at all. Yet, while some officers were content to serve out their careers without ever gaining much understanding of their men's problems or interests, the majority at least adopted a paternal attitude towards them and accepted responsibility for their welfare.

Even so, this sense of responsibility did not lessen officers' basic conception of their men as incorrigibly idle, dissolute and vicious reprobates who required the sternest discipline to deter crime and curb excessive drunkenness. This view was most likely dinned into the young Thesiger while in Halifax, and throughout his career he was known to be 'a strict disciplinarian'.[17] In the 1840s punishment was no longer quite as harsh as it had been, but was fearsome enough. Flogging was the most common sentence handed down by court martial. It was publicly and degradingly carried out during a parade of the regiment drawn up in a hollow square. The offender was stripped to the waist and tied to the triangle with his hands above his head. He was flogged with a whip of nine knotted leather thongs while the drummers stridently played to drown out his screams as his back was flayed and lacerated to the bone. In 1829 flogging awarded by regimental courts for crimes such as desertion, insubordination or theft of Army property was reduced to a limit of 300 lashes, but officers increasingly opposed such punishment as still too brutal. In 1846, soon after Thesiger left Halifax, the number of lashes would be reduced to a maximum of fifty. Later, in 1867, flogging would be restricted to serious crimes such as mutiny and soon thereafter would be outlawed on home service. However, it would be retained as a field punishment until highly publicised incidents of flogging during the Anglo-Zulu War would lead to its abolition altogether by the Army Act of 1881.

In garrison, it was only on the parade ground that most officers regularly encountered their men, while much of the practical daily management, training and disciplining of the other ranks was delegated to the senior NCOs. Clerical staff, paymasters, and colour sergeants attended to the administrative work of the regiment. The most hard-worked officer was the adjutant, a lieutenant selected by the colonel to supervise drilling, duty rosters and disciplinary matters, and to prepare orders, undertake the regimental correspondence and oversee the monthly financial returns. But for an untried subaltern like Thesiger, regimental duties while in garrison were hardly demanding, and far less responsibility was placed on him than on young Royal Artillery and Royal Engineer officers whose specialist and technical training immediately gave them much more real work to do. Thesiger would have spent his time essentially understudying the captain in command of his company who was responsible for inspections, supervising guard duties, drills, parades and canteens, and overseeing the company's accounts. The general slackness among young officers of a garrison, such as the one stationed in Halifax, worked against their developing habits of initiative and responsibility. Nor does it seem that professional discussion about military organisation, tactics and weaponry, which were to be found in military journals, ever percolated down to most ordinary regimental officers, let alone to subalterns like Thesiger who employed their considerable free time in playing sports, hunting and various social activities.[18]

Considering the deep social, educational and cultural gulf between officers and the men they commanded, it must be questioned how loyalty and commitment to the regiment were ever engendered. Yet, the fact is that regiments in the British Army did develop a clan-like loyalty that bound officers, NCOs and soldiers together in a determination not to let their comrades down and inculcated a healthy competitive spirit with other units. The reason why the regiment became the focus of communal loyalty in the Army was that it replaced the lost, pre-existing community of civilian life. The regiment became the man's new family. It gave him a home and a measure of security against the outside world, while the rigid system of drill and discipline instilled a sense of shared pride in military competence, reinforced by the hardships and dangers endured on campaign. As a consequence, soldiers developed their identifiable, life-long military stamp that set them apart from the rest of society. Above all, officers and men were bound together by their common allegiance to the Queen, and by the regimental traditions that framed their lives. All members of the regiment would have been instructed in its history that stressed the continuity of regimental life, and emphasised its past heroic deeds that provided the idealised model for future conduct. The regiment's distinguishing badges, facing colours – and with the Rifle Brigade its distinctive green uniform – along with the practices and traditions peculiar to each regiment, all helped infuse its members with a sense of pride and belonging that marked them off from other units.[19]

The Colours, presented by the Queen herself or by a dignitary on her behalf, were the principal symbol of regimental identity that bound officers and men in a common loyalty. Each infantry battalion of the line carried a Queen's Colour and its own Colour bearing unique regimental devices and battle honours. While the Colours had a practical purpose as the rallying-point for the regiment on the battlefield, their true significance was emotional. They represented the trust vested in each regiment's loyalty by their sovereign and displayed the accumulated honour of the regiment. The Rifle Brigade – and this too helped make it distinctive – did not carry Colours as it was not part of the line, but added battle honours to the regimental badge worn individually by all its members.

As with other imperial garrisons, the role of the one Thesiger joined in Halifax in 1845 was not exclusively military. Besides guarding the Empire, permanent garrisons had a considerable impact on colonial economies and societies. The building of military works, such as the Halifax Citadel, and the prolonged stationing of soldiers with money to spend injected capital into small communities, and colonists certainly gained financially from the military presence. Of the major military stations, Halifax was by far the most popular with troops, who considered Gibraltar on its isolated rock no better than a prison, and who dismissed Malta as unbearably hot and boring. Halifax, on the other hand, offered a notorious and enticing underworld of taverns and brothels in Barrack Street just below the Citadel. Officers such as Thesiger took no part in these low diversions but mixed with the Haligonian elites, contributing actively to their social life and living style. In winter there was skating, curling, excursions by sleigh for dinners and dances with local belles, and tobogganing. In summer officers went yachting and horse racing, and picnicked and played cricket. And all the year round there were dinners, dances (the quadrille was still the most popular dance in Halifax although the waltz was gaining favour) and amateur theatricals and pantomimes mounted in the officers' mess or the private houses of wealthier Haligonians.[20] In later life Thesiger was known to keep up his enthusiastic participation in amateur theatricals, and to have been an accomplished clarinet player – although it is not clear when and where he developed his musical skill.[21]

Lieutenant Thesiger of the Rifle Brigade enjoyed these innocent but pleasurable diversions in Halifax for less than year, because on 28 November 1845 he exchanged by purchase into the Grenadier Guards stationed in London.

CHAPTER 4

Grenadier Guards, London and Dublin, 1845–1855

SOME DEGREE OF MILITARY PATRONAGE, kept in bounds by the requirements of seniority within the regiment, was essential for an officer's advancement. In June 1845 Sir Frederick Thesiger was appointed Attorney General in Peel's Tory administration, and the Duke of Wellington (a Cabinet minister without office) evidently now saw his way to securing a commission for his colleague's son in the Grenadier Guards through exchange from the Rifle Brigade. The matter would have been dealt with through the department of the Commander-in-Chief's Military Secretary (MS) who was the chief channel for correspondence on all matters connected with the appointment, promotion, and exchange of officers.[1] At the time, the MS was Lieutenant-General Lord Fitzroy Somerset, better known as Lord Raglan after he was created a baron in October 1852 and went on to command the British expeditionary force in the Crimean War. He was a younger son of the Duke of Beaufort and had fought with Wellington throughout the Peninsular War and had lost his right arm at Waterloo. Afterwards he had remained very close to Wellington who, as he grew older, leaned increasingly upon him.[2] The practice of exchange between regiments was common until it was much reduced by the Regimental Exchange Act of 1875. It was the regular means by which an ambitious officer advanced his career through joining a more prestigious regiment, thereby escaping a regimental posting to an unappealing location, or securing one that guaranteed active service and the opportunities for promotion that might bring. Sometimes, too, an exchange was a way of escaping the excessive expenses unavoidably entailed by being a member of a fashionable regiment, but which an officer found he could no longer sustain.[3]

The Foot Guards and Household Cavalry were the most fashionable and prestigious regiments in the army, none more so than the Grenadier Guards. The regiment had its origins in 1656 as the exiled King Charles II's Royal Regiment of Guards, and by 1685 had become the First Regiment of Foot Guards. Its title was changed in 1815 to the First or Grenadier Regiment of Foot Guards to honour its rout of Napoleon's Grenadiers de la Garde Impériale at Waterloo, and in commemoration its headgear was changed to the tall, black bearskin cap with a white plume on the left-hand side.[4] The Grenadier Guards were the most aristocratic regiment in the entire Army. Between 1800 and 1849, sixty-nine peers and peers' sons served in the regiment, and fifty-nine between 1850 and 1899. In the same period, however, the strong aristocratic element in the composition of the Guards was being penetrated by officers of rising families like the Thesigers who fully understood that membership of the most fashionable of regiments confirmed aspirant social status.[5]

Frederic Thesiger entered the Grenadier Guards as ensign and lieutenant. (Until the so-called 'dual rank' system was abolished in June 1872, it was one of the privileges of the Grenadier Guards that up to lieutenant-colonel an officer held a concurrent regimental and higher Army rank.) For the next nine-and-a-half years, between the ages of eighteen and almost twenty-eight, Thesiger would play the part of a fashionable and largely ornamental officer in London and Dublin. The purchase of his commission would have been no light financial undertaking for his father. A commission in the Foot Guards cost £1,260, offset by what would have been recouped by the sale of the younger Thesiger's commission in the Rifle Brigade. His son's equipment would have set Sir Frederick back almost as much again since the uniform of the Grenadier Guards was extravagant and the most visible form of their social splendour. Only the most fashionable military tailors could be entrusted with making these uniforms at the staggering cost of £600,[6] and the younger Thesiger's were Henry Poole & Co. of Savile Row, a firm established in 1806 and still going strong.[7] An officer of the Grenadiers wore a scarlet coatee with blue facings and the 'grenade fired proper' badge on the collar, all embellished with gold epaulettes and lace, along with dark blue trousers with a gold stripe down the seam and a towering bearskin cap.[8] Such finery was part of the trend in the peacetime decades after Waterloo for uniforms to become increasingly ostentatious. In 1830 the Coldstream Guards and the Scots

Guards both joined the Grenadier Guards in donning the distinctive bearskin cap, and the Household Cavalry received their sparkling breast-plates.[9]

For a young officer in the ultra-fashionable Grenadiers such as the young Thesiger, burdened by the hardly arduous duties of a subaltern, life while stationed in the capital of the Empire and in heady proximity to royalty was an extravagant round of elegant pleasures. These were governed by the rigid social rules of life in high society involving the ritual of visiting cards, the dancing partner lists at balls, and the nicely graded seating at dinner parties. Officers regularly attended the theatres and opera where all society congregated, and were devotees of the turf. They went off on country house visits where they could indulge in field sports, primarily shooting and hunting, and 'hard-riding' officers were especially admired. Thesiger is known to have been very fond of these pursuits.[10] When not enjoying themselves in London society, or dining at their expensive gentlemen's clubs, officers were involved in the extravagant dinners and exuberant entertainments of their superbly furnished mess when they were expected to drink deep. Some of the racier officers indulged in romantic adventures and frequented courtesans.[11] All officers in the Guards usually employed two servants, and kept a horse or two as well that would have cost upwards of £150 each.[12]

Yet, it must not be supposed that Thesiger was quite like many of his rich fellow officers in the Grenadiers who were not committed soldiers, but who were merely enjoyably whiling away their time with boon companions until they came into their inheritance. It is clear that he took his profession entirely seriously, and during his years in London devoted himself to gaining a better theoretical knowledge of it. He spent many free hours studying in the library of the Royal United Services Institution and attending talks in its lecture room where the intricacies of the military profession were discussed by experts. In later years he was known to be a 'W, although whether he was already one when serving with the hard-drinking Grenadiers is not clear, although peer pressure makes it unlikely.[13] Later, too, he was remembered as setting an example of moderation and frugality that was unusual among officer at the time.[14] Perhaps this was in reaction to the self-indulgent life of his fellow-officers in the Grenadiers, or it might simply have reflected his naturally ascetic, somewhat withdrawn temperament expressed in his habitual way of speaking in 'sharp, rather jerky sentences'. An African auxiliary during the Anglo-Zulu War would later comment on his 'rumbling rasping voice'. Although always maintaining a 'pleasant manner' towards all those with whom he came into contact,[15] it is not hard to suppose that his boisterous mess-mates in the Grenadiers must have found Thesiger with his thin, lanky frame as something of a prig.

Few regiments were as expensive as the Grenadiers with its particularly lavish lifestyle, one that could never be met by an officer's pay alone. Military pay remained low throughout the nineteenth century. This was seen as desirable, not simply because it saved a cheeseparing government money, but because it ensured that those wishing to become officers would be men of substance with a personal stake in the country and a commitment to the preservation of the existing order: men, in other words, who would serve as a matter of honour and not for remuneration. A lieutenant-colonel in a line regiment received £310 a year, £419 in a cavalry regiment, £488 in the Guards, and £522 in the Household Cavalry. But a captain in a line regiment was paid only £211 and a cornet a paltry £95. Granted, officers in the cavalry, Royal Artillery and Royal Engineers received proportionately more than those in the infantry of the line. Nevertheless, this still must be set against the average income of the professional and salaried middle classes that hovered around £300 a year with a successful doctor earning up to £500. Such a sum might have been sufficient to maintain a comfortable standard of living for a respectable middle-class family, but it was certainly not enough for an officer whose failure to match the profligate spending of his brother officers would offend against the etiquette of the mess. Indeed, some regiments required a prior assurance that aspirant officers possessed a private income sufficient to meet obligatory expenses.

The long and the short of it was that a line officer required a private income of about £200 above his pay and a cavalry officer at least £500 (and probably £750 in one of the smarter cavalry regiments). In the Artillery and Engineers, where officers were technically trained professionals and overwhelmingly middle-class, lavish spending over and above military pay was not expected. But in a fashionable regiment a young subaltern required a private income as large as a lieutenant-colonel's pay. The situation was financially most onerous in the Guards where an officer would be expected to spend up to £900 a year above his pay. Many officers who lacked the necessary private means soon found themselves in debt and were either forced to sell out or to exchange into a less fashionable regiment with lower mess bills and fewer social obligations. Scandalously, there were cases of officers unable to sustain the required lifestyle being viciously hounded out of the regiment. And, as we shall see, financial considerations were sometimes the reason for turning down higher commands and their associated expenses. Certainly, as in any other profession, officers had no choice but to keep a wary eye on their income and expenditure and to regulate their career accordingly.[16]

For just over six years Chelmsford sustained the life in London of a fashionable Guards officer while his former comrades in the Rifle Brigade saw active service in South Africa in the Seventh Cape Frontier War of 1846–7, and again in the Eighth Cape Frontier War of 1850–3. Between 1849 and 1853 no promotions were filled in the Guards without purchase, so Thesiger's promotion to lieutenant-and-captain on 27 December 1850 would have cost his father at least a further £525 which was the difference in price between his old and new ranks – although unspecified over-regulation payments of up to double the regulated price were normally agreed upon.[17]

Guards officers regarded it as their right to receive the lion's share of the top and most prestigious appointments in the Army. While they were of more junior rank, they still expected as a matter of course to be offered plumb, socially advantageous ceremonial jobs as ADCs to high colonial officials or staff appointments to generals. This was not on account of any special merits they might possess, but was the consequence of the widespread, customary exercise of patronage working through an officer's network of connections in society, the government and the army.[18]

In February 1852 Sir Frederick Thesiger became Attorney General again in Lord Derby's first Tory administration, and it was no coincidence that his 24-year-old son was simultaneously appointed ADC to the Lord Lieutenant General and General Governor of Ireland, or 'Lord Lieutenant' or 'Viceroy' for short. An officer appointed to the personal staff of a high official or general as an ADC was temporarily withdrawn from his regiment but was still borne on its establishment.

The formal Union in 1801 of the kingdoms of Ireland and Great Britain that allowed Ireland substantial representation in both houses of the British parliament created a hybrid administration that was distinctly colonial. Ireland itself was technically under the direct rule of the Lord

Lieutenant whose powers remained ill-defined and whose office was largely ceremonial.[19] The seat of the British administration in Ireland was Dublin Castle, begun in 1204 under King John but, except for the surviving mediaeval Record Tower, mainly constructed during the eighteenth century. With its throne room and other state apartments it provided the stage for the assertion of British rule over Ireland. It was the social focus of the Protestant Ascendancy, those landowners, clergy, professionals and merchants who were all member of the established Church of Ireland and who dominated the social, economic and political life of Ireland to the exclusion of Roman Catholics.

Thesiger arrived in Dublin Castle in the suite of the newly appointed Lord Lieutenant, a rich Scottish nobleman, Archibald Montgomerie, thirteenth Earl of Eglinton, who was a staunch Tory and close political associate of Lord Derby. Eglinton's main interest was the turf and he played a leading part in turning horse-racing into a popular recreation. He was best known, however, for staging the famous Eglinton Tournament in 1839, an extraordinary (and very expensive) mediaeval re-enactment that caught the public imagination.[20]

Thesiger came to Ireland at a most unfortunate time, because outside the gates of privileged Dublin Castle with its provincial vice-regal pomp where he played out his role as ADC, the notorious Irish Famine that had begun in 1845 was nearing the end of its disastrous course. At the best of times, most people in Ireland lived near the starvation level, and close to four million of them depended for their food on one staple crop, the potato. The worst of the potato blight itself was over by 1847 after two successive and comprehensive failures of the crop, but people continued to die in large numbers from the effects of starvation and disease, perhaps a million in all. The British administrative machinery was unfitted to cope with a catastrophe on such a scale. More than a million desperate Irish emigrated between 1846 and 1851, and another million between 1852 and 1861, almost two-thirds of them to the United States. Between 1849 and 1851 landlords evicted at least 37,000 families of tenants who could no longer pay their rent, and the situation on the land, long characterised by mutual hostility between landlord and tenant, became more explosive than ever.[21]

In these dangerous circumstances, the role of the British Army in Ireland became critical in offering 'aid to the civil power' in suppressing riots, illegal assemblies and rebellious activities generally. Indeed, the size of the Irish garrison during the nineteenth century was exceeded in the Empire only by that in India. Irish nationalists were not far wrong in regarding the Irish garrison as an army of occupation. But Ireland's proximity to the British mainland gave it a particular strategic significance and the argument was constantly made that the military occupation of Ireland was necessary for Britain's security.[22] Outside events would ensure that Thesiger, after serving for just less than a year as Lord Eglinton's ADC, would find himself appointed to the British Army in Ireland.

The Thesigers' long-standing patron, the Duke of Wellington, died on 14 September 1852. On 28 September 1852, General Viscount Hardinge of Lahore, who had been Governor General of India (1844–8) and was a royal favourite, succeeded the Iron Duke as General Commanding-in-Chief.[23] Hardinge was a plain, straightforward man of business. He had been a staff officer of Wellington's in the Peninsular War and had lost his left hand at the battle of Ligny on the eve of Waterloo. Afterwards, he had continued to be closely associated with the Duke, both as his devoted friend and as his loyal political associate.[24] Sir Frederick Thesiger was very much part of their staunchly High Tory political circle. It comes as no surprise, therefore, that Hardinge stepped swiftly and unhesitatingly into Wellington's place as the Thesigers' new patron. A few years later, on 5 August 1855, young Thesiger would write to his brother-in-law Lieutenant-Colonel John Inglis reminding him that 'as long as Lord Hardinge is C. in Chief, my father will almost be able to get anything he applies for'.[25]

So, doubtless with Lord Hardinge's support conveyed through the instructions of Colonel Richard Airey, his MS (on whose staff Thesiger would later serve in the Crimea), on 8 January 1853 Thesiger left the vice-regal court on being appointed ADC to the long-serving CinC in Ireland, Lieutenant-General Sir Edward Blakeney. He was a distinguished veteran who had seen service in many theatres of the French Revolutionary and Napoleonic Wars, including the Peninsular War under Wellington's command, and who had also fought in the War of 1812 against the United States.[26] Still stationed in Dublin, Thesiger would have continued to enjoy the social life centred around Dublin Castle that would have followed the same pattern as in London, but on a less glittering and expensive scale, and with more emphasis in horse-mad Ireland on the turf and riding to hounds. As an ADC he would have received an allowance for two horses. His duties, however, were now purely military, and under the leanly-built General Blakeney's searching gaze Thesiger would have begun to learn how to perform as an efficient ADC on a general's personal staff, attending him at inspections and all public occasions, carrying orders and rendering whatever other services his general required of him. We know from the hours that Thesiger had spent in the Royal United Services Institution in London that he took his military profession seriously, and he doubtless applied himself assiduously. Not that there was as yet such a thing as formal training for young staff officers, and like others in his position Thesiger was simply expected to pick up his duties as he went along. Only after the blatant failures of staff and command in the Crimean War would the decision be taken to found a Staff College.[27]

In accordance with the orders issued through Major-General Charles Yorke, who had succeeded Airey in May 1854 as Hardinge's MS, on 5 August 1854 Thesiger took his farewell of General Blakeney and Dublin and returned to his regimental duties in London. He must have been itching to go because on 27 March 1854 Britain had declared war on Russia, with France following suit the next day, and after months of inaction the two allies were at last on the brink of directly engaging the enemy in the Crimea. Like his fellow Guards officers, Thesiger would have been anxious to play his part, not simply to further his own career on active service, but to prove to the rest of the Army that his conceited regiment could more than justify its privileged existence through its magnificent performance on the battlefield.[28]

CHAPTER 5

In the Crimea, 1855–1856

AT FIRST GLANCE, BRITAIN'S WAR against Russia, fought in alliance with the Ottoman Empire, the French Second Empire and the opportunist late-joiner, the Kingdom of Piedmont-Sardinia, seems an absurdly unnecessary conflict. Yet each of the hostile powers had distinct motives in which nationalism and imperialism combined with religious concerns. The Turks went to war to preserve their crumbling empire in Europe from Russian expansionism; the British and French came to their aid ostensibly to defend them against the Russians but, in reality, to preserve their own commercial and political interests in the eastern Mediterranean, the Black Sea and Central Asia from the perceived Russian menace; while the Sardinians fought to secure future British and French goodwill in expelling the Austrians from Italy. For his part, the Russian Tsar Nicholas I believed it was his God-ordained mission to extend his Orthodox Christian empire to encompass Constantinople and Jerusalem and to free his co-religionists from the Ottoman yoke. To achieve this, with all the hubris exhibited by another Russian autocrat in our own day, he was prepared to go to war with all who stood in his way.[1]

When the Ottomans declared war on encroaching Russia on 5 October 1853, Britain and France both sent expeditionary forces to the eastern Mediterranean ahead of formally declaring war on Russia on 27 and 28 March 1854 respectively. The British force under the command of General Lord Raglan consisted of five infantry divisions and one cavalry one, 26,000 men in all, many of them raw recruits. Thesiger, then still serving as General Blakeney's ADC in Dublin, must have been filled with frustration and envy when he learned that the 3rd Battalion of the Grenadier Guards had embarked for the Mediterranean on 23 February 1854. The 3rd Grenadiers formed part of the prestigious 1st Division which was made up of the Guards Brigade, the Highland Brigade and two batteries of Royal Artillery, and was destined to take part in all the battles of the Crimean War where the British were engaged.[2] Their divisional commander was Lieutenant-General HRH Prince George, the second Duke of Cambridge and Queen Victoria's first cousin,[3] a royal personage destined to play a determining role in Thesiger's career.

In May 1854 the allies concentrated at Varna in Ottoman territory on the west coast of the Black Sea, but when after determined Ottoman resistance the Russians withdrew from the Danubian principalities of Moldavia and Wallachia they had invaded, the British and French were deprived of an obvious military objective. Determined still to curb Russian ambitions and to justify the sacrifices already made, the allies eventually decided in September 1854 to land in the Crimea and capture Sebastopol (now usually spelled Sevastopol) the strategic naval base of the Russian Black Sea fleet. It would prove a grinding campaign for which the British Army was inadequately prepared.

It was once argued that the British Army had atrophied in the long years of peace and financial retrenchment following Waterloo, but it is now accepted that the Army was tentatively beginning to reform itself. Once he became CinC in 1852, Lord Hardinge established a permanent military training camp at Aldershot and the School of Musketry at Hythe. Already, in 1851, the Army had adopted the Belgian Minié rifle, or Rifle Musket Pattern 1851, with a percussion-cap firing mechanism. It had a 39-inch barrel with four grooves of rifling, and fired a pointed, .702-calibre bullet with a hollow base. Accurate to over 300 yards, it was good for volley-fire to more than three times that distance. A hundred were issued to the most expert shots in most regiments. All the infantry battalions that left for the Crimea (with the exception of those in the 4th Division) were equipped with the Minié rifle where it was used alongside the old percussion-cap smooth-bore musket with its meagre effective range of only about 150 yards. The Minié rifle proved a considerably better weapon than the Brunswick rifle that Thesiger would have known in Halifax, but was still not entirely satisfactory. The percussion-cap Enfield Rifle Musket that passed its trials in 1853 was far in advance of any previous firearm issued to the Army, and at Lord Hardinge's insistence it was issued to the troops towards the end of the Crimean War. It was lighter than the Minié rifle because, although the barrel was of the same length, the bore was .577 inch. The rifling consisted of three shallow grooves (these were increased to five in subsequent modifications). Sighted up to 900 yards, the Enfield rifle was infinitely more accurate than the old smooth-bore musket where only one shot in 459 took effect. Now, one shot in sixteen told.[4]

Yet, despite the major technological developments of the percussion cap and the more widespread use of rifled muskets – with the consequent enhancement of weapon-effectiveness – British tactical manuals (of the sort Thesiger was in the habit of studying so assiduously) were still only a refinement of those in use at the end of the eighteenth century. This despite the fact that with a few exceptions – such as the series of conventional battles fought in India during the First and Second Anglo-Sikh Wars of 1845–6 and 1848–9 – most of the Army's practical experience since Waterloo had involved small-scale colonial campaigns where flexible skirmish tactics were required rather than set-piece battles.

The 1833 *Field Exercises and Evolutions* manual laid down infantry tactical formations that were only marginally altered from those employed in the Napoleonic Wars. It advocated close-order formations of the line for firing and then charging with fixed bayonet, compact columns for manoeuvre and the battalion square as a defence against cavalry. Cavalry were expected to furnish the flank- rear- and vanguards of an army, to provide reconnaissance and to skirmish, and to be capable of offensive action in the charge. For 'shock' action the principal cavalry weapon remained the sabre. Some regiments carried the lance, useful in attacking an infantry square and in pursuing broken infantry in flight but an encumbrance in a mêlée. Post-Napoleonic artillery tactics drew away from piecemeal deployment in favour of massed batteries. During the first half of the nineteenth century, the Army's field artillery consisted of 6-pounder and 9-pounder muzzle-loading, smoothbore cannon (the classification described the weight of the projectile) firing solid roundshot or 'canister', musket-balls or large grapeshot in a container that ruptured as it left the gun, spraying the charge like a giant shotgun cartridge; also styled case-shot and used only at close range. Field artillery also included 12-pounder and 24-pounder howitzers capable of indirect fire over the heads of friendly troops or obstacles using exploding 'common shell' or 'spherical case' (also known as shrapnel). These shells, which were filled with musket-balls, were fitted with a burning fuse and were intended to burst in the air over the enemy's heads. The mechanics of siege warfare against defended positions had not changed since the seventeenth century. Zig-zag approach trenches were dug to within range of the fortress's walls where parallel trenches were constructed in which the batteries of heavy 18-pounder and 24-pounder 'position' guns were placed. These smashed a breach in the enemy's fortifications through which the infantry stormed to seize the position.[5]

Thesiger had already returned to his regimental duties in London when, on 14 September 1854, the allied expeditionary force landed at Kalamita Bay in the Crimea and began its advance southwards along the coast towards Sebastopol. In a ferocious encounter the Russians unsuccessfully disputed their advance when they crossed the River Alma on 20 September 1854, the British attacking in the most conventional style possible with two entire divisions in line abreast with two more in support. Each division had its battalions deployed side by side in two ranks screened by skirmishers.

Failing to press on to seize Sebastopol before its defences were ready, the Allies began their investment on 25 September 1854 and only on 17 October unleashed their first bombardment of the sophisticated fortifications protecting the landward side of the port town. As in any classic siege, the besieging force was in danger of being attacked by a relieving army, likely supported by a sortie from the beleaguered town, and the Allies had to throw up their own defence works. As anticipated, the Russian attempted to raise the siege and, to that end, on 25 October 1854 unsuccessfully attempted to seize the Allies' supply base at Balaklava south-east of Sebastopol in a sharp encounter that saw the infamous Charge of the Light Brigade and ended in a stand-off. The following day the allies beat back a Russian sortie from Sebastopol at the Chernaya River (Little Inkerman). On 5 November the Russians made another, very determined effort to raise the siege, but were only just repulsed in the scrambling, hand-to-hand battle at Inkerman, fought for the most part in dense fog over very difficult terrain in which the better discipline and superior armaments of the allies prevailed.[6]

Stalemate followed and the inappropriately clothed Allies (they had anticipated a summer campaign only) spent a miserable winter encamped in inadequate shelters on the wind-swept heights before Sebastopol. Their transport and supply were ill-suited to a distant campaign on such

The Siege of Sebastopol, 1854–1855
Russian batteries
Russian camp
Chernaya River
Battle of Chernaya
16 Aug. 1855
Battle of Balaklava
25 Oct. 1854
British line of defensive works
Highland Division
Harbour
Balaklava
French line of defensive works
Turkish defensive works
Battle of Inkermann
5 Nov. 1854
2nd Division
Turks
9th Division
Light Division
2nd Division
1st Division
4th Division
1st Division
3rd Division
British HQ
Turks
French siege works
British siege works
Harbour
Bridge of Rafts
Fort Paul
Barracks
Little Redan
Malakoff
Mamelon
Hospital
Redan
Inner harbour
Fort Nicholas
Sebastopol
Flagstaff bastion
French HQ
3rd Division
French batteries
French siege works
4th Division
Turks
6th Division
5th Division
French line of defensive works
Black Sea
British
French
Turks
Russians
Supply line
0
4 miles
0
4 km

inhospitable soil (the British faring far worse than the better-organised French), and medical support was entirely inadequate. During the course of the winter there was mounting concern in the British press and Parliament over the army's deplorable plight, for which Raglan's poor administration was blamed. Nor was the criticism unfounded.[7]

No matter how inspired generalship in battle might be (and in the Crimea it was never better than uninspired), the unglamorous task of keeping troops fed and supplied in the field is no less essential to military success. With many years experience as a staff officer, Thesiger would always pay particular attention to this administrative side of the soldier's trade. Yet, for much of the Victorian period the duties of commissariat and supply fell under diverse authorities and the consequences were often chaotic. What formal structures had emerged during the course of the Napoleonic Wars were soon disbanded as part of the government's economy drive during the subsequent years of peace. When the Crimean War broke out, the responsibility for organising provisions in the field fell to the Commissariat Department. This was a civilian body, and no formal establishment existed to supervise the transport of such provisions it might procure. The cool and dignified Major-General Richard Airey, a very professional and efficient officer who since September 1854 had been Quartermaster-General on Lord Raglan's headquarters staff, was unfairly held to account by the British public for the failure to provide sufficient food and forage for the army, even though he had no control over the Commissariat Department.[8] That department's long-established practice was to hire animal-drawn wagons or pack-animals in the area of operations, along with their civilian drivers. The financial advantage was that this transport pool could be dispensed with as soon as the campaign was over. The disadvantage with this improvised arrangement was that it was not reliable. Drivers were not subject to military organisation, and nor was there any guarantee that the necessary transport would even be available. And, if it were, there was a natural tendency for the locals to drive up the price of hire or sale to as much or more than the Army was prepared to pay. Despite various attempts to improve the system of supply and transport in subsequent years, Thesiger would be confronted by precisely the same difficulties when campaigning in Zululand a quarter of a century later.

These self-same shortcomings were cruelly exposed in the Crimea where the Allies found almost no transport available and scant forage for their horses. The occupation of Balaklava provided a landing site for supplies, but there was almost no means of transporting the provisions the eight miles to the allied lines surrounding Sebastopol, and tons of supplies were left in the open to rot in the heavy autumn and winter rains. As a result, throughout the bitter winter of 1854–5 the men in the trenches went hungry – although their officers, who could afford to pay, generally ate well and secured accommodation that was better proof against the freezing weather. The scandalous collapse of the Commissariat Department led to a Royal Warrant in January 1855 that created a new transport body, the Land Transport Corps, to assist in transporting supplies and provisions along the line of communication. Unfortunately, its performance was to prove disappointingly chaotic and ineffective.[9]

For the soldiers in the field, suffering from combat wounds or riddled with illnesses brewed in the insanitary and freezing camps and entrenchments, there was little in the way of Army medical services. Those that existed depended on the regimental medical officer, usually a civilian surgeon paid for out of regimental funds, along with an assistant or two. Bandsmen helped remove the wounded from the battlefield, but there were no properly assigned stretcher-bearers and civilian transport had to be hired in the field for service as ambulances. These terrible shortcomings became widely known, and led to Florence Nightingale's famous mission to the hospital at Scutari across the Bosporus from Istanbul, 300 miles away from the front. Despite her inspiring presence from November 1854, medical conditions remained dire throughout the war.[10]

Chronically under-supplied, in poor, makeshift shelters or on dangerous duty in the trenches, and with barely any medical care, the British soldiers encircling Sebastopol presented a sorry sight that winter of 1854–5, not least because of the state of their uniforms. In colonial warfare there had been a gradual shift towards fighting in undress, especially in the heat of India and Africa and where there was thick bush or jungle. But for conventional warfare against a continental power, it was held that British soldiers should take the field in their most resplendent dress. But what was that to be? Before the army left Varna in September 1854, Queen Victoria had approved wide-sweeping changes in uniform. However, because of delays in manufacturing and issuing the new uniforms, none were yet available. So, when the expeditionary force landed in the Crimea the men fought the battle of the Alma in their existing, old-pattern uniforms. For the infantry, that meant scarlet coatees, bearskins for the Guards and shakos for the rest. Since white summer trousers had been left on board the transports, the soldiers all wore their dark, thick Oxford-mixture ones. The cavalry mostly dispensed with their plumes, pelisses and other flashy adornments. General officers favoured their long, blue undress frock-coats. Some retained their plumed cocked hats, although most replaced this conspicuous headgear with more serviceable forage caps adorned with gold lace. The troops also greatly preferred forage caps as headgear, and in the trenches around Sebastopol they went on duty wearing them.

Uniforms do not survive harsh conditions, and the expeditionary force had not expected to have to campaign over the winter. By the end of 1854 the disliked shakos and bearskins were falling apart, uniforms were faded and torn, and the troops were patching their coatees with the sacking used for sandbags in the trenches. Supplies of warm clothing were sunk in a ferocious storm off the mouth of Balaklava harbour on 14 November 1854, and the troops moved about wrapped in blankets against the bitter cold. Replacement cold-weather clothing finally arrived at the beginning of 1855, and the troops abandoned their tattered coatees for sheepskin coats, hooded cloaks, fur caps, fur mittens and long boots, raiment such as Thesiger would have known in Halifax.

In the spring of 1855, Thesiger learned that, thanks to the military patronage he continued to enjoy through his father's connections, he was at last to experience active service. On 31 May 1855 he joined the 3rd Grenadiers in their camp before Sebastopol. (The Sardinian contingent had arrived just before him, on 8 May.) He would have found that with the warmer weather winter clothing had been withdrawn, and that the British troops had resumed a more conventional military appearance. Officers had almost all adopted shell-jackets, but the men were still restricted to their tattered coatees. Forage caps were almost universal. The new pattern of uniform approved the previous year had at last begun to be issued in April 1855, just before Thesiger's arrival in the Crimea, but few reached the Crimea until the war was nearly over. Some fashion-conscious officers had the latest pattern uniforms specially sent out to them, and Thesiger would have arrived wearing it. The old tight coatee was replaced by a much more comfortable tunic with full skirts all around instead of tails at the back. For the infantry, the tunic remained scarlet with coloured regimental facings and white lace and piping. Officers left off their expensive gold epaulettes and wings, and rank badges were worn instead on either side of the collar opening. Officers' white shoulder-belts were replaced by waist-belts. Infantry regiments were issued with the new 'French' shako, lower than the Albert pattern, tapered towards the crown and tilted forwards The Guards, however, retained their bearskin caps. Undress uniform, as now worn increasingly in the field, remained the shell-jacket and forage cap.[11]

While serving in the Crimea, Thesiger was destined neither to fight in a pitched battle in the field, nor to be among those risking their lives storming the formidable fortifications of Sebastopol. Instead, his role would essentially be that of an onlooker. Very soon after his arrival, on 6 June 1855 he witnessed the Allies' third major bombardment of Sebastopol by 155 British guns and mortars and some 300 French pieces. The elevated Malakoff (or Malakhov) Tower was the key to the Russian system of defences. It was flanked by two other strongpoints, the Redan to it south and the Little Redan to its north. (A redan is a triangular work of which the salient is the apex, with an open gorge to the rear.)[12] Over 8 and 9 June the Allies emerged from their trenches and stormed the Russian forward positions shielding the Malakoff and Redan. In very hard fighting the French succeeded in capturing the Mamelon Redoubt in front of the Malakoff, and the British seized and held on to the Quarries before the Redan. The British 1st Division (which included the 3rd Grenadiers) took no part in the assault on the Quarries but remained as a reserve in the trenches to the rear. Thesiger would have safely watched the battle from there with his battalion, but he would have been acutely conscious of the severity of the fighting that saw 507 British soldiers killed or wounded including thirty-six officers. Afterwards, he would have witnessed the sobering business of burying the dead and retrieving the wounded under flag of truce.[13] Until then, Thesiger had been an ornamental and privileged peacetime soldier, and what knowledge he had of warfare had been gleaned only from military manuals, journals, memoirs and the like. Now, although only a spectator to the fighting at the Quarries, he could have been left with no illusions about the horrifying nature of actual combat.

On 18 June the Allies attacked from their recently seized forward positions. The 25,000 French were to seize the Malakoff, and the 8,000 British were then to attack the Redan. The 1st Division was again kept in reserve and took no part in the fighting. When the French failed in their attack on the Malakoff, Raglan decided to send in his troops against the Redan in a diversionary attack. That too failed, and the Allies withdrew considerably bruised and demoralised. Their casualties were even heavier than on 8 and 9 June: 1,553 British soldiers killed or wounded, 100 of them officers. The total French losses were 4,604.[14] Once again watching the dead and wounded being attended to under flag of truce, Thesiger must have wondered how he would have comported himself under fire if the 1st Division had been sent in to the attack.

Lord Raglan had been suffering from dysentery and was overworked and downhearted after the terrible repulse at the Redan on 18 June. He took to his bed and died suddenly on 28 June, surrounded by all the members of his personal staff.[15] Raglan was succeeded in his command by the senior surviving officer in the Crimea and his Chief of Staff, Lieutenant-General James Simpson. Reputedly the tallest man in the British Army, Simpson was the scion of landed gentry in the Scottish Borders and had served in the Peninsula and also in the Waterloo campaign when he had been severely wounded at Quatre Bras. His appointment was an unfortunate one, for he himself believed he was unequal to the responsibility, and many in the army before Sebastopol felt that, although a good man and a canny Scot, Simpson was indeed 'deficient in firmness and determination, and utterly destitute of military genius'.[16]

Shortly before Raglan's death, on the very same day as the British repulse at the Redan on 18 June, Thesiger was appointed ADC to the GOC 2nd Division, Major-General Edwin Markham, a Royal Artillery officer who had fought in the battles of the Alma, Little Inkerman and Inkerman.[17] After his previous service in Ireland, Thesiger was of course an experienced staff officer and perfectly up to the job, but since the appointment to a general's personal staff was always a matter of recommendation, Hardinge's support, which we know from his correspondence Thesiger had continued to receive, must have been essential. So too must have been Raglan's easy compliance. Nor could it have gone amiss that Markham had long been a close friend of Thesiger's 41-year-old brother-in law, Brevet Colonel John Inglis, who was then in command of the 32nd Regiment of Foot in India. Clearly, he must have put in a word to Markham about his brother-in-law's staff credentials. As for Thesiger, he evidently stood in some awe of Inglis who, although only thirteen years his senior, was already a seasoned warrior who had seen active service in the Lower Canada Rebellion of 1837, and had served with great distinction in the Second Anglo-Sikh War of 1848–9.[18]

From the moment he joined his staff, Thesiger found Markham 'a charming companion', and was able to report to Jack Inglis with some complacency that he and the General 'hit if off very well'. Thesiger rather ingenuously described himself to his seasoned brother-in-law as 'now bearded like a pard' with 'all the appearance of a bronzed veteran'. (During the Crimean War all ranks were encouraged to grow heavy moustaches and full beards, and whenever on campaign thereafter Thesiger did so. On home service he sometimes shaved off the beard on his somewhat receding chin, retaining the moustache that joined his bushy side-whiskers. He parted his luxuriant, slightly wavy hair almost in the middle and generally wore it quite long, although on campaign he sometimes cropped it short.) As Markham's ADC, Thesiger found life decidedly enjoyable. He crowed to Inglis that Markham and his staff lived 'very well' and had the services of a 'fair cook'. Nor were his duties onerous. Thesiger's daily routine entailed going out in the morning for a two-hour ride with Markham, returning at 2 p.m. to do 'ample justice to a very good breakfast, cheese and port wine' (he was evidently not yet a teetotaller), then riding out again on inspection at 3 p.m., with dinner to follow at 7.30 p.m. As ADC, Thesiger was in a position to take critical stock of Markham's subordinate officers in the 2nd Division, and with the impudence of untried youth wrote off some of his brigadiers as 'sad muffs' (bunglers) who 'ought to be comfortably pensioned off' to make way for 'younger, more active officers'.

Thesiger's condign dismissal of Markham's brigadiers was not out of line, though, with popular opinion among many others in the forces besieging Sebastopol; nor was he alone in suspecting that the Allied commanders had no clear idea of what they were about. But, while the generals apparently dithered, the siege went on. During July and August, the British made slow progress in improving their siege works at the Quarries they had captured in early June. Thesiger reported to Inglis that for men of the 2nd Division duty in the trenches came round every third night and that they were beset by such heavy rains that water in the trenches sometimes came up to their waists.[19] Undeterred, they enlarged the trenches to hold stronger bodies of attacking troops and strengthened and improved the parapets so they would be under cover from enemy fire. The advanced batteries were augmented to lay down a future, heavier bombardment. The Russians attempted to thwart these preparations, and the British working parties, including those in the 2nd Division, suffered casualties from numerous small attacks. Meanwhile, the French siegeworks were successfully approaching the salient points of the Russian defences from the Mamelon captured in June, and a parallel with advanced trenches and numerous approaches was created in front of the Malakoff and Little Redan.[20]

Aware of the growing threat to Sebastopol's defences, on 16 August the Russian army encamped outside the town to the rear of the British siegeworks made a determined and desperate attack to relieve the siege. The British were not involved in the ensuing battle of Chernaya where the French and Sardinians repulsed the Russians with heavy losses: 8,141 Russian casualties against 1,761 for the two allies.[21] Despite their success, the allies feared another Russian attack, and Simpson ordered the construction of more earthworks and batteries to defend his supply base at Balaklava, which had been the Russian objective on 16 August. Meanwhile, the siegeworks continued to edge ever closer to the Russian positions.[22]

In the first week of September the French and British made their plans for a decisive assault. The French were to attack the Malakoff and the Little Redan to the right, and the British the Redan to the left of the Malakoff. On the morning of 5 September, the 83 French and 32 British batteries opened with a tremendous combined roar of 803 pieces of ordnance. The bombardment continued over the next two days until the Malakoff was badly battered and the formidable *abattis* (obstacles of interlaced felled trees) in front of it swept away in places.[23] The Redan was left markedly less damaged.[24]

On the evening of 7 September General Simpson issued his final instructions for the British attack to his generals in a long divisional After-Order. The honour of leading the assault was to fall to the 2nd and Light Divisions.[25] Simpson's arrangements were greeted with dismay by many officers who feared the stipulated attacking columns would not be strong enough for the objective set them, and they were concerned that the two divisions making the attack contained too many raw, untried recruits. Yet the plan Simpson had adopted had been drawn up primarily by Lieutenant-General Sir William Codrington whom Raglan had appointed in June 1855 to the command of the Light Division. Codrington was a very short-sighted officer of notably gentlemanly bearing who was too vain to wear spectacles. He came from a very distinguished naval family, but had served for thirty-three years in the Coldstream Guards, never once in that time experiencing action. Even so, in the Crimea he had fought with notable courage and initiative at both the Alma and Inkerman. His command of the Light Division was his reward, no doubt eased along thanks to his family ties to Lord Raglan.[26] Codrington had been assisted in drawing up his plans for the coming battle by his second-in-command in the operation, Major-General Markham of the 2nd Division. As Markham's ADC, Thesiger would have been in attendance when the plan was discussed, but he would have had no say in its adoption.

The Codrington plan laid down that once the French succeeded in capturing the Malakoff, an assaulting column of 1,000 men of the Rifle Brigade, Thesiger's original regiment (was he secretly relieved that day that he had exchanged out of it?), preceded by a covering party of 200 men of the 3rd Regiment (East Kent – The Buffs) of Foot to pick off the enemy's gunners, and 320 men carrying scaling ladders, followed by an armed working party of 200 men, were to storm the Redan. The rest of the Light and 2nd Divisions were to occupy the advance trenches. The Highland Division was to remain in support in the rear trenches to the right, and the 3rd and 4th Division in the rear trenches to the left. The 1st Division was to stand to arms in front of the British camp.[27]

Saturday 8 September was a dull, grey day. A cold, howling wind whipped up clouds of dust. At about 10.30 a.m. General Simpson and his headquarters staff entered the approach trenches and took up station in the second parallel to watch the attack. An eyewitness decided that their appearance was 'neither picturesque nor romantic and did not add to their martial and belligerent aspect'. Lieutenant-General Sir Harry Jones, who commanded the Royal Engineers, was still suffering from wounds received on 18 June, but he was so anxious to be present that, wearing his red night-cap, he was carried down to the trenches on a stretcher. Sir Richard Airey, the QMG, had a white pocket-handkerchief tied over his cap and ears to protect him from the biting wind, while General Simpson sat in the trench with his cloak drawn over his head to protect himself against the cold and dust.

At 11.00 a.m. Codrington, Markham and their staffs took their places in the trenches directly in front of the Redan.[28] From this position Thesiger had a clear view of 'the last and final affair with John Bonsky' (as the Russians were facetiously known). As he later admitted to Jack Inglis, he was understandably dismayed that Codrington irresponsibly 'took it into his head' to go down to the 2nd Division's most advanced parallel with only one ADC. There the commander remained throughout the entire battle with nobody among the staff to his rear 'knowing what on earth had become of him'. The absence of his superior officer put Markham in a 'very awkward position' because he was reluctant to issue any orders of his own for fear the missing Codrington might have commanded something different.

The attacking French troops overran the Little Redan but were then driven out. However, at about 12.10 p.m. the French stormed the Malakoff and raised a flag on the Mamelon to signal their success to Simpson. In response, he ordered a flight of four rockets to catch the attention of his generals and hoisted a square white flag with the red cross of St George as the signal to advance. The designated assaulting column made up of men from the Light and 2nd Divisions at once rushed out of the advance trenches against the salient of the Redan facing them. That required them to advance over 280 yards in the open under the direct flanking fire of twenty Russian guns that had not been silenced in the bombardment of the previous three days. Suffering many casualties from canister and grape, they nevertheless gallantly got over the ditch, up the parapet and into the Redan. The Russians retreated behind their low traverses and breastworks across the triangular Redan's open gorge. There they were strongly reinforced. From this position the Russians poured a galling fire into the salient angle of the Redan where the attacking British were crowded. Colonel Charles Windham, who commanded the men of the 2nd Division in the assaulting column, formed them up with the intention of taking the parapets held by the Russians at the point of the bayonet. But so many officers had been killed or disabled that it was impossible to get enough men together to make a charge. Caught in the salient and suffering heavy casualties, Windham sent three officers in turn to ask Codrington to send up reinforcements, but not one of them got through to the general. At last, Windham himself made it back to Codrington in his forward position. But it was too late. Before the elusive general could ready the requested reinforcements to attack, the men in the Redan were finally driven out in great disarray by a Russian bayonet charge supported by grapeshot.

The unsuccessful fight for the Redan had gone on for over an hour and Simpson decided that it was impossible to renew the assault that day. Not only were the approaches and parallels so crowded with disorganised troops and clogged by the wounded being carried to the rear that the reserves had nowhere to form up, but the uncommitted divisions being held in reserve proved reluctant to come forward because of the cross-fire from the undamaged Russian batteries. Simpson made up his mind to renew the attack the following morning with the Highland Division, but fortunately for the British further sacrifice proved unnecessary. The French hung on to the Malakoff, fighting off repeated Russian attempts to recapture it. With the key to their defences lost, the Russians decided their situation had been rendered hopeless. That night they set about blowing up their magazines and the formidable fort dominating the harbour. Thesiger was woken up in the early hours by the noise and went up a nearby hill to watch the conflagration. He found the sight 'very fine and at the same time very satisfactory'. When dawn broke, the Allies discovered that the Russians had evacuated the town, which had been reduced to rubble by the bombardment, over a precarious pontoon bridge thrown up across the sea harbour to the north shore. Sebastopol continued to burn all through the day and night of 9 September.[29] After breakfast on the morning following the battle, Thesiger rode down with Markham to investigate the field of slaughter in and around the Redan. There they discovered grisly 'heaps of dead'.

Indeed, the Allied victory had been secured at great cost. The carnage on 8 September had been as great as that at the murderous battle of Inkerman. In the day's fighting a total of 21,837 men from both sides had been killed or wounded, or were missing. The British alone lost 390 men killed, 2,043 wounded and 177 missing, with the officer casualties among these amounting to 29 killed, 129 wounded and 1 missing. Thesiger must have been dismayed by the heavy toll, and would little have dreamt that in time to come, at Isandlwana, an even greater disaster would befall the troops under his command.

Although the Russians had abandoned Sebastopol itself, their main army remained strongly posted north of the harbour and to the east of the

Allied encampments, and the Allied commanders could not agree on what concerted action to adopt to drive the Russian forces out of the Crimea. Back in Britain, General Simpson was excoriated for his costly failure at the Redan, and on 22 October the government decided he must be relieved of his command. To save his dignity, Simpson was allowed to resign on grounds of ill-health. But who was to succeed him? The promotion of general officers was normally by seniority, although exception could be made for distinguished service on the recommendation of the CinC.[30] To the surprise of the army in the Crimea, and to the dissatisfaction of many in the field who questioned his part in the failure to capture the Redan, Lord Hardinge appointed Sir William Codrington to take up the command. It was supposed that Simpson had recommended him as the best and most active of the younger general officers in the field, but it was also believed that Codrington's family ties to Raglan and Hardinge's personal favour played a large part. In preparation for his elevation, Codrington was promoted Local General on 29 October, and Simpson handed his command over to him on 11 November.[31]

Thesiger, who would have been well known to Codrington as Markham's ADC, and who still enjoyed Hardinge's patronage, rose with the new commander. On 29 September 1855 he ceased to be Markham's ADC and on 2 November 1855 he was promoted brevet major. A brevet (for which captains and above were eligible) rewarded an officer for distinguished service in the field or for staff work, and conferred on him an Army rank superior to his regimental rank. Confusingly, that meant that while he performed the duties of his lower rank when with his regiment, his duties outside the regiment were at a level commensurate with his higher Army rank. Thus, Thesiger's promotion meant that while he remained a company officer in the Grenadiers, he was now a field officer in the army. Thesiger's promotion also cleared the way to his appointment on 8 November 1855 to the Headquarters Staff, Crimea, which Codrington was assembling under his designated Chief of Staff, the recently promoted Major-General Windham who had won such distinction in the unsuccessful assault on the Redan. Thesiger took up the duties of Deputy Assistant Quartermaster-General (DAQMG) under the command of Lieutenant-General Airey in the QMG's Department which was responsible for the movement and quartering of troops, camps, military positions, reconnaissances, embarkations and so on.[32]

Thesiger relished his highly desirable posting as a member of the HQ Staff until 24 June 1856 and the evacuation of the Crimea. During that time, he was at the army's nerve-centre while the war in the Crimea slowly wound down. Supplies and accommodation improved, the soldiers were kept busy with amusements such as theatre, billiards, hunting and horse racing, and boatloads of tourists arrived to see the famous battle sites and collect grisly souvenirs. Thesiger would have witnessed the widespread drunkenness, insubordination and indiscipline that became a major problem in the British camp after the fall of Sebastopol – between October 1855 and March 1856, 4,000 British troops were court-martialled for drunkenness.[33] One must surmise that this disgraceful behaviour played its part in convincing Thesiger to become a teetotaller. On 29 February 1856 an armistice was agreed, followed by the Peace of Paris on 30 March 1856 and its ratification on 27 April. By the treaty, Russia's expansionism was dealt a temporary blow with the neutralisation of the Black Sea. Yet it was widely held that such a paltry outcome hardly justified Britain's butcher's bill of 19,578 men lost in battle or to disease, of whom 264 were officers. Disease had proved far deadlier than combat. A staggering 81 per cent of the dead rank and file had succumbed to the ravages of disease as opposed to only 21 per cent of the stricken officers.[34] Such statistics might indicate that officers, who were expected to lead gallantly from the front, were proportionately more likely to die in battle than the men they commanded; or, on the other hand, that their superior living conditions and better access to medical care made them less susceptible to disease. Either way, the Army's experience in the Crimea exposed its manifold administrative weaknesses and would accelerate reform.

As far as Thesiger was concerned, however, the Crimean War had been an entirely positive experience. He had finally seen active service, albeit in an entirely conventional war waged between great European armies that had seen great field battles and a prolonged, classic siege. Neither (although he was not to know it) would have any bearing on his future exclusive involvement in colonial warfare. He had been promoted to brevet major, had served on the HQ Staff and had been mentioned in despatches. He was now also a decorated veteran having been awarded the British Crimea Medal with its pale blue ribbon with yellow edges and its ornate clasp for Sebastopol, as well as the fifth (and lowest) class of the Ottoman Order of the Medjidie. Alongside these, he also received the

Turkish Crimea Medal with its dark crimson ribbon with green edges, and the Sardinian Crimea Medal with its blue watered ribbon, bestowed on him by virtue of his position on the HQ Staff.[35] Yet, now that he was to resume his peacetime soldiering in London with the Grenadiers, it would remain to be seen whether his career, like that of many another officer, would stagnate, or whether he could find the means to advance it yet further.

CHAPTER 6

Exchanging into the 95th Regiment, 1856–1858

STATIONED BACK IN LONDON IN 1856 with the Grenadiers, Thesiger had no option but to resume the overly expensive lifestyle of a Guards officer and continued to drain his father's resources. Further career steps in the Grenadiers could only be obtained through purchase, straining the family purse to breaking. Thesiger knew perfectly well from his experiences in the Crimea that distinguished service in action was the surest way to accelerated promotion, but there was no current prospect of the Guards being deployed abroad. However, far away in India a desperate and vicious war was being fought that offered an ambitious officer many opportunities.

The East India Company was a joint-stock company founded in 1600 that by the mid-eighteenth century ruled great swathes of the Indian sub-continent. Pitt's India Act of 1784 had created the India Board to regulate the Company's governance in India under the sovereignty of the Crown, but the Company not only continued to perform all the administrative functions in its Indian territories, but to exercise military power too. For administrative purposes, its territories were divided into the Bengal, Madras and Bombay Presidencies, each with its own army made up of Indian troops (sepoys) commanded exclusively by cadres of British officers, along with European regiments of the Company's armies whose officers and men enlisted for a lifetime's local service. Regiments of the British Army were also stationed in India to support the Company in its wars against still-independent neighbouring Indian states. In 1857 the great bulk of the 36,000 white soldiers were concentrated in the recently conquered Punjab and along the turbulent North-West Frontier. Just over half the Company's 257,000 sepoys were stationed in the Bengal Presidency. And it was there, on 10 May 1857, that they first mutinied in the military cantonment at Meerut and marched on Delhi, the erstwhile capital of the pensioned-off Mughal emperors.[1]

The ensuing conflict that shook British rule in India to its foundations became known to the British at the time as the Indian Mutiny, but it was more than simply that. Undeniably a mutiny by the Company's mercenary troops in the Bengal Presidency against their foreign masters, the revolt drew its strength from widespread disaffection among the civilian population with the Company's increasingly Westernising and Christian evangelising rule, a visceral rejection that combined economic protest by peasants and merchants, religious revival by both Hindus and Muslims, and political opportunism by aristocrats and rulers who had been humiliated or dispossessed. Revolt consequently spread most quickly in those areas where Company rule was in its most recent and most disruptive phase, and clustered around Delhi, Cawnpore (Kanpur) and Lucknow, the formers capitals of recently dethroned dynasties in the Gangetic plain of north-eastern India.

Militarily, the rebels, who been trained to fight exactly like their British counterparts, displayed great determination and skill. It was to their disadvantage, though, that the new Enfield Rifle Muskets with their greater range and accuracy had been distributed less widely among the sepoy regiments than among the British. Moreover, lacking both overarching leadership and a shared vision of the objectives they hoped to attain, they possessed no effective strategic plan and failed to break out of the heavily populated lands lying between the Jumna and Ganges Rivers to raise revolt in other regions. The British, for their part, after their initial shock and disarray, set about ensuring their control over those sepoy armies (primarily in the Madras and Bombay Presidencies) that had not mutinied, and reasserting their authority in those districts where it had been overthrown. At first, they were very much on the defensive on account of their initial shortage of troops in the regions that had revolted. Yet they held the advantage because, while the rebels failed to expand their numbers, they were able to grow their manpower more effectively from elsewhere in the Empire. The continuing loyalty of almost all of the Madras and Bombay sepoys meant that British and Company regiments could be redeployed to the region of revolt. Having secured the loyalty of the Punjab through political accommodation, the regiments stationed there could march south to help crush the uprising, assisted by newly raised units of Sikhs and Gurkhas from the Punjab and Nepal. Furthermore, British regiments already in transit to various garrisons around the globe could be diverted to India. Within a few months the British had greatly built up their forces with fresh troops, along with the artillery necessary to dislodge the rebels from their fortified strongholds. The recapture of Delhi in September 1857 was the turning point of the rebellion, and the fighting thereafter concentrated on reducing the remaining rebel fortresses and dispersing their last armies in the field. By November 1858 the fighting was all but over except for desultory skirmishes in Central India. During its course, almost all the participants had exhibited almost unbelievable savagery and destructiveness. Orgies of violence by the mutineers were more than matched by British demands for pitiless retribution, and in many ways the Indian Mutiny presented all the manifestations of an unforgiving race war.

Besides Thesiger's desire to see action in the field and so further his career, it seems other, more personal considerations were spurring him on to serve in India. His handsome brother-in-law Jack Inglis was the regimental lieutenant-colonel of the 32nd Regiment that was stationed at Lucknow in the former kingdom of Oudh (Awadh) which the Company had annexed in 1856. On 30 May 1857 the sepoys in Lucknow mutinied and on 1 June the British garrison and civilians withdrew to the fortified residency. The following day Sir Henry Lawrence, the Commissioner of Oudh, died of his wounds, and Inglis took charge of the besieged residency. He valiantly defended it for the next eighty-seven days until reinforced on 25 September by Lieutenant-General James Outram to whom he ceded command. The augmented Lucknow garrison was finally relieved on 17 November by Sir Colin Campbell and withdrawn, along with the women and children who had taken refuge in the residency. Thesiger's feisty sister Julia had been with her husband throughout the siege, along with their three small sons, and had comported herself with considerable aplomb.[2] The defence of the residency at Lucknow was seized upon by the British public as one of the very greatest epics of the Victorian era (the defence of Rorke's Drift would be another), and Inglis was hailed as a hero. He was promoted major-general on 26 September 1857 and made KCB for his fortitude and gallantry during the siege.[3] It must be supposed that while greatly admiring Jack and Julia Inglis's courage, Thesiger may well personally have felt somewhat diminished as a soldier by comparison with his brother-in-law, and doubtless desired to measure up to him by proving his own mettle in the field.

There was undoubtedly another reason, too, for Thesiger desiring to serve with a line regiment in India. Life as a Guards officer in London was (as we have seen) exceedingly expensive, one that he (or his father) was finding it more than the family purse could bear. Generous pay and allowances were to be gained by service in India, where the cost of living was lower than in Britain, and officers such as Thesiger from marginally wealthy families habitually sought service there because they could better support the standard of living expected of their high status in British India's rigidly hierarchical society. In sum, India offered Thesiger the opportunity for promotion, profit and adventure,[4] but, as an officer in the Guards, firmly stationed in Britain, how was he to get there?

Thesiger managed to arrange it through his understanding of how the system worked, and through his many military, political and social connections in the metropolis. He began his campaign on 28 August 1857 with a purchased promotion to captain and lieutenant-colonel in the Grenadier Guards, probably at well above the regulated difference of price of £2,750 between his existing and new commission. That outlay was enormous, and Thesiger's father, who was footing the bill, could hardly be expected to purchase the next step up to major in the Guards, when that opportunity became available, for a further difference in price of £3,500. But he would not be called upon to do so, for his son's newly purchased rank was sufficient for the next step in his plan. As a Foot Guards captain, Thesiger was now technically placed to exchange into a less prestigious line regiment at his higher Army rank of lieutenant-colonel, although to do so was most unusual and against Army tradition – besides being a socially retrograde step. Neither did it go unnoticed that Thesiger had been propelled up the steps of promotion with unseemly rapidity, it having taken the thirty-year-old lieutenant-colonel thirteen years to purchase his ascent to that rank instead of the 23½ qualifying years normally required.[5]

In securing his uncommon exchange into a line regiment, Thesiger was able to bring his illustrious connections into play. On 25 February 1858 Sir Frederick Thesiger was appointed Lord Chancellor in Lord Derby's second Cabinet, and was created Baron Chelmsford on 1 March 1858. On 30 April 1858 the Hon. Frederic Thesiger (as he was now styled thanks to his father's elevation to the peerage) exchanged as its junior – effectively supernumerary – lieutenant-colonel into the 95th (Derbyshire) Regiment of Foot, then serving in the Central India campaign. Lieutenant-Colonel Henry Hume, in command of the 95th Foot, had fallen ill in December 1857 at the beginning of the campaign and returned home to England. He was more than pleased to secure his comfortable and socially elevated exchange into the Grenadier Guards, relinquishing actual command of the 95th to Lieutenant-Colonel Julius Raines who exercised it until November 1871. Thesiger, prior to his subsequent staff appointments and promotions, would serve as Raines's second-in-command.[6] As General Sir Garnet Wolseley, who in 1879 had come to hold Thesiger in the greatest contempt, whined jealously in his diary:

> I often think, if I had had for my father a Lord Chancellor, as Chelmsford had, instead of being a poor Major in a marching Regiment, what could now have been my position! How many times in my life might not the authorities have pushed me on . . . if my father instead of being a poor gentleman had been some rich upstart, some snob with a parliamentary interest.[7]

And certainly, as a Cabinet minister, the new Lord Chelmsford wielded considerable influence. He was perfectly placed to promote his son's prospects at the Horse Guards where his 'high interest' secured Thesiger's exchange from the Grenadiers into the 95th despite 'a great outcry and much heartburning.' Indeed, the whole shady business, which it seems was never again permitted, was widely deprecated as bearing 'a striking similitude to a job',[8] where jobbery is understood to mean using public office for personal advantage.

Thesiger's contentious exchange into the 95th Regiment as a surplus lieutenant-colonel would have been handled by the MS to the general commanding-in-chief who (as we have seen) was the channel of correspondence in all matters connected to promotions and exchanges. In April 1858 that figure was Major-General Sir Charles Yorke, a veteran of the Peninsular War and of the Eighth Cape Frontier War. As Lord Hardinge's MS since May 1854, he had not served in the Crimea.[9] Hardinge himself had come under much public criticism for the Army's shortcomings in the Crimea. It had proved too much for the ageing CinC, and on 8 July 1856 he suffered a paralytic stroke to which he succumbed on 24 September.[10]

Yorke had continued to serve as MS to his successor, the second Duke of Cambridge, who took up his post on 15 July 1856.

As CinC throughout the remainder of Thesiger's active career, and as his stalwart patron until Thesiger's disastrous handling of the Zulu campaign obliged him to step away, it is essential to understand where Cambridge stood in relation to the army.

HRH Prince George was the only son of the first Duke of Cambridge, the youngest son of King George III, and succeeded to the title on 8 July 1850. The new duke had been given a thorough military upbringing and held various posts in England and Ireland before being chosen in February 1854 to command the 1st Division in the Crimea. His peace-time soldiering had hardly prepared him, however, for the ferocity and intensity of the battle of the Alma on 20 September 1854 where the 1st Division was engaged; nor had he any experience of field command. His troops were ultimately victorious at the Alma, but under his uncertain leadership their advance had been a hesitant, stop-go affair. Undoubtedly personally brave and popular with the troops, Cambridge was increasingly afflicted by nervous exhaustion brought on by the overwhelming weight of his duties and by his acute dismay at the slaughter of his division in the close-fought battle of Inkerman. Three weeks later, on 25 November 1854, he quit the Crimea. Back home, he recovered his spirits sufficiently to agree to succeed Hardinge as general commanding-in-chief. Promoted general on 28 July 1856, the Queen made him field marshal on 9 November 1862. As a prince of the blood and commander of the Army, over the coming years Cambridge inevitably accumulated a plethora of orders, colonelcies and other honours.[11]

Yet, despite his high titles and honours, Cambridge's position as the general (later field marshal) commanding-in-chief was an ambiguous one. As she was fully aware, his cousin Queen Victoria was *de jure* the commander-in-chief of the Army, while he was the officer commanding-in-chief: a subtle distinction in degree (although Cambridge was usually, if incorrectly, referred to as the CinC). The Queen appeared regularly at military reviews and parades, took a keen, informed interest in military affairs (including promotions), and throughout her life insisted that her soldiers and politicians uphold Britain's military reputation. When she appointed Cambridge CinC in 1856, she took the view that it was her prerogative as sovereign to do so, and that in his office as her representative he would not be subordinate to the Secretary of State for War, and hence to parliamentary oversight. Yet, the situation was not so simple. The unclear relationship between the CinC and the Secretary of State was first defined by Royal Warrant in 1861, yet that still left it ambiguous because it implied that the CinC enjoyed supreme military authority despite being subordinated to the Secretary of State. This meant that in practice military administration was split between Cambridge's headquarters in the Horse Guards – where he was responsible for command, discipline, appointments, and promotions – and the War Department, where the Secretary of State for War of the day exercised overall responsibility for the efficiency and civil administration of the Army. This was the situation when the Horse Guards permitted Thesiger to make his contentious exchange into the 95th Regiment.[12] As we shall see, the powers of the CinC would be modified in future years, but throughout Thesiger's active career he would continue to depend for advancement on the goodwill and support of the Horse Guards. And, the higher he went up the ladder of promotion, the more he depended directly on the good opinion of Cambridge himself, and on his personal support. Happily for him, he found Cambridge a sympathetic and supportive superior – so long, that is, as he did not let him and the service down, as he would do in 1879.

Personally, Cambridge was an endlessly industrious, intelligent, good-tempered, charming man.[13] He was also an emotional one, notably devoted to his widowed mother and his children, though often unfaithful to his wife. True to his obligations as a prince, he diligently shouldered a wide range of royal duties, and with his hearty, forthright manner became much in demand as a public speaker. Indeed, with his penchant for field sports and good living (he became increasingly overweight as he grew older), he was appreciated as the embodiment of the bluff, hearty English gentleman, a veritable John Bull. Yet he also had artistic and musical interests and founded the School of Military Music in 1857.

As CinC, Cambridge gained the reputation in many progressive circles of being an arch-conservative thanks to the efforts of a ring of reformist officers who were energetic and effective publicists and resented the duke's perceived obstruction of the organisational changes they were advocating.[14] Yet, this negative image nurtured by his critics contained only a certain degree of truth. In his early years as CinC, Cambridge was the proponent of many improvements in the Army. He pressed the case for annual military manoeuvres, favoured more thorough military training, supported the creation of a Department of Military Education, and helped found the Staff College in 1858. What he opposed were reforms made from what he considered political expediency, rather than from military necessity, and he believed that when change did become advisable that it should be effected with prudence and consideration. Naturally, such caution could always be written off as conservative stalling, but (as we shall see) it was not always misplaced, and Cambridge saw it as his bounden duty to preserve the customs and traditions of the Army to which he had devoted his life. The Army as a whole appreciated this standpoint – it was, as we have seen, an inherently conservative organisation – and applauded his determined opposition to the perennial reductions in military expenditure required by the politicians, as well as his unrelenting advocacy for increases in the size of the Army. He also won the soldiers' affectionate regard for making it his business to take a personal, hands-on interest in their welfare.

Even his antagonists had to concede that Cambridge, who had a singularly retentive memory, possessed a phenomenal mastery of the whole complex machinery of military affairs. He maintained an immense correspondence in his own execrable handwriting or through his secretaries with generals all over the globe, and had an extraordinarily detailed knowledge of the careers and capabilities of all his senior officers. Indeed, as Thesiger was perfectly aware, his and every other officer's career depended on Cambridge's approval. As Lord Redesdale, a senior civil servant and diplomat, would write of Cambridge, 'During the whole time of his tenure of office no promotion to any rank above that of captain was made without his personal investigation and sanction.'[15] It was with the Duke's approval and support, therefore, that the newly appointed lieutenant-colonel of the 95th Regiment prepared to sail to India to join it in its operations against the rebels.

CHAPTER 7

The Indian Mutiny: Central India Campaign, 1858–1859

THE 95TH (DERBYSHIRE) REGIMENT with its yellow facing colours, into which Thesiger had so controversially exchanged in April 1858 thanks to Cambridge's compliance, was a county regiment raised in 1823. It had been reassigned the number 95 previously held by the regiment that was taken out of the line in 1816 and re-formed (as we have seen) as the Rifle Brigade. Before Thesiger joined it in India, the 95th had served in Malta, the Ionian Islands, Ceylon and Hong Kong before embarking for home in March 1850. It took ship in March 1854 for the Crimean War where it served throughout the campaign as part of the 2nd Division, and it is inevitable that Thesiger, while serving on General Markham's staff, would have become acquainted with many of its officers. The regiment returned to Britain from the Crimea in June 1856. A year later, in June 1857, this seasoned fighting regiment, with a reputation for hard-bitten toughness, embarked for service in the Cape Colony. But the outbreak of the Indian Mutiny disrupted this posting, and the 95th was one of those regiments in relative proximity to India that were redeployed to reinforce the troops engaged there.

No sooner had the 95th arrived at the Cape than it received its orders to proceed immediately to Bombay (Mumbai). The men greeted the news with excited cheers, but they had little idea of what awaited them in India. Within days of landing in Bombay, they formed part of the parade on 13 October 1857 that witnessed the sickening execution of two mutinous sepoys blown from the muzzles of guns to which they had been lashed. In November 1857 the regiment joined the Central Indian Field Force. It remained there in the field until April 1859, during which time it would march nearly 3,000 miles and fight in fourteen engagements. In all, it lost

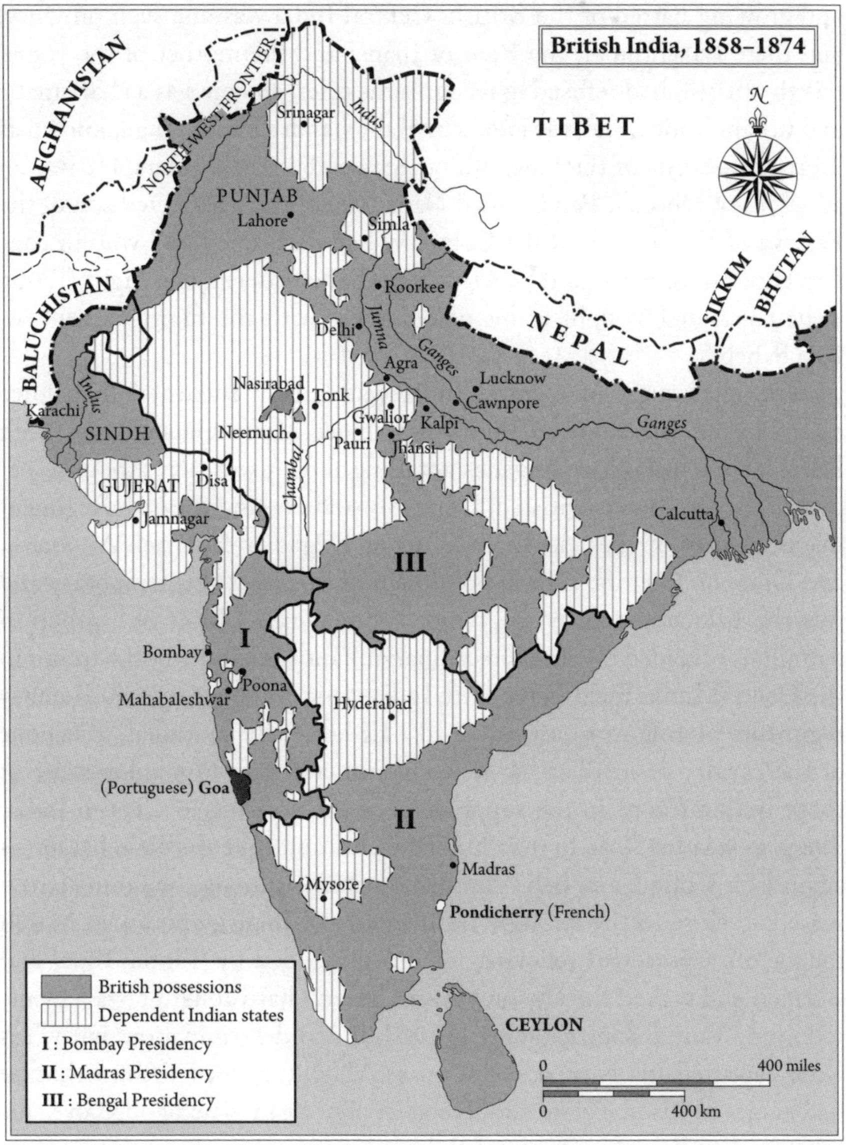

sixty-seven dead and wounded during the course of the campaign, but the conditions were brutal, and on one occasion eighty-nine officers and men were felled by heat-stroke in a single day.[1]

The Indian revolt had spread most quickly in those regions where the traditional elites were being thrust aside by the Company's encroaching rule, and where the political transition was accompanied by social upheaval and growing hatred of the British. Central India was one such province, and there Lakshmibai, the Rani of Jhansi and the mother of the young raja the British had refused to recognise as ruler, emerged as a charismatic and valiant leader. She was joined by Ramchandra Panduranga, known as Tantia Tope, one of the most militarily talented rebel leaders. He was an adherent of Dhondu Pand, called Nana Saheb, the disaffected son of the Peshwa of Bithur, whom the Company had dethroned and who in consequence had rebelled in 1857. After Nana Saheb's defeat and flight, Tantia Tope continued to fight in his name, along with the fugitive's nephew, Rao Saheb.[2]

The reconquest of Central India was largely entrusted to a force assembled in the Bombay Presidency under Major-General Sir Hugh Rose. It consisted of two brigades, totalling about 5,500 men. About 40 per cent of the force were British or Company soldiers, and the 95th Regiment made up part of the 2nd Brigade under Brigadier Michael W. Smith, 2nd Dragoon Guards. (The appointment of brigadier was temporary and was the title assumed by the senior commanding officer of a group of battalions brigaded together on campaign.) The remainder of the troops in the Central India Field Force were Indian, for of the thirty-two Bombay regiments of Infantry only two had half-heartedly mutinied, and none of the cavalry or artillery, so it was considered safe to employ some of these Indian troops in the suppression of the uprising in Central India. The plan was for Rose to march northwards and squeeze the rebel forces against Sir Colin Campbell's command operating along the Jumna River. Rose laid siege to the strongly fortified city of Jhansi, and on 30 March fought off a powerful relieving force commanded by Tantia Tope, and stormed and sacked the city on 3 April. Several hard-fought engagements followed, Tantia Tope showing great skill and determination, but when Rose captured his base at Kalpi on 23 May, it seemed to him that he had achieved his objective and, being in poor health, he handed over his command to Brigadier General Robert Napier. (Brigadier general was a rank, based on a royal commission temporarily promoting an officer for a specific duty.)

However, in a daring and unexpected move, Tantia Tope and the Rani of Jhansi doubled back southwards and seized Gwalior, the most formidable fortress in India and the stronghold of Jayaji Rao Sindhia, the Maharaja of Gwalior, who was a loyal ally of the British. Rose immediately reassumed his command and marched on Gwalior. In the battle of Kotah-ki-serai on 17 June he defeated the rebels and the Rani of Jhansi died in the fighting. Gwalior itself and its enormous fortress were both taken by 20 June. Under Napier's inspired command Tantia Tope's fleeing forces were attacked and dispersed on 22 June at Jaora Alipur. The men of the 95th Regiment distinguished themselves in all these actions, the last major ones of the Mutiny. Rose, his task apparently done, handed his command back to Napier on 29 June and left him to snuff out the last embers of revolt.[3]

In the event, for eight months more Tantia Tope's small but disciplined and lightly equipped army, along with the forces of several other rebel commanders, continued to elude the British columns sent out to pursue and disperse them. Strong in cavalry, these last rebel forces moved at great speed, helped by villagers who refused to betray them to their pursuers. Occasionally they stood their ground for a time before disappearing into the jungle, leading their pursuers ever on. Smith's 2nd Brigade, including the 95th, were engaged in many long, exhausting marches in pursuit of rebels who doubled back and forth through the jungles on either side of the Grand Trunk Road south of Gwalior. Smith's men remained close on their heels, sometimes reaching the enemy's camping grounds only to find them hurriedly vacated with the fires still smouldering, and sometimes engaging them in indecisive, minor skirmishes.[4]

It was while the 2nd Brigade were playing at cat-and-mouse with the remaining rebel forces operating in Central India that, in the first week of November 1858, Thesiger at last joined the 95th in the field. It was just over six months since his exchange into the 95th had been gazetted, and he had apparently taken his time reaching Central India. It would seem, therefore, that he did not travel privately via the so-called 'land route' to Bombay. That entailed sailing from Britain to Alexandria in Egypt, then going up the Nile to Cairo, next being driven across the desert in a horse-drawn van to Suez at the head of the Red Sea, and finally taking one of the paddle-steamers first introduced in 1830 to Bombay – a journey that usually lasted two months. The alternative route to India by sea around the Cape was of longer duration, a voyage that in 1857 had taken the better-built of the two ships carrying the 95th Regiment three months to accomplish, and the other four months. It would seem (taking into account when he finally reached India) that Thesiger must have gone by the slower route, most likely accompanying drafts for the 95th sailing in a troopship.[5]

When he finally caught up with his regiment in Central India, Thesiger would have found them presenting a very motley appearance, quite unlike the polished Guards on parade in London. They were dressed for comfort and convenience during the crushing heat of the summer months in white drill shell jackets and trousers, and went more often than not in their shirt-sleeves. Most were in forage caps with white cloth covers and a long flap protecting the back of the neck, while some favoured civilian sun helmets with a puggaree wound around them. These garments were often stained khaki (after *khakh* meaning dust in Hindustani), but since dyes were neither consistent nor fast, their dull colours ranged through washed-out shades of brown and grey.[6] For their part, when they were confronted by their spic-and-span new lieutenant-colonel, it could not have been easy for the campaign-hardened and battle-scarred men of the 95th to accept this privileged ex-Guards officer and son of the Lord Chancellor. Yet Thesiger does seem to have possessed soldierly and personal qualities calculated to endear him to both officers and men. Critically, it is reported that 'any feelings of resentment which his unusual and swift promotion my have engendered' were quickly buried.[7]

No sooner had Thesiger joined his regiment, than on the evening of 12 November Brigadier Smith received intelligence that a force of about 3,000 rebels had reached the small fort of Gurpiarah. This force was made up of men of the Gwalior Contingent who had deserted their Maharaja, Bengal sepoys who had worked their way south, and the personal adherents of Raja Man Singh, who was in command. Man Singh, the Raja of Narwar, was a feudatory of Maharaja Sindhia of Gwalior who had rebelled against his overlord on 2 August 1858 and seized the important fortress of Pauri, eighty miles south-west of Gwalior. It was typical of the complexity of the Indian Mutiny that this was not a rebellion against the British as such, but a local issue. Pauri had once been part of Man Singh's ancestral possessions, and he was taking advantage of Sindhia's temporary weakness to regain his patrimony. The British understood that, but Sindhia was their ally and they were determined to secure their hold on Gwalior. Man Singh, however, refused to give up Pauri, and Smith's brigade was despatched to dislodge him. Smith found that Man Singh, seconded by his uncle Ajit Singh, was too strongly ensconced in the fortress for it to be stormed without reinforcements. He therefore waited for Brigadier General Napier to come up, and the bombardment of Pauri commenced on 20 August. On the night of 23/24 August Man Singh and Ajit Singh slipped away, an action typical of Indian commanders who saw the advantage of living to fight another day. Napier successfully stormed Pauri on 24 August, and a light column caught up with Man Singh on 4 September and scattered his forces at the Parvati River. However, Man Singh and his uncle escaped once more to rebuild their following and defy the British.[8] Brigadier Smith was consequently delighted to learn on 12 November of their proximity and the opportunity it offered him to deal with the troublesome Man Singh once and for all.

At 4.30 a.m. on 13 November Smith left camp and marched to the fort at Gurpairah where the rebels were reported to be encamped, but found it plundered and deserted. A cloud of dust in the distance showed the enemy to be on the wing.[9] In the early afternoon Smith learned that Man Singh's force had moved on to the village of Uttekairah. Smith led his brigade in pursuit through thick jungle and across a river with precipitous banks. At 7 p.m. he bivouacked for the night three miles short of Uttekairah. His men desperately needed rest after being nearly seventeen hours on the march during which only one man of the 95th had fallen out, and he had been but lately discharged from hospital. How well Thesiger fared during this marathon is not recorded, but that he kept up is evident. To keep his approach secret from the enemy, Smith allowed no camp fires to be lit. It was consequently not possible to cook the men's food but, despite having precious little to eat, they remained cheerful knowing their quarry was close to being run down. During the night Smith learned from spies sent forward by his indefatigable and zealous AQMG, Captain W. S. Bolton of the 2nd Bombay Grenadiers, that Man Singh had left Uttekairah and had doubled back to the village of Koondrye. There his men had made camp and were sleeping, unconscious of the proximity of their pursuers. Smith would generously attribute his success in tracking down and surprising Man Singh to Captain Bolton's efforts, especially since locals were reluctant to give intelligence of the rebels' movements. Indeed, as Smith's superior officers would subsequently note with approval, 'The surprise appears to have been very well managed.'[10]

Smith allowed his troops to sleep until 2.30 a.m. on 14 November when they fell in as silently as they could without sound of infantry bugle or cavalry trumpet. At 3.30 a.m. they marched off for Koondrye, the only sound they made being caused by an occasional striking of a scabbard against a stirrup or spur. After marching for about an hour and a half, Smith's force came in sight of Koondrye and Man Singh's camp fires just as dawn was breaking. Smith halted his column with his men concealed from the foe in fields of head-high crops and prepared to attack. His arrangements were entirely conventional. The experiences of the Crimean War had not formed a watershed in tactical methods, and the 1857 infantry manual continued to advocate the use of column and line, protected by a screen of skirmishers, with volley- or file-firing being advocated for all except skirmishers who were advised to use cover and fire kneeling or prone. Indeed, despite the enhanced powers of the soldiers' Enfield Rifle Muskets, most of the tactics employed in the Indian Mutiny were still virtually 'Peninsular' style.[11]

Smith's force had been marching in column with the baggage in the rear, and he now formed it up for battle as follows. He placed the 95th under Lieutenant-Colonel Raines in column of sections to the right with a company a hundred yards distant protecting their right flank. To the left rear of the 95th he positioned the 10th Regiment, Bombay Native Infantry (BNI), under Captain Pelly in quarter-distance columns. This disposition left the road between the two regiments clear for the six guns and 90 men of the 3rd Troop, Bombay Horse Artillery, under Lieutenant-Colonel Blake to advance since the broken ground on either side of the track was unsuited for their passage. The 1st Bombay Lancers (42 men under Lieutenant-Colonel Curtis) had orders to form in rear of the right flank of the 95th; and the cumbrously titled 8th (The King's Royal Irish) Regiment of (Light) Dragoons (Hussars) (85 sabres under Colonel Rodolph de Salis) were similarly placed in rear of the left flank of the 10th Native Infantry.[12] The military reports of the engagement do not spell it out, but such a disposition ensured that on either flank of the artillery in the centre, units of Indian troops were expected to operate alongside British soldiers and were consequently more likely to remain steady. Finally, Smith placed Thesiger in overall command of the brigade's two infantry regiments – his very first field command of any sort – and summoned the artillery to advance up the road. Some soldiers were detached to the rear as a baggage guard.

In his orthodox opening move, Smith sent forward an advance guard of one company of the 95th and two of the 10th BNI, all three in skirmishing order under Major Vialls of the 95th. They went forward through fields of crops six feet high and commenced firing. When the skirmishers were within a hundred yards of the enemy camp, Raines detached a second company of the 95th from the rear to assist. The remaining companies of infantry began to deploy out of column into line when they came into view of Koondrye and the ground opened up. The artillery galloped up to the front by the road, and when within 300 yards of the enemy camp rapidly formed line, unlimbered their guns and came into action between the two regiments of infantry. The rebels had awoken startled and bemused by the unexpected attack and had collected into large, disorderly masses. The artillery first fired some roundshot into the confused crowd, followed by shrapnel to deadly effect. Meanwhile, the 1st Bombay Lancers had advanced in column of troops and formed up in line on the right flank of the infantry while the 8th Hussars did likewise in front of the left of the line.

Taken successfully by surprise, the rebels offered scant resistance. They fled, leaving behind not only their tents, bedding and cooking vessels, their clothing and camels, but even some children and pet dogs. Food, arms, and burning embers strewed the ground along with discarded pieces of sepoy equipment. The right division of two guns set off at a gallop after the fugitives, getting into action with shrapnel whenever possible. The centre and left divisions of guns proceeded at as slower pace in line with the infantry, their horses being close to collapse from exhaustion. As for the cavalry on the infantry's flanks, this was their moment. On the left, De Salis kept a third of his small force of Hussars in reserve and in reach of the guns while he pursued in skirmishing order at the gallop. The Hussars' pursuit was effective, even though the ground was unfavourable and covered by low jungle, and they sabred or shot a large number of the enemy. The Lancers on the right flank also galloped in pursuit of the enemy who had fled in front of the right of the line, but the ground was covered first in low and then in thick jungle that hampered them and favoured the fugitives. The cavalry pursued for at least five miles, as far as the village of Rajpur – where the brigade would bivouac that night. Then, seeing that the enemy were now scattered over too wide a front for the small number of cavalrymen to cover, Smith ordered the recall to be sounded.

What, meanwhile, of the infantry under Thesiger's command? Raines brought the 95th steadily and rapidly forward through difficult ground, but most of the enemy fled not in front of them, but to their left. Perceiving this, Thesiger took appropriate action. Smith detailed in his report how Thesiger ordered the 10th BNI to move towards their left and then (in copybook fashion) deployed them into skirmishing order with supports to their rear, and sent them off at the double in pursuit, shooting and bayoneting a large number of the enemy who had evaded the Hussars by taking cover in nullahs and clumps of jungle best avoided by horsemen.

Smith despatched the twelve men of Meade's Horse to capture Man Singh himself. But, shocked into action by the first gunshot, he had thrown himself onto his fast and famous cream-coloured horse and galloped away for his life. His uncle and second-in-command, Ajit Singh, was not so expeditious and was among the slain. The number of rebel dead cannot be accurately computed, and it was known that after the fight the surrounding jungle was filled with wounded men. The figure of somewhere over 600, as insisted upon by Smith, was probably not far from the mark. In comparison, Smith's casualties were trifling: twelve men wounded, some severely, including one officer, Captain S. M. Harris of the Horse Artillery. A horse was killed and several others hurt or missing. The British agreed amongst themselves that their casualties would have been more severe had not their surprise of the enemy been so complete that their matchlockmen – many warriors in Central India still carried these obsolete weapons – had been given no time to light their matches. Consequently, the only wounds they had managed to inflict were from swords or musket balls.

The dauntless diarist Fanny Duberly, who had accompanied her husband Henry, an officer in the 8th Hussars, to the Crimea where the regiment took part in the Charge of the Light Brigade, was once again in the field with him in Central India. She noted (although Brigadier Smith did not report it) that the victorious British took between fifty and sixty prisoners at Koondrye. Some of them would still have been wearing elements of sepoy uniform, and she was the horrified witness to their fate:

> We halted for one day after the fight at Koondrye, where nine of the prisoners were shot . . . It seems to me that all this Indian warfare is unsatisfactory work, and although it may be true that in this rebellion severity is mercy, yet, on the other hand, there have been cases of ruthless slaughter, of which perhaps the less said the better.[13]

This subsequent, if not uncommon atrocity aside, Koondrye had been a very satisfactory day's work for Smith's brigade. It was the very first time that Thesiger had fought in the front line rather than remaining in the rear with the staff, as he had in the Crimea. No man can know how he will carry himself in battle until he has experienced its dangers, and doubtless to his secret relief and satisfaction Thesiger comported himself with what became his hallmark sangfroid under fire. And, as we have seen, he had shown decisiveness in redeploying the 10th BNI at the height of the fighting. For this, he earned Smith's approbation, and in his despatch the brigadier mentioned that Thesiger, 'was most active and successful in carrying out my instructions'.[14] This phrasing bears noting because it emphasises that Thesiger had effectively carried out the duties Smith had assigned him, while the planning and execution of the successful operation had remained the brigadier's responsibility. Koondrye, then, demonstrated that Thesiger could keep his head and be relied upon in a subordinate role during a battle. It did not indicate how he would perform as a field commander, and the Central India Campaign that was now winding rapidly down never put him to the test.

Koondrye was the last engagement in which the entire 95th Regiment took part in Central India. Nevertheless, detachments, reinforced by various drafts from home, continued in the field for several more months against the rebels and were involved in various brushes with Tantia Tope. During February 1859 most of the last, dispirited rebels dispersed. Tantia Tope was finally betrayed by Man Singh (who surrendered on 2 April) in return for the British interceding with his overlord, the Maharaja of Gwalior, against whom he had rebelled. Tantia Tope was seized on 2 April by a party of Meade's Horse of the same unit that had failed to capture Man Singh at Koondrye, and hanged on 18 April 1859. His execution marked the effective end of the war in Central India.[15]

During the last lacklustre months of operations, the 95th began preparing to resume its peace-time garrison role. On 15 December 1858 the depot, families and baggage of the regiment, which had been left at Disa in Gujerat during the war, started moving north-east to Neemuch (Nimach), the military cantonment of the princely state of Gwalior. Thesiger had been placed in command of a detachment of the regiment consisting of seven officers and 200 rank and file at Tonk in Rajputana, from where he was ordered on 24 February 1859 to march eighty miles west to Nasirabad.[16] Mrs Duberly described it as a notoriously disagreeable place overrun by mosquitoes with no drinking water nearer than a mile and with no gardens or anything else to make life pleasant.[17] Happily for Thesiger, his stay at this forsaken spot was not for long. At the end of February 1859 Brigadier Smith was invalided to Bombay and Colonel de Salis of the 8th Hussars assumed command of the brigade. On 28 April the brigade was at last broken up at Jamnagar in Sindh and the various regiments left for their summer quarters. Thesiger led his detachment from Nasirabad to Neemuch, his men marching cheerily despite the oppressively sultry weather at the beginning of the hot season. On 12 May Thesiger's detachment was joined by the rest of the 95th who marched in to the cantonment at a swinging pace with Lieutenant-Colonel Raines at their head on his grey Arab, the bugle, fife and drum band playing 'I'm Ninety-five'. They found the cantonment in ruins, having been ransacked by the rebels, and they were hard put to get roofs over their heads before the first burst of the monsoon. Nor were the men in the best of health. Most of them – but not Thesiger to nearly the same extent – had seen an unprecedented period of unceasing service in the field with continual marching and fighting under privations of all sorts, and it had taken its toll on men, horses and camp equipage alike.[18]

On 2 August 1861 Major-General Sir William Mansfield, the CinC of the Bombay Army, presented the silver Indian Mutiny Medal with its white ribbon with two vertical scarlet stripes (each stripe of equal width) and a clasp for 'Central India' to fourteen officers and 527 men of the 95th Regiment. Lieutenant-Colonel Raines was privately disgusted because he believed that a further 236 men had earned the medal, of whom twenty-five were officers.[19] That Thesiger was a recipient of the medal, even though he had taken the field in only the last few months of the war and had fought in only one of its many battles and sieges, says more about his high Army rank and elevated connections than it does about his rather minimal contribution to the campaign.

CHAPTER 8

The Bombay Presidency, 1859–1867

AFTER THE FINAL SUPPRESSION of the Mutiny, Thesiger remained with his regiment in the Bombay Presidency, and there followed a long period of Indian service, extending to 1874. By his own computation, sixteen of his twenty years of foreign service were spent in India.[1] With little doubt, this was surely the happiest and most fulfilling period of his life, during which he consolidated his career, secured influential patrons, married, played an important part in a major campaign, and rose to high administrative rank in the Indian Army. The India in which his career flourished was overshadowed, however, by the poisonous legacy of the Mutiny. The military in particular were slow to recover from the shock of the rebellion and, like the other structures of British rule in India, went through a period of rebuilding in which Thesiger participated.

The end of the Mutiny signalled the demise of the East India Company. On 1 November 1858 the Queen's Proclamation replaced its rule with that of the Crown exercised through the Secretary of State for India with his advisory India Council in London. But the administration of the Indian colony was cumbersome because the viceroy in Calcutta had his own supreme legislative council that made laws for British India. This 'double government' was replicated in India itself with the governors and executive councils of the Bengal, Madras and Bombay Presidencies making their own local laws.

The continued existence of the three Presidencies meant there was to be no unified military command in India, even though in the aftermath of the Mutiny the British were obsessed with security and stability and considered the reconstruction of the military forces in India the most urgent of issues. In each of the three Presidencies there was a CinC who was responsible to the governor. He in turn was subordinate to the viceroy who was advised on military matters by the CinC, India, who was appointed by the Secretary of State for India.[2]

As Thesiger would have appreciated, with the final suppression of the Mutiny there was an immediate need to slash the financial burden of maintaining 250,000 Indian soldiers and 100,000 European troops (now double the pre-Mutiny establishment). Of the latter, 77,000 were members of the British Army with the remaining 23,000 belonging to John Company's European regiments. Since fears about the future loyalty of Indian troops permeated British thinking, a royal commission of March 1859 laid down that the ratio of European to Indian troops must be increased from the pre-Mutiny 1:5 to 1:2, and by the mid-1860s the numbers were set at 60,000 European troops to 120,000 Indian.

It was decided that the European regiments in the new Indian Army (the informal name for the armies of the three Presidencies) would all be drawn from the British regiments stationed temporarily in India, and in 1859 this included Thesiger's 95th Regiment. The Company's European regiments ceased to exist and in 1860 were amalgamated into the British Army with its officers bearing the Queen's commission (although not before it became necessary to put down a short-lived 'White Mutiny' by many of its members who refused to accept the transfer).[3] The Indian regiments of the Company's armies in the three Presidencies were reorganised through the disbandment of some units and the creation of new ones.[4] The Bombay Army was left at about 44,000 strong. The 2,000 or so British officers of the Indian regiments were henceforth appointed to the separate Staff Corps formed in 1861 for each of the three Presidency armies, its members serving until the age of fifty-five with their Indian regiment rather than with the British Army.[5] It became policy that the Indian regiments must never be as well armed as their British Army counterparts in India, and their equipment was deliberately kept a generation behind. In addition, the Indian-manned artillery units of the Company's armies were disbanded. The intention was to handicap the Indian troops if they ever rose again as they had in 1857, but the consequence was to compromise their effectiveness when operating in support of imperial military ventures in Africa and Asia.[6]

The Bombay Presidency, where Thesiger was stationed with his regiment after the Mutiny, was the oldest of the three Presidencies, and had become British in 1661 as part of the dowry of King Charles II's Portuguese queen, Catherine of Braganza. It encompassed the central–western part of the Indian sub-continent and included Sindh to the north-west that had been annexed in 1843, as well as Aden, commanding the entrance to the Red Sea, annexed in 1839. Bombay itself (*Bom Baia*, or 'Good Bay', in Portuguese – but now Mumbai), was an excellent natural harbour that gained in commercial and military importance from the 1840s with the development of railways and the gradual replacement of the Cape route to India by steam travel from the Red Sea. The first paddle steamer from Suez arrived in Bombay in 1830, and once the Suez Canal connecting the Mediterranean to the Red Sea was opened on 17 November 1869, Bombay became India's chief military port.

While Thesiger was stationed there, Bombay was considered the least alluring station in India. The densely populated 'native quarter', as described by Mrs Duberly in 1858, was made up of wooden houses with deep projecting roofs leaning over unpaved streets. The British residents lived outside the town on Malabar Hill in capacious bungalows near the church, club (the social hub throughout British India) and race course. The esplanade along the sea front below the fort was the 'place of fashionable resort' where every afternoon Bombay's elite promenaded in their carriages. The social atmosphere of Bombay was, however, nothing compared to the smart, imperial grandeur of Calcutta (Kolkata) with its palaces, or aristocratic Madras (Chennai). Even so, it had the safe social rhythms of the other two Presidencies. The Bombay government spent the cold weather in steamy Bombay and during the summer heat moved south to Mahabaleshwar in the forested Western Ghats. In June, with the coming of the rainy monsoon, it moved for four months to Poona (Pune), east of Bombay, where a large military cantonment had been established. That was the fashionable time of year to be there, and everyone who was anyone in the British establishment took up residence there for the Poona Season and enjoyed an endless round of entertainments.[7]

From 13 July 1861 to 31 December 1862 Thesiger relinquished his regimental duties to join the staff of the CinC, Bombay, as the Deputy Adjutant-General (DAG) of the British troops stationed in the Bombay Presidency. The CinCs of the three Presidencies all maintained their own staffs with the same structure as that of the CinC, India. The Adjutant-General's branch was responsible for personnel issues, while QMG's department oversaw matters of organisation and equipment. When it came to Thesiger's appointment as DAG, Bombay, the mechanics were as follows. The Viceroy in Council exercised supreme authority over all troops in India, and the CinC, India, who was subject neither to the authority of the CinC in Britain nor to the control of the War Office, was responsible to him. His military secretary had the same powerful functions as his counterpart in the Horse Guards in London, and managed the appointments, promotions and retirements of officers. Yet, in another manifestation of 'double government', the Duke of Cambridge, as CinC, Britain, remained in general control over the British troops serving in India, and took a very close interest in all senior appointments and promotions there. Thesiger, taking into account his past experience as DAQMG on the staff in the Crimea, was clearly qualified for his staff appointment as DAG, but it has to be understood that while jobbery in the army was being progressively restricted in Britain itself, military appointments in India remained rampantly dependent on patronage, influence, family and regimental connections, the comradeship of campaigns, debts for past favours, and promises for the future.[8]

We know Thesiger would have had the support of his firm patron, the Duke of Cambridge, when the question of his appointment arose. But he would also have enjoyed that of the new CinC, India, Lieutenant-General Sir Hugh Rose, who took up his appointment on 4 June 1861. Between December 1857 and June 1858 Rose had been in command of the Central India Field Force with which the 95th Regiment had served. In February 1860 he was appointed CinC of the Bombay Army and he would have made Thesiger's acquaintance. A slender man with a mass of curly fair hair and a Frenchified moustache and beard, Rose was a fine field commander but unpopular with those under his command because he appeared autocratic and uncaring, probably because he was determined to promote army efficiency. It was his fixed policy to reward deserving officers, and it must be assumed that he found the efficient Thesiger such a one. Presumably, shared social class would have helped bring them together. Rose was of the landed gentry in Yorkshire with a number of estates, and was accustomed to moving in London society, as Thesiger had been. Moreover, aristocrats (even if newly minted ones like the Hon. Frederic Thesiger) were thin on the ground in the Bombay Presidency. It must have helped too that Rose had once been equerry to the Duke of Cambridge.[9]

Thesiger did not long remain DAG, Bombay, however, despite making his mark as an able and conscientious military administrator, and in December 1862 he returned to his regiment. It is unclear why his staff appointment proved so brief, but it most likely can be put down to the personality of the new CinC of the Bombay Army, Lieutenant-General Sir William Mansfield, who held the post from 14 May 1860 to 14 March 1865. Tall and wiry with undoubted abilities, Mansfield's contemptuous and arrogant manner made him unpopular with his subordinates. He was a disappointed man, too, because after his stellar performance during the Mutiny he had hoped to be appointed CinC, India, and had to be content with Bombay instead. Certainly, his tenure of command was not successful. He disliked advice, was unable to delegate authority, had several painful and discreditable quarrels with his staff and entirely lacked good temper and judgement in dealing with subordinates.[10] Clearly, the atmosphere at Mansfield's headquarters must have proved too unpleasant for Thesiger to have endured for more than eighteen months. Back with the 95th, on 30 April 1863 Thesiger was promoted brevet colonel, a normal progression in recognition of service on the staff. Thereafter, when with his regiment he continued to carry out the duties associated with his substantive rank of lieutenant-colonel, but when serving outside it, he carried out the duties of a colonel.[11]

During this period, Thesiger formed a fateful friendship with Captain John North Crealock of the 95th, who had served gallantly with the regiment throughout the Central Indian Campaign and had been wounded at the battle of Kotah-ki-serai. Between December 1862 and March 1864, Crealock went on to serve as Mansfield's aide-de-camp. He was a man of many talents and evidently possessed a compelling personality. He excelled at watercolour paintings and sketches of his travels and campaigns, and was an intelligent, capable and brave officer with an intellectual interest in the military profession that he shared with Thesiger, who was clearly drawn to him. Their paths would diverge when Crealock left India for Staff College, but Thesiger evidently kept in touch with him over the years, and when he took up his command in South Africa in 1878, he would appoint Crealock to his staff. But Crealock was a relentlessly ambitious man with a high opinion of his own abilities, a master of sharp, facetious retorts who adopted an overbearing, haughty manner that alienated many of his fellow officers. Perhaps these unpleasant traits were not yet evident when Thesiger first befriended him in Bombay, but Crealock was destined to complicate Thesiger's command in South Africa where, as his constant companion, he was suspected of wielding an undue, and not necessarily beneficial influence over him.[12]

Over the next few years in the Bombay Presidency, Thesiger was in close contact with two other figures who would play a critical role in his future career. The first was Sir Bartle Frere, the Governor of the Bombay Presidency between 24 April 1862 and 6 March 1867. He would be High Commissioner in South Africa when Thesiger took up his ill-fated command there in 1878. Frere came from a family of scholars and statesmen. He had entered the Bombay Civil Service in 1834 and developed a close interest in the languages, human geography, history and customs of its peoples. He also honed his skills as a purposeful administrator, one who was able to palliate his steely firmness with a show of conciliatory manners. His true character revealed itself in his daring horsemanship, and in his endurance and courage as a big-game hunter. In January 1851 he became Chief Commissioner of Sindh, the turbulent territory recently annexed to the Bombay Presidency. His firm and sensible actions during the Mutiny suppressed incipient rebellion in Sindh and he was made KCB for his sterling efforts. In 1859 he was appointed a member of the Council of the Governor General during the period of reconstruction after the Mutiny. On taking up the governorship of Bombay in 1862, Frere energetically set in train grand public works such as he had carried through in Sindh, greatly improving infrastructure and education, and bringing new prosperity to the Presidency. When he retired from Bombay in 1867, he took up a seat on the India Council in London in recognition of his administrative talents. But, as Thesiger would discover to his cost when he and Frere came together again in South Africa, Frere, for all his outward charm, courtesy and scholarship, had a steely inner core, and was prepared – as he had demonstrated in Sindh during the Mutiny – to take independent, measured risks to achieve his objectives.[13]

The second dominant figure with whom Thesiger was closely associated in Bombay was Lieutenant-General Sir Robert Napier who, in March 1865, succeeded Mansfield as CinC, Bombay. Napier was the son of a Royal Artillery officer and had trained as a Royal Engineer. He had enjoyed a distinguished and varied military career in India in which he displayed considerable professional skill as a soldier, engineer and administrator, and was a master of logistics. Even before Napier took up his Bombay command, Thesiger had entered his orbit. Napier took part in the reinforcement in September 1857 of Lucknow where Jack Inglis, Thesiger's brother-in-law, was gallantly holding out in the residency, and was with him until finally relieved in November. During that time Napier became closely acquainted with Thesiger's sister Julia and her three little sons. On 29 June 1859 Napier took over the command of the Central India Field Force from Sir Hugh Rose, and was consequently Thesiger's overall commander when he arrived to take his part in the final operations of Brigadier Smith's brigade. Napier, after exemplary service during 1860 in the Third Anglo-Chinese War that cemented his high reputation, and before he took up his Bombay command, briefly returned to Britain where he met Thesiger's patron, the Duke of Cambridge, and established a lifelong friendship with him. This opportune connection would serve to further Thesiger's career, as did Napier's close working relationship with Frere when both were concerned to improve the living conditions of the British soldiers in India. This was a project that, as a conscientious senior regimental officer, had Thesiger's wholehearted, active support and accustomed him to working closely with both men.[14]

And indeed, the welfare of British troops in India required attention. Before the Cardwell Reforms of 1870–3, British regiments such as Thesiger's could be stationed in India for up to twenty-five years, although the 95th served there for only thirteen before sailing for home in December 1870. British regiments in India had the same composition as those in the United Kingdom, and a battalion consisted of about 800 fighting men. Until 1862 a battalion had ten companies when the two elite flank grenadier and light companies were abolished with the understanding that all companies should be capable of acting as light infantry in skirmishing order. The 1859 infantry manual that Thesiger would have consulted in training his regiment, advocated greater use of 'double time' for skirmishing which previously had been authorised only for the two flank companies. Close-order drill persisted, though, as did volley-fire, but now manoeuvres were performed over greater distances to take account of the enhanced range of improved firearms. In 1857 all the regiments of British regulars in India had received the Enfield Rifle Musket, but in 1864 a Select Committee began to consider how to equip the British Army with breech-loaders, and decided, as an interim measure, on a mechanism that would permit the conversion of the large stock of Enfields held by the army. The Enfield's lock and hammer were retained, but where the percussion cap nipple had been, a protruding striker was inserted that, when struck by the hammer, detonated a centre-fire brass-bodied cartridge inserted by opening the breechblock. The .577 Snider-Enfield as the weapon was known, was sighted up to 1,000 yards and was more effective than any other previous infantry small arm in the British Army. It began to be issued in 1865, and the 95th Regiment received the new weapon and its subsequent 1867 modification. But, in line with the policy of issuing the latest technology only to British units, the Indian regiments of the Bombay Presidency had to remain content with their Enfield muskets.[15]

During the 1860s, improvements in British Army uniforms were also adopted in India. The 1855 shako, with modifications in 1861 and 1869, continued to be worn with full dress, but never in the field. Instead, the troops wore forage caps, and in 1855 a new one was introduced for officers. In an infantry regiment such as the 95th, it was dark blue with a black embroidered band and a flat peak, and was usually worn with the regimental numeral or badge in front. In India, from 1858 the airpipe helmet replaced the forage cap as undress wear, although the latter might still be worn.[16] In 1868 the glengarry bonnet with two ribbons hanging behind and capable of being folded flat, was adopted as undress headgear for all ranks, but many officers continued to prefer their forage caps. From the late 1850s the familiar shell jacket was replaced by a more comfortable five-button red or blue (depending on the unit) frock with full skirts, and at the end of the 1860s added regimental facing colours on collar and cuffs. A white drill version of the frock was issued in India. In 1867 a dark blue patrol jacket was authorised for officers' undress wear and proved very popular. It was loosely cut, fastened down the front with hooks and eyes, and was decorated with rows of braiding across the front, secured at the opening with olivets, oval fasteners through the loops of braid.[17]

British troops and their families – a proportion of British soldiers leaving for India were allowed to take their wives and children with them – were originally quartered in barrack blocks in forts. After the Mutiny, expensive barracks were built for British troops, a project in which both Napier and Frere, who were very concerned to improve living conditions for the troops in the Bombay Presidency, were much involved. The usual layout was a parade ground, surrounded by barrack buildings. Officers and sergeants had messes where they could have meals and socialise, and officers lived in spacious verandahed bungalows outside the barracks, surrounded by dusty gardens. If they were unmarried, groups of two or three would band together to form 'chummeries'. The ensemble of barracks, bungalows and church formed a cantonment – the part of a town or a permanent encampment where British soldiers lived – and by the 1860s there were 175 of them in India, accentuating the social cleavage between the rulers and the ruled and cementing the post-Mutiny British in their attitudes of isolation and superiority.

Disease, not enemy action, presented the greatest danger to British troops in India, and mortality rates were many times higher than at home in Britain. 'Corporal Forbes', water-borne *cholera morbus*, was the greatest killer. There was also a high incidence of venereal disease, and before the 1864 Contagious Diseases and Cantonment Act that provided for the registration of prostitutes and control of brothels, there had been regimental 'bazaars', brothels maintained by the canteen fund.[18] It was alcohol, though, that was the chief curse of the British soldier in India. In cantonments rum or arrack was issued in the regimental canteens, and in the 1860s the price of beer, hitherto imported, was brought down by the emergence of the local brewing industry. There was much obligatory drunkenness in the officers' mess, crimes – including homicides – were committed by both officers and men under the influence of alcohol, and military hospitals were full of drunkards. The close association between drink, crime and disease encouraged official support for regimental temperance societies, and the Soldiers' Total Temperance Association was formed in 1862.[19]

By now a teetotaller, evidently influenced by the campaigners who were encouraging temperance societies within the Army, Thesiger did his best to stamp out the drunkenness under his command that had become worse during the Mutiny and in its angry, uncertain aftermath.[20] He fully subscribed to the changing attitudes of the late Victorian Army that required a greater acceptance by officers of paternalistic concern about their men's well-being, but in setting an example of abstinence, moderation and frugality he went beyond the norm. To combat idleness among his young officers, he urged them (as he himself had done) to study further. He made them welcome in his bungalow where he taught them French, German and music, and encouraged them to read up and discuss military matters such as tactics in order to enhance their professionalism. Officers in India were expected to learn at least one local language, and Thesiger led the way by himself passing the exacting interpreter's examination in Hindustani in 1863.[21]

It seems Thesiger was always appreciated by his men for his unfailingly gentlemanly, courteous and modest behaviour, which he combined with a considerate yet firm manner to his subordinates. He was remembered by contemporaries as always being popular in the Army where his 'upright character and blameless life' earned him widespread 'respect and affection'.[22] Yet he maintained an inherently conservative approach to discipline and punishment, where he was always on the strict side, and was a supporter of flogging.[23]

In March 1868, the British government set up a committee to enquire into military discipline. Flogging had been partially abolished in 1867 following the death of Private Robert Slim from its over-zealous application, but the committee was uncertain about how to maintain discipline and control of the Army in the event of the abolition of corporal punishment. Its report, published in 1869, recommended that flogging remain available as a punishment during peacetime for crimes of violent mutiny or insubordination, and that it continue to be used on active service and even be extended to cover desertion and drunkenness. Branding, whereby the prisoner was 'marked' with a letter 'D' for deserter or 'BC' for bad character, was abolished in 1871, however.

For a decade after the 1869 report the Army employed flogging increasingly sparingly, but its re-emergence as a common punishment in Zululand in 1879 attracted the attention of Liberal politicians, and Chelmsford (as Thesiger was by then known) would be denounced for his favouring of the anachronistic and degrading practice.[24] Chelmsford remained unrepentant, however, and in 1881 assured the committee investigating Army reform that he continued to support flogging as the most suitable punishment on active service since it did not take men out of the field as imprisonment would do.[25] The committee disregarded him, and the resulting annually renewable Army Act of 1881 abolished flogging altogether.[26]

Yet, while he never baulked at soldiers being flogged, Thesiger – as with many men of his upbringing – was compassionate towards animals, so long as he was not hunting them, that is. Soon after invading Zululand in 1879 – and apparently not perceiving the paradox involved – he 'even licked [beat] with his own hand a white-bullock-driver . . . for brutality to oxen'.[27]

Officers in India fitted into a distinctive, stratified society where rigid rules of order of precedence and protocol governed their social lives. At the very top came the small minority of government officials like Frere, and then the commissioned officers of the British and Indian forces in descending strict order of rank from CinC to humble second lieutenant: a hierarchy that placed Brevet Colonel Thesiger very close to the apex. True, as we have seen, it could not be denied that Bombay was something of a provincial backwater where life for officials and officers was carried on in a sedate, decorous, and not overly fashionable manner. It was a world with much time on officers' hands where amateur theatricals, so intrinsic to social life in India, found Thesiger a keen participant. There was much scope for an officer to indulge in India's many and varied field sports and outdoor activities, and Thesiger participated eagerly, always displaying considerable physical energy despite the enervating heat.[28] The quintessential Indian field sport that tested nerve and gave men a feel for the country was pig-sticking, the pursuit of wild boar by mounted men armed with a steel-tipped bamboo spear about eight feet long. This dangerous sport with its regular competitions was controlled by various tent clubs, of which the Poona Tent Club was the oldest in India. Polo too was extensively played, and it is not too much to say that horses were at the heart of British India – although dogs were not far behind, followed by the monkeys and parrots kept as pets.

Officers required several horses and polo ponies, as well as several servants to look after them. At least three or four personal servants were also considered essential, and in this hierarchical society the number of servants reflected the power and status of their employer. A senior officer such as Thesiger required a bevy of them. Then there were mess bills, and the cost of expensive mess dress and appropriate clothes and gear for all the varied sports he engaged in. Procuring the necessities and equipment required when on manoeuvres or campaign was a further heavy financial burden. Thus, although the cost of living in India was certainly lower than in Britain, and an officer could live there in decidedly greater style for the same outlay, Thesiger found that his pay was devoured by the many expenses essential to maintain the way of life expected of a senior officer.[29] And then, there was the matter of the greatly increased expense of a married establishment with at least a dozen servants, a stable of horses and several carriages should he seek the comfort of a wife and family.[30]

Officers over the age of thirty who married were in receipt of a house and marriage allowance. Yet, so that family life should not interfere with military duties, and for reasons of even stronger social convention, officers were expected to follow the unwritten rule that 'captains may, majors should, colonels must' marry. This code left officers, the products of boys-only schools, ill-prepared for communication with equally inhibited women of their own class. Whether they were sexually experienced is another matter for, as we have seen, access to prostitutes was readily available, whether in London or in military stations around the Empire. There has been an increasing historiographical trend to insist that an understanding of an officer's sexual desires and preferences is important for interpreting a career, but the problem is that until private behaviour becomes publicly scandalous, it is not much observed or recorded.[31] Unfortunately for those seeking the sensational or discreditable, there is nothing in what is known of Thesiger's sexual life to suggest it was anything other than thoroughly conventional and uxorious.

Thesiger was a colonel and forty years of age when he finally took the plunge and married on 1 January 1867 while stationed with the 95th Regiment at Karachi, the capital of Sindh. A shortage of suitable wives in India encouraged many officers to go home on leave to find a spouse; Bombay also saw the regular arrival of the 'fishing fleet' from Suez carrying hopeful young women looking for mates among the British officials and officers. Thesiger was obliged to resort to neither expedient, for his bride was on the spot. She was Adria Fanny (20 November 1845–25 February 1926), the eldest daughter of Major-General John Coussmaker Heath of the Bombay Army, who had been born at Poona, the summer hill station of the Bombay elite. Her photograph portrays a self-contained woman with fine, fair hair and soft, demurely pretty features, whose level gaze from her widely spaced eyes hints at a quiet determination of character. The match was a good one from both perspectives, although best from hers. She was of a military family and her father was a senior offer; but her husband was a rising officer whose father was once again Lord Chancellor (this time in Lord Derby's third Cabinet), and he was heir to the Chelmsford barony. True, at twenty-two, she was roughly half her husband's forty years, but such a discrepancy in ages was not at all unusual in the Army where an officer seldom married until older than thirty-five.

Officers' wives automatically assumed their husband's status in the military hierarchy, and in a regiment such as the 95th, none was higher than the colonel's lady. She was expected to be a Christian role model, to be present at Sunday church parade and, in an extension of the paternalistic, squirearchic pattern in Britain, to lead the other officers' wives in helping as unpaid welfare assistants and counsellors with soldiers' domestic and family problems. Brought up as an officer's daughter, Adria Thesiger would have known precisely how to act her part. Besides playing a succouring role in regimental life – one that would be regarded as condescending today, but was then accepted as natural by soldiers and their wives in the hierarchical Army – the colonel's new wife would have been expected to confine herself to the domestic sphere: to overseeing her household of servants, to acting as the gracious hostess to officers and officials when her husband had them to dinner at their bungalow, and to bringing up her children if they came. The wrong sort of wife could mar an ambitious officer's career, while the right sort (one such as Adria Thesiger) only enhanced it. Officers' wives were supposed to keep out of Army affairs, but many were ambitious for their husbands and might use their contacts and influence to lobby those in power for their advancement and promotion. Many Victorian generals' wives are known to have been of this pushy sort, constantly seeking to advance their husbands' careers – none more so than Louisa (Loo), Lady Wolseley and Lady Roberts – but Adria Thesiger does not appear to have been one of them, although (as we shall see) she was capable of leaping staunchly to her husband's defence when his generalship was brought into question.[32]

During the course of 1867, Thesiger took leave from India to sail with his bride for home, there for her to meet her still handsome father-in-law, the famously imperturbable yet relentlessly witty Lord Chancellor. While the newlyweds were still in London, on 30 August 1867 Sir Robert Napier was appointed to command a military expedition to Abyssinia. Such an undertaking took several months to prepare, during which time Napier set about assembling his staff. Thesiger had made his mark as an able and conscientious military administrator in the Bombay Army, and had attracted Napier's 'approval and regard'. It appears, moreover, that Napier had become (and remained) his 'fast friend'[33] and Thesiger had previously served as DAG of the Bombay Army from which the Abyssinian Field Force was to be mainly drawn. Nor would it have passed unnoticed that Thesiger's father was Lord Chancellor and that he was the Duke of Cambridge's protégé. It is no surprise, then, that Napier selected Thesiger to be his DAG on his headquarters staff, the appointment dating from 21 January 1868. Nor is it a wonder that Thesiger leapt at the opportunity and, in Napier's approving words, 'left England at two days' notice to join the Force in Abyssinia'.[34] His wife Adria was pregnant, and Thesiger left her under his father's roof at 7 Eaton Square while he was away at the wars. It was there, on 12 August 1868, that John Napier Thesiger, was born. As Frederic and Adria's eldest son, the day would come when he would succeed his father as the third Lord Chelmsford.[35]

CHAPTER 9

The Expedition to Abyssinia, 1867–1868

THE ABYSSINIAN EXPEDITION, which Thesiger joined with such alacrity, was to prove the pivotal point in his career. In his official report on the campaign to Sir Stafford Northcote, the Tory Secretary of State for India between March 1867 and December 1868, General Napier warmly commended Colonel Thesiger's 'most important service' as his DAG. As he warmly phrased it, Thesiger's 'thorough knowledge of his duties, combined with great ability and untiring energy, render him a most valuable Staff Officer'.[1] The immediate consequences for Thesiger of this public recognition were to be honours and prestigious military appointments. In the longer term, his experiences in Abyssinia introduced him to the considerable challenges of campaigning in Africa and the extent to which success depended on sound logistical arrangements. As Damian O'Connor reminds us, the old maxim that 'amateurs talk tactics but professionals talk logistics' rang particularly true for Abyssinia where the real heroes of the campaign were those responsible for getting the soldiers to the front and supplying them there.[2] This consideration would be foremost in Thesiger's mind when he took up his first independent field command in the Cape Colony in 1878, and when he set about planning the invasion of the Zulu kingdom.

Twenty years after the Abyssinian Expedition, Major Charles E. Callwell, RA's Gold Medal essay, 'Lessons to be Learned from Campaigns in which British Forces have been Employed since the Year 1865' was published in the *Royal United Services Institution Journal.* This was the most important military periodical of Victorian Britain. It reflected the concerns of naval and military officers seriously interested in their profession of arms, and disseminated information within the services.[3] Callwell elaborated his essay into a book, *Small Wars: Their Principles and*

Practice, published in 1896, that went through revised and updated editions in 1899 and 1906, and was taken up internationally as the standard manual on colonial warfare.[4] Callwell defined a 'small war' as encompassing 'all campaigns other than those where both the opposing sides consist of regular troops'. He added that the expression 'small war' did not refer to the actual scale of a campaign. Rather, it was useful in denoting 'operations of regular armies against irregular, or comparatively speaking irregular, forces . . . which in their armament, their organization, and their discipline are palpably inferior'. This sort of fighting, he believed, was 'an art in itself' in which success depended less upon the mass organisation, complex manoeuvre and sophisticated technical skills required in the wars fought between the great industrialised continental powers, than upon firm logistics over difficult terrain, on secure communications and sound intelligence. These underpinned a vigorous offensive strategy in which the overwhelming superiorly of armaments ensured the tactical defeat of the enemy.[5]

Although those commanding the Abyssinian Expedition did not consciously think of it as a 'small war' as subsequently defined by Callwell, that is what it was. Thus, Thesiger's first experience of a colonial campaign in Africa was typical of this type, as would be the Ninth Cape Frontier War and the Anglo-Zulu War where he commanded. Inevitably, his service in Abyssinia and all that it entailed deeply coloured the way in which he conducted his subsequent campaigns in southern Africa. Whether in their course he would fully live up to Callwell's precepts on how to conduct a 'small war' successfully is another matter.

Callwell divided 'small wars' into several classes. There were campaigns of conquest and annexation; others were to suppress an insurrection, which is what the British considered the Ninth Cape Frontier War to be. Some were fought to overthrow a dangerous neighbour, such as 'the crushing of the Zulu power' which Callwell regarded as being 'indispensable for the peace of South Africa'. And finally, there were punitive campaigns to wipe out an insult or to avenge a wrong. These did not culminate in full-blown conquest since the defeat of the enemy did not have to be 'complete and crushing' in order to attain the political or strategic objective.[6] Such a one was the Abyssinian Expedition.

During the course of the seventeenth and eighteenth centuries, royal authority in the Christian Ethiopian kingdom had been progressively weakened by external enemies and by the growing autonomy of the great regional lords. The latter continued to recognise the ritual authority of the ineffectual kings at Gondar and to pay them nominal allegiance, but this chaotic period between 1769 and 1855 came to be known as the *Zamana Masafint*, or 'Era of the Princes'. The warlord who seized the throne as Tewodros II in 1855 attempted to bring the regional lords to heel. His earlier encounters with Egyptian regulars encroaching on Ethiopia from the north convinced him that to safeguard his kingdom he needed to adopt Western statecraft and military technology, and that he furthermore required artillery to reduce the forts of his restive rivals on their flat-topped mountain strongholds. He began importing firearms and foreign technicians and launched a domestic weapons industry. However, within a decade Tewodros began to lose control of his kingdom. The provinces of Tigray in the north and Showa in the south broke away and his attempts at suppression became increasingly brutal.

Tewodros's problems were made worse by his own unstable personality, and by his increasingly desperate attempts to obtain firearms from the French and British. When the British government left his repeated diplomatic overtures insultingly unanswered, he retaliated in 1864 by seizing the British consul posted to Massawa, Captain Charles Cameron, and held him alongside a number of German missionaries and European artisans with their families and servants: sixty-seven persons in all. His intention was to employ the hostages as bargaining chips to secure British diplomatic support and technical and financial assistance.

But Tewodros had seriously miscalculated. Certainly, the British could have defused the situation through diplomatic means, but they chose not to. They could not have cared less about Abyssinia (as they called Ethiopia) itself, and showed little real concern about the plight of the hostages, even if rescuing them provided a useful excuse to the public for intervention. More to the point, the Foreign Office and India Office both feared the adverse strategic consequences if they failed to act and the French of Napoleon III's adventurist Second Empire decided to intervene. In 1839 the Bombay Army had occupied Aden at the entrance to the Red Sea, and the strategic importance of this waterway would be greatly magnified when the French-sponsored Suez Canal opened at the end of 1869 and connected it to the Mediterranean. The French were already showing an interest in the ports on the African side of the Red

Sea, and the Egyptians were pushing down the coast into Somaliland and threatening Ethiopia itself. Consequently, a strike against Ethiopia would serve to assert Britain's sphere of interest in the region and to scare off rivals. Territorial control over the Ethiopian highlands was not envisaged, but an exemplary campaign would demonstrate Britain's determination to respond militarily if its strategic interests were threatened.

And behind this strategic objective there was another, less obvious but no less important one. The campaign would be entrusted mainly to the Indian Army, and military planners were anxious to test their post-Mutiny reforms in the field. More than anything else, they wished to see if the British Army's logistical shortcomings (so cruelly exposed in the Crimea and during the Indian Mutiny) had been overcome, and whether a British army could be mobilised on short notice and deployed where required across the Empire. In this sense, the Abyssinian Expedition was undertaken to 'exercise the troops' in military manoeuvres against a real, if 'savage' enemy where, as Sir Clements Markham complacently expressed it: 'The experience acquired during active service by many young officers is a clear gain to the country.'[7]

Contemporaries regarded the Abyssinian Expedition as an 'engineers' war' *par excellence*, one that they associated with outstanding civil achievements such as the construction of railways, bridges and great irrigation works in India. Indeed, as Brian Bond has reflected, 'perhaps the narrowly military exploits of the "soldiers of Empire" have been given too much acclaim, and their organisational and engineering feats too little'.[8] As we have seen, Sir Robert Napier, the general selected to command the expedition, was himself a Royal Engineer. He had been nominated through the personal influence of the Duke of Cambridge and Sir Stafford Northcote, both of whom believed that the CinC of the Bombay Army possessed the foresight and organisational ability required. And certainly Napier thoroughly understood the immensity of his task and the need for elaborate administrative and logistical planning.[9]

For the coming campaign, Napier selected a largely Indian force, primarily drawn from the Bombay Army. Of five regiments of cavalry, the Bombay and Bengal Armies supplied two each and the fifth was British. Eight battalions of infantry were from the Bombay Army, two from the Bengal Army and four were British. Four companies of Engineers were from the Bombay Army, three more from the Madras Army, and only one was British. In total, there were 9,050 Indian combat troops and 4,114 British. At Napier's special request, he was given permission on 21 January 1868 to arm his Indian troops with the Snider-Enfield rifles already carried by the British troops in place of their less effective Enfields. The combat troops Napier assembled were dwarfed in number by the host of 'followers' deemed necessary to support them in the field. 'Followers', in military terms, were officers' servants, cooks, stretcher bearers, water carriers, labourers and grooms to manage the thousands of draught animals. Mainly recruited in India, their number cannot be accurately ascertained because no proper records were kept. There could have been as few as 19,000 of them, but more likely there were near double that number.[10] Followers aside, for the period this was an exceptionally large army for a colonial campaign. But it would be exceeded by the one Thesiger himself later commanded in the Anglo-Zulu War, and which would be made up of 17,000 British and colonial troops, some 7,000 of whom were black, supported by over 8,000 untrained African auxiliaries.[11]

It took Napier and his assistants several months to put the expedition together. It was an immense task successfully undertaken that vindicated the recent improvements to the Army's logistical system.[12] By the close of the campaign *The Times* believed it could justifiably crow that

> We have really proved ourselves adepts in the art of war . . . The arrangements have been made with skill, and executed with great precision . . . Certainly, we are all aware that without science it would be impossible to overcome the peculiar difficulties of the Expedition.[13]

And indeed, had it not been for the new technology available, the task would have been even harder. Without steam-driven shipping it would never have been possible to move all the troops and equipment required so rapidly. Between December 1867 and April 1868, the government chartered a total of 688 ships for that purpose at a price that amounted to more than a third of the total cost of the expedition.[14] An advance guard of Royal Engineers landed on 21 October 1867 at Zula on the western coast of the Red Sea south of the port of Massawa, then under Egyptian control. There they began to establish a large base by first constructing a stone pier 700 yards long into the deep-water Annesley Bay to allow troops and stores to be disembarked from the shipping. Lighthouses and

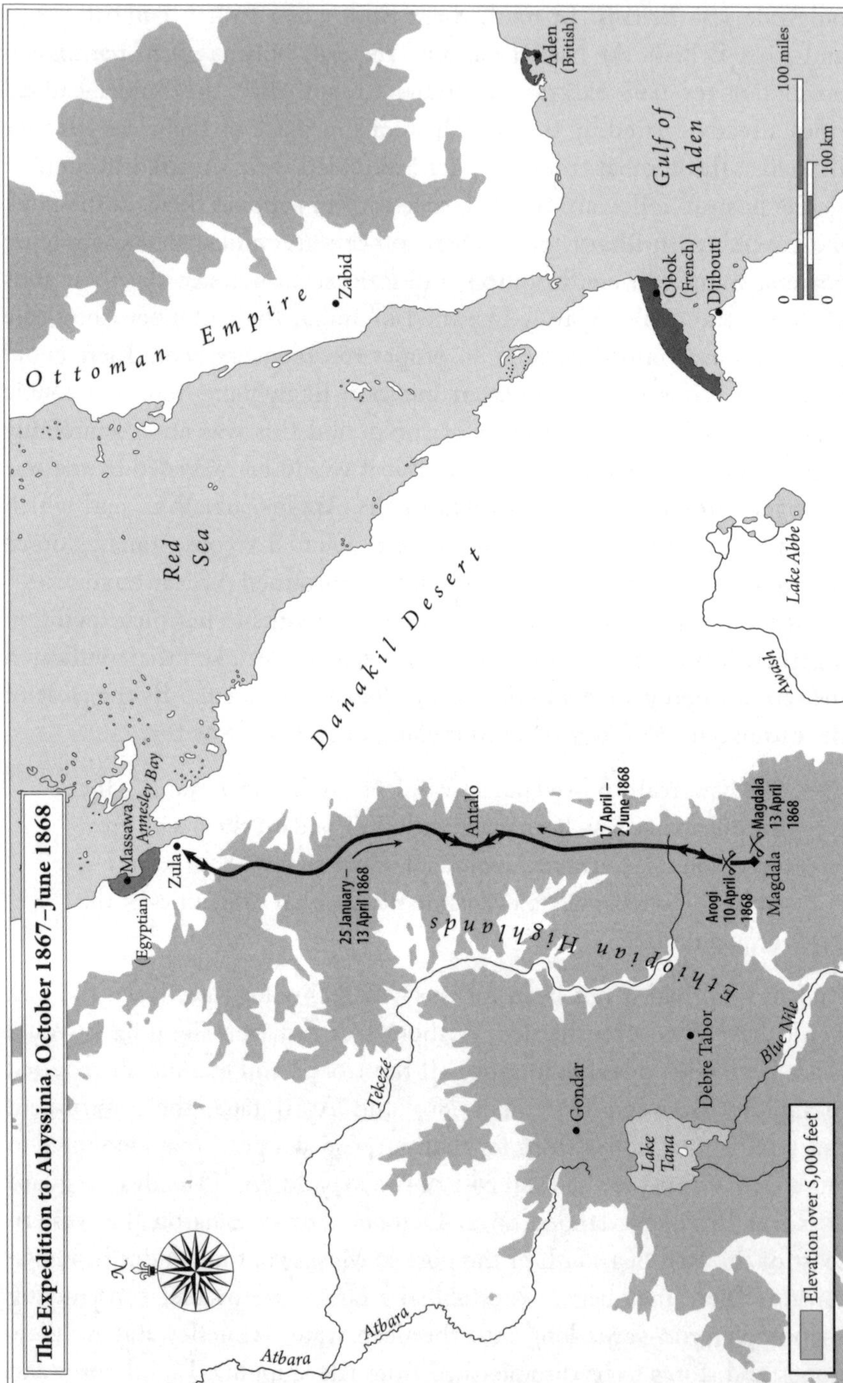

The Expedition to Abyssinia, October 1867–June 1868

warehouses were constructed. The Engineers then built a light railway to carry freight from the harbour across the sandy wastes to the foot of the mountains twenty miles away. Some 230,000 gallons a day of drinking water would be required for the full complement of troops, followers and animals steadily mustering at Zula. But this was an arid, almost waterless place. 'Science' again came to the rescue with condensers on the steamships and on shore distilling fresh water from sea water and with chain pumps bringing up more water from the deep wells that were sunk.[15]

The main body of troops began to land at Zula in December 1867 and Napier disembarked on 2 January 1868 to take personal charge of operations. Tewodros, at the moment when the British officially declared war on him on 19 November 1867, had abandoned and burned his capital at Debre Tabor and retreated eastwards to the fortified heights of Magdala, some 300 miles south of Zula. At the very most, Tewodros had 10,000 men with him. Every one of them at least possessed a firearm, ranging from percussion-cap and flintlock muskets to shotguns, but all of these would be completely outmatched in range and rate of fire by the British Snider–Enfield rifles. The Ethiopians were also armed with their traditional swords, spears and shields. Many were mounted on hardy horses, and all subscribed to an aristocratic code of honour and conspicuous valour. Tewodros also possessed an artillery train of up to fifty guns of almost every conceivable variety and of doubtful effectiveness. His strategy was based on the assumption that the British expeditionary force would never make it to Magdala over the difficult terrain of the highlands. Napier was under political pressure in Britain to make an immediate dash at Magdala but, aware that he had to cross a desert and then nearly 300 miles of roadless mountains to reach the stronghold, he was determined not to begin his advance until he had completed his build-up of stores at Zula and finalised his arrangements for their transportation. He was fortunate that the Duke of Cambridge appreciated the soundness of this approach, and supported him against his armchair critics.[16]

Thanks to the efforts of Colonel Clarke-Kennedy of the Military Train and his staff, who purchased draught animals from all around the Mediterranean, the Persian Gulf and India and shipped them to Zula, by the end of the campaign 2,538 horses (excluding cavalry and artillery horses), 17,943 mules and ponies, 5,735 camels, 1,759 donkeys, 8,075 bullocks and 44 elephants for hauling artillery had been landed at Zula.

Six hundred carts were built at Woolwich and shipped out, but for lack of roads in the rugged highlands could be used to transport supplies only in the short desert stretch between Zula and the mountains, after which pack animals had to be employed.[17] The size of Napier's baggage train in Ethiopia should be compared with the comparably large one Thesiger would assemble for his invasion of Zululand in 1879,[18] the main difference between his and Napier's baggage trains being the great number of wheeled vehicles that could be used in Zululand because the terrain there was much more favourable than in Ethiopia.

The same question, however, can be asked of both the Abyssinian and Zulu campaigns: was such a cumbersome baggage train really necessary, reducing the army itself into little more than what Brian Bond has characterised as an escort for its food?[19] And the answer is that, taking into account the requirements of a British army on campaign in Africa at the time, it was.

Since a British force operating in Africa could not count on living off the land in that thinly populated and sketchily farmed continent (although foraging might bring in some livestock, grain and other supplies), it had to carry its food, the bulky, heavy barrels of pork, boxes of biscuits, crates of compressed potatoes and bottles of essence of beef. Besides food supplies, an infantry battalion of 800 men carried 14,440 pounds of ammunition, another 18,800 pounds of tents (from the two-man triangular model to eighteen-man bell-tents to marquees for the officers), blankets, soap, candles, tobacco, spare boots, extra uniforms and cooking gear, and a further 9,200 pounds of medical supplies. The officers' baggage allowance, including luxuries such as cases of wine and brandy, soda water and cigars, was excessive at 4,700 pounds per battalion, but these items were the first to be jettisoned when necessary. During the Abyssinian campaign, by the time officers reached Magdala, they were down to a waterproof and blanket each and no change of clothing. A cavalry regiment of 400 men needed 16,000 pounds of baggage; while an artillery battery of 200 men required 14,000 pounds, of which over 8,000 pounds was ammunition.

Since (as we have seen) wheeled transport such as Thesiger would use extensively in Zululand found the going too difficult for much of the way in Ethiopia, pack animals were employed instead, but for lack of forage they had to carry their own fodder. This cut down significantly on the weight of supplies they could transport for the troops and the tens of thousands of followers (a mule, for example, consumed twelve pounds a day of the load of 200 pounds it had started out with). Once Napier's army was in the highlands, it had to depend for drinking water on what streams supplied and on what could be shouldered by the water-carriers.[20]

All these difficulties meant that, even though there was a great disparity in the distribution of rations to the expeditionary force – in the Indian Army the commissariat formula laid down that the cost of rations for a British soldier should be eight times that for an Indian soldier, and for a 'follower' half of that – by the time the it neared Magdala, everyone was on very short rations. As a staff officer wrote home:

> We are living in the roughest fashion; we have no sugar, no milk, no butter, no flour, no bread, no liquor of any kind – nothing but water, we get tea though. We get biscuits . . . and tough beef killed just before being taken [with] the muscles still twitching.[21]

On 25 January 1868 the expeditionary force, stretching for seven miles, began its march to Magdala. Rather as Thesiger would do later in Zululand where the war would ostensibly be waged against King Cetshwayo and not his subjects, Napier issued a proclamation stating that only Tewodros and his supporters were being targeted, and that 'no injury was intended to the peoples of Abyssinia, who might remain quietly in their homes'.[22] Anticipating extremes of temperature, the troops took both their warm red smocks and their white drill uniforms which were coloured with improvised dyes to make them a greyish khaki. Headdress was the airpipe helmet with a puggaree wound round it.[23] Progress was slow. A column of infantry might be expected to cover fifteen to twenty miles a day on fair roads but, as an officer wrote home, it was all 'awful marches' over mountainous terrain, so bad that 'old campaigners of the Crimea, Indian Mutiny, and China say nothing ever came up to the fatigue and privations of this'.[24] Consequently, Napier's advance was no more than thirty miles a week or just over four miles a day. The slow pace was of considerable concern because it was essential to storm Magdala and return to Zula before the spring monsoon made the innumerable river gorges across the route impassable. By 14 February the advance guard had only reached Antalo, 140 miles inland. Napier tried his best to reduce the size of the column and to pick up the pace by discarding unnecessary baggage and reducing rations. Yet by 20 March the expeditionary force was still 75 miles from Magdala and halts had to be called to allow the men, exhausted from constructing tracks and digging defensive entrenchments at every camping ground, to rest.[25]

Where was Thesiger all this while? As DAG, Thesiger was Napier's chief of staff. He was universally regarded in the expeditionary force as 'the right-hand man of his chief', conveying his orders as his representative and ensuring they were carried out.[26] Several years later Napier noted disapprovingly that Thesiger was liable to 'a certain imperiousness in communication with others' that rubbed them up the wrong way.[27] But when on occasion Napier's decisions were not popular it seemed Thesiger bore the brunt, notably in the aftermath of an incidence of mass disobedience by the men of the 33rd (The Duke of Wellington's) Regiment of Foot. Disgruntled after a particularly gruelling march between Lat and Dida, they decided they were going to have a rest, jeered at their officers when they tried to move them on, and finally dribbled into camp throughout the night. Napier paraded the regiment the following morning and announced they would no longer have the honour of leading the expedition and that as punishment they were relegated to the rear. To pour salt in the wound, he informed them that their place in the van was awarded to the 4th (The King's Own Royal) Regiment of Foot, their great regimental rival. After the parade, the infuriated Major Cooper of the humiliated 33rd Foot, who had been in command of the regiment since the recent death of Colonel J. E. Collings, publicly addressed some 'intemperate words' to Colonel Thesiger. When he refused to retract them, he was placed under arrest.[28]

In the main, though, Thesiger's chief duty (as Napier later reported) was keeping him 'daily, nay hourly informed of the state of the supplies at every post from Zula to Head-Quarters'.[29] He was considerably helped in this duty by the telegraph line the Royal Engineers had carried as far forward from Zula as Antalo, half-way to Magdala (and which they restored whenever the wire was cut by the enemy). Thus, for much of the advance, Thesiger remained in direct telegraphic contact with Lieutenant-Colonel H. W. Holland, the Controller of Supply and Transport, who had remained at Zula maintaining supplies at the base of operations.[30]

It should be noted that while Thesiger was responsible as DAG for keeping Napier informed about the state of supply, he was not actually responsible for providing logistical support. That was the duty of the QMG's department, and the DQMG on the Headquarters Staff Thesiger headed was Lieutenant-Colonel R. Phayre, the energetic and experienced QMG of the Bombay Army. Phayre had worked closely alongside Napier from the outset in planning the campaign, and was also responsible for providing essential maps and intelligence reports of the area of operations.

It is consequently not going too far to suggest that, despite his superior Army rank and position at headquarters, in many particulars Thesiger would have found himself playing second fiddle to the well-informed DQMG on whose counsel he must have relied. Indeed, it was greatly to Thesiger's advantage that at headquarters he enjoyed the support of many other competent officers from the three Presidency armies, men with invaluable staff experience.[31] Surrounded as he was in Ethiopia by an undeniably competent staff, Thesiger would have been steered away from making any ill-considered decisions of the sort he later adopted in South Africa in 1878–9 when his small staff was of inferior calibre.

On 10 April 1868 (Good Friday), as Napier's vanguard approached to within twenty miles of Magdala, Tewodros's remaining small army of somewhere between 3,400 and 7,000 men under the command of Fitaurari Gabri attacked it at Arogi. Napier hastily ordered forward reinforcements, and a few hundred disciplined British and Indian troops armed with Snider-Enfields and supported by well-deployed 7-pounder mountain guns and Hale rockets easily stood off the Ethiopian attack. With only twenty of their own men wounded, two fatally, the British buried 560 Ethiopians, but estimated 700 killed and about 1,500 wounded.[32] Tewodros's defeated army largely dispersed, and only about 600 fighters returned to Magdala. This debacle was enough for Tewodros, and he turned the hostages he had been holding over to Napier. The official objective of the expedition had thus been attained at the very first armed encounter, at a firefight where Thesiger played no active part. The war was not over, however. Napier believed it still necessary to destroy Tewodros's stronghold on Magdala to underline the comprehensiveness of the British victory.

The defences of Magdala on its flat-topped mountain comprised little more than some large stone gates and high wooden stockades. On 13 April Napier ordered a frontal attack by infantry supported by fire from the rocket brigade and twelve 7-pounders. While Napier, Thesiger and the staff looked on – Thesiger was thus 'present' at the capture of Magdala as he had been at the fall of Sebastopol, although risking his life in the actual assault on neither – their men stormed the fortress with considerable bravery under fire (for which two Victoria Crosses were awarded to men of the 33rd Foot who were anxious to redeem the reputation of their regiment), and only suffered fifteen wounded. In despair, Tewodros committed suicide. The British then razed Magdala. As was customary, the loot they took was sold at public auction and the proceeds went as prize money to the troops. (Magdala was a poor place, and the prize money was as nothing compared to what the troops had garnered during the Indian Mutiny and the Second and Third Anglo-Chinese Wars of 1856–60.) The expeditionary force began its return march to Zula on 17 April. The rain came down in torrents, and the British withdrawal took on something of the aspect of a disastrous defeat with baggage animals dying from exposure, stores blown up or abandoned and crowds of refugees turned away. Napier's force finally reached Zula on 2 June. Thesiger's appointment as DAG officially came to an end on 10 June. By 18 June all the troops had departed, leaving nothing behind but the stripped stone pier.[33]

The purpose of the Abyssinian Expedition had been to secure British strategic interests in the Red Sea region. When withdrawing, Napier presented some of the captured guns, older muskets, ammunition and gunpowder to various chiefs who had assisted in the advance, notably Yohannes of Tigray. The Tigrayan warlord would use this welcome military equipment to seize the Ethiopian throne as Yohannes IV (1868–89), and would then go on to reunite the country and prove strong enough to repel not only Egyptian invasions in 1875 and 1876, but an Italian one in 1887 as well.[34] Ironically, the British thus left Ethiopia more powerful and united than they had found it but, now as a friendly power, it would serve as a bulwark against Britain's rivals in the region.

The underlying aim of the war had been to test out the efficacy of military reforms in the post-Mutiny Indian Army. One of these concerned medical arrangements that had failed so dismally for the British Army in the Crimea. Over nine months in Ethiopia, only thirty-four British or Indian troops died and 333 were wounded or fell ill. While death in action was the professional risk soldiers ran and was seen as a mark of honour, death from disease was considered somehow less honourable. The few fatalities from illness were largely due to sunstroke and to gastrointestinal infections once effective water purification ceased when the advance reached the highlands. That there were no more deaths was a matter for self-congratulation.[35] The effective evacuation of wounded or ill troops was another success. Beyond the railhead at the foot of the mountains, the rough terrain made the use of horse-drawn ambulance carts impracticable. Instead, resort was made to the *dhooly* used by the Indian Army, a heavy stretcher carried by ten bearers, or lighter stretchers, called *dandies*, requiring six porters. Once they reached Zula, ill and wounded soldiers were evacuated for treatment to specially fitted out hospital ships in Annesley Bay – another successful recent innovation.[36]

As Thesiger would have observed during this, his first taste of warfare in Africa, in tactical terms the troops had left no doubt as to the effectiveness and superiority of British discipline and armaments over those of the Ethiopians. Equally striking was the small number of British battle casualties compared to those suffered by the Ethiopians. This marked disparity came to be the expected norm in 'small wars', and was a significant indicator of cultural (if not racial) superiority, while body-counts – such as the careful accounting after the battle of Aroji of the Ethiopian dead – were taken as a reliable measure of the extent of victory. As *The Times* callously expressed it regarding the Abyssinian Expedition: 'A few wounds on our side against a great slaughter on the other duly represents the difference between civilized and semi-barbarous warriors.'[37] None of this would have been lost on Thesiger, and when he returned to Africa ten years later, it deeply coloured his expectation of similarly overwhelming an inferior foe on the field of battle. Where he expected the challenge to lie, as it had in Ethiopia, was in the sphere of logistics. Here, too, the Abyssinian Expedition had convincingly taught Thesiger that logistics could be successfully mastered with thorough and careful planning, even in a country as difficult to operate in as Ethiopia. Whether he would in practice manage the logistical challenges in Zululand as well as Napier had in Ethiopia was another matter.

CHAPTER 10

Adjutant-General in India, 1868–1874

EVERY CAMPAIGN BROUGHT WITH IT promotions for distinguished service in a dangerous venture. It also had its list of honours and awards which officers obsessively pursued as signifiers of success in the keen and often bitter competition for higher status in the military profession. In the nineteenth century the full-size awards were worn for everyday duties, and were integral to an officer's sense of self-worth. Successful commanders and senior officers scrabbled for baronetcies and peerages, and under increasing pressure for decorations and awards in the late Victorian period there was a steady inflation of honours. Nor did officers sniff at the monetary rewards that came with promotion, as well as the pensions that could be granted for meritorious service. Officers who had been wounded also received a pension, and the loss of a limb or an eye was not considered a bar to further service provided the officer could still march and fight.[1]

The Abyssinian Expedition was no exception. As befitted him as its brilliantly successful commander, Napier landed the greatest haul of rewards. He returned to Britain in June 1868 where he was fêted by the Queen and the nation and hailed as one of the finest soldiers of his generation. He was raised to the peerage on 17 June 1868 as the first Baron Napier of Magdala and Caryngton, granted an extravagant pension of £2,000 a year, awarded the GCB and GCSI and showered with many other honours besides.[2] Thesiger would have duly noted the cascade of honours poured over the head of a victorious general, an impression reinforced only a few years later when, after his highly publicised success in the Third Anglo-Asante War of 1873–4,[3] Garnet Wolseley (already a KCMG for his leadership of the Red River Expedition in Canada in 1870) was awarded the GCMG, promoted to major-general backdated five years to enhance his seniority in this rank, and granted a one-off sum of £25,000 in lieu of a smaller annual pension of £1,200.[4]

Gratifyingly, as Napier's DAG with the Abyssinian Field Force, Thesiger was the recipient of such honours as befitted his station and tireless and efficient service. He was one of the 14,000 recipients of the Abyssinian War Medal (established on 1 March 1869) with its scarlet ribbon with white borders. But before that, and much more prestigiously, on 14 August 1868 he was made a Companion of the Military Division of the Most Noble Order of the Bath (CB), the lowest of its three grades and available to officers once they reached the rank of captain. The order in its modern form, established in 1725 by King George I, had been remodelled after the Napoleonic Wars to reward officers who had rendered distinguished service on campaign.[5] On 15 August 1868 Thesiger was appointed an ADC to Queen Victoria, a position he held until 14 March 1877. The sovereign, as head of the Army, was entitled to appoint as many ADCs as she wished in recognition of distinguished war service. Besides entitling the recipient of this honour the right to wear the splendid uniform of a sovereign's ADC with its scarlet tunic with gold embellishments and the braided gold wire loops of an aiguillette with its decorative metal tips hanging from his right shoulder, the appointment carried with it promotion to the rank of full colonel in the army.[6]

Nor was this the last of Thesiger's rewards for his service during the Abyssinian Expedition. When in January 1870 Lord Napier was appointed CinC in India to succeed Sir William Mansfield (he actually held the post from 9 April 1870 – when he returned to India from Britain – until 10 April 1876),[7] he insisted to the Duke of Cambridge that Thesiger, with whom he had worked so well in Abyssinia, be made AG of the Indian Army, succeeding Colonel Errington Longden. The two principal subordinate officers to the CinC on his headquarters staff were the AG and the QMG, the latter of subordinate rank to the former. In 1868 Mansfield had unsuccessfully recommended Thesiger as ideally suited for the vacant position of QMG. Thesiger could console himself for his earlier disappointment when he secured the higher appointment. The AG, as the chief of staff to the CinC and his senior administrative officer, dealt with all military matters except those of movement and supply. This was a prestigious and powerful post, and Thesiger held it for the usual term of five years, from 17 March 1869 until 15 March 1874.[8]

After the Abyssinian Expedition, Thesiger had enjoyed a brief period in Britain before returning to India with his wife Adria and infant son.[9] On his taking up his new duties as AG in India, he and his small family left Bombay for Calcutta, the winter capital of India and Army headquarters. But it was at Simla (Shimla) that their next son, the long-lived Percy Mansfield Thesiger (7 November 1869–3 August 1959) was born. Only a few years before, in 1864, the then Viceroy Sir John Lawrence had declared Simla the summer capital of India, even though it was a thousand miles from Calcutta. In the 1830s the British had first established a hill station there in the cool forested foothills of the Himalayas to escape the baking summer heat of the Gangetic plain. Simla on its seven hills began to grow rapidly, and in the summer was home not only to many departments of government, but to the CinC too. When the Thesigers knew Simla, the viceroys still lived in a rather modest house called Peterhoff, and the grand palace in the Scottish baronial style that replaced it would not be built until 1889.[10] Many of the other government buildings, churches, large houses, luxury shops and hotels would not have been there yet in the Thesigers' time either. Consequently, the annual migration to Simla of the administration of India put a great strain on accommodation, and lodgings were extremely expensive. The viceregal hill station was socially exclusive to a daunting degree, and junior officers and officials had no place there. Social life in Simla was extremely active – including the amateur theatricals Thesiger so enjoyed – and on account of his high position he and Adria would have moved in the most exclusive of circles.[11]

Three more sons would be born to the Thesigers while at Simla. Two of them, Wilfred Gilbert (25 March 1871–31 January 1920) and Eric Richard (17 February 1874 –2 October 1961) survived into full adulthood, but the third, Harold Lumsden (19 May–2 August 1872) died before he was three months old. Infant mortality was high in India with its rampant diseases, and many a parent suffered heartbreak. But for surviving children of the British elite, a privileged Indian childhood surrounded by servants, comforts and the excitements of an exotic land was a time of never-forgotten enchantment, all the more so when replaced by the cold starkness of the boarding school to which they would be consigned when sent back to Britain for their education.[12]

By all accounts, Thesiger was a successful AG, conscientious, even-handed and clear-headed with a notable capacity for work.[13] Indeed, his voluminous surviving correspondence attests to a thorough, even over-meticulous bureaucratic set of mind. During the five years Thesiger was AG there was no major call upon the Indian Army, but there were various minor campaigns that demanded his full administrative attention, notably the Lushai Expedition of 1871–2 in Assam, and the Tochi Valley Expedition of 1872 on the North-West Frontier. These little campaigns were easily dealt with, but they helped Napier resist growing pressure for reductions in the Army of India by the economising and reforming Liberal administration that held power under William E. Gladstone from December 1868 until February 1874.[14]

The enormous cost of the Abyssinian Expedition had unnerved Gladstone's government. Under Lord Derby's previous Tory administration, Parliament had initially approved an expenditure of £2 million, and that had meant a 25 per cent increase in income tax for one year. In the end, the war cost the British taxpayer nearly £9 million, even though the government of India paid the cost of the Indian forces.[15] That was an astonishing sum when it is considered that the major campaign in the Crimea had cost about £80 million, only ten times more than this colonial 'expedition'.[16] Consequently, when in 1870 a Select Committee investigated the prolific expenditure in Abyssinia, it recommended that efficient business training should be part of the military system, and that henceforth it was expected that every colonial campaign should be conducted as economically as possible – a requirement upheld by Disraeli's Tory administration that succeeded Gladstone's Liberal one in 1874. Garnet Wolseley showed this could be achieved with the Red River Expedition in Canada in 1870 that cost less than £1 million, and with the Third Anglo-Asante War of 1873–4 that cost even less, a modest £767,093.[17] One of the major charges that would be held against Chelmsford (as he then was) concerned the excessive expense of the bungled Zululand campaign that amounted to well over £5 million, much more than any British government was happy to spend on a colonial campaign.[18]

During his time as CinC, and with Thesiger at his elbow, Napier continued with his previous efforts in the Bombay Presidency to improve the living conditions of British and Indian soldiers in India. Military reform was in the air in the post-Crimea and post-Mutiny environment, and Napier set about developing his soldiers as a fighting force, ready as possible for action, overseeing improvements in tactics, training and drill, and carrying out frequent military inspections throughout India. Here again he ran into opposition from the cheese-paring government over the cost of the extra training, especially with the number of 'camps of exercise' he initiated during which large-scale military manoeuvres were held. As Napier himself put it: 'I believe I have given a good stimulus and direction to the Field Exercise, leading Commanding Officers not to be glued to their parade grounds, but to shake out their regiments in the open country and to make use of the intellects of their officers,'[19] especially encouraging the initiative of the junior ones.[20] In the winter of 1873–4 Thesiger was selected by Lord Napier to command a camp of exercise at Roorkee north of Delhi, in the flat terrain under the Shivalik Hills of the Himalayas that allowed for full-scale manoeuvres. Thesiger noted complacently in his 'Statement of Service' written in 1881 that he 'Received thanks of Government of India for the manner in which I exercised that command.'[21]

It must be supposed that Thesiger conducted these manoeuvres at Roorkee in a conventional manner that would have been familiar to a veteran of the Crimean War or of the Indian Mutiny, for it turns out that, for all his serious study of military theory, he was a conservative at heart. As we shall see, the 1870s were a period of accelerated reform in almost every aspect of military life, discomposing conservative officers and invigorating reformist ones. The Franco-Prussian War of 1870–1 alerted many military theorists to the need to radically adjust infantry tactical formations to accommodate the range, rapidity of fire and accuracy of breech-loading rifles. From a British perspective, that meant re-thinking the classic two-deep line formation that had been the winning hallmark of the infantry for a century or more, and perhaps replacing it with the skirmisher-swarm formation the Germans had adopted in the recent war against France. How Thesiger approached this debate was publicly revealed in a long lecture he delivered at the Soldiers' Institute, Fort William, Calcutta, subsequently published in 1873 as an article in the prestigious *Royal United Services Institution Journal*, entitled 'Is a Radical Change in the Tactical Formation of our Infantry Really Necessary?'[22]

Thesiger's response to this conundrum is revealing on two counts regarding the nature of his military thinking. Firstly, at this time of theoretical ferment, the intellectual group of officers described as 'continentalists' were primarily concerned with how to fight a war against another European power, and consequently did not consider the 'small wars' of empire, which were conducted with obsolete tactics and strategy, worth serious consideration. Many published their ideas in the *RUSI Journal*, the same vehicle Thesiger chose.[23] Despite his experiences during the Abyssinian Expedition, it is evident that Thesiger's own sights were still set firmly on how best to wage a conventional war against another European power, or one that fought like it, as had the Indian rebels. The nature of 'small wars' did not enter his purview – an unfortunate omission, one might think, considering that the only field command he was ever to hold would require a strong grasp of 'irregular' warfare and how to conduct it effectively.

Secondly, his paper on changes to tactical formations – although clearly and cogently argued, and manifestly based on considerable reading in the literature, including the German authorities – exposes his conventional and cautious caste of mind. Indeed, the line of argument he adopted strongly indicates that he was following that taken by Colonel Edward Hamley in his *Operations of War*, published in 1866. In this monumental work, which rapidly became an established text, Hamley contended that rifled firearms had not in fact introduced radical reforms in warfare and only modified existing conditions. Hamley had dedicated his book to the Duke of Cambridge, and its essential conservatism appealed to a wide military circle that clearly included Thesiger.[24] It is unlikely, moreover, that when Thesiger prepared his paper on tactical reform that he had enjoyed beforehand the opportunity to read Colonel Robert Home's recently published *Précis of Modern Tactics* that subscribed to Prussian military doctrine. This work, prepared to aid officers in passing their examinations for promotion, subsequently achieved the status of a semi-official manual expressing accepted military doctrine.[25]

It is not necessary here to go into all the details of Thesiger's tactical recommendations, except to say that he considered that while the effectiveness of skirmisher-swarm formations remained unresolved, it remained best to instruct soldiers in conformity with 'our *present system*' to attack in two lines of infantry preceded by skirmishers (just as they had at the battle of Koondrye), but with adjustments that were 'merely an extension of our present drill'. He recommended that the attacking troops should lie down to load and fire when within range of the enemy, and that it was 'almost hopeless' to attempt to advance further unless flanking companies had been deployed to suppress enemy fire. These adjustments, he declared, were 'merely an extension of our present drill', and did 'not entail the study of an entirely new system'. In Thesiger's conservative summation, they possessed the merit of enabling soldiers to retain 'that two-deep line formation for attack, which the British army has always looked upon as peculiarly its own'.[26]

Thesiger at last said farewell to India when his term as AG expired in March 1874, and he returned to England with his growing family, most likely on one of the P&O steamers that since 1870 had been passing through the Suez Canal. He was destined never to see India again, although twice in the future he would unsuccessfully attempt to secure a command there. When he sailed from Bombay, he carried with him 'letters from [the] Government of India and [the] Commander in Chief expressing their sense of the ability and success with which I had performed the important and responsible duties devolving on me as Adjutant-General in India.'[27] A home posting could be a drear end to an Indian career,[28] but, with his sterling record and important patrons, Thesiger could be assured of a suitable home command. His military mind-set, as we have seen, was a solidly conservative one, and he would be sucked into the eddies of contention that affected all military careers during the period of Army reform initiated by Gladstone's Liberal administration.

CHAPTER II

Home Commands and the Cardwell Reforms, 1874–1878

ON HIS RETURN TO ENGLAND in mid-1874 with his valise stuffed with letters of recommendation, Thesiger could look forward to a good home posting. Prior to 1889, selection for higher commands and for staff postings was vested solely in the Duke of Cambridge, acting through his military secretary at the Horse Guards. As we have seen, the MS was a key and powerful military functionary, and Cambridge always appointed someone with whom he felt at ease, both professionally and socially. In August 1874 he appointed Lieutenant-General Sir Alfred Horsford, not only because he had a good manner and was widely known socially, but because of his excellent military and administrative record. He had served in the Seventh and Eight Cape Frontier Wars, the Crimean War and the Indian Mutiny, and then held major home commands and filled important staff positions. As MS, Horsford put forward three names as vacancies occurred for senior postings. He then usually notified the nominees to ascertain whether they were willing to be considered.[1]

On 1 October 1874 Thesiger was appointed Colonel on the Staff, commanding Shorncliffe Camp, a post he would hold for nearly two years until 31 December 1876. The camp had been established in 1794 just west of Folkestone on the south coast of Kent facing Revolutionary France with which Britain was at war, and was extended over the following years. A large redoubt, periodically upgraded, guarded the camp to its west. When Thesiger took up his command, the camp still offered only inadequate hutted accommodation for the soldiers, and it was only in 1890 that permanent barracks would be erected in their stead. The redoubt had been converted into a dwelling for the camp commandant, and that is where Thesiger established his family. The earthwork walls of the redoubt on the seaward side had been lowered so that they enjoyed a good view out to sea. It was while Thesiger was at Shorncliffe that his mother Anna Maria died on 9 April 1875 in her seventy-sixth year. Nothing is known about his relationship with her, and a reasonable presumption is that she was overshadowed in her son's life by his dominant father.

On 1 January 1877 Thesiger was given a more senior staff appointment when he was promoted Brigadier General commanding the 1st Infantry Brigade at Aldershot. This was a temporary rank only, bestowed on a colonel or lieutenant-colonel for the duration of a specific command. Thesiger's superior officer was General Sir Thomas Steele who commanded the Aldershot Division of three brigades from 14 April 1875 to 30 June 1880. Steele had much in common with Thesiger, having seen service in India as a young officer, and was a Crimean veteran. The camp on heathland between Aldershot and Farnborough in Hampshire south-west of London had been established in 1854 by Lord Hardinge, then the CinC, as a permanent training camp for the British Army. After the Crimean War, a division of regular troops was permanently based there. To accommodate them, between 1854 and 1859 two camps of around 1,200 wooden huts were constructed on the north and south sides of the Basingstoke Canal. When Thesiger took up his command, there were no married quarters and the wooden shacks were scarcely better than a slum. It would not be until late 1881 that the first steps were taken to convert the hutted camp into permanent barracks, a process only fully implemented with the Barrack Act of 1890.[2]

Soon after his arrival at Aldershot, Thesiger advanced in rank again thanks to the operation of the seniority rule and was promoted to the rank of major-general on 15 March 1877. Until the end of his life the Duke of Cambridge believed that promotion should proceed by seniority unless the officer was manifestly incompetent, and the Royal Warrant of 1877 ensured that promotion to the general-officer ranks was strictly according to seniority. For aspiring generals, however, this depended on those at the top of the list dying off to make room for them. Thesiger was fortunate in this regard, but as a general officer he joined an overpopulated cohort. The Royal Warrant of 1870 had limited the number of British generals, but adding together the effective and retired lists there were 332 of them in 1870, a figure that would increase to 456 in 1880. This represented a considerable surplus of general officers (forty of them in 1877). But general officer rank brought in no pay unless the holder secured an appointment as Thesiger had at Aldershot. It would not be until the end of the century that 'unattached pay' for generals was instituted.[3]

All promotions to the rank of major-general and above had to be formally submitted to the Queen for her approval, and she could (and did) resist the appointment of those she did not like.[4] The courtly and well-connected Thesiger was not one of these. Consequently, at fifty years of age, he evaded the requirements of the Royal Warrant of August 1877 that laid down that any colonel not promoted to major-general by the age of fifty-five would be retired.[5]

For a general officer to turn down the Horse Guard's offer of a command was a risk since it might offend Lieutenant-General Horsford and jeopardise future employment. Yet in 1877 Thesiger declined the offer of the post of DAG, Horse Guards (a position that Horsford himself had held between 1860 and 1866). At first glance it seems odd that the ambitious Thesiger would decline such a prestigious posting. Yet his reasons make sense, and were the same he would provide in 1880, following the Anglo-Zulu War, when he would refuse the command of the Western District. On both occasions he cited his preference for an Indian command because he believed he had acquired a special understanding of India's military requirements over sixteen years of service. Indeed, his years in India had been the most fortunate and satisfactory of his career, and he clearly hankered to resume his life there. Revealingly, though, on the second occasion he gave the additional (and doubtless compelling) reason that such a command required greater expenditure than was offered in pay and allowances, and would be too great for his limited private income.[6] As we have seen, he had previously found the cost of the required lifestyle in the Grenadier Guards too high to sustain. Now, as a married man with four sons to educate expensively at the ancient and prestigious public school, Winchester College, and then to established in their careers, he had to maintain a wary eye on his finances.

When Thesiger took up his command at Shorncliffe in 1874, it was just as a radical and expedited programme of military reform initiated by Gladstone's first Liberal administration took full effect. Edward Cardwell entered Gladstone's ministry in December 1868 as Secretary of State for War. He was a man of great initiative and perseverance but lacked any first-hand knowledge of the Army or war and had a personal distaste for his office, one which was reputedly the least coveted post in the government. Nevertheless, since the new administration was determined that the Empire should be run on a shoestring, his financial and administrative competence was expected to achieve economies in the military budget that accounted for as much as 30 per cent of government expenditure. At the same time, he was expected to combine reduced expenditure with Army reform aimed at increased military efficiency: an almost impossible balancing act.

Cardwell began his reforms in 1870 with the reorganisation of the top command of the Army. As we have seen, with the reforms that followed the Crimean War, the Secretary of State for War had been made responsible for the civil administration of the army. But Thesiger's patron, the Duke of Cambridge, who held his office of Field Marshal Commanding-in-Chief at the pleasure of the Crown, remained responsible for matters of command, discipline, appointments and promotion and retained his separate headquarters at the Horse Guards. This structure was not only cumbersome and inefficient, but Cardwell believed that since the Army was a parliamentary one there should be no division of authority and that the military element should be answerable to the civilian one. To subordinate the Horse Guards to the War Office required an Order-in-Council which Queen Victoria signed with great reluctance on 28 June 1870 since she regarded it as blow struck against the prerogatives of the Crown. The War Office Act of 1870 made clear that henceforth the civilian Secretary of State was the minister responsible to Parliament for the Army, and that the CinC was only his principal military advisor. This new relationship was made plain when the Duke of Cambridge had to vacate his independent office in the Horse Guards building and remove to premises in the War Office in Pall Mall, a move he took badly as a personal derogation. As an act of defiance, he persisted in heading his correspondence 'Horse Guards', and the government jibbed at preventing him from doing so.

Once the dust had settled, it was apparent that the reform of the War Office had merely constructed another form of the old duality. While the Secretary of State was now responsible to Parliament for the supply, equipment and preparedness of the Army, for the conduct of military operations, and for related political and legislative issues, the CinC advised him on military policy, organisation, and preparations for operations, and was still directly responsible for recruitment, appointments and promotions, discipline, education and training – as well as still retaining responsibility for command of the forces. And, in practice, Cambridge, who maintained his long-standing royal authority and prestige, did not necessarily communicate fully with every Secretary of State fleeting in and out of office, or kow-tow to the civilian administrators in the War Office. Ultimately, therefore, the terms of the War Office Act of 1870 made no practical difference to Thesiger and other officers who continued to look to the patronage of Cambridge and the Horse Guards for promotions and appointments.[7] Presciently, in his cartoon in *Vanity Fair* of the Duke of Cambridge published in April 1870, 'Atń' (Alfred Thompson) portrayed him in the driving seat of his carriage firmly holding the reins, while the accompanying text correctly declared that it was not 'likely that any War Minister will gain complete authority over the army while the Duke has the control of its discipline and patronage'.[8]

Thesiger and his fellow officers were much more directly affected by the abolition in 1871 of the purchase of commissions in the cavalry and infantry, the system whereby Thesiger had so rapidly risen to the rank of lieutenant-colonel. This was the most controversial of all Cardwell's reforms, eliciting the hostility of the Queen, the Horse Guards and the majority of officers who had never sought the measure. But there was no denying that purchase was an aristocratic system, favouring those with money and connections over those (no matter how talented) without them. The very fact that almost all officers by purchase – Thesiger included – were members of the deeply conservative, politically powerful class that radical members of the Liberal Party were bent on challenging, was enough to condemn the system in their eyes. That motive of class warfare aside, reformers could validly argue that the system of purchase was an obstacle to the development of more professional standards in the Army, including promotion by merit, and that it focused officers' attention too narrowly on their regiment at the expense of a wider vision of military affairs. Cardwell pushed his Army Regulation Bill through the Commons in June 1871 against stiff and determined opposition, but the Lords immediately rejected it. They were then controversially overruled by the issue of the Royal Warrant of 30 October 1871 that ended the purchase, sale and exchange of commissions with effect from 1 November 1871.

During Thesiger's active career the termination of the purchase system made little change to the social composition of the officer corps.

The hierarchical layering of late Victorian society remained essentially unchanged, and in most regiments the expensive mess traditions and other calls on an officer's pocket still exceeded his pay, thus necessitating a private income. Among the rank and file there was still the expectation that an officer must be a gentleman. And indeed, officers continued to come overwhelmingly from the younger sons of the aristocracy and gentry, the clergy, families with a tradition of military service and the rapidly growing professional and business classes. The majority of officers were increasingly the products of the public schools with their cult of team games that were intended to develop the health, strength, coordination, and quickness of eye essential for an officer, as well as moral virtues like self-discipline and team spirit.[9]

Yet there were other, immediate consequences of the abolition of purchase. The enterprise was an enormous financial burden to the state, costing the taxpayer over time £8 million to compensate officers for the loss of their financial investment and to provide them with pensions in recompense. Thesiger was among those affected. In terms of the Royal Warrant, he might have chosen to be among the 888 officers who between November 1871 and November 1873 arranged that the Treasury reimburse them the purchase price of their commissions and then retired. However, since he had decided to pursue his career and accept promotion, Thesiger's substantial capital investment in purchase was compromised. Fortunately for him, with the acceptance of the recommendations of the Royal Commission of 1875, as a major-general he could expect on compulsory retirement at age sixty-two in 1889 a pension of £700 a year. A further tweak to the system in December 1886 laid down that lieutenant-generals or full generals could retire up to the age of sixty-seven (that would be in 1893 for Thesiger) when the pension would be £850 or £1,000 respectively. It was in Thesiger's financial interest, therefore, to attain the highest general officer rank possible and to serve as long as he could. And, happily for him, the abolition of purchase did not guarantee the triumph of merit over seniority, and patronage remained a critical factor in promotion.[10] The Duke of Cambridge remained Thesiger's patron, and he was thoroughly patriarchal, reputedly knowing almost every officer by sight or name. And as Major-General Dillon assured the CinC's old mother, the Duchess of Cambridge, on 5 September 1880: 'Every promotion, every nomination is his own doing, *his* own decision.'[11]

The Cardwell reforms ensured that the Army over which generals such as Thesiger exercised command was structured rather differently from the one they had long been accustomed to. Not that its principal duties were changed. The Army was still expected to act as a colonial police force, and was required, with the assistance of the Militia and the newly reconstituted Volunteers (whose lack of training and equipment made them almost useless in practice), to deal with civil emergencies at home, and to resist invasion.

However, Cardwell recognised that this dual role was straining the small, long-service Army to breaking point. To overcome this, he looked to recent wars on the European continent. The principal lesson of Prussia's astonishing run of successes in the German Wars of Unification of 1864, 1866 and 1870–1 suggested that a country's military strength would in future be measured not so much by the size of its standing army, but by the number of trained reservists available to swell its ranks when called upon in an emergency. Short service, in other words, seemed the way to go, and had the additional advantage that it would save money, not least on the pensions payable to soldiers after twenty-one years of service. Cardwell's Army Enlistment Act of 1870 laid down that while enlistment would be for twelve years, only six would be spent with the Colours while the remainder would be in the Reserve which, it was intended, would be called out only in time of national emergency. Colonial wars, from which the Empire was never entirely free, would be fought (as they always had been) by garrisons on the spot, supplemented by small expeditionary forces from Britain itself.

This looked good on paper, but brought with it many difficulties. The annual turnover of men on short service was much higher than under long service, so recruiting would have to increase. The problem was that in many quarters the Queen's uniform was still seen as socially degrading, the last resort of the n'er-do-well. Besides, service conditions were not improved sufficiently to compete with civil employment. The infantry private's pay (13*s* 5¾*d* per week) compared badly with that of a lowly railway porter at 15*s*. Moreover, until the mid-1890s soldiers' pay remained subject to the various stoppages Thesiger had first encountered in Halifax in the 1840s – food, clothing, transport and barracks damage – that could leave a soldier with almost no pay at all. Barracks were still in the main bleak and insanitary, or no more than sordid hutments, as at

Aldershot, and the staple rations of bread and meat remained unvarying and unpalatable. Discipline was rigid and severe, though in 1872 Cardwell abolished flogging in peacetime. Except when on campaign, service life in garrison was a monotonous round of drill, parades, fatigues and gymnastic exercises, with recreational activity centred on regimental canteens and local brothels.[12] It is true that some elements of the life of soldiers in the ranks were improving in this period. Many late-Victorian officers – among whom Thesiger was numbered – were infused with gentlemanly and Christian evangelical virtues, and showed increasing concern about their men's conditions. Some (like Thesiger) attempted to stamp out drunkenness and encouraged alternatives like team sports and further study. Indeed, soldiers had to attend school for five hours each week, and promotion to NCO required a basic certificate of education. It is reasonable to estimate that by the 1870s about half the NCOs and private soldiers were literate, and were writing expressive (and uncensored) letters home while on active service.[13]

Even so, a career in the Army remained unattractive for most, and in poor recruiting years the minimum age and physical standards had to be lowered. Experience showed that men under twenty were generally unfit to stand the rigours of active service in tropical climes. But most recruits who came forward were under twenty, so the Army turned a blind eye. The Duke of Cambridge always remained extremely sceptical of the short-service soldier, claiming that the older man was fitter, more robust and more reliable on active service. And certainly, the number of unsuitable youthful recruits made it impossible to send some battalions on foreign service without asking for mature volunteers from other regiments. And as with age, so with physical standards. In 1870, five feet eight inches had been the standard required height, but by 1881 it would fall to five feet four inches. In sum, the short-service system and the failure to secure enough quality recruits to man it, meant that quality was sacrificed to quantity – and that quantity was never enough.[14]

Related to short service was another innovation that did not work as Cardwell intended: the system of linked battalions. Exhausted though he was and his health broken by his enervating parliamentary struggle to push through his reforms, in 1873 Cardwell determinedly rammed through the Localisation Act, the most significant element of his reform package. To his mind, the Prussian model of creating a large reserve seemed, in the interests of efficiency, to require the localisation of units. The Act ensured that the nominal connection of regiments with particular counties, dating from 1782, would be realised – at least in principle. All infantry battalions were affiliated in pairs (although Cambridge insisted that each of the affiliated battalions keep its own number, traditions, uniform and honours), and were localised for the purposes of recruiting and training in specific brigade areas. This in turn entailed dividing the country into sixty-six territorial districts, each to contain two affiliated line battalions, two Militia battalions, and a quota of Volunteers. All of these were to be formed into an administrative brigade, the whole to be centred upon a brigade depot (most of which had still to be built).

The purpose behind linking battalions was to ensure that one of each pair of a double-battalion regiment would normally be stationed at home, and the other overseas. The home battalion was supposed to supply trained reinforcements for its overseas partner, and eventually change places with it. Cardwell hoped thereby to bring order into foreign reliefs and to equalise the periods battalions spent abroad, thus preventing battalions such as the 95th Regiment from serving abroad continuously for decades on end.

In principle, the system of linked battalions seemed a sensible method of providing imperial garrisons in an army based on voluntary service. But there were problems aplenty with it. The numerical balance of linked battalions at home and abroad made no allowance for the demands of the small but frequent colonial campaigns which unbalanced the scales. Decades of parliamentary insistence that British garrisons be withdrawn from colonies of settlement and their defence be placed instead in the hands of the colonists themselves had gone nowhere, and settlers still depended on the Regular Army for their protection.[15] Consequently, by 1879 there were fifty-nine battalions serving at home and eighty-two abroad. This imbalance had further repercussions. The Committee on Army Reorganization of 1878–9 chaired by the AG, Lord Airey, found that the smaller number of home battalions had consequently become mere training units for those abroad, and were being deprived of their best men as drafts. As a result, more than half their establishment was made up of youths and other ineffective recruits unfit to be sent abroad, and Airey's committee found that by 1878 there was not one home battalion it considered ready for active service.[16]

Perhaps the critical fallacy in Cardwell's reforms was that he took as his model the Prussian system based on conscription. Not until midway through the crisis of the First World War would the British government and people countenance conscription, and Cardwell had no option but to attempt to garrison India and a worldwide empire with volunteer soldiers who could never provide the manpower required. When Gladstone and the Liberals lost the general election of 1874 to Benjamin Disraeli's Conservatives, Cardwell left office. Yet for decades to come his Army reforms lived on, albeit with various modifications, and became the prevailing system, ardently espoused by some officers, and viewed with suspicion and disapproval by the majority, not least by the Duke of Cambridge. Thesiger, as we shall see, aligned himself with the critics of Cardwell's system, but that was the structure in place when on 24 January 1878 Whe was offered the command of Her Majesty's Forces at the Cape of Good Hope, Natal and St Helena to replace the GOC South Africa, Sir Arthur Cunynghame, who was being recalled.

PART II

Command in the Ninth Cape Frontier War, 1878

CHAPTER 12

The Nature of the South African Command, 1873–1875

THESIGER'S COMMAND IN SOUTH AFRICA was the apogee of his military career, but also brought its nemesis. To understand the challenges and constraints he would face, it is consequently essential to set the local political and military scene in which he would operate. In March 1878 he stepped directly into the half-finished Ninth Cape Frontier War and into a dynamic situation where the policy-makers were busily in the process of attempting to assert British paramountcy over the sub-continent through suppressing a number of revolts and initiating a sequence of campaigns against still-independent African states. This concatenation of conflicts, several of which overlapped, and in which many of the same officers and military units were repeatedly deployed, number ten between 1873 and 1881. They were the Langalibalele Rebellion of 1873 in Natal, the Diamond Field Revolt of 1875 in Griqualand West, the Ninth Cape Frontier War of 1877–8, the Northern Border War of 1878 in Griqualand West, the First Anglo-Pedi War of 1878, the Anglo-Zulu War of 1879, Moorosi's Rebellion of 1879 in Basutoland, the Second Anglo-Pedi War of 1879, the Gun War of 1880–1 in Basutoland, and the Transvaal Rebellion (First Anglo-Boer War) of 1880–1. British defeats in the final two wars temporarily put paid to the project aimed at uniting South Africa under the Crown, one that would later be successfully consummated through victory in the Second Anglo-Boer War of 1899–1902.

Five of these campaigns between 1878 and 1879 were conducted under Thesiger's watch as GOC South Africa, although he personally took the field in only two of them, the Ninth Cape Frontier War and the Anglo-Zulu War. As GOC he was responsible for protecting British possessions in the whole region, and was bound when called upon to give military implementation to the political agenda of his superior, the High Commissioner. However, he was obliged to do so with the limited and heterogeneous military resources at his disposal. Moreover, the conduct of operations in southern African conditions required adaptability and improvisation that did not come easily to a GOC wedded to the more conventional aspects of military doctrine of the time, whether it was Thesiger or his predecessor.

As GOC, Thesiger succeeded General Sir Arthur Cunynghame, an excellent horseman and shot who, with his dashing mustachios and side-whiskers, strong nose and fine military bearing, along with an easy, bluff manner and disarming relish in his role, seemed to many colonists everything a GOC should be.[1] But, as we shall see, even if he had not actually failed militarily in the on-going Ninth Cape Frontier War, Cunynghame's performance had been lacklustre and his relations with the civilian authorities had been unfortunate. There was much there for Thesiger to ponder upon if he were not in turn to be subjected to the ignominy of Cunynghame's recall. But the circumstances of his command remained unchanged and, just as significantly, it was questionable whether he was the man to adopt an approach significantly different from Cunynghame's. For, in many respects, Thesiger was a pea out of the same pod as Cunynghame, his elder by fifteen years.

Their paths must surely have crossed in India where they both had served, or in London where they would have moved in the same social circles even if Cunynghame was of more established aristocratic lineage. He was the youngest son of Sir David Cunynghame, the fifth baronet, and the Cunynghames of Milnecraig in Ayrshire had been a Scottish landed family since the early seventeenth century. Arthur Cunynghame chose the Army as his profession and (like Thesiger) rose rapidly through purchase, exchange and patronage. Crucially for his essential network of connections in society and the Army, he took as his wife the elder daughter of Viscount Hardinge, the CinC. As an officer in the 1st Division in the Crimean War, he distinguished himself at the battles of the Alma and Inkerman, and earned the commendation of his commander, the Duke of Cambridge, on whose staff he served. When Cambridge succeeded Hardinge as CinC, Cunynghame consequently continued to enjoy the vital patronage of the Horse Guards. The trajectory of his career ensured that Cunynghame was a member of Cambridge's old-school military circle, and was no reforming, modern soldier of the Cardwell school. Yet he was somewhat different from the general ruck of conventional, aristocratic officers of whom Thesiger was a prime example. For Cunynghame was an extensive traveller and a quizzy, intelligent observer, the author of four books based on his military service and travels in China, North America, southern Russia and southern Africa. They reveal him as impulsive and enthusiastic, but unsystematic; his command in southern Africa sorely tested his military and political skills.[2]

Cunynghame had been on half-pay ever since his command of the Dublin District in Ireland had expired in July 1870. The 61-year-old lieutenant-general was aware that the South African command, effective from 5 November 1873, was neither a significant nor a highly prized one. On account of the relative smallness of the imperial garrison it was earmarked for a lieutenant-general and not a full general. Furthermore, a previous dearth of major conflicts in the region meant that the Horse Guards considered it safe to be entrusted to a well-connected if relatively undistinguished senior officer who, though conscientious, lacked experience in conducting independent operations. This low-profile command did not require a thrusting and innovative commander such as Sir Garnet Wolseley, who was currently dazzling the public eye in the Third Anglo-Asante War of 1873–4.[3]

Cunynghame had no sooner set foot on the quayside in Cape Town on 15 November 1873 than he was informed of the uprising in the Colony of Natal (a British possession since 1843) of Chief Langalibalele kaMthimkhulu of the amaHlubi, and the ignominious rout on 4 November at the Bushman's River Pass of a small force of colonial troops under the impetuous Major Anthony Durnford, RE. Cunynghame immediately ensured that Langalibalele was captured, found guilty of treason and imprisoned.[4] At first sight the so-called Langalibalele Rebellion was a small, easily contained matter, but it had significant repercussions. For years now white settlers in southern Africa had been feeling increasingly menaced by the growing quantity of firearms in African hands. Many were antiquated muzzle-loading muskets. However, increasing numbers were more modern firearms that migrant workers had acquired from unscrupulous colonial arms dealers, primarily on the Kimberley diamond diggings (these had opened up on the discovery of rich deposits of the gems in 1867) where tens of thousands of African labourers had converged.

Colonists' fears were growing too that the remaining independent African polities of the region, of which the Zulu kingdom was the most powerful, would join already subjugated Africans in white-ruled territories in rising up to extirpate the colonial presence – a chimera referred to as the 'black conspiracy'. The Langalibalele Rebellion seemed to give substance to these fears (unjustified as we know them with hindsight to have been) and led to urgent calls for the formulation of a common policy in the sub-continent aimed at disarming all Africans before it was too late.[5]

The shrill fallout of the Langalibalele Rebellion inevitably shaped the freshly arrived Cunynghame's perception of the dangers confronting his command. What particularly concerned him was the apparent lack of coordination and the confusion of command between the colonial and imperial forces deployed in the affair that (he believed) could easily have led to disaster.[6] Nor was this the only problem he discerned in undertaking his command effectively. As Thesiger would discover when he replaced Cunynghame, the position of GOC was a complicated one. The demarcation of British military authority in southern Africa had been tricky from the outset. After much indecision the imperial government had ruled that it reposed in the hands of the High Commissioner (who was always simultaneously the Governor of the Cape Colony, British since 1806) and in 1846 that official was designated CinC.[7] As the imperial agent in southern Africa directly responsible to the Secretaries of State for both the Colonies and for War, the High Commissioner's office enabled him to assert British paramountcy over the interior of southern Africa beyond the Cape Colony, including African kingdoms and the two Boer republics. His authority also overrode that of governors or lieutenant-governors of other British colonies in southern Africa, especially in frontier matters. Therefore, as CinC the High Commissioner could claim that the framing and implementation of defence policy throughout southern Africa was his preserve alone.[8] But did this mean the High Commissioner exercised actual control over all military planning and operations, or did these fall within the sphere of the GOC? That officer, whose command extended beyond the Cape to encompass all the South African High Commission territories, was himself responsible to the Secretary of State for War who framed imperial military policy. But (as we have seen), to complicate matters further, thanks to the unwieldy division of authority between the Field Marshal CinC at the Horse Guards and the Secretary of State for War, the GOC was also answerable to the Duke of Cambridge.

This is where a GOC's temperament and local standing came into play. Inevitably, if he were not a powerful personality in his own right, he would tend to lean on the High Commissioner for support when dealing with his superiors in London. That in turn could lead to the GOC effectively surrendering his autonomy to the High Commissioner, who might then assume the lead in military planning and the conduct of operations.[9] This proved to be the case with Cunynghame, but would it also with Thesiger once he took over?

If this were not challenging enough for a GOC unsure of his footing, Cunynghame also had to contend with the civilian government of the Cape. The High Commissioner, Sir Henry Barkly (December 1870–March 1877), saw to it that Britain annexed the diamond diggings and surrounding territory on 27 October 1873 as the Crown Colony of Griqualand West. Large-scale speculators with international finance behind them had commenced extracting diamonds on an industrial scale. Southern Africa, previously considered little more than an agricultural backwater, was rapidly being transformed economically and socially by what historians have dubbed the 'mineral revolution'. The exploitation of diamonds, combined with a boom in wool and ostrich-feather exports, meant that revenues in the Cape Colony began to rise steeply. For Gladstone's economising Liberal ministry, this indicated that the Cape could now pay for its own defence and administration, relieving the imperial government of the financial burden. A vociferous faction of colonists from the western regions of the colony under the leadership of John C. Molteno, the member for Beaufort West, was likewise eager to gain control over their own affairs. The answer was the granting of responsible government in June 1872 with Molteno as the Cape's first prime minister. Henceforth, the Governor of the Cape and GOC had to work with a colonial prime minister and his cabinet responsible to the elected legislative assembly.[10] This posed a fresh, untested question: what would be the proper respective spheres of military authority should the GOC and the Cape government – both of them effectively subordinate to the High Commissioner – come into dispute? It was Cunynghame's misfortune that this conundrum would become a crucial matter of policy while he was in command at the Cape.

South Africa, 1878–1879
British possesions
Independent Boer Republic
Portuguese Possessions
African 'Great Places'
(e.g.) Bapedi African chiefdoms/kingdoms
Fort
N
BECHUANALAN
Kalahari Desert
Batlharo
Batlhap
GRIQUALAND WEST
Griqua
Orange (Garieb)
CAPE COLONY
ATLANTIC OCEAN
Victoria West
Graaff-Reinet
Oudtshoorn
Robben Island
Cape Town
Stellenbosch
Swellendam
Simon's Town

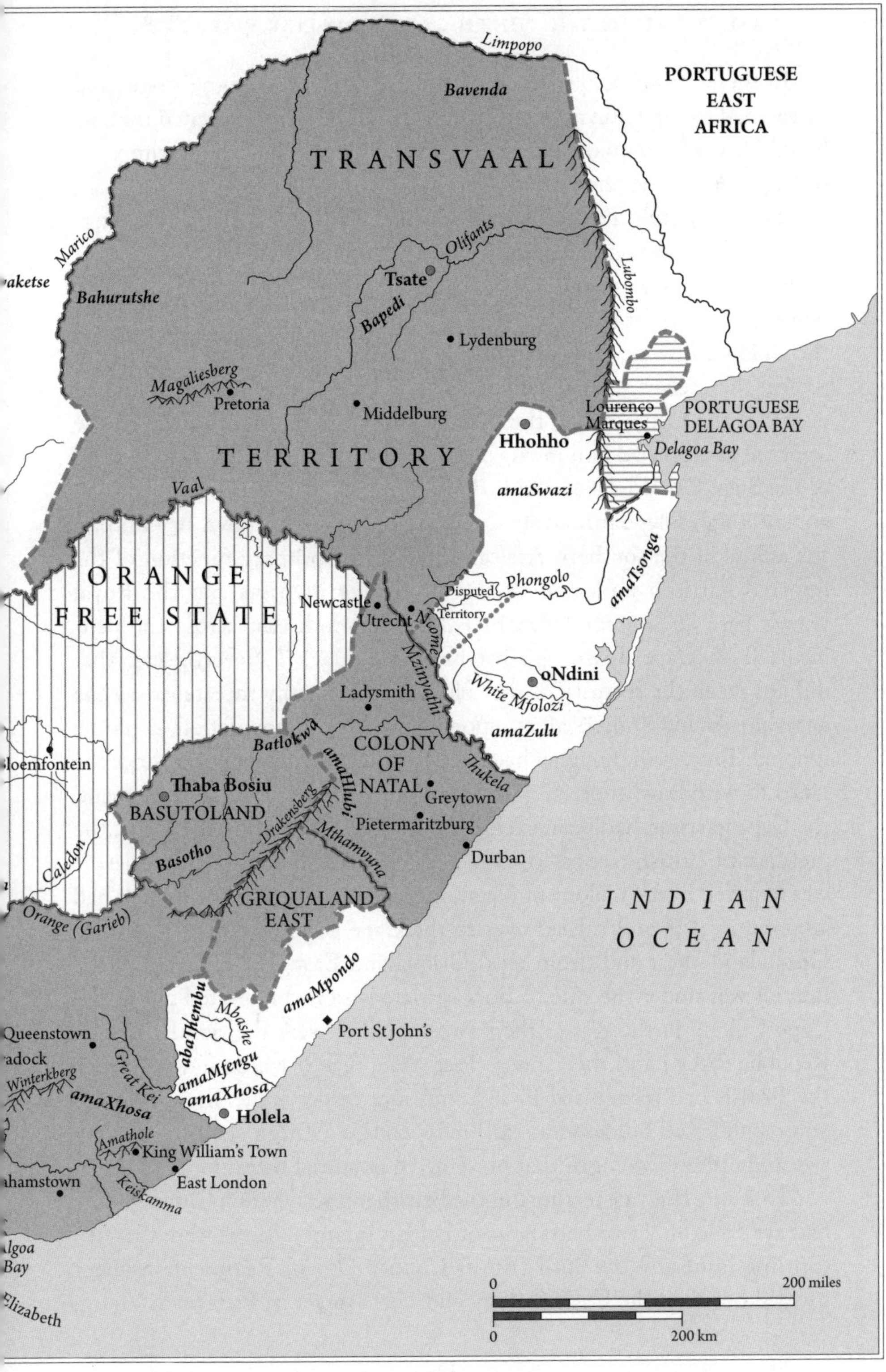

Limpopo
PORTUGUESE EAST AFRICA
Bavenda
TRANSVAAL
TERRITORY
Marico
Bahurutshe
Olifants
Tsate
Bapedi
Lydenburg
Lubombo
Magaliesberg
Pretoria
Middelburg
Lourenço Marques
PORTUGUESE DELAGOA BAY
Delagoa Bay
Hhohho
amaSwazi
Vaal
ORANGE FREE STATE
Newcastle
Utrecht
Disputed Territory
Phongolo
amaTsonga
Ncome
Mzinyathi
oNdini
White Mfolozi
Ladysmith
amaZulu
Batlokwa
amaHlubi
COLONY OF NATAL
Thukela
Thaba Bosiu
BASUTOLAND
Greytown
Pietermaritzburg
Drakensberg
Mthamvuna
Durban
Caledon
Basotho
GRIQUALAND EAST
Orange (Garieb)
INDIAN OCEAN
amaMpondo
abaThembu
Mbashe
Port St John's
Queenstown
Great Kei
amaMfengu
amaXhosa
Winterkberg
amaXhosa
Holela
Amathole
King William's Town
East London
Keiskamma
0
200 miles
0
200 km

If these complex questions of divided and overlapping command threatened to trip Cunynghame up and any GOC who succeeded him, he found himself potentially hamstrung by the sheer size of the territory his scattered and inadequate troops were supposed to defend.

'Her Majesty's Troops', stated Colonel William Bellairs (Cunynghame's DAG and a veteran of the Crimea with considerable staff experience in the West Indies, Ireland, Canada and Gibraltar), 'may be said to occupy South Africa (1) for the protection of Imperial interests, and (2) to assist the Colonials, who, from weakness in numbers may be unable wholly to protect themselves against native attacks.'[11] Indeed, ever since Britain had occupied the Cape during the Napoleonic Wars, its significance in the imperial context had lain in its control of the route to India. The opening of the Suez Canal in 1869 did little to diminish its strategic importance, and although safeguarding the Cape had increasingly drawn Britain into the affairs of the southern African interior, the primary function of the imperial garrison remained that of protecting its ports and the Royal Navy's base at Simon's Town in False Bay, south-east across the peninsula from Cape Town, against maritime attack.[12] Nevertheless, that did not mean the security of the colonists, perennially threatened by the antagonistic and numerically preponderant African population, could be ignored. Thus, even though it had been British government policy since the 1860s to withdraw imperial garrisons from colonies of white settlement, the Cape garrison had been exempted. Besides garrisoning the Cape, the presence of British troops – or the possible need to deploy them there – was required in the Colony of Natal, in Basutoland which the British had annexed in 1868 and turned over to the Cape administration in 1871, in Griqualand West and (from 1874) Griqualand East. The highveld of the interior was under the rule of Boer settlers who had migrated out of the Cape Colony in the 1830s. Their two republics were the South African Republic (SAR) and the Orange Free State (OFS) whose independence the British had recognised in 1852 and 1854 respectively. These colonies and republics all bordered on still independent African states of varying size and military strength that presented a potential threat to all of them.

To secure this vast territory in the British interest, in 1873 Cunynghame had available only two battalions of British infantry. These were the 75th (Stirlingshire) and the 86th (Royal County Down) Regiments of Foot divided between the Cape Colony and Fort Napier in Pietermaritzburg, the capital of Natal, where a garrison had been stationed since 1843.[13] At the beginning of 1875 the British garrison in South Africa was relieved. The 1st Battalion of the 24th (Second Warwickshire) Regiment of Foot arrived in Cape Town from Gibraltar in January. Its commander was a stocky 44-year-old, Colonel Richard Glyn, a veteran of the Crimea and of the Indian Mutiny whose passion was the hunting-field. Seemingly irascible, he was in fact a steady and dependable officer, if somewhat hide-bound and unadventurous, and (like Cunynghame and Thesiger) a beneficiary of the purchase system. The 1/24th was followed into harbour by the 1st Battalion of the 13th (1st Somersetshire) (Prince Alfred's Light Infantry) Regiment of Foot from Malta. While the headquarters of the 1/13th proceeded to Fort Napier in Pietermaritzburg, the rest of the regiment – along with the 1/24th – remained stationed for the moment in the Cape.[14]

The British forces in South Africa under Cunynghame's command were organised – on paper at least – in a clear-cut fashion.[15] The standard infantry tactical unit was the battalion, which on service was made up of a headquarters and eight companies, with a nominal complement of 30 officers and 866 men. A battery of six guns, each with its own limber, ammunition-wagon and crew, was the RA's usual tactical unit, but was often broken up, if necessary, into three divisions of two guns, each worked by two officers and 45 men. No regular cavalry were then stationed in South Africa, but mounted infantry were deployed instead. Experience had taught the British of the need to combine the mobility of cavalry with the infantry's firepower for scouting and fighting. The first South African dedicated mounted musket unit had been raised in the Cape Colony in 1827. Thereafter, mounted infantry were regularly raised from volunteers among the infantry battalions, and it was accepted even by conservative soldiers that they were particularly suited to colonial warfare. A squadron of mounted infantry, made up of two troops, usually consisted of three officers and 110 men.[16]

In addition to these troops, British generals of this period regarded the Royal Navy as a ready source of manpower and artillery in support of land operations. Cunynghame therefore knew that in an emergency he could always count on a Naval Brigade. This was a landing party of sailors and Marines trained in the use of small arms and light artillery that would come ashore with their ordnance from whatever warships might be in harbour at the naval base at Simon's Town, at Port Elizabeth or riding offshore at East London in the Eastern Cape, or anchored outside Durban Bay in Natal where large ships could not get over the sandbar.[17]

When Cunynghame took up his command, the standard overseas field dress for British soldiers was the undress uniform of a single-breasted five-buttoned unlined serge frock with white trefoil piping on the cuffs and around the shoulder straps and the bottom of the collar.[18] The frock was scarlet for infantry and RE, and blue for all others with the exception of the Rifles, whose frock and trousers were dark green. The traditional, coloured regimental facings were still worn on cuffs and collar. Trousers were dark blue with a scarlet welt down the outside seam for infantry, or a wide red stripe for RA, and were tucked into black leggings above the black leather boots, which were all too often of poor quality. Officers wore either the scarlet undress frock with a collar of the regimental facing colour and with gold lace on the cuffs, or a dark blue patrol jacket, which was the preferred choice in the field. Mounted infantry wore their regimental frocks with dark buff corduroy trousers tucked into their boots. Scarlet as a battledress would only be officially discredited by the Colour Committee of 1883, and it was not until 1897 that khaki was finally adopted as service wear on all overseas postings.[19]

The infantry were fitted with accoutrements of the Valise pattern introduced in 1871 consisting of a black waterproofed canvas sack, or valise, supported in the small of the back by leather shoulder straps whitened for parade (those of the Rifles were black). The straps were attached to a waist belt to which were fitted three black leather ammunition pouches (in 1874 these were replaced by buff leather ones) holding in total 70 rounds. The rolled greatcoat and D-shaped mess-tin were secured above the valise and the wooden, barrel-shaped 'Oliver' pattern water bottle was worn over the left shoulder. The bayonet was carried in a frog attached to the left rear of the waist belt. Mounted infantry carried their ammunition in leather bandoliers. Head-dress in South Africa was the light cork sun helmet covered in white canvas that replaced the blue helmet worn in Europe, and in 1877 was adopted for overseas service everywhere. The shiny brass shako-plate badge was usually removed on active service, and the white helmet was stained light brown with tea, coffee, mud or boiled mimosa bark, as were the equipment straps and pouches. Undress head-dress was the 1855 pattern forage cap for officers and the glengarry for other ranks.

On active service uniforms hardly met the requirements of the parade ground. They were seldom replaced, and after a prolonged campaign or a rapid series of them, as occurred in South Africa between 1877 and 1881, a regiment might be wearing a tattered assortment of garments, some of them civilian clothes, with everything patched and worn, including accoutrements that were missing straps and other elements. Their scarlet frocks were faded to the colour of brick-dust and their helmets were misshapen from having been slept in throughout months of campaigning. As an officer in the Second Anglo-Pedi War of 1879 wrote home, 'you would laugh if you saw the state of rags our men are in'.[20] Officers in the field tended in any case to adopt an idiosyncratic assortment of non-regulation dress, drab civilian shooting tweeds being especially favoured. Many of the officers and men also sported full beards on campaign, completing their wild appearance.

British infantry in South Africa were armed with the single-shot Martini-Henry rifle, weighing 9 pounds, that had replaced the Snider-Enfield. The Mark I was issued to the troops in 1874, and Mark II, with minor modifications, followed in 1876.[21] These rifles with their grooved barrels that made the bullet spin and fly more accurately, were a product of the breech-loader revolution of the late 1860s. The breech block was dropped when an external lever behind the trigger-guard was lowered, allowing a cartridge to be inserted into the rifle's chamber. (The British Army did not adopt a magazine rifle until 1888, when the Martini-Henry was replaced by the .303-calibre bolt-action Lee-Metford Mark I.) The metal cartridge, which was wrapped in waxed paper, contained the .450-calibre hardened lead bullet of 1.1 ounces, the black powder and cap. It was detonated when it was struck by the firing-pin released by the trigger, and the exploded propellant gave off dense white smoke. The fired lead bullet flattened on impact causing massive tissue damage and splintering bone lengthways, stopping its victim in his tracks.[22] After firing, the spent cartridge-case was extracted when the lever was lowered again, and the empty chamber was ready for the next cartridge. Improved breech-loading rifles such as the Martini-Henry made it possible to fire more rapidly (about six shots a minute) and very accurately up to 500 yards, and to do so while standing, kneeling or lying down. This flexibility encouraged open-order skirmishing tactics rather than close-order formations.

The Martini-Henry rifle, an improvement though it was over previous models, had several shortcomings. The paper-covered cartridge was difficult to insert, and the thin rolled-brass case could become stuck when the chamber was fouled and heated by exploded propellant and was often torn by the ejector lever. Fouling also lodged easily in the seven, deep-cut grooves of the rifled barrel. This significantly increased the rifle's already severe recoil, bruising the firer's shoulder, and made the barrel too hot to touch after repeated firing. The fouling also affected accuracy because the bullet would no longer spin properly.

By the 1870s marksmanship was taught and encouraged in the British Army, though not practised regularly enough, and sufficient emphasis was not given to individual fire. Volley firing was still considered effectual in the open field and was generally delivered by section because that way officers found it easier to control the rate of fire and prevent wastage of ammunition. In broken terrain, though, it was better for men to fire independently, selecting their own targets. Whatever the situation, it was important always to avoid premature firing until the enemy was within sufficient range and, when there was time to do so, range markers were put in place to assist in judging the distance and adjusting the rifle's sights. It was considered equally essential to maintain fire discipline, as slower, deliberate, better-aimed fire was more effective than blazing away.

The Martini-Henry rifle was supplied with a triangular socket bayonet, twenty-two inches long, that became universal issue in 1876. It was known as the 'lunger' because, when combined with the four-foot-long rifle, it gave a formidable reach of over six feet in hand-to-hand combat. However, its blade was of poor quality steel and too often bent or broke.[23] Officers still put considerable faith in the demoralising effect on the enemy (who were assumed to have no stomach for cold steel) of a well-timed bayonet charge. Even so, it was courting disaster to attempt a charge before the enemy had been thoroughly mauled by artillery and musketry fire and were on the verge of breaking.

Mounted infantry were equipped with the Swinburne-Henry carbine. Officers carried privately owned swords, those in the infantry being of the 1822 pattern with a gilt half-basket guard and a steel scabbard introduced in 1866. It remained in service until 1892. Officers in Highland regiments carried the 1865-pattern broadsword.[24] Officers also carried double-action .45 revolvers (usually the Mark II Adams model of 1872 or the Webley

Royal Irish Constabulary model of 1867 using .450-calibre centre-fire ammunition) which were not accurate at more than twenty-five yards at best.[25]

Both infantry and mounted troops conventionally depended on artillery to provide close fire support in combat, but the limited number of guns in South Africa at this time meant that the artillery never operated as a decisive force in its own right. The artillery weapons deployed in southern Africa in the 1870s were of several varieties, all firing explosive shells. The standard field piece was the 9-pounder Rifled Muzzle Loaders (RML) introduced in 1871 and sighted at between 1,690 and 2,780 yards. The lighter, 7-pounder RML Mark IV steel mountain gun came into service in 1873. It was mounted on a light, low-slung carriage, with a maximum range of 3,200 yards. The small bursting power of the shell fired by the mountain gun rendered its destructive effects insignificant, and case-shot (or canister) could only be employed effectively at ranges of less than 280 yards. These mountain guns, being more mobile, were considered better suited to local conditions than 9-pounders, but they capsized easily in rough ground. In addition, there was the 6-pounder Armstrong RBL (Rifled Breech Loader) introduced in 1859 with its unsatisfactory and unreliable breech-closing mechanism.[26]

Besides British regulars of the Cape garrison and the occasional Naval Brigade, Cunynghame had to rely on whatever settler units or African levies could be raised locally. In the Cape the most professional of these was the Frontier Armed and Mounted Police (FAMP), a paramilitary force which was the colony's only regular military unit and that had operated against Langalibalele in Basutoland. Created in 1855 and numbering some 1,000 men on paper, but only about 200 in peacetime, it accepted only whites into its ranks. Since 1866 its men were armed with breech-loading Snider-Enfield rifles and were dressed in loose suits of variously coloured Bedford cord and slouch hats. This costume was undoubtedly suitable for bush warfare, but was deplored as disreputable by British regulars. At Cunynghame's instigation an artillery unit was added to the FAMP's establishment in 1874, although this amounted only to one 9-pounder RML and two RML 7-pounder mountain guns mounted on poor, locally made carriages that broke under the smallest strain. Cunynghame considered the FAMP's weapons, training and discipline so seriously neglected over the last decades of peace that he despaired of their being effective in the field, even if the settler raw material was strong and robust.[27] In Natal, Cunynghame could call upon the white Natal Mounted Police (NMP), created in 1874, a small standing body of 170 quasi-military police in smart black corduroy uniforms who were stationed at various strongpoints in the colony to provide mobile defence.[28]

The dozens of exclusively white volunteer units of urban militia that had sprung up in Britain's South African possessions – as they had across much of the Empire – were of questionable military value. They were based on the British regimental system and were formed predominantly by English-speaking settlers. The first of such units in the Cape was raised in 1855, and by 1877 there were forty-nine of them. Unfortunately, most were little more than social clubs – often only several dozen strong – with few training sessions and low standards of drill and musketry. In Natal the 750-strong Natal Volunteer Corps, which had been established in 1854 for the protection of the colony and consisted of one artillery, two infantry and eleven mounted 'corps', mirrored the composition and training of the Cape volunteer units and was of equally questionable military value.[29] Nevertheless, the Cape and Natal units of mounted infantry were potentially invaluable for scouting, screening and raiding across the limitless terrain in conjunction with British mounted infantry. Mounted infantry and mounted colonial units usually dismounted in action to make best use of their firearms.

Additional mounted infantry were available in the form of the commandos of essentially rural volunteers who mustered during emergencies. Commandos had been first instituted in 1715 in the Cape when the Dutch East India Company sought mobile defence against Khoisan raiders, and the system had been carried with the Voortrekkers to their short-lived Republic of Natalia (1838–42) and to their two republics on the highveld. The British inherited the commando system and attempted to formalise it in the Cape in 1855 and in Natal in 1863. However, these Burghers, as they were called, consisted predominantly of poorly armed, rural Dutch-speaking settlers (and mixed-race men in the Cape) who resisted British-style military organisation and discipline and were, at best, undependable.[30]

And then there were African levies. Since the late fifteenth century, it had been the standard practice for the severely out-numbered colonial armies operating in Africa to raise African levies under the command of white officers for combat and logistical support. For Africans, serving the colonial power militarily was a means of maintaining their warrior traditions and sense of masculine honour – as well as reaping the rewards of fighting on the winning side.[31] Such especially was case of the amaMfengu of the Eastern Cape frontier (and to a much lesser extent, the neighbouring abaThembu) whom the colonial authorities rewarded with extensive grants of land taken from their defeated common enemies, the amaXhosa. The amaMfengu first entered colonial service in the Sixth Cape Frontier War of 1834–5 when they proved their worth as light troops operating in bush fighting which white troops found difficult work.[32] They subsequently fought in the Seventh (1846–7) and Eighth (1850–3) Cape Frontier Wars, carrying increasing numbers of firearms and confirming their expertise in irregular warfare and their mastery of remorseless scorched-earth operations. Besides their fighting skills, the amaMfengu were more economical than white troops because they were paid less and were disbanded after each conflict. The British consequently raised more and more Mfengu levies in each succeeding frontier war, so that by the time Cunynghame took up his command he could expect that in case of war they would make up the majority of the Cape military manpower available to him.[33]

Campaigning in southern Africa was conducted across great distances along rudimentary tracks (or none at all), in difficult terrain ranging from dense forests to semi-deserts, from rugged mountain ranges to bare, open plains. And always, the extreme climate was unforgiving. The essential logistical support for troops was consequently usually perilously close to breaking down. Nevertheless, this was an area where the Army habitually tried to save money. Logistics were in the hands of the chronically under-staffed and over-worked personnel of the Commissariat and Transport Department, the Ordnance Store Department and the Army Service Corps. Medical care was likewise provided on a shoestring. The Army Medical Department dated from 1873 when the existing regimental system of medical officers was abolished and the department assumed responsibility for trained surgeons of officer rank, station hospitals, and the trained orderlies and bearers of the Army Hospital Corps. The too limited personnel were always over-stretched, grievously so during a campaign when the number of wounded and ill soared.

Communication between headquarters and military units and posts was still by mounted despatch rider or flag signal. Both were slower but more reliable than the recently introduced field telegraph whose line was vulnerable to being cut by the enemy, and the Mance pattern heliograph, devised in 1869. This sent its signals by reflecting sunlight towards the recipient with a mirror mounted on a tripod, the beam being keyed on and off with a shutter or tilting mirror, thereby transmitting Morse code at the rate of up to twelve words a minute, depending on the skill of the operator. Under good conditions a flash could be seen from a vantage point thirty miles away with the naked eye and up to fifty miles away with a telescope. But of course, its flashes were halted every time the sun went behind a cloud or went down at night.[34]

CHAPTER 13

The Ninth Cape Frontier War, 1875–1878

GENERAL CUNYNGHAME SAW IT as his 'duty as a soldier' to advise his superiors that the best way to secure the scattered British territories of southern Africa from attack would be through federating them all under the Crown.[1] However, the notion of bringing the British colonies and two Boer republics under unified British rule was not Cunynghame's brainchild, and he was merely falling in with the dominant policy initiative of the moment. Some form of federation had long been in the air, as had the idea that the dangerously warlike independent African kingdoms of the region – most particularly the Zulu one – should be disarmed and politically neutralised. Gladstone's first Liberal administration had seriously toyed with the idea, but when Disraeli's Conservative ministry came to power in February 1874 it gained sudden momentum. The driving force was the new Secretary of State for the Colonies, the Earl of Carnarvon, who in 1867 had overseen the creation of the self-governing Dominion of Canada. He believed that if a prosperous, stable dominion could similarly be established at the strategically vital tip of Africa, not only would that secure the route to India, but it would lead to the economic integration of the whole area and bring the endemic, expensive little wars of the region to an end. The new 'Dominion of South Africa' would consequently be able to manage its own affairs and shoulder the costly burden of its own defence.[2]

Because the self-governing Cape Colony was by far the largest and richest white-ruled territory in southern Africa, with twice the settler population of the Colony of Natal and the two Boer republics combined,[3] it would inevitably have to take up the chief burden of confederation. And there was the rub. Carnarvon would have to persuade the prickly and parochial Cape Legislative Assembly to go along with him. Unfortunately for Carnarvon, the Molteno ministry did not share his imperial vision. For while it held that it was the obligation of the British garrison stationed in the Cape to defend the colony, it considered it quite another matter that the Cape should be required to pay for British troops furthering the confederation project beyond its borders.[4]

While the policy-makers began to clash pens over confederation, in March 1875 Cunynghame was faced by the need for military action in Griqualand West to put down an uprising by the unruly diamond diggers against British authority. The Diamond Field Revolt kept Cunynghame engaged until October 1875.[5] Meanwhile, Carnarvon despatched the thrusting Sir Garnet Wolseley as his Special Commissioner to Natal where, appointed as Administrator between April and September 1875, he pushed through constitutional amendments (the colony enjoyed limited representative government) that would make it easier for the Colonial Secretary to compel Natal to go along with his confederation plans.[6]

Wolseley, who had no high opinion of Cunynghame's abilities, used his time in Natal to make his own assessment of the military situation in South Africa. The War Office accepted his recommendations to redeploy the British garrison, and told Cunynghame to reinforce Natal by sending the 1/13th stationed in King William's Town (the administrative hub of the Cape Easter Frontier) to join its headquarters already at Fort Napier in Pietermaritzburg. Cunynghame moved two companies of the 1/24th from Cape Town to King William's Town to take the departing battalion's place. Wolseley also urged the reinforcement of the Cape garrison and the War Office complied, despatching the 2nd Battalion of the 3rd (East Kent) (The Buffs) Regiment of Foot. The 2/3rd landed in the Cape in November 1876 and took up position on the Eastern Frontier.[7]

Such were the British military disposition in southern Africa when in July 1876 the South African Republic went to war against the Bapedi, its independent African neighbours along its unsettled eastern frontier ruled by Sekhukhune woaSekwati, the resourceful and determined Maroteng paramount. The Boer campaign was ill-managed and mortifyingly unsuccessful, and alarmed settlers around South Africa predicted it would surely encourage other African societies to resist white rule. The Boers and the Bapedi eventually signed an inconclusive peace treaty on 15 February 1877,[8] but the Boer–Pedi War had already opened a new chapter in the affairs of the sub-continent.

The humiliation the Bapedi had inflicted on the anarchic SAR provided Carnarvon with an unforeseen but God-sent excuse to push forward with his stalling confederation ambitions. How better to reassure the Cape, reluctant about being drawn into troublesome frontier wars, than by annexing the SAR and then sending in British troops to deal conclusively with the Bapedi? This démarche required prior parliamentary sanction in Britain, secured through the passing of the South Africa Act of 1877 (the Permissive Federation Bill), and then the commissioning of a local agent to execute it. Carnarvon found him in Sir Theophilus Shepstone, a retired but experienced Natal colonial official. Shepstone entered the SAR in January 1877 with a small force of twenty-five NMP, and after negotiations annexed the bankrupt and demoralised SAR on 12 April 1877 as the British Transvaal Territory.[9]

At the same time, Carnarvon decided to entrust his revitalised plans for confederation to an imperial statesman capable of carrying them into effect, and to whom he would entrust considerable discretion to act as he saw fit. The instrument he selected was Thesiger's patron and friend from his days in the Bombay Presidency, the great Indian administrator, Sir Bartle Frere. A personal friend of Queen Victoria and of her heir, Edward, Prince of Wales – who like him, was a crack shot – there was no doubting Frere's intellectual powers and forceful personality any more than his ruthless ambition. Nevertheless, to the small number of those determined to be unimpressed, his outstanding qualities were somewhat obscured by his unctuously hypocritical and 'oily, almost old womanly manner and appearance'.[10] A more typical response was that of a susceptible young staff officer who wrote of the tall, dapper High Commissioner with his brown eyes, sharp nose and chin, greying hair and thick moustache:

> He had a wonderfully quiet, deliberate manner of speaking, never hesitating and never at a loss for the right word, giving you the idea that whatever might be the subject of the conversation he knew much more about it than any of his audience.[11]

Frere's multiple offices as High Commissioner and Commander-in-Chief in South Africa and Governor of the Cape gave him considerable discretion to act as he deemed fit in southern Africa because Carnarvon and the permanent officials in the Colonial Office depended on the advice of their senior administrator on the spot. And Frere was a man in whom the government was inclined to place implicit trust because of his unparalleled experience and vision as a celebrated administrator in British India. Moreover, Frere's responsible posts in India had trained him to act on his own initiative and he never drew back from taking vigorous executive action once he considered it necessary. A committed evangelical Christian, Frere saw it as his moral duty to bring British civilisation to benighted savages. Consequently, to this high-minded proconsul of empire South African confederation was an exalted goal, one that he intended should crown his distinguished career with his appointment as the first governor-general of the new South African Dominion and with his elevation to the peerage.[12]

On 31 March 1877 Cunynghame welcomed Frere ashore at Cape Town. The new High Commissioner knew his mission to consummate confederation would not be an easy one. Before he had even arrived in South Africa, the Cape parliament rejected in principle the draft Permissive Federation Bill, and the still-independent OFS would follow suit in May 1877.[13] The very annexation of the Transvaal would make Frere's task harder because Molteno and his supporters came out against the legally dubious subjugation of their brother Afrikaners by the perfidious British.[14] Undeterred, and while he waited for circumstances to arise that would favour the prosecution of his agenda, Frere strove to ensure that when they did, he would have sufficient troops available to ensure success.

The annexation of the Transvaal had an immediate ripple effect on the South African garrison and its deployment, and with Frere vigorously at the helm, more troops steadily became available. The 1/13th marched out of Natal to occupy posts across the recently annexed Transvaal. The 2/3rd stationed at East London and the newly arrived 80th (Staffordshire Volunteers) Regiment of Foot replaced them at Fort Napier.[15] The 88th (Connaught Rangers) Regiment of Foot would arrive in Cape Town in July 1877 and free the companies of the 1/24th still there to join the rest of the battalion on the Eastern Frontier.[16] Backed up by Frere, Cunynghame insisted that the Transvaal garrison must have a unit of Mounted Infantry and at least a division of 7-pounder guns. The War Office concurred and undertook to send out more artillery so that Cunynghame soon had at his disposal in South Africa three batteries of 7-pounder guns and a battery of 6-pounder Armstrong RBLs: a total of twenty-three pieces.[17]

With a greatly enhanced imperial garrison under his command, Cunynghame decided that he must embark on a tour of inspection of Britain's new bases in southern Africa.[18] On 3 May 1877 he sailed for Durban. There he found the Natal garrison under-strength after reinforcing the Transvaal, and he ordered up a half company of the 1/24th from the Cape. Cunynghame then travelled to the little village of Newcastle in northern Natal, strategically important as a forward base for the Transvaal and the Zulu kingdom. He instructed the companies of the 80th stationed there to build a barracks and a permanent fortification (named Fort Amiel after their lieutenant-colonel) on the heights above the town.[19] At Standerton to the north across the Vaal River in the Transvaal Territory he set up a cavalry station in the healthy high country free from horse sickness. Journeying on to Pretoria, the capital of the Transvaal, Cunynghame ordered the establishment of a military cantonment consisting of barracks, a hospital, bathing houses and a fort. On 21 June he travelled to the Eastern Transvaal and its gold diggings and acquainted himself with the villages and other bases from where in April 1878 the British would mount their own offensive against the Bapedi.

On 13 April 1877 Cunynghame attained the rank of full general through seniority. Technically, according to the rules of the service, in ordinary circumstances he was now of too high a rank to retain his South African command. However, it was 'intimated' to him that it was intended to leave him at the Cape to complete his period of a lieutenant-general's command.[20] This was just as well, because in September 1877 Frere summoned him urgently to proceed to King William's Town where trouble was brewing on the Eastern Frontier.[21] At the age of sixty-five and after forty-seven years in the Army, this was to be Cunynghame's first opportunity to demonstrate in a full-blown colonial campaign – and not a military promenade such as the Diamond Field Revolt had turned out to be – that he possessed the qualities of a field commander. It somehow seemed unlikely that he would. Lieutenant Nevill Coghill of the 1/24th, who was appointed his ADC in August 1876, wrote describing him as 'a highly enthusiastic soldier' but – unsurprisingly considering the nature of his career and social contacts – 'of the old school' with an obsessive over-emphasis on organisation and logistics.[22]

The Eastern Cape frontier zone, where Thesiger too would conduct his first campaign, was an extensive, summer-rainfall region, stretching between the Sundays River to the west and the Mbashe River to the east. Looming mountain chains covered by a thick mantle of forest and bush bounded it to the north, and to the south the lush coastal bush came down to the Indian Ocean. Many rivers and streams flowed erratically down from the mountains and hilly uplands, and it was in the river valleys that possessed the best soils and pasturage where people preferred to settle.[23]

Between 1779 and 1853 eight increasingly destructive wars had been fought along this fluctuating frontier that pitted white settlers, along with British troops and their African allies, against the amaXhosa people. Fatally for their ability to mount a unified armed response against the forces of colonialism, the amaXhosa never developed into a unified state akin to that of the amaZulu and were politically fractured into several chiefdoms. The rulers of both the amaNgqika and amaNdlambe west of the Kei River in the Ciskei were of the royal Tshawe clan, with the head of the amaNgqika being the senior of the two. Both conceded precedence in ritual matters to the chief of the amaGcaleka who lived east across the Kei River in the Transkei because he was of the senior Tshawe line. They also acknowledged him as their paramount chief, but his real authority ended at the Kei River, and instead of being a powerful monarch, he was merely the accepted figurehead of the Xhosa nation.[24]

The national weapon of the amaXhosa was the throwing-spear, but during the course of the nineteenth century they had abandoned shields and added more and more muzzle-loading muskets to their arsenal.[25] Nevertheless, firearms played an uncertain role in Xhosa warfare because the amaXhosa remained doubtful about their effectiveness and regarded them as ancillary to their conventional weapons, except for hunting.[26] Traditionally, the amaXhosa favoured pitched battles, in which they deployed into a chest and two enveloping wings with two further columns positioned in support on either flank. But by the time of the Sixth Cape Frontier War of 1834–5 the amaXhosa knew better than to risk frontal attacks against the British with their superior firearms, and were increasingly resorting to irregular warfare with ambushes and sudden raids. Finding it difficult to defeat the Xhosa warriors in the field, especially when they resorted to guerrilla tactics, the British and Cape troops increasingly adopted a brutal, total approach to frontier warfare that targeted the homes, livestock, fields and lives of civilians in order to break the spirit of the amaXhosa and bring about their submission.[27]

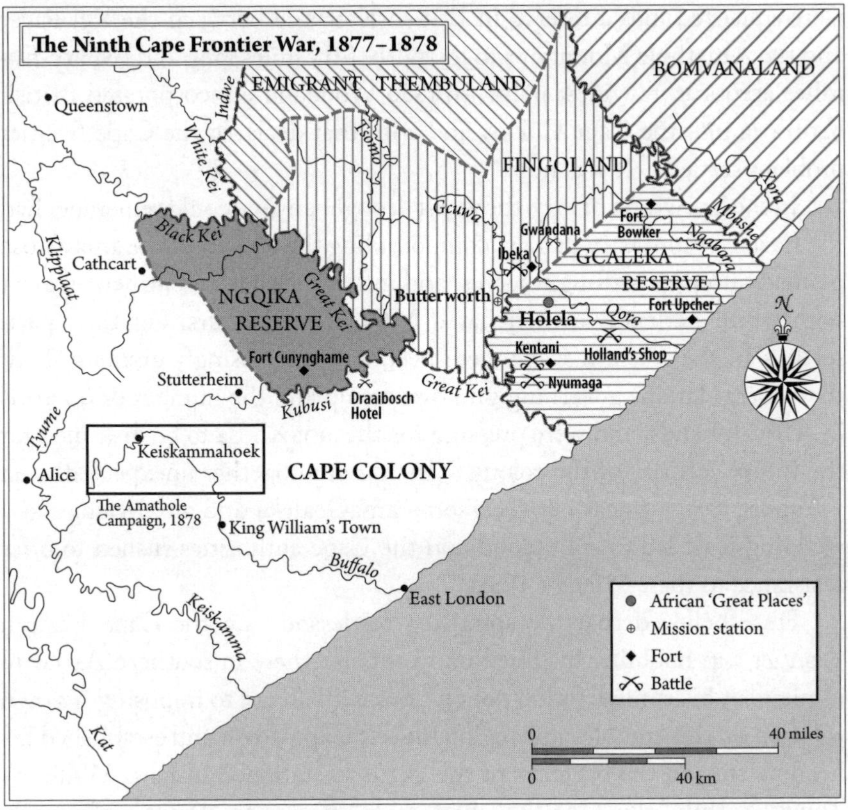

In 1865, as part of his general settlement of the frontier after the devastations and mass expulsions of the Eighth Cape Frontier War of 1850–3 that opened up British Kaffraria (the territory between the Keiskamma and Great Kei Rivers) to white settlement, the Governor of the Cape, Sir Philip Wodehouse (1862–70), settled the amaGcaleka in a stretch of territory between the Great Kei and Mbashe Rivers. It was little more than forty miles long and twenty miles across. This reserve constituted only a third of the former Gcaleka domain. The Thembu chiefs, who had fought as British allies in the late war, were resettled in the northernmost third of the former chiefdom, to be known as Emigrant Thembuland. Wodehouse made over the central third to the main British allies in the late war, the amaMfengu. Although not officially part of the Cape, Fingoland (as this territory was named) was placed under colonial military protection because it was accepted that it constituted a particular affront to the amaGcaleka whose 'dogs' or vassals the amaMfengu had once been. The amaNgqika were squeezed into a reserve in British Kaffraria between the Kei River and the Amathole Mountains to its south, fifty miles long and twenty-five miles across at its widest point. In 1866 Wodehouse incorporated British Kaffraria into the Cape Colony and with that declared the Cape frontier problem settled.[28] It was not.

In the late winter of 1877, the worst drought anyone could remember had the Eastern Frontier in its grip, compounding the despair of the amaXhosa penned into their stifling reserves, and inflaming their resentment against both white settlers and their hated Mfengu neighbours. For their part, settlers in the Eastern Cape were becoming increasingly anxious about the lax regulations governing gun ownership and the number of firearms in African hands, and were pressing for the amaXhosa to be disarmed for the future security of the colony.[29] Then, not altogether unexpectedly, on 3 August 1877, a fracas between some amaGcaleka and amaMfengu at a wedding feast led to spilt blood and the Cape authorities rushed to offer assistance to their Mfengu allies.[30]

Frere believed that the spiralling restlessness on the Cape Eastern Frontier was hobbling his freedom to act elsewhere in southern Africa to implement his confederation policy.[31] So, with an eye to imposing his own solution on this troublesome region, he left Cape Town and established his headquarters in the barracks of the garrison stationed in King William's Town. Sarhili, the Gcaleka chief and Xhosa paramount, reluctantly prepared for the unequal conquest, fatalistically declaring: 'I intend to fight the English. I am in a corner. The country is too small and I may as well die as be pushed into a corner.'[32]

Frere convened an informal war council where wrangling immediately broke out between him and Cunynghame on one side, and two ministers of Molteno's cabinet on the other, over their respective spheres of authority in the impending campaign. It was eventually agreed that while the general was to be in formal command of all the troops, whether imperial or colonial, the actual conduct of operations in the Transkei was to be left exclusively to colonial troops – even though Frere and Cunynghame were decidedly sceptical of the Cape's military ability to handle a campaign on its own. As for Cunynghame, he regarded himself as the High Commissioner's obliging military instrument whose duty it was to carry out Frere's policy in his day-to-day military arrangements, and he made no significant decisions without consulting him.[33]

The upshot was that while Colonel Richard Glyn, who commanded the British garrison stationed in King William's Town, distributed his troops in military posts along the Kei River to secure the Cape frontier, the colonial forces marched off towards the Gcaleka Reserve. Under the command of Colonel Charles Griffith, a tough frontiersman who had fought in the Eighth Cape Frontier War, had suppressed the Langalibalele Rebellion and was currently the Cape Government Agent in Basutoland, they consisted of the 180 FAMP and 2,000 Mfengu levies. On 29 September a Gcaleka army of 7,000 or so warriors armed with spears and muzzle-loaders, and under the command of the famous war-leader Khiva, attacked Griffith at his fortified headquarters in a small trading store at Ibeka on the west bank of the Qora River, just within Fingoland. In two days of fighting the amaGcaleka were repulsed by the heavy fire laid down by Griffith's garrison and finally routed in a mounted counter-attack.[34]

Following this crushing defeat, Sarhili attempted to negotiate a settlement, but Frere decided that the time had come to annex the Gcaleka Reserve and include it in his South African confederation. On 18 October Griffith began his advance through the Reserve in three lightly equipped columns, comprehensively devastating it as they went. The columns encountered little opposition because the Gcaleka warriors deliberately fell back eastwards with their families and livestock across the Mbashe River into the sanctuary of neutral Bomvanaland. In mid-November Griffith called off the colonial campaign. His commissariat, which he had entrusted to the hands of inexperienced colonials rather than to the Army's professional Commissariat and Transport Department, had failed as (Cunynghame predicted it would), and his ill-disciplined volunteer forces were simply packing up and going home to enjoy their loot. Nevertheless, it appeared that his campaign had achieved its objective. On 13 November notices went up offering grants of land in the conquered territory, and on 1 December 1877 Frere designated the Gcaleka Reserve a Cape magistracy. The war, it seemed, was over.[35]

In fact, far from being extinguished, the flames of war were about to burst into a furious blaze that would still be burning when Thesiger took up his command. During Griffith's campaign in the Gcaleka Reserve, some amaGcaleka had sought sanctuary west of the Kei. Frere decided these refugees on Cape soil must be disarmed. When they took flight to the Ngqika Reserve, the nearby settlers panicked, and Cunynghame attempted to cordon off the Ngqika Reserve with a thinly stretched line of imperial troops. The amaNgqika did not resort to arms as it was feared they would, but the military presence along their borders deeply unsettled them. Some began to urge war as a last chance to regain their lost independence. The amaGcaleka, however, anticipated them. With their families and herds stowed away beyond the Mbashe, their warriors resumed the struggle. Griffith had now only 500 FAMP available to patrol the long Mbashe River border with Bomvanaland. On 2 December 1,000 or more Gcaleka warriors under the formidable Khiva slipped undetected over the Mbashe and attacked an FAMP patrol at Holland's Shop on the west bank of the Qora River. The skirmish was inconclusive,[36] but the over-stretched FAMP were near exhaustion and Griffith called for reinforcements. At this juncture Frere decided he had had enough of colonial dithering and incompetence. Ignoring colonial sensitivities, on 8 December the High Commissioner placed Cunynghame in active command of the imperial troops he intended to send into the Transkei to deal with the amaGcaleka. At the same time, he placed the general in direct control of the colonial troops, which he pulled back to monitor the Ngqika Reserve.[37]

Colonel Glyn, whom Cunynghame characterised as 'a straightforward man of great energy, and good common sense',[38] was gazetted Commander of the Army of the Transkei with the acting rank of Brigadier General with his headquarters at Ibeka. There he was reinforced for the planned offensive by six companies of the 88th Regiment from Cape Town and a Naval Brigade of 196 men – forty-two of them Royal Marine Light Infantry – from HMS *Active*, a 3,078-ton 270-foot corvette built in 1873 of iron and sheathed wood. The 'Bluejackets' of a Naval brigade (as opposed to the 'Redcoats' of the infantry and Royal Marines) wore blue frocks and trousers with leather-bound tan canvas gaiters. Their officers wore a double-breasted blue frock or a single-breasted five-buttoned blue tunic with blue or white trousers and white canvas leggings. Headgear was a blue foreign-service helmet, a blue cap or broad-brimmed straw sennet hat for sailors, or peaked blue cap with white cover for officers.

Men of the Royal Marine Artillery with the Naval Brigade, dressed in their dark blue tunics with red collars and blue trousers with a broad red stripe, manned one of the new-fangled Gatling guns that had come into service in 1871 and had first been employed in the Third Anglo-Asante War of 1873–4. Mounted on a carriage similar to that of a field gun, it could fire 200 Boxer .250 rounds a minute from ten rifle barrels rotated around a fixed central axis by a manually operated crank. The bullets were fed by gravity from a revolving upright case holding forty cartridges which was replaced after every four revolutions. Though highly effective up to 1,000 yards, causing terrible casualties to an exposed enemy, the Gatling was an unreliable weapon on account of its tendency to jam. More traditionally, the Naval Brigade also had two rocket tubes. They fired the Hale's rocket with explosive head, approved in 1867, that came in both 24-pounder and 9-pounder versions and had a hand-lit fuse. The Royal Artillery, when they employed rockets, preferred to fire them from a V-shaped trough on a stand rather than from a tube, which was more suitable for shipboard service.[39]

Because so few of the Cape volunteer units came forward for Glyn's campaign, and virtually none of the Boer commandos, two new formations were created under British – not Cape – command. One was infantry (sardonically nicknamed 'Pulleine's Lambs' after their commander, Major Henry Pulleine of the 1/24th);[40] and the other was mounted infantry, the Frontier Light Horse (FLH), raised by Lieutenant Frederick Carrington, another officer of the 1/24th. Both units were made up of the dregs of railway gangs, diamond diggers and the like. The colonial roughs of the FLH had no specific uniform, but usually wore yellow or buff corduroy with black trimmings and a wideawake hat with a red puggaree. Under Carrington and Major Redvers Buller, who succeeded him in command in April 1878, they were forged into a tough and efficient unit, invaluable for scouting and raiding.[41]

While Glyn, on Cunynghame's orders, waited at Ibeka for reinforcements and concentrated his supplies, Khiva himself with a small escort slipped past Cunynghame's patrols and through the cordon surrounding the Ngqika Reserve. On 22 December Khiva brought Sandile, the Ngqika chief, a personal message from Sarhili in which the paramount begged him to bring all his adherents into the war. Despite his misgivings, the day after Christmas Sandile's war parties broke out of their location to raid and ambush settlers as well as amaMfengu, and some went on to blockade the forts along the Cape's side of the Kei. Thrown into panic, the white farmers and their families fled to the military posts or villages for protection, just as they had done in so many previous frontier wars.[42]

Cunynghame, meanwhile, arrived at Ibeka on Christmas day to superintend operations in the Gcaleka Reserve. He had had a narrow squeak on the way when he and his small escort only just evaded an encounter with Khiva's party on its way to the Ngqika location.[43] Aware that the Ciskei was bursting into flame behind him, Cunynghame decided that the best way of containing the conflagration was to deploy his troops in the Transkei to prevent the amaGcaleka from joining hands with the amaNgqika.

Cunynghame was almost obsessively thorough concerning logistics, but his approach to strategy was ploddingly conventional and lacking in vision, and he never contemplated the option of irregular operations against an elusive foe. Instead, he fell back on the usual procedure – familiar to him from operations on the North-West Frontier of India – of mounting cumbersome sweeps through enemy territory, seeking decisive pitched battles and building lines of fortifications to contain the foe. Consequently, in a futile repetition of Griffith's strategy in October, on 27 December he ordered three columns to commence a drive to the coast, and then to swing east to the Mbashe. For two weeks Glyn's columns, wilting badly in the heat of midsummer, traversed most of the Gcaleka Reserve but made little contact with the enemy. Presuming that the Gcaleka warriors had fallen back into Bomvanaland as they had during Griffith's campaign, Glyn had a series of earthworks constructed along the Mbashe intended to keep them safely bottled up east of the river.

But Glyn had been duped. While his columns were grinding east towards the Mbashe, the main body of Sarhili's forces slipped past them in the opposite direction, crossed the Kei, and joined forces with the amaNgqika. Precisely what Cunynghame had planned to prevent had disconcertingly occurred. The combined Xhosa army was now concentrated to Glyn's rear in the densely wooded valley of the Tyityaba River that ran into the lower Kei River from the south-west, about fifteen miles from the coast and five miles west of the Kei River. There the amaXhosa kept the scattered British forces in the area fully occupied. Guarding the approaches to Bomvanaland had been rendered embarrassingly pointless. Badly wrong-footed and his campaign a failure, Cunynghame had no choice but to order Glyn to pull his columns back to Ibeka. Once concentrated there, Glyn was to march them westwards towards the Kei preparatory to engaging the combined Xhosa forces in the region of the Tyityaba valley.[44]

At this tense juncture, Molteno, the Cape premier, arrived at Frere's headquarters on 8 January 1878. In lengthy, stormy meetings he rejected Cunynghame's sole command over all the forces on the Cape frontier – not least because he found the GOC over-cautious as a commander and an unbearable old chatterbox to boot – and insisted that the colonial forces would undertake their own independent military campaign in the Ciskei under the command of Griffith whom, on 15 January, he appointed Commandant-General. Frere and Cunynghame were both outraged.[45] As Frere later explained to Sir Michael Hicks Beach (an aloof but strikingly handsome man – a veritable 'scagliola Apollo'[46] – known as 'Black Michael' for his biting tongue,[47] who in February 1878 replaced Carnarvon at the Colonial Office), he strongly believed that it was 'the constitutional duty of the Governor and Commander-in-Chief to guard against such a dangerous anomaly as a divided command of military forces . . . in one area of operations'.[48]

Cunynghame, with his eyes anxiously on the military situation, had pressed Frere to write on 31 December to Carnarvon urgently requesting that two regiments be sent out immediately to the Cape as reinforcements, and that a battery of field artillery accompany them. Carnarvon, who firmly believed he had to act to rescue the confederation project from the 'black conspiracy' against the white presence in southern Africa that he imagined was being stirred to violent life by the unresolved war on the Cape Eastern Frontier, responded with the immediate despatch of the 90th (Perthshire Volunteers, Light Infantry) Regiment of Foot, followed by the 2nd Battalion of the 24th Regiment.[49]

Meanwhile, far away from the political wrangling in King William's Town, Glyn's campaign in the Transkei was faring well. On 13 January 1878 about 1,000 Gcaleka and Ngqika warriors attacked the camp of Glyn's Right Column near a small river called the Nyumaga, nineteen miles to the south of his headquarters at Ibeka and about six miles from the Kei.[50] For defence Glyn had two infantry companies (one each of the 1/24th and the 88th), two troops of the FAMP, fifty Bluejackets of the Naval Brigade with two rocket launchers, and two 7-pounder guns of the Royal Marine Artillery. Critically, these white troops were augmented by a strong force of Mfengu levies under Veldtman Bikitsha, some of them mounted.

In deploying his small force for battle, Glyn was acting in the spirit of the new flexible battlefield training adopted by the War Office and printed in the 1877 edition of *Field Exercise and Evolution of Infantry* – recommendations that made Thesiger's urging in his *RUSI* article of 1873 (*see* Chapter 10) that existing tactical formations be retained distinctly old-fashioned. All the dispositions were Glyn's to make for, as an officer who fought in the campaign put it, 'The men are not supposed to know anything about strategy, and not much about tactics, except *Fire low, fire slow, and obey orders*.'[51] The key to the 'bush-fighting' of small wars – according to this manual that for the first time officially recognised their existence alongside conventional campaigns against other continental powers – was a loose skirmishing order in an extended firing line with the troops making the most of the terrain and natural cover since they could kneel or even lie down when firing their Martini-Henry rifles. A section on 'Extended Order' allowed an interval of at least three paces between each file in a skirmishing line, and permitted extension to ten paces depending on circumstances. When a company was extended as a fighting line, another was supposed to act in support about 150 yards to the rear. Any part of the extended line could be reinforced by throwing forward supports. If forced to retire, the extended firing line would fall back through the supporting line, and the two would continue falling back by alternate portions, each company covering the retreat of the other.[52]

At Nyumaga Glyn adopted an apparently winning tactical formation that would influence Thesiger, as we shall see, in his future field dispositions against African enemies. Glyn positioned his infantry in skirmishing lines on either side of the fixed anchor of field guns with a second line (as recommended by the *Exercise and Evolution of Infantry*) in support. The mounted troops and African levies hovered on the flanks to foil an enemy attempt to envelop the formation and to act as a mobile force in counter-attack and pursuit. The potential flaw in this formation was that the Martini-Henry rifle depended for its effect on both range and volume, and on average it took forty or fifty rounds to kill a single enemy. The recommended rate of fire, even in a hot action, was only four shots a minute, and it remained to be seen whether a thin skirmishing line, even at point-blank range, could develop the necessary volume of fire to stop a determined charge. At Nyumaga it did, and in what became essentially a firefight the the amaXhosa were routed and dispersed west across the Kei River into the bush of the nearby Tyityaba valley. Follow-up operations, however, achieved very little despite some sharp skirmishes, and the amaXhosa easily eluded the plodding British who were overcome by the summer heat. With no resolution in sight, Cunynghame decided to suspend operations until Glyn had built up more supplies and until the promised British reinforcements had arrived.

At his headquarters in King William's Town, Frere was seething at Molteno's denial of his authority as High Commissioner over the Cape forces. Matters reached a head at a stormy meeting on 31 January. Frere decided to have done, and on 6 February 1878 dismissed Molteno's uncooperative ministry. Beaconsfield's government subsequently endorsed Frere's coup, convinced that Molteno's parochial insistence on separate and independent colonial operations was both absurd and dangerous. Meanwhile, Frere wasted little time in appointing a prominent Eastern Frontier politician, J. Gordon Sprigg, to replace the insubordinate Molteno as prime minister. The High Commissioner at last had a ministry he could rely upon to be sensible about military matters, and to insist on African disarmament so essential for the cause of confederation.[53]

The very day after Frere dismissed Molteno, on 7 February 1878, the amaGcaleka were knocked out of the war. At the end of January Glyn had decided to establish a forward supply and operations base deep in Gcaleka territory to support further sweeps across the Transkei. Captain Russell Upcher of the 1/24th was placed in command and pitched his camp on some high ground 300 yards from the southern slope of a high hill called Kentani, twelve miles south of Ibeka. To defend the position, Upcher laagered his wagons and built a strong earthwork surrounded by trenches and rifle-pits. The 600 white troops who held the defences consisted of 200 British regulars of two companies of the 1/24th, 25 Bluejackets of the Naval Brigade, 90 mounted men of the FAMP and 70 of Carrington's FLH. They also had two guns – a 7-pounder and a 9-pounder – and a rocket tube. Some 560 Mfengu levies were deployed on the flanks outside the defences.[54]

The crops had failed in the Eastern Cape because of the prolonged drought, and Upcher's patrols had destroyed whatever stores the amaXhosa had left. Made desperate by their people's plight, the Xhosa leadership – just as Glyn had intended – decided they must risk all in a decisive battle.

Glyn had advance word that a Xhosa attack was imminent, but being unsure whether it would be on Ibeka or Kentani, with good strategic foresight he positioned a strong reserve column of infantry, horsemen and guns at the mission station at Tutura, midway between the two bases. As he anticipated, though, Sarhili, having brushed aside Sandile's counsel that guerrilla operations would be the more effective strategy, decreed that Kentani was to be the objective since it posed a greater strategic threat than Ibeka.

Early on the wet, misty morning of 7 February a joint Gcaleka and Ngqika Xhosa army of about 5,000 warriors advanced on Kentani. The 2,000 or so amaGcaleka were under Khiva and under Sarhili's son, Sigcawu. Sarhili himself harangued his warriors before the battle, reminding them that he 'was the tree their fathers had lain under, safe and sheltered, and for whom their fathers had often fought the white man. To-day they could show if they were the white man's dogs, or if they were their fathers' sons.'[55] Unfortunately for them, the amaGcaleka hearkened to their war-doctors who admonished them to fight in the heroic style of their ancestors, and to attack in traditional massed columns. The Ngqika contingent, however, preferred to advance in the skirmishing order they had learned to adopt in previous wars.

British skirmishers went out to meet the amaXhosa and deliberately stung the Gcaleka contingent into committing themselves to the attack without waiting for the amaNgqika to come up in support. Once in range of the fortified British camp, the amaGcaleka were cut down in swathes by the defenders' concentrated, disciplined firepower. After less than twenty minutes the Gcaleka attack faltered, and Glyn's mounted men charged out and routed them. The Ngqika contingent finally came on in their open order. They skilfully held their ground in the ensuing firefight until Sandile's scouts warned him that the strong reserve Glyn had posted midway between Kentani and Ibeka was marching towards the battlefield. Sandile thereupon broke off the engagement and the amaNgqika retired in good order, hotly pursued by the British mounted troops. In the course of the battle the British lost only two amaMfengu and four horses killed, along with nine men wounded. In stark contrast, an estimated 400 amaXhosa perished, mainly men of the Gcaleka contingent.

The triumphant British celebrated Kentani as a model action. The key to success had been Upcher's strongly fortified position defended by concentrated firepower that held off the enemy. Once the worsted foe had disengaged, mounted troops, supported by levies on foot, had been essential in converting a withdrawal into a rout. This was the winning tactical formula against African foes, but Thesiger would not adopt it in Zululand until after the disastrous battle of Isandlwana, which had been fought more or less following the dispositions Glyn had made previously at Nyumaga.

As for the amaGcaleka, their fighting spirit was utterly broken by their rout at Kentani, and they would never again appear in the field deployed as an army. Quite daunted, Sarhili fled over the Mbashe to the sanctuary of Bomvanaland. With the crumbling of Gcaleka resistance, the amaNgqika were left to carry on the war alone. Their forces were as yet relatively unscathed and they pulled back across the Kei to pursue their tried and trusted guerrilla tactics in the Amathole Mountains to the south of their reserve in the Ciskei.[56]

Despite his troops' victories at Nyumaga and Kentani, General Cunynghame would not long remain in charge of the Ciskei campaign. For a few heady days he believed that, following on the convincing defeat of the amaGcaleka, he was set to crown his career by subduing the amaNgqika as well. The promised reinforcements were marching in: the 90th had already arrived in the Ciskei; the 2/24th was on its way (it would land in March), and the 200-strong volunteer Diamond Fields Horse had cantered in from Griqualand West. With a line of posts established along the railway that now connected King William's Town to East London, Cunynghame was ready to march.[57]

But politics would trip him up, and Cunynghame never quite grasped that dealing effectively with political problems was as much part of a commander's brief as was winning battles. He simply did not see how his public record of 'want of cordiality' with the Cape ministry over the direction of military policy would make him an embarrassment to his political masters in London who were trying to mend fences with the colonial government.[58] If Cunynghame had proved himself to be an outstanding commander it might have been different, but as a merely adequate one he was dispensable, and he was offered up as a placatory sacrifice. Unbeknown to Cunynghame – and at Carnarvon's insistence during his last days in office before his resignation on 23 January 1878[59] – the British government had already decided on his recall.[60]

It would prove no consolation that Cunynghame's long-time patron, the Duke of Cambridge, assured him on his return to England that in his opinion he had committed 'no fault whatsoever',[61] and had earlier gone so far as to write to G. Gathorne Hardy, the Secretary of State for War, in support of his 'poor old friend'.[62] But Cambridge felt he could not intervene because the reasons for Cunynghame's recall were not purely military ones. As for Cunynghame, overwhelmed by indignation, there was no palliating 'the grievous injury' he had suffered when he was superseded 'by a junior officer in command of an army in the field when in the midst of a successful command'.[63] The irony is that his successor was likewise destined to believe he had been betrayed by his political superiors at the very moment he had achieved victory in the field.

CHAPTER 14

General Officer Commanding South Africa, 1878

WHO WAS TO REPLACE CUNYNGHAME as GOC South Africa and what were the criteria for his selection? As we have seen, prior to 1889 selection was vested solely in Cambridge as CinC acting through his MS, Sir Alfred Horsford, although the Secretary of State for War's approval was required. In gauging an officer's capabilities there was little for the Horse Guards to go on besides the annual confidential report that provided information on his technical competence, leadership ability and personal qualities such as tact, intemperance or bad temper. By the mid-1870s over 6,000 annual reports were reaching the Horse Guards and most were tactfully noncommittal or spuriously enthusiastic, and it was not always easy to determine which officers should be advanced. When considering an officer for higher command, there were further considerations besides laudatory reports and how well he was known to the Horse Guards. His state of health was a consideration, as was his social standing. Indeed, there was a distinct correlation between high command and smart regiments – a disproportionate number of higher appointments were drawn from these. Royal interest too was a factor in disposing of commands. Both the Queen and the Prince of Wales had their favourites and did not hesitate to put pressure on the Horse Guards to appoint them. By the same token, they exercised their influence to block the careers of those they held in disfavour.

Promotion and selection to higher command was further complicated by the so-called 'rings' – personal cliques of officers determined to have their own way with appointments. Cambridge was surrounded and supported by his own circle of conservatively minded officers of the Horse Guards party such as Horsford and General Sir Charles Ellice, AG to the Forces since 1876. Cambridge was especially prejudiced against appointing officers who were members of Wolseley's ring, thrusters who (in his opinion) had already been over-promoted at the expense of other deserving officers.[1]

For his part, Wolseley – ambitious, self-seeking and dictatorial – wrote off the conservative old fogeys around the Duke who, he was firmly convinced, were determined to undermine the military reforms Cardwell had inaugurated.[2] He therefore saw it as his mission to demonstrate that the Cardwell reforms did work, and on his various campaigns assembled a staff equally committed to that end. This select coterie of officers, first formed for the Asante expedition of 1873–4 and known subsequently as the 'Ashanti Ring' (or 'Mutual Admiration Society', as its detractors dubbed it) was made up either from decorated veterans of distinguished service, or from intelligent Staff College graduates who showed promise.[3] They, in turn, benefited from their successful service with Wolseley that gained them public recognition and rapid promotion.

Cambridge was probably correct, however, in his disapproving concern that the elite Ashanti Ring depressed morale elsewhere by denying excluded officers of promise the opportunity to shine. It also encouraged emulation that further fractured the service. In India, the ruthless careerist Sir Frederick Roberts's rival ring formed a similar coterie of favoured officers grouped around a charismatic commander who believed that the Horse Guards never favoured those on Indian service. In direct opposition to the members of Wolseley's ring, who determinedly touted the effectiveness of the new system of short service, Roberts and his circle were convinced of its many flaws (as were Cambridge and his clique) and campaigned determinedly and fruitlessly against it.[4]

The agendas and ambitions of these rival military factions – the Duke's, Wolseley's and Roberts's – prevented the emergence of a common military doctrine in the British Army, a single imperial strategy or the creation of a general staff on the successful German model that might have challenged Cambridge's authority as CinC (which is why he opposed its formation). The rival rings accentuated the inevitable rifts within the Army that were played out in the immensely complex internal manoeuvring concerning command.[5]

It is in this context that Thesiger's appointment to the South African command must be considered. One candidate canvassed was the squint-eyed Lieutenant-General Sir John Jarvis Bisset. He had considerable local experience, having fought in the Sixth, Seventh and Eighth Cape Frontier Wars before pursuing his military career in India. The problem was that as a seventeen-year-old ensign in the Cape Mounted Riflemen, Bisset had been of the party that had pursued the escaping Hintsa, the Xhosa paramount, to his death on 11 May 1836 and then mutilated his corpse. At the subsequent court of inquiry he had given blatantly contradictory evidence. Then, in October 1847, he had played a duplicitous role in the surrender of Sandile, the Ngqika chief. Consequently, even though Cambridge considered him well suited to rough colonial warfare, Frere warned that his rather discreditable record in the Cape had not been forgotten there. Moreover, Frere feared that Bisset, who had been brought up in the Cape, and who had gone on to marry the daughter of Sir Theophilus Shepstone, the new Administrator of the Transvaal, would align himself too closely with the settler interest. Besides which, Bisset was very much a colonial rough diamond, and as Colonel since 1875 of the undistinguished 106th Regiment of Foot (Bombay Light Infantry) which had been integrated into the British Army in 1861, he lacked connections with a smart regiment. Frere believed that the GOC, with whom he would work closely, must be of acceptably high social and military standing, and Bisset simply did not fit the bill.[6]

Lord Carnarvon then suggested that Brevet Colonel George Pomeroy Colley, currently Private Secretary (PS) to the Viceroy of India, replace Cunynghame. Colley, who had passed through Staff College with unusual brilliance, had held a number of military academic posts and served with distinction on Wolseley's staff during the Third Anglo-Asante War. He had served again with him in Natal in 1875, and was one of the leading reforming officers of the day. That alone was enough to damn him in Cambridge's eyes, compounded by the fact that he was one of Wolseley's foremost protégés. In any case, Cambridge considered that Colley was far too junior in rank for the post of GOC, and Gathorne Hardy, the Secretary of State for War, concurred.[7]

A temporary possibility that came under consideration was General Sir Daniel Lysons, a veteran of the Crimea and former AAG at Horse Guards, but he was altogether too distinguished for the post. Another name that was very briefly considered was that of the Welsh Major-General Sir Arthur Herbert, but Gathorne Hardy rejected him as simply too lacklustre. Nor did he view Lieutenant-General Sir Patrick MacDougall – in his day a leading exponent of the conservative but realistic school of military theory[8] – as sufficiently physically fit for a command in Africa's unhealthy climate, although MacDougall subsequently survived his five-year appointment in 1878 as Commander of the British Troops in Canada despite its harsh winters. Cambridge briefly contemplated Colonel Glyn, Cunynghame's successful second-in-command at the Cape and the victor at Nyumaga, but like Colley he was deemed too junior in rank. A very likely candidate was Major-General the Hon. Henry Clifford, who had won the Victoria Cross at Inkerman. He had a military record at the Cape, having fought in both the Seventh and Eighth Cape Frontier Wars, and also possessed considerable administrative experience. Currently, he was the AAG at Horse Guards and ADC to Cambridge himself.[9] He probably would have been the best choice for the South African command, and during the course of the Zulu campaign Cambridge would send him out in May 1879 as Chelmsford's effective minder and the successor to the command should he die or break down. But in 1878 Clifford seemed too senior, and was in any case too valuable to Cambridge at Horse Guards.[10]

So, in the event, and not necessarily as the first choice, on 24 January 1878 Major-General Thesiger was informed that he had been selected to replace Cunynghame in the South African command with the local rank of lieutenant-general (which he held from 25 February 1878 to 16 July 1879).[11] His appointment was thanks in no small part to his acceptability to Cambridge who, as Wolseley acerbically put it, delighted 'to honour those of the old cut-and-dry model from whom nothing new is ever to be expected'.[12] And certainly, Thesiger, was well known to Cambridge and trusted by him, a general officer with a very solid and successful – if conventional – career behind him and with the elevated social standing Frere considered essential in a GOC. Yet the *imprimatur* of the Horse Guards brought with it its own peril. For it was in the nature of the rivalry between the rings that should a commander associated with one of them fail, then the members of the other rings would gleefully grasp the opportunity to discredit him and, by association, the military doctrine of the circle to which he was affiliated.[13] Wolseley was never likely to miss the golden opportunity to excoriate both Chelmsford (as he was by then) and the Horse Guards when, as Cambridge's man, he stumbled badly in Zululand.

A few days before his official appointment as GOC South Africa that commissioned him with bringing the Ninth Cape Frontier War to a speedy and successful conclusion, Thesiger received an unsolicited brace of letters and a memorandum advising him on how to conduct the campaign in the Eastern Cape. These missives were sent by General Sir John Michel, CinC Ireland, who was a distinguished soldier of considerable combat experience in the Crimea, India and China, and who had served in the Seventh and Eighth Cape Frontier Wars.[14]

Thesiger was bound to take Michel's counsel most seriously. He warned Thesiger that his was 'a command of great danger to your reputation' and reminded him that two excellent generals, Sir Peregrine Maitland and Sir Harry Smith, had been ignominiously superseded towards the end of the Seventh and Eighth Frontier Wars respectively[15] – as of course Cunynghame had been during the course of the Ninth. It must have been somewhat chilling to read that Michel wished him 'better fortune' and that he undertook to put in a helping word if Thesiger found 'events placed to your discredit'. In the same lugubrious vein, Michel promised him 'a long and tedious campaign' and commiserated that the 'want of efficient Mounted Infantry will be a sad thorn in your side' and that he should make 'every exertion' to raise more. The reason he must do so was, Michel explained, that in the difficult warfare he would have to conduct in the Cape bush, mounted men were essential for pursuing the only successful *modus operandi*, one adopted ever since the Sixth War and carried out by Michel himself in the Seventh and Eighth, namely 'tormenting the Caffres' by capturing their cattle, burning their homesteads and destroying their crops when they were nearly ripe. And to wage this war of attrition with safety required 'judicious skirmishing thro' the bush'. Warning Thesiger that he must expect a guerrilla war of ambushes, he strongly urged him never to move without flanking parties under reliable officers first taking control of the high points overlooking his advancing columns. 'If you pursue my tactics,' concluded Michel, 'and have no butcher's bill, you will probably lose kudos and perhaps credit. But you will know that you are right.'[16]

And so, indeed, it would turn out. For Thesiger was destined to fight no decisive, pitched battle in the Eastern Cape such as Kentani, but would have instead to conduct protracted, unglamorous operations against elusive irregulars who could only be defeated through the systematic destruction of their homes and means of subsistence. And that meant, as would subsequently be the case in the Zulu campaign, waging war on civilians who supplied their menfolk in the field, and whose sufferings demoralised them and helped induce their surrender. To look a quarter of a century ahead, this was the self-same strategy the British would adopt in the guerrilla phase of the Second Anglo-Boer (South African) War of 1899–1902 to induce the surrender of the Boer commandos still in the field. Only this time, because so many of the civilian victims were white settlers and not Africans, their ill-treatment would elicit an international outcry.

In his covering letter, Michel firmly advised Thesiger: 'Do not hamper yourself with staff, they are useless, as Colonels of Regts. do all the work, with an efficient D. Assistant, or Brigade Major.' Point 7 of the enclosed memorandum expanded on this injunction: 'Staff officers of rank, without Caffre experience, are not valuable, active young, intelligent D.A.G.'s more useful.'[17]

Although he himself had been a staff officer, Thesiger seems – to an extent at least – to have accepted Michel's dismissive views of their usefulness and hearkened to his advice not to burden himself with too large a staff. Quantity should not be confused with quality, however. The problem is that Thesiger seems not to have made any special effort to seek out outstanding officers to fill the role. In this he was the direct opposite of Wolseley who preferred to work with a staff of officers of proven talent and professional knowledge in whose abilities he had implicit trust and who became his personal friends. Wolseley had no scruples in selecting the same set again and again (this was the genesis of his ring) and so earned the resentment of those he excluded and the ire of the Horse Guards. It was noticeable, too, that Wolseley favoured officers with the *psc* qualification (Passed Staff College) over those without. Cambridge was hostile to the Staff College, dismissing its graduates as a pushy, dissatisfied bunch, a minority who saw the *psc* qualification as a means of advancement rather than attending to regimental duties that were in themselves valuable as staff training.[18]

It was only after the blatant failures of staff and command in the Crimean War, and after studies by several committees and much debate in parliament, that the decision had been taken in 1858 to found a Staff College at Camberley in the same grounds as the Royal Military College.

The Staff College initially offered a two-year course with an instructing staff of nine, of whom four were serving officers styled 'professors'. Admission was by competitive examination and thirty students from the Army were admitted, five of whom were from the Royal Artillery. The course (taught in the most pedantic, boring fashion) included military history, military law, drawing, fortifications and reconnaissance, with a foreign language, science or mathematics as options. The study of military administration (one hour per week) was thought sufficient instruction in matters of supply and movement, even though a grasp of logistics was so essential for a staff officer. Following criticism, the course syllabus was slightly expanded in 1870 with the inclusion of road-making and military telegraphy. More, but still insufficient, attention was given in military administration to the transport of men, casualties, animals, stores and field encampment. The continuing problem with Staff College was that while it attracted a few officers of keen intellect (along with those wishing to get married or to avoid a posting overseas), it made only a limited appeal to officers who were mainly focused on a conventional regimental career of the sort that had Cambridge's approval. Indeed, the reluctance to attend Staff College was made worse by the dislike in which it and its graduates was held by many senior generals, such as Michel, who preferred officers who had not been at Staff College for staff appointments.[19]

On 2 March 1878 a General Order was published naming the three officers Cambridge had approved to serve on Thesiger's personal staff: his Assistant Military Secretary (AMS; this was a rank and there was no MS as such to assist), Major John N. Crealock, 95th Regiment, and his two ADCs, Captain Matthew W. E. Gossett, 54th Regiment, and Lieutenant William C. F. Molyneux, 22nd Regiment.[20] Thesiger had cast no wide net in making his selection; nor does there seem to have been the clamour to be chosen, as there always was with Wolseley's expeditions. Unimaginatively, all three officers had served under Thesiger when he commanded the 1st Infantry Brigade at Aldershot. Crealock had been the Deputy Assistant Adjutant-General (DAAG) at Aldershot, Gossett a brigade major and Molyneux his ADC. Molyneux seems to have had nothing special to recommend him except that Thesiger was comfortable working with him. Gossett had at least fought in the Indian Mutiny, had passed Staff College and been an instructor in tactics at the RMC, Sandhurst. Even in Wolseley's exacting book he was qualified for a staff appointment. The same went even more so for John Crealock, Thesiger's old comrade in the 95th in India. Between 1862 and 1864 Crealock had been ADC to Lieutenant-General Mansfield, Bombay Army, had passed Staff College in 1868 and between 1870 and 1878 had held a series of staff posts culminating in his appointment on 30 September 1877 as DAQMG Intelligence Branch of the War Office at Adair House in Pall Mall facing the War Office.[21] Before Cardwell established the Intelligence Branch on 1 April 1873, the collection of military intelligence had been very haphazard, but he had seen that a single office was required to process information and to produce reliable military intelligence on which to base military and political decisions. As yet, the Intelligence Branch was small, but it would steadily rise in importance as the only military staff element at the War Office with defence and intelligence planning responsibilities.[22]

Of the three members of Thesiger's staff, it is certain that Crealock applied to be selected, although the others may have done so too. As Thesiger later wrote to Major-General Sir Archibald Alison, the Deputy Quartermaster-General (DQMG) for Intelligence at the War Office and Crealock's immediate superior, Crealock's wife Marion appeared 'under the impression' that he had 'entrapped her husband' into serving on his staff, 'whereas the real truth is that I had never thought of him as my military secretary until he wrote and asked me to take him'.[23] The duties of an AMS encompassed all matters concerning promotions and appointments, as well as his general's confidential correspondence, imbuing him with considerable influence behind the scenes. Crealock was of course qualified to be appointed as Thesiger's intelligence officer entrusted with examining all information collected by spies, scouts and informants and questioning prisoners. Thesiger was content, however, to allow these critical functions to be carried out by his regular staff officers as part of their other duties such as conveying his orders to his subordinates. Only in the later stages of the Zululand campaign would he appoint colonials with specialised local knowledge to his staff as intelligence officers.[24]

As it transpired, the original three members of Thesiger's small staff, who sailed with him to the Cape on 31 January 1878 in the mail steamer *America*, proved very loyal to him throughout his time in South Africa. Molyneux, who was invalided home in July 1878 at the end of the Ninth Cape Frontier War, rejoined his staff in Zululand in March 1879 with the rank of captain as his senior ADC for the rest of the campaign. Gossett stayed on as his ADC after the end of the campaign in the Eastern Cape, and was with him during the first invasion of Zululand and on the disastrous day of the battle of Isandlwana.[25] It was he, by then a major-general, who (as we have seen) after Chelmsford's death in 1905 carefully classified and authoritatively annotated his military correspondence, now conserved as the Chelmsford Papers in the National Army Museum, in honour of his chief's memory and in the hope that his efforts would one day serve to rehabilitate his reputation.[26]

Crealock, who gained a reputation for haughtiness, facetiousness and sharp retorts while serving as the General's AMS (he was promoted to MS in May 1879), was rather more ambivalent than Gossett about his conduct of operations, and was downright critical when reporting back to his previous chief, Sir Archibald Alison, at the Intelligence Branch. Yet, when it came down to it, Crealock always defended him loyally, and wrote to Alison at the very end of the Zululand campaign:

> I have never left Lord Chelmsford since we left Waterloo Bridge [for the Cape] and have worked with him for eighteen weary months, not always agreeing with him and with many disappointments – but never varying appreciation of his qualities and high character.[27]

From the comments of his staff and those who knew him, there is no denying that Thesiger showed cool courage under fire and possessed enough personality to inspire his men in the field, and that he cemented their personal loyalty with human sympathy and his demonstrable care for their welfare. No one disputed his commendable – if conventional – personal qualities as an individual, and his genuine commitment to his profession of arms. Yet more is demanded of a successful senior commander. Such a one must ensure that he secures the intelligence necessary to gauge the nature of the terrain where he is to fight and to evaluate his foe's fighting methods and likely intentions. To counter these, he must possess the vision to formulate an effective strategy of his own, and be prepared to employ the most appropriate tactics when armed encounters take place. He must possess the flexibility and quickness of mind to respond to unanticipated challenges and to take advantage of unexpected opportunities. More prosaically, but critically, he must be the master of logistics, meticulous in his planning so that his army in the field has the transport it requires, is properly supplied at all times, and remains in good communication. He also has to possess the toughness of mind to sanction extreme measures should the success of the campaign depend upon them. And beyond these purely military requirements, a general in the field must possess the diplomatic skills necessary for negotiating with enemy leaders, as well as the political sensibility vital for cooperating with the senior officers under his command. He must also be able to work harmoniously with often mistrustful civilian authorities (something Cunynghame had signally failed to do). And beyond all of that, a commander in the late Victorian era had to be aware that his performance was subject to critical review, not just in the Horse Guards, but in the popular press and in Parliament, and that it behoved him to play cannily to the gallery, as Wolseley always did with such success. But did Thesiger, outward bound on the *America* with his small staff, possess these necessary qualities? Would this perfect gentleman and conventional soldier of the old school rise to the myriad, demanding challenges awaiting him in South Africa?

CHAPTER 15

Finishing the Ninth Cape Frontier War, 1878

ON 25 FEBRUARY 1878 THESIGER and his small staff landed in Cape Town. On 2 March he officially superseded Cunynghame in command of the troops in the Cape, Natal, Transvaal and St Helena, with the local rank of lieutenant-general, and proceeded to headquarters in King William's Town.[1] Despite his deep chagrin, Cunynghame carried himself very correctly. He wrote to Gathorne Hardy that he would 'make it my study to place upon him [Thesiger] all the information which I possess' regarding the South African territories.[2] In company with Frere he gave Thesiger 'a cordial welcome' when he arrived on 4 March in King William's Town by special train from East London, which he had reached by ship.[3]

Frere immediately took Thesiger in hand, proffering him copious advice about local conditions, and from the very first the new GOC found himself beholden to the High Commissioner and dependent, as he informed Cambridge, on his 'full support' in assisting him to 'bear the weight' of his new responsibilities.[4] Clearly, Thesiger appeared to be content, as Cunynghame had been, to play second fiddle to the domineering Frere, and to act as his military instrument in implementing his policies.

Thesiger's first impulse on taking command was to write introducing himself in the friendliest manner possible to his senior subordinates, and especially so to Commandant-General Charles Griffith, for he understood the need to mend the strained relations he had inherited from Cunynghame with the colonial forces.[5] Thesiger's charm offensive bore fruit, and there would no longer be any question of a divided command in the campaign. He was soon able to report to Gathorne Hardy with considerable satisfaction that with the full approval of J. Gordon Sprigg's new Cape ministry he would enjoy 'the entire direction of the Colonial as I have already of the Imperial troops'.[6]

That was a distinct plus, but it still remained to be seen just how effectively the new GOC would employ the forces under his command. In his letter to Griffith, Thesiger made it clear that although he could only make his plans 'through the medium' of his own 'military experience, without being able to bring any local knowledge to bear upon the situation', that he had nevertheless already determined upon the strategy he intended to adopt. Edward Spiers has written that one of the real strengths of Victorian soldiers when conducting one of their many small-scale colonial campaigns was their usual readiness to adjust their military doctrine to local conditions.[7] Thesiger, however, had clearly devised his strategy while on board the *America* and before he had put so much as a foot on Cape soil. The War Office had supplied him and his staff with official records, histories, travel books, dictionaries and every sort of literature aimed at familiarising them with the situation in the Cape. Not, though, as Captain Molyneux later wryly commented, that this book learning did much to familiarise them with the actual situation.[8]

Undeterred, as Thesiger informed Griffith on 5 March soon after he had landed, he intended to send in several strong columns against the amaXhosa with the intention of surrounding them and bringing them to a decisive battle.[9] This conventional strategy – one that he would employ again in Zululand in 1879 – differed little from Cunynghame's equally conservative one in his campaign against the amaGcaleka in the Transkei. Whether it would serve against the amaNgqika in their mountain fastnesses remained to be seen.

King William's Town, a flourishing commercial centre with a bank, hospital, two churches and a jail had been made pestilential thanks to a water shortage, undisposed waste and recent overcrowding.[10] The town was teeming with refugees when Thesiger stepped off the train, because every farm within a radius of seven miles to the north and east had been burnt out by Ngqika war bands that Sandile, the Ngqika chief, had pulled back across the Kei after the disaster at Kentani. Even so, Thesiger was confidently informed by the officials and soldiers who welcomed him that the war was virtually over.[11] But only five days later, on 9 March, Sandile and the bulk of his forces eluded the patrols sent by Griffith to contain them. Leaving a trail of smouldering settler farms behind them, they made for their strongholds in the Amathole Mountains.[12] There, among the graves of their ancestors, they were prepared to fight and die.

Sandile, long given over to drink, now abjured it and steeled himself to take on the role of stalwart warrior. He deeply regretted deferring to Sarhili and taking part in the disastrous pitched battle at Kentani because he understood well from experience in the two previous frontier wars that only guerrilla warfare in the bush could prolong resistance. His amaNgqika accordingly made for their traditional fighting-ground, known as the Pirie Bush. This was a rugged region of the south-eastern Amathole some twenty miles long, and a similar distance from King William's Town. A fractured plateau fell away to deep clefts and ravines filled with great rocks through which meandered treacherous, stony stream beds. All was overgrown by impenetrable bush through which reared enormous forest trees strangling in wiry creepers. In awestruck tones Captain Molyneux described the difficulty of operating in this region: 'The Bush is the primeval forest. Enormous trees overhead keep off the sunshine, while dense undergrowth with multitudes of creepers, or monkey-ropes, and wait-a bit-thorns make movement difficult and limit the view to a few yards.'[13] Even so, what hope was there for Sandile and the Ngqika fighters? Were there enough of them to put up an effective resistance, and would not the British be able to contain the area of operations and systematically snuff them out?[14]

Ominously, as Captain Henry Hallam Parr, Frere's MS, noted, even those amaNgqika who seemed to have been fully acculturated, and had worked all their lives on white farms or in government service, were now readily exchanging 'their clothes for a blanket, their pen for a rifle' and going off to join the warriors in the bush.[15] Thesiger understood he must act swiftly to prevent the fighting spreading further across the eastern frontier and threw together a major offensive.[16] He gave the command of 3,000 imperial and colonial troops – including the 90th Regiment, the 2/24th (which had landed through the heavy surf in East London on 9 March) and some companies of the 1/24th[17] – to the ambitious, experienced and capable Colonel Evelyn Wood of the 90th, one of the five Special Service officers who had accompanied him to South Africa in search of action and promotion.[18]

Wood had been the AQMG at Aldershot at the same time Thesiger had been in command of his infantry brigade quartered there, and so was already known to him. Popular, energetic and very deaf, with a tendency towards valetudinarianism and so notoriously vain that it was later said that he wore his many decorations to bed, as a commander Wood was dynamic and self-confident, eager to act on his own initiative. He had begun his career in the Royal Navy in 1852 before joining the Army in 1855. Thereafter he proved a gallant soldier, serving with distinction in the Crimean War before earning the VC in 1859 when fighting in the last stages of the Indian Mutiny in Central India – the same theatre where Thesiger had seen action, albeit less gloriously. Wood was also an intellectual soldier, passing very successfully through Staff College in 1862–4, and in 1877 turned down the position of Commandant at the RMC, Sandhurst in the hope of seeing more active service. Service in the Third Anglo-Asante War had brought him Wolseley's patronage and the membership of his 'ring'. That might have prejudiced Thesiger against him, as might his reputation earned at Aldershot of being a reformist and innovator, but Wood was an intuitively political soldier, well able to navigate the shoals of military patronage and the competing 'rings'. His excellent service in the Eastern Cape would cement Thesiger's trust in him and elicit his open admiration of him as an energetic and successful commander.[19]

Major Crealock, Thesiger's AMS, was by his elbow throughout the campaign, sharing his exhausting rides through difficult country and his uncomfortable bivouacs, and observing alongside him from some vantage point as the general directed operations. Over the next three months he kept a copious journal of his experiences between 4 March and 3 June 1878.[20] His entries amply bear out Charles Low's characterisation of Thesiger's operations in the Ciskei as being 'of a desultory, and not very stirring, character'.[21] It would serve little purpose, therefore, to follow this essentially repetitive campaign in minute detail, but its main contours can be discerned and these are sufficient to permit an assessment of how well Thesiger performed in his first independent command in the field.

In Crealock's word's, the moment Thesiger had 'the reins of the team in his grasp', he issued 'distinct instructions' to all his commanders to move their forces to the points from which he planned to launch his offensive. While he waited for them to reach their posts, Thesiger who, with his hallmark over-meticulous attention to detail, had been 'from daybreak to midnight . . . since his arrival hard at work revising administrative details with his staff in the one bare barrack room that formed his reception room, office and bedroom', looked with longing eyes towards the mountains where the fighting was to take place.[22]

On 14 March Thesiger, who while in South Africa would always be determined to see the terrain for himself, led his staff out on a personal reconnaissance of the area of the coming operations. All was ready to his satisfaction by 18 March when he ordered Wood's three columns to converge on the Pirie Bush in a wide arc from Bailie's Grave in the south through Keiskammahoek around to Stutterheim in the north-east and commence a sweeping pincer movement to squeeze the amaNgqika out of the bush onto the plain below where, it was intended, they would be brought to battle on the open ground and destroyed.[23]

The amaNgqika probably numbered no more than 2,000 fighters in three main groups, but they were in their element in the Amathole wilderness, staying out of sight and always two jumps ahead of the blundering British forces. They lured one British column into an ambush and the badly demoralised troops had ignominiously extricate themselves in the driving rain, heavy mist and freezing temperatures of the early Cape winter. Thesiger, who had posted himself at Hayne's Mill, a position from which he could do little but gaze at the forested height around him, was for long unaware of what had occurred.[24] Heavy shelling of the forests achieved nothing at all, and soon the offensive was in complete disarray. On 20 March, the third day of the offensive, Thesiger decided to move his headquarters to Mount Kempt, a high bleak mountain that afforded a clearer sight of the proceedings and from which he intended to direct the final attack in person.[25] But when he arrived there on 21 March, he found that many of the colonial volunteers had decided to give up and go home.

It was not surprising that recently arrived British regulars should be at a loss in this completely unfamiliar environment, but the colonial forces fared little better. The white volunteers were reluctant to risk themselves in the densely overgrown twilight of the rocky ravines, and adopted the practice of first sending in the 1,000 Mfengu levies (who had been recruited locally from within the Ciskei) to locate the elusive amaNgqika and flush them out. But the amaMfengu also hung back, and were only persuaded to move in when they were promised all the livestock they could lay their hands on and £500 if they captured Sandile. Their failure to achieve tangible results disillusioned the already reluctant volunteers and eroded their confidence in Thesiger. Their period of employment had not quite expired but, to add to their reluctance to commit themselves, they were discontented by the chronic shortage of rations because of the commissariat's difficulties in bringing them up over the exceedingly rough terrain, and simply disintegrated as a force Thesiger could call upon.[26]

Thesiger was consequently left with no option but to abandon his offensive on 22 March. As he ruefully admitted to Gathorne Hardy, as a result of the Cape volunteers' defection the 'difficulties of command' were 'enormously increased', and he had been 'placed in an embarrassing position'.[27] But Thesiger was undeterred – and wiser. In preparation for the next round, and on Crealock's advice, he ordered paths cleared through the bush in an east–west direction to facilitate the movement of supplies, and to coordinate operations better and leave his commanders with less independence of action, he introduced flag-signalling between the units.[28] It seems that this was also the moment when he ordered the issue of a booklet entitled *Regulations for the Colonial Forces Now in the Field* with the purpose of enforcing tighter and more uniform control over them.[29]

On 24 March Frere left King William's Town for Cape Town. On account of the war, he had been away from the seat of the colony's administration for nearly seven months, and needed to pick up the reins. Although Thesiger had as yet achieved no tangible results, Frere had seen enough of him to believe he could safely leave the conduct of the campaign in the GOC's hands. Indeed, despite his setback over the Cape volunteers, Thesiger did not repine long. On 29 March he launched a limited new offensive onto the high Lotutu plateau across the Gwili Gwili Range and the Rabula Heights in the Pirie Bush.[30] The amaNgqika effortlessly melted away once more. Not surprisingly, the regulars were also becoming dispirited with the interminable hardships of the war, and as Private George Morris of the 1/24th Regiment complained to his father: 'My clothes are worn to rags, and I have not a boot to my feet . . . God knows I have had enough of campaigning this last few months; the weather has been very bad and wet, and many of our poor fellows have died of dysentery.'[31]

The defection of the volunteers persuaded Thesiger to bring in another 1,000 Mfengu levies from Fingoland in the Transkei. They arrived on 3 April and the general was unimpressed by their lack of firearms and by their poor motivation. They were indeed unwilling recruits because

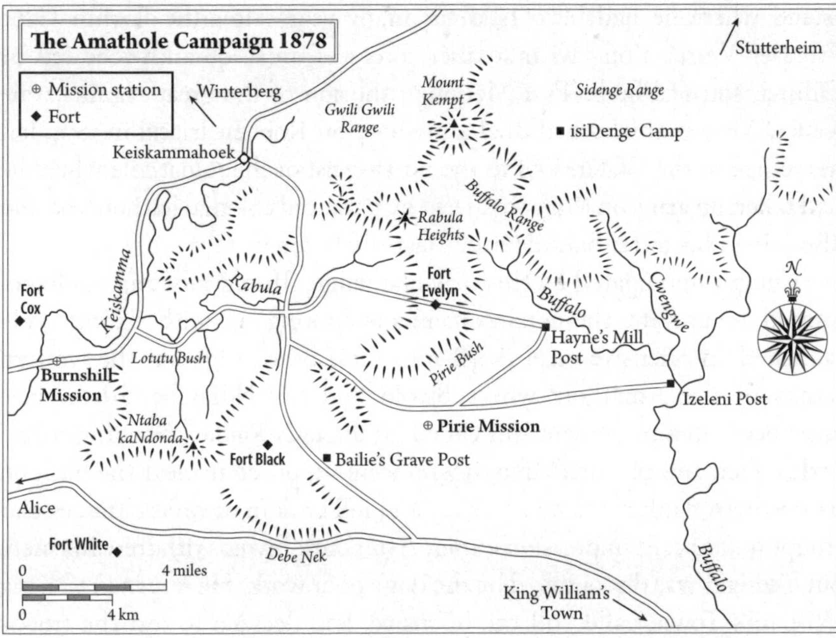

The Amathole Campaign 1878

they had become rich on the spoils of the Transkei campaign against the amaGcaleka and were unwilling to risk their skins so far from home.[32] Even so, Thesiger used them on a new sweep beginning on 4 April in which they were to scour the bush from Mount Kempt to Hayne's Mill and identify Ngqika hideouts for follow-up action by regular troops.[33] Their performance was uninspiring, and on 5 April Major Crealock disparagingly recorded that the amaMfengu fired 'wild volleys before they came to a thick bit of bush to warn the Caffres . . . At 5.30 they began to emerge, firing volleys of valuable ammunition into the air! and singing the most magnificent war songs!' In stark contrast, Crealock had nothing but admiration for the way the amaNgqika were conducting themselves, writing that the 'Caffres were conspicuous in their pluck and leaving the Bush a yard or two would from behind a stone fire into us'.[34]

Despite his lack of success thus far in corralling the amaNgqika, Thesiger could not afford to let up the pressure. Sandile's intrepid stand in the Amathole was inspiring warriors of other Xhosa chiefdoms between the Buffalo and Keiskamma Rivers in the Ciskei to throw in their lot with him. These reinforcements comprised 2,000 fighting men led by the veteran Ndlambe chief, Siyolo, who had been released from Robben

Island where he had been held for many years after the Eighth Cape Frontier War,[35] along with smaller forces of amaGqunukhwebe led by Dilima, son of Phato. Tini Maqoma, the son of the great Ngqika war-leader, Maqoma, who had died a prisoner on Robben Island in 1873, left his refuge in the Waterkloof to the north-west of the Amathole where he had taken up arms on threat of arrest by paranoid colonial authorities, and also joined his uncle Sandile in his last-ditch defiance.[36]

Caught unprepared by this new challenge, Thesiger swung his forces around to prevent these reinforcements linking up with Sandile. He launched an offensive on 6 April into the Lotutu Bush on the western flanks of the Amathole where Siyolo and his Ndlambe forces were ensconced on a prominent hill called Ntaba kaNdonda.[37] Shelling it had little effect, and the amaMfengu who were supposed to clear the bush on its northern flank made no headway and fell back in disorder. The regular troops made scant impression either. After dark Siyolo withdrew his men, but Thesiger was discouraged by the day's poor work. He returned to King William's Town, called off the offensive, and decided to rest the troops for three weeks, refit and garner new reserves. The Mfengu levies were sent home in disgrace for mutinous conduct and plundering. Since they had proved unreliable when they fought in return for loot, when Thesiger recruited a new contingent to replace them, he made sure that this time they would be paid for their services, even if that unambiguously turned them into mercenaries rather than notional allies.[38]

The amaXhosa grasped this respite to strengthen their positions in the Lotutu Bush where Siyolo was concentrated, and also in the Pirie Bush to the east where Sandile remained ensconced. On 15 April Thesiger set out on a tour of inspection of the area of operations and noted that the enemy were well established. He determined that a renewed attack was required to drive them out, but was stymied when the Cape volunteers who had been returning to the field and the amaMfengu again dispersed home to recoup. As he reported to the new Secretary of State for War, Colonel the Hon. Frederick A. Stanley (Gathorne Hardy had been elevated to the House of Lords as Viscount Cranbrook and appointed Secretary of State for India),

> This lull in active operations has been most distasteful to me, feeling as I do [and here he was reiterating the advice given him

> by General Michel] that the only way to bring this War to an end is to constantly harass the Kaffirs cutting of their supplies, and preventing their obtaining fresh recruits.[39]

So Thesiger persevered, and by the last week of April he had succeeded in concentrating 1,600 white and 2,400 African troops for a renewed offensive.[40] His plan was first to root Siyolo out of the Lotutu Bush and then to turn east to deal with Sandile in the Pirie Bush. Accordingly, on 30 April, four columns formed a cordon around the Lotutu plateau and advanced in a tightening noose. With much effort and sweat artillery was positioned on high ground to fire case-shot and shrapnel down the forested gorges which were then laboriously swept by the plodding infantry who found the going extremely trying. Captain Molyneux recalled: 'What a race it was! Into holes, out again, hands and faces bleeding from thorns, knees punctured, and shirtsleeves in ribands, till after about an hour of it [we] came out on the open plateau.'[41] Yet, even though the new flag-signalling made for better coordination between the converging columns over the broken country, the results were still disappointing for the British. They killed about 140 amaXhosa, but the rest had no difficulty in breaking up into small groups and stealing through the British lines. In that way Siyolo, Tini Maqoma and other leaders all succeeded in slipping away and joining Sandile in the Pirie Bush.[42]

Still, even if he had not cornered and eliminated the amaXhosa in the Lotutu Bush, Thesiger had at least cleared it, and was free to concentrate on Sandile's strongholds in the Pirie Bush. On 8 May 1,122 imperial troops, 920 colonial volunteers who had once again drifted back into the campaign, and 2,890 Mfengu levies commenced their new sweep. The intention was to drive the amaXhosa into the arms of the troops deployed along the rim of the plateau and the edges of the Pirie Bush, and to seize as many of their cattle and as much of their food supply as possible. With Thesiger commanding the attack from Hayne's Mill, his forces enjoyed some minor successes, but failed in their main objective of driving the amaXhosa out of their sanctuary.[43] As Crealock observed with disgust after another day of scrappy, futile operations in this 'most miserable' of little wars, 'it was becoming rather like a rat hunt'.[44]

It could no longer escape Thesiger that despite mounting five large-scale offensives he had failed to extinguish Xhosa resistance, and that he was fast becoming the 'laughing stock of the colony'.[45] He was a stubborn man, and wedded to the strategy he had plotted out while on board the *America*. Yet, he could no longer deny that attempting to manoeuvre mass formations in column through the broken terrain and dense bush of the Amathole was both impracticable and ineffective, and that if he persisted in this strategy the war would drag on for many more months. Moreover, for weeks his colonial commandants, all veterans of warfare in the Eastern Cape, had been urging him to adopt an alternative strategy.[46] Finally, Thesiger swallowed his pride and took their advice, effectively adopting the counter-insurgency methods successfully employed in 1852 during the closing stages of the Eighth Cape Frontier War by Lieutenant-Colonel William Eyre (known to the amaXhosa as 'Four-Eyes' on account of his spectacles), a specialist in irregular warfare.[47]

The new approach required Thesiger to divide the Amathole theatre of operations into eleven military districts.[48] Both a mounted and an infantry force was stationed in each one of them. Two strongly garrisoned earthworks – Fort Evelyn and Fort Black – blocked favoured Xhosa routes along which they manoeuvred and brought in supplies, and constant patrols scoured the country at will, never venturing too far from their supply depots. The objective of these patrols was to pursue any Xhosa parties they encountered up to the border of their military district when the garrison in the next district would take up the remorseless chase afresh. Much depended on the effectiveness of tough, colonial district commandants who knew the terrain, and on their determination never to ease up the pressure on the amaXhosa. This meant sending their men out on dangerous missions such as night attacks to surprise the enemy, or into caves to search out amaXhosa hiding there. It also entailed capturing what pitiable supplies of food the amaXhosa still had left, and destroying their wretched shelters. This was harsh, merciless warfare in which no prisoners were taken and the amaXhosa were systematically mopped up in detail.

This ruthless, redesigned campaign ground remorselessly on without a pause throughout the last three weeks of May.[49] Winter was beginning to bite and the defenders were cold, wet (this is a winter-rainfall region) and quite famished. By mid-May many amaXhosa could take no more punishment and began trying to wriggle through the iron British grid. Siyolo made his escape to the Fish River valley, and Tini Maqoma crept back to the Waterkloof. Starved and desperate, the shattered Xhosa bands would not give themselves up as a matter of honour, but would fight when they could neither hide nor escape. The British became increasingly embarrassed by destitute Xhosa women and children from the devastated Ngqika Reserve and from the Amathole who flocked into the military camps for succour and had to be fed from military supplies.[50] The winter brought much hardship and sickness to the British garrisons in the Amathole highlands as well, but their sufferings were as nothing compared to those of the Xhosa fighters still pathetically lurking in the sunless ravines.

During late April and May, concurrently with the launching of Thesiger's new strategy in the Amathole, the British opened a new offensive beyond the Transkei to finish off any residual Gcaleka resistance. Several companies of imperial infantry, along with some troops of the FAMP and 3,000 Mfengu levies, all under the command of Colonel Glyn, crossed over the Mbashe into Bomvanaland from the former Gcaleka Reserve and pursued Sarhili and the remnants of his forces as far east as the Qora River. They took little booty (the amaGcaleka had few livestock or other possessions left to relinquish), but the operation brought the fighting in that sector to a definitive end.[51] Since his new strategy was progressing well in the Transkei, Thesiger took the opportunity to tour the Transkei between 23 May and 6 June to make sure with his own eyes that soon it would be unnecessary to maintain the large garrison stationed there since December 1878 under Glyn's command.[52]

The campaign in the Ciskei was also drawing to its cruel conclusion. On 31 May 1878 Sandile and his Ngqika bodyguard attempted to break out from the Buffalo River valley where they had been hemmed in. Near isiDenge hill in the north-eastern plateau country of the Pirie Bush they ran into a small patrol. Sandile was mortally wounded in the ensuing fire-fight. His surviving companions carried him away, but he died on 5 June. A British patrol found his corpse on 7 June and brought it back into the isiDenge camp. There, Mfengu warriors were allowed to dance past the corpse, jeering, laughing, chanting and shaking their weapons in victory over their reviled enemy, the 'Tiger of the Forest'. On 9 June the British finally gave Sandile a decent burial and his grave is still tended by the local Xhosa community.[53]

After Sandile's death desultory mopping up continued for several weeks more.[54] Mfengu patrols killed other Xhosa notables including

Siyolo, who was shot in the Fish River Bush in early June. Many Xhosa warriors, rightly fearful they would be killed out of hand, continued to lurk in the Pirie Bush. Colonial forces including the volunteers were sent in to flush them out, and they performed their task with vengeful callousness, tracking the amaXhosa down and shooting them as if they were little more than vermin. Embarrassing reports began to trickle out of the abuse and summary execution of prisoners.

Moved by compassion, and convinced it would not interfere with the patrolling still being carried on by the colonial forces, Thesiger wrote to Frere on 21 June urging him to pressure the Cape government to proclaim an amnesty that 'would but give an opportunity to the poor wretches who are now hiding and starving, to come in without fear of being shot or put in prison'.[55] The Cape government finally complied, and on 2 July proclaimed an amnesty for any fighters still in the field, and the killing ended. The poor remnant of Xhosa warriors knew they had comported themselves as true men, and little honour would be conceded in surrendering when all was lost. In July, Sandile's sons, Edmund and Mathanzima, who had fled to Emigrant Thembuland, gave themselves up, and were sentenced to prison for life. Tini Maqoma, who also surrendered, was sentenced to death for treason, but the sentence was commuted to life imprisonment.[56]

In early August Glyn finally brought his forces back from Gcalekaland, thereby signifying the territory pacified and the war officially over. Sarhili, nevertheless, was still at large. With a reward of £1,000 and 500 cattle on his head, the Xhosa paramount remained in hiding like 'a baboon in a hole' in an inaccessible refuge deep in Bomvana territory. He declined to emerge even when offered a free pardon in 1881, but eventually acquiesced and accepted British rule, dying in 1892 at eighty-three.[57]

The Cape government set aside Thursday, 1 August, as a day of public thanksgiving throughout the Colony for victory over the amaXhosa.[58] An estimated 3,680 amaXhosa warriors died in the Ninth and last Cape Frontier War, something like an appalling 50 per cent casualty rate. This number does not include other warriors who died off the battlefield of their wounds or privations, or Xhosa non-combatants who perished of starvation. Only 171 men were taken prisoner, testifying to the ruthlessness of the campaign. More than 45,000 cattle and some 579 horses were lost to the conquerors. Most painful of all, perhaps, was the fate of the 4,000 Xhosa women who had taken refuge with the British. They were taken off by steamer from East London to earn a bare living labouring in the environs of Cape Town.[59] In startling contrast, British and colonial casualties numbered no more than 60 white and 133 African soldiers killed.

The settlement the Cape government imposed on the defeated amaXhosa was unrelenting. In September 1878 all the amaNgqika, even pro-government chiefs and those of Sandile's adherents who had not taken up arms, were expelled from their lands, which were sold to white settlers, and the dispossessed relocated across the Kei in the western half of the former Gcaleka Reserve. The remnants of the amaGcaleka were settled in a location next to them.[60] Their century of armed resistance against the unremitting colonial advance finally defeated, the amaXhosa as a people were diminished, scattered and impoverished, hemmed into inadequate reserves and left to eke out an existence as labourers for white colonists on land that had once been theirs.[61]

The amaMfengu anticipated they would be accorded privileged treatment for the loyal and vital role they had played in the recent war, but were rapidly disabused. Sprigg, the new Cape premier and Frere's willing instrument, was determined that the frontier would never again experience a war between the races, and that the peace – unlike those that had imperfectly concluded previous frontier wars – must be no patched-up affair. Africans therefore had to be left in no doubt that they were conquered, and that the whites were now the unassailable masters of the land.[62] There would be no place in future for African levies, not even for loyal allies like the amaMfengu, and the colonial forces defending the Cape would be exclusively white. It was therefore essential to disarm without exception all Africans under Cape rule. Frere and Sprigg made disarmament the cornerstone of their native policy, passed into law by the Peace Preservation Act of 2 August 1878, known as the Gun Act.[63]

As for Thesiger, he could conveniently put the ineffectual, conventional strategy he had employed during the first part of the campaign behind him. He had, after all, eventually adapted his plan of campaign to local conditions and the requirements of irregular, bush warfare, and could bask in his success and the approbation of his superiors and the colonial public. In an impressive ceremony on 3 July, he received the formal, relieved thanks of both houses of the Cape legislature for 'suppressing the late rebellion'.[64] As he had already complacently reported to Cambridge, 'I believe everyone is now thoroughly satisfied that the work has been effectually completed.' In the same despatch, he concluded with undisguised satisfaction: 'I cannot be sufficiently grateful to Your Royal Highness for having given me the opportunity of commanding a force which by its excellent conduct has enabled me to bring a difficult war to so speedy a close.'[65] Shortly thereafter, on the recommendation of the satisfied government in London, Thesiger was promoted in the Most Honourable Order of the Bath from Companion to Knight Commander. Henceforth, he would be the Hon. Sir Frederick Thesiger, KCB, entitled to wear the breast star of the order, a stubby eight-pointed silver cross pattée with three crowns in the centre surrounded by a red ring with the motto in gold '*Tria Juncta in Uno*', flanked by two gold laurel branches above a scroll with the motto of the Military Division of the Order of the Bath '*Ich Dien*'.[66] Thesiger could not know it, but this accolade was the last time he would receive the unalloyed commendations of the Horse Guards, the government and the public at large. Flushed as he was with success at the termination of the Ninth Cape Frontier War, he little expected his next steps as GOC South Africa to be so fraught with peril and disgrace.

PART III

Command in the Anglo-Zulu War, 1878–1879

CHAPTER 16

Establishing Headquarters in Pietermaritzburg July–August 1878

ON 25 JULY 1878, THESIGER SET SAIL from Cape Town for Durban on HMS *Active* to prepare for likely military operations against the Zulu kingdom.[1] With the final subjugation of the amaXhosa, Frere was convinced that the moment had come to defeat and disarm the remaining nodes of African resistance to British hegemony in southern Africa in order to complete the confederation project. There was no doubting that the amaZulu, with their fearsome warrior reputation, presented the greatest challenge, and as a military commentator expressed it at the time, 'no rational being believes in the struggle with that military nation being postponed much longer', and that when it came they would have to be 'struck down with an iron hand'.[2] Yet, before trying conclusions with Cetshwayo, Frere knew he had first to clear his decks by finishing with Sekhukhune and the Bapedi in order to secure the Transvaal. He was aware that Africans were reported to be knowingly asking of each other: 'If the bull-calf [Sekhukhune] has to be let alone, what will happen when the elephant [Cetshwayo] attacks the white man?'[3]

Also requiring attention was what Thesiger characterised as a 'very troublesome rebellion' that broke out in Griqualand West in April 1878 over the harsh land settlement the British administrators of the colony had imposed on the indigenous inhabitants.[4] This campaign, officially called the Northern War, persisted over six gruelling months of ambushes, skirmishes and indecisive firefights waged over a harsh, unforgiving terrain of stony, arid, limitless plains, and in deep gorges surrounded by rocky ridges. Most of the fighting took place during the bitter winter months with nights of hard frost and intense cold that made camping in the open miserable for all the combatants. Major Owen Lanyon, the melancholic

Administrator of Griqualand West – who was nevertheless an ambitious and efficient officer who had served with Wolseley in the Third Anglo-Asante War and was reckoned a member of his 'ring' – prided himself that the volunteer corps of settlers he raised in Griqualand West performed so well that never once did he have to request the aid of imperial troops in putting down the rebellion. Since Thesiger was still fully engaged in chasing the amaXhosa, this came as a relief. By the end of June Lanyon had largely defeated the insurgents, although desultory fighting would continue until he finally signed an amnesty on 13 November. With that, the Griqua, Batlhaping, Prieska amaXhosa, Korana and Khoisan were firmly subjected to British rule, Frere could slot Griqualand West securely into the confederation edifice, and Thesiger as GOC was relieved of an annoying distraction.[5]

Critically, as insignificant a campaign as the Northern War had been, it was nevertheless viewed by Frere, as well as by Lanyon, as yet another manifestation of the widespread black conspiracy threatening to sweep away white supremacy everywhere in southern Africa. As Lanyon put it to Frere,

> There is much evidence of concert between distant and apparently unconnected outbreaks here [Griqualand West] and elsewhere, and if there is anything like a combination among the evil-disposed in different Kafir tribes, there is no surer means of encouraging its spread than by delaying the complete reassertion of the authority of the Government.[6]

It was the perceived 'combination' between Sekhukhune and Cetshwayo that particularly alarmed Frere, and there were two intertwined reasons for solving the Pedi problem before tackling the Zulu one. Sekhukhune was resisting the authority of Sir Theophilus Shepstone, the Administrator of the Transvaal Territory, 'a crafty-looking and silent man, who never used an unnecessary word or gesture' and whom the recently annexed Transvaal Boers believed to be 'utterly insincere'.[7] But if the British could bring Sekhukhune to heel after the SAR's humiliating failure to do so in the Boer–Pedi War of 1876–7, then the disgruntled burghers might be persuaded to acknowledge the benefits of British rule.[8]

The second reason for dealing with Sekhukhune before attacking Cetshwayo was more convoluted, but had implications far beyond the borders of the Transvaal. Shepstone dinned into Frere's ear his unwavering conviction that the Boers' previous lack of military successes against the Bapedi had done enormous harm to the prestige of the white man throughout the region, not least because Sekhukhune was acting 'as a kind of lieutenant' to the baleful King Cetshwayo.[9] In fact, that was not the case, and historians now agree that Sekhukhune and Cetshwayo never formed an active alliance. Rather, Sekhukhune's 'old councillors' were strongly advised him 'to arrange his own affairs' and to avoid becoming involved in Cetshwayo's separate disputes with the imperial power.[10] What mattered at the time, however, was that Shepstone and Frere, along with most self-styled local white experts – settlers, missionaries, officials – were absolutely convinced that Cetshwayo and Sekhukhune were hand in glove. Thus, even if (in Frere's words) Cetshwayo was 'the head and moving spirit' of this alarming combination,[11] it was essential to crush his so-called 'lieutenant' first to reassert British military prestige.

In addition to which, the ultimate elimination of the Zulu 'threat', which Charles Brownlee, the Resident Commissioner of Native Affairs in the Cape Colony, saw as the key to solving the South African 'native question',[12] was likewise essential for placating the restless Boers of the Transvaal. Although the southern end of the frontier between the Zulu kingdom and the SAR had been recognised in 1854 as the Ncome (Blood) River, the frontier to the north about the headwaters of the Phongolo River remained very hazy. For decades Boers had been taking advantage of this uncertainty to infiltrate deep into north-western Zululand, a region of excellent grazing, highly desirable to both Zulu and Boer pastoralists. The amaZulu and the SAR very nearly went to war in 1861 over what had become known as the Disputed Territory, and there were further crises in 1864, 1869 and 1870. The Boers even went so far as to allot farms to settlers and unilaterally proclaimed in 1875 that Cetshwayo had ceded the territory to them – an assertion the Zulu king strenuously rejected.[13] When in mid-1877 a series of incidents in the Disputed Territory brought the issue to the boil again, Shepstone resolved to assert the Transvaal's claims in order to demonstrate to the sceptical Boers the advantages of being under British rule.[14] However, his meeting on 18 October 1877 with a large Zulu delegation on a flat-topped hill (subsequently called Conference Hill) in the wide plain overlooking the west bank of the Ncome River, proved a disaster when Chief Mnyamana kaNgqengelele Buthelezi, Cetshwayo's chief councillor, refused on behalf of the Zulu nation to abandon any Zulu land claims whatsoever.[15]

Shepstone's humiliation on Conference Hill reinforced his belief that 'The sooner the root of all evil, which I consider to be Zulu power and military organization is dealt with the easier our task will be.'[16] Frere could not have agreed more, although, on account of the Ninth Cape Frontier War he was not yet quite ready to attempt a military solution.[17] Instead, he stepped up a diplomatic offensive against Cetshwayo to force him into making concessions over the Disputed Territory, but was thrown off balance by the unexpected intervention of Sir Henry Bulwer, KCMG, since 28 August 1875 the Lieutenant-Governor of Natal. Born into the landed gentry and educated at Cambridge University, Bulwer had gained extensive experience in the colonial service. He did not follow the pack in believing that Cetshwayo posed an imminent threat and feared that, if Frere too openly supported the Transvaal in the border dispute, war with the Zulu would follow, and he wanted to keep Natal out of the fray. He therefore offered to mediate and Cetshwayo, who was equally desirous of avoiding war, eagerly agreed. The Boundary Commission began sitting at Rorke's Drift on 17 March 1878. Three months later, on 15 July, just as the Ninth Cape Frontier War was being wound up, Frere received its scrupulous report. To his dismayed frustration its findings in large measure vindicated Zulu territorial claims and threatened to cause a political explosion in the increasingly truculent Transvaal. Frere believed the report would be read there as proof positive that the British could not guarantee their security against hostile African neighbours, and he feared this would finally spark off a Boer rebellion in the Transvaal. It was his fevered nightmare that such an uprising would draw in the Boer Republic of the OFS as well as anti-British Boers in the Cape and Natal, and that hostile Africans would be encouraged to fall upon the whites while they fought each other. And naturally, to his way of thinking, the amaZulu would be the leaders in the general uprising.

Frere believed it was therefore essential not to make the findings of the Boundary Commission public until he had found a way to neutralise them, and had been able to concoct another plausible *casus belli* against the amaZulu. Events played into his hands. A series of minor incidents between July and October 1878 along the jittery borders of Zululand with its colonial neighbours alarmed settler opinion and provided Frere with opportune justification to the Colonial Office for taking military action. And disastrously, because the recent Ninth Cape Frontier War had proved a relatively inexpensive victory in terms both of casualties and treasure, Frere remained in thrall to the mirage of cheap and swift military intervention that would finally clinch the confederation deal.[18]

Thesiger reported to the Duke of Cambridge on 1 July 1878 that since the war against the amaXhosa had been 'brought to a close', he had arrived back in Cape Town. There he would spend the remainder of the month as Frere's guest at Government House in the formidable company of his politically acute wife and four unmarried, intellectual daughters (the two eldest, along with Lady Frere, acted as the High Commissioner's private secretaries). 'It is still more than probable,' Thesiger went on to add, 'that active steps will have to be taken to check the arrogance of Cetywayo, Chief of the Zulus.' In 'talking the situation over' with Frere, he had already gathered that the High Commissioner's views were 'identical with what I have just expressed'.[19]

Understanding the sequence of military initiatives to be adopted, with a campaign against Sekhukhune preceding one against Cetshwayo, on 2 June 1878 Thesiger had already divided the hitherto joint military command of Natal and the Transvaal Territory. He left Colonel Charles K. Pearson, CB, of the 3rd Regiment, a veteran of the Crimea, as Commandant of Natal, which was not yet intended as a base of operations. Pearson had been with his regiment in South Africa since 1876, but Thesiger had yet to meet him and had no report concerning his military capabilities. He therefore entrusted the more immediately significant command of all the imperial and colonial troops in the Transvaal to the Welshman, Colonel Hugh Rowlands, VC, CB, of the 34th Regiment, who had distinguished himself at the battle of Alma in the Crimean War. Rowlands had travelled out to the Cape with Thesiger as one of his Special Service officers, and on arrival the General had appointed him his Inspector of Colonial Forces.[20]

Rowlands would only take up his appointment in the Transvaal on 13 August 1878, but in Cape Town Thesiger was already tentatively formulating a plan of campaign. Rowlands was to proceed first against Sekhukhune and was then to invade the Zulu kingdom from the north-west in conjunction with a force of allied amaSwazi recruited from that kingdom to the north of Zululand, and its traditional enemy.[21] By the end of July, after Frere had received the disappointing report of the Boundary

Commission while he was staying with him in Cape Town, Thesiger was gearing himself up to take the field himself against the amaZulu. As he informed Shepstone:

> If we are to have a fight with the Zulus, I am anxious that our arrangements shall be as complete as it is possible to make them – Half measures do not answer with natives – They must be thoroughly crushed to make them believe in our superiority and if I am called upon to conduct operations against them I shall strive to be in a position to show them how hopelessly inferior they are to us in fighting power, although numerically stronger.[22]

On 9 August 1878 Thesiger arrived in Pietermaritzburg, the colonial capital of Natal, where he intended to set up his headquarters to plan for what he assumed was the impending Zululand campaign. On the low hill overlooking the little town – laid out in a grid pattern of wide streets lined by small houses and a scattering of public buildings – was Fort Napier, established on 31 August 1843 as the HQ and supply and remount centre of the British garrison. The strongest fortified post in Natal, it consisted of a rectangle of brick-built barracks enclosed by earthworks constructed in 1876 and strengthened by stone redoubts and gun emplacements.[23]

From the moment of his arrival in Pietermaritzburg, Thesiger made it clear to the local officials that although he was personally inclined to go along with Frere's bellicose plans, he was nothing more than the military agent of the policy initiated by his superior – and theirs – the High Commissioner.[24] He was initially Bulwer's guest at Government House, an unpretentious and rather cramped residence built of shale with a red tiled roof, under the lee of Fort Napier.[25] It was an uncomfortable experience for both of them.[26] As Lieutenant-Governor of Natal, Bulwer was responsible to the British government and not to the elected Legislative Council and nominated Executive Council of colonists that made up Natal's representative government. His goodwill and cooperation were therefore essential. However, he was wary and resentful of the sudden rush to a 'quite unnecessary' war against the amaZulu with whom his government had always attempted to maintain good relations;[27] he was dubious about the justice of forcing it on; and deplored the likely risks and cost for Natal. Although at first Thesiger and Bulwer were able to discuss several issues 'in the most friendly spirit and without reservation',[28] and although Thesiger came to appreciate the well-read Bulwer's 'private character as a gentleman', and learned to respect his 'honesty of purpose and earnestness as a governor',[29] relations between the two men rapidly soured.

For his part, Bulwer found the general's 'official manner . . . not always an agreeable one', especially when Crealock, whom he found 'a sort of military wasp' and 'rather snobbish' was present.[30] (At the time, a 'snob' was taken to be a person who lacked good breeding and carried himself with a disagreeable air of superiority.) Bulwer also resented that the military habitually 'pooh-poohed' his opinions.[31] Nor did it help matters that Bulwer did not altogether trust Thesiger's military acumen. As he later confided to Wolseley, he swiftly came to the conclusion that Thesiger 'was very much inflated by the idea of his own ability as a general: in fact that easy successes in Kaffraria had turned his head'.[32] He would only have been confirmed in this assessment, and furthermore seen evidence of Thesiger's fundamental military conservatism, if he could have read the general's letter to Shepstone, written the day after he arrived in Pietermaritzburg: 'The broad principles of tactics hold good in Africa equally as well as in Europe, and the idea of South African colonists that there is a specialité in African fighting is quite a mistake.'[33] Indeed, as we have seen, although not entirely closed to military innovation, Thesiger was indubitably a prosaic product of the system and remained inherently reluctant to adapt orthodox military practices to colonial conditions unless absolutely pressed, as had finally been the case in his campaign against the amaXhosa.

Thesiger's initial view of Bulwer was reciprocally unflattering. With his tufty red hair, bushy moustache and little imperial, and with his pot belly overbalancing his thin legs, the lieutenant-governor was not an entirely prepossessing figure, especially when in didactic mode with index figure wagging.[34] Thesiger's military associates rapidly came to regard Bulwer as 'a very obstinate and arrogant man in public affairs' with an essentially 'small mind' who looked 'on every question from a small standpoint'.[35] Thesiger reported to Frere that, while Bulwer appeared to be a man of justice and ability, he was self-opinionated, obstinate and ill-tempered and had been misled by the artfulness of the African chiefs. Thesiger's problem was that as GOC he did not have the authority to interfere with the Natal government or override the lieutenant-governor. He therefore urged Frere to hurry to Natal as soon as he could to compel Bulwer to obey him as High Commissioner.[36] As it was, Thesiger was destined to become ever more frustrated by Bulwer's obduracy and the stalling tactics adopted by his government. By the end of the campaign, he would be complaining bitterly to Cambridge that 'Sir H. Bulwer from my first arrival in Natal has thrown every obstacle in my way.'[37]

It was unfortunate, to say the least, that the dispute between the military and civil authorities in the Cape that had bedevilled the first phase of the Ninth Cape Frontier War and had ultimately led to Cunynghame's supersession, should have to be played out again in the Zulu campaign. It was not, though, that Thesiger had not learned from Cunynghame's mistakes, and he had done his best in the Cape to get along with the colonial authorities. Rather, much of the fault lay in the convoluted system of imperial governance and the entangled lines of authority.[38] Besides, as in all human affairs, personalities played their part. Thesiger had got along perfectly well with Sprigg, the Cape premier, because their objectives in the war against the amaXhosa had coincided. The difficulty with Bulwer was that not only did he have a strong, annoying personality and a high sense of his position as lieutenant-governor, but that he most definitely did not go along with Frere and Thesiger in seeing the necessity for war against Cetshwayo. As a consequence, his support for the coming campaign would never be better than lukewarm, and Thesiger would be commensurately irritated and resentful.

While still in the Cape, Thesiger had evinced concern that no real preparations had been made in Natal for the defence of the colony should there be war with Zululand.[39] That deficiency would have to be addressed urgently. Meanwhile, only days after his arrival in Pietermaritzburg, Thesiger was informing Shepstone that he was endeavouring to convince the Natal colonists that 'their interests in respect to the Zulu difficulty' were 'identical with those of the Transvaal', and that his first priority was to settle quickly with Sekhukhune so that the forces in the Transvaal could be redeployed to assist in his projected invasion of Zululand.[40] But before he could take further action, on 23 August he had to sail on HMS *Active* for the mouth of the St John's (Mzimvubu) River in the territory of the Mpondo kingdom between the Cape's recently pacified Eastern Frontier and Natal. Frere had resolved to secure the natural harbour at the river's mouth and to establish a fort and garrison there to overawe the amaMpondo and secure Natal's southern border. Thesiger superintended the disembarkation of a company of the 1/24th Regiment and on 31 August proclaimed nine miles of the west bank of the Mzimvubu British territory.[41]

Two mountains, the Gates of St John, guard the entrance to the river. The great flat-topped sandstone mountain on the west bank that looms over the little town of Port St John's is still called Mount Thesiger. The peak on the opposite bank is known as Mount Sullivan, named after Captain F. W. Sullivan, the commodore of the South African Station and commander of the *Active*. Today, very few people indeed know why these mountains bear the names they do, those of an obscure British general and a forgotten admiral. It is only a matter of time before they are renamed in the drive to expunge all topographical names deemed relics of the colonial past, and Thesiger will have been deprived of his one memorial.

CHAPTER 17

Readying the Invasion Force, August 1878–January 1879

IT IS NOT TO BE SUPPOSED that the obsessively conscientious Thesiger allowed the greater matter of the Zulu question to slip his attention while he was establishing the fortified post at the St John's River. While on board the *Active* he began drawing up detailed plans encompassing every military aspect of the coming campaigns in the Transvaal and Zululand, including the contribution to be made by colonial forces.[1] As for the political aspects and the diplomatic machinations necessary to bring on a state of war, these he left in Frere's hands.

On 5 October 1878, two months after Thesiger had established his HQ in Pietermaritzburg, his father, the first Lord Chelmsford died in his eighty-fourth year and was buried next to his wife in a heraldically ornate tomb in Brompton Cemetery in London that proclaimed his elevation to the peerage. His heir would not know until four weeks after his sire's demise that he had succeeded him, and continued until 5 November to sign his correspondence as 'Thesiger'. It took him so long to learn that he was now the second Baron Chelmsford because of the unsatisfactory nature of communications between Britain and South Africa, a shortcoming that was to play a significant part in the unfolding of the Anglo-Zulu War.

Communication between South Africa and Britain had been entirely by sea until the laying in 1874 of a trans-Atlantic undersea telegraph cable connecting Brazil to Europe by way of São Vicente in the Cape Verde Islands off the west coast of Africa, and then via the island of Madeira 1,300 miles to the north.[2] But that was only half the story. Once a telegraphed message from London reached either Madeira or São Vicente, it languished there awaiting the weekly mail steamer that was to carry it to Cape Town, a slow sea voyage that took about three weeks from the former island and a fortnight from the latter – and longer if the weather were poor. In April 1878 Cape Town was linked overland by copper telegraph cable to Durban which since 1864 had been connected to Pietermaritzburg by the same means. Pietermaritzburg was in turn connected by telegraph to Pretoria in the Transvaal Territory. Official telegraphic messages were often sent in cypher, and if they were of any length this could take secretaries or officials several hours to formulate and decypher, thus delaying their immediate transmission. All this meant that a telegraphed message from London to Pietermaritzburg took at best two weeks but often as many as four to reach its destination. Yet this was rapid compared to the time it took despatches too lengthy to telegraph to arrive in London, weighty missives of the sort that the general, an indefatigable penman, would produce in such quantity. They went the entire way by sea from Durban, and this would take about five weeks. The upshot was that even the most urgent official business sent by sea between the GOC in South Africa and the Horse Guards or the War Office, or between the High Commissioner or the lieutenant governor of Natal on the one hand, and the Colonial Office on the other, required ten weeks or more to turn about. Consequently, the British government's decisions concerning the distant region were unavoidably all too often scarcely more than belated responses to events that had already taken place.[3]

When he finally learned of his father's death, the new Lord Chelmsford, was deeply affected. As he wrote on 7 November 1878 to Colonel Wood, who had commiserated with him, 'My father's death has been a great blow to me. Up to the last his constitution was so vigorous that I had every reason to hope I might have found him alive and well on my return from this country.'[4] Nevertheless, dedicated as he was to duty, Lord Chelmsford (as he would now be known until his own death, and will henceforth be referred to throughout the rest of this book) did not permit his genuine personal grief to interfere with his task as GOC in preparing for the coming campaigns against the Bapedi and amaZulu.

As soon as he was settled in Pietermaritzburg, Chelmsford took stock of the troops at his disposal.[5] In Cape Colony there were two batteries of Royal Artillery (N Battery, 5th Brigade and No. 11, 7th Brigade); 7th Company, Royal Engineers; and the 1st and 2nd Battalions, 24th (Second Warwickshire) Regiment and the 88th Regiment (Connaught Rangers). The 2nd Battalion, 3rd Regiment (East Kent, The Buffs) and the 80th

Regiment (Staffordshire Volunteers) were stationed in the Colony of Natal. Two more battalions of infantry were now in the Transvaal Territory. The 1st Battalion, 13th Regiment (First Somersetshire) Prince Albert's Light Infantry, initially formed the garrison in Pretoria, the capital of the Transvaal Territory, but soon proved insufficient for the task. Shepstone had consequently appealed to Frere for reinforcements. On 12 March 1878 the 90th Perthshire Light Infantry, which had recently arrived in Natal from the Cape, accordingly moved up to Utrecht in the southern Transvaal.

Since Chelmsford intended to settle the Pedi issue first, he ordered the 80th in Natal to join the 1/13th and 90th in the Transvaal under the command of Colonel Hugh Rowlands. The Natal garrison was kept up to strength by the arrival by sea of the 2/24th from the Cape, freed up by the conclusion of the Ninth Cape Frontier War. The forces in the Transvaal were further reinforced by the FLH, a colonial mounted force some 200 strong which had been raised in the Cape Colony during the Ninth Cape Frontier War, and which Chelmsford increased to 300 with freshly raised recruits.[6] They were under the command of the outspoken Brevet Major R. W. Buller, CB, 60th Rifles who would receive his brevet lieutenant-colonelcy on 11 November 1878. Born into the Devonshire squirearchy at the family seat of Downes, and with considerable estates in Devon and Cornwall, Buller had served in the Second Anglo-Chinese War of 1856–8 and with Wolseley in the Red River Expedition of 1870. Wolseley, who had learned then to appreciate Buller's fearlessness and resourcefulness, had appointed him his chief intelligence officer during the Third Anglo-Asante War. After four years as DAAG, Horse Guards, on 30 January 1878 Buller was appointed a Special Service officer and sailed with Thesiger for the Cape. There he relished being in the field again and, although brusque and tough, he was also an accessible and sympathetic commander who earned the deep trust and admiration of the roughnecks of the FLH for sharing every hardship with them and for fearlessly leading from the front.[7] Although Buller was technically a member of Wolseley's 'ring', Chelmsford greatly appreciated him as a soldier and would rely on him increasingly.

While reinforcing the Transvaal, Thesiger continued to build up his forces in Natal for the impending Zululand campaign. The battalions already in Natal and the Transvaal were brought up to full strength, and the two batteries of Royal Artillery were despatched from the Cape. During September and October seven companies of the 1/24th arrived in Natal from the Cape ('B' Company was left to garrison Port St John's). Concerned that the British troops he had at his disposal were too scattered and altogether insufficient in number for the intended invasion of Zululand, during September 1878 Chelmsford urgently requested Colonel the Hon. Frederick. A. Stanley, the Secretary of State for War, for more Special Service officers and reinforcements.[8] But, already embroiled in the Second Anglo-Afghan War that had begun in June 1878, the British government was hesitant to comply. As Stanley later told the House of Commons, 'While it [the Second Anglo-Afghan War] was going on I think I should have been unworthy of the position I hold, if my attention had not been directed to the reinforcements which might be required there.'[9] Indeed, besides the troops of the Indian Army already deployed in Afghanistan, six regiments of British infantry were also fighting there, along with a regiment of cavalry and batteries of the Royal Horse, Field and Garrison Artillery.

It was with reluctance, therefore, that on 25 November 1878 the government embarked 1,190 infantry and 240 Royal Engineers for South Africa. Hicks Beach, the Colonial Secretary, sternly informed Frere that 'It is my duty to impress upon you that in supplying these reinforcements it is the desire of Her Majesty's Government not to furnish means for a campaign of invasion and conquest, but to afford such protection as may be necessary at this juncture to the lives and property of the Colonists.'[10] His warning had no deterrent effect on Frere's plans, however, and when in early January the 99th (Duke of Edinburgh's Lanarkshire) Regiment and the 2nd and 5th Companies, Royal Engineers, disembarked in Durban, they were added to Chelmsford's army of invasion. The 2nd Battalion of the 4th (King's Own Royal) Regiment, however, would not arrive in Natal until a few days after the war had already begun to run its course.[11] To supplement this small force of regular troops, a Naval Brigade was landed in Durban on 19 November from HMS *Active* consisting of 170 sailors and Royal Marines, with two 12-pdr Armstrong guns, one Gatling gun and two rocket tubes. The Naval Brigade was reinforced on 6 January by 50 more men from HMS *Tenedos*.[12]

Chelmsford's ultimately successful formula in the Ninth Cape Frontier War had required African auxiliaries who were invaluable for undertaking garrison and convoy duties in place of the militarily more valuable British troops, and were also useful in scouting and in following up the enemy once they had been broken by the British regulars' disciplined firepower. On 17 August 1878 Brevet Colonel Anthony Durnford addressed a memorandum to Chelmsford suggesting the raising of African levies, ultimately known as the Natal Native Contingent (NNC). Durnford was a lean, energetic Royal Engineers officer sporting distinctive Dundreary whiskers who had been posted to Natal in 1873. There he had been the acting colonial engineer in 1873–5 and had served on Bulwer's Boundary Commission earlier in 1878. During this period, he had become intimate with the family of the humanitarian Anglican Bishop of Natal, John Colenso, and become involved in a close sentimental friendship with Frances Ellen Colenso, the bishop's second daughter – a relationship that would have fateful repercussions for Thesiger in the years to come. Durnford consequently believed he understood the colonial dynamic well. Unfortunately for his military record, he had been the officer in command on 2–4 November 1873 during the debacle at the Bushman's River Pass during the Langalibalele Rebellion. His military leadership was subsequently severely criticised, even though his personal courage was acknowledged. The disastrous encounter left him with a crippled left arm and with an intemperate determination to redeem his military reputation. That quest conflicted with his genuine humanitarian concern for the downtrodden Africans in Natal that he shared with the Colenso family and further forfeited him the goodwill of many colonists. It contrasted, too, with his sincere deprecation of a war of aggression against the amaZulu. His desire for military renown won out, however, and he would throw himself into the raising and training of African auxiliaries and into zealously advising Chelmsford in planning for the Zulu campaign.[13]

Chelmsford took up Durnford's August memorandum with enthusiasm and over the next three months pressed its suggestions on the Natal government. As the Supreme Chief over Africans living in Natal, the Lieutenant-Governor had the right to exact *isibhalo* – or compulsory labour and military service – from them, but Bulwer had strong reservations about doing so on a number of counts. He was reluctant to cede the control of Natal African levies to the military; he shared most colonists' concerns about training and arming Africans who so menacingly and comprehensively outnumbered the settlers; and he believed that the levies, if raised, should retain their traditional military organisation and fighting methods and not be forced into the mould of British soldiers as insisted upon by Chelmsford on Durnford's urging.

Chelmsford nevertheless prevailed on all counts, and on 23 November 1878 he was able to issue a General Order setting out the regulations for the NNC. This was accompanied by a minutely detailed pamphlet issued on his orders by Colonel William Bellairs, reminiscent of the one he had produced during the Ninth Cape Frontier War entitled *Regulations for the Colonial Forces*. The title spoke for itself: *General Instructions for Management of Natives for the Guidance of Officers appointed to the Natal Native Contingent*.[14] From early November the Natal resident magistrates began raising Africans for military service from the chiefs of the Native Reserves, encouraging recruitment with inducements of regular rations and pay of twenty shillings a month, and with promises of captured cattle. Bulwer duly transferred the NNC to Chelmsford's command, making it an imperial, rather than colonial force. The men received no uniform except a red cloth to be tied around the head to distinguish them from the amaZulu, and were issued with a blanket (a different colour for each battalion). They were formed into three regiments with three battalions in the 1st Regiment and two each in the 2nd and 3rd Regiments. Each battalion consisted of ten companies with a nominal establishment of 1,100 officers and men. Three white officers and six white NCOs led each company which consisted of one African officer, ten African NCOs and ninety men. The 1st Regiment received the best officers, local men who spoke isiZulu, but the 2nd and 3rd Regiments made do with men who had served with the Mfengu levies in the Cape and spoke no isiZulu, or possibly some isiXhosa, a closely related language. This led to great dissatisfaction among the men they led. Some of the officers were seconded or former British officers who were preferred for senior command. The white NCOs were generally colonial riff-raff, men of inferior military calibre.

Since there was considerable settler resistance to Africans receiving firearms, only the African officers and NCOs were issued with Enfield rifles, and the rest of the men carried their traditional spears and shields. The white officers and NCOs were issued with Martini-Henry rifles. In all, poorly armed, indifferently commanded and ineffectually trained in unfamiliar British military discipline, drill and tactics, the NNC promised to be of doubtful morale and effectiveness.

In addition to the NNC, Chelmsford raised the Natal Native Pioneer Corps (NNPC) of about 250 men organised into three companies, each under five white and four black officers, to construct earthwork fortifications and maintain the rudimentary tracks. They were issued with uniforms consisting of an outdated scarlet military frock with facings removed, knee-length white cotton trousers, and a blue forage cap with a yellow band. Each man carried a digging implement but firearms were restricted to their officers.[15]

Even more essential to the success of colonial campaigning than locally raised auxiliaries were mounted troops. They had proved pivotal in the later stages of the Ninth Cape Frontier War, and would be crucial in Zululand for reconnaissance and raiding purposes, and vital in the pursuit of a broken enemy when they would convert a withdrawal into a rout. Yet, as Chelmsford was uncomfortably aware, he had not nearly enough for his purposes.[16] Regular cavalry would not be made available until the closing stages of the campaign, and he had to rely on what mounted men he could raise locally. These consisted of several different elements. Firstly, there were two squadrons of some 200 Mounted Infantry raised from volunteers from the regiments of infantry in South Africa, who exchanged their blue trousers for brown cord riding-breeches, their rifles for carbines, and took to the saddle – often rather insecurely.[17] The main difference between cavalry and mounted infantry was that while the latter would likewise undertake reconnaissance and screening, and perform advance guard, sentry and escort duty, they would not be required to take part in a charge with the *arme blanche*, the sword or lance. That was left to the cavalry that, on this account, considered themselves socially and militarily superior. It would not be until the later 1880s that the concept of mounted infantry was fully accepted in the British Army.[18]

In addition to the Mounted Infantry, Chelmsford had at his disposal various colonial units of horsemen who fought as mounted infantry. There were the 80 troopers of the paramilitary Natal Mounted Police, and about 370 men of the ten out of eleven corps of the Natal Mounted Volunteer Corps that signed up in October 1878 for active service outside the borders of the colony (the Mounted Volunteers were obliged only to defend Natal itself), and would be called out for active duty on 26 November 1878. The Mounted Volunteers consisted of men drawn from the more established elements of primarily English-speaking colonial society, and wore a

'Isandula'. Major-General Sir Frederic Thesiger, second Baron Chelmsford, GCB, in the House of Lords. *Vanity Fair*, 3 September 1881. By Spy (Leslie Wood).

Left: The Halifax Citadel, Nova Scotia, where Second Lieutenant Frederic Thesiger, Rifle Brigade, was stationed in 1845.

Right: The first Baron Chelmsford. *Vanity Fair*, 5 February 1870. 'Statesmen No. 39', by ATn (Alfred Thompson).

Left: A watercolour of soldiers of the Rifle Brigade *c.* 1850. Thanks to the influence of the Duke of Wellington, the Colonel-in-Chief of the Rifle Brigade, in 1844 Sir Frederick Thesiger purchased his son Frederic a commission as second lieutenant in the regiment.

Below: Dublin Castle and Chapel, which Thesiger would have frequented in 1852–3 as ADC to the Lord Lieutenant of Ireland. Pictured in 1903.

An ensign of Grenadiers, *c.* 1850 carrying the Queen's Colour. Print by R. Akermann.

Frederic Thesiger's younger brother Captain Charles Wemyss Thesiger of the 6th (Inniskilling) Dragoons, photographed in 1858. He would complete his successful career as a lieutenant-general.

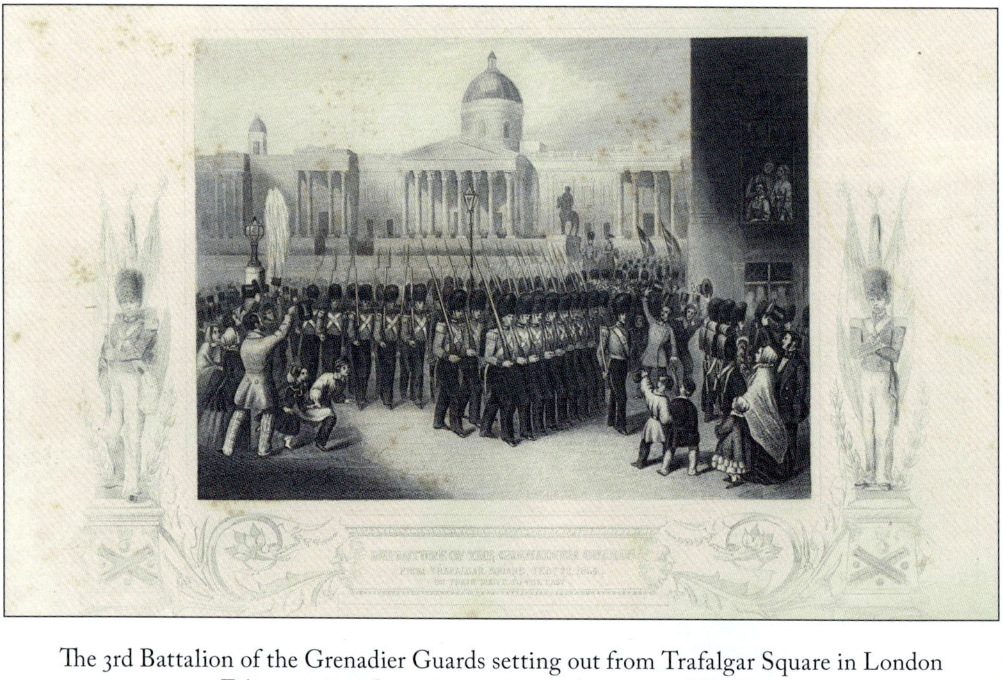

The 3rd Battalion of the Grenadier Guards setting out from Trafalgar Square in London on 23 February 1854, for active service in the eastern Mediterranean.

The Gwalior fortress, a key stronghold in the Central India Campaign of 1858–9 during the Indian Mutiny in which Lieutenant-Colonel the Hon. Frederic Thesiger took part.

Lieutenant-Colonel the Hon. Frederic Thesiger with officers of the 95th (Derbyshire) Regiment, while stationed in the Bombay Presidency, 1859–69.

Left: HRH Prince George, Duke of Cambridge, KG, Field Marshal Commanding-in-Chief, by ATn (Alfred Thompson). 'Statesmen No. 47', *Vanity Fair*, 23 April 1870. His enduring patronage was critical for Frederic Thesiger's military career.

Below: Lieutenant-General Sir Robert Napier and the Headquarters Staff of the Abyssinian Field Force. The bearded Brevet Colonel Thesiger, Napier's Deputy Adjutant-General, sits to his left looking at the map on the table.

Right: Frederic Thesiger's 'fast friend' and patron in India, General Sir Robert Napier, Baron Napier of Magdala and Caryngton, GCB, GCSI, Commander-in-Chief, Bombay, commander of the Abyssinian Expedition and subsequently Commander-in-Chief in India. Painting by Lowes Cato Dickinson.

Below: The HQ Staff pictured at Simla in 1874 while Brevet Colonel the Hon. F. Thesiger ADC, CB, was Adjutant-General of the Indian Army. Seated, from left to right are five colonels, Rattray, Wright, Thesiger, Arbuthnot and Gordon.

Major-General the Hon. Frederic Thesiger, ADC, CB in March 1877. This carte-de-visite was corrected by pen to reflect his higher rank and orders after the Anglo-Zulu War.

Brigadier General Evelyn Wood, VC, CB. He was commander of No. 4 Column, subsequently the Flying Column, and the victor at the critical battle of Khambula. 'The Flying Column', *Vanity Fair*, 15 November 1879. By Spy (Leslie Wood).

Lord Chelmsford and the portion of No. 3 Column not engaged at Isandlwana approach the stricken camp on the evening of 22 January 1879. Note the columns of red-coated British infantry, artillery and the Natal Native Contingent. An eye-witness sketch by Lieutenant-Colonel J. N. Crealock in which the looming bulk of Isandlwana Mountain is greatly exaggerated.

A watercolour by Lieutenant William Lloyd of British soldiers of the 2nd Division crossing the Ncome River at Harrison's Drift on 1 June 1879. The proliferation of natural obstacles such as this go part of the way to explain the slow progress of the British columns invading Zululand.

Major-General Henry Hope Crealock, CB, commander of the 1st Division, known derisively as 'Crealock's Crawlers'. 'Second in Zululand', *Vanity Fair*, 15 March 1879. By Spy (Leslie Wood).

Lieutenant-Colonel Crealock's watercolour of Lord Chelmsford, painted a few days before the battle of Ulundi.

Lieutenant William Lloyd of the 2/24th Regiment marched with the 2nd Division towards oNdini. He depicted the column as it passed Siphezi Mountain on 18 June 1879. Note the ox-drawn wagons, the ranks of red-coated soldiers, and the burning Zulu *imizi* on the slopes of the mountain.

The charge of the 17th Lancers at the height of the battle of Ulundi (*detail*). Note the infantry square in the background, and the burning *amakhanda*. Watercolour by Charles Fripp, special artist for the *Graphic*, who was with the 2nd Division.

Left: After the battle of Ulundi, British troops look on while oNdini, King Cetshwayo's great *ikhanda*, is consigned to the flames. Note the 9-pounder guns and the members of the NNC bearing away the British wounded in litters. *Illustrated London News*, 23 August 1879.

Lieutenant William Lloyd witnessed triumphant soldiers of the NNC taunting Zulu prisoners being brought into the British camp at the White Mfolozi after the battle of Ulundi.

A late nineteenth-century photograph of the Guards Crimean War Memorial in Waterloo Place in London, close by the United Service Club to the left where Lord Chelmsford died on 9 April 1905.

General Lord Chelmsford's grave in Brompton Cemetery, London.

variegated array of smart uniforms. Their military training, however, was mediocre, as had been made manifest at the Bushman's River Pass debacle.[19] Besides the veterans of the FLH, Chelmsford had recourse to the equally rough-and-ready Baker's Horse that had served in the Ninth Cape Frontier War and were now also stationed in the Transvaal, along with several other smaller units being raised in the Transvaal itself for service under Rowlands, such as Raaff's Transvaal Rangers and Weatherley's Border Horse.[20]

Besides these colonial units of white men mustered as mounted infantry, Chelmsford raised several units of African irregular cavalry comprising the Natal Native Mounted Contingent, the counterpart to the infantry of the NNC. Some 400 keen and effective volunteers from the Natal Native Reserves and from the Christian community at Edendale outside Pietermaritzburg formed three troops of Sikali's Horse and one each of Hlubi's Troop, Jantze's Native Horse and the Edendale Horse They were maintained by the War Office and commanded by white colonial officers. The troopers supplied their own horses but were armed with a variety of breech-loading carbines (some men also carried traditional weapons) and were given uniforms of yellow or brown corduroy and brown broad-brimmed hats with a red puggaree. Only the Edendale Horse elected to wear the boots issued them and the rest rode barefoot. Jantze's Native Horse refused to wear the trousers issued them.[21]

While fully engrossed in building up his forces for the coming confrontation with Cetshwayo, Chelmsford adhered to his strategic agenda by attempting to settle with Sekhukhune first. He knew that by the end of October wasting 'horse sickness' would bring the campaigning season to an end,[22] but he hoped for a rapid, decisive blow before then and had been reinforcing the troops in the Transvaal to that end. In all, by early September Rowlands had 1,216 infantry and 611 mounted men under his command for the Pedi campaign.[23] By 19 September he was encamped at the Spekboom River near Fort Burgers in the eastern Transvaal and was readying to advance on Tsate, Sekhukhune's stronghold on the flanks of the Leolo Mountains. On 3 October, Rowlands marched with 130 men of the 1/13th Regiment, 338 men of the FLH and Mounted Infantry, and the two 7-pdr Krupp guns of the mule battery. Tsate was twenty-five miles to the west, and the Bapedi determinedly skirmished with the British as they scrambled through the very rugged country. The season was exceptionally hot and dry and the watercourses had ceased to flow. They country was consequently denuded of pasture for the column's horses, mules and slaughter oxen. As so often in colonial warfare, Rowlands had underestimated his enemy and the harshness of the inhospitable terrain. Disconcertingly, his horses were beginning to die of the dreaded, wasting horse sickness. All things considered, there was no option but to retreat before reaching Tsate, and all his officers concurred.

At dawn on 6 October Rowlands pulled his weary, dispirited troops back the way they had come. It was an awful march. Exhausted and dehydrated, they and their surviving horses reached their base at Fort Burgers late in the afternoon of 7 October. Human casualties were negligible with only one man wounded, but the blow to British prestige was considerable.

Before suspending further operations, though, Rowlands needed at least one success to burnish the dented British image. On 27 October he targeted a Pedi stronghold only about five miles away from his camp at Fort Burgers, so logistical problems would not again upset his plans. His men stormed and burned the place, and with that last, futile flourish the First Anglo-Pedi War came to an end. With horse sickness gaining hold and with supplies still an intractable problem, Rowlands abandoned Fort Burgers and all other advanced posts. Following Chelmsford's orders, he withdrew his troops to various garrisons in the Transvaal, concentrating them along the Swazi and Zulu borders for the anticipated campaign against the Zulu kingdom.[24] Even if these troops were not diverted within the next few months to the Zululand theatre, Rowlands held out no hope that the next campaigning season against Sekhukhune could open again before late April 1879.[25]

Shepstone was naturally taken aback by the humiliating outcome of the campaign and admitted to Rowlands that with chastened hindsight he had miscalculated, and that 'Sikukuni's powers to resist or to defend himself were underrated from the beginning.'[26] For his part, Rowlands was broken by his failure and indicated to Chelmsford that he wished to resign his command. Chelmsford was not a vindictive man and had no wish to destroy a fellow soldier's career, so he wrote to Rowlands not to do so since it would be a mistake 'from a professional point of view'. However, Chelmsford was not willing to put his trust in an officer who had failed as a field commander and had dislocated his plans at the very outset, and was resolved to sideline Rowlands in his continuing arrangements for the invasion of Zululand.[27]

Chelmsford entertained no doubts that his forces would defeat the amaZulu in any armed encounter, as had been the case against the amaXhosa, but his problem (as we shall see) was how he could make sure of bringing them to battle and so avoid the desultory and time-consuming irregular warfare he had experienced in the second phase of the Ninth Cape Frontier War. Whatever strategy he adopted, though, the first step in ensuring a swift, decisive campaign such as Chelmsford and Frere envisaged depended upon firm logistics. Unfortunately for Chelmsford, the Anglo-Zulu War exemplified one of the fundamentals of colonial warfare: it was a campaign against distance and natural obstacles as much as against an enemy, and problems of supply would overshadow its entire course. The challenge was that Chelmsford could not depend on obtaining supplies from the theatre of operations, so they would have to be carried, as they had been during the Abyssinian Expedition. That meant that his invading army would have to be turned into an escort for the soldiers' provisions and draught animals' fodder, let alone for the prodigious quantity and variety of baggage carried as a matter of course by a Victorian army on campaign in Africa. Besides officers' personal baggage and much of the soldiers' kit, all normally carried in the wagons when on the march, baggage included camping equipment, tents, engineering and signalling equipment, medical stores, camp kitchens, field bakeries and shoeing smithies. Transport was also required for the artillery and rocket batteries, and for the critical reserve ammunition.

Logistics were supposedly Chelmsford's area of expertise and, as we have seen, he had performed very well as the DAG Abyssinian Field Force in 1868. The challenges he faced in this area in Natal in 1878–9 were therefore not new to him, and with all his experience as a staff officer he knew precisely how to proceed. As his voluminous correspondence concerning logistics attests, for months before the invasion he was personally engrossed in collecting and organising supplies and transport. However, if he had succeeded in establishing better relations with the Natal government, and in particular with Bulwer, the cooperation of the colonial officials would have eased his logistical problems considerably. Unfortunately, as we have seen, he and his staff had alienated them, and the Natal civil authorities consequently volunteered little in the way of help. Chelmsford had therefore to proceed largely on his own, By January 1879 he had assembled 977 ox-wagons and 56 carts along with 10,023 oxen, 803 horses and 398 mules to draw them, and 1,910 civilian conductors, drivers and leaders to manage them.[28]

The ponderous ox-wagon, drawn by a team of ten to eighteen oxen yoked in pairs, was capable of carrying up to 8,000 pounds but, in the event, because of the wretched tracks in Zululand, was never loaded with more than about 3,000 pounds. The carts drawn by eight mules or horses carried at the very most about 2,000 pounds and usually half that weight, and the draught animals' fodder took up an appreciable part of each load.

There was a practical limit to the size of a convoy. The wagons and carts required all-round protection on the march, particularly on the flanks. Mounted patrols had to move parallel or in advance of the column to give early warning of enemy movements. Yet, since a single wagon in full span took up about sixty yards and a cart some twenty yards of road, a lengthy train of several hundred wagons and carts dangerously thinned out its escort, exposing it to ambush. The vulnerability of an already extended column was increased at drifts (fords) across rivers or passes up steep hills where wagons usually had to proceed in single file, creating protracted traffic jams. In open country, however, wagons and carts could proceed more rapidly at about eight abreast, ignoring the rutted tracks and driving across the veld in a more concentrated formation easier to escort effectively.

Even in the best of circumstances, the progress of a convoy was sluggish in the extreme. Draught oxen grazed the veld and did not depend on fodder as did the mules and horses, but they needed abundant time to do so and remain in good condition. Nor could they be kept in the yoke for more than three or four hours at a stretch without a rest. The mules and horses also needed breaks to recover. The dirt roads in Natal and the Transvaal were poor, and in Zululand were no more than unsurveyed traders' tracks cut across by drifts and dongas (gullies) that collapsed under the volume of traffic. As a result, twelve miles a day was the utmost convoys could achieve, and when the terrain was broken or wet, they could often cover only a quarter of that distance. The advance of a convoy was further inhibited by the need to halt at intervals to establish and garrison forward fortified depots for reserve supplies along its line of march. Before resuming its march, a convoy then had to wait until wagons and carts shuttling backwards and forwards between the rear supply base and the new depot had fully stocked it.

Chelmsford's task in assembling this transport was made all the more frustrating by the under-staffed Commissariat and Transport Department under Commissary-General Edward Strickland, CB, a hide-bound veteran of numerous campaigns who sported a long ginger beard and sweeping mustachios.[29] His department's inexperience in purchasing and in looking after its draught animals in South African conditions provided an unexpected windfall for colonists who shamelessly hired out or sold their animals, wagons and carts at exorbitant prices.[30]

There was unfortunately nothing new about this situation on campaign, and Chelmsford would have witnessed precisely the same ad hoc and wasteful practices during the Crimean War. The dispiriting thing was that he found himself unable to improve on them when preparing for the Zululand campaign. He was only too aware of the Commissariat and Transport Department's inadequacies but, to his repeated exasperation, he came up against the jealously held service prerogatives of the Victorian Army. Strickland was going to do things his own way despite Chelmsford's fretful exhortation for the 'working of transport' to engage his 'serious attention' since it was 'absolutely essential that there should be a proper system established'.[31] Consequently, despite repeated attempts, Chelmsford failed to impose a remedy on the department's unwilling personnel, and ultimately left them to their own inadequate devices.[32] Perhaps, if he had attached more importance to assembling a larger, better trained group of staff officers they might have augmented the overstretched officers in Strickland's department. As it was, Chelmsford had no option but to second 'combat officers', men with no trained expertise in logistical matters, to assist lest the department 'break down utterly under present arrangements'.[33] Even then, the officers of the department refused to cooperate willingly with the seconded officers and Chelmsford was soon complaining to the War Office of their virtual insubordination.[34] It was thus only with great difficulty and expense that Chelmsford gathered the transport necessary to supply his army assembling to invade Zululand.

CHAPTER 18

Planning the Invasion, August 1878–January 1879

CHELMSFORD'S DEPENDENCE on slow-moving and vulnerable supply trains meant put a limit on the size of the columns they were to support and compromised their manoeuvrability. The larger the convoy, the slower it moved, so Chelmsford decided that he must adopt the strategy of sending in a number of smaller columns. That echoed his initial, unsuccessful deployment in the Ninth Frontier War, but nevertheless seemed appropriate for the impending Zulu campaign.

Military wisdom holds that a division of forces is bad strategy. Yet in Victorian 'small wars' it was considered excusable because of the problems of supply and mobility that Chelmsford faced, and because a separate number of invading forces had the advantage of seeming more formidable to an unsophisticated enemy than a single one.[1] Besides, Chelmsford calculated that with smaller columns sufficient grazing would be available for the draught animals of each. Strategically, a number of supporting columns promised to reduce the chances of being outflanked, and presumably would discourage Zulu counter-thrusts against the British frontiers. And, by invading simultaneously at several points, he hoped to force Cetshwayo to keep his forces fully mobilised in order to face the diverse threat, and so present his enemy with supply problems no less daunting than his own.[2]

At all costs Chelmsford wished to avoid the desultory, protracted warfare he had experienced in the Eastern Cape, and intended to conclude the campaign expeditiously with a decisive battle.[3] The experience of 'small wars' proved beyond doubt that those which were the most decisive were marked by pitched battles where all the advantage lay with properly trained troops carrying superior armaments. Upcher's victory at Kentani on 7 February 1878 that had knocked the amaGcaleka out of the Ninth

Cape Frontier War was a recent case in point. Chelmsford's strategic objective, therefore, was for his columns to converge in a pincer movement on oNdini in the Mahlabathini plain, Cetshwayo's chief *ikhanda*, or royal military homestead. Chelmsford reckoned that the Zulu king would be forced into a pitched battle to defend it, a risk he was more than likely to take because of the strong Zulu military culture. Chelmsford took his victory in the battle for granted, and expected it to lead to the collapse of the Zulu kingdom. Certainly, there was the danger that by reducing the size of his converging columns each might become more at risk if attacked, but he was confident that they would nevertheless all be strong enough to fight off any size of Zulu force. Indeed, Chelmsford's division of his army into several deceptively vulnerable columns was no more than a conventional gambit intended to entice the amaZulu into risking the pitched battle he desired.[4]

Old colonists, harking back to their experience in 1838 during the Voortrekker–Zulu War when their forces suffered several defeats at Zulu hands when fighting in the open instead of from behind a prepared position, urged him to make each column form a defensive wagon-laager every time it halted in Zulu territory.[5] But laagering was a time-consuming and complicated procedure and it had not been Chelmsford's practice to laager temporary camps when on the march against the amaXhosa. Chelmsford persisted therefore in supposing that for his well-armed columns laagering would prove an unnecessary delay, and that partial entrenchments around their temporary camps would suffice instead.[6]

Chelmsford believed that his strategy of converging columns possessed a further great advantage. He knew that when he advanced into Zululand, he would leave Natal and the Transvaal to his rear vulnerable to raids not only by the amaZulu, but, thanks to Rowlands's failure in the First Anglo-Pedi War, by the still-undefeated Bapedi as well. Nevertheless, as we have seen, he assumed that invasion by a number of supporting columns would discourage any enemy counter-thrusts, even if the possibility of the attempt could not be discounted. He found the colonial attitude to this danger curiously ambivalent. Many white settlers dreaded the possibility of Zulu raids, especially since they anticipated that the colony's Africans might rise up in support.[7] Yet, to Chelmsford's exasperation, the Natal government continued to be insouciant in the face of what he considered this real threat. Bulwer's contingency plans were limited to advising settlers to take refuge in the scattered urban and rural government laagers in the process of improvement or construction about Natal and in the southern Transvaal, or in the private laagers being hurriedly thrown up by some local communities of farmers. These permanent fortifications were merely stone and sod enclosures, sometimes with bastions at opposite corners.[8] There was no provision for accommodating the unfortunate black population in them, except for a handful of servants and retainers, and these people were to be left at the mercy of Zulu raiders. Faced with the common attitude held by members of the Natal government that the very idea of a Zulu invasion was 'absurd', Chelmsford set about chivvying them out of their 'fool's paradise'. At a crucial meeting of the Natal Executive Council's Defence Committee on 10 September 1878, he at last persuaded the Natal authorities to follow all his suggestions and take appropriate action.

On 26 November Natal was divided into seven rural Defensive Districts and two Sub-Districts comprising the main towns of Durban and Pietermaritzburg. Each was placed on 3 December under a Colonial District Commander who had charge of the colonial forces in his district as well as of the public laagers and the government arms and ammunition stored there. However, since many men would be absent serving with the Natal Mounted Volunteers (NMV) or NMP, it was up to the remaining members of the various Rifle Associations and other volunteers to defend the laagers as best they could. Small garrisons of imperial troops would remain in Durban and Pietermaritzburg, as well as along Chelmsford's lines of communication and supply to Zululand at the villages of Stanger, Greytown, Ladysmith and Newcastle. But who would defend the countryside in between the various strongpoints?

There was available a very small and uncertain number of essentially untrained Mounted Burghers who were liable to turn out for commando duty if called upon by their local field cornet, but at best they would only be of use patrolling and giving warning of Zulu movements. The Africans of the Special Border Police, stationed under white border agents along the Thukela and Mzinyathi (Buffalo) Rivers, amounted to only 190 men, and their primary task was to gather intelligence and not to deter a Zulu incursion.[9] It was obvious that the Natal government would have to raise African levies for the defence of the countryside. But Natal was a poor colony and its government could not afford to maintain a large standing force. So, it devised a system that came into effect on 20 December whereby every chief in the border Defensive Districts (Nos. I, VI and VII) would furnish a quota of fighting men who would take the field under white levy-leaders when a Zulu raid threatened. Otherwise, they would remain at home busy with their normal occupations. Besides these part-time levies, or Reserve, the government provided for a small standing force of several hundred Border Guards in each Defensive District. They were to be stationed at strategic drifts from which they could move to any threatened stretch of the river frontier. The system was in operation by the time Chelmsford placed the entire border region under military control on 11 January 1879.[10]

Nevertheless, Chelmsford knew that these arrangements would not be sufficient if the amaZulu decided to make a determined incursion, and he had no further alternative but to fall back on the terrain and climate to assist. On account of the summer rains, the rivers between Natal and Zululand were generally unfordable between January and March except at a limited number of defensible drifts, and so formed a natural line of defence. As Bulwer admitted once the invasion had begun, he feared that the border had been 'left a little too weak', so that 'our best friend is the river'.[11] The Transvaal border country was more open than Natal's broken terrain and had no great rivers to cross, but Chelmsford considered that a Zulu force would on that account be easier to intercept than in Natal.

Chelmsford did not reach his conclusions about the defence requirements of Natal and the best points from which to invade Zululand by remaining at his desk in Pietermaritzburg, any more than he had kept to his office in King William's Town during the Ninth Cape Frontier War. As he wrote when deprecating Colonel Rowlands's habit of sitting in his tent and writing all day, 'That way will not do in S. African warfare – A commander must ride about and see the country for himself, or he will never be able to handle his troops properly.'[12] Not that Chelmsford did not devote many hours a day conscientiously – almost obsessively – writing detailed missives to the government in London, to the High Commissioner, the Lieutenant-Governor of Natal, the Administrator of the Transvaal and to his various commanders. But he did regularly 'see the country for himself'. On 23 October 1878 he returned from a fortnight's tour of inspection of the north-eastern border of Natal during which he rode a distance of 370 miles over rough country.[13]

Yet Chelmsford's desire to see everything for himself, and his practice of bombarding his commanders with fussily over-detailed written instructions, were both aspects of his already noted disinclination to delegate. That unwillingness caused him on occasion to lose sight of the wider picture while spending time and energy on routine duties more appropriately performed by his subordinates. This tendency was observed by the ambitious Major Cornelius Clery. He had passed Staff College in 1870, been an instructor and then professor of tactics at the Royal Military College, Sandhurst (1871–5), and had held various staff appointments before coming out to Zululand as a Special Service officer and being appointed Glyn's Principal Staff Officer. He was a close friend of Sir Archibald Alison at the Intelligence Branch to whom he penned many frank and catty letters.[14] In one of these, he wrote of Chelmsford: 'his energetic, restless, anxious temperament led him into very minor matters for he used even to detail the patrols and constantly gave orders direct to commanders' that should have been for his staff to undertake and left them uncertain of their responsibilities.[15]

However, as we have seen, Chelmsford's staff was in any case barely up to the mark. Crealock was made brevet lieutenant-colonel in November 1878 in recognition of his services during the Ninth Cape Frontier War, and continued on Chelmsford's Personal Staff as his AMS, even though he was not conspicuously efficient, and the spiky penmanship of his despatches nigh on illegible. Nevertheless, Crealock continued to eclipse the other members of Chelmsford's small Personal Staff in the General's esteem. Captain Ernest Buller, Rifle Brigade, served as Commandant at Headquarters. Lieutenant Molyneux had been invalided home, but the heavily bearded Gossett, now a brevet major, continued as one of Chelmsford's two ADCs. The other was the handsome, sleek-haired and beardless Lieutenant Archibald Berkeley Milne, RN, the well-connected son of the First Sea Lord serving with the Naval Brigade from HMS *Active*. The white-haired Brevet Colonel William Bellairs, CB, who had served in the Crimea and had held a series of staff appointments around the globe, headed the Headquarters Staff as DAG and QMG.[16]

Crealock himself acknowledged that Chelmsford's Personal Staff remained 'miserably weak',[17] and would have liked to have filled the more responsible role of the General's chief of staff. But that was never on the cards in the opinion of that sharp observer, Major Clery. In his view,

Chelmsford was confident in his own organisational abilities and persisted in imagining that he 'could do without an immediate staff'.[18] Thus, while there were many who deplored the undue influence Crealock had apparently obtained over Chelmsford, Clery was not one of them. He did not believe 'that the general really took advice much from anybody, for he certainly seemed . . . to discourage anything in the way of suggestion'.[19] Indeed, as Jeff Mathews has concluded, Chelmsford's diffident manner discouraged discussion with his staff, although he too easily allowed his habitually snap decisions to be swayed by contrary advice.[20] Not surprisingly, as the Zululand campaign unfolded, the deficiencies of Chelmsford's poorly trained and structured staff became increasingly apparent. As Crealock would report in 11 April 1879, 'We know Lord Chelmsford does not appreciate the importance of staff, and I can see in half an eye in 2 days, how chaotic all that part is.'[21] The critical difference between him and General Wolseley, who would supersede him in Zululand, was that while the latter likewise depended largely on his own judgement in planning and conducting operations, thereby effectively acting as his own chief of staff, he nevertheless looked to his carefully chosen staff for efficient administrative support.[22]

It should be noted that, as with Wolseley, Chelmsford was not blind to the advantage of taking advice from knowledgeable colonists, even if, until later in the war and after the Isandlwana disaster, he did not appoint them officially to his staff. One was Henry Francis Fynn, Jnr, the Resident Magistrate of the Umsinga Division in northern Natal. He was the son of the famous pioneer of 1824, had been born and bred in Natal and was absolutely fluent in both isiZulu and Dutch. In colonial circles he was acknowledged as an authority on Zulu customs and institutions. At the start of the invasion of Zululand, when Chelmsford began to feel the need for a knowledgeable interpreter and guide, he asked Bulwer to permit Fynn to hand over his duties as a magistrate and join him in an advisory capacity.[23]

Fynn returned to his magisterial duties after the Isandlwana debacle, but other individuals whom Chelmsford initially attached informally to his staff would go on to serve throughout the coming months. The first of these was the Hon. William Drummond, the third son of the ninth Viscount Strathallan. As a younger son he had to seek his own fortune, and at the age of seventeen began his life in south-eastern Africa as a transport rider and professional hunter. Still in his early thirties and clean-shaven (unusual in that age of exuberant masculine facial hair), he offered his services to Chelmsford as an interpreter, guide and adviser on Zulu customs, and the General was only too pleased to take on the experienced and well-connected fellow aristocrat. Drummond went on to serve officially in the Intelligence Department on Chelmsford's Staff during the relief of Eshowe, where he was joined by John Dunn (of whom more later), a hunter and trader living in Zululand. Chelmsford then placed Drummond in charge of his Intelligence Department during the final stages of the Zululand campaign when he was responsible for interrogating Zulu deserters and captives and compiling reports on their testimony.[24]

Drummond's subordinate throughout the campaign was Chelmsford's personal interpreter, the 29-year-old William Longcast, whom he promoted from second- to first-class interpreter after the battle of Ulundi. Fully bearded with deep-set eyes under heavy brows, Longcast was a settler orphan brought up by the Anglican missionary community in Zululand. Like Drummond, he earned his living as a transport rider and hunter, and was well known to King Cetshwayo. Once he had married Alice, a Zulu convert, in 1870 and brought up a family of seven children in Zululand, however, he put himself outside settler society and became (like John Dunn) what is known as a transfrontiersman. It is uncertain who recommended him to Chelmsford, but their duties brought them continuously into each other's company. The General came genuinely to appreciate the ever-cheerful Longcast, who was an efficient and conscientious interpreter, and to value him particularly as a guide.[25]

Chelmsford had done his best in planning for the defence of Natal and the Transvaal once he invaded Zululand, and had determinedly overcome colonial reluctance and inertia in the process. Nevertheless, the likely inadequacy of his arrangements continued to haunt him. As a further precaution he resolved to send the five invading columns he had decided upon into Zululand in precisely those sectors of the border country he believed most vulnerable to Zulu attack.[26]

From south-east to north, No. 1 Column, consisting of 4,750 men (of whom 2,256 were men of the NNC and 622 were non-combatant drivers of 384 wagons and 24 carts), along with four 7-pdrs, a Gatling gun, two rocket tubes and one rocket trough, was under the command of Colonel Pearson, previously Commandant of Natal. This column would protect the Natal coastal plain. Brevet Colonel Durnford's No. 2 Column of 3,871 men of the NNC (excluding 63 drivers of 30 wagons), with three rocket troughs, would shield central Natal, as would Colonel Glyn's No. 3 Column to their left. This column of 4,709 men (of whom 2,566 were NNC, and 346 were drivers of 220 wagons and 82 carts) was accompanied by six 7-pdrs and two rocket troughs. Brevet Colonel Wood's No. 4 Column would guard the Utrecht District of the south-eastern Transvaal. This open frontier of the Phongolo region, where Zulu, Swazi, Boer and German settlers contended for supremacy, was the most volatile of Zululand's border areas.[27] Wood would be hard-stretched to secure it with his 2,278 men, of whom 387 were NNC and 48 were drivers of 41 wagons and 2 carts. His artillery consisted of six 7-pdrs and two rocket troughs. Colonel Rowlands's No. 5 Column of 1,565 men (including 338 NNC and 25 drivers of the 17 wagons and 2 carts) would protect the volatile eastern Transvaal that abutted the unpacified Pedi, Swazi and Zulu kingdoms.[28]

The seven battalions of British infantry that constituted the main striking force of each of the columns (except for Durnford's No. 2) numbered 5,128 men. They were parcelled out as follows: No. 1 Column: the 2/3rd and 90th Regiments; No. 3 Column: the 1/24th and 2/24th Regiment; No. 4 Column: the 1/13th and 90th Regiments; and No. 5 Column: the 80th Regiment. The NNC amounted to nearly double their number. However, the white mounted troops (1,193) were almost four times as many as their African counterparts (315 troopers).[29]

Chelmsford intended the invading columns to converge on oNdini, Cetshwayo's 'capital' as he thought of it, but as the day of invasion approached, the prospects for successful coordination, let alone mutual support, seemed ever less likely. A major obstacle was the lack of any accurate map, although at the time Chelmsford did not appreciate just how out of scale those available were, how full of empty, uncharted spaces, and how often just plain wrong. In his typically methodical fashion, on 29 September 1878 he forwarded to the Horse Guards a tracing of Lieutenant-Colonel Anthony Durnford's inadequate sketch map of Zululand for immediate lithographing so that 100 copies could be hurried back to him for use by his officers when they took the field.[30] The Intelligence Branch of the War Office did its best to assist with the issuing of a booklet in January 1879 titled *Précis of Information Concerning the Zulu Country*, and included a map. It was a curious ragbag of information, some of it current and some based on reports from several years back, listing books of reference on Zululand and the best maps available, and providing information on the kingdom's geography, topography and climate, as well as vital information on landing places, roads and fords across the many rivers.[31]

The problem with the available maps and other information was that none of it was necessarily reliable. Later in the campaign, and with hindsight, Chelmsford would querulously complain that 'The maps of Zululand are almost useless for military purposes as the country has never been surveyed with any pretensions to accuracy; and even the trading tracks . . . have been inserted more by guess work than from any real knowledge of their direction.' Lamely, he admitted that 'At the outbreak of the Zulu war in January last I was not aware of the untrustworthy character of the maps, or of the information regarding the country, furnished by traders and others . . . being so inaccurate.' Rather too late, he explained that:

> It was only by degrees . . . that we discovered how dangerous it would be to lay down any plan of operation [*sic*] which was based upon any information other than that afforded by our own officers gained by bold reconnaissances.[32]

This was a critical, if not fully acknowledged, intelligence failure, and the consequence was that the commanders of the invading columns would have to rely as best they could on mounted patrols, supplemented by the NNC, to relay information about the terrain to be traversed, and to locate the enemy. But the dire lack of sufficient horsemen for comprehensive intelligence-gathering was a particular concern;[33] while the dearth of properly trained intelligence officers to process it was another. This was another consequence of Chelmsford's reluctant to delegate or to see the need for surrounding himself with a competent staff, and meant that overburdened, unspecialised staff officers had to do their inadequate best to deal with the intelligence brought in as a normal part of their many other duties. Overworked local experts, such as Fynn, Drummond or Longcast, were too few in number to make up the shortfall. The consequence, of course, was that Chelmsford had only the vaguest knowledge of the routes along which he intended to send his columns, and once they were committed in Zululand, the column commanders would be hard-put to locate each other, let alone coordinate their advances.

By the first week of January 1879, only days before the commencement of hostilities, Wood's no. 4 Column, which had advanced south-east from Utrecht, was encamped at Bemba's Kop, just east of the Ncome River in the Disputed Territory. It was thus thirty-five miles north of Rorke's Drift on the Mzinyathi River where Glyn's No. 3 Column – which Chelmsford planned to accompany with his staff – was intending to cross into Zululand. Pearson's No. 1 Column was concentrated on the southern bank of the Thukela near its mouth, and was well over a hundred miles to the south-east of Glyn's column across extremely broken country. Halfway between those two columns, at Middle Drift, was Durnford's No. 2 Column, and at the last moment Chelmsford decided to hold it back on the defensive since the remote and difficult terrain of the middle Thukela invited a surprise Zulu attack. Concerned about the intentions of the unsubdued Bapedi and uneasy that Transvaal Boers unreconciled to British rule might make trouble, Chelmsford concluded that Rowlands's No. 5 Column at Derby in the Transvaal, sixty miles to the north of Wood, must also stay put.

Uncertainty about Swazi intentions when war broke out reinforced Chelmsford's decision to keep Rowlands on the defensive. During the mid-nineteenth century King Mswati II had firmly established the Swazi state, which was closely related culturally to the neighbouring Zulu kingdom to its south. However, he and his successors had to cope with the expansive tendencies of the Boers of the SAR who asserted their sovereignty over Swaziland, but lacked the means to put it into effect.[34] Mbandzeni, the current Swazi king, consequently suspected that the British, as the new rulers of the Transvaal, would make good their claims over his kingdom. Yet the amaSwazi were also longstanding foes of the amaZulu who had raided them many times in the past. Caught between two potential enemies, Mbandzeni had consequently prevaricated when Norman MacLeod, the Swazi Border Commissioner, made repeated overtures to him in late 1878 to take the field on the side of the British and protect Rowlands's left flank. The long and the short of it was that Mbandzeni (as Chelmsford indeed suspected) did not intend to commit himself until he could be certain of securing his own best interests by backing the indubitably winning horse in the coming war.[35]

Once the already widely dispersed Nos. 1, 3 and 4 Columns (often referred to at the time as the Right, Centre and Left Columns) advanced into Zululand, it would be challenging, to say the least, to keep communications open between them. Distance, cloudy summer weather and hilly terrain made flashed messages by mirror either impracticable or intermittent. In any case, no proper flashing apparatus was available until later in the war when the Mance pattern heliograph was shipped out with the reinforcements after Isandlwana. Even then, its flashes could be read from no more than fifty miles away, even with the aid of a telescope.[36] That meant messages between the column commanders had to be sent by mounted couriers or by African runners. These messengers had not only to seek out where to deliver their despatches, but along the way they had to brave hostile terrain, swollen rivers and potential enemy patrols.[37] Before the invasion even began, Wood at Bemba's Kop was already some eight hours' ride away from Glyn at Rorke's Drift,[38] and Pearson at the Thukela mouth was at least twenty-four hours' ride away from Glyn via Greytown, and even longer in practice because Chelmsford instructed Pearson to communicate with him via Frere in Pietermaritzburg.[39] Chelmsford had consequently to accept that the columns to the left and right of the Centre Column, where he resolved to set up his headquarters, would be only tenuously in communication with him for much of the time. And that meant that their commanders would have to act on their own authority without reference to him, especially if they had to make rapid tactical decisions when engaging the enemy.

Appreciating all the many difficulties that confronted him, as the day of the invasion drew close Chelmsford began increasingly to obsess in his letters to his commanders about deficient logistical arrangements, difficult terrain and insufficient mounted troops for effective reconnaissance. It is noteworthy how his tone varied in these communications. When writing to Glyn, Pearson, Rowlands, Strickland and the others, Chelmsford was straightforward and matter-of-fact, the commander giving orders. But Wood, with whom he had worked closely during the Ninth Cape Frontier War, had emerged as his confidant. Whether they were ever truly friends is another matter, for Wood, a member of Wolseley's 'ring' and intensely ambitious, was always ambivalent in his loyalty to Chelmsford. Nevertheless, he was the one commander with whom Chelmsford regularly and openly discussed issues and from whom he would elicit advice.

With almost painful attention to detail, Chelmsford sent his commanders exhaustive instructions concerning the routes they should follow into Zululand once war was declared – routes, as we have seen, about which he had little reliable knowledge. Despite the odds against doing so successfully, he anxiously exhorted them to coordinate operations and establish lateral communications by every means possible, whether by postal runner, mounted courier, heliograph or even telegraph wire (although that last was unlikely).[40] That Chelmsford nevertheless understood that it was never going to be easy to maintain communications was made manifest in his fretful letter to Wood on 4 January 1879 when the Left Column was on the march to the Zulu frontier:

> I am exercised in my mind as to how to come and see you – In the first place it is doubtful, if you cross the Blood river (Ncome) [towards Bemba's Kop], where you will make your halting place – Until I know that I cannot of course come across the Buffalo (Mzinyathi) [where the Centre Column was concentrating]. Then secondly when I know where you are, how can I find you? And how am I to get across the river?[41]

No wonder that as the date of the invasion of Zululand approached, the strain began to tell on Chelmsford. Bulwer tried to calm his own disquiet by stoutly affirming that Chelmsford's military arrangements were 'good and sure to succeed', and that the GOC was 'a good general officer, very, very careful, very painstaking, very thorough'.[42] But Crealock reported that 'Our general looks sadly fagged and weary, and no wonder; it is worry from morning to night and he never spares himself. However,' he continued more optimistically, 'when we are moving we shall all be very fit.'[43] Bulwer and Crealock made these observations about Chelmsford only days before 13 December when the General announced that his preparations for the invasion of Zululand were complete.[44] It was now up to his civilian counterparts to finish manufacturing the grounds for going to war.

Frere had arrived in Pietermaritzburg on 28 September 1878 to chivvy Bulwer, whom he found 'almost fanatically just and loyal' but sadly unknowledgeable of military affairs,[45] into assisting Chelmsford with his military preparations. The unfortunate Lieutenant-Governor, whose salary was unequal to covering the expense, put Frere up at Government House along with Chelmsford. The High Commissioner settled down in dreary, hot, provincial Pietermaritzburg determined once and for all to solve the so-called 'native question' that was bedevilling his confederation plans. That entailed settling with Cetshwayo, the apparent moving force behind the mythical 'black conspiracy'. As Frere informed Shepstone, he was determined therefore to 'draw the Monster's teeth and claws',[46] and that could not be effected while the dreaded Zulu military system remained intact. And since he was convinced that destroying it would take brute force, not fair words, he was not (as he put it) prepared to 'decline the contest'.[47] He therefore forged ahead with the military plans Chelmsford was conscientiously implementing, knowing that the Cabinet in London would not readily sanction them.

Towards the end of 1878, when it slowly dawned on Hicks Beach, the Colonial Secretary, that Frere was determinedly forcing on a war with the Zulu kingdom, he made it abundantly clear in a series of increasingly alarmed messages that the headstrong High Commissioner must desist.[48] Hicks Beach was mindful of Britain's over-stretched global reach, and the last thing he desired was an unnecessary and distracting war in Zululand. The vexatious 'Eastern Question' remained unresolved, and in late 1878 the Royal Navy took up station in the Dardanelles. Relations between Russia and Britain were consequently dangerously strained to the point of war. To add to which, the Second Anglo-Afghan War was already promising to be an onerous undertaking, and would indeed see several drastic British defeats before final British victory in 1881.[49]

Despite Hicks Beach's orders to desist, Frere encouraged Chelmsford to continue with his warlike preparations. Frere knew that he risked his own distinguished career, but he was confident that any censure for disobeying explicit instructions would be wiped away by his triumphant clinching of South African confederation. So, even while he continued to prime the engine of war, he used his experience as a seasoned administrator to play the system and coolly exploited the sluggish communications with London to keep the Cabinet off balance and a step or two behind the fast-moving crisis he was orchestrating. By late 1878 he had also worked out how a disarmed Zululand would be slotted into the new British order in South Africa. Drawing on his extensive administrative experience in India, he did not envisage Zululand being annexed. Rather, he saw it taking its assigned place in the confederation like an Indian 'subject ally', or princely state, ruled indirectly through a compliant chief under a British resident.[50]

Supremely confident in his objectives, Frere took the final, diplomatic steps to war. With the advice of Shepstone, Bulwer and other colonial administrators, he drafted an ultimatum to the Zulu king.[51] It was delivered to Cetshwayo's emissaries on the Natal side of the Thukela River on 11 December 1878. The Zulu delegation was first apprised of the Boundary Award that favoured their territorial claims, but which Frere had been duplicitously keeping under wraps. Their jubilation was swiftly snuffed out when they absorbed the terms of the ultimatum that followed. Among other stipulations, it demanded that the Zulu military system be abolished and that the king submit himself to the control of a British resident. Cetshwayo's representatives understood as well as the colonial officials delivering these terms that they could never be accepted by their king, and that he would never give up his sovereignty without a fight. Frere placed Chelmsford under orders, therefore, to 'take the matter in hand' once the period of grace stipulated in the ultimatum had expired on 11 January 1879, and to secure Cetshwayo's compliance through force of arms.[52]

It must be understood, though, that the timing of the expiry of the ultimatum was anything but arbitrary, and had everything to do with military considerations. As we have seen, the rivers along Natal's frontiers with Zululand were usually unfordable from January to March, forming a line of defence against Zulu raids, and Chelmsford confidently expected the campaign to be over before the waters subsided and the frontier became more vulnerable. Chelmsford also understood that after the late spring rains the grazing that so many of his columns' draught-animals needed would be plentiful, but would cease to be so in the dry winter months. For these reasons, January was the ideal month for launching the campaign.

Fending off Hicks Beach with slow-moving, obstructive despatches while urging Chelmsford on in his military preparations while he waited for the ultimatum to expire, took its stressful toll on Frere. He began to suffer from neuralgic headaches that Chelmsford, who, as we have seen, was also experiencing considerable pressure, had no doubt were brought on by all the 'perpetual worry and annoyance' the High Commissioner was being subjected to.[53] In the end, though, Frere's machinations seemed to have paid off. When Chelmsford invaded Zululand on 11 January 1879 on the expiry of the unanswered ultimatum, Frere was able (as he always intended) to present his superiors with a *fait accompli*. All that remained was for his general to secure a quick, easy victory that would mollify London and transform potential official censure into approbation. Speedy success would also take the wind out of the sails of Bulwer, who was proving so unenthusiastic about invading Zululand, and also those of John Colenso, the outspoken and schismatic Anglican Bishop of Natal, who believed war with Cetshwayo was unnecessary and unjustified. As for Chelmsford, he entertained no qualms or doubts about the rightness of his mission, or of his ability to bring it off. As he assured Frere on New Year's Day, 1879:

> I trust that before long the troops under my command may have an opportunity of settling, once and for all, the Zulu question –
>
> I have every confidence in those under my command and I am satisfied that they will do credit to their cloth – Our cause will be a good one, in spite of all the Colenso party may say, and I hope to able to convince them all before many weeks are over that for a savage, as for a child, timely severity is greater kindness than mistaken leniency.[54]

CHAPTER 19

Opening Moves of the Zulu Campaign, January 1879

WITH THE EXPIRY ON SATURDAY 11 JANUARY 1879 of the unanswered ultimatum to King Cetshwayo, Lord Chelmsford's forces began their invasion of Zululand.[1] The Centre (No. 3 Column) under Colonel Glyn, accompanied by Chelmsford and his staff, had been concentrated at Rorke's Drift on the Mzinyathi River by 9 January, leaving garrisons along its line of supply through Helpmekaar, Greytown, Ladysmith, Pietermaritzburg and Durban. Anticipating likely Zulu resistance, it began its advance across the Mzinyathi at 4.30 a.m. on 11 January in thick mist under the cover of the battery of artillery positioned on a knoll overlooking the crossing-places. The mounted men and the 1/3rd NNC crossed at the drift itself where the rain-swollen river came up to the men's necks. The 2/3rd NNC crossed at a drift higher upstream, while the two battalions of British infantry were ferried across on two ponts. The amaZulu made no attempt to dispute the crossing, and by 6.00 a.m. the entire column was on Zulu soil. Once across, the mounted men were sent out in front to screen the bridgehead, and the foot soldiers were deployed in skirmishing order in a line nearly three miles long with reserves to the rear. During the day all the wagons, stores and camp equipment were carried across the river on the ponts, and the soldiers then formed camp. A company of the 2/24th Regiment and a company of the 2/3rd NNC were left behind on the Natal side of the river to secure the depot at Rorke's Drift.[2] There was a general – if misplaced – feeling among the cock-a-hoop invaders that crossing the river without opposition was 'a moral victory', and that 'it was 'an established fact that . . . they [the amaZulu] are afraid to meet our forces in a fair fight'.[3]

Chelmsford had supervised the crossing personally because his decision to accompany the Centre Column had the effect of reducing

Glyn to a mere cypher. Barely consulted by the general and left with unimportant, routine duties, the gruff colonel withdrew into his shell and let Chelmsford dictate the movements of the column, even making the small directives that should have been Glyn's as the column's commander, such as the sending out of patrols.[4]

Colonel Durnford's No. 2 Column remained positioned on the defensive at Kranskop on the high escarpment above Middle Drift in the valley of the Thukela below. The Right (No. 1) Column under Colonel Pearson, drawing its supplies through Stanger and Durban, began on 12 January to cross into Zululand on ponts drawn over the Thukela at the Lower Drift. The crossing was commanded from the high bluff on the Natal bank by Fort Pearson, a strong, leaf-shaped earthwork thrown up in November 1878 following the contours of the ground and garrisoned by two companies of the 2/3rd Regiment.[5] Once across the river, on the days between 13 and 17 January the troops set about building Fort Tenedos, named in honour of the Naval Brigade. It was sited 600 yards from the river bank directly opposite Fort Pearson and was intended as a depot for the distribution of stores and provisions to No. 1 Column during its advance deeper into Zululand. However, when he first saw Fort Tenedos on 11 February, Crealock was far from impressed. In its embellishments such as 'useless wire entanglements' he found nothing but the pointless 'dandyism of a course at Chatham'. Even worse in his eyes was the fort's site, 'completely open to the fire of a long, strong, stony hill 300 yards off!!'[6]

Apparently unaware of these defects, on 18 January the column, escorting 130 wagons, began its advance in two mutually supporting divisions, leaving behind a garrison of one company of the 99th to garrison Fort Tenedos. Its objective was the Norwegian mission station at Eshowe, some thirty miles away, which the missionaries had abandoned in 1878 for fear of being attacked by Cetshwayo. Pearson intended to use the deserted church and other buildings as a depot for the column's further advance on oNdini.

During early January 1879 Wood had assembled his No. 4 Column at the Balte Spruit laager in the Utrecht District of the Transvaal, drawing his supplies from Utrecht and Newcastle. Colonel Rowlands's No. 5 Column remained on the defensive at Derby in the south-eastern Transvaal. That placed him fifty miles to the north-east across the Assegai River from

Luneburg, a tiny settlement just north across the Phongolo River in the Disputed Territory which King Mpande had permitted a community of German settlers of the Hermannsburg Missionary Society to establish in 1869. Luneburg lay between Wood's and Rowlands's commands, an inconvenient thorn in the sides of both. Fearing that Cetshwayo would attack them, the Luneburg settlers had built a stone-walled laager around their little church. Frere was concerned for their safety and pressed Chelmsford to do something to succour them, but the General was reluctant to weaken Wood's column.[7] After a scare of a Zulu attack in late 1878 that actually came to nothing, Wood, on his own initiative, detached two companies of the 90th on 19 October 1878 to strengthen the Luneburg laager and to build an earthwork – Fort Clery – close by. Chelmsford, concerned about the security of the more significant posts at Utrecht and Newcastle, tartly reprimanded Wood for his action, reminding him that 'Charity begins at home', and (in the in the words of a derogatory 'Paddy' joke of the time) that he 'had rather imitated the Irishman who, finding his sheet too short, cut off a piece from the bottom and sewed it on the top'.[8] The irrepressibly confident Wood was never disconcerted by Chelmsford's grumbles, however, and continued to make his own arrangements in his sector. In December 1878 he ordered two companies of the 1/13th and the Kaffrarian Rifles – tough volunteers of mainly German stock whom Commandant Frederick Xavier Schermbrucker had raised in the Eastern Cape and dressed in smart black corduroy uniforms with a white puggaree around their wideawake hats[9] – to relieve the two companies of the 90th in Luneburg so that they could re-join No. 4 Column for the invasion of Zululand.[10]

Colonel Wood's Left Column crossed the Ncome River on 6 January to encamp at Bemba's Kop. This position was in the Disputed Territory, and therefore arguably did not constitute an invasion of Zulu territory – although the amaZulu would hardy have agreed. This was a region of open grassland between deeply incised river valleys and granite, flat-topped mountains, country ideal for the effective operation of Buller's FLH. On 10 January, in misty, rainy weather, Wood led the bulk of his column down the left bank of the Ncome in the direction of Rorke's Drift in the belief that the Zulu army might contest the crossing of No. 3 Column and that it would require his support. The going was very difficult over the marshy ground cut by many streams, and his men had not made much progress when Wood received Chelmsford's orders to meet him for a consultation. Accordingly, on 11 January, Wood pressed on only with a flying column consisting of the FLH and Wood's Irregulars (African levies made up from labour tenants on white-owned farms in the south-eastern Transvaal who had been pressed into service).[11] For his part, once the Centre Column had safely crossed the Mzinyathi into Zululand, Chelmsford hurried forward on the same day with an escort consisting of the bulk of his mounted men (mounted infantry, NMP and NMV). He met Wood at Nkonjeni Hill, nine miles from Rorke's Drift, where the two commanders had a satisfactory discussion. During their advance, Wood's men had captured large numbers of Zulu livestock, and on his return journey to Rorke's Drift Chelmsford could not resist emulating them and seized several hundred head of Zulu cattle grazing the hillsides.[12]

Wood returned to Bemba's Kop on 13 January from where his patrols became engaged in several skirmishes with local Zulu irregulars. The dominant group in north-western Zululand where Wood was operating was the abaQulusi people. They were attached to the ebaQulusini *ikhanda* which King Shaka had established on the northern flank of Mashongololo Mountain, five miles east of the huge, flat-topped Hlobane Mountain with its coronet of cliffs and freshwater springs the abaQulusi used as a place of refuge for themselves and their herds. The abaQulusi fell under the direct rule of the royal house and the men formed a distinct *ibutho* (age-grade regiment) drawn only from males in the surrounding locality. The region around Luneburg was the territory of Mbilini waMswati. He was an exiled Swazi prince who had lost a succession conflict in 1865 and had put himself under Cetshwayo's protection, building up a strong personal following and forging close relations with the abaQulusi and with the nearby Kubheka people of the Ntombe River valley close to Luneburg. The *inkosi* (chief) of the amaKubheka was Manyonyoba kaMaqondo, who also owed allegiance to Cetshwayo and the obligation to assist him in war.[13]

On 18 January Wood resumed his advance, and on 20 January his column halted on the western bank of the White Mfolozi River where he built Fort Tinta. On that day a mounted patrol led by Buller was forced to retire from Zungwini Mountain, about four miles west of Hlobane, when it skirmished unsuccessfully with the abaQulusi under their *induna* (appointed headman), Msebe kaMadaka, and with some of Mbilini's

OPENING MOVES OF THE ZULU CAMPAIGN, JANUARY 1879

adherents. In retaliation, Wood led out the column on 22 January and dispersed the enemy on Zungwini, capturing much of their precious livestock, and forcing them to take refuge on Hlobane. Two days later, on 24 January, Wood's troops broke up another Zulu concentration between

Ntendeka Mountain and Hlobane just to its east, once again forcing the amaZulu to seek sanctuary on the latter mountain's defensible heights.[14]

As for Centre Column, Chelmsford exuberantly reported on 12 January that 'We have had our first fight today.' A reconnaissance in force, accompanied by Chelmsford and his staff, advanced for about five miles from the camp opposite Rorke's Drift until reaching the ravine of the Batshe River, at the head of which stood kwaSogekle, the stronghold of Sihayo kaXongo, the Qungebe chief and a particular favourite of Cetshwayo's. Encountering some Zulu resistance, Colonel Glyn advanced up the valley with three companies of the 1/24th and the 1/3rd NNC, the African levies experiencing some embarrassing moments of panic and confusion during the encounter. After half an hour's skirmishing among the huge boulders and in the caves that punctuated the steep hillside, the amaZulu withdrew. Four companies of the 2/24th and the 2/3rd NNC (whom Chelmsford was pleased to note 'behaved very well') then advanced further up the valley to clear the caves and burned kwaSogekle itself. Meanwhile, No. 1 Squadron, Mounted Infantry, and other mounted men of the column advanced over the high ground above kwaSogekle and dispersed some amaZulu concentrated there. In the fighting, which was punctuated at midday by a very heavy thunderstorm, the amaZulu lost about thirty men, and the British two men of the 1/3rd NNC.[15]

The scrambling style of fighting that day proved very reminiscent of that Chelmsford and his staff had become accustomed to in the Ninth Cape Frontier War.[16] The Zulu failure to make a determined stand seemed to confirm that they would make no better a showing than had the amaXhosa in the Amathole. Accordingly, when Major Clery, Glyn's Principal Staff Officer, had wished to send in the mounted men 'rather widely to flank', Crealock had checked him in what Clery termed 'a remonstrating way': 'Do not do that as it will cause what actually happened in the last war – the enemy to take flight and bolt before we can get at them.' Indeed, Chelmsford issued an order that 'artillery was never to open fire until the enemy were within 600 yards of them for fear of frightening them, and so deterring them from coming on, or making them bolt'. Not surprisingly, Clery was left with the firm impression that their experience of warfare in the Eastern Cape would not allow Chelmsford and his staff to admit that in Zululand they were fighting with 'anything more than a superior [perhaps?] class of kafir, who had only to be hunted'.[17]

Noting with satisfaction that the British troops involved in the short, sharp and well-executed skirmish in the Batshe valley had suffered minimal losses in dislodging the amaZulu, Chelmsford declared himself 'in great hopes that the news of the storming of Sirayo's stronghold . . . may have a salutary effect in Zululand & either bring down a larger force to attack us or else produce a revolution in the country'. The advance was then resumed eastwards towards oNdini. But, as Chelmsford went on to explain to Frere, the country was in 'a terrible state' from the incessant rain. The rudimentary tracks required considerable work to make them passable and more oxen were urgently required to drag the wagons through the mud. Nevertheless, as the General concluded, 'The soldiers are in excellent health & spirits and do not seem to feel either physically or mentally the continual ducking which they get from the daily thunderstorms – Yesterday & todays work will do both British & Native a good deal of good.'[18]

Still, progress was painfully slow, and it was only on 20 January that the Centre Column halted at Isandlwana Mountain, only five miles on, a dozen miles short of Siphezi Mountain, Chelmsford's original objective. The distinctively shaped mountain, an unmissable landmark for questing mounted patrols returning to base, was perceived by the amaZulu as 'something like a small house' (*sa* – 'something like' – and *ndlwana*, the diminutive of *indlu* – 'house' – a name they also gave to the second stomach of a cow). The British saw Isandlwana quite differently. To them, the mountain resembled a sphinx, by apparently happy coincidence portrayed on the badge of the 24th Regiment.[19] There, on the gently sloping ground on its eastern flank, Chelmsford established his HQ camp.

In November 1878, Chelmsford's DAG, Colonel Bellairs, had issued *Regulations for Field Forces*, always facetiously alluded to by the headquarters staff as 'Bellairs's Mixture' (a patent cure-all medicine).[20] The *Regulations*, which bore the imprint of Chelmsford's micro-managing, laid down exhaustive instructions on how British troops should be managed in the field, covering everything from encampments through transport, field hospitals, sanitary precautions and postal arrangements, to cattle and other prizes, conditions of service, monthly returns and an almanac.[21] Yet, in disregard of his own *Regulations* that laid down that a camp be 'partially entrenched on all sides' and that a wagon laager be constructed to hold the oxen at night,[22] Chelmsford did neither at Isandlwana. His reason for breaking his own rules was that the camp was intended to be only a temporary one. This, as he later explained, apparently made the backbreaking task of excavating entrenchments in the rocky soil unnecessary, as it did the laborious business of forming a laager.[23] When Glyn approached Chelmsford with the suggestion that he laager, 'the general pooh-poohed the idea altogether, remarking in a jocular way, "why it would take a week to make one."'[24] After all, it had not been the practice to laager temporary camps when on the march against the amaXhosa, and Chelmsford regarded a laager as providing protection for oxen, rather than as serving as a redoubt for soldiers.[25] It is not as if J. J. Uys, a farmer from the Utrecht District with experience fighting the amaZulu, had not exhorted Chelmsford on 16 January always to laager, but 'The General smiled, and said that he thought it was not necessary.'[26] In any case, the wagons were required to bring supplies up from Rorke's Drift, and they could not do that if they were laagered. In earnest of the camp's temporary nature, patrols continued to be sent out to ascertain the movements of the amaZulu and to find a suitable site for the next camp forward.

With the advantage of hindsight, the very siting of the camp, which was overlooked by a spur of the Nyoni hills to the north that obscured the Nquthu heights beyond, and with dongas and much dead ground before it, was severely criticised by armchair generals such as the newspaper correspondent, Archibald Forbes.[27] But its positioning had Chelmsford's approval because its defensive potential was a subordinate consideration to the availability of drinking water and wood for fuel.[28] It was Major Clery who laid out the camp along much the same lines as the previous one in the Batshe valley,[29] but several officers, both British and colonial, apparently expressed misgivings both about its unnecessary extent, stretching for some 1,300 yards, which would make it difficult to defend, and (along with Glyn) worried about the lack of a laager.[30] After all, as Glyn would have been perfectly aware, the key to Upcher's victory at Kentani during the Ninth Cape Frontier War had been his laager and well-fortified earthwork,

These considerations,' declared the 2/24th's official record of the campaign, were 'not afterthoughts' that surfaced only in the wake of the disastrous battle.[31] Yet it was not that Chelmsford was out of step with the perception of the enemy common among his officers. As Clery later explained, Chelmsford's attitude was bound up with his and his staff's chronic underrating of the enemy, so that the 'idea was never entertained of being apprehensive that the enemy would come on and attack, but on the contrary, that . . . we should have to hunt him up'.[32]

Chelmsford employed the enforced leisure of his bogged-down advance to give thought to a future settlement of a defeated Zululand that would ensure a 'permanent peace'. He assumed that the only way to secure Natal from future Zulu attacks would be to maintain control of both sides of the river frontier (and he had precise suggestions on how the border should be 'rectified'); while he held that, to break the Zulu power once and for all, the country should be 'parcelled out into small divisions under small chiefs' ruling independently, yet under overall British control.[33] Although seldom acknowledged, this solution precisely prefigured the settlement Wolseley was to impose on Zululand in September 1879.

But that was to put the cart before the horse, and Chelmsford had first to win the war. Almost immediately, he had to reconsider the strategy he had arrived at before the invasion was under way, for the rain-sodden ground made the rapid, coordinated advance he had envisaged impossible. As he wrote to Frere on 16 January, he had devised a new plan, 'not so ambitious a one as a rapid march upon Ulundi' (as the British always referred to oNdini), but one he was 'certain' was 'the only safe one under the circumstances'.[34] The General's new plan required that the toiling, slowly advancing columns should halt once inside Zululand and only resume their march when conditions had improved sufficiently. Meanwhile, the stationary columns would send out mobile flying columns to drive the amaZulu away from the Natal and Transvaal borders and to occupy and devastate as much of Zululand as they could, constantly threatening those districts remaining under Cetshwayo's control. They were to target in particular the *amakhanda* (military homesteads) that were the nodes of the king's authority, the rallying-points for the *amabutho* (age-grade regiments) and the depots for Zulu supplies. Their systematic destruction was designed to reduce Zulu ability to resist militarily, and Chelmsford calculated that by also destroying the homesteads of ordinary amaZulu and capturing their livestock (as had been the practice in the Ninth Cape Frontier War), the king's increasingly desperate subjects would be driven up into the inhospitable north-eastern corner of Zululand and be provoked into deposing him and then surrendering. As far as Chelmsford could see, the only potential military problem with this politically motivated strategy was that mounted troops were essential for carrying it out, and the number of horsemen he had available was limited.[35]

However, Chelmsford's revised strategy brought up vexed issues other than purely operational ones. The widespread devastation he envisaged was one. The British officially had no quarrel with the Zulu nation, only with its king,[36] and Chelmsford initially forbade excesses against the civilian population. On 31 December 1878 he sent out a memorandum to the following effect:

> Officers commanding columns are requested to have it clearly explained to the native portion of the force under their command that any native convicted of wilfully killing a woman or child or a wounded man, will render himself liable to be hanged. No huts in Zululand are to be burnt except under the special orders of the officer commanding the column –
>
> Any soldier, European or native, transgressing this order will render himself liable to a flogging.[37]

On 10 January 1879, when No. 3 Column was concentrated at Rorke's Drift for the invasion the following day, Chelmsford himself addressed the three battalions of the 1st NNC in turn, forcefully reiterating these instructions and reminding the men that they were associated with Her Majesty's troops and must comport themselves as such.[38]

Fine sentiments which Chelmsford seemed determined to enforce (as we have seen, he did not flinch at administering floggings), but were they practicable? Surely, they were at variance with the strategy of widespread destruction he had actually adopted? As the General's father, the first Lord Chelmsford, had put it to his old legal colleague Biggs Andrews, QC, when earlier discussing his son's campaign against the amaXhosa, one of the most effectual ways of defeating a people such as they was 'through the stomach'.[39] The General had seen this policy work well in the Eastern Cape, and could see no reason why it should not in Zululand as well. In thinking along these lines, Chelmsford was no different from other commanders in Queen Victoria's 'small wars' who accepted civilian suffering as an unfortunate prerequisite for victory, and could shrug off the criticism received as unmilitary sentimentalism.[40] It is significant that in his memorandum forbidding the burning of Zulu huts, he left it to the discretion of commanders to permit it. And, as we shall see, the strictures against the killing of civilians and the wounded would be abandoned after Isandlwana had changed the whole tone of the war.

Chelmsford's policy of sowing widespread devastation supplemented his objective of fostering political disarray and fatally undermining Cetshwayo's authority as king. This was to be brought about in two complementary ways. Firstly, Cetshwayo was to be cut out of any parleys because Frere was of the opinion that there could be little room for 'pacific negotiations' until the Zulu king had tasted military defeat and was no longer in a position to wrangle over the terms of surrender.[41] Until then, any Zulu peace feelers emanating from Cetshwayo were to be regarded with suspicion, and all his emissaries were to be considered potential spies. Chelmsford unreservedly endorsed Frere's position on this. He made it axiomatic that no Zulu emissaries were to be admitted into British camps or fortifications,[42] and marched into Zululand determined not to treat with the Zulu king until he capitulated unconditionally. To ensure that, Chelmsford issued strict orders on 17 January laying down that any Zulu royal emissaries must communicate exclusively with him, and no other commander. Significantly, he stressed that no peace overtures could even be considered that were not 'preceded by . . . the unconditional acceptance of all demands [in the ultimatum] as before notified'.[43] By this order he slammed the door on any compromise settlement Cetshwayo might attempt to negotiate.

On the other hand, Chelmsford was very open to any overtures ventured by Zulu notables. Shepstone had convinced Frere that under the pressure of war internal opposition to Cetshwayo would grow, fracture resistance and bring the kingdom to its knees. Chelmsford was therefore heartened by intelligence of existing rivalries and tensions among the Zulu elite, and knew that some of the king's counsellors, family and chiefs were opposed to the war and hoped for an accommodation with the British. Consequently, from the outset he actively attempted to detach likely notables and their adherents from their loyalty to the king by appealing to their political ambitions and by playing on their fears of a British occupation. By winning over men of power and authority along the British line of advance, Chelmsford would also be creating a pool of collaborators from whom to select compliant chiefs to rule over the partitioned Zululand he envisaged in his suggestion for a final settlement.[44]

With this in mind, on 10 December 1878 Chelmsford issued Wood with orders to which he intended that the Centre Column should also adhere: 'When you advance every effort should be made to induce those Zulu tribes, who are averse to war, to come under our protection – They should be sent to the rear as soon as they come in, and a special civil officer told off to locate them and feed them.'[45]

Chelmsford, as we have seen, had no doubt that when any of his columns encountered the amaZulu in battle that they would easily prevail. Even if he seemed content to make do with a skeleton staff and inadequately processed intelligence, he did fully understand that it was essential for a field commander to study and understand beforehand the military system of his prospective foe, just as he had done before taking up his command in the Cape in 1878. Accordingly, he had a booklet prepared for his officers on the Zulu military system. *The Zulu Army and Zulu Headman*, compiled by the Administrator of Native Law and Natal Border Agent, Lower Tugela Division, Frederick B. Fynney, supplied detailed (if considerably over-schematised) information on the Zulu way of war, military organisation and command structure.[46] Despite all the painstaking information *The Zulu Army* contained – which reflected Chelmsford's own genuine intellectual interest in the profession of arms and willingness to be immersed in military minutiae – it is nevertheless clear that neither he nor his officers seem actually to have believed what they read in it about the fighting qualities of the amaZulu, and were not prepared to accept that their prior estimate of an enemy's fighting qualities might be confounded in practice.[47] Naturally, their well-ingrained sense of racial, cultural and technological superiority to 'savages' would have played its usual, seductive role in forming this undervaluation,[48] but it is also clear that their recent experiences in the Ninth Cape Frontier War contributed greatly to their over-confidence.

In the first phase of the war, the Cape colonial forces under Griffith had won a major action at Ibeka on 29 September 1878, and Glyn enjoyed equal success at Nyumaga on 13 January 1879 and Upcher at Kentani on 7 February 1879. In all of these engagements, the FAMP in the first, a disciplined British force of regulars in the next two, supported by colonial horsemen and African auxiliaries (the same sort of mix Chelmsford commanded in Zululand) was professionally positioned and handled so as to give maximum effect to the destructive weight of fire of modern armaments against poorly armed and dislocated mass attacks. In two cases, the troops were anchored on prepared all-round defensive positions – the fortified store at Ibeka and the wagon laager and earthworks at Nyumaga – which proved the most effective way of concentrating fire and stemming the enemy's rush. Once the repulsed amaXhosa had attempted to disengage, the mounted troops, supported by the African auxiliaries, had attacked and converted the Xhosa withdrawal into a rout. At Kentani, Glyn had deployed a skirmishing line on either side of an anchor of artillery, and that formation had put down a sufficient weight of fire to see off the enemy. So the tactical lesson seemed obvious: whether deployed in the open or fighting from behind prepared defences, the British forces were more than a match for their African foes. Yet whether a skirmishing line – no matter how superior its armaments – would be as proof as a prepared defensive position against a determined, coordinated mass charge of amaZulu manoeuvring to outflank it remained to be seen.

All too many generals seem cursed to fight the current campaign based on the flawed assumption that it will somehow be a repetition of the last, and Chelmsford was no exception. His experiences in fighting the amaXhosa in the second phase of the Ninth Cape Frontier War, and those of his staff and many of his officers too, indicated that the enemy were always inclined to melt away to evade a pitched battle. The lesson these officers drew was that the foe was not to be much respected or feared. Unimaginatively and arrogantly, while they expected the amaZulu to be tougher adversaries than the amaXhosa, they nevertheless assumed that they would be essentially in the same league – an expectation apparently confirmed by the skirmish at kwaSogekle on 12 January. As Major Clery later put it, 'the easy promenade' in the Cape made 'all go into this business with light hearts'.[49] The consequence, he explained, was that:

> The general and his staff not only did not anticipate that the enemy would venture to attack him, but if they should do so that the only thing to be apprehended was that the fire of our people would frighten them so much that they would never come near enough to suffer any serious loss. So that to take any precautions against an attack, such as entrenching, etc., such a thing was never dreamt of.[50]

CHAPTER 20

Zulu Preparations to Resist, January 1879

VIOLENCE DEFINED THE ZULU KINGDOM which rose and fell within the span of a long-lived person's lifetime, from the reign of King Shaka in the 1820s to King Cetshwayo's in the 1870s.[1] The vital instruments of royal power holding together the political structure of the Zulu kingdom were the *amabutho* (age-grade regiments) of warriors. They collected tribute, participated in great hunts, enforced internal control (which included quelling recalcitrant regional chiefs) and served as the king's army against external enemies. When going on campaign they wore a much-abbreviated version of their precious and constricting festival attire, although officers might sport some feathers and other conspicuous items as a sign of their rank. All carried a selection of the basic traditional weapon, the spear. The deadliest variety was the short-handled, long-bladed stabbing-spear, or *iklwa* (plural *amaklwa*), intended for close fighting. A warrior would also carry several throwing-spears with long shafts. Used primarily for hunting, the *isijula* (plural *izijula*) could find its target up to thirty yards away. Many fighting men might also heft a brutal wooden knobbed stick or *iwisa* (plural *amawisa*) to beat out an enemy's brains. The *amabutho* also carried a great war-shield of cattle-hide, the *isihlangu* (plural *izihlangu*), two-thirds of the height of a man. Despite the tantalising description in Fynney's *Zulu Army* detailing the uniform colours and markings of shields that supposedly identified each *ibutho*,[2] this was not necessarily adhered to in practice because Zululand's herds had diminished through the ravages of lung-sickness and trade with the neighbouring colonies, and only two shields could be cut from the hide of a single beast. All that could be said for certain was that younger *amabutho* carried predominantly black or reddish *izihlangu* and married *amabutho* mainly white ones.[3]

These Zulu warriors enjoyed a fearsome military reputation across southern Africa subscribed to and propagated by Frere. But was it entirely deserved? The *amabutho* were a militia, after all, that served the king for several months a year or during a national emergency, and were not professional soldiers like those of the British standing army.[4] When the campaign experience of the *amabutho* in January 1879 is examined, what strikes one is the lack of it. The last Zulu military campaign against whites had been in 1838 during the Voortrekker–Zulu War, forty-one years before. The record against neighbouring African states was little different, and the last time the amaZulu had raided beyond their borders had been against the amaSwazi in 1852. Ironically, the most recent campaign the amaZulu had waged had been the civil war of 1856 when Cetshwayo had secured the royal succession against his rival brothers. But that was twenty-three years before, a considerable hiatus in active service, one might say, for such an apparently ferocious warrior nation. Compare that record with that of the men of the 24th Regiment or the FLH who were battle-hardened veterans of the Ninth Cape Frontier War only the previous year.

Naturally, this does not mean that many warriors who had fought in earlier campaigns did not do so again in 1879, and the senior commanders in 1879 had previously seen action, albeit in a more junior capacity. Four of the older *amabutho* aged between forty-one and forty-seven who would fight in 1879 had fought in the 1856 campaign. Two even older ones, aged between fifty-six and fifty-eight, were considered too elderly for active campaigning and were mainly kept in reserve to protect the king. Otherwise, not one of the other twelve *amabutho* who fought in the Anglo-Zulu War, men aged between their early twenties and mid-thirties, had seen the field of battle: this was to be their very first campaign.

None of this is to suggest that the *amabutho* were not desperately eager to face the British in battle and were not confident of beating them. But that is precisely the problem. Who among them possessed any experience in facing disciplined soldiers armed with modern rifles, rather than with the muzzle-loading flintlock or percussion-lock muskets of previous wars? Could courage and tenacity in traditional hand-to-hand combat hope to prevail against Chelmsford's forces bristling with breech-loading rifles, artillery, rockets and even Gatling guns?

Compared to the amaXhosa and Bapedi with whom the British had recently done battle, the amaZulu permitted firearms to play only a very tentative part in their military culture. Unlike a firearm which is used at a distance, the *iklwa* was wielded only at close quarters, when an underarm stab – normally aimed at the abdomen – was followed before withdrawing by a rip. This was the weapon of the hero who cultivated military honour and proved his personal prowess in single combat. This valiant, warrior ethos pervaded male Zulu life, and was played out most fully in battle.[5] There the tactical intention was to outflank and enclose the enemy in a flexible manoeuvre, evidently developed from the hunt, which could be readily adapted to a pitched battle in the open field or to an ambush. This attack formation, likened to the encircling horns of a bull, was illustrated in Fynney's *Zulu Army* for the edification of Chelmsford's officers.[6] The amaZulu did not attack in a solid body, shoulder-to-shoulder, but advanced in open skirmishing order. They only concentrated when upon the enemy, casting a shower of *izijula* to distract the foe as they rushed in to engage in hand-to-hand fighting with their *amaklwa* or *amawisa*. After a few vicious minutes of frenzied stabbing or clubbing they would fall back and regroup before re-engaging as many times as was necessary before the enemy broke. No quarter was given to a defeated foe who was instead pursued to his complete destruction.[7]

Even though the amaZulu were remarkably resistant to the new firearms technology and remained essentially wedded to their traditionalist military ethos and its weaponry, they could not but see how firearms were spreading rapidly throughout South Africa and were being increasingly adopted by their African neighbours such as the Bapedi and Basotho.[8] But how were the amaZulu to keep up in this arms race since no man was permitted to leave the kingdom because he had to serve the king in his *ibutho* and could not therefore earn the money as a migrant worker to buy a firearm, as did the amaXhosa and Bapedi? Cetshwayo decided he must therefore import firearms through traders. The enterprising hunter–trader John Dunn, who gained Cetshwayo's ear as his adviser, cornered the lucrative Zulu arms market, buying from merchants in the Cape and Natal and bringing in the firearms (mainly antiquated muskets) through Portuguese Delagoa Bay to avoid Natal laws against gun trafficking.[9] The Zulu paid mostly in cattle that Dunn then sold off in Natal.[10] Conservatively, 20,000 guns entered Zululand during Cetshwayo's reign, of which only one in forty was a modern breech-loader.[11]

It was the Zulu elite, rather than ordinary warriors, who monopolised most of the many firearms in the kingdom and who valued them for the mystique of power they conferred upon the possessor.[12] These men of status had the ammunition to improve their marksmanship with practice. So too did a select handful of men recruited and trained in the use of firearms by white hunters such as John Dunn or Drummond, who needed them to procure the tusks, hides and feathers of their lucrative trade.[13] Otherwise, they were not widely dispersed into the hands of ordinary warriors, and many had little (if any) practical training in their use. This being the case, we cannot wonder at the oft-repeated British assertions made during the Anglo-Zulu War about the very poor quality of Zulu marksmanship. Naturally, part of the reason for this doubtless lay with the known ineffectiveness of the many obsolete and inferior firearms in Zulu possession, with the unskilled way in which they were maintained, with the usually poor quality of their gunpowder and shot and with shortages of percussion caps and cartridges. But these mechanical shortcomings were exacerbated by lack of musketry instruction. For example, the amaZulu were accustomed to the curving trajectories of thrown spears, and aimed firearms high with the not unnatural expectation that bullets would drop similarly.[14] Put simply, most amaZulu did not shoot well because they had scant practice in it. Unsurprisingly, therefore, the bulk of *amabutho* continued to regarded firearms in the same light as throwing-spears, and regularly cast both aside before getting down to the real business of fighting hand-to-hand – the only form of combat celebrated down the generations when a man's descendants declaimed his praises.

Zulu tacticians in 1879 were aware of these constraints and the effectiveness of British weaponry. From distant experience fighting the Voortrekkers in 1838, and from what they had learned of the more recent disasters that had befallen the amaXhosa when confronting the British in open battle, they understood the dangers involved in trying to storm prepared positions such as laagers or forts. They knew their greatest chance of success lay in forcing the British to give battle in the open field, where they ought to overwhelm their enemy with their superior numbers deployed in their traditional frontal mass attack.[15] Thus, before Cetshwayo sent his armies off to war in 1879, he issued his generals with careful tactical instructions.[16] He categorically forbade them to attack any form of entrenchment. Instead, his commanders were to bypass defensive works and to threaten the British lines of supply and the territory to their rear. That, it was believed, would force the enemy out of their fortified positions to protect them. Then, Cetshwayo instructed, 'if you see him out in the open you can attack him because you will be able to eat him up'.[17]

The impending war would reveal how successfully this 'savage' Zulu army would contend tactically with the invaders, but before hostilities began Cetshwayo and his advisers had to concert their strategy. From spies in Natal, the Transvaal and Portuguese Delagoa Bay, Cetshwayo learned the precise strength and intentions of the British columns poised to cross his borders.[18] Zulu kings habitually employed spies to keep then apprised of what was occurring throughout their kingdom, and in time of war the king expected his subjects to report on the enemy's movements and gather intelligence in hostile territory. The British were aware even before they crossed the border that they were under constant Zulu surveillance, but it took them some time before they realized that the deserters and refugees they succoured or even employed as camp servants were actually spies.[19]

Knowledge of the extent of the threat to his kingdom and the limits of his own resources caused Cetshwayo to cast around for allies. If he really had been the prime mover of the 'black conspiracy' so dear to Frere's heart, it should have been no challenge to summon up aid from across southern Africa. However, although African rulers maintained diplomatic relations with each other, sectional advantage continued short-sightedly to be placed before wider, common interests. Consequently, despite Cetshwayo making some friendly overtures in late 1878, there was never any prospect of aid from Swaziland.[20] King Mbandzeni looked forward eagerly to the elimination of Zulu military might, as did Muhena, the regent of the Mabhudu-Tsonga, the dominant chiefdom across Zululand's trade routes north to Delagoa Bay. Despite some activity by his emissaries in late 1878, Cetshwayo had absolutely no success with the Basotho who had been under Cape administration since 1871, or with the amaMpondo on the southern borders of Natal.[21] There *is* evidence that Cetshwayo and Sekhukhune of the Bapedi were considering a common anti-British front but, in the end, no active alliance was ever formed. Sekhukhune seems to have decided that it was too dangerous to allow his unresolved conflict with the British in the Transvaal to be sucked into Cetshwayo's major war against them. In any case, he was aware that Colonel Rowlands's No. 5 Column was strategically positioned between his territory and the Zulu kingdom.[22]

Knowing then that no other African state would rally to their cause, and unsure of being able to wage a successful aggressive campaign over their borders, in January 1879 Cetshwayo and his advisors opted for a defensive strategy. This conformed with his political programme of presenting himself as the pacific victim of unwarranted attack, prepared only to fight in self-defence within the borders of his own kingdom.[23] He knew that the British possessed the resources overseas to reinforce their army until it was ultimately successful. The campaign had therefore to be swift and limited, and the hope was that, if the Zulu armies were able through victory in battle to menace the borders of Natal, the British would be pressured into concluding a peace favourable to the amaZulu before reinforcements could arrive.[24] As he would declare to Cornelius Vijn, a trader detained in Zululand with the outbreak of hostilities:

> It is the Whites who have come to fight with me in my own country, and not I that will go to fight with them. My intention, therefore, is only to defend myself in my own country.[25]

Having decided on this defensive military strategy determined by policy objectives, the next issue was how best to deploy Zulu forces for the coming war. The problem was that the kingdom faced attack from every quarter, and with a total Zulu population of about 300,000 people there were not enough fighting men of military age to go around. The numerical strength of the *amabutho* is difficult to estimate with any certainty. Chelmsford and his staff made their plans with Fynney's figure of 41,900 warriors in mind.[26] In fact, the Zulu army probably did have a nominal strength of about 40,000 men, but actual effectives – those who were in an age-band between their early twenties and late forties – were unlikely to have numbered more than 29,000.[27] In addition, Cetshwayo could count upon an approximate 5,000 irregulars joining the *amabutho* on campaign. These included the people of the Tsonga chiefdoms to the south of the Mabhudu-Tsonga who were in a strong cultural and tributary relationship with the neighbouring Zulu kingdom, as well as various petty chiefdoms living in the disputed north-western region of the kingdom who owed Cetshwayo a shadowy allegiance, such as the amaKubheka and Mbilini's followers.

In making his dispositions, Cetshwayo correctly decided to discount the possibility of a sea-borne invasion.[28] By January 1879 it was clear the British were not intending to land troops at Portuguese Delagoa Bay or at St Lucia Bay to its south. Nor were they going to attempt an amphibious landing further down the Zululand coast despite a serious effort in August 1878 to identify a suitable landing-place along a shoreline frustratingly deficient in natural harbours north of Durban.[29] The king was far less confident in leaving his borders with Swaziland undefended. Nevertheless, he gambled rightly that Mbandzeni would not risk committing his warriors to the conflict allied to the British until he was absolutely certain they would win.[30]

The upshot was that Cetshwayo believed he could safely ignore his northern border and also the coastline to concentrate on the British forces to the south and west. His spies correctly informed him that the Centre Column operating out of Rorke's Drift was the strongest, and confirmed that Chelmsford himself was accompanying it. This intelligence persuaded Cetshwayo that this must be the main British force and that the maximum effect would be gained by defeating it. He consequently resolved to direct his main army against it, while a subsidiary force would confront Pearson's Right Column advancing up the coast. Local irregulars in the Nkandla Forest in southern Zululand would oppose No. 2 Column if it crossed the middle Thukela. The king also sent some reinforcements to support the irregulars in the open grasslands of the north-west who were confronting No. 4 and No. 5 Columns.[31]

In early January Cetshwayo sent out orders for his *amabutho* to assemble at oNdini to prepare for war. During several days following the expiry of the British ultimatum on 11 January 1879 the *amabutho* already mustered in the *amakhanda* in the Mahlabathini Plain were ritually 'doctored' for war.[32] Much remained uncertain, however. If the British could not be caught in the open outside prepared defences and brought swiftly to decisive battle, then the Zulu armies would founder for lack of logistical support. When a Zulu *impi* (army) marched off to war, boys older than fourteen (*izindibi*) accompanied it as carriers of sleeping-mats and other equipment, and also as drovers of cattle to be slaughtered for consumption on the march. Daughters and sisters of the *amabutho* bearing supplies kept up with the *impi* for a few days until their stocks were exhausted. The warriors themselves carried iron rations in a skin sack. But these varied sources of food soon began to give out. The hungry *amabutho* tried to spare their own civilian population along the line of march as far as possible, and camped whenever they could at *amakhanda* where stores of food had been amassed. Nevertheless, the *amabutho* could not afford to be squeamish about pillaging their own people when out of supplies, and Zulu civilians took the same precautions against them as against an enemy, removing their grain, vital as seed for the next season's planting, driving off their cattle and taking refuge themselves out of the *impi*'s path in forests, caves or on mountain tops. Cetshwayo knew as well as Chelmsford did that such disruptions to the lives of his people could not long be borne, and that a war waged on Zulu soil must of necessity be short.[33]

Of course, unless it was also a victorious war, everything would have been ventured in vain. But, whatever the outcome, Cetshwayo and his people were determined to resist the British invasion. Morale was high, for the *amabutho* believed in their cause and were exuberantly confident that they would scatter the red soldiers.[34] Nzuzi of the uVe *ibutho* recalled that before the *impi* finally marched out to war on 17 January, the king addressed it as it stood around him in a great circle:

> 'I have not gone over the seas to look for the white men, yet they have come into my country and I would not be surprised if they took away our wives and cattle and crops and land. What shall I do?' . . . 'Give the matter to us,' we replied. 'We shall go and eat up the white men and finish them off. They are not going to take you while we are here. They must take us first.'[35]

Then, after parading past the graves of Cetshwayo's royal ancestors to secure their spiritual blessing, the main Zulu *impi* of 24,000 men began its march. Two commanders strode out in front on foot, rather than riding horses as many other men of status did, thus associating themselves closely with the men they led, as well as setting a comfortable pace that did not exhaust the army.

The senior of these two generals was Ntshingwayo kaMahole, the *inkosi* of the Khoza people in central Zululand, regarded by Cetshwayo as his CinC. He was a stocky, powerful man of seventy with greying hair and a considerable paunch. As a member of the uDlambedlu *ibutho* he had doubtless fought in the Voortrekker–Zulu War as well as in the Swazi campaigns of King Mpande, Cetshwayo's father. Mpande had recognised Ntshingwayo's charismatic leadership qualities, oratorical skills and soldierly flair and had raised him up to be the *induna* of the emLambongwenya *ikhanda*. Cetshwayo also put his trust in him, and on his succession made him *induna* of the kwaGqikazi *ikhanda* and of the *ibutho* quartered there. Ntshingwayo was a close friend and associate of Mnyamana, Cetshwayo's experienced and canny chief *induna*, or leading counsellor, and with him served on Cetshwayo's *umkhandlu*, or council, second only to him in rank. There, precisely because of his astute military knowledge, he was one of those who had advised strongly against war with the British. But once the conflict became inevitable, he threw himself with all his considerable energy into planning the campaign.

Ntshingwayo's associate commander and junior in age and status was Mavumengwana kaNdlela, the *inkosi* of a section of the Ntuli people in south-eastern Zululand between the Thukela and amaTigulu rivers. His father, Ndlela kaSomipisi, had been the chief *induna* of Dingane, Mpande's half-brother and predecessor on the throne. Still in his late forties, Mavumengwana had been enrolled with Cetshwayo in the uThulwana *ibutho*, had served with him in the Swazi campaign of 1852, and remained his close friend. Mavumengwana was one of the greatest men in the kingdom, the principal *induna* of the uThulwana *ibutho* and (as was Ntshingwayo) a member of the *umkhandlu*. Like his fellow commander, Mavumengwana had been a leading member of the peace party who now committed himself wholeheartedly to winning the war once it became inevitable. It seems that his appointment to the joint command with Ntshingwayo reflected the king's desire to have a royal favourite and a man of his own generation in a leading position at the head of his army.

The day after the Zulu *impi* marched out, on 18 January, a force of about 4,000 men detached itself from the main body and marched off south-east to confront Colonel Pearson's No. 1 Column. Its commander, Godide kaNdlela Ntuli, tall, thin and with a dark complexion, was nearly seventy years old and had been enrolled in the iziNyosi *ibutho*. Most likely he had fought the Voortrekkers in 1838. He was Mavumengwana's elder brother, hereditary *inkosi* of the Ntuli people along the middle Thukela, and already a leading *isikhulu* (nobleman) under King Mpande and member of the *umkhandlu*. He had continued in Cetshwayo's favour and was the senior *induna* of the uMxhapho *ibutho*.[36]

On the evening of 20 January the main *impi* under Ntshingwayo and Mavumengwana bivouacked by Siphezi Mountain, just over twelve miles east of Isandlwana where the Centre Column was settling into its temporary, unentrenched encampment, entirely unaware of the menacing proximity of the Zulu army.

CHAPTER 21

Isandlwana: The Division of Forces

INEVITABLY, THE ISANDLWANA DISASTER has overshadowed all subsequent accounts of the Anglo-Zulu War and has formed the pivot for all discussions of Chelmsford's problematic generalship.[1] It might be contended that it was Chelmsford's singular misfortune to be remembered primarily for a military defeat at which he was not even present. But the troops the Zulu overran at the Isandlwana camp were under his direct command; he had divided his forces in the face of an enemy whose massed presence he had failed to detect; and he was out of communication scouting for much of the time while the battle was in progress.

When Chelmsford began establishing his camp at Isandlwana on 20 January, he had no inkling that the main Zulu army that had bivouacked during the preceding night on the table-land near Babanango Mountain was marching westwards that day to Siphezi Mountain, just over twelve miles to the east of Isandlwana, where it intended to bivouac. His attention was focused on 'the two Matyanas', the Sithole *inkosi*, Matshana kaMondisa in the Qudeni Bush north of the Mzinyathi River, and the Mchunu *inkosi*, Matshana kaSitshakuza in the valley of the same river. Intelligence had led him to believe that they might be gathering a force in the broken country of the Qudeni Bush and the Mangeni River to the south-east of Isandlwana with the intention of interrupting his column's line of supply once it advanced further into Zululand.[2] With that in mind, after lunch on 20 January Chelmsford himself led out a reconnaissance from the Isandlwana camp as far as the flat-topped Malakatha Mountain six miles away to the south, but observed nothing more threatening than a few fleeing Zulu women. Shortly after his arrival back at Isandlwana at 6.30 p.m., he received intelligence from a scouting party of NMP that a big Zulu army was approaching from the direction of the Nquthu heights to the north. But Chelmsford and his staff were convinced that the only real Zulu threat was likely to come from the region they had been scouting earlier that day and brushed aside the inconvenient (but accurate) intelligence of Zulu military activity in the opposite direction. Instead, the General decided he must probe the terrain to the south-east of the camp once again before resuming his advance, and the following morning, 21 January, he sent out a reconnaissance-in-force to investigate more thoroughly. In doing so, he unwittingly set in motion the chain of events that led directly to the Isandlwana disaster.[3]

The reconnaissance-in-force consisted of most of the NMP and half the NMV under Major John Dartnell (150 troopers), as well as the bulk of the two battalions of the 3rd Regiment, NNC, under Commandant Rupert Lonsdale (1,600 men). Lonsdale, a retired officer who had served in the 74th Highlanders and who had settled in the Eastern Cape, had earned a formidable reputation during the Ninth Cape Frontier War as a dynamic and inspiring commander of Mfengu levies. However, a fall from his horse just before the invasion began had given him a bad concussion, and he was still suffering from the after-effects.[4]

The plan was for Dartnell's mounted men to proceed towards the Mangeni River, some eight to ten miles south-east of the camp and to probe the mountains overlooking it to the north and east where Matshana kaMondisa was understood to have his stronghold. Meanwhile, the 3rd NNC was to sweep Malakatha, the 1st Battalion going in skirmishing order across its flat summit and the 2nd Battalion proceeding in parallel along its western slopes. Both battalions rounded up several hundred head of cattle from the *imizi* that dotted the countryside (which they sent back to camp under escort), and by late afternoon had joined up and ascended Hlazakazi Mountain to the east of Malakatha. There they waited to rendezvous with Dartnell's force before returning to camp. But things were not going quite as planned with Dartnell's mounted troops. During the afternoon some 2,000 amaZulu under Matshana kaMondisa had skilfully retired eastwards before them, and by evening were massed on the Magogo heights some four miles to the east of Hlazakazi. When Dartnell attempted to approach them from the Mangeni valley below, the amaZulu proficiently deployed into two horns in skirmishing order, and the mounted men had to withdraw to avoid being enveloped.[5] Darkness was now falling, and to forestall an advance by Matshana's force on

Isandlwana, Dartnell and Lonsdale decided to bivouac in a hollow square for the night on the eastern eminence of the Hlazakazi heights, westwards across the valley from Magogo and the Zulu watch fires.[6]

Meanwhile, Ntshingwayo and Mavumengwana, the joint Zulu commanders, who had indeed been considering a flank march to Chelmsford's east to join with Matshana and cut the British column off from Natal, decided instead to take advantage of the General's rash and poorly conceived division of his forces. They detached some men to reinforce Matshana, but on the same evening of 21 January and during the next they transferred most of their army north-west across the British front from Siphezi Mountain to the deep shelter of the Ngwebeni valley. The *amabutho* moved rapidly in small units, mainly concealed from the Isandlwana camp nine miles away by the Nyoni heights. The British mounted patrols sighted some apparently isolated Zulu units but had no inkling an entire army was on the move. This was indeed a masterful manoeuvre, facilitated by the local topographical knowledge of Sihayo, the Qungebe *inkosi* and of his spirited senior son, Mehlokazulu, a favoured *inceku* (personal attendant) of Cetshwayo's and a junior *induna* of the iNgobamakhosi *ibutho*.[7]

During the moonless night of 21–22 January there was a false alarm in Lonsdale's and Dartnell's bivouac on Hlazakazi. The disgruntled and fearful NNC panicked, the square collapsed and sleeping officers were trampled by their bolting men who bore many horses with them down the hillside. With many kicks and blows the officers eventually managed to force the demoralised mob back into formation, but Dartnell was left distinctly rattled and sent a note back to camp urgently requesting support.[8] Major Clery, Glyn's Principal Staff Officer, received the note at 1.30 a.m. and carried it straight to Glyn. But Glyn told him to take it to Chelmsford because, as he later huffily explained, the General had effectively usurped his position as commander of No. 3 Column and he 'was in the habit of receiving instructions from the Lieutenant-General Commanding as to the movements of the columns'.[9] Clery made his way into Chelmsford's tent, roused him, and lying on his face and hands close by his camp-bed read him the message written indistinctly in pencil on a piece of crumpled notebook paper.[10]

Ian Knight conjures us to pause at this critical moment when Chelmsford weighed his strategic alternatives and reached a fateful decision that would cost the lives of well over a thousand of his men and bring about a defeat that would sully his reputation ever after.[11] In fact, as Clery recorded, 'the general did not hesitate much'. Dartnell's message confirmed for Chelmsford that the enemy movements in his vicinity indicated that the main Zulu army was pushing down the Mangeni valley to the east of the Isandlwana camp and threatening to invade Natal downstream of Rorke's Drift. It was always Chelmsford's intention to force on a major battle with the amaZulu – a battle he was confident he would win – but if he drew all his forces in on the Isandlwana camp the Zulu commanders would probably conclude that the position was too strong to attack and the opportunity would be lost. On the other hand, if he waited until daylight to move forward with his entire column and its lumbering baggage train, the amaZulu would have time either to disperse or to outflank him by moving down the Mangeni.

He therefore decided that his best option was to move out immediately with about half the force still encamped at Isandlwana, not simply to reinforce Dartnell against attack, but to intercept the Zulu army and bring on the decisive general engagement he sought. This column had to be strong enough to fight off any threat it might encounter, and he accordingly ordered Colonel Glyn to be ready to march at daybreak at 4.30 a.m. with four out of the six guns of N/5 Battery, RA, six companies of the 2/24th Regiment in light marching order with a day's prepared rations, a detachment of No. 1 Squadron Mounted Infantry and men of No. 1 Company, NNPC. Mobility was required for this flying column, so no wagons would accompany it. The green Regimental Colour of the 24th Regiment had been left at Helpmekaar, and only the Queen's Colour had accompanied it into Zululand. It was left in the camp because experience in the Ninth Cape Frontier War had shown it was impracticable to carry Colours in the rough bush-fighting that was anticipated.[12]

The departure of Glyn's flying column, which Chelmsford intended to accompany with his staff, would leave the camp with its stores, oxen and wagons under the protection of a reduced garrison consisting of a division of two 7-pounder guns, five companies of the 1/24th Regiment and one of the 2/24th, the balance of mounted troops not already deployed, two companies each from the 1/3rd NNC and the 2/3rd NNC and small details from other units.

After the event, Chelmsford would be lambasted for dividing his forces in the face of the enemy. But, in the light of his experiences in the

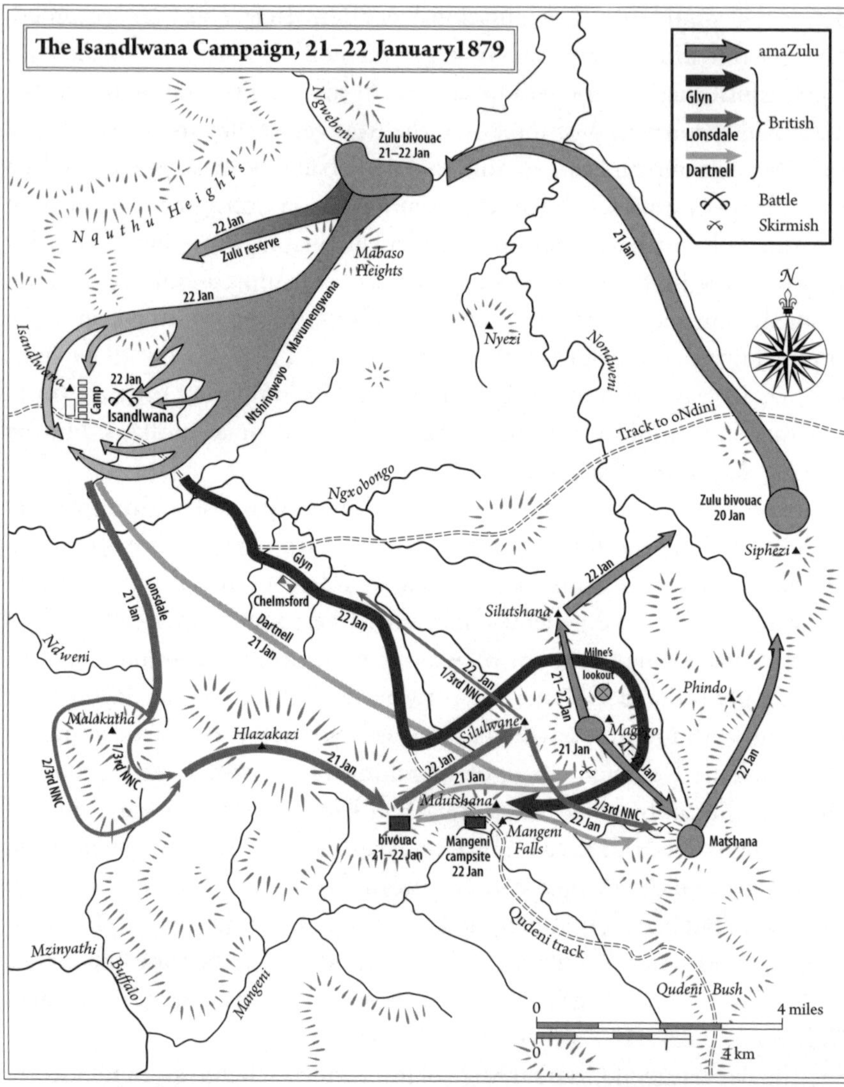

Amathole campaign, there seemed nothing unusual in a flying column moving out of its lightly defended camp to make a sweep through enemy territory. In this regard, it should be noted that, on the very same day as the battle of Isandlwana, Colonel Wood left his weakly garrisoned camp at Fort Tinta to make a sweep towards Zungwini Mountain with the bulk of No. 4 Column. It was his good fortune (which seemed always to attend him) that in performing this manoeuvre made standard in the Ninth Cape

Frontier War, that there was no great Zulu army in the vicinity waiting to overrun his camp during his absence.

It must not be supposed, though, that Chelmsford was unconcerned about the defence of his camp while he was operating to its east. Aware that the depleted garrison at Isandlwana ought to be augmented against what he nevertheless considered the unlikely possibility of a Zulu attack, Chelmsford decided to summon Colonel Durnford from Rorke's Drift to Isandlwana with those elements of No. 2 Column he had available. Durnford's earlier redeployment to Rorke's Drift had not been without is problems. On 11 January Chelmsford had ordered him to move up to Rorke's Drift from his position at Kranskop above Middle Drift with the mounted men and Rocket Battery of his No. 2 Column. There, they were to join the Centre Column. The 2/1st NNC under Major Harcourt M. Bengough (a Special Service officer) was also to advance towards Rorke's Drift with the objective of crossing the Mzinyathi downstream of the post to support the Centre Column when it advanced. The two remaining battalions of Durnford's 1st NNC were to remain above Middle Drift, and only to advance into Zululand once Pearson's Right Column had reached Eshowe.[13]

However, Durnford had not complied with his orders. On 13 January, receiving unsubstantiated information that the amaZulu were going to invade Natal by way of Middle Drift, he took it upon himself to prepare to march down from Kranskop with all of No. 2 Column to repel the phantom incursion.[14] But Chelmsford did not take kindly to his commanders flouting his orders. As we have seen, in October 1878 he had rapped Wood over the knuckles for reinforcing Luneburg without permission to do so. However, while Wood was his closest associate and an officer he was reluctant to offend, Chelmsford had no such scruples regarding Durnford. Before the truant commander of No. 2 Column could begin his advance down the escarpment to Middle Drift, on 14 January he received a stinging reprimand from Chelmsford, threatening to remove him from his command if he persisted in disobeying his orders and acting on his own initiative. There was a rider, though, in Chelmsford's note to Durnford that had unintended consequences. He wrote:

> When a column is acting <u>separately</u> in an <u>enemy's country</u> I am quite ready to give its commander every latitude, and would

> certainly expect him to disobey any orders he might receive from me, if information which he obtained, showed that it would be injurious to the interests of the column under his command.'[15] This ambiguous formulation, one that did not make precisely clear when a column commander was acting separately and when he was not, was to have critical consequences during the battle on 22 January when Durnford might well have believed that he was entitled to act independently.[16]

That is to look ahead. Duly chastened, Durnford moved forward as originally ordered with a detachment consisted of 11/7th Brigade, RA (a rocket battery of three 9-pounders), five troops of the Natal Native Mounted Contingent, and two companies of the 1/1st NNC. On 19 January Chelmsford ordered him once he had arrived at Rorke's Drift 'to co-operate' with the Centre Column in his further operations against Matshana. The 2/1st NNC under Bengough was to remain further downstream by the Mzinyathi, preparing in three days' time to cross the river at the Mazomgeni (kwaMahamba) Drift six miles south-west of Malakatha to support Chelmsford's right flank,[17] a disposition that unintentionally left them uselessly stranded during the coming fighting, unable to assist in defending either the camp at Isandlwana or the post at Rorke's Drift.

From the neighbouring tent, in the early hours of 22 January, Crealock overheard Chelmsford telling Clery to 'Order up Colonel Durnford with the troops he has to reinforce the camp.' Since Durnford's was an independent command, and Clery was Glyn's staff officer, Crealock insisted that it was his place as the General's AMS to write the order, and Chelmsford concurred.[18] In the brief missive he penned, Crealock ordered Durnford 'to march to this camp with all the force you have with you of No. 2 Column . . . [P.S] If Bengough's Battalion has crossed the river . . . it is to move up here.' The message, which Crealock copied into his notebook which was later recovered from the battlefield, neither stated that Durnford was to reinforce the camp, nor to take command of it.[19] However, in his evidence to the Court of Inquiry held after the Isandlwana debacle, Crealock (who did not know that his notebook would ever be found) gave a much more detailed version from memory, stating that he had written: 'Move up to Isandula Camp at once with all your mounted men and Rocket Battery; take command of it.'[20] We know from Clery that it was Chelmsford's intent that Durnford reinforce the camp. But for Crealock not to have put that in writing, only telling Durnford 'to march to this camp', gave an impetuous and vainglorious commander such as Durnford – one who was aching to wipe away his humiliating defeat at the Bushman's River Pass in 1873 – all the latitude he required for independent action, especially if he believed that, in terms of Chelmsford's letter of 14 January, as a column commander he was 'acting separately in an enemy's country'.

When issuing his orders about the formation of a flying column and summoning Durnford from Rorke's Drift, Chelmsford did so, wrote Clery, 'in a decided kind of way, as he was in the habit of doing to me, that discouraged any suggestion'.[21] The decision, therefore, to further divide the already fractured Centre Column in the near but yet unfixed proximity of the enemy was Chelmsford's, and his alone, and the dreadful consequences that stemmed from it were his sole responsibility. Yet, lulled by his experiences in the Amathole campaign, Chelmsford never imagined that his dispositions might be a recipe for disaster. Nor did he conceive that the garrison he left in camp would not be strong enough to defend it if attacked; nor would it have been (it can be argued) had the troops been better deployed in the fighting.

It was 'pitch-dark' when Clery delivered the General's orders to the various commanders around the camp. While he was doing so, it occurred to him that, because Chelmsford 'had not the smallest apprehension about the camp being attacked', he had not thought to leave specific instructions for its defence. Clery grasped that this oversight was 'a mistake' that must be remedied, but Chelmsford was not to be found in the darkling confusion of night-time preparations. Clery doubted that he was himself at liberty to issue the necessary orders to Lieutenant-Colonel Pulleine, the senior officer who would be left in the camp when the flying column marched out, since the general 'had assumed such complete control of all actions of the force' that he feared he 'was running some risk of being found fault with' if he did so.[22] He nevertheless went ahead with issuing the necessary orders to Pulleine knowing that it was not unusual for a senior staff officer to anticipate his commander's intent and issue orders in his name.[23]

With regard to his written instructions to Pulleine, in his evidence before the Court of Inquiry Clery stated that they read:

> You will be in command of the camp during the absence of Colonel Glyn; draw in (I speak from memory) your camp, or your line of defence – I am not certain which – while the force is out; also draw in the line of your infantry outposts accordingly, but keep your cavalry vedettes still far out advanced.

Clery further declared that before leaving the camp he checked with Pulleine that he had received the orders and 'again repeated them verbally to him'.[24] Crealock confirmed that at the time he had heard Clery declare that he had 'left precise instructions' to Pulleine 'to defend the camp'.[25] Lieutenant Berkeley Milne, Chelmsford's Naval ADC, in his statement written in late January 1879, but not submitted by the Admiralty to the Colonial Office until 11 September 1879, confirmed that 'Orders were left with Colonel Pulleine that should the camp be attacked, the camp was to be reduced and defended.'[26]

These orders would become of paramount importance in the aftermath of the battle of Isandlwana when the responsibility for the disaster was being investigated. Suspiciously for some, Clery's written orders were never found. Still, as Mike Snook has argued, it is unlikely that Clery, known to be a true professional and a man of honour, would have invented such a lie;[27] and, in any case, both Crealock and Berkeley Milne independently corroborated Clery's account. The day after the battle, once the remnants of No. 3 Column had returned to Rorke's Drift, Clery informed Chelmsford that he had left precise written orders for Pulleine detailing how he was to defend the camp, orders that he had fatally disregarded. The General, who had signally neglected to issue the vital orders himself, and had left it up to the initiative of a staff officer to do so, instantly grasped how their existence would save his reputation. He turned to Clery and exclaimed, 'I cannot tell you what a relief it is to me to hear this.'[28] Nor did it take him long to appropriate Clery's fortunate initiative. In his official despatch to the Secretary of State for War reporting on the battle, Chelmsford would imply through canny use of the passive voice that he had himself seen to the matter, writing: 'Lieutenant-Colonel Pulleine . . . was left in charge of the camp, and received strict instructions that he was left there to defend it.'[29]

The issue of the command of the camp also became pivotal in the post-battle enquiry and during the escalating recriminations. As we have seen,

Clery's orders to Pulleine (which we must take on trust as the original was lost) flatly stated that he was to be in command of the camp. On the other hand, when Crealock ordered Durnford up to Isandlwana from Rorke's Drift, his written instructions (which survived) made no mention of the issue of command, even if, when recollecting the contents of the order, he stated that he had ordered Durnford to take command. This discrepancy requires examination. As a substantive lieutenant-colonel and brevet colonel, Durnford outranked Pulleine who held his rank of lieutenant-colonel by brevet only. Besides, he was a column commander, which Pulleine was not. Thus, when Durnford arrived at the Isandlwana camp he would automatically have taken command as the senior officer present. Perhaps this was so obvious to Chelmsford that Crealock did not state it in his written orders, but expressed it as his remembered *intent*. Yet Clery's orders to Pulleine placing him in command contradicted this assumption. Usefully, as we shall see, Durnford's refusal to take orders from Pulleine on the day of the battle and his independent actions that compelled the latter to disregard his instruction regarding how the camp was to be defended, allowed Chelmsford to place the blame for the disaster on Durnford. However, that such an incoherent situation should ever have arisen is an indictment Chelmsford's command style and of the uncoordinated measures of his staff.

Once the flying column marched out, and until Durnford came up, the troops left in the camp under Pulleine (a veteran of the Ninth Cape Frontier War when he had raised and commanded two units of mounted irregulars, but an officer who had never commanded in battle) numbered 67 officers and 1,707 men (approximately half of whom were African). As Lieutenant-Colonel Harness later reflected,

> there are few who will not agree . . . that the force left to guard the camp on January 22 was a sufficient one for the purpose; and had that force been kept together, as was ordered by the Brigadier-General [Chelmsford] through his principal staff officer [but see above for Clery's initiative], and formed for defence, with its ammunition at hand (which there was ample time to do), there is little doubt that the Zulu army would have been completely defeated at Isandhlwana, in spite of its overwhelming numbers.[30]

That indeed was the common perception among officers. As Crealock later stated, 'It did not occur to me that the troops left in camp were insufficient for its defence.'[31] Not that there was any expectation that they would be called upon for, as Clery recollected, 'Nobody from the general downwards had the least suspicion that there was a chance of the camp being attacked.'[32] Indeed, many of those not forming part of the flying column 'were terribly disappointed at the thought of being left behind in Camp and lose [*sic*] the chance of a fight', Lieutenant Henry Harford (a regular officer seconded to the NNC) noted in his journal, 'and begged hard to be allowed to find substitutes'.[33] Even when early on the morning of 22 January a thousand or more amaZulu appeared on the hills to the east of the camp, no officer was disconcerted. For, as Lieutenant Henry Curling, RA (one of the few officers to survive the battle) later explained to his mother: 'We none of us had the least idea that the Zulu contemplated attacking the camp and, having in the last war [Ninth Cape Frontier War] often seen equally large bodies of the enemy, never dreamed they would come on.'[34]

It was with no fears for their camp, therefore, that the men of the flying column (also known as the relief force) set off at the first glimmer of light.[35] At 4 a.m. Chelmsford rode off quickly with his staff and an escort of twelve Mounted Infantry, along with several officers who were not on duty at the camp that day 'and had just come out for the ride'.[36] Glyn and the flying column followed on, reaching Hlazakazi some eight miles away at about 6.30 a.m., bringing the troops operating in the area to about 2,500 men. Meanwhile, the amaZulu on Magogo had broken away. Some had withdrawn south-east onto the Phindo heights and others north onto the Silutshana heights, both apparently with the intention of eventually pulling back north-east to Siphezi and thus drawing the British after them, away from the camp. Chelmsford took the bait. The 3rd NNC advanced from Hlazakazi in skirmishing order to take Silulwane hill to the west of Magogo, only to find no amaZulu there. Meanwhile, the flying column moved eastwards up the valley between Magogo and Silutshana while Dartnell's mounted men advanced up the Mangeni valley towards the Phindo ridge with its dense bush and cliffside caves. There Dartnell became involved in a heavy skirmish with Matshana's men, and the 2/3rd NNC moved forward in support while the 1/3rd NNC remained on Silulwane.[37]

Chelmsford, unaware of falling into a Zulu trap, and never even considering the need to concentrate the flying column and Dartnell's and Lonsdale's forces in order to make a united stand should the amaZulu attack in force, revealed his contempt for the enemy by scattering his forces yet further. He decided to let Dartnell and the 2/3rd NNC get on with taking the Phindo heights while Glyn and the flying column cleared the area to his rear around Silutshana and along the Nondweni River valley between the Magogo and Phindo heights. While these operations were under way, Chelmsford intended to utilise the opportunity to personally select a suitable new campsite for the whole Centre Column in advance of the existing one at Isandlwana.

At 9.30 a.m., while Chelmsford was dismounted and breakfasting picnic-style with his staff near Magogo, a trooper of the NMP brought him a short message that Pulleine had despatched at 8.05 a.m. Written in black ink on a half-sheet of blue foolscap, it read: 'Report just come in that the Zulus are advancing in force from left front of camp.'[38] No one with Chelmsford enjoying their scratch meal dreamt for a moment that this could be the main Zulu army they believed to be somewhere to the east of them; besides, there was no note of urgency in Pulleine's brief message. Chelmsford himself, when Clery asked him what should be done, tetchily replied, 'There is nothing to be done on that.' The General's staff did not pursue the matter because (Clery later revealed) the micro-managing but stressed General had become 'particularly touchy about suggestions being made to him'.[39]

Yet Chelmsford did not brush Pulleine's report entirely aside. He sent his ADC, Lieutenant Berkeley Milne, accompanied by Captain William Penn Symons of the 2/24th, scrambling up the slopes of Magogo to observe the camp twelve miles away through his powerful naval telescope. For upwards of an hour Milne kept scanning from his perch below a cabbage tree. He noted clusters of amaZulu on every hilltop watching the British movements, but saw nothing particularly untoward unfolding in the camp, besides that the oxen had been driven in among the tents. Fatally for the British that day, he did not realise that the southern shoulder of Silutshana cut off his view of the plain to the east of Isandlwana where the Zulu army was deploying in battle array.[40] So, soon after 10 a.m., Milne reported back to Chelmsford's satisfaction that all seemed quiet at the camp.

By this stage the General had concluded that his hope of bringing on a major engagement in the vicinity of the Phindo heights would not be realised. Therefore, at about 10.30 a.m., he summoned Captain Alan Gardner of the 14th Hussars with his heavy cavalry moustache, a Special Service officer attached to No. 3 Column, to carry orders back to Pulleine at Isandlwana 'to send on the camp equipage and supplies of the troops camping out, and to remain himself at his present camp, and entrench it'. In the best of circumstances, Pulleine would have found it taxing to comply with that order because the despatch of tents and rations would have required a small convoy of ox-wagons and a military escort, and it was hardly likely that the operation could have been completed before nightfall. But the practicality of Chelmsford's order would never be put to the test. With the dozen Mounted Infantry that had previously been serving as Chelmsford's personal escort, and accompanied by the officers who had ridden out that morning for the adventure, Gardner reached Isandlwana between noon and 1 p.m. There he found the garrison already hotly engaged with the attacking Zulu army and the delivery of camp equipage and supplies the very last thing on Pulleine's mind. Gardner sent an urgent note to Major Clery:

> Heavy firing near left of camp. Shepstone [Captain George Shepstone, Durnford's Political Agent or senior staff officer] has come in for reinforcements, and reports the Basutos falling back. The whole force at camp turned out and fighting about 1 mile to left flank.

This critical message never reached Clery, but seems to have been received by Major Gossett at about 3 p.m.[41] Caught up in the fighting before the camp, Gardner was fortunate to be one of the very few survivors, and those light-hearted officers who had accompanied him back to Isandlwana all perished.[42]

Having sent Gardner with his orders to Pulleine, Chelmsford next ordered the 1/3rd NNC under Commandant George Hamilton-Browne (known as 'Maori' Browne), a swashbuckling adventurer and the self-proclaimed hero of many an unattested exploit in his melodramatic memoirs, to move down from Silulwane. When he reported to Chelmsford, the General ordered him to march his men back to Isandlwana to assist Pulleine in bringing up the camp equipage and supplies. Furthermore, he was to flush out any amaZulu lurking along the way who might interfere with the operation. Hamilton-Browne's 800 or so African levies (whom he held in the utmost racial disdain) and 50 white officers and NCOs were already exhausted by the skirmishing and marching, and had not been fed for the last 24 hours. He knew they were hardly in a condition to face off a strong Zulu attack, but when he asked what he should do if he came across the enemy in strength, Crealock airily replied: 'Oh, just brush them aside and go on.'[43]

Soon after his started his march back to the camp, Hamilton-Browne learned from a captured Zulu scout that a large Zulu army was behind the Nyoni heights, the range of hills on the left flank of the camp. He immediately sent off a note off carried by Lieutenant B. Pohl to inform Chelmsford and then resumed his advance. About an hour later, looking through his field-glasses, Hamilton-Browne saw puffs of smoke from bursting shells and a 'huge black shadow' moving across the hills. This, he realised, must be a Zulu army advancing to attack. He at once sent off a second message to Chelmsford carried by Sergeant G. Turner. At that very moment, the first messenger, Lieutenant Pohl, returned with the information that he had delivered the note to an unnamed staff officer, who was most likely Lieutenant-Colonel Cecil Russell of the Mounted Infantry,[44] who told him to order Hamilton-Browne to continue pushing on towards the camp. At about midday Hamilton-Browne was about four miles from the camp, close enough to see through his field-glasses that the amaZulu were sweeping around the line of defenders who nevertheless still seemed to be holding their own. He therefore sent off a third urgent written message to Chelmsford to inform him of the camp's peril.

At about 1.30 p.m. Hamilton-Browne spied the defensive British line collapse and the amaZulu storm into the camp. Realising everything was lost, and with no time to write, he ordered Captain R. Develin, a fine horseman, to ride as hard as he could in Chelmsford's direction and to tell every officer he met, 'For God's sake come back, the camp is surrounded and must be taken.'[45] Hamilton-Browne, believing he was now himself in danger of attack from large bodies of amaZulu on the move in the vicinity, and with only about fifteen rounds of ammunition for each man, ordered his battalion to retreat slowly. It was fortunate that its withdrawal went undetected by the amaZulu, or was ignored by them. About five miles from the camp Hamilton-Browne found a rocky position he believed he could hold. There he halted and, after ordering each company to form a defensive circle, waited on events.[46] After an anxious pause, Captain Develin returned alone and reported that he had given the verbal message to Lieutenant-Colonel Harness who was moving slowly in Chelmsford's direction at the head of his four 7-pounder guns with an escort of two companies of the 2/24th and a number of mounted men. Develin added that Harness had responded to the urgency of his plea, and that he had turned his guns and escort about and begun to march in the direction of Isandlwana. When Hamilton-Browne urgently enquired where they were then, Develin replied: 'Why sir, as we were marching back we met the staff and the troops were ordered to go back again, so I came on alone.'[47]

That morning 'dreadfully rough country' had slowed the advance of Harness and his four guns, an ambulance and a wagon, and Chelmsford had detached two companies of the 2/24th to escort them to his newly-selected Mangeni camping ground (see below) by an easier route.[48] On the way, soon after midday Harness had heard gunfire coming from the direction of the Isandlwana camp. About an hour and a half later, looking though his field-glasses, he spotted a large force of NNC close to the Isandlwana camp and two horsemen galloping towards him. They were Captain Develin and another NNC officer, and they conveyed Hamilton-Browne's verbal warning that unless help was immediately sent to the camp, it must fall.[49] As we have seen, Harness instantly decided to return to Isandlwana. He had barely set off before Major Gossett, Chelmsford's ADC, arrived on the scene and called a halt, reputedly declaring: 'It is all bosh: I do not hear big guns. You had better continue your march [to the Mangeni campsite] as ordered.'[50] Harness was not to be deterred, and sent Gossett back to Chelmsford accompanied by Lieutenant C. S. B. Parsons, RA, who was to explain the situation. That done, Harness resumed his march back to Isandlwana. His guns and their escort had covered two or three miles in good spirits when they were stopped again.[51] Harness wrote to his sister that the General himself 'came up' and ordered him to proceed as originally ordered and join Glyn at the new camp Chelmsford had selected for the Centre Column. Chelmsford had not been persuaded by Parsons because (so he informed Harness) the report he had himself received about the camp was 'nothing like so strong as the message I [meaning Harness] had received'.[52] Neither Chelmsford nor Crealock mentioned this episode in their subsequent reports, and Lieutenant-

Colonel Edward Durnford (Colonel Durnford's brother) believed it was deliberately suppressed although, to Chelmsford's embarrassment, it subsequently seeped out.[53] And although one may speculate, it cannot be known what the outcome might have been had Chelmsford permitted Harness and his force to continue their march back to Isandlwana.

To understand why Chelmsford and his staff were so determined to prevent Harness from returning to Isandlwana and were insistent that he proceed to the new campsite, we must follow Chelmsford's movements earlier that day. Having given his orders to Gardner and Hamilton-Browne, he had remounted at about 11.45 a.m. and ridden off with members of his staff and a small mounted escort to scout further for a suitable camping site. For the next few hours his whereabouts were consequently unpredictable, and messengers carrying ever more desperate reports of unfolding events at Isandlwana found it nigh on impossible to locate him. Insouciantly unaware, therefore, of the disaster unfolding at the Isandlwana camp, at about 12.30 p.m. Chelmsford hit on a suitable new campsite on level ground eleven miles to the south-east of it, just east of Hlazakazi on the Mangeni River above its spectacular horseshoe falls. Satisfied, he ordered the flying column under Glyn (including Harness's detachment, as we have seen) to concentrate there, and during the course of the early afternoon its weary units began to straggle in.

At about 1.00 p.m. intelligence from Zulu prisoners being questioned by Chelmsford's staff at the Mangeni campsite indicated that a great Zulu army was expected to arrive in the vicinity, and during their interrogation artillery-fire was distinctly heard from the direction of the Isandlwana camp. The amaZulu immediately said: 'Do you hear that? There is fighting going on at the camp.'[54] Clery afterwards wrote that he heard Crealock superciliously exclaim: 'How very amusing! Actually attacking our camp! Most amusing!'[55] Indeed, Crealock later admitted that 'Not a suspicion had crossed my mind that the camp was in any danger.'[56] About an hour later more cannon fire was heard, and one of Dartnell's mounted Africans appeared on a hill above the Mangeni campsite gesticulating wildly and calling out that firing had been going on around the camp. This was most disquieting. As Crealock later affirmed, neither he nor Chelmsford 'had up to this time received any information but that I have mentioned' concerning the state of the camp, and that any other messages, such as those sent by Hamilton-Browne, had never reached them.[57] It was only after Chelmsford had started back to Isandlwana that Lieutenant-Colonel Russell of the Mounted Infantry came into the Mangeni camp and informed Crealock and Glyn that two of Hamilton-Browne's messages had reached him, but had apparently never found the General.[58]

As it was, the African rider's shouted message was enough to send Chelmsford and his staff galloping up the Mdutshana hill just north of the new campsite at about 1.15 p.m. From this vantage-point every pair of field-glasses was levelled at the camp. Charles Norris-Newman, the *Standard*'s war correspondent, was with them. He recorded that all seemed quiet, that sun was shining on the white tents, no signs of firing were seen, and the bodies of men descried moving about the camp were put down to British soldiers or 'friendly natives'. As he admitted, 'not the faintest idea of disaster occurred to us'.[59] It seemed particularly telling that the tents had not been struck as regulations dictated during an engagement. Consequently, as it was put in Ashe and Wyatt-Edgell's history of the campaign published in 1880: 'One and all of Lord Chelmsford's escort came to the conclusion that an attack had been made and repulsed.'[60]

Chelmsford had spent quite some time on the ridge scanning the camp, and it was not until about 2 p.m. that he returned to the Mangeni campsite and had the HQ bugler sound the general assembly, summoning officers in the vicinity to receive his orders. Lieutenant Harford of the 2/3rd NNC was one of them, and was ordered to get his men whom he had dispersed to rest and forage together again and to bring them up to the new campsite. Harford fell into conversation with Major Wilsone Black of the 2/24th who, along with other officers, was still scanning the ground towards Isandlwana through his field-glasses and 'was evidently in a great state of anxiety'. Harford asked him, '"What's happening Major?", and he replied, "The camp has been attacked and something very serious has occurred."'[61] Chelmsford himself was less anxious. As he later informed Frere, 'At that time I had no doubt but that the reported attack was of small importance and that the force in camp would be quite sufficient to beat it off.'[62]

Nevertheless, he finally decided to return to Isandlwana to investigate. At 2.45 p.m. he gathered up his staff and some forty NMV and Mounted Infantry under Lieutenant-Colonel Russell to act as his escort back to Isandlwana and set off at a leisurely pace. He ordered Glyn, who was left in command of the troops concentrating in the area at the Mangeni to prepare the camp for the night.

Well into the afternoon, at about 3.15 p.m., Hamilton-Browne saw Chelmsford and his escort riding towards the position he had prudently fallen back to earlier that afternoon with the 1/3rd NNC. In his memoirs Hamilton-Browne described his encounter with Chelmsford whom he had ridden forward to meet:

> He looked very surprised when he saw me and said, 'What are you doing here, Commandant Browne? You ought to have been in the camp hours ago.' I replied, 'The camp has been taken, sir.' He flashed out at once, 'How dare you tell me such a falsehood? Get your men into line at once and advance.' I did so and led my 700 miserables supported by the staff against the victorious Zulu army.[63]

Apparently believing that he could punch his way through to the camp with this inadequate force, Chelmsford advanced until he had a good view of the camp about four miles away. He then called Hamilton-Browne to him, and said 'in a kindly manner, "On your honour Commandant Browne, is the camp taken?"' Hamilton-Browne affirmed that it was indeed so and that the amaZulu were burning some of the tents. Clutching at straws, Chelmsford suggested 'That may be the Quartermaster's fatigue burning the debris of the camp.' Hamilton-Browne tartly responded that 'Q.M.'s fatigues do not burn tents, sir.' Chelmsford could not argue with that and ordered Hamilton-Browne to halt his men and rode back to consult his staff.[64]

At that moment (it was then about 3.30 p.m.) the shattered Commandant Lonsdale approached from the direction of the Isandlwana camp leading his exhausted pony, 'Dot'. Still suffering from concussion, at about 2 p.m. he had nonchalantly ridden into the Isandlwana camp to arrange for supplies to be brought up, and had barely escaped the triumphant amaZulu who were already in possession.[65] When Lonsdale made his irrefutable report, Chelmsford was appalled, exclaiming in disbelief: 'But I left over 1,000 men to guard the camp.'[66] Berkeley Milne loyally reported that despite the 'fearful news', Chelmsford 'never showed any trace of the anxiety he must have felt'.[67] This observation was not endorsed by Clery who later described 'the look of gloom and pain' on

Chelmsford's 'expressive' countenance which clearly mirrored his inner turmoil.[68] Indeed, an anonymous soldier wrote home that the General was 'very near crying'.[69] But Chelmsford never 'flunked' his duty and saw there was nothing for it but to advance on the Isandlwana camp and, if the Zulu held it, to fight his way through to the river and his base at Rorke's Drift.

CHAPTER 22

Isandlwana: Return to the Camp and Rorke's Drift

'THE TRUTH WAS NOW KNOWN, and every man drew his own conclusion' about the fate of the camp, recalled Crealock.[1] One who did so was Trooper Fred Symons of the Natal Carbineers. He recorded in his diary:

> The suspense became maddening. I cannot describe my feeling at that time. Anger at the delay in returning to camp when the guns had warned us in the morning that the camp was being attacked; foreboding as to the fate of the garrison for I knew the Zulus would give no quarter (that's not their way); and grief at the thought that we could do nothing to help.[2]

Chelmsford sent Major Gossett galloping back to the Mangeni camp, now about five or six miles to his rear, which he reached at 4.05 p.m. There he told Glyn and his incredulous staff: 'The General's orders are that you are to saddle up and to march on Isandhlwana at once; the Zulus have got into our camp. The General is waiting for you with the mounted men.'[3] While Glyn set about concentrating his exhausted and scattered forces at the Mangeni campsite and preparing them for action, Chelmsford advanced another two miles or so. The 1/3rd NNC were deployed in three ranks with the white officers and NCOs and those levies with firearms to the fore, while the NMV and Mounted Infantry rode on either flank with scouts sent out forward. At about 4.45 p.m. Chelmsford halted when within about two miles of Isandlwana. Two ridges lay between him and the camp and made it impossible to see what was happening there, although the amaZulu were observed retiring in their thousands over the hills to the right with a good many captured wagons. Russell went forward to reconnoitre with some Mounted Infantry, and returned at about 5.45 p.m. He reported that 'All was as bad as it could be', and that an estimated 7,000 amaZulu were swarming like bees in the camp itself and in the plain to its front.[4]

Meanwhile, Glyn had been pushing on as fast as he could, and 'The men of the 24th, weary as they were, stepped out well.'[5] Even so, the time he was taking seemed very long to the General and his staff as they remained stationary and watched the sun sinking behind Isandlwana. Glyn finally arrived with his men at 6.10 p.m., shortly after Russell had delivered his report, with the apprehensive 2/3rd NNC making up the rear of the column. Anticipating Zulu resistance when he advanced, Chelmsford, normally not an inspired orator, addressed his dismayed troops with determination:

> Men, the enemy has taken our camp. Many of our friends must have lost their lives defending it. There is nothing left for us now but to fight our way through – and mind, we must fight hard, for we will have to fight for our lives. I know you, and I know I can depend on you.[6]

Berkeley Milne reported that 'He was answered by three hearty cheers, which were taken up by the Natives.'[7] Then Chelmsford, always one to follow the book, deployed his men in regulation fighting formation, very much the same one he had seen Brigadier Smith adopt in the battle of Koondrye during the Indian Mutiny twenty years before: guns in the centre in column with room to form line for action; three companies of British infantry in line on either flank of them; a battalion of the 3rd NNC to each flank of the regulars; and the mounted troops in advance of the NNC. Skirmishers were thrown out in front and a small guard looked after the wagons and ambulances in the rear.[8] Then, shortly after 6.15 p.m. in the gathering darkness of a moonless night, Chelmsford (in Crealock's words) 'advanced to the camp prepared to attack anyone found on our path back to Rorke's drift'.[9]

At about 8 p.m. Chelmsford's force neared the camp. Harness described what happened next to his younger sister, Caroline, or 'Co':

> About a quarter of a mile from the neck we halted and I fired about a dozen shells as well as we could in the dark and the infantry on our left went forward to take one of the little hills,

> which they did without resistance. We then all advanced and found out the enemy had gone, but could see in the dark the complete wreck and slaughter which had taken place.[10]

Indeed, the victorious Zulu had already withdrawn except for a few stragglers when Chelmsford reoccupied the camp at about 8.30 p.m. Once the fighting at Isandlwana had died down somewhere after 2 p.m., the exultant *amabutho* had set about comprehensively looting the camp in the sickly light of a partial solar eclipse.[11] Firearms and ammunition were the most highly prized booty, especially the modern Martini-Henry rifles, about 800 of which fell into Zulu hands. Pillaging had continued until the *amabutho* saw the dilatory Chelmsford at last approaching when (as the British had observed) they pulled back with their loot to their bivouac in the Ngwebeni valley.

Consequently, when Chelmsford's force reached the camp, no enemy were seen and Chelmsford determined to remain the night there. The sight of several large fires seemed to indicate the proximity of the enemy and their intention to attack, but it later turned out that all these fires were on the far side of the Mzinyathi where the amaZulu were raiding the Natal bank and attacking the post at Rorke's Drift. Not realising this, Chelmsford urgently drew up a hollow square surrounding the ambulance wagons and gun limbers. The infantry formed ranks two deep in front; the guns were positioned pointing to the rear about sixty yards away and were defended by all the mounted men; and the NNC were stationed on either flank between the infantry and the guns, completing the defensive formation.

What then followed was what Clery described with quintessentially British understatement as 'not a pleasant night',[12] bivouacked, as Chelmsford laconically informed Frere, 'among the bodies from dead soldiers and of the enemy'.[13] Undoubtedly, though, he must have felt the dreadful situation deeply. As the military historian Major Elliott expressed it in his book of 1882 prepared for the *Deeds of Daring Library*, he could only imagine 'what Lord Chelmsford must have mentally undergone at that solemn moment of frightful solitude, as he stood amongst the dead victims of misplaced confidence in his own arrangements'.[14] Nevertheless, always mindful of his duty, Chelmsford 'remained just behind the front ranks all night, watching and encouraging the men not to lie down and sleep; it was hard to prevent them as they were tired out.'[15] The troops spent all that pitch-dark night among the heaped bodies of slaughtered men, oxen, horses and mules in a foul miasma of blood, excrement, spilled guts and chemicals from the shattered contents of the Army Hospital Corps wagon. Sergeant W. E. Warren wrote home: 'You could not move a foot either way without treading on dead bodies.'[16] Most of the men had not eaten for very many hours. Lieutenant Harford joined one of the small parties of officers sent out to forage in the wrecked commissariat wagons, among the burned, shredded tents and in the hospital lines for what food the Zulu had not carried off or deliberately spoiled, 'stabbing or smashing up all the tinned articles'.[17] Enough was found for a rough meal for the troops (even if some of the more selfish officers kept the more desirable items like unbroken bottles of port and packages of tobacco for themselves).[18]

Berkeley Milne recorded that several times during the long hours of the night false alarms were given by the nervous NNC 'rushing through our ranks' and that the British soldiers opened fire although no enemy appeared.[19] Some men of the 2/3rd NNC tried to creep away and soldiers had to drive them back at bayonet point into their position in the square. Chelmsford was so angry that he posted British sentries with orders to bayonet the first man who again tried to leave.[20] Making his rounds, Chelmsford approached Harford and asked whether he thought the amaZulu would attack or not. The young officer responded that he 'felt pretty certain that they would as soon as it was daylight'.[21]

Chelmsford and his staff were of the same opinion and fully expected that the Zulu army that had overrun the camp the previous day 'would be on our backs' if they did not get away. 'Moreover', as Major Clery explained, 'we had no food or ammunition, except what the men carried of the latter, so we fully expected to fight our way to the river.'[22] Chelmsford therefore gave the welcome order to march at 4 a.m., not only to make a head start on the enemy, but because it was also his intention to get his men away in the grey light of the pre-dawn to spare them a clear view of the horrible devastation in the sacked camp and of 'the mutilated remains of some of the 24th, some naked, others only in shirts and all without boots'.[23] In his haste to be gone, Chelmsford left the British dead unburied – a decision that would cause an indignant storm in Natal and back in Britain, and one that would continue to pursue him.

As Chelmsford had intended, the head of the column, marching four abreast with the 2/3rd NNC in the lead (so Lieutenant John Maxwell of the NNC remembered), was on the road to Rorke's Drift – some three or four miles away in a straight line, although twelve miles by road – 'before objects could be clearly seen'.[24] However, the 1/3rd NNC who were the last foot soldiers to quite the ground, and the Mounted Infantry, NMP and NMV who formed the rearguard and provided flankers for the column, had all too clear a sight of the abundant horrors in the light of early morning.[25] Sergeant Warren wrote home: 'Oh, father . . . I could not help crying to see how the poor fellows were massacred.'[26] And what particularly horrified him and his comrades was that the amaZulu had disembowelled all the dead. The amaZulu believed that when the blood of the slain in battle spurted over the killer, it ritually contaminated him and formed a fearsome occult bridge between the living and the world of the dead. All sorts of special ritual precautions then became necessary to gain ascendancy over the vengeful spirits of the slain and to be ritually cleansed.[27] One essential ritual was to slit open the belly of a dead foe so that *umnyama* (or evil influence) would not affect the killer and make him swell up like the dead.[28] The British did not understand these rituals – or would not have condoned them even if they had – and viewed the mutilation of their killed comrades as an abomination, one that changed the whole nature of the war and justified all future excesses against the Zulu 'savages'.

Soon after the retreating column had passed over the Manzimnyama stream and was within three miles of Rorke's Drift, Harford with the NNC at the rear was 'dumbfounded' at the 'extraordinary spectacle' of hundreds of Zulu warriors who 'sat and stood within a few yards of us on the right of the road, simply gazing at us like sightseers at a review'. He assumed that a trap was being laid since a few hundred yards to his left he saw great masses of amaZulu, several thousand strong, pulling back from Rorke's Drift through the valley of the Batshe River and potentially threatening the straggling British column. Since the British column was 'hurrying along at a great pace', Harford thought that Chelmsford at its head might not have seen the amaZulu in the valley below and rode forward as fast as he could to report. But he found that the General was perfectly aware of the Zulu presence. He commanded that unless they attacked, the column was to push on with all haste to Rorke's Drift where, to their alarm, all could discern a thick pall of smoke clinging ominously to the side of Shiyane hill that overlooked the post. In the event (and this must surely have been the most extraordinary occurrence of the war), since the British were almost out of ammunition and both they and the amaZulu were exhausted, hungry and demoralised, the two forces passed by each other close enough for some provocative verbal exchanges, but neither fired a shot and both continued on their separate ways.[29]

On the British column coming in sight of Rorke's Drift, it was observed through field-glasses that the hospital and part of the storehouse had been burnt and that there were men moving about the post. Chelmsford's attention was drawn to a man seen waving a flag, and to everyone's intense relief the figures were made out to be British. Russell and some Mounted Infantry crossed the river and galloped up to the station. 'Much to our delight and relief,' wrote Norris-Newman, 'we were greeted with a hearty English cheer.'[30] At about 8.15 a.m. the rest of the mounted men crossed at the drift and Chelmsford and the infantry went across the river by the ponts the amaZulu had neglected to destroy. It was not until 9.30 a.m. that the General's staff arrived at the post, where Chelmsford was received with three cheers. Berkeley Milne saw dead amaZulu lying in heaps and heard the firing still going on at wounded ones attempting to escape.[31] Trooper Symons recalled with a shudder that many of the dead amaZulu were burnt to ashes and that 'a strong smell of roasting flesh pervaded the place'.[32] Chelmsford's first words to the garrison were, 'I thank you all for your gallant defence.'[33] Private Henry Hook recollected that the General then asked to hear the story of the battle from some of those who had distinguished themselves. While his staff sought them out, the rest of the garrison wandered about elaborating details of their gallant defence of the post to their rescuers.[34]

Indeed, the defence of the post had been a desperate one. When the Centre Column had advanced across the Mzinyathi on 11 January, it left behind a small garrison of a company of the 2/24th under Lieutenant Gonville Bromhead, a company of the 2/3rd NNC and various detached personnel to secure the depot at Rorke's Drift. Not anticipating a Zulu attack, the British had neglected to fortify the post. Shortly after 3 p.m. on the afternoon of 22 January, fugitives from the battle of Isandlwana brought warning that a large Zulu force of between 3,000 and 4,000 men under Dabulamanzi kaMpande, Cetshwayo's half-brother, was rapidly approaching. This was the Zulu reserve that had not been engaged in the fighting at Isandlwana and burned to prove their mettle by invading Natal, ravaging the plain between the Mzinyathi and the heights at Helpmekaar to its south, and seizing the lightly defended depot at Rorke's Drift full of tempting supplies. This Zulu incursion into Natal territory was directly contrary to King Cetshwayo's strict orders, because it was his policy to present his kingdom as the victim of British aggression, fighting only in self-defence.[35] As he feared it would, Dabulamanzi's rash move presented the British with the useful pretext that they were fighting to repel a Zulu invasion, and cut the diplomatic ground from under Cetshwayo's feet.

Lieutenant John Chard, RE, the senior officer present, resolved that the small garrison must attempt to hold the post and hastily established an improvised defensive perimeter. At about 4.20 p.m. the horsemen who had escaped the Isandlwana battlefield and were keeping watch at the river, made off for the safety of the British post on the heights of Helpmekaar, followed by the demoralised company of NNC. Their flight deprived Chard of about 200 men, leaving fewer than 150 defenders (the official, although contested, number was 8 officers and 131 men, 35 of whom were invalids in the hospital) to hold the now over-extended perimeter. Before it could be effectively reduced in size, the amaZulu attacked at about 4.30 p.m. A brutal struggle ensued well into the night, much of it hand-to-hand, and it seemed at times that the attackers must prevail. During the course of the fighting two companies of the 1/24th Regiment stationed at Helpmekaar advanced down the escarpment to within three miles of the post, but withdrew when they saw the hospital in flames and presumed the garrison had been overwhelmed. But it had not been, and their successful defence demonstrated conclusively that an all-round position could be successfully held against overwhelming odds, just as Boers in their wagon-laagers had time and again repulsed Zulu attacks in the war of 1838. In the case of Rorke's Drift, repeated attacks, although pressed with determination, were uncoordinated, and although the attackers steadily pushed the garrison back from one defensive position to another, they could not finally dislodge them and capture the post. After about 9 p.m. the amaZulu made no further full-scale attacks, and during the course of the night the fighting gradually died down and ceased altogether at about 4 a.m. At daybreak, instead of renewing their attack as the anxious defenders feared they would, the amaZulu, demoralised by their heavy losses and lack of success, and aware that Chelmsford's column was advancing from Isandlwana, began their withdrawal.[36]

As soon as the men of the relieving British column had eaten some food from the stocks at Rorke's drift, they were set urgently to work improving the rudimentary defences around the post. Chelmsford sent Russell and a few of his Mounted Infantry straight off up the escarpment to Helpmekaar where on the night of the battle the troops stationed there had constructed an entrenched laager of wagons and mealie bags around the storehouse. They carried a letter for urgent delivery to Frere in which Chelmsford baldly stated: 'I regret deeply to have to inform you that No. 3 column has maintained a terrible disaster . . . I cannot yet give details of losses, but they are very serious indeed.'[37] Russell then returned to Rorke's Drift where the traumatised troops spent another anxious night punctuated by several false alarms of a Zulu attack. Many members of the two battalions of the 3rd NNC began to slip away under cover of darkness.

At 9 a.m. on 24 January Chelmsford and his staff with a small escort of NMP set off for Helpmekaar. They were followed by the artillery and the rest of the mounted men, leaving at Rorke's Drift the company of the 1/24th that had defended the post and the six companies of the 2/24th that had not been engaged at Isandlwana. All were under the command of the dispirited Colonel Glyn. No sooner had the artillery and mounted men departed for Helpmekaar, than the remaining members of the 3rd NNC began to desert. Commandant Lonsdale, believing he could no longer rely on his men, disbanded the regiment and rode to Helpmekaar for further instructions. During his absence, the white NNC officers and NCOs succeeded during the course of the afternoon in disarming the men without provoking their resistance and stripped them of all their government issue. The men then bolted for home, sowing panic wherever they went.[38]

At Helpmekaar, Chelmsford found that Bengough's 2/1st NNC that had missed all the fighting had made its way safely there from the banks of the Mzinyathi. The men were extremely shaken by the British defeat and were being encouraged to desert by the disbanded 3rd NNC streaming home. It was Chelmsford's plan that the 2/1st NNC make for Umsinga, fifteen miles to the south of Helpmekaar, there to protect the magistracy and to deter any Zulu incursion over the border in that direction. However, Bengough reported that his men were flatly refusing to go and that he was disarming them prior to sending them home. Chelmsford was extremely rattled by the Isandlwana disaster and could no longer maintain his habitually courteous demeanour. He became extremely angry with Bengough who he insisted had no right to dismiss anyone without his permission. (He certainly would never have countenanced Lonsdale's earlier disbandment of the entire 3rd NNC, and Lonsdale, belatedly realising this, allowed Chelmsford to remain under the impression that they had all deserted.)

As for the 2/1st NNC, Chelmsford ordered Bengough to recall it before the men had a chance to disperse. Then, following the procedure he had seen employed against mutinous sepoys during the Indian Mutiny, the General paraded them without their weapons. He had them form three sides of a square while the fully armed British soldiers of the Helpmekaar garrison made up the fourth side. Chelmsford then grimly warned the NNC that they must march to Umsinga as ordered, that he would permit no alternative, and that 'if he thought they were all cowards, he would shoot them on the spot'. To make good his threat, he thereupon gave orders to the British troops to shoot any man of the NNC who attempted to leave his regiment. Thoroughly cowed, Bengough's NNC set out for Umsinga without further demur. They reached the place on the evening of the following day and immediately started erecting a fort to protect it.

Having regained control of the 2/1st NNC, at 2 p.m. Chelmsford started out for Pietermaritzburg. He believed there was little more he could achieve at Helpmekaar, and he needed to discuss the military situation with Frere and take charge of the defence of Natal against an anticipated Zulu invasion.[39] He and his small escort went the longer route by way of Ladysmith because refugees from the fighting and the disbanded 3rd NNC had been spreading panic among the African working parties and wagon drivers employed by the Natal government along the shorter Helpmekaar–Greytown road. They had either deserted or were refusing to work because that route was so dangerously close to the now exposed border. Consequently, for the time being the Greytown–Helpmekaar road ceased to be the line of supply to the garrisons remaining at Helpmekaar, Umsinga and Rorke's Drift.[40]

The 2/4th (The King's Own Royal) Regiment of Foot had disembarked at Durban at the beginning of the year, and five companies were on the way towards the front when they learned of Isandlwana. One company remained to garrison Greytown and four went on to reinforce the garrison at Helpmekaar. Half of No. 5 Company, Royal Engineers, was also stationed at Helpmekaar where Captain W. Parke Jones built a proper earthwork fort to replace the wagon laager protecting the stores. Colonel F. C. Hassard of Chelmsford's HQ Staff was left in command and effectively shut himself up in the new fort. Indeed, bracing themselves for a Zulu offensive, all the elements of the now broken-up Centre Column assumed a purely defensive stance behind their fortifications, not only at Helpmekaar and Umsinga but at Rorke's Drift too. There the other half of No. 5 Company, Royal Engineers, began properly fortifying the post on 29 January under the direction of Lieutenant R. Porter.[41]

The defeat at Isandlwana comprehensively shattered Chelmsford's invasion plans. The heavy loss of life, weapons, ammunition and transport meant that he could make no further advance until his forces had regrouped and been reinforced, and fresh transport assembled. Until then, he would have to stand on the defensive and do his best to rally the defences of Natal, where panicking colonists were in daily expectation of a Zulu invasion. Meanwhile, how was he to explain away the disaster that had overtaken the Centre Column under his command?

CHAPTER 23

Panic in Natal and the Despatch of Reinforcements

'A PANIC IS SPREADING BROADCAST over the Colony which is difficult to allay,' Chelmsford telegraphed Stanley from Pietermaritzburg on 27 January 1879.[1] For many weeks he continued to subscribe to the general alarm, informing Cambridge that 'Natal is daily expecting an inroad of Zulus and I cannot but feel that such a contingency is not only possible but probable.'[2] His fears seemed to have been well grounded when, on the evening of 3 February, intelligence that later proved false reached Pietermaritzburg that the Zulu had crossed the border in force. The citizens flocked into the improvised town laager of fortified buildings connected by barricades, while Bulwer and his staff had their bedding and the government records moved to the sturdily built gaol where they intended to make a last stand.[3] The alarm spread to Chelmsford and the military secure behind the walls of Fort Napier overlooking the city, and it was said that Chelmsford stayed up all night, his horse saddled for any eventuality.[4]

Indeed, in the panic-stricken days after Isandlwana, Chelmsford's was not a calming presence and his arrival in Durban on 6 February had a disturbing effect that reflected his own sense of apprehension. Accompanied by Crealock, Gossett and Rear Admiral T. V. Sullivan, the commodore at the port, he was there to inspect the town's defences. The members of the civilian Defence Committee were clamouring for Durban to be entirely encircled by fortifications, but Chelmsford sensibly dismissed the scheme as impracticable. Instead, he endorsed the suggestion of the Colonial Commandant of Durban Sub-District, Major J. W. Huskisson, that the accepted military procedure for the defence of an open town be adopted by preparing certain buildings for defence and erecting a stockade across the Point behind which non-combatants could take refuge.[5] That was all well and good, but unfortunately the jittery Chelmsford also advised the Defence Committee that a Zulu raid was a real possibility, and he and his staff were at pains to emphasise the gravity of the situation to the appalled citizenry. As John Robinson (a Member of Natal's Legislative Council) reflected, 'It must be admitted that his presence did not tend to allay alarm . . . What else could the arrival of the Commander of the Forces, and his words of warning while inspecting the town, portend than some sudden and appalling crisis.'[6]

Certainly, the Isandlwana disaster seems to have brought Chelmsford to the verge of a nervous breakdown. Nor was such a reaction uncommon. His old chief in the Crimea, Lord Raglan, had fallen into a deep depression after the needless slaughter of so many British soldiers during the failed assault on the Redan on 18 June 1856. When Raglan died ten days later, it was believed to have been of 'acute mental anguish' rather than of cholera.[7] Chelmsford's psychological condition was poor, if not quite as severe. He admitted to Cambridge on 27 January that he was 'in daily dread' of learning that a similar fate had overtaken either Woods's or Pearson's columns. He went on: 'I am at the present moment inwardly inclined to view everything "au noir" altho' I need scarcely assure your Royal Highness that I do not allow anyone here to perceive it.'[8] He deluded himself, however, for his distress was painfully obvious. In early February his ADCs reported that 'they have serious fears about him. He is still so depressed refused all stimulants and mopes his life out . . . No one feels this as he does.'[9] Indeed, as he admitted to Cambridge on 10 February, while he did not 'anticipate breaking down', he still felt that 'the strain is very great on me in every way'.[10] Chelmsford considered himself 'fortunate' that once in Pietermaritzburg he was able to talk calmly over the dismal state of affairs with Frere who exhibited 'so cool a head and so stout a heart' that he was finally able to take a better grip on himself.[11]

He first concern was for the defence of Natal where the panicking colonists were flocking into the existing laagers, extemporising defences in the towns or trekking over the Drakensberg to the perceived safety of the OFS. Chelmsford arrived in Pietermaritzburg from Helpmekaar on the evening of Sunday, 26 January. That morning during divine service the churches in the city had been hung in black in mourning for those who had died at Isandlwana. Despite his own deep despondency, Chelmsford dutifully set about coordinating the defensive policies of the civil and military authorities, although he was never able to make them work quite in step. In its pre-war preparations for defence, the Natal government had been most concerned to protect settlers living in the countryside or in the small villages like Greytown, Ladysmith and Stanger. (No arrangements were made for the African population.) Perhaps the presence of imperial garrisons in the two big towns of Pietermaritzburg and Durban, or the notion that the townspeople there could be quickly be organised to take up arms, meant that no prior defensive preparations had been made there. Emergency efforts were now put in train, even in the southern districts of Natal far from any possibility of a Zulu incursion, and by the second week of February had proceeded sufficiently for Chelmsford to believe that further settler panic would be prevented.[12] He was on the whole unimpressed by what he observed of the efforts of the colonists, privately complaining that 'The townspeople [of Pietermaritzburg], although in a fright, are however terribly apathetic, and give little or no assistance.'[13] By early April when the laagers finally emptied of their refugees and the various civilian *ad hoc* defence corps stood down, a total of twelve government laagers, nine settler laagers, and sixteen improvised posts and stockades had been put into use.[14]

Ensuring that the colonists had fortified places of refuge in the event of a Zulu invasion was one thing. But, much worse for him, Chelmsford had to report his shocking, personally humiliating defeat both to the British government and the Horse Guards. He had also to request reinforcements, not only for the defence of Natal, but without which he could not resume the offensive in Zululand.

Accordingly, on 27 January, Chelmsford telegrammed Stanley: 'I regret to have to report a very disastrous engagement which took place on the 22nd between the Zulus and a portion of No. 3 Column . . . The effects of the reverse have already been very serious.' He went on to state that 'Additional reinforcements must be sent out. At least three Infantry Regiments and two Cavalry Regiments with horses are required and one more Company of Engineers.' He then concluded with what, in the circumstances, was a bizarrely detailed stipulation that 'The Cavalry must be prepared to act as Mounted infantry and should have their carbines slung on their shoulder, and a sword shorter than the regulation pattern fastened to the saddle.'[15]

Chelmsford followed up this telegram with an abject letter to his patron, the Duke of Cambridge:

> The sad disaster which has occurred to a portion of the force under my command will, I know well, distress Your Royal Highness extremely – It has thrown back the subjugation of Zululand to an indefinite period & must necessarily entail sacrifice of men & money in far larger proportions than was originally expected.[16]

Chelmsford's telegram to Stanley reached the War Office in the early hours of 11 February. Stunned, 'with the deepest regret' Stanley immediately apprised Cambridge of 'the news of a serious reverse at the Cape [*sic*]',[17] urgently summoned Sir Charles Ellice, the AG, and Sir Daniel Lysons, the QMG, to meet him and Cambridge later that morning. After conferring, they requested Beaconsfield to hold a Cabinet meeting shortly after 1 p.m. that same afternoon. There the decision was taken not only to despatch the reinforcements Chelmsford had requested, but to increase their number substantially to double the total of British regulars already deployed in South Africa.[18] In doing so, they anticipated Chelmsford's subsequent letter to Cambridge informing him that his 'first demand for three infantry regiments was clearly not enough', and that 'we should certainly want double the number if Zululand is to be properly occupied'.[19]

Two days after learning of Isandlwana, and still in a state of consternation, Cambridge wrote to Frere that,

> This has come like a clap of thunder upon us and is very distressing, so much so indeed as to upset all our hopes and calculations for a speedy issue of the war. We are most anxiously waiting for details to understand clearly how it has all come about, for at present there is much that is quite inexplicable to us.

Being still in the dark about Chelmsford's role in the debacle, he optimistically concluded, 'I know you have a good man in Lord Chelmsford and able officers to back him with gallant troops under their command and for the rest we must place our faith in God's providence.' Cambridge went on to inform Frere of the reinforcements being despatched, and lamented that 'it will be long before they can be with you and the intermediate suspense is very anxious and distressing'.[20]

Embarkation of the reinforcements began immediately on 12 February, and thirty-four ships were eventually required to transport them to Natal. Those setting out from English ports included two regiments of cavalry, the 1st (The King's) Dragoon Guards and the 17th (The Duke of Cambridge's Own) Lancers. There were also two field batteries of Royal Artillery, M Battery, 6th Brigade (six 7-pdr guns), and N Battery, 6th Brigade (six 9-pdr guns). Royal Engineers were included among those embarking, comprising 30th Company, RE, and the Right Half of C Troop, RE. Five battalions of regular infantry were embarked: the 2nd Battalion, 21st (Royal Scots Fusiliers); the 58th (Rutlandshire) Regiment; the 3rd Battalion, 60th (The King's Royal Rifle Corps); the 91st (Princess Louise's Argyllshire Highlanders); and the 94th Regiment. Various supports were added in the form of Nos 3, 4 and 5 Companies, Army Service Corps, as well as personnel of the Army Hospital Corps, Army Medical Department, Veterinary Department, Ordnance Store Department, and Commissariat and Transport Department. Drafts for the regiments already in South Africa were included. The total came to 387 officers, 8,895 men and, 1,866 horses, along with 238 wagons and carts. The 57th (West Middlesex) Regiment was shipped from Ceylon. No. 8 Battery, 7th Brigade, RA (two 7-pdr guns of garrison artillery) was sent from St Helena. No. 10 Battery, 7th Brigade, RA (three 7-pdr guns) and one company of the 88th Regiment sailed from Mauritius. Altogether, this was a further tally of 31 officers, 1,101 men and just 2 horses. The great majority of these reinforcements embarked only in the last quarter of February, with some drafts not taking ship until 5 May. The first reinforcements disembarked in Durban on 6 March, but the majority came ashore during the second half of March and the first week of April.[21] They did not arrive in South Africa without incident. The *City of Paris* with the 2/21st on board ran aground off Simon's Town on 23 March and the troops had to be transferred to HMS *Tamar*; while on 3 April the *Clyde*, carry a large draft for the 1/24th, struck a reef about seventy miles from Simon's Town and sank, but not before the troops took to their boats in calm weather and made it safely to the shore.[22]

The reinforcements brought with them a field telegraph requested by Chelmsford on the grounds that, as he put it, 'In a country of vast distances, with so few facilities for transmission of news, it would be of great value & in the future will supplement the main lines of telegraph according to the importance of the post.'[23]

Naturally, the despatch of so many reinforcements was not without its problems. As Cambridge bemoaned to Frere:

> We have done all that we could to back up Lord Chelmsford in his military requirements . . . but it is no easy task. We are on a poor establishment; we have had to meet the cost of two armies in the field [the other was fighting in the Second Afghanistan War]. We are not allowed by law to touch the reserves; then how are we to find men? We can only send boys, and these are not the elements necessary for carrying on a war such as we have on our hands in South Africa.[24]

Indeed, having to rake the bottom of the barrel for reinforcements revived the controversy over Cardwell's Short Service reforms. The Duke, who was to spend the second half of February in snowy weather conscientiously inspecting troops embarking for South Africa, noted in his diary on 18 February: 'To Aldershot to inspect several corps for service at the Cape . . . The troops looked well, but there are a very large number of volunteers and young men, which is certainly a great disadvantage.'[25] It remained to be seen how well these unseasoned troops would comport themselves in South Africa.

In his letter of 13 February to Frere, Cambridge also informed him that the reinforcements sailing for Natal would be accompanied by

> Major-Generals [Henry] Crealock, [Edward] Newdigate and [Frederick] Marshall – excellent men, very intelligent, reliable and active. They are all junior to Chelmsford in whom I have the greatest confidence and who [he added hopefully] no doubt will do, and has been doing, all that is prudent and right.[26]

Throwing in three major-generals – a fourth, the Hon. Sir Henry Clifford, VC, was added at the last moment – was in direct response to Chelmsford's letter of 1 February to Cambridge suggesting the 'advisability of sending out a Major General who will be competent to succeed me not only as Commanding the Forces, but also as Lt Governor & High Commissioner should anything happen to Sir B. Frere . . . None of the senior Colonels out here possess in our [his and Frere's] opinion the requisite qualities.'[27] That was indeed so. The officer next senior to Chelmsford and his obvious successor was Colonel Fairfax Hassard, RE, whom he had left in command of Helpmekaar after Isandlwana. But, overcome by events, Hassard rapidly succumbed to a nervous collapse more serious than Chelmsford's, surrendered his command to Colonel Edward Bray and was invalided to Cape Town where he remained in command until the end of the war. Of the remaining colonels, the energetic and effective Brevet Colonel Wood would have been the obvious choice had he not been low in seniority on the list of colonels. Moreover, in Cambridge's view he had already been over-rewarded for his service in the Ninth Cape Frontier War with promotion in November 1878 to substantive lieutenant-colonel.[28]

A major-general it had to be then. But why four? Partly, it was because the large number of troops being sent out required senior officers. But it was also because of the large pool of general officers eager for active employment and Cambridge's desire to accommodate as many as he could. The four finally selected were all his own choices and met the criteria he considered important. Every one of them had served in the Crimea where Clifford had won his VC at Inkerman. Crealock had fought in the Indian Mutiny like his younger brother, Chelmsford's AMS. Both the elder Crealock and Clifford had served in the Third Anglo-Chinese War of 1859–60, while Newdigate had been on the Red River Expedition of 1870. Clifford alone had previous experience in South Africa, fighting in both the Seventh and Eighth Cape Frontier Wars. All were very much part of the military establishment and were personally known to Cambridge, in the same way as Chelmsford, on account of the senior administrative posts they had held. Crealock, a vain and arrogant military courtier, had been military attaché at both St Petersburg and Vienna, and most recently had served as DQMG Ireland. Newdigate had held a series of home staff appointments, while Clifford had been the AAG at the War Office. Furthermore, both he and Marshall had been Cambridge's ADCs and were thus on very close terms with him. Cambridge had an especially close association with Clifford with whom he kept up an extensive correspondence. Inevitably, opinion in military circles on the merits of the four major-generals Cambridge had selected was mixed. Considering that they were all Cambridge's protégés, it was hardly surprising that Wolseley and the jealous, unchosen members of his 'ring' declared themselves to be contemptuous of them as a set of feeble old ladies, not fit for field command.[29]

Whether or not there was some truth in this assertion will be seen when the four major-generals' performance in Zululand comes to be assessed, but Clifford was clearly a cut above the other three and Cambridge envisaged him taking on the herculean logistical task of transport and supply. As Cambridge informed Frere on 27 February:

> We have added one general officer for the base of operations in the person of Major-General Clifford, an officer of great knowledge and experience in former Cape wars, and moreover a most agreeable and satisfactory man to deal with. He will aid Lord Chelmsford in sending to the front and landing the large amount of supplies and stores sent out from England, will communicate with the Naval people as to the transport, etc., and will make himself generally useful. Major-General Crealock is junior to him but it is clearly understood that he will join Lord Chelmsford in the field and be looked upon as next senior while Clifford takes charge of the base of operations.[30]

How well Clifford would work with Chelmsford remained to be seen, and his anomalous situation *vis-a-vis* Major-General Crealock regarding their respective commands promised future difficulties.

Unfortunately for Chelmsford's reputation, he did not leave his request of 1 February to Cambridge for an additional major-general there. Crealock had reported to Alison on 2 February that Chelmsford, although 'better in the last 24 hours' was

> . . . still not himself and the authorities ought to realize the chance of his not being able to stand up against a long continuance of his present duties. He has pulled through so far very well, physically and mentally, but reaction comes, and a long year's hard work is telling I can see.

A week later, on 9 February, Crealock admitted to Alison that his 'remarks on the general's health have been fully borne out since I wrote last'.[31] It is in this context of confirmed mental distress that on the very same day Chelmsford, who did not know as yet that Cambridge was despatching four major-generals with the reinforcements, wrote to Stanley urging that 'an officer of the rank of Major-General should be sent out to South Africa without delay'. He unguardedly gave as his reason the damning information that: 'In June last I mentioned privately to His Royal Highness the F.M. Comd in Chief that the strain of prolonged anxiety & exertion, physical & mental was even then telling on me – What I felt then, I feel still more now.' Chelmsford's apparent admission that the strain of the Ninth Cape Frontier had also proved too much for him was not mitigated by his lame assurance that 'it will be my earnest desire to carry on my duties for Her Majesty's Service up to the fullest extent of my powers'.[32]

Since this disquieting confession was made in an official despatch to the War Office, and not in a 'private and confidential document' as he later protested it was, Chelmsford should have realised that it would be published and exposed to intensely embarrassing public scrutiny. Doubly unfortunately for Chelmsford, it caused his long-time patron, the Duke of Cambridge, seriously to doubt him. To make matters worse, Cambridge was put in the humiliating position of having to rise in the House of Lords on 24 March to assure his sceptical peers that until the War Office's receipt of Chelmsford's disastrous despatch of 9 February he had always believed that, 'A more robust man, or a man in all respects more capable of doing his duty in trying circumstances, could not be found than my noble and gallant Friend Lord Chelmsford.' To his further embarrassment, Cambridge was obliged to insist that he was 'in total ignorance' of any letter from Chelmsford sent in June 1878 reporting he was then feeling the strain of command, lamely suggesting that if such a one existed it 'might have miscarried in some way'.[33]

Once the damage had been irreparably done, Chelmsford insisted privately to Major-General Martin Dillon, who had been one of those prepared to defend him in public, that

> The dispatch in question was written by Crealock, at my request . . . I must have given Crealock a completely wrong idea of what I had said in my private letter to the Duke, alluded to in my dispatch . . . I could not have written anything that would imply my state of body and mind was not what it ought to be.

He then went on to insist unconvincingly that he must have 'signed the dispatch without noticing the misquotation of my private letter and can only attribute having done so to pressure of work and to constant interruptions during a busy day of persons anxious to see me'.[34] These excuses ring very hollow. We know from Crealock's letters of 2 and 9 February that the despatch accurately reflected Chelmsford's pessimistic and disturbed state of mind at that moment; while it is unlikely that an officer accustomed to paying such meticulous attention to every military detail would have signed an important despatch to the Secretary of State for War without reading it. One can only assume that at the time Chelmsford meant what he ordered Crealock to write on 9 February, and only disowned it once his own metal health had improved and the negative repercussion in Britain became apparent to him.

Chelmsford's reputation took a further, simultaneous battering over another issue that would continue to haunt him for many months to come. In reporting the 'sad disaster' of Isandlwana to the Duke of Cambridge on 8 February, he was at pains to explain why he had not buried the British dead, as was expected of a commander left in command of the field. He wrote:

> The question no doubt will be asked as to why I made no effort to bury the dead bodies, and why having obtained possession of the Camp again I did not retain it – The answer is clear. I had no supplies and no spare ammunition nearer than 10 miles, and at a post which was very open to attack, and I could not afford to delay as the troops wanted food and rest – The terrible massacre which had taken place precluded all possibility of my being able to bury those that had fallen, and to do so partially could only have the effect of bringing home to the troops the full extent of the disaster, of which to a certain extent they were kept in ignorance, owing to the darkness –
>
> I felt that there was much to lose and nothing to gain by delaying the march, and I consequently did not hesitate.[35]

Aware nevertheless of how he would be criticised for the perceived dereliction of his duty, on 16 February he ordered Wood to attempt to 'bury decently the bones of those poor fellows', but not to proceed if there should be any attendant risk.[36] In the event, Wood did not permit Buller and his mounted men to make the hazardous journey and perform the task. Chelmsford, it turns out, was relieved, not only because he feared the effects of the horrible task on Buller's men, but because he had come to realise that if they had gone ahead, it would 'have been immediately seized upon as a slur upon No 3 Column who are not really able to undertake the task'. If Glyn's men were to be accorded the honour and obligation of interring their dead comrades, he informed Wood, then the task would have to wait until reinforcement had come out.[37] Meanwhile, Chelmsford was able to salve his conscience on receiving the report of Major Wilsone Black of the 2/24th who had led a reconnaissance to the Isandlwana battlefield on 14 March, and who described 'the stench as very sickening'. Chelmsford could therefore conveniently conclude that 'it would not do' to 'attempt any burying for some time even if I could manage it'.[38]

CHAPTER 24

Regrouping, January–April 1879

LORD CHELMSFORD, REPORTED CREALOCK on 9 February, 'very naturally does not wish to risk anything until the reinforcements come out, but with such a vast frontier and the important centres of preparation being so far apart it is a fair puzzle to know what best to do'.[1] Certainly, with the Centre Column shattered after Isandlwana and with the Right and Left Columns stranded in Zululand, for a time Chelmsford remained at a loss, and in a private letter called on Wood for his advice:

> The situation of affairs does not appear to me to improve, and I am fairly puzzled when I contemplate our future operations . . .
>
> When you have thought over the situation kindly let me know what your views are regarding it – Let me know particularly what you think you and your column can do, when reinforced, and how I can assist you . . . The advance to Ekowe [Eshowe] shows that it is a mistake to move in farther than you can get back from easily, or that you can be regularly fed –
>
> I wish I saw my way with honour out of this beastly country, and had you as my travelling companion. Best love to Buller – You two will have to pull me out of the mire.[2]

As he recovered his mental equilibrium and became more assured concerning the security of the Natal settlers, Chelmsford began to look ahead. He was greatly heartened when the Cape government 'behaved with great spirit' in immediately sending to Natal the three companies of the 2/4th left in garrison in Cape Town and the three companies of the 88th stationed in King William's Town.[3] Their arrival made that of the reinforcements promised by Cambridge somewhat less urgent. By

20 February Chelmsford felt sufficiently confident to draw up a memorandum laying out the way forward. He accepted that the troops were 'at present compelled to remain on the passive defensive', and that Pearson's column (as we shall see) was immobilised in Eshowe where he hoped it would nevertheless hold its own and that the 'moral effect' of its presence would be felt by the amaZulu. Even so, Chelmsford was adamant that 'Nothing can be so demoralizing to both European and Natives as remaining on the passive defensive – It at once admits an inferiority on our part, and a superiority on the side of the Enemy.' He therefore hoped that the Natal colonial forces would eventually be in a position to mount punitive raids into Zululand. Meanwhile, Chelmsford pinned his hopes on Wood's column which he believed would soon be reinforced by 'mounted volunteers from the Cape Colony and the Free State' that would enable it 'to resume its former activity'.[4] It was most important, he reiterated, 'that we should resume the offensive as soon as possible, and my best efforts are being directed towards that end'. His recent defeat had taught him caution, however, and he reminded himself that 'it would be folly to attempt it with inadequate means'.[5]

Meanwhile, Chelmsford trusted to Wood, assuring him that 'I have however no anxiety about <u>you</u>, as I have in other directions,'[6] and was seriously alarmed in mid-February when he learned that Wood had been delirious with a fever brought on by want of sleep and consequent neuralgia, and had been confined to bed for thirty-six hours. 'I was so relieved to hear that you have got over your bad attack,' Chelmsford wrote, for 'If you shut up I don't know what I should do.'[7]

As we have seen, on 22 January, the day of the battle of Isandlwana, Wood had divided his forces as had Chelmsford, and had led out a column from Fort Tinta to Zungwini Mountain where he dispersed the abaQulusi concentrated there and captured many cattle.[8] On 24 January the column broke up another Qulusi concentration between Zungwini and Ntendeka Mountains. During the course of this operation Captain Gardner, one of the few survivors of Isandlwana, who had then gallantly undertaken a daring, marathon ride from Helpmekaar, brought Wood word of the disastrous battle. On learning of this 'mishap', as Chelmsford chose to refer to his crushing defeat in perhaps the oddest, most self-deluding lines he ever penned to Wood,[9] the latter withdrew his column north-west via Fort Tinta towards Khambula Hill between the Old Hunting Road and the Ncome River. There, on 31 January, he laagered and formed a strong entrenched camp.

From that well-defended base, and thanks to his energy and the number of experienced irregular horse at his disposal under Buller's proactive command, Wood retained the ascendancy in north-western Zululand despite several setbacks. On 1 February a patrol under Buller burned ebaQulusini, the *ikhanda* that was centre of Zulu resistance in the area, and on 10 February raided Hlobane where many Zulu had taken refuge. The patrols captured great herds of cattle on both occasions and the amaZulu in the neighbourhood began to submit or move eastwards out of range. But Manyonyoba kaMaqondo's amaKhubeka, the abaQulusi and Mbilini kaMswati's adherents hit back, ravaging the Ntombe valley north of Luneburg on 10–11 February. Counter-raids by Wood's forces during the course of February were not effective in subduing that sector.[10]

Meanwhile, Colonel Rowlands's No. 5 Column remained in garrison on the Phongolo frontier to protect Wood's left flank. It did not advance beyond its posts at Derby and Luneburg, but supported No. 4 Column in skirmishing with the amaKubheka in the Ntombe valley. Chelmsford had lost any confidence in Rowlands since his defeat in the First Anglo-Pedi War the previous year, but felt that at his distance from the area of operations he was 'quite unable' to tell him what to do. He therefore delegated, and instructed Rowlands to be guided entirely by Wood since, in Chelmsford's estimation, Wood was 'the only person who really understands the situation'.[11] It was not long, though, before Chelmsford was being made 'uncomfortable' by the suspicion that the unenterprising Rowlands was hampering Wood in their joint operations. He therefore assured Wood that he was 'quite prepared to order him away, if you find him a nuisance'.[12] Wood indeed did so, and on 26 February No. 5 Column was attached to Wood's command. Rowlands was sent back to Pretoria to deal as best he could with the disaffected Boers who, ever since Isandlwana, had been encouraged by the exposure of British military vulnerability to believe that it was far from impossible to overthrow their British rulers.[13]

Not that all went well in the sector now under Wood's single command. Supplies for the British garrison stationed at Luneburg continued to be forwarded from Derby and the route remained vulnerable to attack. On 7 March Captain David Moriarty was sent out with a company of the 80th Regiment to escort in a convoy of eighteen wagons. The convoy closed up on the banks of the rain-swollen Ntombe River on 9 March where Moriarty formed a sloppily arranged laager. On 12 March, Mbilini, the enterprising leader of the Zulu irregulars in the vicinity, attacked the sleeping encampment under cover of thick mist. His men overran it and withdrew with 250 head of cattle and the contents of the wagons. The British lost an officer and sixty men in the disastrous affray, along with a civil surgeon, two white wagon conductors, and fifteen black wagon drivers. Mbilini's successful strike was more than a demonstration that Wood still had a way to go before he could confidently claim that he had succeeded in subduing north-western Zululand. Damagingly, it was yet another shocking blow to British military prestige with an unacceptably high tally of casualties for an encounter in a colonial campaign.[14] Chelmsford's reputation was further diminished by this, the second catastrophe to have befallen the troops under his command. Cambridge was appalled when he learned of the 'disaster', characterising it as 'lamentable in the extreme' and calling for Chelmsford to furnish a full explanation. He pointedly concluded his missive with the hope that some good news would soon emanate from Natal.[15]

If not wholly successful in his operations, Wood was at least actively taking the war to the enemy. To Chelmsford's disappointment, the same could not be said of Pearson.[16] During the initial invasion of Zululand, No. 1 Column had been plagued by rainy weather, swollen rivers and muddy tracks, and had made slow progress. On 22 January – the same day as the battle of Isandlwana – a Zulu army of about 6,000 men under the command of Godide kaNdlela ambushed the column when half of it was across the Nyezane River and the rest was trying to catch up. The amaZulu failed to envelop the British as they had planned, while the troops of Pearson's leading section were able to seize a commanding position while the rest of the column closed up. With their rifles, four 7-pounders, Gatling gun and rocket tube the troops poured a devastating fire into the amaZulu, finally dispersing them. During the course of the firefight, Pearson's men were deployed in skirmishing order, exactly as the troops were at Isandlwana. The different outcome can be attributed to several factors. While Pearson's column was some 300 men stronger than the garrison defending Isandlwana camp, Godide's army was a quarter the size of the main Zulu army fighting there and was made up of a high proportion of irregulars and fewer seasoned *amabutho*. Godide found it impossible to coordinate his attack with his less-trained forces, and they never succeeded in coming close enough to the British to engage in hand-to-hand combat. It goes without saying that if the main Zulu army had fallen on Pearson's column instead of fighting at Isandlwana, that the outcome would most likely have been very different. As it was, the fortunate Pearson's encounter with the amaZulu was never more than a firefight and cost him very few casualties.[17] Chelmsford was very aware of Pearson's lucky escape, not least because he had fought in skirmishing order. Chelmsford, to give him some credit, had learned from Isandlwana how vulnerable that deployment was to Zulu attack. Consequently, when giving Pearson his 'best thanks' for 'the very good business' at Nyezane, he went on to exhort him to keep his men together in the event of another encounter because 'The Zulus are sure to attack in heavy masses and close order is the one to meet it.'[18]

Having brushed aside Godide's attempt to intercept him, the following day Pearson occupied the deserted Norwegian mission station at Eshowe. It was not a good defensive position and had only been chosen because the existing building could be used for storage of supplies. Nevertheless, over the next two months it was converted into a strong earthwork fort that deterred the amaZulu from even contemplating making an attack on it.[19]

On 28 January Pearson received Chelmsford's telegram of the previous day from Pietermaritzburg informing him of Isandlwana. In a telling abrogation of his authority, Chelmsford gave him permission to 'make the best arrangements' he could, to consider all the general's 'instructions as cancelled', and to act 'in whatever manner' he thought 'most desirable'.[20] Unsure what best to do, Pearson immediately held a council of his senior officers. By a small majority it was decided not to retreat to the forts at the mouth of the Thukela, but to hold fast in Eshowe to divert Zulu attention away from invading Natal.[21]

Concerned that he would be short of supplies unless rapidly relieved, on 29 January Pearson sent back all the Mounted Infantry under Major Barrow to the Thukela and most of the men of the two battalions of the 2nd NNC. The next day his remaining men, 1,339 whites and 355 blacks, of whom 337 were non-combatants, took up position in the fort. Believing that there was not enough pasturage for his livestock, Pearson sent 1,000 draught oxen back to the Thukela. He provided an inadequate escort, and to Chelmsford's annoyance the amaZulu captured 900 of them.[22]

Without his draught oxen, Pearson was effectively marooned in Eshowe where he reckoned he had supplies to hold out for two months.[23] The Zulu leadership considered his presence so deep in Zulu territory a great affront, and Cetshwayo had the garrison blockaded and its communications to Natal cut by members of all the *amabutho* living in the coastal country, and by local irregulars. Constant watch was kept on the fort by about 500 men in parties of forty or fifty, while the remainder – perhaps as many as 5,000 under the command of Dabulamanzi kaMpande and Mavumengwana kaNtuli – were quartered in small groups at local *imizi* (homesteads) and *amakhanda*. There they held themselves ready to re-form to repel a sortie by the garrison, or by British forces marching to its relief.[24]

Chelmsford had now to work out what to do with the beleaguered garrison. Early in February he decided he must soon set out for the Lower Thukela to see for himself what should be done until sufficiently reinforced to take the initiative himself.[25] Meanwhile, he urged Pearson not to take any risks with the troops in Eshowe, and (fearing he would run out of supplies) began to attempt to persuade him to fall back on the Thukela with the bulk of his forces, leaving a reduced garrison to hold Eshowe until relieved.[26] But on 6 February Pearson's senior officers decided not to split their force and so risk exposing the withdrawing column to another Isandlwana.[27]

Thus far, Chelmsford had kept in communication with Eshowe, but by mid-February no messages were getting through, and he lamented that 'Native runners have been intercepted & killed, & my letters may have been lost.'[28] Chelmsford's growing concern prompted him to leave Durban where (as we have seen) he was inspecting the fortifications, and move on 11 February to Fort Pearson. But with no way of knowing what Pearson intended to do, he had temporarily to shelve his tentative plan to coordinate an orderly withdrawal from Eshowe. The one consolation, he informed Wood, was that Pearson had 'foodstuffs for his whole force up to the second week of April', so he had no immediate cause 'to feel uneasy for him'.[29]

With that, Chelmsford set off back for Pietermaritzburg. On the way he drew up a memorandum reassessing the strategy he intended to pursue. In it, he decided that until solid information reached him that Pearson was withdrawing part of his force to the Thukela, or until sufficient reinforcements arrived, it would not be advisable 'to make any effort to engage the enemy offensively on this line – or to occupy any intermediate position between Lower Tugela and Ekowe' because there 'would be no commensurate advantage gained by such a move, as the force would not be large enough to act boldly and its advance prematurely would therefore be no assistance to the Garrison of Ekowe'.[30] This did not mean that Chelmsford had abandoned his intention to withdraw the Eshowe garrison, but for lack of communication it was impossible for the moment to coordinate a timetable for the joint operation.[31]

In early March messages began to be relayed to Fort Eshowe from Fort Pearson by 'sunflashing' from an improvised heliograph, but the garrison had no means of replying. As a result, it proved impossible to confirm plans to link up with a relief force on 13 March. Soon thereafter, though, the garrison managed to contrive a heliograph of its own out of iron tubing, a small mirror and two pieces of paper,[32] and communication by flashing signals was securely established. Meanwhile, in Fort Eshowe there was an alarming increase in the number of men falling prey to typhoid fever and dysentery. Food rations had to be drastically reduced, and Pearson feared that his ammunition supply would also run out. Chelmsford was left in no doubt that he must relieve Eshowe as soon as he could arrange it and that he must withdraw the entire garrison and abandon the fort. As Chelmsford informed Stanley on 17 March, 'Colonel Pearson instructed that it would be desirable to relieve the whole of the garrison as Officers and men were generally sickly and that any relieving force should bring a convoy and be prepared to fight.'[33]

While Chelmsford awaited the arrival of reinforcements and prepared to evacuate the Eshowe garrison, he had to consider the future role of the NNC. He had written to Cambridge on 1 February that 'the Native Contingent can never be of any use again, except for work inside the Colony'.[34] At that stage, with white settlers rushing into laager, thus leaving the countryside open to Zulu raiders, it seemed both to Chelmsford and the Natal government that black levies were essential to hold the frontier line. But the NNC was in some disarray. After Isandlwana the two battalions of 3rd NNC with the Centre Column had been disbanded. The two battalions of the 2nd NNC with the Right Column had left Eshowe and returned to the bases by the lower Thukela. The 1st and 3rd Battalions of the 1st NNC remained at Kranskop on the middle border, and Bengough's 2/1st NNC was still at Umsinga.

During February Chelmsford set about reorganising these units so that the three battalions of the 1st NNC became respectively the 1st, 2nd and 3rd Battalions, NNC, while the two battalions of the 2nd NNC became the 4th and 5th Battalions, NNC.[35] Chelmsford's restructuring of the NNC immediately ran into Bulwer's opposition, however. On 29 January, Bulwer reminded him that from the first he had been opposed to imposing a 'regimental system' on the levies instead of maintaining their 'native system' of military organisation. His reasoning was that the 'regimental system' led to his authority 'as supreme chief of the native population' being 'superseded by the military authority'.[36] This line of argument would have reminded Chelmsford of the vituperative debate during the Ninth Cape Frontier War between the civil and military authorities that had terminated General Cunynghame's career, and he confided in Wood that Bulwer was 'making himself very disagreeable over the matter'.[37] Rattled, Chelmsford reminded Frere that 'Troops in the field must be commanded by the supreme *military* chief who is present with them at the time,'[38] the very same conclusion that the government had finally reached in Cunynghame's case. In a strong memorandum of 4 March Chelmsford restated this position at great length, and insisted that he was 'unwilling to continue the controversy regarding the tribal and regimental systems as adopted in the Natal Native Contingent'.[39] Chelmsford had a firm ally in Frere whose practical concern was 'how to get the native force required as auxiliaries to Her Majesty's troops in the field',[40] and when forwarding Chelmsford's memorandum to Bulwer, urged 'that instead of discussing the past, the rules under which the Native Levies may be called out for future service should be laid down . . . by joint consent'.[41] Bulwer duly backed down, assuring Frere that with regards to the 'raising and management' of the NNC, when he and Chelmsford met in Pinetown in the hills north-west of Durban on 11 March, 'nothing will be wanting on the part of the Government to meet as far as possible the views of the Lieutenant-General'.[42] And indeed, after the Pinetown conference Bulwer believed he was justified in reporting to Frere that he and the general had 'arrived at a satisfactory understanding as to what was required and what could be furnished' by Bulwer as Supreme Chief.[43]

Bulwer might have believed that the matter had been ironed out, but he was misled. He had certainly conceded that any black troops raised by the military and paid for by the imperial government, such as the

NNC, were, as confirmed by the legal opinion of the Attorney General of Natal, Michael Gallway, liable to perform 'any military service which the General Commanding in Chief may assign to them or order them to engage in'.[44] But what of the African border levies raised and maintained by the Natal government, rather than by the military authorities?[45] Concurrently with Chelmsford's restructuring of the NNC, the colonial government had set about augmenting the existing Border Guard in Colonial Defensive Districts I, VII, and VI by additional levies brought up mainly from the defensive districts to the south. By the end of April they would number somewhere around 8,500 men, including the 600 men of the Weenen Contingent made up of former members of the disbanded 3rd NNC, and the Ixopo Native Contingent raised in District No. IV that consisted of some 800 foot and 500 horse.[46] With regard to their deployment, it should be remembered that on 13 January Chelmsford had placed the three defensive districts along the Zulu border under his overall military command.[47] Recognising this, Bulwer had conceded on 28 February that Chelmsford had the right to dispose of the colonial troops in these districts for whatever 'military reasons may at the time appear necessary'.[48]

So far, so good, but how did Chelmsford intend to 'dispose' of these colonial levies? Frere had already made it clear on 11 February that he feared the 'raw' border levies would be 'next to useless' for cross-border sorties and should be reserved entirely for the 'passive defence' favoured by Bulwer.[49] He also early reminded Chelmsford that Bulwer very much disliked the idea of raids into Zululand.[50] Indeed, it was the opinion of the members of the colonial government that the levies should act exclusively on the defensive, and not become involved in the 'active defence' advocated by Chelmsford. On 1 March the Executive Council furthermore resolved that 'raiding expeditions' were 'an impolitic and undesirable system of war . . . calculated to provoke retaliation'.[51] Yet Chelmsford's unshakeable position was that the adoption of the 'active defence' would eventually force the Zulu to abandon the border zone, disrupt their military plans and secure Natal from invasion. In the shorter term, he was convinced that demonstrations along the Thukela–Mzinyathi border by all the forces stationed in the border defensive districts, including the colonial levies, would create a diversion in favour of the Eshowe Relief Column when it at last began its advance, and that some cross-border raids would add

The Turning-Point in the Zulu Campaign, 16 February–6 April 1879

greatly to the effect. As he wrote to Wood on 3 March, he hoped when he was in a position to march on Eshowe 'to send in large raiding parties with a hooroosh'.[52] In other words, Chelmsford was determined to use the border levies as he thought fit, and that included cross-border raids. If he acted without Bulwer's prior sanction, then he was prepared to face the consequences. Indeed, he seems to have convinced himself that if duplicity were required, the circumstances warranted it.

It appears that at the Pinetown meeting on 11 March Chelmsford gave the impression that he had bowed to Bulwer's insistence that the levies should not raid into Zululand. He let Bulwer know that he might require the levies to create a diversion by demonstrating along the border, but made no reference to sorties across it. In the days following the meeting, Bulwer fulfilled his part of the bargain by ordering the border levies to be prepared to make demonstrations along the Natal bank when Chelmsford marched out to relieve Eshowe. However, behind Bulwer's back Chelmsford bluntly informed Wood that he would 'tell the border Commandants to make demonstrations all along the line . . . and if the river permits to raid across'.[53] Once Bulwer found out, to his vociferous indignation, that Chelmsford had deliberately duped him at Pinetown,[54] and that without his prior knowledge raids had been launched across the Thukela on 2 and 3 April,[55] the Pinetown meeting would become a matter for intense recriminations that (as we shall see) helped destroy Chelmsford's credit at the War Office.

Chelmsford had been fortunate while regrouping and waiting for reinforcements to arrive that the amaZulu had not fulfilled his fears and invaded Natal but, instead, had remained (as he put it) 'perfectly quiet'. Intelligence received during early February confirmed that, despite their victory at Isandlwana, the amaZulu 'had been much disheartened' by 'the heavy losses inflicted on them' and by their defeats at Nyezane and Rorke's Drift.[56] That was true enough, and the *amabutho* had moreover refused to stay in the field while they performed their post-combat purification rituals. Consequently, although Cetshwayo had brought the British invasion to a halt, and the British forces still on Zulu soil were neutralised or contained for the moment, he had been unable to exploit the military advantage gained at Isandlwana. He knew he ought to take the field again before the British brought in more reinforcements, but it would be some time before he had reassembled his *amabutho*. He therefore decided to employ the lull in operations to attempt to secure a negotiated settlement, hoping that the British would be prepared to talk.[57]

Diplomacy, however, would prove futile. Cetshwayo never quite grasped that after Isandlwana it was essential for the continuance of British hegemony in South Africa that the might of British arms be speedily and conclusively vindicated. The irony of the Zulu victory at Isandlwana was that now nothing short of complete military victory was acceptable to the British, along with the overthrow of the Zulu kingdom. As Frere would minute on 4 April, 'no overtures of any kind must be allowed to delay military operations', at least until 'complete command of Zululand was secured'. After that, the British could dictate any terms they wished since they were no longer bound by the terms of the ultimatum Cetshwayo had rejected. In his same minute, Frere reaffirmed the complementary policy pursued since the beginning of the war that laid down that 'overtures for peace' would be acceptable from any chief, but not from the king himself, so long as they served to sever that chief's allegiance to Cetshwayo.[58]

Unaware that his peace feelers would be futile, Cetshwayo sent two emissaries who crossed the Thukela Middle Drift on 1 March and went to the Norwegian mission station at kwaNtunjambili.[59] There, through Bishop Hans Schreuder, a longstanding friend of Cetshwayo's, they begged the British in their king's name to withdraw from Zululand and to resume talks.[60] Although not properly grasped by the British until much later in the war, there was a real limitation to all Zulu peace feelers because, in accordance with Zulu custom, emissaries had no authority to talk about actual terms of peace, only the king's desire to negotiate. If the other side were willing, it was their duty to arrange a meeting of the 'chiefs' who alone had the power to discuss terms.[61] What made Zulu overtures doubly pointless was not only Frere's obdurate refusal (as he informed Chelmsford) to consider any message that did not come 'in a form to bind' Cetshwayo – which they never could – but his insistence that he would not accept anything short of an unconditional Zulu surrender.[62]

Yet Frere was as prepared as was Chelmsford to employ duplicity when it served his purposes. Unofficially, he welcomed Zulu peace feelers because they kept the enemy's 'attention occupied', and by spinning out the process gave time for reinforcements to build up preparatory to a renewed offensive.[63] On this occasion, though, Chelmsford's reaction to the Zulu emissaries at kwaNtunjambili could not have been more straightforward. He was convinced that no message from the Zulu king could be anything else but 'humbug', and that he would be 'doing the most foolish thing to accept this Zulu's protestations'.[64] As he explained to Wood,

> I hope to be able to give him his answer next week by sending in a column to Ekowe – Sir B. Frere is not prepared to approve of any reply but that of unconditional surrender and general disarmament, coupled with the conditions already laid down.[65]

If the British were not being straightforward in their dealings, Cetshwayo found that he too had to resort to deception when his hand was forced by growing signs of disloyalty in his kingdom. Hamu kaNzibe, a member of the Zulu royal house who was the *induna* of the uThulwana *ibutho* and chief of the Ngenetsheni people in north-western Zululand, had long entertained designs on the Zulu crown, and had been opposed to risking war with Britain. He had been in communication with the British since November 1878, and finally defected. He reached Wood on 10 March, joined by many of his adherents. From behind the British lines, he prepared to await his half-brother Cetshwayo's defeat, and then to claim his reward from the British. His betrayal was a severe blow to morale across the Zulu kingdom and a clear indication to Cetshwayo that more defections were likely to follow. Realising that only another military victory could forestall such a development and restore his credibility, Cetshwayo decided in mid-March to recall his *amabutho* for a fresh offensive against the British. By 22 March the veterans of Isandlwana had reassembled at oNdini for ritual war preparations. Since Wood's raids in the north-west were presenting a greater threat than Pearson's inactivity at Eshowe, Cetshwayo decided to direct his army against him. Under the command of no less a personage than Mnyamana, the king's chief *induna*, the army began its march towards Khambula on 24 March. While his army was mustering, and even while it was on the march, Cetshwayo tried to disguise his intentions by stringing the British along with new, but now insincere, negotiations.[66]

Not that the British welcomed further emissaries, darkly presuming they must be spies. On 21 March two messengers reached Schreuder but were sent packing. Two days later another brace of envoys approached Fort Eshowe where they were promptly clapped into irons. On 28 March, the very day the advancing Zulu army soundly defeated Wood at Hlobane, three further messengers crossed at Middle Drift and were detained at Fort Buckingham pending Chelmsford's instructions. The General laid down that all communications from Cetshwayo must be sent directly to his HQ camp wherever that might be.[67] By that stage it was in Zululand, for Chelmsford was at last on the march to relieve Fort Eshowe. He was unaware that on the same day he had set out from the lower Thukela, 29 March, Wood had redeemed his debacle at Hlobane by winning his great victory at Khambula that transformed the whole dynamic of the war.

CHAPTER 25

Failing to Shift the Blame, January–April 1879

IT WAS ONE THING FOR CHELMSFORD to retrieve the military situation by seeing to the defence of Natal, by regrouping, and by readying himself to relieve Pearson's blockaded column in Eshowe once reinforcements had arrived. All these things fell within the range of his practical responsibilities as GOC. It was another matter entirely to explain away the catastrophe that had overtaken the Centre Column operating under his command to the satisfaction of the War Office, the government, Parliament and the public at large. Dealing with the political and public relations fallout of Isandlwana thus presented Chelmsford with a personal challenge every bit as demanding as prosecuting the war with Zululand. After all, his reputation and career were at stake.

When reporting by telegram to Colonel Stanley on 27 January that 'a very disastrous engagement' had taken place at Isandlwana, he further informed the Secretary of State for War that, 'A court of enquiry has been ordered to assemble to collect evidence regarding this unfortunate affair, and will be forwarded to you as soon as received.'[1] Chelmsford had swiftly established the court at Helpmekaar on 24 January before he set off for Pietermaritzburg, and it assembled on 27 January and sat until 29 January. Colonel F. C. Hassard, RE, the officer next senior to Chelmsford in South Africa served as its president, and its members were Lieutenant-Colonel Francis T. A. Law, RA, and Brevet Lieutenant-Colonel Arthur Harness, RA.[2] The court's proceedings were, according to Colonel William Bellairs, the DAQG, restricted to investigating 'the loss of the camp' and not the wider 'circumstances' of the disaster. That remit amounted to ascertaining from the eight individuals whose evidence was recorded what orders were given for the defence of the camp and how the orders were carried out.[3] Moreover, as Colonel Hassard explained: 'The court has refrained from giving an opinion as instructions on this point were not given to it.'[4]

In his article of February 1880 that excoriated Chelmsford's conduct of the Zululand campaign, Archibald Forbes, the combative and critical war correspondent of the *Daily News*, complained that the Court of Inquiry 'did *not* inquire into the circumstances' of the disastrous battle, and that 'the tribunal was a solemn mockery'.[5] Harness, who had taken a more active role in 'the tribunal' than had Hassard (who was on the verge of a nervous collapse and would soon surrender his command at Helpmekaar), or than the indolent Law who did as little as he could, riposted in a lengthy article published in April 1880. In it, he pointed out that 'Mr Forbes is evidently not aware that the instructions were given to the Court to inquire into the "*loss of the camp on January 22*," and *not* "into the circumstances of the disastrous affair of Isandlwana".' Harness reiterated Bellairs's statement that the duties of the court were to 'ascertain what orders were given for the defence of the camp and how these orders were carried out', and confirmed that the court 'was not called upon to give an opinion'. Indeed, as Harness understood it, the court 'was assembled solely for the purpose of assisting the General commanding in forming an opinion', that is, in 'collecting evidence for his own information'.[6]

What Chelmsford planned to do with the evidence contained in the proceedings of the court was another matter. When he forwarded the report to Stanley on 8 February,[7] he stated that the court had 'very properly abstained from giving an opinion, and I myself refrain also from making any observation or from drawing any conclusions from the evidence therein recorded'.[8] A month later, when writing to Cambridge, Chelmsford tried to rationalise this unusual reticence on his part, loftily explaining that he had 'studiously avoided giving any opinion as to the cause of the disaster at Isandlwana' because he 'considered it more becoming and more dignified to forward all the evidence that I could collect and to allow the evidence to speak for itself'.[9]

Yet Chelmsford was being intentionally disingenuous, and his apparent neutrality was a deception. Ron Lock and Peter Quantrill, when writing darkly of a deliberate cover-up to shield Chelmsford from having to take responsibility for the Isandlwana disaster, were not far off the mark.[10] It is very clear that Chelmsford's staff and close associates were quick to rally around their chief to protect his reputation – along with their own – and in the process were willing discreetly to suppress any private reservations they might have harboured about the calibre of his generalship.[11] Between them, they deployed the evidence collected at the Court of Inquiry to concoct a version of events that let Chelmsford off the hook, and were not squeamish in identifying scapegoats on whom they could pin the blame instead. They were not unsuccessful in this, for it is their version that was eventually enshrined in the War Office's official *Narrative of Field Operations*[12] – a convenient, whitewashing version that saved the honour of the British Army, but one that (as we shall see) the War Office did not finally buy.

Durnford was immediately identified as the ideal fall-guy. He was disliked by the military establishment for being too closely aligned with the colonial viewpoint after years in Natal, and for being too closely associated with the Colenso faction that was opposed to the war. Nor did it help that he had earned Chelmsford's ire for intending to take independent action at Middle Drift with No. 2 Column. And, most usefully, being dead he could not defend his actions.[13]

In Chelmsford's own holograph notes on the findings of the Court of Inquiry (from internal evidence he seems to have completed making them only in April, after the relief of Eshowe), he made no bones about identifying Durnford as the chief architect of the disaster. He took the line that Durnford had been ordered to take command of the camp, that he had ignored his instructions to remain strictly on the defensive when he moved out to confront the Zulu army, and that by doing so he had compelled Pulleine to over-extend the British defensive perimeter in his support, thus bringing on the ensuing calamity.[14] The section on 'Extended Order' in the 1877 edition of *Field Exercise and Evolution of Infantry* laid down that when a company was extended as a fighting line, another was supposed to act in support about 150 yards to the rear to throw forward supports if required. If the firing line was forced to retire, it would fall back through the supporting line, and the two would continue falling back alternately, each company covering the retreat of the other.[15] Thanks to Durnford's precipitate advance, Pulleine had not enough regulars available to make the prescribed dispositions with companies in support of the firing line. Besides which, their far-flung deployment meant they could not concentrate to defend the camp itself. That failure, Bellairs insisted in his report to Chelmsford on 5 February, 'clearly established' the cause of the disaster:

> Had Lt Colonel Pulleine not been interfered with [by Colonel Durnford] & been allowed to carry out the distinct orders to defend the camp, it cannot be doubted that the result would have been different. As it was, the camp was never defended but the companies and Battery were sent forward at long distance from the camp, more or less detached from each other & were slaughtered in detail without having been able to offer any really effectual resistance to the enemy.

Bellairs advised Chelmsford to publish the proceedings of the Court of Inquiry 'to remove many erroneous impressions since entertained'.[16] Chelmsford scarcely required any prodding, and on 27 January he had already acquainted Cambridge with his analysis of the debacle: 'The garrison of the camp appears to have been scattered about one mile and a quarter in front of the camp it was ordered to defend, and of course fought at a very great disadvantage by not being together and by having both of its flanks unprotected.'[17] Writing on the same day to Hicks Beach, Frere did not mince his words either in placing the blame for Isandlwana squarely on Durnford:

> There appears . . . to be no doubt that the Zulu force . . . took the camp by surprise. That, in disregard of Lord Chelmsford's instructions, the troops left to protect the camp were taken away from the defensive position they were in at the camp . . . [and] that they were then surrounded and fairly overwhelmed by force of numbers.[18]

Blame could conveniently be apportioned to Pulleine too, who also was no longer alive to explain his actions. But in fact, his contentious forward deployment at Isandlwana had not departed substantially from the instructions Chelmsford had issued column commanders in December 1878, a deployment very similar to that Glyn had successfully adopted at the battle of Nyumaga: guns forward with supporting flank companies of British troops thrown back; the NNC clear of each flank and to their rear in echelon; mounted infantry covering the flanks; and a reserve of British infantry.[19] Yet, in writing to Wood on 16 February, Chelmsford went back on these instructions when he declared: 'I do not believe that they [the amaZulu] would have got the better of the force left for the protection of the camp had it been brought together with its back to the precipitous sided hill, where their flanks could not have been turned and where they would have had an unlimited supply of ammunition.'[20] Of course, in retrospect it could be questioned whether an extended firing line was ever the most appropriate deployment at Isandlwana – although at the battle of Nyezane on the same day, that was precisely the deployment Pearson had employed. In any event, with hindsight, it quickly became the military orthodoxy that in like circumstances a skirmishing line was inappropriate. As Colonel T. Lyndon Bell explained in a lecture given to the Royal United Services Institution in February 1881, in both the Zulu and Afghan campaigns, it had been 'generally found impracticable or impossible to retain infantry sufficiently long in extended order to break the force of rushes of irregulars or fanatics,' and that to attempt to do so was particularly 'fatal' in a skirmishing line with 'its inability to resist a flanking dash'. In other words, a skirmishing line with intervals of at least three paces or as many as ten could not develop the necessary volume of fire at six shots a minute to stop a determined charge, and only a concentrated, all-round formation without flanks to be turned could keep its 'ground against the rush of the masses'.[21] Indeed, such had been the formation Griffith had adopted at Ibeka and Upcher at Kentani when they won their battles in the Ninth Cape Frontier War.

In his letter to Wood, Chelmsford also referred obliquely to the inadequate ammunition supply at Isandlwana. This issue would prove to be another canard that long served to help explain the British defeat without impugning the calibre of the British troops at Isandlwana. It was contended that the imperfect design of the wooden Mark V ammunition boxes made them difficult to open and so impeded the vital supply of ammunition to the firing line. In fact, the sliding lid to the ammunition box was secured by only one screw and was easy to remove. When the special screwdriver issued to quartermasters was not available, a sharp kick or blow from a rifle butt was sufficient to open the box. The real problem, as Chelmsford's letter made clear he understood, was that of the great distance between the firing line and the reserve ammunition in the camp at Isandlwana, a problem that a concentrated formation would have obviated.[22]

Integral to the inappropriate deployment of an extended firing line at Isandlwana was the presence of the NNC that made up part of it. In his notes on the findings of the Court of Inquiry, Chelmsford stated categorically that 'the Natal Native Contingent gave way, and the Zulus swarmed into the camp on the left through the gap between the two bodies of British infantry, who vainly endeavoured to retire and take up a final position inside the camp.'[23] In fact, recent research has shown that the British line was making a measured retirement on the camp and was holding its own until its flanks were turned by the Zulu advance. Its withdrawal thereupon lost cohesion, but that was the consequence of being outflanked, and not because its centre had disintegrated because of the craven conduct of the NNC.[24] But the NNC were conveniently neither white nor regular British infantry, and to load the blame for military failure on them spared the honour of the British regulars and their officers. So the official history duly declared that the NNC 'turned and fled', leaving the fatal 'gap in the line'.[25]

Besides doing his best to shift the blame for Isandlwana to a combination of Durnford's disobedience, Pulleine's faulty dispositions, the failure of the ammunition supply and the cowardice of the NNC, Chelmsford and his supporters also attempted to deflect attention away from the disastrous battle by drawing attention to the valiant defence of Rorke's Drift and its positive consequences. When forwarding Lieutenant Chard's report of 25 January on the defence of the post addressed to Colonel Glyn,[26] Chelmsford assured Stanley that:

> The defeat of the Zulus at this post and the very heavy loss suffered by them has to a great extent neutralized the effects of the disaster at Isandhlwana and it no doubt saved Natal from a serious invasion –
>
> The cool determined courage displayed by the gallant garrison is beyond all praise, and will I feel sure receive ample recognition.
>
> As at the present moment the lesson taught by this defence is most valuable I have thought it advisable to publish for general information the report in question.[27]

Yet Chelmsford's efforts to deny, or greatly minimise, his direct responsibility for Isandlwana, and indeed to downplay the disaster itself, failed to convince either the military and political establishments, or the public at large. The news of Isandlwana came as a terrible shock, although the full extent of the catastrophe was not known in Britain until mid-February. When it was, the press and the Liberal opposition in Parliament joined in a vitriolic campaign demanding the recall of both Frere and Chelmsford. Of course, as *The Times* pointed out on 12 February, there was 'little room for doubt that if Lord Chelmsford's invasion had been successful, Sir Bartle Frere's conduct would have been condoned.'[28] But, as it was, scapegoats were required on whom to fix the blame. Beaconsfield was stunned by the disaster, resented having to accede to Chelmsford's urgent request for costly reinforcement, and was privately furious with both Frere and Chelmsford for laying his administration open to searing criticism.

In the interest of the Army's reputation, and the government's credibility, Chelmsford's patron, the Duke of Cambridge, initially stood by him in public. But there was much criticism within the walls of the Horse Guards. An internal War Office memorandum was swift to ascribe blame to Chelmsford for not fortifying his camp, for not keeping in contact with the enemy, and for being decoyed by the amaZulu. And to Cambridge's frustration, Chelmsford's limp attempts at self-justification did little to throw sufficient light on what had actually happened to materially help his cause or to allay censure.[29] Chelmsford was himself uneasily aware that Cambridge would 'hardly be satisfied with the proceedings [of the Court of Inquiry] as they stand'.[30] On 6 March the AG, Major-General Sir Charles Ellice, wrote to Chelmsford requesting acceptable replies to seven searching questions on issues not covered satisfactorily by the Court of Inquiry.[31] And in an effort to compel Chelmsford to help himself, Cambridge wrote to Frere:

> We have received the dispatches [on 1 March] by the last two mails and I must honestly tell you that Chelmsford's account of the whole proceedings of 22 January have left us in much perplexity as to what actually occurred and how it all happened. This is most unfortunate . . . for the public excitement is very great and the criticism of the public of the dispatch is not favourable from the fact that so many points are omitted or left in doubt and uncertainty . . . I am most anxious to be in a

> position with the government to defend what the general has done, but we cannot do this if his dispatches do not give us the means or material for doing so . . . But pray impress upon him the necessity for writing carefully worded and good clear dispatches, for the public at home and parliament in particular require this.[32]

The problem for Chelmsford, though, was that his oblique defence depended upon obfuscation and evasion. In late February Chelmsford's HQ Staff attempted another ploy, sensing that their previous attempts to shift the responsibility for Isandlwana away from Chelmsford were failing to convince either the authorities or the public.[33] Crealock, abetted by Gossett, took the lead. On 24 February Crealock wrote to Alison, disingenuously suggesting that although 'the general is the last person to desire to shift responsibility from his shoulders,' it was Glyn who was in command of No. 3 Column in all respects.[34] This, as Archibald Forbes scathingly put it, was 'an effort to fix on Colonel Glyn the responsibility for Isandlwana, on the grounds that Lord Chelmsford was but a visitor with that officer's column – an attempt which was frustrated by the wary provision of Major Clery.'[35] Indeed, it was Clery, Glyn's principal staff officer, who, when Chelmsford's HQ presented him with a series of 'apparently ordinary enquiries as to how certain regulations had been carried out' in No. 3 Column, twigged that they were an insidious attempt, 'entered upon with a certain amount of skill', to entrap Glyn. Under Clery's guidance, the 'guileless' but 'very upright and scrupulously truthful' Glyn 'accepted responsibility for details, but declined to admit *any* responsibility *for the movement of any portion of the troops in or out of the camp*'. When Chelmsford eventually became aware of his HQ Staff's shabby manoeuvring, he was deeply embarrassed and, to his credit, hastened to disassociate himself. He wrote to Cambridge on 27 March assuring him that he had 'no desire to cast any blame upon Colonel Glyn'.[36] According to witnesses, he hauled Crealock over the coals for not behaving as a gentleman, and sent Glyn 'a private letter . . . practically repudiating what had been attempted'.[37] All in all, it had been an unsavoury and dishonourable affair. As Captain J. F. Maurice later expressed it: 'Crealock certainly comes out in a very unpleasant light and I am afraid deservedly so in some particulars. The attempt to turn on

Glyn, after all power had been taken out of his hands, was as feeble as it was unfair.'[38]

Meanwhile, in Britain the growing political row over Isandlwana was leading up to a major parliamentary debate over the war in Zululand. But before it could take place, both Frere and Chelmsford received formidable support from a highly influential quarter. Directly after breakfast on 11 February, Queen Victoria received a telegram from Colonel Stanley 'telling of a great and most unfortunate disaster at the Cape, or rather more Natal'. She was initially stunned by the news. 'How this could happen we cannot yet imagine,' she admitted in her journal. Nevertheless, she quickly rallied, and through her Private Secretary Major-General Sir Henry Ponsonby requested Stanley to telegraph both Frere and Chelmsford expressing her continuing confidence in them. With regards to Chelmsford, she wished Stanley to assure him 'that she sympathises most sincerely with him in the dreadful loss . . . and that her Majesty places entire confidence in him and in her troops to maintain our honour and our good name'.[39] Frere and Chelmsford gratefully grasped at this royal support, Chelmsford writing effusively to Cambridge that 'I cannot tell you with what feelings of pride and gratitude I received the gracious message from Her Majesty.'[40] The pair of them, along with Frere's politically astute wife and daughters, bombarded the Queen with further missives thanking her for her support, and stressing the political and strategic importance of Rorke's Drift as vindicating their war against the amaZulu.[41]

The Prince of Wales also jumped into the fray, making clear that he accepted the line that Durnford alone was responsible for the debacle at Isandlwana. During the course of the heated debate in Parliament he wrote to Lady Frere, assuring her that 'I have however never ceased exonerating Lord Chelmsford from the blame which many here attach to him. Alas! He who fell and led the attack was in my mind the only culprit.'[42]

It was not, though, that the Queen was entirely uncritical of how Frere and Chelmsford had managed the Zulu business. But she robustly resisted the mounting demands for their recall because she felt compelled to defend two loyal servants of the Crown who she felt were in danger of being abandoned by a craven government. She kept up the pressure on Beaconsfield, who tetchily informed her on 12 March that 'with the exception of Sir Michael Hicks Beach' his 'whole Cabinet had wanted to yield to the clamour of the Press and Clubs for the recall of

Lieutenant-General Chelmsford'.[43] But instead, it fudged the matter and unsatisfactorily neither sacked nor backed Frere and Chelmsford, leaving the Queen rightly, but uncharacteristically, displeased with her favourite prime minister.[44]

Before the debate on the Zulu War opened in the Lords on 25 March, Hicks Beach pre-empted the anticipated attack on Frere by reprimanding him in an extraordinarily contradictory document. On the one hand, he deplored that Frere had begun a war without the government's 'full knowledge and sanction' and against his specific instruction to avoid doing so. On the other hand, as the Colonial Secretary assured Frere, the government had 'no desire to withdraw, in the present crisis of affairs, the confidence hitherto reposed in you'.[45] The government's pledge of support would not save Frere from savage criticism in the forthcoming parliamentary debate, but for the present he was secure in his office. Chelmsford, also facing parliamentary censure, had no such guarantee. Prefiguring what was to come, on 14 March J. Edward Jenkins, MP, rose in the Commons to enquire whether the government was going to place the 'supreme command of the forces in South Africa in other hands?' since 'It is the almost universal opinion that the conduct of Lord Chelmsford shows great military incapacity'.[46]

The news of Isandlwana had indeed stunned the country, and the press struggled to find an explanation for the disaster. In doing so, it generally followed party political lines, the Liberal press condemning the unjust and unnecessary war, and the Conservative papers emphasising the need to restore Britain's military prestige. Where there was consensus was in mercilessly questioning Chelmsford's competence as a general in editorials, cartoons and biting parodies.[47] Cambridge was very aware of the power of the domestic press fuelled by the reports of war correspondents and by the deluge of letters sent to the newspapers by soldiers serving in Zululand and giving their version of events.[48] As public criticism of Chelmsford mounted, the Duke (as we have seen) repeatedly encouraged him to state his case in carefully crafted despatches aimed at reassuring the general public and Parliament.[49] Distance and poor communications, however, for a time saved Chelmsford from the coming daily mortification of learning what was being said of his military incapacity in the printed media and in Parliament. Evidence is lacking, but his immediate family would not have been spared. His four surviving sons, the eldest eleven and the youngest five years of age, probably would have learned little, but Adria, Lady Chelmsford would have been only too aware that her husband's name was being dragged through the mud, as would his two sisters and three brothers. We can imagine that Chelmsford was profoundly relieved that his ambitious and demanding father had not lived to witness his public humiliation.

The Marquess of Lansdowne moved a resolution in the House of Lords on 25 March deploring the unnecessary war begun without the approval of the government and regretting that Frere should remain in office. After a reasonably decorous debate, the resolution was defeated by 156 votes to 61.[50] On 27 March Sir Charles W. Dilke moved an identical motion of censure in the House of Commons.[51] Alongside Frere, Chelmsford immediately came under Liberal attack that was not deflected by J. Chamberlain Starkie MP's distinctly weak defence that 'the accusation against Lord Chelmsford . . . amounted to this – he had failed to take the necessary precautions in an enemy's country. He had paid dearly for that error, and no one imagined he would be likely to repeat his mistake.'[52] Nor was he, but that was hardly the point.

It was during the second night of the debate that discussion of Chelmsford's culpability became really nasty. Sir Robert Peel reminded the House that on 4 January Frere had given 'the entire responsibility' of military policy in Zululand to Chelmsford, 'and that policy . . . as we all know, resulted in the great disaster of Isandlana'. Despite angry interjections from the Tory benches, Peel insisted that soldiers were killed at Isandlwana

> through the gross incompetence of a General upon whose head rests the blood of these men ['No, no!'] Upon whose head it rests, until he has been tried by court martial . . . People in this country are not surprised that the spirits of Lord Chelmsford are depressed at this disaster . . . He is not the first General by a great many who has been out-generalled, out-manoeuvred, surprised and defeated; but I venture to say he is the first General who has ever been surprised with compliments on the bloody results of a defeat.[53]

Peel was making ironic allusion to Chelmsford's defenders in the House, many of them fellow officers. Sir Charles Russell rose in a lengthy speech to 'defend 'an old comrade and an absent man', going on to stand up for his military performance and to draw attention to his distinguished military record and 'great capacity'.[54] Russell was supported by Evelyn Ashley who acidly added that, 'In cases like the disaster at Isandlana the tendency was to find a scapegoat, and the one selected on this occasion, he regretted to say, was Lord Chelmsford.'[55] But it was Colonel Stanley, the Secretary of State for War, who, on behalf of the government and the Horse Guards, rose to 'vindicate, as far as possible, the character of an officer whose reputation I believe has thus been unduly aspersed', a 'chivalrous' officer, moreover, of whose friendship of twenty-five years, he assure the House, he had 'never been more proud'. Stanley proceeded to dilate on Chelmsford's 'brilliant services' that had 'earned the love, respect, and esteem' of those with whom he had served. In an aside intended to protect the Horse Guards that had selected him for his command, he reminded the House that 'the representations of officers who have been his [Chelmsford's] superiors have invariably been in his favour'. Stanley drew his peroration to his end with the ringing declaration that 'If an officer were to be selected for the command in South Africa, Lord Chelmsford would still be the man to select.'[56]

It may be questioned how many members on the Government benches – let alone in the Cabinet – would honestly have agreed with Stanley; certainly, the opposition members did not. Nevertheless, when the House divided after the third day of debate at 2 a.m. on 30 March, Dilke's motion was defeated by 306 votes to 246.[57] Frere continued as High Commissioner, and Chelmsford was not recalled. But their reputations had taken a terrible, prolonged and very public battering, and Beaconsfield's administration and the Horse Guards had also been bruised and embarrassed in the process. Neither body was left in any mood to tolerate further failures by the two men who remained in office purely on sufferance.

Frere and Chelmsford could still count on royal patronage, however. A few days after the Commons debate on South Africa had ended, on 4 April, the Prince of Wales wrote to Frere 'earnestly' hoping that, despite all that had been said against him, he would 'stick' to his 'post and not think of resigning'. The Prince sympathetically added: 'Poor Lord Chelmsford has also come in for his share of abuse at home, but I feel convinced that we shall soon hear of a brilliant victory that will soon alter the tone of those military men who live at home at ease.'[58] His Royal

Highness would not have known that, two days before, Chelmsford had indeed secured a victory in the field against the amaZulu at Gingindlovu. But whether it would prove enough to redeem his reputation or confirm him in his command, remained to be seen.

CHAPTER 26

The Eshowe Relief Column, March–April 1879

SINCE 11 FEBRUARY NO RUNNER from the British forts at the lower Thukela had made it through to Fort Eshowe, but on 20 March one finally arrived carrying a despatch informing Colonel Pearson that the Eshowe Relief Column would start its advance on 29 March.[1] Besides heavy rains, several other factors had delayed the start of the operation.

Firstly, Chelmsford was prudently prepared to wait until the disembarkation at Durban on 20 March of six companies of the 3/60th (The King's Royal Rifle Corps) Regiment of Foot completed the reinforcements he considered necessary for the relief.[2] The 3/60th joined the column assembling near Fort Pearson that by 23 March also comprised the 57th, the 91st Highlanders, five companies of the 99th, two companies of the 2/3rd, a Naval Brigade made up of sailors drawn from HMS *Shah*, *Tenedos* and *Boadicea*, and the 4th and 5th Battalions of the NNC. In addition, there were 150 white and 130 African mounted troops in several small units, as well as 150 Native Foot Scouts. The total strength of the column came to 3,390 white troops and 2,280 African ones with two 9-pounders, four 24-pounder rocket tubes and two Gatling guns.[3]

Secondly, there was the question of transport for the assembling column. In the weeks following Isandlwana, Chelmsford had unavoidably found little time to spare from his other concerns to devote to the transport requirements of his forces. Yet it is also evident that he had somewhat petulantly distanced himself from the problems of the understaffed Commissariat and Transport Department and had left it to the touchy Commissary-General Strickland and his overworked colleagues to muddle along as best they could without his interference, cavalierly writing off the transport system as being in a state of disarray.[4] However, when

Chelmsford learned in mid-March that Pearson's food supplies would be depleted by 4 April and that the relief of Fort Eshowe was urgent,[5] he recollected himself and called on his many years as a highly placed staff officer to good effect. Even so, he experienced many difficulties and frustrations in assembling sufficient transport and the necessary supplies, querulously complaining to Wood that 'An ox-waggon transport is enough to destroy the reputation of any number of commanders!'[6] The problems he was encountering led to his telegraphing on 25 March to Hicks Beach requesting the power in future to impress all the transport he needed from the colonists,[7] a prerogative destined to raise a fresh quarrel with Bulwer who was determined to protect Natal interests.

Once Chelmsford had assembled the relief column and the necessary transport and supplies, he was then faced with planning how the operation was to be successfully carried out. From his HQ Camp on the Lower Thukela, he wrote nervously to Stanley on 25 March, seeking justifications in advance should he be met with failure:

> A force moving . . . with ox transport through a difficult country is heavily hampered, if attacked determinedly by large numbers, and whilst feeling every confidence in the ability, courage and determination of those under my command I trust that should our efforts fall short of what is no doubt, expected of us, that circumstances may be duly taken under consideration.[8]

Indeed, Chelmsford faced real enough challenges. To move rapidly he needed to reduce his transport and supply requirements and decided to take no tents (except one or two bell tents for hospital purposes) and only ten days' provisions. Even so, ninety-four wagons and forty-four carts were required, and his advance could not be as swift as he had hoped.[9] Moreover, a convoy of wagons and carts was extremely vulnerable to attack while on the march. Chelmsford evidently gave the matter considerable thought, and in his best bureaucratic military style he caused to be published the snappily titled *Special Instructions Regarding the Management of Ox Transport on the Line of March, and for Conducting the Line of March When Troops March with Ox Wagon Transport, and for Forming Wagon Laagers.* The printed copy in his papers is heavily annotated in his own hand, likely in response to his practical experiences during the Eshowe campaign, and indicates that he continued to fuss and tinker over how best to handle a wagon convoy securely.[10] The critical point in *Special Instructions* was that (as the battle of Nyezane had demonstrated) it was 'essential' that 'the length of a column on the march should . . . be kept as short as possible, and that the troops should be so distributed as to be ready to act in *compact formation* whenever required'.[11]

Related to this pamphlet and underpinning its main points, was the memorandum he drew up on the eve of the advance providing instructions for his officers on how the campaign was to be conducted – instructions that heavily reflected the lessons of Isandlwana. Whatever else might be said of him, Chelmsford cannot be charged with not learning from his mistakes. There were to be no more vulnerable skirmishing lines, and he insisted that 'Companies must be held together in close order – Files must loosen out, but will not be extended.' With the issue of the faulty distribution of ammunition at Isandlwana firmly in mind, he laid down that 'Each wagon and cart with the convoy must have some ammunition boxes placed on it in such a position as to be easily got at – The regimental reserve boxes must have the screw of the lid taken out.' The memorandum also contained detailed instructions on how the column was to conduct its march: 'The troops will be under arms at 4 am every morning, and the column will prepare for its further advance, so soon as it is daylight, and so soon as the scouts (which should be pushed forward when the force gets under arms) have reported that the enemy is not in force in the immediate neighbourhood.' If attacked, the column was immediately to close up in defence. When the column halted after the day's march, Chelmsford specified that 'The force will form a square laager of the wagons every night with a shelter trench around it, 9 ft from the wagons, & will bivouack, as far as possible in the order of march – The European portion of the force will bivouack between the wagons and the shelter trench; the natives, cattle and horse will be inside the laager.' At night 'outlying sentries' with 'Native scouts' were to be 'pushed forward at least a mile'. Finally, no bugle sounds were to be permitted 'except the "alarm" which will be the signal for every man to stand to his arms'.[12]

The emphasis in Chelmsford's memorandum on forward scouting and sentries was another response to the deficiencies of the Isandlwana campaign, and it is for this reason that he recruited the Native Foot Scouts, otherwise known as Dunn's Scouts. John Dunn was the quintessential transfrontiersman. He had entered Zululand as a hunter and trader in 1853 and later succeeded in gaining King Cetshwayo's confidence, becoming his adviser and supplier of firearms. Cetshwayo rewarded him liberally with a large chiefdom in south-eastern Zululand. In 1878 Dunn strongly cautioned Cetshwayo against risking war with Britain, and this led to his being accused of treachery by other members of the royal council. Fearing for his life, in December 1878 Dunn crossed over into Natal with his adherents and livestock. There he intended to sit out the war as a neutral. But Chelmsford would be advancing to Eshowe through Dunn's erstwhile chiefdom, and his adherents were naturally very familiar with the terrain and could provide effective forward reconnaissance. It was essential, therefore, to induce them to join the Eshowe Relief Column.[13] Chelmsford sent Captain Molyneux of his Staff to tell Dunn that the General wished to see him, and his wooing of Dunn exemplifies how his charm and courteous manners could be deployed to cloak his ruthlessness in getting his way.

Molyneux found Dunn a 'handsome, powerful man . . . a perfect rider and rifle-shot . . . [who] had the best of saddlery, breeches, boots and other clothes' imported from Britain where he had never been. Except for his broad-brimmed wideawake hat, he could have been 'taken for an English country gentleman'.[14] Apprised of Chelmsford's desire to meet him, Dunn set off for HQ and was met by the General on the road. According to Dunn's account, Chelmsford politely got off his horse and insisted on joining him in his horse-drawn trap because he wanted 'some private conversation'. Once seated next to Dunn, Chelmsford admitted confidentially that 'he had been greatly misled by people who knew nothing of Zululand, and that he would be glad if [Dunn] would give him [his] advice and assistance'. Won over, Dunn promised to raise 150 scouts from among his own men, with these each to be issued with an identifying red handkerchief to be worn around his head.

Having spoken with Dunn and been impressed by him, Chelmsford saw how useful he himself could prove during the coming operations. Chelmsford therefore wrote to him on 25 March, asking Dunn to accompany him during the relief of Eshowe 'as an advisor', making clear that he did not expect him to 'do any work' with the scouts. Chelmsford backed up his polite letter by sending the rebarbative Crealock to 'induce' him to comply. Dunn entertained considerable qualms about taking up arms against his old patron, Cetshwayo, but during his long interview with Chelmsford on 26 March, the General applied the carrot and the stick, and pressured him by saying:

> Well, Mr. Dunn, I feel sure you can be of much service to me, which, if you will render, you will receive the thanks of Her Majesty's Government, to say nothing of my own personally, but if you do not, you know what will be thought of you for withholding the assistance you can give, and you can expect nothing after the war is over.[15]

Given the night to mull the matter over, it is understandable that Dunn decided nothing was to be gained by remaining neutral and that much was to be lost by doing so. The next day Chelmsford was 'very much pleased' when Dunn indicated he was willing to comply.[16] He therefore joined Drummond who, alongside him, was officially appointed to the Intelligence Department on Chelmsford's staff.

Chelmsford had assumed command of the Eshowe Relief Column assembled at Fort Pearson on 23 March. As Mathews notes, until the four major-generals arrived in Natal, there was no suitable alternative to Chelmsford himself as commander in the field, and he could not afford to delay his advance further on account of the dwindling supplies in Fort Eshowe. Yet there can also be little doubt (despite his nagging fear of failure) that Chelmsford was eager to disprove his critics by leading the relief column to victory in battle.[17] And indeed, in his official despatch to Stanley describing the battle of Gingindlovu and relief of Eshowe (a document that hums with a deep sense of personal vindication) he would lay considerable emphasis on the fact that the operation has been under his 'personal command'.[18]

While Chelmsford was completing his arrangements, not only troops were assembling at Fort Pearson. At the time of the outbreak of the war, only one of the influential London dailies, the *Standard*, had considered it worthwhile to send out a war correspondent. Charles Norris-Newman, who also acted as a stringer for local South African newspapers that drew in addition on anonymous soldiers with the forces and on well-placed colonists to file vivid, detailed reports, had consequently scooped his rivals by being the only British journalist present during the Isandlwana campaign. But, after that disaster, the war in Zululand had become international news, Britain's military reputation had been brought under scrutiny, and Norris-Newman and local correspondents no longer had the field to themselves. Consequently, the reinforcements requested by Chelmsford had been accompanied by a small flock of professional war correspondents from the leading British newspapers. As Norris-Newman ruefully put it, during March 'many accessions had been made to the noble army of "Specials"' including Francis Francis of *The Times*, Melton Prior of the *Illustrated London News*, Charles Edwin Fripp of the *Graphic*, and W. Peace of the *Daily Telegraph,* later joined by Phil Robinson from Afghanistan.[19]

These Victoriawar correspondents and artists, slung about with military-style paraphernalia and flaunting foreign decorations, were known respectively as 'special correspondents' or 'special artists'. They formed a glamorous, self-conscious elite among journalists, closely bonded by their shared wartime dangers and hardships. War news greatly increased newspaper sales, so editors were prepared to bear the heavy costs of supporting 'specials' with their hugely expensive telegraphed reports or field sketches that required engraving for the printing process. Smaller and provincial newspapers who could not afford 'specials' were out of the hectic and costly race to get the news home before competitors, and made do with reprinting the despatches that appeared in the major papers. Whether first- or second-hand, their reports and images ensured that news of Britain's colonial campaigns was published in the fullest detail, bringing them vividly home to an increasingly insatiable public. Written for civilians and armchair critics at home, the nature of the reportage wired back by the 'specials' reveals as much about popular culture in Britain as it does about military events in distant lands. Even so, comment by the 'specials' was usually informed, trenchant and sometimes highly critical, but that was the inevitable consequence of a free press in Britain and its colonies. Possible military concerns at the potential security risks of uncensored reporting were normally brushed aside, not least because foes in 'small wars' were hardly equipped to pick up intelligence from British newspapers.

In the field, 'specials' enjoyed an ill-defined quasi-officer status. They were often made honorary members of officers' messes and tended to relate closely to the officer ethos. Thus placed, they would have learned from companionable officers how they rated the performance of their commander. As for their own relations with the commander in question, that tended to depend on the extent to which their reporting was laudatory or unfavourable. Ambitious officers such as Wolseley cynically but wisely cultivated the 'specials' to ensure a favourable press that brought him into the public eye, boosted his reputation and furthered his career. In return, he cooperated fully with those embedded in his military expeditions, even if he privately deplored them. However – as in Chelmsford's case – when commanders were subjected to stinging criticism by war correspondents, they generally responded with hostility and non-cooperation. It was also true that the military establishment tended to close ranks against insolent journalistic upstarts when one of their own was too severely pilloried. Even so, it was difficult to shrug off a negative public image once it was established in the popular press, and (as Chelmsford was to discover) it could prove very damaging to career prospects.[20]

In preparation for the advance of the Eshowe Relief Column, Chelmsford ordered his forces stationed along the Thukela and Mzinyathi Rivers to mount demonstrations to create a diversion, and (despite his assurances to Bulwer that they would not) to raid where feasible into Zululand. On 24 March Major A. C. Twentyman demonstrated at Middle Drift and raided across the Thukela on 2 and 3 April. In his turn, Captain G. A. Lucas demonstrated on 27 March along the Lower Thukela.[21] The amaZulu, noting the increased British activity, realised that an attempt to relieve Eshowe must be in preparation. They accordingly strengthened their forces blockading Fort Eshowe until there were more than 10,000 men under Somopho kaZikhala, the *induna* of the emaNgweni *ikhanda*, concentrating in the vicinity. Thanks to the indefatigable work of the spies deployed by Drummond and Dunn, Chelmsford had a good knowledge of Zulu dispositions around Eshowe and of the probable number of warriors he would have to face once they had concentrated to oppose him.[22]

Chelmsford and his staff crossed over from Fort Pearson on the morning of 29 March and joined the column that had assembled at Fort Tenedos on the Zulu bank the previous day.[23] Crealock was acting as his senior staff officer since Colonel Bellairs had been left behind in Durban to perform his duties as DQMG. The advance immediately commenced with the column divided into two supporting brigades. Determined to rectify the deficiencies that had led to the Isandlwana disaster, Chelmsford not only insisted on effective forward scouting by Drummond's and Dunn's men, but threw out mounted patrols under the command of

Major Percy Barrow that were effective in shrouding the movement of the column from the amaZulu so they were left unsure of its strength and intentions. On the advice of John Dunn, Chelmsford followed a route much closer to the coast than had Pearson in order to keep to more open terrain in order to avoid being ambushed as No. 1 Column had been at Nyezane. While on the march, Chelmsford painstakingly laagered every night according to the procedures he had laid down in his memorandum.

Heavy rain had started falling on 27 March, and it continued to pour every night. For lack of tents, the soldiers slept miserably in the open between the laagered wagons and the surrounding shelter trench or, as Chelmsford himself did, picked out the driest spot under a wagon that he could find.[24] Without fresh dry clothes to change into, the men remained wet through while on the march. The rain hampered the column's progress, and on 29 March it advanced only ten miles from Fort Tenedos, laagering at the Nyoni River. On 30 March the column moved forward only another nine miles to the right bank of the flooded Matigulu River and laagered there. All of 31 March was spent bringing the column across the fast-flowing river, each wagon requiring thirty-two instead of the usual sixteen oxen to pull it across the swollen stream and up its steep banks. A fresh laager was finally established a mile and a half beyond the Matigulu. Dunn observed these laborious proceeding with a sardonic, and over-critical eye. He concluded that Chelmsford was 'a thorough gentleman and a good and brave soldier, but no General' because Dunn assumed that 'his personal pluck led him to have no regard for the safety of his men', carelessly selecting 'any spot for a night encampment without studying the surroundings'. This assessment seems particularly unfair because it appears that Chelmsford only ever hit on the site for a laager on Dunn's advice. However, there may have been more heft to Dunn's criticism when he charged that Chelmsford, in contravention of his own *Special Instructions*, 'did not keep his men sufficiently together on the line of march, so much so that if the Zulus had been properly led they would have given us much trouble, and cut many a column up'.[25]

If that were indeed the case, it is fortunate for Chelmsford and the men he was leading that the amaZulu were not yet sufficiently concentrated to make such an attempt. On 1 April the column struggled forward another six miles, halting (on Dunn's recommendation) on a slight eminence about a mile south of the Nyezane stream and the burnt-out remains of the kwaGingindlovu *ikhanda* Pearson had torched on 21 January. There was a belt of bush and high reeds on either side of the Nyezane, and the undulating and boggy surrounding countryside was covered with very high grass, interspersed with clumps of palms and thick undergrowth that would provide excellent cover for the amaZulu should they attack. The entrenched laager Chelmsford ordered to be established on the low knoll was in sight of Fort Eshowe. Contact though 'flash signalling' was at once established with the beleaguered garrison confirming that relief was imminent – provided that the large Zulu forces concentrating to oppose the Eshowe Relief Column could be repulsed.

CHAPTER 27

The Battle of Gingindlovu, 2 April 1879

A HEAVY THUNDERSTORM CAME ON while the British laager was being manoeuvred into position, and the surrounding shelter trench, 156 yards square and 15 yards in front of the wagons, was completed only after dark. Rain continued to pour down throughout the night. The laager itself, formed of carts and wagons, was about 130 yards square to give sufficient room inside for the 2,000 draught oxen and 300 horses with the column. Molyneux described how this livestock, along with the men inside the laager, churned the very sodden ground into a horrible, stinking compost.[1] Sleep in these conditions was impossible for the defenders.

During the day and evening of 1 April the amaZulu previously bivouacked around Eshowe under the overall command of Somopho kaZikhala steadily concentrated in the vicinity of the laager until they numbered between 10,000 and 11,000 men. Any assault on it would be spearheaded by the seasoned *amabutho* that had been bivouacked at the old oNdini *ikhanda* some fifteen miles north-east of Fort Eshowe. However, they arrived in the main Zulu camp in the hills five miles to the north of the laager only well after dark. They were tired and hungry and in no state to launch an immediate attack. The Zulu commanders decided to hold off until the following morning when they intended to employ their traditional enveloping tactics which they felt the broken terrain at the battle of Nyezane had disrupted. The plan was that they would not push home their attack until they had the laager surrounded on every side.[2]

The Zulu campfires on the hills to the north were clearly visible to the defenders of the laager. And even though there seemed no imminent danger of a Zulu attack during the course of the night, tension rose.

At midnight Chelmsford anxiously ordered the shelter trench to be strengthened. Then, between 2 a.m. and 3 a.m. Chelmsford and two of his staff went quietly around the laager on a tour of inspection. Here and there he made trifling changes and explained his plans to the more senior officers. On the way he made known that he was 'extremely satisfied with how his arrangements had been carried out', and 'the low murmur of gratification, which even discipline could not suppress, showed how much his men were devoted to their chief'.[3]

After a night of incessant rain, the morning of 2 April broke surprisingly clear, although a dense mist still hung in the valley of the Nyezane stream. The British stood to arms at 4 a.m. in accordance with Chelmsford's 'invariable rule'. At 5.45 a.m. scouts reported the amaZulu to be advancing to the attack. At 6 a.m. the amaZulu to the north on the far side of the Nyezane, and those on top of Misi Hill five miles to the west, came in sight of the laager. Swarms of their skirmishers professionally drove in the British picquets and mounted scouts.[4]

A strong Zulu column crossed the Nyezane with their left division advancing at the north-eastern corner of the laager where it could take advantage of some dead ground, and with the right division making for the northern face. Slightly later, a somewhat weaker column came forward from north of Misi Hill west of the laager, one part of the column threatening its western face and the other its southern side. Two large bodies of reserves waited on the hills beyond the Nyezane. The two Zulu columns deployed in open order and at the double, and within ten minutes of being sighted were formed in a classic crescent around the northern, western and southern sides of the laager. Once the enveloping Zulu crescent was in position, the amaZulu broke into three distinct lines and advanced skirmishing towards the laager in knots and groups of between five to ten men, creeping up under the cover of the long grass, bushes and anthills in splendidly disciplined style. Captain Alan Hart thought the Zulu approach 'the most splendid piece of skirmishing eye ever beheld'.[5] At a distance of about 750 yards, they opened up a brisk but ineffective fire. Contrary to British expectations gleaned from Fynney's manual on the Zulu army published on Chelmsford's orders,[6] they did not wear their elaborate ceremonial dress, but were stripped for action to their loin-covers, just as (unbeknown to the troops in the laager) the bulk of the Zulu army had been four days earlier when it attacked Wood at Khambula.

The Eshowe Relief Column was ready for the Zulu onslaught, and Chelmsford had prepared his ground well. The troops manned the enclosing shelter trench while marksmen and colonial wagon-drivers – many of whom were experienced hunters – were stationed along the tops of the wagons and carts forming the laager. Reserve troops remained within the laager ready to move forward to reinforce the firing line when required. John Dunn joined these snipers and his accurate shooting would prove deadly that day. Two 24-pounder rockets tubes reinforced the north-west corner of the shelter-trench, a Gatling gun the north-east corner, two nine-pounder guns the south-west corner and a Gatling gun and two 24-pounder rocket tubes the south-east corner. The 4th Battalion, NNC (800 men) and the 5th Battalion NNC (1,200 men) remained squatting in a block inside the wagon laager, and the personnel of the Medical Department also took cover there. However, Dunn's Scouts were stationed between the wagons and the troops manning the south face of the shelter-trench. Six companies of the 3/60th held the north face, flanked to left and right by detachments of Royal Marines from HMS *Boadicea* and *Shah* and two companies of the Naval Brigade contingent from HMS *Boadicea*. The east face was held by seven companies of the 57th with two companies of *Shah*'s Naval Brigade on their right. Eight companies of the 91st Highlanders were ranged along the south face. Five companies of the 99th held the west face, flanked on their left by two companies of *Shah*'s Naval Brigade, and on their right by two companies of the 2/3rd Regiment. Two troops of Mounted Infantry and the Natal Volunteer Guides (a unit drawn from volunteers among the NMV) were stationed inside the north face of the laager; while No. 1 Troop, Natal Horse (made up of NCOs of the disbanded 3rd Regiment, NNC), No. 2 Troop, Jantze's Native Horse (raised in March), and Mafunzi's Mounted Natives (raised in February) were stationed likewise inside the east face.[7] Chelmsford's orders to the troops were few and simple: 'Stand to your arms – saddle up – no independent firing – volley by companies when they are within three hundred yards.'[8]

This indeed was a soldiers' battle, and once the fighting began there was little for Chelmsford to do. He would be called upon to make several tactical decisions during the course of the action, but for the main part it fell on his officers to control and direct their men's fire. Idiosyncratically still wearing his red nightcap, he paced on foot around the trenches encouraging the men, directing their fire and telling them to fire steadily and low. As he made his rounds he gave 'an occasional kind and complimentary word when a particularly good shot was made or an especial coolness was observed'.[9] His AMS and two ADCs followed their chief on horseback, a dangerous position considering the wild nature of the shooting. Crealock was hit in the arm by a spent bullet which he later found among his clothes, Molyneux had two horses shot under him, and Berkeley Milne had a bullet pass through his sleeve, grazing his arm. Not that Chelmsford was entirely out of harm's way even on foot, and the unfortunate Lieutenant George C. F. Johnson of the 99th, a scion of the Anglo-Irish Ascendancy and, ironically, his regiment's Instructor of Musketry, was shot dead through the breast while sniping only a yard or two away from the General.[10]

The Zulu assault on the north-eastern and northern faces of the laager developed first because the attacks on the western and southern face, where the terrain offered less cover, were more hesitant. As the amaZulu converged on the laager their concentrations became denser and therefore more vulnerable to the British fire. The Gatling guns began the engagement at 1,100 yards, and firing became general when the amaZulu were 450–350 yards from the laager. The amaZulu doggedly held their ground, taking cover behind fallen comrades but, despite several desperate charges, never came closer than twenty yards from the shelter trench, and were never able to break through the wall of concentrated British fire. That was so, even though the British fire was not always nearly as effective and accurate as it might have been because of the inexperience of many of the short-service troops, especially the men of the 3/60th holding the laager's north face.

The blond, curly-haired 23-year-old Lieutenant A. C. Baskerville 'Bunny' Mynors, an old Etonian whose first battle this was, found that 'Our men were awfully frightened and nervous at first, could not even speak and shivered from funk so we – the officers [of the 3/60th] – had enough to do to keep the men cool.'[11] Indeed, the wavering men of the 3/60th were as untried as the young 'Bunny' Mynors. The battalion had been quartered at Colchester in Essex and was significantly under-strength. Numbers had had to be made up with raw recruits, and although the 3/60th included several senior NCOs, most of the men in the ranks were between the ages of nineteen and twenty-three.[12] The heavy Zulu fire, even though it was

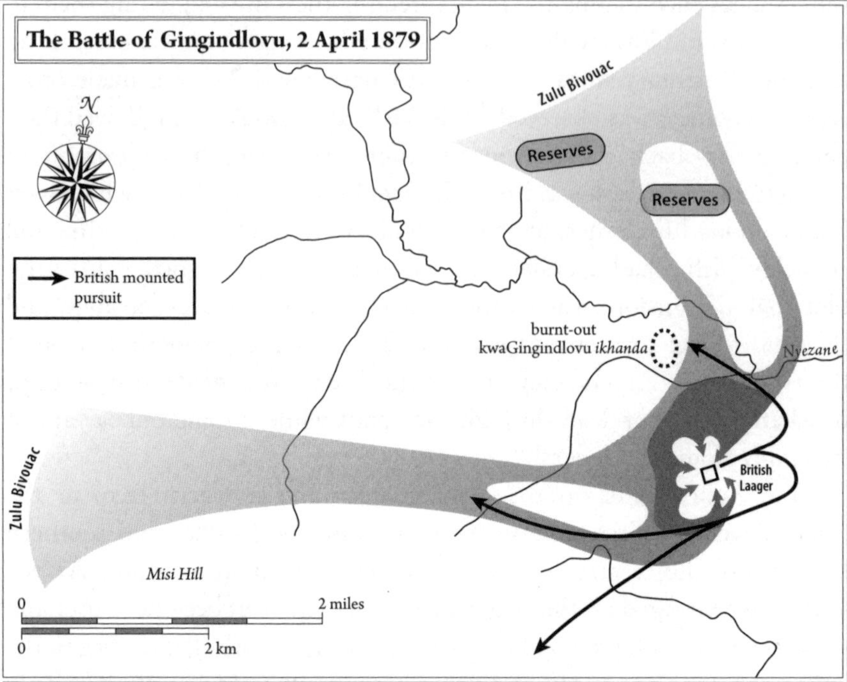

The Battle of Gingindlovu, 2 April 1879

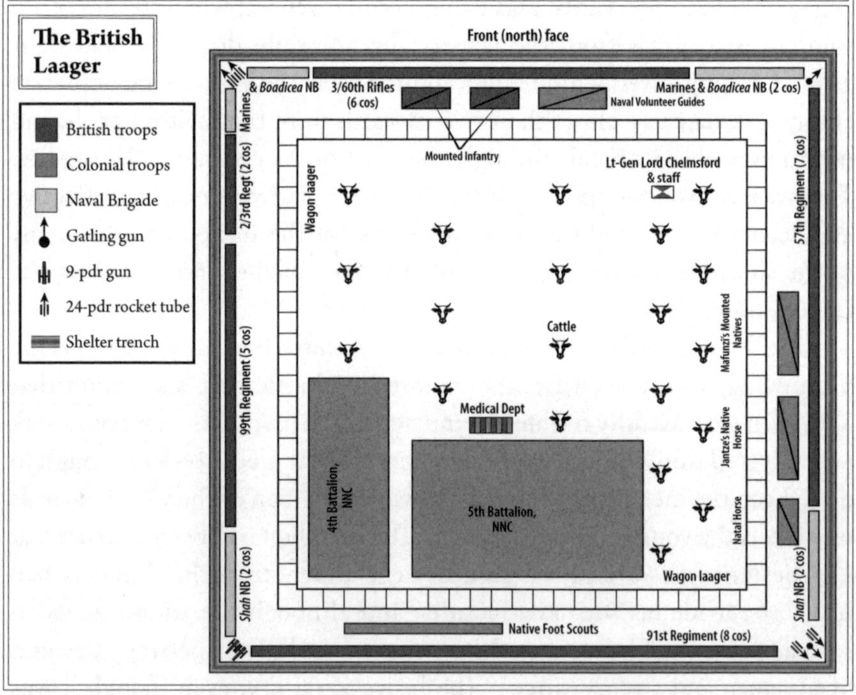

The British Laager

high and inaccurate, was enough to severely unsettle the men who found the three-foot rampart of the shelter trench was only just high enough to provide cover for a man kneeling. Their morale was further shaken when their commander, Lieutenant-Colonel Francis Northey, an old Etonian and ardent cricketer, was mortally wounded in the head.[13] Hamilton-Browne (who had joined the relief column) observed that 'the half-baked nervous boys' became 'worse than wobbly'.[14] For a moment it seemed the square might cave in and the men started firing wildly. But the officers (as Mynors reported) managed to steady them. They stood their ground and the crisis passed.[15]

The unreliable deportment of the 3/60th under fire contrasted adversely with that of the disciplined sailors and Marines of the Naval Brigade either side of them, and fuelled the debate about Cardwell's short-service soldiers. Hamilton-Browne, for one, reflected that the engagement 'caused every officer, of any experience, who witnessed the action, grave anxiety, as the conduct of the young troops engaged was far from creditable and their behaviour [as we shall see] did not improve'.[16] The 'special', Norris-Newman, stoutly contended, though, that 'The firing in our ranks was throughout very fair, taken all in all, and considering the many young soldiers.' Nevertheless, he had to concede that 'The officers were especially earnest in restraining the men from too rapid firing.'[17] John Dunn, perched with his rifle on an ammunition wagon (a buck wagon, that is, one without a tent), noticed that the 3/60th had their long-range sights up. With the contempt of a professional hunter for the inferior marksmanship of soldiers, he noticed that they were 'firing wildly in any direction', and that the bullets of their volleys were striking the ground far beyond their mark. He urgently called He urgently called on Chelmsford to order the lowering of their sights since their officers were failing to do so, and the men's firing then became more effective. Even so, Dunn noticed that when his own sights were down to 100 yards, the soldiers still had theirs up to 300 yards. Overall, Dunn reflected that he 'was much disappointed in the shooting of the soldiers. Their sole object seemed to be to get rid of ammunition or firing so many rounds per minute at anything, it didn't matter what.'[18]

And certainly, there could be no denying that even among the most experienced soldiers manning the laager there was a dearth of good marksmen. That meant independent firing was ineffectual and only controlled volley-firing answered. Molyneux noted approvingly that when the 57th stationed along the east face became engaged, their volleys 'rang clear as if they had been at Aldershot'. With the short-service soldiers of the 3/60th in mind, he sourly wished that 'every regiment had possessed such seasoned men'.[19] Yet, volley firing, even when well conducted, was not properly suited to stop an enemy rapidly advancing in skirmishing order, and (as we have seen) rifles were in any case often incorrectly sighted and fired high. And if the shooting of the troops was frankly disappointing, that of the rockets and guns seems to have been little better. Only the Gatling guns were handled really successfully. During the battle they fired 1,200 rounds, while the 9-pounders fired about forty rounds of case and shrapnel. The average number of shots fired per regular soldier was 6.2, while the average for the whole force including the irregulars was ten. These figures were well within the normal range of ammunition expended in a pitched battle in a 'small war'. They demonstrate that, for all the relative ineffectiveness of some of the British firing at Gingindlovu and the criticism levelled at it, it was still sufficient to create a zone of fire too hot for the amaZulu to penetrate.

The crisis along the north face of the laager passed when the 3/60th rallied, and at 6.40 a.m. the amaZulu confronting them began to retire into the long grass. Chelmsford believed the moment had come for a counter-attack and ordered Major Barrow's mounted troops stationed at the north side of the laager – the two troops of Mounted Infantry and the Natal Volunteer Guides – to make a sortie. The movement was premature and Chelmsford had miscalculated. The amaZulu quickly rallied in turn, and fearing that Barrow's men would be cut off, Chelmsford sent out Molyneux to recall them. He was only just in time, and the horsemen had to fight their way back to the shelter of the laager. Barrow was slightly wounded, as were two of his men. Molyneux's horse was shot under him and foundered, although he managed to make his way back to safety.[20]

The right division of the Zulu column attacking the laager's north face then circled to their right to reinforce the left division of the column from Misi Hill assailing the laager's western flank. Concurrently, at about 7 a.m., the right half of the Misi column began its assault on the laager's southern face under the energetic leadership of Dabulamanzi kaMpande himself. This proved to be the most determined and furious attack of the day, and Chelmsford was compelled to order two companies of the 3/60th out of the north face, which was no longer seriously threatened, to support the hard-pressed 91st Highlanders. Despite the desperate courage of his men, Dabulamanzi's attack eventually stalled under the heavy British fire. It then rolled right around the laager for a brief but unsuccessful attempt on the eastern face where his warriors were met by the controlled volleys of the 57th Regiment that so impressed Molyneux.

The Zulu attacks had now been arrested on every side, but although the warriors were pinned down under fire, they showed no signs of retiring; instead they stayed put on their stomachs in the cover of the long grass. The soldiers in the trenches could not see them, but those on the wagons could, and kept up their sniping. The first mounted sortie Chelmsford had ordered out had proved premature, but he decided that the correct moment had now come to unleash his mounted men and force the amaZulu to retreat. Barrow's men were already mounted in anticipation, and Chelmsford ordered them to sortie out of the laager's largely unengaged eastern face. Barrow, with one troop of the Mounted Infantry in the leading line and with Jantze's Native Horse and Mafunzi's Mounted Natives in a second line in support to rescue any of those in front who were unhorsed, charged the flank of the wavering Zulu on the right of their crescent formation. After standing for a moment the Zulu sullenly gave way, and this was the moment for the mounted men to transform a retreat into a rout. In their efforts to escape, the amaZulu abandoned weapons and accoutrements. The British later collected up about 435 discarded firearms, almost all of which, with the exception of five Martini-Henry rifles and a revolver (the spoils of Isandlwana), were obsolete flintlock or percussion-cap muskets. The Mounted Infantry had been issued with cavalry sabres on Chelmsford's insistence and used them to great effect, killing between fifty and sixty of the fleeing amaZulu with them.

Wheeling to his right, Barrow kept up the pursuit westwards for about one-and-half miles towards Misi Hill, while some of his horsemen peeled off and drove others of the flying amaZulu southwards towards the Matigulu River. Meanwhile, the remainder of the mounted troops – the second troop of Mounted Infantry and the Natal Volunteer Guides – wheeled left out of the laager to attack the amaZulu retiring from its north face. They too kept up a merciless pursuit, driving the amaZulu before them towards the flooded Nyezane and the burnt-out kwaGingindlovu *ikhanda* beyond. Then, at about 7.15 a.m., Chelmsford ordered the two battalions of NNC and Dunn's Scouts, led by Dunn himself, to join the pursuit. They advanced with loud cheers out of the southern side of the laager to mop up after the mounted men and (as was their practice) kill all the Zulu wounded they encountered. In case the Zulu retreat should prove to be a feint, Chelmsford ordered all the other troops to remain at their posts around the laager. But the amaZulu had suffered enough. Their reserves on the hills beyond the Nyezane retreated when they saw their army in flight, and fire from the 9-pounders dispersed those amaZulu who attempted to rally on Misi Hill. Finally convinced that the amaZulu had been comprehensively repulsed, Chelmsford ordered the ceasefire sounded about an hour and three-quarters after the advance of the Zulu army had first been sighted. The exhausted, sated pursuers straggled back to the laager, the NNC singing victory songs as they came, rejoicing in their second victory over the amaZulu (the first had been at Nyezane). From Fort Eshowe, the garrison saw long lines of dispirited warriors making their way northwards up the coast towards the Mlalazi River. From Fort Eshowe Pearson flashed his congratulations to Chelmsford who replied in high spirits.

Indeed, to his intense satisfaction Chelmsford had overcome severe logistical difficulties and poor weather, and his caution, born of his bitter experiences in the Isandlwana campaign, had paid dividends. As always, his calm manner and personal bravery under fire had boosted the morale of his men. Above all, under his personal command he had at last secured a thorough-going victory. Not only was the Zulu army in full retreat and abandoning the blockade of Fort Eshowe, but it had suffered at least a 10 per cent casualty rate. The British buried some 470 amaZulu within 500 yards of the laager, 250 of whom had fallen in front of the western and southern faces. A further 200 dead were found nearby. Many more lay within a radius of five miles along the Zulu line of flight, especially along the banks of the Nyezane where the fleeing amaZulu had abandoned their wounded to the merciless NNC. Lieutenant Julius Backhouse went over the field 'where the dead Zulu were lying', and found it 'a ghastly sight, such fine men too, they were as thick as peas in some places'.[21] Most of the Zulu wounded who did manage to make their way home would have succumbed to their vicious, bone-shattering bullet wounds, although those with sabre cuts might well have survived. In all, the amaZulu probably lost nearly

Photograph taken on 20 June 1879 of the Isandlwana battlefield with wagons and other debris in the foreground, and a burial party in the distance at the site of the British camp which the Zulu army had overrun on 22 January 1879.

Lord Chelmsford was much criticised for leaving the British dead unburied when he hastily withdrew to Rorke's Drift on the morning after the battle. Major-General Marshall led a reconnaissance-in-force that hurriedly interred some of the bodies on 21 May 1879, but most of the remainder were buried during late June 1879 by Major Wilsone Black's forces stationed at Rorke's Drift. It was not until March 1880 that all the dead finally received proper burial.

The Grenadier Guards in the trenches before Sebastopol.

Queen Victoria receiving the 3rd Battalion of the Grenadier Guards at Buckingham Palace in July 1856 on their return from the Crimea. Note the change in style of uniform from 1854.

Thesiger much admired his brother-in-law Sir John Inglis, KCB, husband of his sister Julia. Inglis was the hero of the siege of Lucknow (June–November 1857).

Adria, Lady Chelmsford (1845–1926).

EXECUTION OF MUTINEERS AT PESHAWUR; BLOWING FROM THE GUNS, ETC.

British retribution after the Indian Mutiny: The execution of captured mutineers at Peshawar in the Punjab by blowing them from the guns or by hanging. *Illustrated London News*, 1857.

The Abyssinian Field Force, its artillery carried by pack animals, picks its way in column through the mountains. *Illustrated London News*, 4 July 1868.

The storming of Magdala by the Abyssinian Field Force on 13 April 1868.

Benjamin Disraeli, first Earl of Beaconsfield and British Prime Minister, 1874–80.

Colonel the Hon. Frederick Stanley, Secretary of State for War, 1878–80.

Sir Bartle Frere, Governor of the Cape, in King William's Town in late 1877 with British officers and Cape officials. Seated second from left to right are Frere, Lt.-Gen. Sir Arthur Cunynghame and Col. Richard Glyn. Standing fifth from left is Capt. H. Hallam Parr. Lt.-Col. Henry Pulleine stands eighth from left. Lt. Nevill Coghill sits on the ground to the left.

Above: Lt.-Gen. Thesiger at King William's Town in 1878 with his staff. (*L to R*) Maj. J. N. Crealock, Lt. William Molyneux, Col. Evelyn Wood, Thesiger (*seated*), Lt.-Col. Redvers Buller and Brevet Maj. Mathew Gossett.

Left: The repulse of the Gcaleka army on 29 September 1877 by the garrison of Colonel Charles Griffith's fortified headquarters at Ibeka in Fingoland.

Left: British regulars, African levies and colonial mounted volunteers in the Lotutu Bush, 6 April 1878, during the Ninth Cape Frontier War. *Illustrated London News*, 11 May 1878.

Right: 'A hot corner'. Major J. N. Crealock's drawing of Mfengu levies skirmishing in the broken terrain and dense bush of the Amathole Mountains in April or May 1878 during the Ninth Cape Frontier War.

Below: The earthwork Fort Evelyn on the Gazo heights in the Pirie Bush was constructed in April 1878 during the final stages of the Ninth Cape Frontier War.

Lieutenant-General Thesiger on his pony in the field in the Eastern Cape in mid-1878 with a trooper of the Cape Mounted Rifles as escort, drawn by Major J. N. Crealock, who was a talented watercolour artist.

Sir Henry Bulwer, Lieutenant-Governor of Natal, 1875–80. He clashed with Chelmsford over transport and supply and the role of the Border Guard.

Lt.-Gen. Lord Chelmsford (*centre*) in January 1879 with three members of his Personal Staff: (*seated right*) Brevet Lt.-Col. J. N. Crealock; (*standing*) Brevet Maj. M. Gossett (*left*) and Lt. A. Berkeley Milne, RN. Acting Capt. H. J. F. Campbell, RN, CO of HMS *Active*'s Naval Brigade is seated left.

Brevet Col. Anthony Durnford, RE, CO of No. 2 Column, killed at Isandlwana. Chelmsford attempted to fix the blame for the disaster on him.

The first engagement of the Anglo-Zulu War. On 12 January 1879 elements of No. 3 Column stormed kwaSogekle, the stronghold of Sihayo kaXongo. *Illustrated London News*, 1 March 1879.

A drawing done on the spot by Trooper N. Nelson of the Natal Mounted Police of Lord Chelmsford marching away from the stricken field of Isandlwana on the morning after the battle. Note the disembowelled corpses of the British dead.

Above: Louis Napoleon, Prince Imperial of France, on the eve of his departure for Zululand in February 1879. His death on 1 June 1879 was a major embarrassment for Lord Chelmsford.

Below: The funeral service for the Prince Imperial was held near Thelezi Mountain on 2 June 1879. The gun-carriage bearing his body halted in the square formed by the troops for Father Bellard, Catholic Chaplain, to offer prayers. Lord Chelmsford stands alone to the right, ahead of his Staff.

Above: Commissariat stores for the 1st Division accumulating below Fort Pearson on the Natal bank of the lower Thukela River during the last months of the Anglo-Zulu War. Note the trestle bridge spanning part of the river beyond Mr Smith's house in the centre of the photograph.

Right: Charles Fripp's sketch of Wood's Flying Column on the march towards oNdini. Note the cased Colours carried by the infantry (*centre*) and the trooper of the Frontier Light Horse (*right foreground*). *Graphic*, 16 August 1879.

Dabulamanzi kaMpande, the Zulu commander at Rorke's drift, photographed in 1873 with the hunter-trader John Dunn who supplied firearms to the Zulu kingdom, but who threw in his lot with the British in 1879.

The depot at Rorke's Drift sketched immediately after the battle of 22–23 January 1879, and its relief by Lord Chelmsford.

Right: An engraving of the final repulse and pursuit of the amaZulu at the battle of Gingindlovu on 2 April 1879, based on an eye-witness sketch by Lt.-Col. J. N. Crealock. Published in *Illustrated London News*, 24 May 1879.

Right: Chelmsford's HQ, 3 July 1879. 'Shall we have a fight tomorrow?' *Illustrated London News*, 6 September 1879.

Below: Melton Prior, special artist for the *Illustrated London News*, accompanied the 2nd Division and made this eye-witness watercolour of Chelmsford and his Staff inside the square at the battle of Ulundi.

A pensive Major-General Lord Chelmsford, sporting the star and sash of the GCB reluctantly conferred on him at the conclusion of the Anglo-Zulu War. A photograph taken in *c.* 1880 when he was facing much public criticism of his conduct of the campaign.

General Sir Garnet Wolseley, GCMG. The British government appointed him in May 1879 as High Commissioner in South Eastern Africa, Governor of Natal and the Transvaal, and Commander-in-Chief of the Forces.

The first Viscount Chelmsford (1868–1933), *c.* 1924. He outshone his father in a stellar career of public service that included being Viceroy of India and First Lord of the Admiralty

In this *Fun* cartoon, Chelmsford's critics, led by Lord Beaconsfield himself, hasten to clean up his reputation in the aftermath of his victory at Ulundi.

'I only went and gave Mr. Forbes a kick,' complains Chelmsford to 'Grandpa' Beaconsfield in this *Fun* cartoon, 'and he's been and gone and hit me back again!'

This *Punch* cartoon in the wake of the Isandlwana disaster sums up the lesson to be absorbed by the British Army when conducting a 'small war'. Lord Chelmsford would have taken the message very personally. *Punch*, 1 March 1879.

A gilded retirement: General Lord Chelmsford as Gold Stick-in-Waiting, *c.* 1900.

1,200 men. In stark contrast, two British officers were killed, along with seven British soldiers and five black troops. Four officers, twenty-six white and seventeen black troops were wounded. Chelmsford was undoubtedly correct in believing that had it not been for the cover of the broad shelter trench his losses would have been heavier.

On the day after the battle, Chelmsford reduced the laager to 100 yards square by taking out the forty-four carts. These he added to the relief column when, leaving behind a small garrison to hold the laager, he marched the fifteen miles over difficult country to Fort Eshowe. As the column approached the fort, Pearson and a mounted escort came out at a smart canter to greet it. Chelmsford and several of his staff galloped past the toiling column to meet them. When Chelmsford grasped Pearson warmly by the hand, 'The respectful silence of the General's escort was broken by a cheer such as only English throats can give.'[22] The column then marched to their bivouac outside the fort, and the pipers of the 91st Highlanders played them in to loud cheers.[23]

The next morning, 4 April, any stores of value in the fort were placed in the 120 wagons Pearson still had with him. The garrison then evacuated the fort they had held for seventy-two days and began its march back to Fort Tenedos on the north bank of the Thukela. The Eshowe Relief Column was scheduled to follow on the next day. In the interim, spies informed Chelmsford that Dabulamanzi, whom the British held in detestation for the leading part he had played at Rorke's Drift and in operations around Eshowe, had returned to eZuluwini, his *umuzi* in the Ntumeni hills eight miles west of the fort. Chelmsford thereupon seized on the opportunity to show that 'he too had a long arm to strike with',[24] and ordered out a patrol of 225 mounted men under Major Barrow to destroy Dabulamanzi's home. The General rode with the patrol, paying Barrow the 'high compliment' of allowing him to take active command while he 'remained more a spectator'. Chelmsford's staff came along too 'to see some fun'. A small force of some forty amaZulu, commanded by Dabulamanzi himself mounted on a black horse, kept up a fire on them from a neighbouring hill, and a shot whizzed just over the head of one of Chelmsford's ADCs. The Zulu sniping was insufficient to prevent the torching of eZuluwini, however, and Chelmsford returned to the fort in good humour.[25]

The following day, 5 April, the Eshowe Relief Column began its march back to the Thukela. Once it was out of sight, the amaZulu wasted no time in setting fire to the buildings of the abandoned fort, but did not harm the British graves, two of them inside the fort, and twenty-six in the military cemetery outside.[26] At first glance it might seem odd that after so much effort, privation and loss Chelmsford should have abandoned this fortified forward position deep in Zululand. Yet his was a calculated decision, for he had resolved that the future operations he intended to entrust to Major-General Crealock against the two most significant coastal *amakhanda*, the old oNdini and emaNgweni, would best be effected by way of the coastal road that avoided the difficult ascent to Eshowe. When reporting to Cambridge, Chelmsford justified his decision by pointing out that it was 'an intense relief . . . to get the garrison out of Ekowe' since 'It would have been madness to have clung onto Ekowe and General Crealock on his new line of operations along the lower or Coast road will have the benefit of a fine open country.'[27]

Being lightly equipped, the Eshowe Relief Column overtook Pearson's encumbered column on the road, but their paths diverged when Chelmsford led his men back to the vicinity of the Gingindlovu laager and bivouacked for the night at the eMvutsheni ('Imfuchini') Mission. At 3.30 a.m. on 6 April, a sentry of the 91st Highlanders fired a shot at what he took in the darkness of the night to be the enemy.[28] On hearing the report, a picquet of the jittery 3/60th on the opposite side of the entrenched enclosure retired on it without being ordered to do so, together with some of Dunn's Scouts from further out. It was bright moonlight, and for what happened next Chelmsford could offer Stanley 'no excuse or explanation . . . beyond the youth of the men of the 60th'.[29] The main body of the 3/60th was lining the entrenchment, and seeing the picquets and scouts running towards them, panicked and opened fire. Five men of the 3/60th were severely wounded, and eight of Dunn's Scouts were bayonetted as they attempted to gain the shelter of the laager, one subsequently dying of his wounds.[30] Dunn was horrified, recalling that, 'I recognised the voices of some of my unfortunate native scouts, calling out "Friend! Friend!" which they had been taught to respond to the challenge of the sentries.'[31] But it was of no avail, and the short-service soldiers had once again shown that they were not sufficiently steady for active service.

With the coming of daylight on 6 April after this shameful episode, Chelmsford resumed the march. Rather than halting at the laager at Gingindlovu where the vicinity of the battlefield was tainted by the Zulu dead, many still lying unburied, he established a new encampment a mile to its south. The small garrison of the old laager moved into the new entrenchment on 7 April, and settled down there with the rest of the erstwhile Eshowe Relief Column, soon to be re-designated the 2nd Brigade, 1st Division, to await the resumption of the advance up the Zulu coast. Chelmsford himself, accompanied by his staff, left them there and reached the Thukela at noon on 7 April, just as Pearson's column was arriving. The following morning he left Fort Pearson, and on 9 April arrived in Durban which, with all the transports and troops arriving daily, was then the busiest place in South Africa.[32] Two days later, he sat down to report in modestly expressed but crowing terms to the Duke of Cambridge 'after what I trust your Royal Highness will consider a successful 10 days operations'.[33] But now, with all four of the promised major-generals and the bulk of the reinforcements disembarked in Durban, he was faced with the daunting challenge of planning and implementing the renewed invasion of Zululand.

CHAPTER 28

Preparing for the Second Invasion, April–May 1879

EVEN BEFORE CHELMSFORD SECURED his victory at Gingindlovu, the Zulu veterans of Isandlwana had been comprehensively defeated on 29 March at Khambula, Colonel Wood's fortified camp far away in north-western Zululand. The previous day, Wood had raided Hlobane Mountain, the base of Mbilini kaMswati, the most effective leader of irregulars in the region. By attacking Hlobane with his mounted units and African auxiliaries, Wood had hoped to create a diversion in favour of the Eshowe Relief Column, as well as to capture the herds of cattle the amaZulu had concentrated there for safety. In the event, Mbilini's irregulars and the abaQulusi ensconced on the flat-topped mountain thoroughly worsted the British raiders in their sloppily planned and poorly executed operation, and the fortuitous arrival of elements of the main Zulu army advancing towards Khambula under the command of Mnyamana kaNgqengelele transformed their disordered withdrawal into a headlong rout back to Khambula. The British lost fifteen officers and seventy-nine men killed in this disastrous affair, along with well over 100 of their African auxiliaries. This was a casualty list second only to that at Isandlwana, redeemed only by individual acts of gallantry for which five Victoria Crosses were subsequently awarded. Buller, one of the recipients, especially distinguished himself during the retreat. Wood, whose erratic movements throughout the day compounded the British difficulties, clearly lost control of the battle, but he was not slow to pin the blame for the debacle on two of his subordinate officers. Commandant Frederick A. Weatherley of Weatherley's Border Horse (like Durnford) conveniently perished in the affray; while Lieutenant-Colonel John C. Russell, an officer whom Wood had long disliked, found himself ignominiously transferred by Chelmsford on his commander's urging to Pietermaritzburg as Commandant of the Remount Establishment.[1] It was nevertheless extremely fortunate for Wood's reputation that his decisive victory the following day at Khambula blunted criticism of his badly bungled raid on Hlobane with its division of forces every bit as culpable as Chelmsford's dispositions before Isandlwana.[2] As it was, at Khambula he routed the main Zulu army of up to 20,000 men or more (on a par with the army that fought at Isandlwana) in a ferocious pitched battle determinedly waged from 1.30 p.m. until nightfall. For the loss of twenty-eight men killed and fifty-five wounded, the British inflicted well over a thousand Zulu casualties – no fewer than they had suffered at Isandlwana, and probably more.[3]

The battle of Khambula, therefore, and not Gingindlovu, marked the true turning-point of the war. With the disastrous repulse of their main army, Zulu morale slumped grievously. Khambula proved (a realisation confirmed at Gingindlovu) that no Zulu army, not even their best, could prevail against the British if they failed to catch them in the open as they had at Isandlwana and Hlobane, and that it was hopeless to attack them in prepared positions. Cetshwayo's *amabutho* nevertheless declared themselves willing to fight on, but the king abandoned any hope of winning the war in the field, and accepted that his only salvation lay in negotiating with the British.[4]

It might be supposed that Chelmsford, arrived back in Durban from the relief of Eshowe, and having to deal with the formidable task of planning the second invasion of the Zulu kingdom, would have responded to the news of Khambula with acclaim. After all, Wood's victory was sure to make his undertaking considerably easier and assure it of success. Yet, for once the punctiliously courteous Chelmsford could not bring himself to rise to the occasion. Perhaps he did not quite appreciate the extent of Wood's success – or, more likely, he did only too well. After several days he finally wrote tepidly to his far too successful subordinate whose glory was likely to eclipse his own won at Gingindlovu: 'One line to congratulate you upon your successful repulse of the attack made upon Kambula laager – I am up to my ears in work & cannot say as much as I could wish, but I know you are aware how fully I appreciate all your good work.'[5]

Grudging as his congratulations to Wood were, Chelmsford could not but be buoyed up by the overwhelming victories at Khambula and

Gingindlovu that indicated that the British had conclusively regained the initiative in the war. Crealock noticed with relief that he was '*quite himself* again'.[6] Yet it was not immediately clear to Chelmsford what strategy he ought to follow in order to bring the war to an end. He seemed embarrassed by the large number of reinforcements rushed out to him by the anxious government, and was presented by immense organisational problems. He was swamped by Special Service officers anxious for action and promotion and, with the memory of the wavering, short-service troops at Gingindlovu still fresh, complained to Wood that 'Drafts will not be of much use, as they are certain to be composed of boys.'[7] He also had to allocate suitable commands for the four major-generals Cambridge had selected to accompany the troops.

At the same time, Chelmsford was short of staff officers to assist them. In mid-March Crealock had foreseen that a more comprehensive and better structured staff organisation was essential for launching the second invasion, but he had failed to persuade Chelmsford to take any concrete steps.[8] It is true that on 20 April Chelmsford did eventually request additional staff officers to be sent out from Britain as soon as possible,[9] but it was very late in the day. Meanwhile, Chelmsford continued to go his own way, apparently undervaluing the routine but necessary duties his headquarters staff were required to perform in order to 'oil the cogwheels'. Crealock bemoaned that the General expected his staff 'to rattle along' as best they could in his wake as he indefatigably moved about Natal to inspect military preparations, and that 'Under these circumstances the use of a headquarters staff disappears.'[10] Over a month later, on 23 May, Chelmsford wrote to Cambridge from the little village of Utrecht in the south-western Transvaal where he had set up his temporary headquarters on 5 May,[11] excusing the perplexing lack of information in his despatches and promising in future to do his best to send in daily reports. (This letter crossed with that of the exasperated Duke, repeating that unless Chelmsford supplied the Horse Guards with full details, they 'cannot assist you . . . as we could wish'.)[12] The reason Chelmsford gave for his inadequate despatches could hardly have mollified Cambridge for it spoke of his poor use of his staff and his reluctance to delegate: 'I have had no general officers to whom I could delegate full powers to act as my correspondent and I have been forced to travel about myself in order to see with my own eyes and to ascertain in the open what was required.'[13] All in all, as the exasperated Clery commented somewhat later in the campaign: 'The general is apparently incapable of realizing what the necessity of an efficient staff is, i.e. to allow him to think while they carry out his ideas, so he has no faculty for selecting men.'[14]

It should be noted, though, that with his typical courtesy and sense of *noblesse oblige* Chelmsford paid attention to the creature comforts of his personal staff and other officers messing with him. During March and April, besides the cutlery, table linen, cooking equipment and carbolic soap he ordered from Pietermaritzburg merchants, Chelmsford – although himself a teetotaller – purchased no less than ten cases (or 120 bottles) of whisky and four cases (forty-eight bottles) of Bass Pale Ale for his guests.[15]

Within days of his return to Durban, Chelmsford was settling on the strategy he intended to adopt for the second invasion. Both Wood and Major-General Crealock advocated advancing a single column to place less strain on the Commissariat and Transport Department, but Chelmsford decided to send in two widely spaced columns to advance on oNdini from opposite directions, supposedly screening the Transvaal and Natal from a possible Zulu counter-blow.[16]

The 1st Division of 7,500 men under Major-General Henry Crealock, the most senior of the three major-generals conducting operations in the field, was to advance on oNdini up the coast from the lower Thukela, burning the old oNdini and emaNgweni *amakhanda* as they went. The rationale was that Cetshwayo would be pressured into dividing and thus weakening his forces to protect these two *amakhanda* and the people of the coastal plain.[17] The 2nd Division of 5,000 men under Major-General Edward Newdigate, which Chelmsford intended to accompany with his HQ, was to be made up of the balance of the troops already in the area, and from reinforcements landed in Durban. To it was attached the Cavalry Brigade allocated to Major-General 'Handsome Fred' Marshall, a famous cricketer and captain of the United Eleven of England, and the most junior of the major-generals. The 2nd Division was to march on oNdini from the north-west, and was to concentrate at the tiny village of Dundee in northern Natal where its main depot would be formed. Chelmsford selected this place over Helpmekaar, the Centre Column's depot in the first invasion, because the roads were better by way of Ladysmith than by Greytown, and were less exposed to the Zulu border and the Qudeni Forest where the enemy might be lurking. Moreover, Dundee was

The Second Invasion of Zululand, 6 April–8 July 1879

closer to the southern Transvaal and the OFS from which considerable supplies would be drawn.[18] Above all – and this was the most powerful if unspoken consideration – this route avoided the ill-fated road by way of Isandlwana and the still-unburied British dead. But advancing into

Zululand from Dundee rather than from Helpmekaar meant adopting a route that was 100 miles longer and was unfamiliar, so that considerable and time-consuming reconnaissance would be required.[19] Wood's forces at Khambula were restyled the Flying Column (3,200 men) on 13 April, but remained under his independent command. The Flying Column was to cooperate in its advance from the north-west with the 2nd Division, entrusting the protection of the Transvaal border to the small garrisons it left behind to its rear.[20]

While Chelmsford began to put these plans into effect, he took action – what he regarded as 'the active defence' – to ensure that the amaZulu would not disrupt them by striking into Natal. On 7 April he sent orders from Fort Pearson for continued raids to be made across the Natal–Zululand border wherever feasible, disregarding what Bulwer had understood at the Pinetown meeting to be his undertaking not to do so. In the event, the flooded state of the Thukela prevented Major Twentyman and Captain Lucas from doing more than hover menacingly at the unfordable drifts. It was different at Rorke's Drift, and on 9 April Major Dartnell led 2,000 men over the Mzinyathi River on a major raid up the Batshe River valley, burning a dozen of Sihayo's *imizi* and all the standing crops. The raid achieved its objective, for the amaZulu evacuated the whole region.[21]

The growing concentration of troops in Natal preparing to move up to the Zulu border put intolerable strain on the Commissariat and Transport Department.[22] It had already shown itself all but unequal to providing the transport and supplies required for the relief of Eshowe, and Chelmsford was right to fear that it would not prove 'equal to the occasion'.[23] Yet unaccountably, considering his extensive experience as a staff officer, he shied away from tackling the problem. Frustrated by his reticence on the subject, Cambridge wrote to him declaring: 'I fear that Transport will be your greatest difficulty, and one thus far you have really told me *nothing*.'[24] Nevertheless, despite the critical seriousness of his logistical problems, Chelmsford seemed content to leave their solution to others, principally to Major-General Clifford who disembarked at Durban on 9 April, the same day that Chelmsford arrived there from Fort Pearson. Within a few days Chelmsford was lauding him to Cambridge, writing that Clifford 'has already done much to systematize the work here, and will be perfectly valuable as my locum tenens when I again cross the border'.[25] Accordingly, when Chelmsford set off on 22 April to join the 2nd Division in Dundee, Clifford set up his headquarters in Pietermaritzburg in his capacity as the Inspector General in command of the base, of the lines of communication between it and all the forces operating in Zululand, and of all the troops (both imperial and colonial) left to defend Natal.[26]

In other words, it was up to Clifford, along with Commissary-General Strickland, to grapple with the host of problems associated with keeping Chelmsford's forces supplied in the field, and he expected them to cooperate in solving them.[27] It was not long, though, before Clifford, a notably conscientious and efficient administrator who was under Cambridge's orders to limit expenditure as much as he could, was declaring himself 'very, very anxious about the state of transport and supplies',[28] and was bewailing that 'Every day . . . fresh evidence appears before me of the entire want of system and organisation in the Commissariat Department and the abuses and extravagance and waste of public money have gone so far, to an extent that they are almost beyond control.'[29] Chelmsford was placed in the deeply embarrassing position of having to report to Stanley on 1 May that 'The difficulties to be overcome are very great, and the advance of the troops into Zululand cannot take place until the Transport has thrown a sufficient amount of supplies into our present advance depots, and has moreover, provided the requisite amount of wagons, etc. for that advance.'[30] A fortnight later he was forced to admit that the troops, although in position, were still not able to advance because of a lack of supplies.[31] Nine days on, the situation had not improved, and he sheepishly admitted to Cambridge that 'I am afraid the people in England will become very impatient at our long inaction, but to advance before our supplies were up was simply impracticable.'[32]

When reporting to his superiors in the War Office, Chelmsford naturally had to find plausible reasons for the breakdown in logistical arrangements that let him personally off the hook. He backed up Clifford in blaming the Commissariat and Transport Department, declaring that he had 'no hesitation in saying that our transport has broken down completely for want of officers who have been properly educated to that branch of the service'. He hastened, though, not to put the blame on Strickland himself (as Clifford had not shied away from doing), insisting that he been badly let down by his subordinates, 'poor creatures afraid of responsibility, of no resource and without proper energy'.[33]

For his part, Strickland did not dispute that there were insufficient trained officers in his department to superintend transport, but pointed out an additional complication. As early as 20 April Chelmsford had recognised that, 'Our great difficulty everywhere is still the want of drivers and leaders' for the wagons and carts,[34] and Strickland repeatedly brought to his attention that civilians, especially African ones, were afraid to join the wagon teams because of the ill-treatment often meted out by military officers.[35]

This problem brought to the fore another, critical issue. When Chelmsford defensively informed Stanley that 'Every effort is being made by all under my command . . . to tide over our present difficulties,' but that they were contending with 'circumstances over which they themselves have no real control,' he was referring to Bulwer's lack of 'any real power to help us'.[36] When Chelmsford met Bulwer in Pietermaritzburg face-to-face for the last time before departing for the front, he failed to secure the lieutenant-governor's committed cooperation concerning transport.[37] Indeed, the civil authorities in Natal seemed unable or unwilling to work harmoniously with the military, while the Natal government proved reluctant to intervene actively to ensure that the colonists assisted the war effort. Clifford was consequently deeply concerned about the exorbitant prices he claimed grasping colonists were forcing the military to pay for transport as well as for provisions and other stores.[38] Frere too was alarmed, writing to Hicks Beach that, 'Unless all the material resources of Natal are heartily and unreservedly placed at the disposal of the military authorities, the Lieutenant-General cannot be expected to bring the present war to a speedy and satisfactory conclusion.'[39] But, as Gerald French put it in his biography of Chelmsford, 'the almost inconceivable difficulty experienced in procuring natives, animals, and vehicles for transport purposes' continued to dog the progress of the second invasion.[40] At the very end of the campaign, in mid-July, a journalist could still point to the appalling wastage of stores thanks to the poor supervision of the Commissariat and Transport Department: 'Loads upon loads of precious stores, conveyed long distances . . . have been left exposed to the rains, and have been thrown into the river to get rid of them, their place being supplied by other stores . . . recklessly pitched down among mud, to be destroyed in like manner.'[41]

CHAPTER 29

Launching the Second Invasion, May–June 1879

APRIL WAS SPENT BRINGING UP convoys of supplies to the 1st Division concentrating at the lower Thukela and in strengthening Forts Pearson and Tenedos. To prepare depots on the Division's planned line of advance, on 23 April its 1st Brigade began work on the earthwork Fort Crealock on the north bank of the Matigulu River; while the 2nd Brigade, which had been stationed where Chelmsford had left it at the new Gingindlovu laager, started the construction of another earthwork further north. Dubbed Fort Chelmsford, it was sited on the south bank of the Nyezane.[1] By mid-June the lower Thukela was spanned by two trestle and pontoon bridges to augment the pont plying between its two banks; while a gunboat taking soundings fifty miles up the coast at Port Durnford (nothing more, in fact, than an empty stretch of sandy beach) had established it as a feasible place for landing supplies once the Division eventually advanced that far. Finally, on 20 June the entire 1st Division concentrated at Fort Chelmsford where supplies had been accumulating,[2] and Crealock was ready to move forward in earnest.[3] But his over-methodical preparations had meant that his advance thus far had been painfully slow. His lack of progress, instead of forcing Cetshwayo to divide his forces as Chelmsford had intended, allowed the Zulu king to ignore the presence of the 1st Division and to concentrate his *amabutho* to meet the joint advance of the 2nd Division and the Flying Column on oNdini from the north-west.[4]

When Chelmsford had arrived back in Durban after the relief of Eshowe, he found Prince Louis Napoleon, the Prince Imperial of France, who had come ashore on 31 March, eagerly awaiting him. The 23-year-old Prince and his mother the Empress Eugénie had sought refuge in Britain following the defeat and capture in 1870 of his father the Emperor

Napoleon III in the Franco-Prussian War and the subsequent collapse of the Third Empire. The Emperor's death in 1873 made his only son the Bonapartist pretender to the French throne, and thus the figurehead of a sizable faction that did not accept the insecurely established Third Republic. Beginning his career in the same way as his famous great-uncle, the exiled young Prince had entered the Royal Military Academy at Woolwich, graduating in 1875. As a foreigner, however, he could not take a commission, although he was permitted to join an artillery battery at Aldershot in an honorary capacity where, unofficially, he much enjoyed the military life.[5] The stirring events of the Anglo-Zulu War inspired him to volunteer for service in Zululand in search of adventure and military renown in the Napoleonic tradition.[6] His mother was anxiously opposed to his placing himself in danger, and Beaconsfield and his government had considerable reservations. The Prince finessed them by appealing directly to Queen Victoria who was won over,[7] although she wrote to Cambridge that, 'He *must* be careful not unnecessarily to expose himself, for we know he is *very* venturesome.'[8] Cambridge, although he could not permit him to join the army in the field, sanctioned his accompanying the campaign 'in the capacity of a spectator'. Like his cousin the Queen, Cambridge found Louis Napoleon a likable young man and commended him to Frere's and Chelmsford's care as 'a charming young man, full of spirit and energy' who also possessed the advantage of 'speaking English admirably'.[9]

The last thing Chelmsford needed at this time was the added burden of looking after the feisty young prince whose safety was so essential to the Bonapartist cause. It must have given him pause that in Cambridge's letter carried to him by the Prince, in which he requested Chelmsford to 'help him on in any way', the Duke admitted that his 'only anxiety on his account would be that he is *too plucky* and *go-ahead*'.[10] Nevertheless, it was an honour to 'show him kindness', as Cambridge requested as a personal favour, and complying was calculated to cement Chelmsford's relations with the royal family. He permitted the Prince to wear the uniform of an artillery officer and invited him to mess with his staff as an officially designated 'Extra Aide-de-Camp'. Chelmsford unctuously informed Cambridge in words that would soon ring horribly hollow:

> I have asked the Prince Imperial to accompany my Head Quarters, which I am glad to find is what he himself was anxious

> for – I should feel much obliged if Your Royal Highness would assure the Empress that I will look after the Prince to the best of my ability, and that I am convinced I shall find him a very valuable addition to my Staff.[11]

Paul Deléage, a young journalist with *Le Figaro*, had at his own request followed the Prince out to South Africa to report on his adventures, and has left an invaluable outsider's take on the British in Zululand, rather different in perspective from that of the many British 'specials' with the army. He was there to observe with some shock the determined stoicism of four British soldiers in the camp at Dundee, found guilty of insubordination and drunkenness under arms, when each received twenty lashes on his bare back while tied to the wheels of a wagon.[12] Flogging as a military punishment on campaign was, as we have seen, favoured by Chelmsford, but it did not enter Deléage's head to task him with it when he interviewed him in Pietermaritzburg on 21 April. What we have is a closely observed but somewhat awe-struck pen portrait of the General at the moment when he was about to take the field for the second invasion:

> Lord Chelmsford is still a young man, about forty years old at most [in fact, he was fifty-two]. A few months before, his hair and his beard had been black but were now grizzled after the disastrous first days of the Zululand war. Tall and lean, Lord Chelmsford is the epitome of the great English nobleman. His glance is forthright and honest, his manner engaging without arrogance or restraint, yet also without undue familiarity. Had it not been for the pressure of grievous anxieties which was apparent at certain moments beneath an expression whose character is one of composure and resolution, I could have wished to engage freely with [him] on a great many things.[13]

On his arrival in the last days of April at the camp in Dundee to join the 2nd Division, Chelmsford was shocked by the lack of defensive measures. Incensed he wrote to Wood that 'The camp here shows that neither he [Glyn] nor Clery have learned anything from Insandlwana!'[14] He insisted that a strong fort be built to protect the supplies and serve as an anchor for defence. The earthwork Fort Jones was accordingly begun on 28 April, and the three galvanised iron commissariat sheds were removed from

Helpmekaar and re-erected within its walls.[15] On 2 May a new camp in advance of Dundee was established on the western bank of the Mzinyathi at Landman's Drift, and three earthwork forts were thrown up in a kind of echelon. The cavalry and artillery camps, the cattle laager (formed of the Division's wagons) and the hospital were all sited under the protection of their guns. Now that the Division was approaching the margins of Zulu territory, Chelmsford was taking these elaborate precautions with the dread fate of the unentrenched camp at Isandlwana very much in his mind.[16] Over the next few weeks, the 2nd Division massed at Landman's Drift while convoys were escorted back and forth to fill the depot with supplies.

Between 13 and 21 May the Division mounted extensive and repeated patrols and mounted raids with NNC support to ensured that the country to Chelmsford's front and immediate right was clear of Zulu forces when he resumed the advance. The military thinking was that systematic pillaging in the area of operations denied the opposing Zulu forces bases, shelter and supplies and created an extensive zone free of Zulu forces around the vulnerable columns, dangerously extended on the march. Great numbers of *imizi* were accordingly burned in an arc of fire stretching from the Mzinyathi between Landman's Drift and Rorke's Drift eastwards towards Babanango Mountain, and large numbers of cattle and other livestock captured. To secure his right flank further and clear the Thukela border of Zulu forces that might threaten Natal, Chelmsford required further cross-border raids over the Thukela.[17] On 20 May Major Twentyman made the border forces' most extensive incursion of the war into Zululand at Middle Drift; while downstream Lucas also raided on 28 May.[18]

These destructive raids against the Zulu population along the 1st and 2nd Divisions' lines of advance were undertaken not only for tactical reasons.[19] In late April Chelmsford stated that his strategy was to drive 'all of the Zulu population into the North East portion of Zululand' precisely because he believed it was 'unhealthy and not over well cultivated'.[20] This was in accordance with the strategy he had formulated in November 1878 whereby, by pushing the increasingly hungry, shelterless and desperate amaZulu into this inhospitable countryside, he might provoke them into deposing Cetshwayo and surrendering. This strategy proved particularly effective along the coast with its disheartening record of repeated Zulu military defeats. The laboriously advancing 1st Division regularly sent out ruthless mounted patrols to burn *imizi* and *amakhanda* and to drive off livestock with the specific and successful intention of demoralising the civilian population and encouraging defections and submissions.[21]

In authorising and encouraging these methods, Chelmsford cannot be accused of being unusually cruel, and John Crealock would write of him that the General did 'not wish to prolong the war or in any way inflict any unnecessary hardships on the Zulus; but war can't be made with kid gloves'.[22] Indeed, in destroying Zulu homesteads and crops and running off their livestock in order to induce them to submit, Chelmsford was following the normal practices of 'small wars' in the conquest of Africa.[23] Nor was he unfamiliar with this military doctrine. He had adhered to it in the Ninth Cape Frontier War, believing himself militarily justified in targeting Ngqika civilians to diminish their ability to sustain their fighting men in the field, to break their morale and so end resistance. However, it cannot be denied that after Isandlwana and the perceived 'atrocities' the amaZulu committed there, that the British were conducting their campaign against them with especial animosity. When Britain went to war in Zululand, it officially had no quarrel with the Zulu people, only with their king. This distinction no longer held. As Norris-Newman wrote in the heat of the immediate aftermath of Isandlwana:

> The fallacy of fighting with an uncivilised race with the same feelings of humanity that dictate our wars with civilised races was thoroughly proved; and it thus was shown that in Zululand neither men, kraals, cattle, nor crops should be spared on any pretence whatsoever, except on the complete submission and disarmament of the whole nation.[24]

As a consequence, no restrictions were henceforth placed on the ruthlessness of military operations, and war correspondents who witnessed the raiding could not help recommending a 'little sympathy' for the enemy, even if 'In campaigns of this kind one is apt to look lightly on the sufferings of the enemy who, happening to be of a darker hue, is often supposed to be utterly devoid of the gentler feelings possessed by the superior white man.'[25] Charges began to be laid in Britain of unnecessary destruction being visited upon Zulu civilians, and Ashe and Wyatt-Edgell complained that 'Accusations of shooting down women and children were not infrequently brought against our troops.'[26] Sensationalist reports of this kind have led the historian Michael Lieven to claim that 'the British campaign, while stopping just short of the demands of genocide, amounted to total war'.[27]

Now, genocide is defined by Article II of the 1948 United Nations Convention on the Prevention and Punishment of the Crime of Genocide as 'various acts committed with intent to destroy, in whole or in part, a national, ethnic, racial or religious group'.[28] And in Zululand in 1879, *pace* Lieven, there was the scantiest verifiable record of atrocities being perpetrated against the Zulu population with the intent of destroying them, whether in whole or in part. In most cases Zulu civilians were able to flee in good time if a British patrol appeared, abandoning the open country for their mountain fastnesses or forests where they took refuge until the war had passed by, or simply falling back with what they could of their goods and livestock out of range of the advancing columns. The worst that befell those that fell into the hands of British patrols was the loss of their homes and possessions, for there was little or no danger of being killed by their captors.

There is no denying, however, that even if they did not lose their lives, many civilians did suffer privation and considerable material loss, and that in their offensive operations (as was typical of 'small wars' in Africa and had certainly been the case in the Ninth Cape Frontier War) the British did blur the distinction between soldiers and civilians, thus visiting what certainly could be described as 'total war' on Zululand. Yet, the extent of the devastation should not be exaggerated. Beyond the range of the British patrols, the amaZulu escaped with little or no harm or loss, and damage was concentrated to the coastal plain as far north as the Mhlathuze River, to the countryside around Luneburg and Khambula in the north-west, limited localities facing Rorke's Drift and Middle Drift, and the route taken through west-central Zululand by the 2nd Division and Flying Column. British records make mention of only 211 *imizi* burnt out of a probable 21,250 in Zululand, and even if we were to double or treble this number, that comes to no more than 3 per cent of the whole. Likewise, British tallies of captured livestock arrive at 5 per cent of the approximately 300,000 cattle in Zululand, 6 per cent of the 200,000 goats and 8 per cent of the 40,000 virtually hairless African sheep. Double or even treble the figure, and the number would still have been less than catastrophic for the Zulu people except in those limited zones where losses were concentrated.[29]

One major raid, or reconnaissance-in-force, undertaken in the third week of May had as its dual objectives a military exercise for the as yet untried Cavalry Brigade and the long overdue interment at Isandlwana of the British dead. As Chelmsford put it: 'The move will have a good effect in a military point of view, over and above that which will be produced in the colony and in England by our doing what many think ought to have been done long ago.'[30] Chelmsford had originally intended to accompany the 'burying party', not least because it would have given him the opportunity to see for himself 'the first part of our line of advance.'[31] As it was, he left it to Major-General Marshall to lead the expedition. Evidence is lacking, but it is more than likely that Chelmsford jibbed at revisiting the horrible field of slaughter, brought about – even if he would never bring himself to acknowledge it – by his culpable strategic blunder four months before.

Marshall set out on 19 May for Rorke's Drift with the King's Dragoon Guards and the left wing of the 17th Lancers. On 21 May, with the support of the Rorke's Drift garrison under Major Dartnell, he advanced to Isandlwana. Nervous of Zulu resistance and taking no chances, the cavalry were accompanied by several units of the NMV, the NMP, Bengough's 2nd Battalion, NNC, and a thousand Border Guards. Four companies of the 2/24th Regiment protected the column's rear. As it turned out, no enemy were encountered and the locating and burial of the dead commenced undisturbed. The dreadful stench of decay had largely dissipated, but desiccated bodies and wreckage lay all around. Most of the dead officers were identified by their 'rings, necklaces, medals, bracelets' (and Deléage noted that 'the wearing of bracelets was very common among the English officers').[32] Marshall did not linger long, retiring that evening with forty wagons still found to be serviceable, and by 23 May all the units that had taken part in the expedition were back at their posts. Chelmsford was not satisfied, and guiltily wrote to Stanley that he could not 'but regret that . . . the burying of the dead was not carried out in the fullest extent possible,' and that 'the earliest opportunity will be taken to complete this sad duty'.[33] It was left to the Border Guards to carry on with the arduous and grisly task for six more weeks. They left the bodies of the men of the 2/24th for interment by their own regimental comrades stationed at Rorke's Drift, and that was carried out on 20, 23 and 26 June. Even then, some bodies still eluded the detection of the burial parties because of the long grass which was not yet dry enough for burning, and it was not until March 1880 that the job was finally completed.[34]

The mounted reconnaissances undertaken during May from Landman's Drift had established that the shortest route for the 2nd Division to follow to oNdini was across the Ncome River below Koppie Alleen.[35] This necessitated creating a new depot on 28 May called Fort Whitehead with two supporting earthworks built by the 58th Regiment and named after their colonel. Fort Whitehead replaced the forward base Chelmsford had already established twenty miles to the north at Conference Hill, adding to the pressure on the already overworked and enfeebled Commissariat and Transport Department that was not geared to adapt its operations to such changes.[36] Embarrassed by the delays such reconsiderations of strategy imposed on his advance and the need to explain them to his superiors in London,[37] Chelmsford was compelled to make a virtue of necessity and fell back on the 'good' but distinctly uninspiring proverb: 'slow and steady wins the race' to justify his slow forward progress.[38]

There is no doubt that his many problems preparing the second invasion were at that time taking their mental and physical toll on Chelmsford. He snapped back at Wood when he dared dispute his arrangements, reminding him that 'I am the one to be hanged if anything goes wrong.'[39] And tellingly, when Chelmsford assured Cambridge on 23 May that his health had improved and he was confident of success, he nevertheless added that once he had finally defeated the amaZulu he would immediately hand over his command to Clifford and return to England.[40] Captain William Montague, the Brigade Major of the 2nd Brigade, 2nd Division, observed Chelmsford closely and perceptively during these anxious days when he appeared far less assured than he had to Deléage only a few weeks earlier in his office in Pietermaritzburg:

> From under a rather low white helmet his anxious face peered out; a nose long and thin, and, if anything, hooked; the principal feature black bushy eyebrows, from under which his dark eyes seemed to move restlessly, ever on the watch for something sudden, coming. A pleasant manner, sharp, rather jerky sentences; and a general air of watchfulness pervading all his actions. He gave one the idea of a man pre-occupied, under a

spell, and glad to get rid of his thoughts by an incessant attention to detail.[41]

On one typical occasion, Montague saw Chelmsford personally supervising wagons experiencing difficulties crossing a stream, 'endeavouring to put some little method into the obstinate drivers. And the men passing looked at him with some astonishment, and asked one another, "Where is the staff?"'[42]

At last, on 27 May the 2nd Division began to move forward from Dundee, Landman's Drift and the Doornberg to concentrate at Koppie Alleen, and Chelmsford dourly noted that 'Newdigate is going to buy his first experience of S. African marching – I hope it will open his eyes to the necessity of attending to transport details.'[43] Indeed, the advance would prove unduly laboured. The columns would move only once cavalry had reconnoitred the route ahead to ensure that there were no Zulu concentrations capable of threatening them while extended on the march; and wherever they camped for the night they undertook the laborious and time-consuming procedure of forming laager. There was disagreement among Chelmsford's staff over the form this should take, and the complex initial design was soon abandoned in favour of a simple oblong one that continued to be adopted during the advance.[44] Moreover, Chelmsford periodically halted to build fortified depots along his line of communications, and convoys had to be escorted back and forth to fill them with supplies.

When planning the advance, Chelmsford had to find a suitable role for the Cavalry Brigade under the hard-riding and hide-bound Major-General Marshall. As Deléage observed, while the 'easily-handled, light horses of the Lancers' were adapted to every sort of terrain, 'the large horses, heavily accoutred' of the Dragoons were 'an embarrassment'.[45] Cavalry chargers, moreover, were used to plentiful fodder of oats and hay, and its lack, thanks to the logistical deficiencies that beset the Cavalry Brigade, meant they were soon losing condition. Chelmsford crossly noted that 'The Cavalry Officers . . . have been slow to recognize the necessity of adopting colonial customs as regards the horses, and have hesitated to run them loose to graze.' In time they would learn to do so, but not before the poor state of the regular cavalry's horses had slowed down the advance.[46]

Since the ponderous Dragoons were altogether less mobile and adaptable than the Lancers, Chelmsford decided they would be detached and not continue with the advance. Rather, two squadrons would be posted at Conference Hill to patrol constantly to cover the left flank of the columns moving towards Babanango and to escort the convoys going back and forth; while the remaining two squadrons would be stationed at Rorke's Drift to watch over Sihayo's country and the column's right flank.[47] Marshall was having none of this. He angrily put it to Chelmsford that it would be a personal insult to him if, as the general in command of the Cavalry Brigade, he was actually to command only one regiment in the field. Chelmsford placated him for the moment, Deléage sardonically reflected, 'to save the appearance of the importance of a cavalry general', and conceded that one squadron of the Dragoons would join the Lancers in their advance into Zululand.[48] Lieutenant John Jervis of the 17th Lancers (who would soon succeed his father as Viscount St Vincent) noted at this time that 'All the generals seem to be fighting amongst themselves,'[49] and were especially jealous of the favour Chelmsford always showed Wood in terms of the provision of armaments and supplies and in the exercise of an independent command.

On 31 May Chelmsford wrote to Major-General Crealock revising his strategic role. Only too aware that 'Crealock's Crawlers', as the men of the 1st Division were coming to be derisively known, were still far short of their original objective, Chelmsford advised Crealock that 'I do not think it would be of any use your attempting to move on Ulundi, as our force will be quite sufficient to meet any force Cetywayo may send against us.'[50] Instead, the 1st Division was to confine itself to diverting Zulu forces from confronting the 2nd Division by raiding and burning *amakhanda* along the coast, always an element of its function as envisaged by Chelmsford in his memorandum of 12 April for Major-General Crealock's guidance.[51]

On 31 May, in rainy weather, the 2nd Division crossed over the Ncome River into Zulu territory proper. Immediately, a quite unnecessary disaster cast a blight on the advance when on 1 June the impetuous Prince Imperial was ambushed and killed while out on patrol (*see* Chapter 30 for details). Wood had begun his movement south from Khambula on 5 May with the Flying Column, marching by way of laagered encampments at Wolf Hill and Munhla Hill. He entrusted the security of the Transvaal border to the garrisons he left behind at Utrecht, Luneburg and various posts in between. Not that they could do much outside their entrenchments if challenged. Between 7 and 21 June Zulu raiders in the region of Luneburg would sweep off thousands of cattle and sheep over the Phongolo and burn settlers' farms, assisted in their depredations by disaffected Boers from the Wakkerstroom District of the Transvaal.[52] However, these raiders were not such a threat that Wood was diverted from his march, and he effected his planned junction with the 2nd Division at the Tshotshosi River on 3 June.[53]

On 5 June the mounted men of the Flying Column and the 2nd Division had a stiff and chastening encounter with the amaZulu that underscored Chelmsford's concerns over the efficacy of the Cavalry Brigade. Some 300 irregular horse from the Flying Column under Buller made a reconnaissance towards Zungeni Mountain on the two columns' left flank. Coming into contact with about 300 amaZulu stationed at eZulaneni, a cluster of four large *imizi* on the west side of the mountain, they charged and scattered the defenders and put eZulaneni to the torch. They then nimbly withdrew under fire from the amaZulu who were shooting at them from under cover and were trying to outflank them. Three troops of the Lancers, the squadron of the Dragoons and two colonial mounted units (some 500 men in all) were stationed in support of Buller's troopers who had by now successfully pulled back. The cavalry had not yet seen action in Zululand, and Marshall was eager to put them to the test. He therefore quite unnecessarily ordered them to charge towards eZulaneni. The horsemen became entangled in the difficult terrain and ignominiously fell back under brisk fire from the amaZulu who were skirmishing effectively around their flanks. The cavalry were finally extricated under the covering fire of Buller's contemptuous irregular horse. Lieutenant F. J. Cokayne Frith, the promising and popular young adjutant of the 17th Lancers, was shot dead in the pointless affray and was buried that same evening, followed lugubriously to his grave by Chelmsford, his staff, and most of the officers in the camp.[54]

Marshall, who Wolseley was later informed had embarrassingly 'fainted from excitement' when Frith was killed,[55] was left to ponder the superiority of the tactical skills of the colonial horse over his regular cavalry. Within a few days, on 13 June, Chelmsford managed to side-line him, relegating him to being 'in charge of the whole line of communication in the enemy's country and such portion of the garrisons which are left in the frontier posts for the purpose of patrolling'.[56] Colonel Drury C. Drury-Lowe of the 17th Lancers was left as the senior cavalry officer with the joint column, an officer whom most – even Chelmsford – regarded as 'useless' since (in Wolseley's contemptuous words) he was 'a Hyde Park Colonel who would always have his Regt. well turned out, but dislikes working his horses as it pulls them down in condition'.[57]

The next day, 6 June, the joint force resumed its advance. The difficulties it was encountering crossing steep drifts and marshy streams and the time it was spending in constructing laagers were severely delaying the march. Chelmsford realised he would have to halt to build up more supplies and construct depots to hold them. Accordingly, Fort Newdigate, a supply depot between two stone-walled redoubts, was constructed on the east bank of the Nondweni River. That clear moonlight night, while the fort was still being completed, one of the jittery infantry outposts started firing volleys at what was assumed to be the enemy, and set off a panic among the many young and inexperienced soldiers who started firing wildly, expending thousands of rounds of ammunition, and the artillery fired off a round of case. Bugles sounded the alarm; tents were struck and there was pandemonium.[58] The camp was riddled with bullet holes. Several soldiers were wounded and a number of animals killed in the firing. Chelmsford and his officers at last restored order and deployed their troops in a proper defensive formation. This false alarm was all too reminiscent of the almost identical incident at the Gingindlovu laager on 6 April, and did little to bolster Chelmsford's confidence in the steadiness of the troops under his command.[59]

The 2nd Division halted from 7 to 17 June at Fort Newdigate, now known to the men as 'Fort Funk',[60] while the Flying Column escorted a convoy of 660 wagons back and forth to Koppie Alleen to bring up supplies.[61] While waiting, the 2nd Division went out to gather wood for fuel and improve the tracks. Several raids were mounted to clear the area, and Buller patrolled on 14–15 June as far north as Ntabankulu Mountain, burning about thirty *imizi*, inflicting a few casualties on the amaZulu and capturing about 300 cattle and some 100 sheep and goats.[62] Charles Fripp of the *Graphic* recalled that,

> . . . columns of black smoke rose from burning kraals . . . [and] the country was being thoroughly scoured of the enemy . . . Our

> native allies revelled in the glory of burning and destroying without any risk to their black skins, and returned to camp chattering and singing, laden with mealies, strips of meat, and Zulu utensils.[63]

Chelmsford reported on the joint force's progress to Stanley on 16 June, informing him that it would resume its advance in the direction of Babanango Mountain on 18 June from a new depot on the east bank of the Ntinini River established under the protection of the earthwork Fort Marshall.[64]

Cetshwayo, meanwhile, faced with increasing numbers of defections (especially along the Zulu coast), and uncertain how best to prosecute the increasingly disastrous war, in mid-May summoned the principal men of the kingdom to oNdini to give of their advice. It seems that they opposed the continuation of the war and urged the king to seek peace with the British. Even though his *amabutho* who were beginning to muster in the Mahlabathini plain were still full of brave fighting words, Cetshwayo, unnerved by the disaffection of his nobles and despairing of fighting off the British, consented to attempt a fresh peace initiative.[65]

It was to prove a hopeless undertaking for (as have seen) Frere's minute of 4 April had starkly laid down that, in effect, only unconditional surrender could be entertained.[66] Cetshwayo did not know that, and during the last weeks of May, Major-General Crealock began to complain that he was 'in a state of chronic messengers from the King and his indunas'.[67] However, as instructed by Frere, Crealock referred all their messages to Chelmsford for his sole attention.[68]

Chief Ndwandwe, the first of this series of messengers, came into Fort Chelmsford on 15 May with Cetshwayo's plaintive message: 'What have I done? I want peace – I ask for peace.'[69] Chelmsford responded to the report he received of this message by evolving addition terms of surrender over and above those contained in the original ultimatum of 11 December 1878. All captured weapons and prisoners were to be surrendered, 10,000 stands of firearms were to be handed over, as well as at least 10,000 cattle and 20,000 sheep.[70] These were impossible terms surely designed to elicit resistance until the final British victory. Frere capped Chelmsford's new conditions with his harsh directive that the king's messengers were to be told that unless acts were 'substituted for words' and genuine efforts made to comply with the British terms, then their land would be devastated.[71]

A further relay of Zulu emissaries arrived in the 1st Division's camp in the last days of May and Crealock packed them off to find Chelmsford.[72] Meanwhile, Cetshwayo also attempted to negotiate directly with the 2nd Division. Three messengers, Mgcwelo, Mtshibela and Mphkothwayo, reached Wood's camp on 4 June, carrying a message that Cetshwayo had given them personally in the presence of his councillors.[73] The following day, 5 June, the three emissaries had a formal interview with Chelmsford. They made a bad impression on the British who found them 'villainous-looking scoundrels'.[74] For his part, Chelmsford was firmly resolved that 'there could be no permanent peace until the king was deposed.'[75] He therefore laid down fresh conditions that were a refinement on those additional ones he had insisted upon in May.

Chelmsford first stated that, in light of developments along the coast, he no longer believed that the king was being obeyed. Therefore, unless Cetshwayo could provide proof of his authority, he would rather continue negotiating with the chiefs alone. Chelmsford went on to warn that he would continue his advance unless the king, in earnest of his power and genuinely peaceful intentions, sent in to the British camp all the oxen at his royal homestead, along with the two 7-pounder guns captured at Isandlwana. He also required Cetshwayo to promise that all the firearms in Zululand would be collected and given up to the British. Furthermore, an *ibutho*, to be designated by Chelmsford, was to come into the British lines and lay down their arms. Then, and only then, would the General even entertain peace discussions.[76]

The disconsolate three messengers left the British camp on 6 June bearing with them Chelmsford's written statement of his impossible terms. It is hard not to regard this punctilious sop to correct diplomatic procedure (for who in Cetshwayo's council did Chelmsford imagine could read his words?) with deep cynicism. His conditions (in writing too!) were for the record. His intention was to fight and destroy the king whose warriors had ruined his reputation at Isandlwana, and he would brush aside intelligence that Cetshwayo was indeed calling on his people to send cattle to help him buy off the invaders.[77]

In stark contrast to his dealings with the king's emissaries, on 16 June he offered the chiefs easy terms, laying down only that, on their submission, they must give up their arms and the royal cattle in their keeping. In return, their people were to be spared and protected.[78] Only the king, then, could not hope for Chelmsford's mercy. On the same day as his emollient message to the Zulu chiefs, Chelmsford despatched a Zulu captive to Cetshwayo with a further directive reinforcing his demands of 6 June:

> Until the King sends an Ambassador and complies with the preliminary conditions, the army under my command in every part of Zululand has orders to advance and make raids.[79]

CHAPTER 30

Misfortunes and Disputes, June 1879

CHELMSFORD'S LONG-DELAYED ADVANCE into Zulu territory with the 2nd Division was met immediately by an ill-fated incident and was bedevilled by festering disputes that again brought his suitability as commander seriously into question.

In great haste and distress, from his camp near Thelezi Mountain seven miles beyond the Ncome River, Chelmsford composed a letter at dawn on 2 June. When it finally reached Britain on 19 June, it was destined to throw the Queen, her government and the public at large into utter consternation. The missive baldly stated:

> Prince Imperial acting under orders of the Assistant Quarter Master General [Colonel Richard Harrison] reconnoitred on 1st June road to camping ground of 2nd June accompanied by Lieutenant [Jahleel Brenton] Carey 90th Reg. D.A. Quarter Master General and his six white men and friendly Zulus all mounted. Party halted and offsaddled the road about 10 miles from this camp, but as the Prince gave the order to mount a volley was fired from long grass around the Kraals.
>
> The Prince Imperial and two troopers are reported missing by Lieut. Carey who escaped and reached the camp after dark. From the evidence taken there can be no doubt of the Prince being killed. 17th Lancers and ambulance are now starting to recover the body but I send this off at once hoping to catch mail.
>
> I myself [Chelmsford was at pains to emphasise] was not aware that Prince had been detailed for this duty.[1]

Chelmsford, who was totally preoccupied with mounting the second invasion, had not asked for the burden of being responsible for the

Prince's safety but (as we have seen) he had done his best to see that he was accommodated. The Prince, however, was not content to be a passive observer. While accompanying military patrols in May – during one of which he had come under Zulu fire – he exhibited a strong streak of recklessness and bravado. Alarmed, Chelmsford had attached him to the QMG's Department under Colonel Harrison where his map-making duties should have been less hazardous. But on 31 May the Prince obtained Harrison's permission to make a reconnaissance of the route which the 2nd Division intended to follow the next day. The patrol was in fact nothing more than a jaunt, thought up by the Prince as an excuse to escape the boredom of camp routine. Harrison indulged him in his whim because he considered he faced little risk, and was disarmed by the Prince's considerable charm and vivacity. When Harrison gave Lieutenant Carey permission to accompany the Prince, he made it clear that, for safety's sake, they were not to set off without an additional escort of Shepstone's Native Horse. However, in their keenness to be gone on 1 June, the Prince and Carey disregarded Harrison's orders, and left accompanied only by a Zulu guide and six troopers of No. 3 Troop of the Natal Horse (Bettington's Horse). Harrison, who joined Chelmsford soon after issuing his orders to the Prince and Carey, assumed all would be well and did not even mention the patrol to him.[2] Nor, according to Chelmsford, did the Prince say a word about his planned reconnaissance to any members of his staff.[3]

Although Carey, as a serving officer, was technically in command of the patrol, he deferred to the Prince on account of his royal status. It was therefore the Prince's decision during the mid-afternoon to halt the patrol at Sobhuza's *umuzi* near the Tshotshosi River where the men dismounted for an hour's rest and brewed up coffee. Unaccountably, no precautions were taken against a possible ambush. A party of between thirty and sixty *amabutho* had been tracking the unwary patrol, and the Zulu guide alerted the Prince that he had observed amaZulu moving in the vicinity. It was clearly time to move off, but it took a while to round up and saddle the horses and, just as the patrol was about to mount, the attackers let loose an unexpected volley. In the ensuing panic and confusion Carey and five of the troopers threw themselves onto their saddles and galloped off without attempting to help the Prince who failed to mount his restive horse. One of the escaping troopers was shot off his horse; the sixth, who had failed to mount, was killed, as was the Zulu guide. The Prince, whose courage was never in doubt, died fighting to the last.[4]

Carey and the survivors of the patrol reached the 2nd Division's camp at about 7 p.m. when it was already dark and too late to take any action. When the news spread that the Prince had probably been killed, the men stood about gloomily discussing the matter, and many expressed sympathy for Chelmsford in this, his latest setback.[5] Indeed, he was only too aware how it would further blight his reputation, and that night Major F. Grenfell, the DAA and DQMG, saw him 'in his tent with his head on the table in a state of absolute despair'.[6]

Chelmsford's worst fears were realised the next day. Newdigate noted down in the official diary of the 2nd Division:

> The body was found by a party of Lt Colonel Buller's Horse which moved out from Br Genl Wood's Column . . . and was carried into camp by the 17th Lancers – The funeral attended by all the troops off duty in the Division took place in the evening.[7]

The Prince had suffered eighteen spear wounds including one through his right eyeball, and the amaZulu had ritually slit his belly open. His body was stripped naked except for a gold chain around his neck with a medallion and a locket of his mother. When at about 2 a.m. the body was deposited in a tent in the HQ camp, Lord Chelmsford was observed to turn 'quite a deathly colour, and but for his catching the wheel of the ambulance, would . . . have fainted, so much was His Excellency affected'.[8] Chelmsford's initial intention was to bury the body at the camp, and a burial party was detailed to dig the grave, but his staff persuaded him to change his mind. Instead, late that afternoon at 5 p.m., the Prince's body was wrapped in a horse blanket, draped with a *Tricolore*, placed on a gun-carriage and brought to where three companies from each regiment formed three sides of a hollow square with arms reversed. Chelmsford and his staff walked behind the body in the funeral procession following a Roman Catholic priest. The Royal Artillery officers, many of whom had been fellow students of the Prince at Woolwich, were the pall bearers.[9] During the memorial service when the troops off duty were gathered round, Deléage observed Chelmsford standing further off, 'leaning sadly on his cane, his eyes red rimmed and his heart full of bitterness . . . the unfortunate general who had known every possible misfortune since the day of his arrival in South Africa'.[10] The Prince's remains were embalmed, and the following day were transported under cavalry escort to Durban where they were put on board HMS *Boadicea* on 11 June, and transferred in Cape Town on 15 June to HMS *Orontes* that carried them to Britain. Queen Victoria and her court went into mourning between 22 June and 2 July for 'His late Imperial Highness the Prince Napoleon',[11] and he was finally interred in the Bonaparte mausoleum at Chislehurst on 12 July, the Queen herself attending the funeral.

With the Prince's remains despatched to Durban, along with what was left of his already tattered reputation, Chelmsford had still to deal with Lieutenant Carey. Carey was openly blamed by his fellow officers for cravenly abandoning the Prince to his fate. In an attempt to clear his name Carey requested an official inquiry. Chelmsford convened it on 4 June, and on its recommendation Carey's trial by General Court Martial was held on 12 June at the British camp on the Phoko (Ntinini) River under the presidency of Colonel Glyn. Major Philip Anstruther, who served as Judge Advocate and was 'very sorry for poor Carey', reflected that 'whatever way the verdict goes we shall be called fools or rogues as the case may be. I only know that I thank God that I was not placed in his position. I hope I should have done differently but really one cannot say.'[12] In the event, Carey was found guilty of 'misbehaviour before the enemy' in that he galloped away without attempting to rally the Prince's escort.[13] But neither the court nor Chelmsford himself could decide on an appropriate punishment, and sentence had in any case to be confirmed by higher authorities in Britain. The humiliated Carey was therefore deprived of his sword and sent home under arrest to learn his fate. Chelmsford – with considerable generosity and fair-mindedness considering what harm the debacle was likely to do to his standing – wrote on 19 June arguing for mercy for 'an officer of considerable promise . . . zeal and ability' who was 'not wanting in personal courage' but who, he believed, had 'lost his head'.[14]

Chelmsford was right to fear the repercussions once the news of the Prince's death reached Britain. As Norris-Newman reflected, 'considered per se,' it could 'only be regarded as a minor episode of the campaign . . . But various causes combine to invest it with a special pathos and interest, almost world-wide.'[15] Certainly, the death of the young and gallant Bonapartist pretender caused an uproar every bit as vehement as the news of Isandlwana. Any sympathy felt for Chelmsford, especially in military circles, was outweighed by the battering he received in the press,[16] and from probing questions in Parliament.[17] Cambridge was appalled and informed Chelmsford privately on 26 June that the news of the Prince's death 'has filled all hearts with grief & sorrow'. His first impulse was to shift the blame away from himself and obliquely place it on Chelmsford's shoulders, writing disingenuously that 'I was in hopes that it had been distinctly laid down that the Prince was to be looked upon as a Spectator & Volunteer in camp, that the possibility never occurred to me of his being sent out on such a very dangerous expedition.'[18]

Meanwhile, the popular impression gained ground that Carey was being made a scapegoat for the ineptitude and folly of his military superiors.[19] This appeared to be confirmed when the Judge Advocate General, James Cornelius O'Dowd, found on 16 August 1879 that there was 'no evidence legally to justify' the conviction of the court martial since, although Carey was the senior combatant officer present, the command of the patrol was in fact distinctly exercised by the Prince 'up to the last moment'.[20]

The Horse Guards simply could not permit the quashing of Carey's court martial to rest there. On the very same day as O'Dowd delivered his judgment, General Sir Charles Ellice, the AG, responded with an official despatch reflecting the Duke of Cambridge's views. While accepting that the charge against Carey could not be sustained, the Duke offered a stiff rebuke to all those involved, especially to Colonel Harrison for not displaying 'more firmness and forethought in his instructions' to Carey and the Prince. Identifying this new scapegoat (whose career, it should be noted, suffered no ill effects) conveniently allowed Cambridge to reverse his initial blaming of Chelmsford and to absolve him of any responsibility for the disaster. In fact, Ellice went so far as to declare:

> His Royal Highness desires it to be known that he entirely approves of Lord Chelmsford's arrangements for the reception and occupation of the Prince; and that he considers the orders issued for his protection were marked with judgement and adapted to the occasion.[21]

The Queen was also inclined to absolve Chelmsford of direct culpability, passing on to Frere that the Empress Eugénie herself 'thinks [Chelmsford] is blameless, which *she cannot* consider others under his command to be'.[22] However, overall the Queen was far from pleased, especially with how the court martial had been conducted, and Ellice relayed her oblique reprimand to Chelmsford on 10 October: 'The queen regrets the charges laid and the imperfect evidence adduced should have led to what the queen considers a very unsatisfactory conclusion. Her Majesty cannot help expressing the wish that a more perfect investigation had been made.'[23]

In the event, the death of the Prince Imperial occurred too late in the campaign to have any effect on Chelmsford's supersession which the government had already decided upon, and Chelmsford had in any case been officially exonerated of any blame. Nevertheless, it served to further tarnish his reputation and, like Isandlwana, would continue to be associated negatively with his name.

If public opinion in Britain and Natal held Chelmsford in increasingly low esteem, many of the troops he was commanding were of the same mind. Clery, while conceding that Chelmsford 'has certainly had no *luck*' and had been dogged by misfortune at every turn, nevertheless attributed many of the problems being encountered in the advance of the two divisions to unsound strategy and lack of direction from the top.[24] Others were even less circumspect. Captain James McSwiney wrote to his mother that 'Everyone is becoming fearfully disgusted, for we never know when we shall get on and Lord Chelmsford does not know either.'[25] An anonymous Gunner was even blunter in his letter to the press at home in Wales, asserting that 'Lord Chelmsford is most unpopular amongst the men who look on him as a very inferior general – and so he is, for now he is over-cautious as he was before over-rash, and the delays in advancing are most vexatious.'[26]

What made it worse for Chelmsford was that he was constantly being compared unfavourably to Wood. It is not clear how aware Chelmsford was of this. He continued to lean on Wood for advice and confide in him, never quite accepting that his trusted lieutenant was an instinctively political and self-serving officer who contrived to disassociate himself from those aspects of Chelmsford's leadership which attracted criticism while remaining on close personal terms. There was no doubting, though, that Wood, not Chelmsford, was the man of the hour. Deléage visited him at the Flying Column's camping ground at Munhla Hill and enthusiastically reported that Wood was 'dressed in a grey greatcoat and wearing a soldiers' little fatigue cap', and

> . . . would not have been recognised as the famous general except for the respectful deference that everyone showed as the energetic figure passed by . . . If ever a man lived up to his legend, it was he. The sun-tanned face bore testimony to every hardship and act of daring. His amazing energy justified the blind confidence which his soldiers placed in him.

Tellingly, with the troubled mood in Chelmsford's headquarters obviously in mind, Deléage added: 'There prevailed in this camp an atmosphere quite lacking in anxiety which was a pleasure to experience.'[27] A subversive riddle going the rounds of the camps of the invading army (and gleefully recorded by Wolseley) summed up the current assessment of Chelmsford and of his all too popular lieutenant: 'Why is it that the men with Lord Chelmsford's Column cannot be regarded as Xtians? Because they made an idol of Wood (Evelyn) and do not believe in the Lord."'[28]

John Crealock was sufficiently aware of the prevailing mood to be both concerned and defensive. If 'soldiers of all sorts', he wrote with indignation,

> and the gentlemen of the press . . . instead of this constant carping and gossiping and crabbing their general . . . would imitate a little his unselfishness, his unswerving sense of duty, his unwearying efforts for the good of the service and his temper under daily trials – and utter want of appreciation – we should all of us be more worthy of the colour of the coats on our backs . . . If I could only get people to understand just a *little* of the untiring work for the good of the service Lord Chelmsford has done.[29]

But many of the 'specials' with the army were not prepared to give Chelmsford any leeway, and the misgivings of the troops were echoed by local and overseas correspondents, none more so than Archibald Forbes of the *Daily News* who was unfailingly critical of Chelmsford's conduct of operations. Only a small scattering of the colonial newspapers, such as the *Times of Natal* of 13 June and *Natal Mercury* of 16 June, were willing to point to Chelmsford's difficulties in acquiring supplies, building forts and keeping open the lines of communication, and were prepared to blame delays on logistical problems and poor morale among the troops. What made matters worse was Chelmsford's inept handling of the unwelcome war correspondents who were joining his forces in ever-growing numbers. Determined self-publicists like Wolseley cultivated them to ensure a laudatory press, but Chelmsford found it went against the grain to do so. He did try on occasion to be amenable, as when on a patrol to the Ncome River on 26 May he graciously invited Deléage and Francis of *The Times* 'to share his rustic luncheon'.[30] But he exposed his true sentiments when he advised Wood to treat the 'specials' in the same way as he did, 'with silent contempt'.[31] The problem was that Chelmsford was increasingly smarting at the criticism levelled by war correspondents he considered 'generally hostile' to him and prepared, 'either intentionally or ignorantly' to 'distort the truth, or misrepresent it' in order to damage his reputation. Consequently, he simply could not bring himself to work positively with the 'specials' he despised and mistrusted, and querulously informed Stanley on 10 June that,

> Their presence in the camp will make no difference to myself, and you may depend upon my pursuing 'the even tenour [*sic*] of my way' uninfluenced by the knowledge that I am surrounded by those who will not be sparing in their criticism if everything is not rearranged exactly to their liking.[32]

Chelmsford's deteriorating relations with Clifford, his Inspector-General of the Line of Communication, added to the malaise affecting his command. Initially, the two men had worked well together, but friction soon arose, not least because Clifford, who was both zealous and hard-working, was not easy to get along with at a personal level.[33] It did not help that Clifford developed a strong antipathy towards Colonel Crealock, promoted in April to be Chelmsford's MS rather than AMS. Clifford (as did many others) believed that Crealock was exercising an undue influence over his chief and cutting him off from those who would give him good counsel. He therefore took it upon himself to address Chelmsford in long and frequent letters of advice and complaint, adopting a peremptory tone that did not fall far short of impertinence, and was certainly inappropriate towards his superior officer. Nevertheless, Chelmsford continued to exercise much forbearance towards Clifford, even if he was exasperated by his continual, insubordinate carping.

What Chelmsford did not know was that one of the reasons Cambridge had sent Clifford to South Africa was to keep the Duke informed of events through a confidential correspondence, and specifically to report on Chelmsford's conduct of the campaign.[34] On occasion Clifford went too far in denigrating Chelmsford to Cambridge, and at the war's end the Duke rebuked him in terms that provide an illuminating window into how he conceived his officers ought ideally to comport themselves:

> I must frankly tell you that I am rather surprised at the very severe remarks contained in your letters on Lord Chelmsford. You cannot think what serious mischief must arise in an army [in] which these sort of sentiments are entertained in the highest quarters – and whatever shortcomings there may have been I had rather they had been left unremarked upon than they have been.
>
> It is the tone and spirit of the service which must suffer in this way and I hope you will give such sentiments no encouragement.[35]

Wolseley suffered from no such finer scruples, and once he had landed in South Africa in late June he predictably proved only too receptive to Clifford's disparagement of his commander. He relished Clifford's malicious revelation that, 'Chelmsford had really no plan of campaign when he left Maritzburg for Dundee & said he could not form one until he had seen & consulted Wood.'[36] Eventually, Chelmsford became aware that Clifford was deliberately undermining him in his superiors' estimation, and was deeply affronted by his disloyalty.[37]

One issue in particular exercised Clifford. He was especially irked by Chelmsford's appointment of Marshall on 13 June to take command of the lines of communication inside Zululand itself.[38] This meant that Clifford's command now ended at the Natal border and not, as previously, wherever the forces were operating in the field. He wrote to Chelmsford, testily declaring that should a breakdown of communication between the frontier and the advancing columns now occur, he could not be held responsible.[39] Chelmsford was finally stung in a memorandum he penned on 2 July to expostulate: 'General Clifford seems to imagine that when sitting at his desk at P.Mburg [300 miles to the rear] he is capable of looking after my lines of communication in the enemy's country. I am satisfied that he can do nothing of the sort.'[40] Chelmsford was doubtless right, but the dispute was enervating and further damaged morale at his headquarters.

Unfortunately for Chelmsford's tottering standing with his superiors in London, Clifford was only too aware of the General's ongoing and unseemly dispute with Bulwer over the employment of the border levies. He self-righteously reported to Cambridge on 21 April:

> I regret to say that there appears to be anything but a good understanding between the two Heads, and I fear to a great extent it has been caused by Lord Chelmsford not placing himself in more direct communication with Sir Henry. Long letters have passed between them when a few words might have resulted in a satisfactory understanding.[41]

It was the trans-border raids conducted by Twentyman and Lucas on 7 and 9 April that had ignited the inflammatory correspondence.[42] The moment he learned that they had taken place, Bulwer wrote to Chelmsford to complain. Chelmsford, determined to have his way, and knowing that Cambridge deprecated civilian interference in military matters, sent him a letter on 11 April complaining that Bulwer's interference with his arrangements to secure the border from incursion was 'quite indefensible' and requesting Cambridge to give him his 'full support' in the matter.[43] Chelmsford followed up by informing Bulwer that he had referred the whole question of military command in South Africa to the Home Government.[44] Bulwer indignantly responded to Chelmsford on 15 April, pointing out that sending in the levies to raid was 'at entire variance' with the understanding they had reached in Pinetown on 11 March.[45] Thoroughly aroused, Chelmsford pursued his battle of words with Bulwer on 18 April, vehemently denying that he had ever agreed at Pinetown to the border levies' 'exclusive employment *within* the border' and reasserting his right, if he was 'to be considered fit to be entrusted with the conduct of the war' to employ them 'in whatever manner I may consider best in the interests of the Colony'.[46] Meanwhile, Bulwer had sent an enormous, eleven-page despatch to Hicks Beach on 16 April insisting that he had never authorised the deployment of levies over the border, and that in doing so Chelmsford had 'exceeded his powers and acted without due regard for the authority of this Government'.[47]

By this stage, although it had become a matter of principle to Chelmsford that it was his prerogative as CinC to deploy the border levies as he saw fit, he was beginning to doubt the advantage of using them at all.[48]

Picture Bulwer's astonishment when, after all of Chelmsford's previous vehemence over the absolute necessity of adopting the 'active defence' with the levies, he received Chelmsford's letter of 7 May informing him that with troops of such inferior calibre 'it would be absurd to attempt any military operations across the border'.[49] Yet, even then, Chelmsford was not being consistent. As we have seen, in late May he ordered the border forces to raid Zululand once more as a diversion for his second invasion. And, as Bulwer had always feared they would, the raids of 20 and 28 May provoked Zulu retaliation. A thousand warriors drawn from the Zulu border population launched a major raid into Natal at Middle Drift on 25 June 1879. They victoriously carried off 678 cattle and 771 goats, torched seventy-three *imizi* and killed thirty of the African border population, along with a Border Policeman and two River Guards.[50] The success and intensity of this raid exposed the weakness of Natal's border defences and confirmed, in Wolseley's words, that Chelmsford's advocacy of the 'active defence' had been 'objectionable and mistaken in policy'.[51]

Not that Wolseley did not believe that Bulwer had 'made the mistake of rather trying to interfere with military matters', and that his 'conduct on this point was silly'. Nevertheless, he considered that Bulwer had been 'so bullied' by Frere and the military over the issue of the border levies that he could be forgiven for having 'lost his head'.[52] Yet, if Bulwer did not emerge unsullied from his shrill dispute with Chelmsford, the consequences for the latter were far more serious. True, the Duke was inclined to blame Bulwer for not surrendering his authority on military matters to Chelmsford, and Hicks Beach finally telegraphed Bulwer on 19 May 1879 informing him that 'The full command of any forces whether European or Native, which are called out for service, must of course be with the General, with whom the responsibility for the operations rests.'[53] This was a victory for Chelmsford, but a Pyrrhic one. Unfortunately for him, the government in London could only regard his unnecessary dispute with the civil authorities in Natal – one that had consumed so much needless ink and energy – as further proof (should it be required) that, as had been the similar case with General Cunynghame in the Cape in 1878, he was a liability and not suited to his command.[54]

CHAPTER 31

Supersession, May–June 1879

ADDING TO CHELMSFORD'S WOES as he finally got the advance of the 2nd Division under way, was a growing sense that the Horse Guards and the government were fast losing confidence in his leadership. Indeed, although he had survived thus far in his command thanks to Cambridge, who had initially stood staunchly behind him, the Duke's support was becoming ever more grudging. The main reason for his waning confidence was that Cambridge was anxious to understand better what had gone wrong at Isandlwana so as to present a credible explanation to the government and the public, but Chelmsford's obfuscations (as we have seen) did not make this possible. Losing patience, on 6 March the AG, Major-General Sir Charles Ellice, wrote to Chelmsford requesting satisfactory replies to seven searching questions on issues not covered properly by the inadequate Court of Inquiry.[1]

Chelmsford responded testily to Cambridge on 11 April, declaring: 'I trust that my replies to the questions put to me by the Adjutant-General will be considered sufficient – I believe that most of them have already been answered by the evidence which I have already submitted.'[2] But Chelmsford's replies failed to convince Cambridge, who could not understand why the camp at Isandlwana had not been fortified according to Chelmsford's own field regulations, and the Duke was left more perplexed and irritated than ever. Meanwhile, on 19 March, in a letter to Cambridge he must surely have come to regret, Chelmsford had made the most candid avowal he would ever pen of his responsibility for the faulty strategy he had adopted for the campaign – even though, as always, he was at pains to justify himself as best he could:

> I must candidly express that I had underestimated the difficulties of a campaign in Zululand, owing to the inaccurate information

> which I had obtained regarding the physical difficulties of the country. I had calculated upon working in an open country over which wagons could pass without difficulty, but I at once discovered that colonial information was not to be depended upon. I believe, and still believe, that two British Infantry Regiments armed with the Martini Henry, should in open country be able to successfully resist any attack of the Zulus, assisted of course by the force of mounted infantry attached to each column – and, if entrenched, or in a strong defensive position where the rear was secure, that one regiment would be equal to the occasion. Events, lamentable as they have been, have not disproved this assumption of mine; but with the knowledge that I now possess of Zulu courage and determination, I should not consider myself justified in putting so small a column into the field. Those who criticize my division of the forces at my command into four parts forget that I had the responsibility of the defence of the Natal and Transvaal border thrown upon me, as well as the invasion of Zululand.[3]

Cambridge replied on 1 May and let Chelmsford know that he rejected the arguments he had put forward in his defence.[4] The implications of this rebuttal and implied censure would hardly have escaped Chelmsford, but Cambridge did not pursue the matter further until after the General had returned from Zululand.

If Cambridge believed the Horse Guards' official censure of Chelmsford for Isandlwana could wait until a more opportune moment, then an assessment of how effectively he was conducting the second invasion of Zululand could not. And what Cambridge adduced thoroughly alarmed him. Not only was it taking Chelmsford an unconscionably long time to wind up the campaign, but, as Cambridge confided to Frere, 'The cost of the war is also something terrible.'[5] Indeed it was, and it was eventually put at £5,230,328, considerably more than the government was willing to countenance for a colonial campaign.[6] The upshot was that Cambridge was losing the will to save Chelmsford in his command. So too was the frustrated government.

On 10 June, while encamped at the Phoko River in advance of Fort Newdigate, Chelmsford received two letters, both posted from London on 8 May. One was from Stanley and the other from Cambridge. Both severely criticised his current conduct of operations in similar terms, and it must be assumed that they had been drawn up after consultation between the War Office and the Horse Guards. The letters found fault with Chelmsford's risky deployment of two widespread columns and his failure to provide detailed plans for the second invasion, and took him to task for allowing the war to drag on for too long.[7]

While neither letter could have come as surprise, they certainly caused Chelmsford considerable alarm, and in his reply to Stanley – written on very same day he received the Secretary of State for War's epistolatory bombshell – he wretchedly admitted that he could not conceal that it had 'distressed me very much'. What affected him most was the paragraph in Stanley's letter that put forward the possibility of 'an officer of superior rank' being sent out to supersede him, an eventuality that Chelmsford angrily took 'in the light of a threat'. Nevertheless, he bethought himself in time to avoid any charge of insubordination, assuring Stanley that he would 'be quite ready to serve in a more subordinate capacity under whomsoever may be selected to succeed me'. (Just how genuinely this assurance was made, future events would reveal.)

For the rest, Chelmsford querulously defended his record at length at every point, citing difficulties such as faulty maps, difficult terrain, inefficient Transport and Commissariat Department officers and carping war correspondents. Whipping himself up into an indignant froth, he rhetorically enquired:

> Do people at home imagine that a country so large as Zululand, and peopled by such warriors as the Zulus have proved themselves to be, can be conquered off-hand . . . Looking to all the difficulties which surround military operations in this country, I cannot but consider in spite of the untoward results of the Insandlwana, Intombi and Inhobani affairs, that the forces under my command have made as much progress towards a final result as could reasonably be expected.[8]

Chelmsford was far more circumspect and measured in his response to Cambridge, written on the same day as his reply to Stanley. In it, he carefully explained that, although his deployment of two columns in the second invasion had exacerbated his logistical problems, he had been obliged to implement this strategy to screen Natal and the Transvaal from Zulu incursions.[9]

As he sat in his tent and feverishly composed these two impassioned letters of self-justification Chelmsford did not suspect that it was already too late for them to have the slightest effect on either Stanley or Cambridge. For, unbeknown to him on account of the laggardly transmission of communications between London and his camp in Zululand, he had already been superseded and was no longer in command.

Stanley's letter of 8 May to Chelmsford had encapsulated all the concerns of the Tory administration that had come to perceive him to be demoralised, uncertain of his strategy, and unable to bring the increasingly expensive war to a speedy conclusion. Lord Beaconsfield had at first been disinclined to make changes to the command structure in South Africa. But he was fast losing any confidence in Frere, who had been in the Transvaal Territory throughout March and April but had failed to make any progress in reconciling the Boers to British rule.[10] As for the equally unsatisfactory Chelmsford, he complained that although he had 15,000 troops under his command he seemed 'cowed and confused'.[11] Beaconsfield subsequently confided to Wolseley that Chelmsford's misfortunes were 'partly mismanagement & partly ill-luck, for ill-luck always attends upon mismanagement,' and that thus far he had retained his position only as a result of the influence of the Horse Guards.[12] But by mid-May the Cabinet knew that Chelmsford no longer enjoyed the full support of the Horse Guards. Beaconsfield wrote a long letter to the Queen on 30 May outlining the Cabinet's growing uneasiness regarding Chelmsford's conduct of the war. The initial reluctance to replace him, he explained, had changed with the arrival of a new batch of Chelmsford's despatches on 22 May 'revealing such a state of affairs – of anarchy and impotence – that your Majesty's Ministers absolutely refused to bear the responsibility of indifference'.[13]

In these circumstances, Chelmsford's protracted and wearying dispute with Bulwer over the deployment of the border levies was but the last straw. As Stanley would put it to Chelmsford on 29 May when explaining why he had been superseded: 'I must express my sorrow that you should have been unable to settle this question amicably with his Excellency by personal or friendly communication without the necessity of resort to the Home Government.'[14] Consequently, although the government confirmed on 19 May that Chelmsford exercised full command over all the forces –

both imperial and colonial – deployed in the war with Zululand, it decided to remedy the root cause of the discord between the competing authorities in the theatre of hostilities by creating a single, unified civil and military command. Chelmsford, Bulwer and Frere were all considered unsuitable to fill the new post with its greatly enhanced powers. But who was?

At the Cabinet meeting on 12 February immediately after receipt of the shocking news of Isandlwana, the Marquess of Salisbury, who was the Foreign Secretary, had been the most adamant for Chelmsford's instant dismissal and supersession. He had Wolseley firmly in mind as his replacement, and Wolseley himself was blatantly eager to be given the South African command. Nevertheless, Salisbury had to concede that, although he honestly wished that Wolseley 'were in Zululand at the moment', 'those who are in authority' did not agree with him.[15] Even so, he continued to lobby for Wolseley as Chelmsford's replacement, and Stanley, ever more disenchanted with the General's performance, began to support him.

As the pre-eminent and most go-ahead general of the day in the public's eye – even if Cambridge's circle in the Army held a distinctly jaundiced view of his reformist zeal and unashamed ambition – Wolseley seemed in Salisbury's and Stanley's estimation to be the ideal person to pull the government's chestnuts out of the fire in Zululand. But Wolseley, who had been promoted substantive lieutenant-general on 25 March 1878, was not immediately available. By the Cyprus Convention of 4 June 1878 the Ottoman Empire had ceded the administration of the island to Britain in exchange for a guarantee that the British would use it as a base against possible Russian aggression in the eastern Mediterranean. With that in mind, on 22 July 1878 Wolseley was appointed first High Commissioner and Governor-General of Cyprus. But with the signing of the Treaty of Berlin on 13 July 1878 between the great powers, the war-scare over the Eastern Question was brought to a close, and the point of having Wolseley stationed in Cyprus fell away. But Wolseley remained trapped in his now dead-end posting. Fretting that he was missing the Second Anglo-Afghan War where the fighting began in November 1878, as well as the Anglo-Zulu War, he set about canvassing for high military command in either India or South Africa.[16]

His efforts did not fall on deaf ears. On 27 April Stanley summoned Wolseley back to London, ostensibly to sit on a nebulous committee at the War Office considering the short service system. But, as Stanley would later admit to Wolseley, it was a ruse to get him back to London because the Secretary for War had decided he wanted him to exercise both civil and military command in South Africa.[17] As a ruse, though, it was a particularly transparent one. When Stanley informed the House of Commons on 26 May that 'It has been found that it was a most fortunate circumstance that Sir Garnet Wolseley's presence at home has enabled the Government to avail themselves of his able services,' he was greeted by knowing and derisive laughter.[18]

The decision to supersede Chelmsford and reduce Frere's powers was made after three rapid Cabinet sittings in successions between 19 and 23 May. At the first of the sittings only five members gave Chelmsford their qualified support. They were Hicks Beach (Colonial Secretary), the Duke of Richmond (Lord President), Lord John Manners (Postmaster General), the Duke of Northumberland (Lord Privy Seal) and Stanley who seems to have felt some embarrassment at being seen to be too keen to throw over a general he had originally appointed and supported. Beaconsfield too felt some compunction. As we have seen, he had left the first Lord Chelmsford out of his Cabinet in 1868 because he considered he had proved a poor Lord Chancellor. It distressed him now to have to supersede the son as well for being an incompetent general.[19]

By the end of the third Cabinet meeting Chelmsford had lost what little support he had initially enjoyed.[20] The Queen, however, was inclined to support Chelmsford, and was 'much annoyed' by Beaconsfield's suggestion, which she thought 'was very wrong', that he be superseded.[21] But Beaconsfield stood firm and explained to the Queen: 'No one upheld Lord Chelmsford. Even the Secretary of War gave him up, and spoke as if the military authorities had done the same. His quarrel and controversial correspondence with Sir H. Bulwer seemed the last drop. Perhaps also the dissentions in his staff.'[22]

The Cabinet's reverse judgement of Solomon was to create a single, unified civil and military command in South Africa and, strongly urged by Salisbury and Stanley, they resolved unanimously to appoint Wolseley. In an attempt to convince the dubious Queen of the wisdom of the Cabinet decision – she was much annoyed and would only ever sanction rather than approve of Wolseley's appointment which she feared would lead to the embarrassing resignations of both Frere and Chelmsford[23]

– Beaconsfield consulted Cambridge on 23 May. The very same day Wolseley had a long interview with the Duke but skirted around the issue of replacing Chelmsford since 'It was not my business to find fault with the strategy or tactics of a commander who had been selected by the C. in C.'[24] The following day Cambridge had a long discussion with his mother (the Dowager Duchess of Cambridge, born Princess Augusta of Hesse-Kassel) about 'the *dangers* of him [Wolseley]! and his being at the bottom of the whole Cardwell system!!' Not that Cambridge cavilled at either Chelmsford's or Frere's demotion, but he wanted Chelmsford's old chief in Abyssinia, Lord Napier of Magdala, to be selected rather than Wolseley. He went to see Beaconsfield about it on 25 May, and Salisbury the following day. Wolseley, who knew Napier was being considered, was on tenterhooks, anxiously consulting with Ellice, Stanley and Salisbury. But Cambridge was told firmly that Napier was too old (which he would not admit), and conveniently Napier would not make himself available. So, Wolseley it was.

Writing to his son Adolphus on 4 June, Cambridge crossly declared: 'Wolseley's appointment was not pleasant to me though I think it was necessary to do something at once as matters at the Cape were going on badly . . . I cannot see why he should be the *only* man in the Army we have left for duties requiring energy.'[25]

Finally, on 26 May Wolseley went to Downing Street where Beaconsfield told him the Cabinet had decided on his appointment. Asked when he could leave, he assured the Prime Minister that he would be ready to do so on 29 May. As his wife Loo (Louisa) told Wood, Wolseley's appointment was 'sharp work I assure you, just as it *always* is, only told of it on Monday & sent off on Thursday leaving me to sweep up the debris'.[26] Exalting in his South African command, Wolseley left Downing Street for Westminster to hear the long debate in the House of Commons about the nature of his instructions.[27]

In the House, Sir Robert Peel on behalf of the Opposition wanted to know if 'the confidence of the Government has been withdrawn for the General Commanding-in-Chief, Lord Chelmsford?'[28] Sir Henry Havelock (son of the Indian Mutiny general) then rose to enquire

> . . . whether Lord Chelmsford's position would be that of second in command, or would he revert to the command of one of the

> two main columns, or would he revert to the command of the troops in Cape Colony . . . or would he be entirely superseded and set aside?'[29]

In his fudging reply that dodged the question, Colonel Stanley stated:

> Sir Garnet Wolseley is in the Army senior to Lord Chelmsford, and though it is true that Lord Chelmsford at the present moment holds a local rank which gives him the position of lieutenant-general, he is still in many degrees junior to Sir Garnet Wolseley; and by the sending out of a senior officer he will naturally have to subordinate his plans and his general action to the superior officer who may be on the spot.

Stanley went on to declare that giving Wolseley 'the general direction of affairs, military as well as civil, must not be held to imply censure on Lord Chelmsford's proceedings. It is simply that we have found it necessary at the present time to place the direction of affairs, civil and military, in one pair of hands'. Wolseley, Stanley assured the House, was being sent out to South Africa with instructions 'to bring this war to a conclusion'.[30]

Wolseley finally received his three official commissions on 28 May. He was to go out to South Africa as High Commissioner in South Eastern Africa and Governor of the Transvaal, thus confining Frere's authority to the Cape Colony. As Governor of Natal, he out-ranked Bulwer. And as CinC of the Forces in South Africa with the local rank of full General, he out-ranked Chelmsford.[31] After dutifully saying farewell at Gloucester House to Cambridge, who was predictably 'very indignant' that Wolseley had interfered with his patronage and was taking with him Special Service officers and staff of his, rather than the Duke's choosing, Wolseley took train from London with great, cheering crowds to see him off at Paddington Station. Arriving in Dartmouth, he went on board SS *Edinburgh Castle*, which steamed out of harbour at noon on 30 May, bound for the Cape.[32]

On 28 May, the same day that Wolseley received his commissions, Hicks Beach telegraphed both Frere and Bulwer informing them that the chief civil and military authority in South Africa had been placed in Wolseley's hands. Stanley telegraphed Chelmsford to the same effect on the same day.[33] The three telegrams were carried from St Vincent by an Australian steamer to Cape Town where Frere, who received them on 15 June, sent them on to Clifford in Pietermaritzburg.[34] He in turn, transmitted them on 16 June to both Bulwer and Chelmsford.[35] Chelmsford received his in his camp on the banks of the Phoko River.[36] It read:

> Her Majesty's Government have determined to send out Sir Garnet Wolseley as Administrator in that part of South-Eastern Africa in the neighbourhood of the seat of war, with plenary powers, both civil and military; Sir Bartle Frere instructed accordingly by Colonial Office. The appointment of a senior officer is not intended as a censure on yourself, but you will, as in ordinary course of service, submit and subordinate your plans to his control.[37]

Less than a week before, in his letter of 10 June, Chelmsford had assured Stanley that he would be 'quite ready to serve in a more subordinate capacity' under any officer of superior rank sent out to supersede him. Yet, when push came to shove, Chelmsford baulked. He affected to find the text of Stanley's telegram ambiguous, and continued to act as if he were still GOC in South Africa. His headquarters staff knew otherwise. When Crealock wrote to Alison on the very same day that the fatal telegram came into Chelmsford's hands, he was in little doubt that it was 'meant to be a supersession of Lord Chelmsford'.[38] Frere understood for certain that it was. He wrote to Chelmsford on 18 June confiding how affronted he had been by the totally unexpected telegrams 'intimating, as all the world read it, that he [Wolseley] was coming out to supersede you, Bulwer and myself'.[39] That certainly was how colonists in South Africa saw it. Major Frank Russell, who had only just arrived in Durban and had still to join the army in the field, reported to Alison that, 'The prospect of Sir Garnet's coming here was indeed most startling . . . The colonists are of course delighted, but there is no abuse too violent with them for the present command-in-chief. One cannot help feeling that it will be a terrible blow for him, poor fellow.'[40] So indeed it was, but Chelmsford maintained an imperturbable front and persisted in the charade of still being in command, '*deliberately so*', as Crealock reported,[41] refusing (as we shall see) to be swayed until he received some unspecified but more explicit official notification of his supersession.

Crealock, who understood full well that Wolseley had superseded Chelmsford in his command, observed to Alison that 'There is one consolation to us old Africans, however, that the two wars [the Ninth Cape Frontier War and the Anglo-Zulu War] will have been ended before England's one soldier [Wolseley] was called on to assist.'[42] And that was the whole point of Chelmsford's apparently obtuse failure to accept the import of Stanley's telegram.

The rebarbative but unpredictable Clifford, who had repeatedly crossed swords with Chelmsford, thought so too, and wrote to him the moment word came of Wolseley's imminent arrival hoping that he won the war first.[43] When Frere wrote to Chelmsford on 18 June, he added a telling postscript: 'I cannot tell you . . . how confidently I hope that you will have a brilliant success before anyone comes to share the fruits of your labours, trials and sufferings.'[44]

That was certainly the hope of Adria, Lady Chelmsford, ever her husband's staunch champion, and fully informed concerning the problems he was encountering in the exercise of his command. While Chelmsford was as yet unaware that his nemesis was already on the high seas, steaming towards the Cape, she already knew that he been superseded. From Bath, she wrote an impassioned letter to Wood on 3 June expressing her intense umbrage and concern:

> I know you would feel for my husband. He certainly has been most cruelly abused, & I am sure you will feel still more for him now, when you hear he is superseded by Sir Garnet & thrown over by the Govt. without a word of thanks for all his hard work . . . It is quite insulting to a man who has worked & slaved under intolerable difficulties as my husband has done, & thwarted at every tune by a petty jealous man like Sir Henry Bulwer. *He certainly* deserves to be superseded. Sir Garnet & his partisans have been moving heaven & earth to go out to the Cape, & have succeeded. I only pray the war may course to an end before he arrives to reap another man's harvest – but I fear it is impossible, tied & bound as my husband is by his transport difficulties. Sir Garnet will of course proclaim 'martial law' & bring difficulties to an end. Then they will cry 'What a clever General is Sir Garnet.' Forgive this very bitter letter.[45]

Had she had knowledge of it when she wrote, Lady Chelmsford would have applauded her hard-done-by husband's determination to prevent the thrusting Wolseley from reaping his 'harvest'. Indeed, Chelmsford was galvanised by Stanley's telegram. He immediately ordered Wood, who was unloading the wagons he had escorted to Fort Newdigate, to move the Flying Column forward immediately, even though his men and oxen were exhausted.[46] Then, on the very same day, 16 June, he sat down to write to Stanley. Studiously avoiding any mention of the fateful telegram he had just received, he reported on the progress of the forces under his command and confirmed his intention to advance on Ulundi as speedily as possible with the 2nd Division and the Flying Column.[47] The next day, Crealock reported to Alison:

> The intention appears to be to 'rush' Ulundi. In fact the season is now so advanced that there is nothing else left to do. So now apparently matters have come to this, that there will be a scramble to get to Ulundi and back again. If the Zulus won't then make peace I can see nothing for it but the very cheerless prospect of waiting till next season to begin the thing over again.[48]

CHAPTER 32

The Advance to the White Mfolozi, June–July 1879

CHELMSFORD ORDERED A GENERAL ADVANCE on 18 June with the Flying Column marching slightly ahead of the 2nd Division. After completing the construction of the earthwork Fort Marshall to guard the next supply depot, the joint column began the slow and difficult slog to the top of the steep Babanango Mountain range. Once finally there on 20 June, Chelmsford found it necessary to halt four miles beyond the Mhlathuze River to form yet another supply depot under the earthwork walls of Fort Evelyn, constructed on 22–3 June.[1] From there, Chelmsford's objective, the distant Mahlabathini plain with its cluster of *amakhanda*, including oNdini, could just be made out.[2] Progress forward over the following week was slow. Although the terrain along the Babanango ridge was reasonably level, there was much thick bush to be cleared and drifts across numerous streams to be improvised. As a precaution against Zulu attack, once Fort Evelyn was left behind the joint column laboriously formed laager every night when it halted. Cavalry and the colonial mounted units cautiously reconnoitred the route ahead and continued to burn Zulu *imizi* and drive off livestock. Large bodies of amaZulu kept watch on the advancing British from the crests of the hills. On 20 June there was a skirmish with 500 amaZulu in the Mphembheni valley, and another in front of the column on 24 June. The amaZulu attempted to burn the drying winter grass along the British line of advance to deny their animals forage, but mounted patrols were mainly successful in preventing this.[3]

On 26 June Wood led a strong patrol down into the emaKhosini valley on the south bank of the White Mfolozi and destroyed nine of the *amakhanda* clustered there.[4] Before they set off at daybreak, the force was drawn up for Chelmsford's inspection which, 'as was usual with him, was, though rapid, most carefully minute'.[5] The emaKhosini valley was a particularly sacred spot for the amaZulu since Cetshwayo's royal ancestors were buried there. Unbeknown to the British, Wood's patrol had perpetrated an act of the greatest symbolic significance to the amaZulu when the *inkatha yezwe yakwaZulu* was consumed in the flames of the esiKlebheni *ikhanda*. Handed down from King Shaka himself, this sacred grass coil was the symbol of Zulu unity and nationhood, and its destruction was seen as a dire portent of the imminent fall of the Zulu kingdom.[6]

On 27 June the joint column reached the foot of the flat-topped Mthonjaneni heights. To reach the summit, it required a stupendous effort with three spans of oxen hitched to each heavy wagon and teams of soldiers straining on the drag ropes. But once having gained the heights, oNdini was only some sixteen miles away in the plain far below, north across the White Mfolozi River. It had taken the 2nd Division twenty-eight days to advance the sixty-five miles from Koppie Alleen to this vantage point. To any outside observer this would have seemed an extraordinarily slow pace and, anticipating criticism, Chelmsford defensively tried to explain to Stanley that, 'As considerable difficulties in road making have had to be overcome, the progress has not been as great as might be expected perhaps by those ignorant of the country.'[7] But, regardless of whether he could have advanced faster or not, Chelmsford knew that he was at last in striking distance of his objective. He called all his senior officers together, and informed them that the time had come for a final blow against the enemy, putting them 'in the highest possible spirits'.[8] The joint column formed laager on Mthonjaneni on the evening of 27 June. The days were warm but the nights were chilly, especially on the misty, drizzly heights. Crealock grizzled that,

> The general, as usual, likes being badly off as the private soldier on every occasion, and has always succeeded in being worse off than any officer, so we are not to be permitted to pitch our patrol tents even if we carry them on our packhorses. Stores of any sort have long since disappeared from our meals.[9]

On 27 June, while the combined column was laagering on Mthonjaneni, a patrol under Buller intercepted a party of Zulu emissaries and escorted them into camp. King Cetshwayo, although being forced into a situation where he must fight to the last, was nevertheless attempting more urgently than ever before to negotiate.[10] Chelmsford's written conditions that the king's three messengers, Mgcwelo, Mtshibela and Mphokothwayo, had carried off with them on 6 June still required the king's response. As Cetshwayo could not read the message, it had been necessary to fetch Cornelius Vijn, a trader whom the war had detained in Zululand, to do so for him. But Vijn was living at a distance, and it was not until about 17 June that he had translated the note and sat down to translate and pen Cetshwayo's dictated response.[11] Affronted by Chelmsford's impossible demands, the king's reply, although dignified in tone, rejected negotiations while British armies were advancing into Zululand and plundering as they went.[12] This letter never reached Chelmsford. The four messengers to whom it was entrusted were turned back at Fort Marshall and, fearing they would be shot, returned to Cetshwayo with the note undelivered.[13]

Vijn consequently wrote again. This time, Mgcwelo, Mtshibela and Mphokothwayo were sent off again in search of Chelmsford carrying Vijn's second letter in a cleft stick. Their retainers bore two great tusks of elephant ivory, symbolic of tribute to a superior, and as a peace offering drove along with them a herd of 150 of the cattle captured at Isandlwana. It was they whom Buller intercepted on 27 June and brought before Chelmsford.[14] The General did not yet know that he no longer possessed the authority to treat with them. On 29 May Stanley had written to him that 'the responsibility placed upon you' by Frere to enforce his demands on Cetshwayo 'will therefore be terminated upon the arrival of the High Commissioner, and any overtures for peace will henceforth be transmitted for decision by him'.[15] But Chelmsford was not yet in receipt of this letter or of future communications from Wolseley on the wide scope of his commission, and continued to lay down terms as he before.

Even though the tone of the letter presented by the three Zulu envoys was, unbeknown to Chelmsford, more placatory than the undelivered one, it did not engage with the conditions the general had previously laid down on 4 June and amended the next day. He therefore declared he would continue his advance and rejected the elephant tusks. However, in order to give Cetshwayo a last chance to comply, he undertook in his reply written on 27 June not to cross the White Mfolozi immediately; furthermore, he kept the cattle as a sign he was still willing to make peace.[16] The three messengers left the next day telling the interpreter as they went that the amaZulu 'would have to fight now' since it was impossible for the king to comply with Chelmsford's terms.[17] For his part, the general was equally unshakable. It was not that he did not credit the king and his councillors with a genuine desire to end the war, but (as Crealock explained) because he believed they still obstinately clung to doing so solely on their own terms.[18]

Meanwhile, Wolseley had landed in Cape Town on 23 June. During the voyage he had been ruminating on Chelmsford's 'ignorance of his trade',[19] and was especially critical of his two-pronged invasion strategy. He was determined to take an immediate and firm grasp of the conduct of the Zululand campaign, uniting the 1st and 2nd Divisions and provisioning the single column from a coastal base. Then, at its head, he intended to finish off the war himself, cutting Chelmsford out. Wasting no time in his hurry to reach the front, he sailed from Cape Town the day after he landed and reached Port Elizabeth on 26 June.[20] From there he sent out a slew of telegrams to all the generals conducting operations imposing his control.[21] His journal entry sums up their content:

> I have telegraphed orders to Crealock and Chelmsford desiring them in future to report in every instance to me as I must at once stop this system of everyone communicating direct with the Authorities at home. I have also informed Chelmsford that I have full powers to make peace & that all communications regarding peace must be made to me. I shall have some trouble in making this team pull together and answer to one whip.[22]

In addition, Wolseley instructed Chelmsford to supply full details of his intended strategy with the joint column.

Wolseley disembarked at Durban on 28 June (the day after Chelmsford encamped on the Mthonjaneni heights) and proceeded at once to Pietermaritzburg where, at 5 p.m. that very same evening he was sworn in as Governor of Natal. While in Pietermaritzburg, Wolseley closely consulted with Clifford who informed him that Chelmsford's joint column was made up of about 6,000 imperial and 2,300 colonial personnel, along with 700 wagons, 10,600 oxen and 450 mules; Crealock's 1st Division was slightly smaller with 5,200 imperial and 2,300 colonial military and support personnel, an unspecified number of wagons (about half as many as in Chelmsford's column) drawn by 3,400 oxen and 40 mules. Crealock's oxen were reported to be dying at the rate of 400 a day, while Chelmsford's were doing well.[23]

A few days before, on 24 June, Clifford had telegraphed Chelmsford criticising his arrangements of 13 June for the lines of communications that divided them between him and Marshall.[24] Clifford had sent off this message with the deliberate aim of gaining Wolseley's ear. When he met him in Pietermaritzburg, Clifford imparted that there had been no direct communication from Chelmsford since 21 June, even though the telegraph connected Pietermaritzburg with Landman's Drift, from where signals could be flashed by heliograph to and from Chelmsford's latest camp. This revelation confirmed Wolseley suspicion that Chelmsford had deliberately cut himself off from his base to prevent his new commander from communicating with him so that he could 'do something brilliant' before the new CinC joined the troops in the field. When consulted, Bulwer (with whom Wolseley found he could work easily) showed himself of like mind and was convinced that Chelmsford was doing his best to 'rush it' to gain a great victory of his own.[25]

Wolseley's response was to telegraph Chelmsford peremptorily on 28 June:

> Concentrate your force immediately and keep it concentrated. Undertake no serious operations with detached bodies of troops. Acknowledge receipt of this message at once and flash back your latest moves. I am astonished at not hearing from you.[26]

When he finally read this telegram on 2 July, Crealock scathingly commented: 'Sir Garnet now appears on the scene, orders that nothing is done except through him, that he disapproves of there being 2 columns and that they are to join – *how* I don't know, unless he can give No. 1 Division wings to advance to us.'[27]

Furthermore, since he accepted Clifford's critique, Wolseley ascribed the break in communications to the 'divided control of the lines of communication' set up by Chelmsford, an arrangement 'fatal to a proper conduct of operations'. He therefore placed Clifford back in command over the full extent of the lines of communication, expecting 'much good from this change'.[28] Having thus vindicated Clifford and done his best to set his military house in order, Wolseley reported to Hicks Beach that he intended next to join the 1st Division. After that, he would 'proceed westward as rapidly as possible, with the view of effecting a concentration of the two divisions under my command'.[29] At the same time, he wrote to Stanley expressing his amazement that Chelmsford had not yet replied to his telegram of 26 June.[30]

In fact, at 3 p.m. on the afternoon of 28 June, Captain H. Stewart, Marshall's efficient brigade major, had ridden into Chelmsford's camp on the Mthonjaneni heights from Rorke's Drift. He carried with him Wolseley's telegram of 26 June sent from Port Elizabeth informing Chelmsford that he was subordinated to his command. Stewart had found the men of the joint column busy at work on erecting a laager but, as Crealock testily put it, 'We had immediately to set everyone down to clerical labour . . . and the poor general to a long, long letter which I copied.'[31] In it, Chelmsford responded fully to Wolseley's request for details of his proposed movements. 'Plan of operations in this part of Zululand almost developed,' he wrote. He went on to state that he intended to leave a strong garrison on Mthonjaneni while he advanced on Ulundi with the rest of the joint column. As for the 1st Division, which he lamely explained had been slowed down by unforeseen difficulties, he was 'at such a distance from General Crealock' that (as he expressed it), 'it would have been impossible for me to control his movements, even had I desired to do so'. (In fact, that same day he finally received intelligence by telegraph through Natal of the 1st Division's activities up to 22 June, and sent off two African runners with a cypher letter informing Crealock of his plans.)[32]

Chelmsford went on in his despatch to admit to Wolseley that once he had destroyed oNdini and the surrounding *amakhanda* it would be 'difficult to write confidently' of what he intended next. He continued:

> I very much question being able to hold on to the Ulundi valley even if it were advisable, which I doubt. Our supplies will not last beyond a certain time, and it would be difficult to replenish them from such a distance as Landman's Drift. The grass will also be getting scarce and dried up, and much of it is sure to be burnt. It will be desirable, therefore, to decide upon some advantageous position which can be permanently occupied in the enemy's country, which will command as much of it as is possible, and for which supplies can be safely and speedily carried.

Chelmsford believed that Kwamagwasa, the abandoned Anglican mission of the Rev. R. Robertson situated on elevated ground south of Mthonjaneni, would be the most advantageous spot for such a depot. But it would be required only 'on the supposition' that he did not inflict such 'a decisive defeat upon the enemy' that Cetshwayo would be obliged to 'agree to any terms that may be imposed upon him'. And that conclusive victory he intended to secure. As he concluded: 'I am, however, hopeful the enemy will stand, and thus give the troops under my command the opportunity they are longing for.'[33]

On 1 July Wolseley left Pietermaritzburg for Durban, and with his customary despatch went on board HMS *Shah* that same evening and set sail for Port Durnford where, as he scathingly put it, Crealock was 'apparently engaged in making roads, and not advancing'.[34] Just before he embarked, he received Chelmsford's despatch dated 28 June which had been carried to him by a relay of mounted officers riding through day and night. When he grasped that Chelmsford must already be advancing on oNdini to force on a decisive battle, Wolseley understood that he was now engaged in a desperate race to get to the front in time to take the command of the joint column out of Chelmsford's hands before he could engage the amaZulu. It was imperative, therefore, that he go ashore at Port Durnford without any delay.[35] Before setting sail, he sent a telegram to Chelmsford, ordered him, if compelled to fall back, to retire on the 1st Division by way of Kwamagwasa and St Paul's missions. He added: 'Wish you to unite your force with the First Division, as I strongly object to the present plan of operations with two forces [acting] independently of each other, and without possibility of acting in concert.'[36]

By 1 July the 1st Division was encamped at Port Durnford where it was supplied by sea with stores landed on the open beach from lighters when the surf was not too heavy, or by convoy from Fort Chelmsford. 'Crealock's Crawlers' had been making slow, over-methodical headway,[37] and it was only on 20 June that the 1st Division had finally concentrated at Fort Chelmsford for its further advance up the coast. Its lack of progress seemed to have borne out the criticism of those who, like Wolseley, opposed the independent operations of a second column. On the other hand, it was proving effective in securing the surrender of most of the coastal region, even before the battle of Ulundi was fought. Overawed by the large British military presence, local chiefs began to negotiate their submission, encouraged by the easier terms Chelmsford had promulgated on 16 June. Among those giving up the struggle were local luminaries and former military commanders such as Dabulamanzi and Mavumengwana. The 1st Division finally advanced from Fort Chelmsford, threw a pontoon bridge across the Mlalazi River, and commenced building Fort Napoleon on 25 June to cover the crossing. Mounted patrols raided between the foot of the Ngoye hills to the west and the coast, and as far north as the Mhlathuze River, burning many *imizi* and capturing much livestock. There was little, if any, resistance for the Zulu men along the coast were responding to Cetshwayo's summons to gather at oNdini to face Chelmsford's combined column.

HMS *Shah* anchored off Port Durnford at 7.30 a.m. on 2 July, but over that day and the next strong winds and heavy surf made it too dangerous for Wolseley to go ashore by steam tug. With the weather showing no signs of improvement, on 4 July – the same day Chelmsford fought the battle of Ulundi – the *Shah* sailed back to Durban with a fretting Wolseley still on board. Indefatigable as ever, the moment he landed Wolseley started out to join the 1st Division by land. By the evening of 5 July, he was at Fort Pearson. There he found a telegram awaiting him from Archibald Forbes, the war correspondent of the *Daily News*, informing him that the previous day Chelmsford had inflicted a severe defeat on the Zulu army. The following day, 6 July, when Wolseley reached Fort Chelmsford, he received Chelmsford's telegraphic despatch officially confirming Forbes's report.[38] And with that, Wolseley had to concede that all his frantic, frustrated hurrying had been in vain.

In planning his final push on oNdini (as he had explained to Wolseley in his despatch of 28 June), Chelmsford had decided that because of the steep and difficult terrain ahead that the troops should advance lightly equipped without 'all spare impedimenta' and without tents. They would bring ten days' provisions in 200 ox-wagons, and mule-carts would carry the reserve ammunition. Some of his transport train was on the road to the rear, bringing up supplies, but this arrangement would still leave some 500 wagons and 8,000 oxen on the Mthonjaneni heights. During 29 June these wagons were formed into two laagers flanking a central kraal for the oxen and were surrounded by a breastwork. This strong base, commanded by Major R. Upcher of the 24th Regiment (the victor of the battle of Kentani), was garrisoned by about 500 men made up of two companies of the 1/24th, one NCO and two privates from each company in the joint force, the 'weakly' likely to 'knock up from exposure', a troop of Shepstone's Native Horse, a few of Baker's Horse and forty European wagon conductors armed with rifles.[39] At 8.45 a.m. on 30 June the rest of the joint column began its march down to the Mahlabathini plain with the more experienced Flying Column in advance of the greener troops of the 2nd Division. At 3.30 p.m. the joint column bivouacked by a small stream on the sandy, bush-covered flats at the base of Mthonjaneni.[40]

At about midday, while the joint column was still laboriously making its way down Mthonjaneni, those two well-travelled Zulu emissaries, Mfunzi and Nkisimana, approached. They carried a third letter written by Vijn, as well as the sword of the Prince Imperial in earnest of their mission. Moreover, they promised the speedy arrival of the two 7-pounders captured at Isandlwana and yet more cattle.[41] Unbeknown to them, the letter they put into Chelmsford's hands carried Vijn's duplicitous postscript in which he correctly assured the General that the Zulu people, if not the king and his chiefs, intended to fight on.[42] Even so, Chelmsford responded by modifying his earlier terms somewhat. He was now prepared to accept a thousand rifles captured at Isandlwana in lieu of the surrender of an *ibutho*. He also gave Cetshwayo until noon on 3 July to comply with his terms, and undertook to keep his troops on his side of the White Mfolozi until that moment.[43] Yet, lest we are tempted to perceive these slight concessions as an indication that Chelmsford wished to avoid further bloodshed, we should understand that they were nothing more than a ploy on Chelmsford's part to keep up parlaying. Crealock certainly understood this, and later wrote that it was 'lucky indeed for us the Zulus did not attack us on the line of march – diplomacy helped us through that difficulty'.[44] Major Robinson was even more explicit: 'Cetywayo was given time because we could not well make our preparations complete until the 4th [July].'[45] The employment of insincere negotiations for strategic objectives in warfare is common enough, even if hardly ethical, and it is difficult to think well of Chelmsford for his underhand ploy. As it turned out, Chelmsford's disingenuous new terms never reached Cetshwayo because his councillors, who no longer saw any point in prolonging fruitless negotiations, did not allow the emissaries to report back to the king.[46]

At 7.30 a.m. on 1 July the two British columns continued their advance through difficult country cut by streams and covered in long grass, euphorbias, thorn-trees and mimosa bush. At about midday the Flying Column in the lead began forming an irregular, four-sided laager in a loop of the White Mfolozi about half a mile from the drift across the river. In the Mahlabathini plain beyond, *amabutho* were seen being drilled and doctored in preparation for the fighting to come, but the experienced officers of the Flying Column correctly believed that they were not intending to attack that day. But while the 2nd Division to the rear was still on the march, a sudden Zulu movement towards the river at about 1.30 p.m. convinced an edgy Chelmsford that an attack was imminent, and he over-hastily ordered both laagers to be completed within half an hour. Considering how long it took to form a laager correctly, it was unrealistic to expect the 2nd Division to do so from scratch in the time stipulated. Instead, it parked its wagons on a hill about a mile to the rear of the Flying Column's nearly completed laager and threw up a breastwork around them. Fortunately for the alarmed troops of the 2nd Division who were in a state of great confusion, the *amabutho* did not attack, and by about 5 p.m. had withdrawn to their *amakhanda*.

That night it poured with rain and there was a panic in the 2nd Division when a sentry fired at an officer who had not answered his challenge. The 2nd Battalion, NNC, who were sleeping as was customary outside the improvised laager, stampeded inside it in fright, trampling over the sleeping soldiers and the indignant HQ staff. Captain Molyneux, who had been present on 6 April during the panic at the bivouac at the eMvutsheni Mission near Gingindlovu, commented that it said something for the discipline of the soldiers that this time they did not shoot down and bayonet the NNC.[47] The following morning, Wednesday 2 July, the 2nd Division moved forward to park its wagons in triangular formation beside those of the Flying Column. The day was spent in forming a secure double laager and in building a small stone fort on a hillock at its southern apex to command the position. Behind its design was the intention that this fortified camp would be strong enough to be held by a small garrison when the main force finally advanced across the river to do battle.

During the afternoon of 2 July, the band played while the troops carried on fortifying their camp, and Zulu snipers opened fire on British bathing and watering parties at the river before being suppressed by British return fire. In the midst of these activities Cetshwayo made his final attempt to negotiate with the invaders. He ordered 100 or so of his own royal white cattle to be driven towards the double laager as a sign of submission. But the young men of the uKhandempemvu *ibutho* drove them back, insisting they would fight at all costs. Their gallant insubordination told Cetshwayo that the decision on whether to continue to resist had been taken out of his hands. So, even though he expected to be defeated, he gamely issued his final instructions for the decisive battle. The *amabutho* were not to attack the British when they were stationary, for that suggested they were entrenched. Bitter experience at Rorke's Drift, Khambula and Gingindlovu had taught them the consequences of attacking the British in prepared positions. Instead, every effort had to be made to manoeuvre and catch the British in the open as they had in their victories at Isandlwana and Hlobane.[48]

While he was busy that same day, 2 July, with overseeing the construction of the double laager and fort at the White Mfolozi, Chelmsford finally received Wolseley's telegram of 28 June ordering him to 'undertake no serious operations'. But it was too late to deflect him now. Chelmsford therefore advised Clifford by telegraph that he had formed camp at the drift across the White Mfolozi, and that, unless the king accepted his proposed terms of 30 June, at noon the following day, 3 June, he intended to make a strong reconnaissance across the river towards Ulundi.[49] Crealock, weary and sensing the end-game, and perfectly aware that Chelmsford was deliberately disregarding Wolseley's orders not to fight, wrote the same day:

> I trust, fight or no fight, that this business will be closed as far as soldiering goes before Sir Garnet appears, and it is the devout wish of everyone I hear speak; and then I hope Lord C's anomalous position may cease and we may be permitted to leave South Africa.[50]

Chelmsford now indeed had the bit between his teeth. During the course of 3 July, he received Wolseley's telegram of 1 July ordering him that 'if compelled to fall back' he was to retire by way of Kwamagwasa and St Paul's Mission in order to unite his force with the 1st Division. Wolseley testily concluded by insisting that Chelmsford 'communicate news to me daily' and that he acknowledges receipt 'immediately'.[51] Molyneux recalled that Wolseley's order 'made us all laugh' since it would have been 'a great military error' to fall back at this stage, and that Chelmsford, 'as the one on the spot who knew most of the game . . . wisely declined to alter his plans'.[52] Chelmsford disingenuously responded by telegraphing Clifford that the 'Weather has prevented flashing . . . Communication by this means very uncertain.' Having thus put the lid on any possible counter-orders, he went on to add that the die was irrevocably cast: 'Tomorrow I propose moving all available men up to Ulundi, and expect to fight with strong forces of the enemy.'[53]

CHAPTER 33

The Battle of Ulundi, July 1879

CHELMSFORD HAD RESOLVED that he would demonstrate to the amaZulu, who were taunting the British from across the White Mfolozi that they were afraid to attack them in the open, that he was fully capable of achieving a victory in the field instead of hiding behind entrenchments. As he said to Wood, 'They will be satisfied if we can beat them fairly in the open. We have been called ant-bears long enough.'[1] It seems, moreover, that he believed a decisive victory in the open would not only end Zulu resistance, but would underpin his contention that had the troops at Isandlwana adopted a more concentrated deployment, they would have won the battle.[2]

At noon on 3 July Chelmsford's undertaking to Cetshwayo not to cross the White Mfolozi expired without the Zulu king tendering his submission. Therefore, in preparation for his advance into the Mahlabathini plain to do battle on 4 July, Chelmsford ordered Buller to make an immediate reconnaissance in force across the river with all the mounted men of the Flying Column, some 500 officers and men.[3] Buller's objectives were threefold. First, he was to drive off the troublesome Zulu snipers posted on the bluff above the wagon drift across the White Mfolozi. Second, he was to approach as near as possible to oNdini to find the best position for Chelmsford's army to fight the next day. And third, he was to provoke the amaZulu into responding to his sortie so as to give away their points of concentration and likely tactics.

Accordingly, at about 1 p.m., the two squadrons of Baker's Horse, supported by two 9-pounders of the 2nd Division, crossed at the wagon drift and made straight for the Zulu snipers. Simultaneously, Buller led the greater part of the mounted men – a squadron of Mounted Infantry, two squadrons of the FLH, a squadron of the Natal Light Horse, a squadron of Raaff's Transvaal Rangers, and two troops of the Natal Native Horse – across the lower drift downstream. They then wheeled left to take the Zulu snipers in their flank. The snipers scattered and fled, pursued by Baker's Horse who then halted and regrouped. Buller, meanwhile, had continued across the plain with his men. Zibhebhu kaMaphitha, the most innovative of the Zulu commanders, had devised a strategy for luring the mounted men into a trap. A group of Zulu scouts drew Buller's men forward as far as the kwaNodwengu *ikhanda*. There they were relieved by another party of amaZulu driving a large flock of goats over the very ground where the next day's battle would be fought. Galloping Zulu horsemen, led by Zibhebhu himself, then took over and enticed Buller's men into the valley of the Mbilane stream, just short of oNdini itself. Several thousand *amabutho* were stationed there in ambush and poured an ineffective volley into the horsemen. Buller's troopers beat a hasty retreat, firing by alternate ranks. The Transvaal Rangers, who had halted to investigate kwaNodwengu, were able to give them covering fire. Baker's Horse were in their turn able to do the same. Further concentrations of amaZulu in the plain tried to cut off the flying horsemen and pursued them in fine skirmishing order right down to the river's edge, disregarding the shrapnel and grape fired from the two guns on the opposite bank and the heavy rifle-fire from three companies of the 1/24th that were hastily brought up in support.

It had been a desperate situation for the mounted men, who performed various feats of gallantry in rescuing unhorsed companions, for which three Victoria Crosses were subsequently awarded. The amaZulu were buoyed up by their apparent victory, but Buller had lost only three troopers killed and four wounded, and had in fact achieved all his objectives. When Chelmsford marched the next day, he had to hand all the necessary intelligence for fighting his battle.

Chelmsford's troops slept ill that bitterly cold, clear, moonlit night. Beginning at about 11 p.m. the roar of voices from thousands of *amabutho* in the plain preparing for the last great battle in defence of their kingdom, and the shrill cries of the women as they sang and danced, kept them kept them awake and unnerved the younger soldiers. At one stage the *amabutho* approached the river, but they did not go on to attack and marched away, still singing their *amahubo* (battle anthems), to take up the positions for the next day. Even so, as a precaution Chelmsford ordered the British cavalry to saddle up, and by about 2 a.m. they were crammed with the oxen in the laager where they spent the rest of the night. British nerves were not calmed by the sight of Zulu campfires and signal lights, not only across the river, but behind them as well.[4]

Chelmsford's forces began their preparations at 3.45 a.m. on 4 July for their advance into the Mahlabathini plain.[5] It took some time for the troops to eat breakfast, and the sun was already breaking through the early morning mist when they marched down to the river. Buller's mounted men of the Flying Column crossed at the lower drift at 6 a.m. They then took up position commanding the wagon drift across which the Flying Column and the 2nd Division, under Chelmsford's watchful eye, passed in parallel columns shortly after 7 a.m. and then formed up on higher ground on the opposite bank. The men carried only their greatcoats and two days' rations, and wheeled vehicles were restricted to a few carts carrying ammunition, water and entrenching tools. The amaZulu did not attack the British at the river crossing, for their plan was to surround and fight them in the plain and cut off their retreat to their fortified camp across the river. Chelmsford was awake to the danger of the amaZulu attempting to seize the double laager while his forces were committed in the plain, and detailed a garrison of some 600 men under the command of Colonel William Bellairs – one company of Royal Engineers, five companies of the 1/24th Regiment and other small detachments – to hold it against such a possibility.

The 2nd Division, Major General Newdigate commanding, numbered 132 officers, 1,725 white troops, 540 African troops and 39 camp followers; while the stronger Flying Column, Brigadier General Wood commanding, was made up of 122 officers, 2,159 white troops, 465 African troops and 108 camp followers. In the advance across the Mahlabathini plain, the Flying Column took the lead, as it had on the march down to the White Mfolozi. Once it had moved out of the riverine bush onto open ground, it halted at about 7.30 a.m., one and a half miles from the drift. There it formed the front half of a hollow square, which was completed by the 2nd Division marching up behind it. An infantry square was an archaic formation in European warfare, devised originally to repel cavalry. But in colonial warfare, where the enemy rapidly manoeuvred in a manner not unlike cavalry, and where they had no artillery and their marksmanship with what firearms they possessed was poor, the infantry square continued to be an effective formation. Showing a fighting front in every direction, it was proof against having its flanks turned as at Isandlwana; while the closely packed troops delivered a far more concentrated fire than had the extended firing line in the same disastrous battle.[6] Chelmsford had previously made known his intention to form square so the men got into position quickly. The six 9-pounder guns, six 7-pounder guns and two Gatling guns were positioned at regular intervals at the angles and faces of the square. At this stage all the mounted men remained outside the square, but the Royal Engineers, NNPC, 2nd Battalion, NNC, Wood's Irregulars and the medical personnel, along with all the carts, took cover inside it. In the event of an attack, the infantry were to face outwards in four ranks, the two front lines kneeling and the two rear ranks standing. Before the square advanced, Chelmsford ordered a practice drill to ensure that they would deploy efficiently when the moment came. He then ordered the troops to fix bayonets, and with the band of the 13th Regiment striking up an inspiring march, shortly before 8 a.m. the troops stepped out with regimental colours unfurled.

The formed-up square began its march north-east across the plain in rather loose order because it was a clumsy formation to manoeuvre. Chelmsford and his staff rode in the centre, behind the front face. Buller's men fanned out in advance and also about half a mile on the flanks to keep Zulu skirmishers away. The colonial horse of the 2nd Division (Shepstone's Native Horse and No. 3 Troop, Natal Horse [Bettington's Horse]) made up the rearguard. Approaching kwaNodwengu, Chelmsford ordered the *ikhanda* to be put to the torch. Then, 'in his clear, sharp, soldier-like voice' which 'rang out like a trumpet to the men', he gave the order: 'The square will wheel to the right.'[7] At about 8.30 a.m. Chelmsford brought it to a halt on the level top of the slight knoll Buller had selected during his reconnaissance the previous day. KwaNodwengu was on the square's right rear flank and it directly faced oNdini about one and a half miles away across the Mbilane stream. The guns were got into position and the ammunition boxes were opened so there would no repetition of the difficulties reputedly experienced with the ammunition supply at Isandlwana. As Buller had foreseen, the square's position afforded it an excellent field of fire with little dead ground and few dongas and trees, although the grass was high in places. However, the clouds of smoke issuing from burning kwaNodwengu obscured the surrounding area, and Chelmsford ordered the flames to be doused.

The Zulu forces that had concentrated in the *amakhanda* on the plain, numbering between 15,000 and 20,000 men, consisted of elements of all the *amabutho* save for two elderly ones detailed to guard the king. Cetshwayo himself, after giving his battle orders to his commanders at oNdini, had departed the previous day with his entire household for the nearby emLambongwenya *ikhanda*. On the morning of the battle, he moved further north-east still, to the kwaMbonambi *ikhanda* somewhat over four miles from oNdini. There he would stay throughout the battle, receiving regular reports of its progress. The Zulu forces were commanded in the field by his favourite brother, Ziwedu kaMpande who, along with other Zulu princes and great chiefs, was stationed on Mcungi hill a mile to the east of oNdini. At about 8 a.m. the Zulu forces in the plain began to manoeuvre with the aim of enveloping the newly formed British square that was beginning its advance. By about 8.30 a.m. when the square halted and took up its battle position, the amaZulu had completed their encirclement. The *amabutho* then began to close in on the stationary square in loose undulating lines about four deep with large masses in file in support behind. They were preceded by waves of skirmishers (just as modern tactics required, the British noted admiringly) who opened a desultory and inaccurate fire at great range. For the recent British reinforcements who had never before met the amaZulu in battle, their splendid manoeuvring in half-open order was a revelation.

Meanwhile, while the British square was forming up and beginning its advance, about 5,000 amaZulu in two separate bodies moved towards the fortified laager on the opposite side of the river. Bellairs's garrison went on the alert at 8.10 a.m. as the amaZulu approached the wagon drift. Some crossed the river to within 500 yards of the laager. But, as it turned out, this forced never seriously contemplated attacking the formidable British position, and it was not long before they melted away to join the battle developing in the plain.

The infantry square was a defensive formation, dependent on a great development of fire that could mow down an enemy charge and bring it to a standstill before getting close enough for hand-to-hand combat. For fire to be effective and achieve its objective of deterrence, it had not only to be accurate and disciplined, but it had to be reserved until the enemy was well into range, no further than about 600 yards away. At the battle of Khambula Buller's irregular horse had been very effective in provoking the amaZulu into effective range. This was not the role of regular cavalry which was to charge the enemy once they were broken and to transform their retreat into a rout. Chelmsford therefore ordered the regular cavalry of the 2nd Division (the five troops of the 17th Lancers and the small detachment of the 1st Dragoon Guards) to enter the rear of the square until their moment came. It was now up to the irregular horse of both the Flying Column and the 2nd Division to bring the amaZulu on. Between 8.35 and 8.45 a.m. they vigorously engaged the advancing amaZulu, pouring in volley after volley while conducting a measured withdrawal, drawing the irritated amaZulu forward. Finally, they took refuge within the square, the front and rear ranks of infantry opening to receive them.

Chelmsford then enquired of Newdigate and Buller, if the mounted men were all in? On being assured they were, Chelmsford pronounced: 'Then give the enemy a round or two of shrapnel.'[8] So, at 8.45 a.m. the six 9-pounder guns of the 2nd Division opened up with shrapnel shells. The artillery and infantry volley fire from the square became general at 8.50 a.m. as the great circle of amaZulu surrounding the square contracted to within 250 yards of the square, that is, to within close range of the rifles and Gatling guns. Many amaZulu would afterwards refer to what the British called the battle of Ulundi as oCwecweni, the battle of the corrugated-iron sheets. This was because the flashing of the bayonets, swords and gun barrels along the four sides of the compact square gave rise to that impression. Some amaZulu, including King Cetshwayo himself, afterwards insisted that the British had fought from behind iron shields. Others were convinced that the British had hung red coats on iron palings in front of them, off which the Zulu bullets harmlessly bounced.[9]

Such tales undoubtedly arose from the Zulu desire to explain why, having at last caught the British in the open, they were not able to defeat them. After all, following several previous battles it was not as if they lacked experience in facing British firepower. At Ulundi they consequently advanced at a run, keeping low in crouching positions behind their shields, taking every advantage of natural cover, and of the dense white smoke emitted from the British weapons. Nevertheless, despite great courage and determination, the amaZulu were finally pinned down within 100 yards of the square, and were unable to penetrate the zone of point-blank fire from mass rifle volleys and the Flying Column's two lethal Gatling guns. Nor, manoeuvre as they might, could they find a flank to turn as they had at Isandlwana.

It has been asserted that the Zulu attack was half-hearted because they entertained no hope of success, and Wood was at pains in his autobiography to claim that 'the hurried, disorderly manner' in which the *amabutho* attacked at Ulundi compared unfavourably with their 'methodical, steady order' at Khambula.[10] But Wood was not disinterested, for he was at pains to minimise Chelmsford's victory at Ulundi compared to the magnitude of his earlier one at Khambula. Frances Colenso, who was romantically attached to Colonel Durnford and was as zealous to restore his reputation as she was to sully Chelmsford's, also did her best to discount the extent of the British victory at Ulundi – a line uncritically adopted by several modern historians.[11] She deduced from what she considered the low rate of British fire that the amaZulu were easily repelled. In fact, the British infantry alone (there is no tally for the colonial mounted units) fired between 6.4 and 7 rounds per soldier; while 90 rounds of artillery ammunition were expended. Callwell has demonstrated that in 'small wars' a heavy expenditure of ammunition was unusual, and that in a typical battle under ten rounds per man was the norm.[12] At the battle of Gingindlovu, where no one accused the amaZulu of a half-hearted attack, the expenditure of British ammunition was even less than at Ulundi, at 6.2 rounds per man.[13] The battle of Ulundi, therefore, was a 'normal' one in the history of British colonial warfare. Chelmsford himself, when reporting to Cambridge on the battle, described the fire from the square – 'while it lasted' – as 'very heavy', and ascribed the moderate expenditure of ammunition to the men having been 'under perfect control'.[14]

Rather, then, than assert that Zulu conduct at Ulundi was lukewarm, it would be fairer to say that the amaZulu had acquired a better appreciation of the effectiveness of close-range, concentrated fire. If they were less reckless than in previous battles, it was because they possessed a more realistic sense of when it was pointless to persist in an attack. That does not mean that they did not hope for victory and failed to drive in their attack with great tenacity. Indeed, the ferocity of the initial Zulu onslaught caused the British considerable alarm. The amaZulu were hard targets to hit because of their open order and use of cover, and the volley-fire by company from the square was often aimed too high. Moreover, on occasion the volume of smoke from their weapons made it impossible

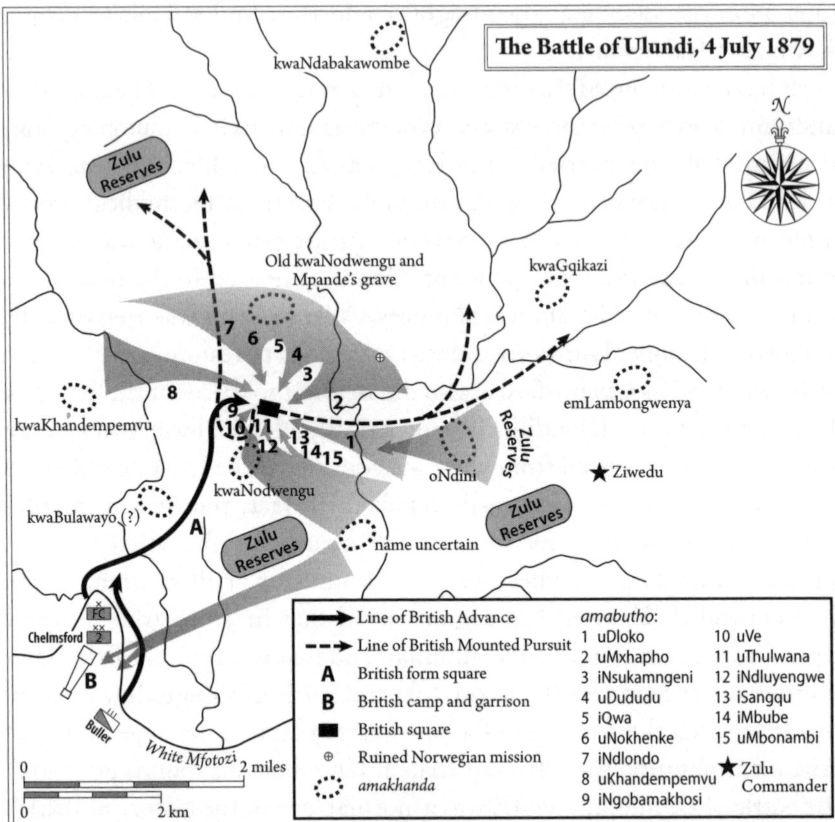
The Battle of Ulundi, 4 July 1879
N
kwaNdabakawombe
Zulu Reserves
Old kwaNodwengu and Mpande's grave
kwaGqikazi
7 6 5 4 3
8
2
9
10 11
12 13 14 15
1
kwaKhandempemvu
emLambongwenya
Zulu Reserves
oNdini
Ziwedu
kwaNodwengu
kwaBulawayo (?)
A
Zulu Reserves
name uncertain
Zulu Reserves
FC
2
Chelmsford
B
Buller
White Mfotozi
0
2 miles
0
2 km
Line of British Advance
Line of British Mounted Pursuit
A British form square
B British camp and garrison
British square
Ruined Norwegian mission
amakhanda
amabutho:
1 uDloko
2 uMxhapho
3 iNsukamngeni
4 uDududu
5 iQwa
6 uNokhenke
7 iNdlondo
8 uKhandempemvu
9 iNgobamakhosi
10 uVe
11 uThulwana
12 iNdluyengwe
13 iSangqu
14 iMbube
15 uMbonambi
Zulu Commander

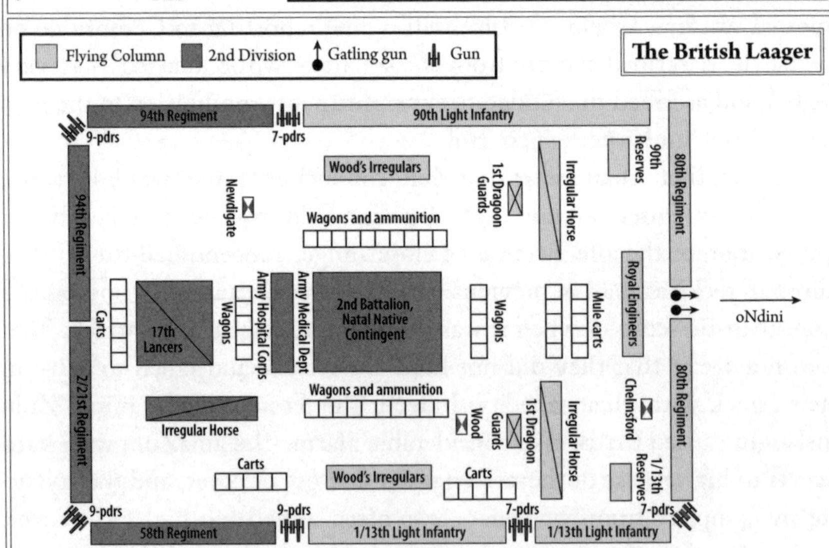
Flying Column
2nd Division
Gatling gun
Gun
The British Laager
94th Regiment
90th Light Infantry
9-pdrs
7-pdrs
Wood's Irregulars
90th Reserves
80th Regiment
Newdigate
1st Dragoon Guards
Irregular Horse
Wagons and ammunition
94th Regiment
Royal Engineers
Carts
17th Lancers
Wagons
Army Hospital Corps
Army Medical Dept
2nd Battalion, Natal Native Contingent
Wagons
Mule carts
oNdini
Wagons and ammunition
Chelmsford
80th Regiment
2/21st Regiment
Irregular Horse
Wood
1st Dragoon Guards
Irregular Horse
Carts
Wood's Irregulars
Carts
1/13th Reserves
9-pdrs
9-pdrs
7-pdrs
7-pdrs
58th Regiment
1/13th Light Infantry
1/13th Light Infantry

for the British to see many yards in front of them. Every now and again bugles had to sound the cease-fire to allow the smoke to clear away, and the amaZulu exploited the lull to creep closer. The two Gatling guns, although deadly when they worked, frequently jammed. Despite Chelmsford's intention of defeating the amaZulu in the open, the men of the 90th Light Infantry and the 80th Regiment of the Flying Column holding the leading portion of the left side of the square and its front face, hastily constructed rudimentary shelter trenches.

For their part, the *amabutho*, many of whom had captured British rifles, opened up a hot fire on the square. Yet the amaZulu generally either fired when not yet in range, or aimed too high. As a result, even though the formation was an enormous, closely packed target, Zulu fire was unexpectedly ineffective. Most of those falling as casualties to Zulu fire were shot in the back by bullets coming over the opposite side of the square. Still, enough bullets found their mark for the hospital within the square to be kept busy. As a cavalryman wryly commented, the square 'was hardly a place for a nervous old gentleman to take a stroll'.[15] Chelmsford, who in the days before the battle had often seemed nervous, undecided and depressed, was transformed by the excitement and peril of combat. To obtain a clear view of the battlefield (so his aide-de-camp, Captain Molyneux remembered), 'The Chief refused to dismount, so all staff-officers, including Newdigate's and Wood's, remained on horseback throughout the action.'[16] Fortunately, although dangerously exposed to the dropping Zulu fire, only one of Chelmsford's personal staff was slightly wounded when Lieutenant Berkeley Milne had his coat torn from the elbow to his shoulder by a bullet.

Chelmsford moved rapidly around the square issuing orders in a precise and deliberate manner.[17] Indeed, as at Gingindlovu, the heat of battle brought out the best in him and he acted coolly and decisively. Through the thick pall of smoke Charles Fripp of the *Graphic* saw Chelmsford at the climax of the battle 'quietly sitting his horse as he watched the men rapidly handle their Martini-Henrys and discharge a terrific storm of bullets.'[18] Even his arch-critic, Archibald Forbes of the *Daily News*, had to concede that he comported himself most creditably, although in his report of the battle he managed to draw acidulous attention to the general's shortcomings when not in combat. He wrote:

> Lord Chelmsford's soldierly coolness and decisive clearheadedness in action go far to redeem the passiveness and peevish vacillation which are his characteristics when no battle is raging. One might wish him a military Rip van Winkle, only wakening to direct a battle.[19]

The attacking amaZulu, soon finding they were making no progress against the front and sides of the square, decided to make a determined attack on its rear where they made good use of the shelter provided by the huts and stockade at the half-burned kwaNodwengu and by the depression in the terrain that ran along the rear of the British position. The angle of an infantry square is its weakest point because less fire can be developed there. Instinctively grasping this, between 2,000 and 3,000 men of the iNgobamakhosi and uVe *amabutho* came nearest to breaking through the cordon of British fire at the right rear corner of the square. Although the two 9-pounders at the corner fired seven rounds of case shot (which was used only at the closest quarters), and although the infantry (the 58th and the 2/21st Royal Scots Fusiliers) poured in rifle fire, they failed at first to slow the charge. Chelmsford who, with Newdigate, had been watching the Zulu build-up to the rear of the square with growing alarm, came galloping up and ordered the 5th Company, Royal Engineers to move to the rear of the square to bolster the endangered sector. This was certainly the critical moment of the battle, for the amaZulu charged to within thirty yards of the corner, and when some of them got to within nine paces of the troops it seemed they would soon be close enough to engage the British hand-to-hand. Newdigate drew his revolver and several officers unsheathed their swords. For the first and only time, Chelmsford lost his composure and, according to Melton Prior, called out to the troops: 'Men, fire faster; can't you fire faster?'[20] They coolly responded with such controlled and heavy fire that the *amabutho* were stopped in their tracks. When they finally fell back in disarray, the British troops burst into a cheer. The iNgobamakhosi's traditional rival, the uKhandempemvu *ibutho*, fared less well at the left rear corner of the square, and were repulsed by the two 9-pounders and the 94th Regiment with greater ease. This seemed to some of his staff the moment to unleash the cavalry, but Chelmsford – doubtless with the premature sortie at Gingindlovu in mind – decided to delay doing so until the Zulu withdrawal was more universal.

With the Zulu assault thrown back and pinned down, the main Zulu reserve, several thousand strong and composed of members of the older *amabutho*, made a final effort to break the deadlock and advanced out of oNdini in a dense column to attack the front of the square. In this crisis the Gatlings jammed, but Chelmsford ordered the two 9-pounders at the left rear of the square to be brought up to support the two 7-pounders at the front right corner. Their bursting shells, supported by rifle fire from the 80th Regiment, dispersed this last assault. Further reserves posted on the hills to the north and between the British square and the river never came into action.

At about 9.15 a.m. the amaZulu, increasingly disheartened at not being able to find a way around or through the British zone of fire, began to falter. By 9.20 a.m. a disorderly withdrawal was in progress, although it was not yet a rout and the commanders of the *amabutho* were still making every effort to rally them. But Chelmsford perceived that an air of Zulu demoralisation had set in. At 9.25 a.m., after hesitating for a few minutes to give the order until he was entirely satisfied the Zulu retreat was general, he decided that the moment had finally arrived to unleash all the mounted men. Infantry could not deliver an effective counter-thrust against an enemy as mobile as the amaZulu, but a well-timed cavalry charge over the open plain was sure to throw the disordered *amabutho* into a panic and transform retreat into a rout, just as it had at both Khambula and Gingindlovu. A cavalry officer recorded that 'We heard Lord C. say, "Now Colonel Lowe – the lancers."'[21] As the cavalry formed up for their long-anticipated charge, Chelmsford raised his helmet to them in salute and shouted to Drury-Lowe: 'Go at them colonel, but don't pursue too far!'[22]

To ringing cheers from the infantry who opened their ranks in the rear of the square, the cavalry charged out towards kwaNodwengu and then, wheeling right, ploughed into the amaZulu concentrating to the north-west of the British formation. Avoiding as best they could the deadly thrusts of the 1868 pattern lances with their nine-foot-long bamboo poles and triangular steel points as well as the slashing sabres, the *amabutho* dodged and ducked, some standing in places to fight and stabbing the cavalry's horses: twenty-eight chargers were killed and forty-five wounded. Having scattered the amaZulu at the rear of the square in their furious charge, the regular cavalry pursued them to the lower slopes of the hills two miles away to the north. There the *amabutho* rallied and set up a galling fire. With their horses blown, and heeding Chelmsford's admonition not to charge to far, the cavalry gave up the chase and retired out of range. Meanwhile, the Mounted Infantry of the Flying Column had galloped out of the left side of the square in support of the cavalry, and after taking the amaZulu in the flank had merged into line with Lancers. Buller's irregular horse sallied out of the right front corner of the square a few minutes after the cavalry and relentlessly pursued the amaZulu beyond oNdini and as far as the hills to the north-east. There the amaZulu rallied and, like the cavalry had done, the irregular horse fell back in turn. At 9.40 a.m. the six 9-pounders – even though they were out of effective range – fired shrapnel into the main body of the amaZulu who were retreating in great masses over the hills 4,000 yards to the north and accelerated their flight. At 10.07 a.m. the guns then fired on oNdini and dispersed a large concentration of amaZulu sheltering there.

With the broken *amabutho* fleeing over the hills, the British were left in full control of the plain. It remained for them to flush out any amaZulu who had concealed themselves in the long grass and dongas, or were lying wounded. For hours after the fighting around the square had ceased, the firing of the irregular troopers' carbines continued to be heard as they went about their horrible and pitiless work. The NNC and Wood's Irregulars emerged from within the square to assist them in flushing out and despatching as many amaZulu as they could find. Zulu losses in the battle are estimated to have been about 1,500. Between 500 and 600 were killed within close range of the square, while the regular cavalry took credit for 150 more and the irregular horse (and the African auxiliaries) for at least another 450. Many hundreds of the wounded would have died subsequently of their shattering bullet injuries or of exposure in the cold, wet weather as they tried to reach home.

As soon as it was evident that the amaZulu were beaten, remembered Molyneux, 'We all at once crowded round to congratulate the Chief; the soldiers cheered their generals, and everyone rejoiced.'[23] Indeed, Chelmsford was openly elated by his success, and as Guy Dawnay, the intelligence officer on Marshall's staff observed, 'The difference in Lord Chelmsford, before and after the fight, was something to see.'[24] There still remained much for him to do, however. Sixty-nine men had been wounded in the battle and they had to be properly attended to. Three officers and ten men had been killed and they had to be buried where they had fallen. Once that had been done to his satisfaction, at 11.30 a.m. Chelmsford ordered the square to move forward to the Mbilane stream. There the infantry rested and ate their dinner while the mounted troops and African auxiliaries continued with their work of destruction, burning all the *amakhanda* in the plain.

When at the Mbilane stream, Chelmsford ordered the mounted men who had returned for a short rest to go out again at once and burn oNdini. So began a race between mounted officers for the honour of being first at Cetshwayo's capital. The race was won by Captain Lord William Beresford, Buller's staff officer and a notorious bruiser and all-round sportsman who had earned the VC the previous day for his gallantry during the reconnaissance across the White Mfolozi. These impetuous lone horsemen encountered scant resistance, and that made it even more unfortunate that the Hon. William Drummond, who was in charge of the Intelligence Department on Chelmsford's staff, should have joined the race and have been killed by some amaZulu still lingering in oNdini when he lost his way among the maze of huts.[25] At 11.40 a.m. Buller ordered oNdini to be fired, although it seems that the amaZulu had already set it alight themselves to deny it to the enemy. For lack of wind the fire did not burn freely, however, and oNdini smouldered sullenly for four days. Even then, not all the huts were consumed. Yet the columns of smoke from oNdini and the other burning *amakhanda* that enveloped the entire Mahlabathini plain in a thick black haze signalled to the amaZulu watching from afar that their defeat was final and that the Zulu kingdom had fallen.

At about 2 p.m. Chelmsford ordered his victorious but exhausted troops to begin their march back to their secure camp at the White Mfolozi. They progressed in high spirits and in easy stages with the bands playing, arriving in separate detachments between 3.30 a.m. and 5.30 p.m. That night the British triumphantly agreed that the Zulu challenge to fight them in the open had been fairly answered and British arms fully vindicated. Over the next few days many expressed what they felt in despatches and letters home. Chelmsford reported to Stanley with relief and evident pride that:

> It appears that [the amaZulu] considered they would have no difficulty in defeating British Troops if they advanced in the

> open, away from their wagons. I feel I have a right in saying that the results of the Battle of Ulundi, gained by the steadiness of the Infantry, the good practice of the artillery, and the dash of the Cavalry and Mounted Troops will be sufficient to dispel this idea from the minds of the Zulu Nation and of every other tribe in South Africa for ever.[26]

Chelmsford's officers looked on the battle with equally great satisfaction, Major Russell believing that 'So far as my opinion goes, nothing could have been more perfect than both the arrangements of the march and the measures for the defence of the laager; the success was well merited.'[27] Major Robinson was fully aware that, 'Our having gone out and fought and beaten the Zulus . . . fairly in the open, has had an immense effect on our natives and morally has done 10 times as much good for our prestige with them as a victory from a laager would have.'[28] Beyond having taken part in a great victory, there was another cause for satisfaction amongst practically all the officers who had served with Chelmsford during the campaign. Lieutenant-Colonel Harness expressed it succinctly in a letter to his sister: '*I am so glad for Lord C.* He has quite taken the wind out of Sir G. W.'s sails and I hope recovered a little of his reputation.'[29] Joining Harness in his delight that the thrusting Sir Garnet had been thwarted in his desire to snatch the prize from Chelmsford's hands, Robinson astutely observed two days after the battle: 'Lord C. is ten years younger now; I suppose he feels he is not a failure as it were after his success. Before this he was anxious and fidgety to a degree.'[30]

CHAPTER 34

Resignation, July–August 1879

THE DEEP SENSE OF VINDICATION and new-found confidence Chelmsford gained from his victory at Ulundi were very quickly spoiled by the unforgiving politics of command and by the unremitting pressure of having to make decisions about the future conduct of operations. And nothing Chelmsford ever did now went unquestioned or without a hitch.

The troops spent the night after the battle in the laager at the White Mfolozi. Chelmsford and his staff could take little rest, however, for despatches announcing the victory had to be prepared. Back in the laager by 3.30 p.m., Captain Molyneux, his ADC, 'commenced the drudgery of writing'. However, all were so buoyed up that they did not resent it; besides (as he put it) 'We all felt so light-hearted at having completed the business without interference'[1] – that is, before Wolseley could steal Chelmsford's thunder.

But Chelmsford was not the only one keen to get the news out. The special correspondents were also anxious to do so and to scoop their rivals as well, none more so than Archibald Forbes of the *Daily News*, whom Lieutenant Curling described at the time as a 'great, strong, coarse-looking man, able to undergo any amount of fatigue and to put up with any amount of snubbing'.[2] Forbes and Chelmsford had repeatedly clashed, and even Wolseley, himself a dedicated self-promoter, considered Forbes an unprincipled 'paid penny-a-liner' dealing in 'sensational untruth'.[3] The nearest telegraph line to Mthonjaneni was at Landman's Drift, and Forbes asked Chelmsford whether he might send his account of Ulundi back by official despatch rider. Unwilling to accommodate him, Chelmsford dismissively replied that he would not be sending off his official communiqué until the next day because he was waiting for the exact returns of casualties. Forbes thereupon histrionically announced that he would go himself. He set off at 5 p.m. with his report and a packet of private telegrams from the General's staff. After a ride of 110 miles in twenty hours he reached Landman's Drift at between 2 and 3 p.m. on 5 July and telegraphed his report to Frere and Wolseley to gain the kudos of being the first to break the news of Chelmsford's victory to the top civil and military officers in South Africa. The cult of personality was grist to the mill of the 'specials', and Forbes later published his adventure in the *Daily News* of 21 August 1879 where it was billed as 'The Ride of Death', although the risks he had run were much exaggerated.[4] As we shall see, this episode would be given a sour twist when Forbes claimed his ride entitled him to the Zulu War campaign medal and Chelmsford refused his support.[5]

Forbes was not alone on the road to Landman's Drift. He had not been gone ten minutes before Chelmsford had second thoughts. He sent for Guy Dawnay, the intelligence officer on Marshall's staff, and asked him if he could go after Forbes once the moon was up? The official despatch to Stanley was ready by 8 a.m. – a second one in continuance with further reports and returns, followed the next day.[6] Dawnay's ride took five-and-a-half hours longer than Forbes's – not least because at the various posts along the way the latter had commandeered all the best horses ahead of him – and he reached Landman's Drift at 9.45 p.m. on 5 July.[7]

Forbes's telegram that brought the news of the battle to Wolseley on the evening of 5 July reached Frere in Cape Town on the same night.[8] Frere telegraphed Hicks Beach: 'I congratulate Her Majesty's Government on decisive victory vouchsafed to Her Majesty's forces under Lord Chelmsford in a fair fight in the open on July 4th.'[9] Frere's telegram was received by the government on 23 July 1879. Hicks Beach responded with great relief the following day, pointedly adding: 'I trust that the proof thus afforded of the superiority of the British forces may induce a speedy submission on the part of the Zulus, and result in the early conclusion of peace on satisfactory terms.'[10] The government immediately shared the news of Ulundi with the Queen, and Wolseley was informed that 'Her Majesty received this intelligence with very great satisfaction and thankfulness, and is proud of the conduct of her brave troops.'[11] Critically for Chelmsford's future, the Queen and Royal Family were determined to give him full credit for his victory. The Prince of Wales (the future King Edward VII) telegraphed at once to Lady Chelmsford, then staying in Bath, offering his 'most sincere congratulations' on her husband's 'great victory', and sympathetically commenting that it must come as a great relief 'after all the severe trials and anxieties' he had experienced.[12] The Queen herself was not far behind, and on 28 July commanded Colonel Stanley to communicate to Lady Chelmsford 'her Majesty's congratulations on the victory at Ulundi'.[13] As for Chelmsford's family, an indication of the intense pressure they had all been under can be found in the telegram his brother Alfred Thesiger, QC, Lord Justice of Appeal, immediately sent his sister-in-law Adria on learning of Ulundi: 'My heart felt thankful congratulations.'[14] Sir Bartle Frere's sense of relief was no less, and Lady Frere hastened to telegraph Lady Chelmsford: 'All well. Lord Chelmsford has great victory on fourth July.'[15]

In Zululand meanwhile, on Wolseley's impatient prompting, the 1st Division was being more proactive. On 4 July – the same day as the battle of Ulundi – Major Barrow crossed the Mhlathuze River with a mounted patrol and burned emaNgweni. No resistance was offered at the *ikhanda*, and many cattle were taken. That same day, more local Zulu chiefs, responding to the favourable terms offered them, made their submissions at Port Durnford. Crealock moved his forces forward on 5 July to a camp on the lower drift of the Mhlathuze, and there more of the important local chiefs surrendered. Barrow led out another patrol on 6 June and burned the old oNdini *ikhanda*, before returning to Port Durnford on 7 July. Thus the 1st Division's objectives, as originally laid down by Chelmsford, had been accomplished, but by then they had been rendered largely irrelevant by his victory at Ulundi that had put an end to organised Zulu armed resistance.[16]

Wolseley finally rode into the camp at Port Durnford on 7 July. He had been pre-empted by Chelmsford's victory, but he was now determined to take personal command of all the forces in the field, as was his right in terms of his commission. Chelmsford, however, was still acting as if he were in untrammelled command of the troops encamped at the White Mfolozi. On 5 July he marched the joint column back to the earlier camping ground of 30 June at the base of Mthonjaneni. The Flying Column bivouacked there for the night, but he ordered the 2nd Division to continue up the heights to the Mthonjaneni laager where Chelmsford and his staff joined Newdigate later that day.[17]

That evening, Chelmsford received two missives. The first was a telegram sent by Wolseley on 1 June and brought by runner from Port

Durnford. It had been overtaken by events, for it contained Wolseley's order for Chelmsford to retire and unite his forces with the 1st Division. Nothing was said about what he was to do if his current operations were successful.[18] The second document placed in Chelmsford's hand had an infinitely greater impact. This was Stanley's long-anticipated despatch of 29 May informing Chelmsford of his 'supersession' by 'an officer senior' to him.[19] Chelmsford immediately wrote back resigning his command since he considered the 'appointment of a senior officer' as a censure on himself. He went on to request that he and his personal staff be allowed to return to England, and (if Wolseley did not object) to do so in anticipation of Stanley's 'sanction'.[20] The next day, 6 July, Chelmsford wrote again to Stanley reiterating his request to be allowed to resign his command and return home.[21] On the same day he wrote to Cambridge asking him to support the application he had made to Stanley. Sensing that Cambridge, with whom he had a closer relationship as his longstanding patron, would be more sensitive to his hurt feelings than Stanley was likely to be, he went on to add candidly: 'I cannot but consider that I have been treated very badly altho' the Secretary of State is good enough to say in his telegram that Sir Garnet's appointment implies no censure upon myself.' Explaining his desire to resign, he stated that, 'So long as there was any useful work to be done . . . I was quite ready to accept the position and do my best for the public good.' But with the amaZulu decisively defeated, that no longer pertained. Exhausted and humiliated, Chelmsford concluded his painful letter with a frank admission: 'I have had 18 months of very hard work and of great anxiety and I consider that I have earned some rest.'[22]

Yet, if Chelmsford did the correct thing on receipt of the fatal despatch of 29 May by requesting Stanley and Cambridge to permit him to resign his command, at the same time he could not bring himself to accept that Wolseley had really superseded him. His staff knew perfectly well that such was the case,[23] but as yet it was not known to the troops under his command, at least not in official published form. Until it was – and even though he had tendered his resignation to Stanley and Cambridge – Chelmsford resolved to carry on as if he were still in command and to bring the operations he had initiated to a conclusion. Accordingly, on the same day that he confirmed his request to resign, he issued General Order, No. 124 of 6 July 1879: 'The Lieutenant-General Commanding desires to place on record his hearty appreciation of the gallantry and steadfastness displayed by all ranks of the force under his command at the battle of Ulundi.'[24] He then ordered Wood and the Flying Column up to the Mthonjaneni heights to camp next to the 2nd Division. The laager was broken up since, with the dispersal of the Zulu forces and little danger of attack, it was no longer deemed necessary.

Having issued his orders, Chelmsford then sat down to answer Wolseley's telegram received the previous evening. Of course, since it had been sent on 1 June, Ulundi and the dispersal of the Zulu army had entirely changed the situation. Obliquely acknowledging Wolseley's superior position, he informed him that, 'with your approval', he intended to send the 2nd Division with all the wounded back to Fort Newdigate in the Phoko valley where food, wood for fuel and grass for grazing were available. The Flying Column was to join the 1st Division at St Paul's Mission, halfway between Mthonjaneni and Port Durnford. Chelmsford went on to explain that it was not possible 'to strike another blow' at present against the dispersed enemy. Even so, he told Wolseley that 'A hasty evacuation of the country I now occupy seems to me inadvisable at the present moment, and I await your further instructions before carrying it out.'[25]

Before Chelmsford could receive a reply from Wolseley, a storm of bitterly cold wind and rain began on the night of 6 July on the cloud-wrapped Mthonjaneni heights and lasted throughout 7 and 8 July. Its intensity rendered all further movement impossible. The men's kit was all wet through,[26] and the losses from exposure of horses, and even more so of oxen, were very heavy. Chelmsford warned Wolseley on 7 July that the oxen were in too bad a way to bring up a fresh convoy of supplies. Despite what he had written only the day before, he now doubted 'the advisability of keeping too large a force in this part of the country'.[27] During 8 July the weather began to clear, and having received no countermand from Wolseley, Chelmsford commenced preparations to move his troops off Mthonjaneni as he had proposed on 6 July.

Then, that night of 8 July the post brought in Orders, No. 62 from Wolseley. At 9 p.m. Crealock entered Chelmsford's tent and put the official paper into his hands. And the game was finally up. The orders read: 'Lieutenant-General Lord Chelmsford, K.C.B, will till further orders, command the Force consisting of the 2nd division, under Major-

General Newdigate, and the Flying Column, under Brigadier-General Wood, V.C., C.B.'[28] The import of the orders was clear: Chelmsford was no longer commander of all the British forces in South Africa.

Mortified and seething, Chelmsford had no option but to grasp the nettle and resign at once, and not to wait for Stanley and Cambridge to give him their permission to do so, as he had requested they do in his letters of 5 and 6 July. Crealock, who was privy to these two letters, now saw only too clearly that the General had been wrong in asking to resign a command that was in fact no longer his to relinquish, and that as a consequence he was placed 'in a very false position'.[29]

Chelmsford sent his letter of resignation to Stanley from Mthonjaneni on 9 July. At the same time he sent Wolseley a telegram repeating in condensed form the reasons he had given Stanley for his resignation and that of his personal staff, and informing him, 'I propose . . . to leave by the earliest opportunity for P'M'Burg *en route* to England.'[30] In his letter to Stanley, Chelmsford capitulated with ill grace, writing querulously that 'You will see that I have been deprived by this General Order of the position given to me by Her Majesty of Lt General commanding the Forces in S. Africa, altho' the Commission which I hold conferring upon me that command has never, to my knowledge been cancelled.' This General Order, he went on, 'certainly does not agree with the instructions contained in your despatch of 29 May'. He assured Stanley that he would have been quite prepared to 'submit and subordinate' his plans to Wolseley's 'control',

> . . . but I could not accept the inferior command to which he has considered it within his power to reduce me, except under a firm conviction that such sacrifice of dignity & position was required in the public interest . . . Since however the recent battle of Ulundi such necessity has ceased to exist; and I feel that under present circumstances I am not called upon to make any self-sacrifice.

In a nutshell, he refused to accept an inferior command and was left with no alternative but to resign. He bitingly concluded his letter of resignation with a phrase that echoed Crealock's above and proves they had discussed the matter together:

> I shall thus extricate myself from a false position, in which, I am inclined to think, it was not the intention of H.M. Govt to place me in; and I shall moreover relieve the army estimates of the charges due on arrival of my pay and allowances as Lt General commanding the Forces in S. Africa and those of my personal Staff – I trust that this step will meet with your approval and with that of H.R.H. the commander in chief.[31]

The next day Chelmsford wrote to Cambridge as well, reiterating 'how anxious' he was 'to withdraw from a false position'.[32] As it turned out, the Duke, who was only too pleased that Chelmsford had secured his victory before Wolseley got to the front, believed that his decision to return home had been only wise. He was in no doubt that Chelmsford's position, if he had opted to remain in South Africa in a subordinate command, would have proven 'difficult, not to say embarrassing'.[33]

Having finally surrendered his command, it remained for Chelmsford to make it known to the troops. On the morning of 9 July, he ordered a grand parade of all arms that he might take formal leave of them. At 9 a.m. they formed three sides of a hollow square and Chelmsford, his staff and the commanders of the 2nd Division and Flying Column made up the fourth. A witness recorded that 'in a few warm-hearted, well-chosen and soldier-like sentences' Chelmsford 'bade them farewell and thanked them for the manner in which their duty to their Queen and country had been performed'.[34] Until his resignation had been received and accepted, however, Chelmsford had to continue with his duties. That same afternoon, 9 July, he told Wolseley by telegram that the Flying Column was beginning its march to St Paul's, which it hoped to reach on about 14 July. In accordance with his communiqué of 6 July, Wood's column would be parting from the 2nd Division that was due to begin its march to Fort Newdigate the following day, 'unless', Chelmsford repeated once more, 'instructions to the contrary are received from you'.[35]

Wolseley, meanwhile, was deciding what steps he should take to bring the campaign speedily to a conclusion. He was becoming aware that in the days immediately after Ulundi, the Zulu army had speedily dispersed all over the country. The British, wherever they were stationed in Zululand, detected no organised Zulu force still in the field, although they did notice warriors returning home crossing their lines of communication.[36]

As Wolseley wrote to Chelmsford on 9 July when 'heartily and sincerely' congratulating him on his victory (and courteously suppressing his own disappointment), he believed that Ulundi had indeed 'ended the war', and that it was 'now merely a matter of arranging the terms upon which "peace with honour" is to be secured'.[37] And that, as Wolseley confided to his journal, made him 'anxious to maintain the forward position the troops now occupy as long as I can possibly feed them there'. 'This', he added, 'is very desirable for political reasons.'[38] In writing to Stanley the following day, he reiterated how essential it was to 'maintain the troops in their advanced positions' in order 'to make a peace upon satisfactory terms'. And to ensure that, he told Stanley that he had ordered Chelmsford to leave Wood and a strong brigade of infantry and artillery at Mthonjaneni and to fall back with the remainder of his force to St Paul's Mission Station.[39]

The problem was that when Chelmsford broke up his combined column on 9 July and retired from Mthonjaneni, he had not yet received Wolseley's orders to that effect. The next day he and his staff joined the Flying Column in their new camp, and on 11 July reached the deserted mission station at Kwamagwasa where work began on erecting Fort Robertson (later renamed Fort Albert).[40] For his part, Wolseley had not received Chelmsford's telegrams of 6 and 9 July informing him of his intended movements. Chelmsford and Wolseley were therefore at cross-purposes. While at Kwamagwasa on 11 July, Chelmsford finally received a memorandum from Wolseley's MS, Lieutenant-Colonel Henry Brackenbury, a long-standing member of the Ashanti Ring. It was dated 8 July, and contained the orders Wolseley went on to report to Stanley on 10 July. Guessing that Chelmsford might have already begun his retrograde movement, but not anticipating that he had split his combined force up and sent the 2nd Division westwards instead of to the coast, Brackenbury concluded: 'In case you have fallen back with your whole force to or towards Kwamagwaza [*sic*] before you receive this message, you need not send Brigadier-General Wood back towards Entonjaneni, but he may occupy any suitable position near to the place where this message finds him.'[41]

Chelmsford wrote back at once that the movements had begun before receiving Brackenbury's memorandum. In any case, he argued, it seemed better that the 2nd Division should escort back the wounded and baggage wagons while the Flying Column was 'best suited' for any operation proving necessary before it joined the 1st Division. There was no going back on these arrangements, and Chelmsford notified Wolseley that he would proceed to St Paul's and there await his further orders.[42]

Foiled in his strategic intentions by Chelmsford's withdrawal from Mthonjaneni, Wolseley embarked on a skilful disinformation campaign blaming Chelmsford entirely for the position he found himself in. Typical of his many despatches to members of the government hammering home the point is that of 27 July to Hicks Beach. Asserting that, 'The Zulu nation are amazed at our retreat from Ulundi after Lord Chelmsford's victorious action,' and that it was likely that they thought the British were driven away by 'fear and weakness', he went on to reassure Hicks Beach that he would 'reverse these sentiments' once he had rectified Chelmsford's miscalculation.[43] These oft-repeated half-truths bore the fruit Wolseley intended. Bulwer's comments after having spoken to Wolseley at length encapsulate the line Wolseley was propagating:

> There has been rather a rush to the conclusion that the success at Ulundi has ended the war. I think it might have done so if they had followed it up at once. But the fact is that Chelmsford advanced to Ulundi before he was ready to hold his ground there. He advanced prematurely. Everyone says he did it because of Sir G.'s coming out and I fancy they are right . . . [H]e had to retire again at once and Sir G. has to make up again for all the ground and all the time that has thus been lost.[44]

The War Office also accepted Wolseley's gloss on events. Chelmsford would discover this to have been the case when in late February 1880 he received a copy of the latest *British Parliamentary Papers* (C. 2482). Much of the vital correspondence between him and Wolseley concerning the withdrawal of the troops from the vicinity of Ulundi, both before and after the battle, was omitted. As Chelmsford indignantly put it to Stanley, leaving out these letters fostered the impression that the withdrawal of Chelmsford's forces had never been contemplated by Wolseley, and 'that I had committed a very serious mistake, and that Sir Garnet Wolseley was unable to rectify it in time to prevent its consequences being such as to complicate materially the final pacification of Zululand'.[45] Stanley saw the justice of Chelmsford's complaint, and his letter and the missing documents were subsequently presented to Parliament and printed in the

British Parliamentary Papers (C. 2584) in June 1880.[46] The damage, however, had been done. The impression had indeed been established that the talented Wolseley had been hamstrung in his sensible plan of operations by the bumbling Chelmsford's mistakes, whereas the truth was far more nuanced, and much of the reason for the mutual confusion between the two commanders lay in the inadequacy of the lines of communication.

On 12 July Wolseley received Chelmsford's despatch of the previous day informing him that he had fallen back and dispersed his combined column. At the same time, Wolseley was handed Chelmsford's telegram of 9 July saying that he was resigning his command and wished to go home. While Wolseley found the tone of both communications 'very objectionable', he was at last fully informed of the whereabouts of the troops under Chelmsford's command and could plan accordingly. Besides, he was anything but dismayed by Chelmsford's resignation, and was prepared to be magnanimous. He wrote in his journal: 'Since his fight he is all cock-a-hoop. Poor fellow, I can understand his feeling and am anxious to let him down easy.'[47] So Wolseley immediately wrote to Chelmsford a superficially complimentary but slyly ambiguous letter of valediction. 'I have no wish to find fault,' he declared. 'I did not come here to do so, but to command the troops and make the best I could of the position as I should find it.' He concluded:

> You can now return home with the halo of success around you, and I am sure you will find all the authorities at the Horse Guards and War Office ready to receive you with the utmost cordiality, for although men may not approve of the way the war has been conducted . . . as far as you personally are concerned, no one could have devoted himself with greater zeal for the public service . . . than you have done.[48]

Wolseley's implied censure of his conduct, carefully swathed in apparent compliments as it was, did not escape Chelmsford and his inherent stubbornness asserted itself. He wrote back while on the march to St Paul's in the prickliest and most stiff-necked of terms, haughtily affirming, 'With regard to my plan of campaign, it is of course, like any other, fair ground for criticism. I am anxious, however, to let you know that had I to begin operations again, I should make no change whatever in my operations or in the distribution of my troops.'[49]

Wolseley arrived with his staff at the camp of the 1st Division at the lower drift of the Mhlathuze on 14 July, and Chelmsford and the Flying Column reached St Paul's on the following evening. The two generals were now close enough to arrange a meeting. Wolseley informed Chelmsford that he would ride up to St Paul's on 15 January, and requested an escort to come out and meet him. Chelmsford courteously decided to ride out seven miles himself to greet him, but it was typical of the continual, unfortunate mis-communication between the two that they missed each other on the road. Chelmsford finally galloped back only to find Wolseley already in the camp at St Paul's.[50] Wrong-footed from the start, Chelmsford doubtless suspected that Wolseley saw in the botched rendezvous yet another indication of his incompetence. For his part, Wolseley must have known that his appearance was not entirely welcomed by Chelmsford's officers. As Clery expressed it: 'There is one universal feeling of extreme satisfaction that Lord C. fought the battle of Ulundi before his successor arrived. However one's opinion of him as a general may be shaken, everybody's regard and sympathy for him is as strong is it can be.'[51]

It comes as no surprise, therefore, that Wolseley could not say that he found his meeting with Chelmsford 'a pleasant one'. While the deeply resentful Chelmsford did his best to maintain his dignity, Wolseley for his part was inwardly fuming that Chelmsford had been persistently ignoring his military authority over him and derailing his plans. Nevertheless, he reminded himself that he should 'make every allowance' for Chelmsford's raw feelings at being superseded. Wolseley's presence certainly changed the dynamic in the camp at St Paul's. Wood and Buller, whom Chelmsford considered his best and most loyal lieutenants, but who were also longstanding members of the Ashanti Ring, lost no time in informing their old chief that Chelmsford was 'not fit to be a corporal'. Not that Chelmsford proved any more loyal regarding his subordinate officers, and before long he was telling Wolseley that both the fatherly Newdigate (who was very popular with his men) and Drury-Lowe were 'no use'. This was balm to Wolseley's ears who was only too happy to hear commanders selected by Cambridge being dissed. Yet, for all the backbiting and embarrassment of the situation, Wolseley found Chelmsford 'in good spirits, & I think glad to think he is going home: I never saw him looking better'. Wolseley duly approved of Chelmsford proceeding at once to Britain with his personal staff, and Molyneux rejoiced that they were 'all homeward bound together'. They were to be joined by Wood, returning home 'on medical certificate', and by Buller 'for well-earned rest.'[52]

The next day, on Wood's request, Wolseley inspected the Flying Column and presented the VC to Major Chard, the recently promoted senior officer at Rorke's Drift – 'a more uninteresting or stupid-looking fellow I never saw', commented Wolseley who did not approve of the wholesale award of the decoration to the defenders of the post.[53] During heavy showers on 17 July Wolseley set off back to his camp by the Mhlathuze. Chelmsford and his staff accompanied him part of the way before turning off and heading towards the lower Thukela and Natal. Back at his camp, having at last found out what Chelmsford had done with his troops, Wolseley informed Stanley that 'I consider it necessary to make preparations to return to and to occupy Ulundi as a visible sign of our power; and I think it desirable that I should dictate what are to be the terms of settlement of the country at the King's kraal itself.'[54] With that objective in mind, he set about ordering the reduction and redistribution of his forces.

Wolseley received the formal surrender of the coastal Zulu chiefs on 19 July at his camp on the lower drift of the Mhlathuze, but it still remained to capture the fugitive Cetshwayo to ensure a final peace. To that end, he ordered the dispersal of the 1st Division on 23 July. Some of the troops went home, while the remainder were formed into a reduced column under Lieutenant-Colonel Charles Clarke with orders to march back to the Mahlabathini plain from where patrols were to be sent out in search of Cetshwayo. On 26 July the 2nd Division was formally broken up at Fort Marshall and the troops sent home. The Flying Column was likewise broken up on 31 July at St Paul's, and Lieutenant-Colonel Baker Russell was put in command of a second reduced column that was required for the final pacification of north-western Zululand.[55]

Wolseley himself moved back to Port Durnford where on 21 July he went on board the SS *City of Venice* bound for Durban. He landed there the next day, and with his staff proceeded straight to Pietermaritzburg where Chelmsford was already in residence in the Royal Hotel. Wolseley was hardly pleased to find him there, and had already decided that his 'line was to get Chelmsford out of the country as soon as possible'. Even then, Wolseley's feelings towards him were ambivalent, and tinged with pity. 'Although I have the poorest opinion of his ability as a general or a public servant,' he wrote, 'I have a feeling for the position in which he finds himself. Why kick a dead horse?'[56]

Chelmsford had arrived in Durban from the lower Thukela on the evening of 20 July where, Captain Molyneux recalled, 'The town had turned out to meet us with a guard of honour and a regular ovation. There was a great dinner at the club [the Durban Club], with much speechifying.'[57] In Pietermaritzburg the next day, Chelmsford was received with the 'utmost enthusiasm'. He was carried shoulder-high to his hotel, repeatedly raising his helmet to the crowds deafeningly cheering the 'Hero of Ulundi'. Responding to Mayor Wesley Francis's congratulations on his 'brilliant and decisive victory', Chelmsford adopted the somewhat querulous, defensive tone that would become the hallmark of his public speeches. He thanked the citizens 'for their kindness and sympathy, and could not but feel that they appreciated what some others seemed not to appreciate, namely – the difficulties which had to be contended against'.[58]

Major-General Clifford who witnessed the scene was (as we have seen) no admirer of Chelmsford, and he could not resist telling Wolseley that he had 'made rather an injudicious speech'. Wolseley duly jotted down that 'I look upon Chelmsford as a goose, capable of any stupid folly,' adding that he wished he had 'gone quietly home without stirring it here'.[59] Obviously, his presence was an embarrassment to Wolseley, who was compelled to accept invitations to the same official functions where the resentful Chelmsford, and not he, was 'the hero of the hour'.

But Crealock caught the public mood of the colonists when he wrote: 'The fact is, the feeling is very distinct that Lord C. has been very scurvily used all round (including ourselves *I* think) and their conscience smites them, and their love of fair play made one and all anxious that he should have the credit that another was so *very nearly getting*.'[60] At a dinner given for Chelmsford on 24 July by the Mayor and Corporation, in his speech of thanks Chelmsford said:

> There is a saying very frequently quoted that 'nothing succeeds like success,' but gentlemen, if I thought that you asked me to dinner simply because I had been successful, it would be as water from the Dead Sea placed in my mouth; but from what the

> Mayor has said, it is clear you sympathise with me not because I succeeded, but because under circumstances of extreme difficulty I endeavoured to do my duty (cheers).[61]

Wolseley, who was present, privately reflected that the speech was made well, and that Chelmsford 'is a gentleman and a very nice fellow'. But, he caustically went on, 'The Lord forbid that he should ever again have command of troops in the field.'[62] Yet, despite private gripes, the social niceties were kept up by all. Wolseley made a deliberate point of avoiding all controversial subjects with Chelmsford. Likewise, Bulwer, who sat next to him at the Mayor's dinner, reported that, 'We are on very good terms, but of course we did not touch on the subject of our differences.'[63]

Leaving Wolseley in Pietermaritzburg, Chelmsford returned to Durban on 26 June where he had promised to attend a public ball in his honour that was considered the most 'brilliant affair' of its kind ever held in the colony.[64] On 28 July, he prepared to go on board the transport ship *Queen Margaret* bound for Cape Town. Nearly all the vessels in the harbour were flying their flags and at the Bluff the flagstaff was covered in bunting. For the last time Chelmsford addressed the Durban crowd come to see him off. He began with his now customary plaints, but this time managed to air them in a more light-hearted manner that pleased the crowd: 'I have always endeavoured in facing my difficulties to put my head straight at them', he declared, 'and have got out of them somehow or other (hear, hear, and laughter).' But then, he went on reveal the deep religious principles that underpinned his actions, a system of belief that would have been fundamental to his upbringing in the early Victorian age, and which still resonated strongly with the great majority of the colonists he was addressing, and who cheered his words heartily. 'I have felt throughout the campaign,' he affirmed, 'that I have been sustained by your prayers and also those of the people at home. I am one of those who believes firmly and implicitly in the efficacy of prayer and in the intervention of Divine Providence.'[65]

That was not all Chelmsford would have to say before quitting South Africa for good. From 1 to 5 August, he stayed in Government House in Cape Town where he and Frere had much to say to each other about the blows fortune had dealt to their plans and ambitions. Again, there were receptions in Chelmsford's honour, but now, with no official position or responsibilities, and believing himself to be what Molyneux termed 'a free agent', he gave a final speech aimed squarely and uncompromisingly at all his critics. At the outset, he complained about 'the serious misrepresentations regarding my conduct of the war which have appeared from time to time in the public press' and which had had the bad effect of lowering him 'in the estimation' of those he commanded. He denied the public accusations 'of hesitation and vacillation' on his part, and that he had 'lost the confidence of all but my personal staff'. He denied the charge 'that the advance on Ulundi was . . . a desperate undertaking made against the express orders' of Wolseley, and defended his withdrawal from Mthonjaneni, insisting that after 'the crushing defeat inflicted upon the Zulus at Ulundi, and their subsequent complete dispersion' there had been no point in staying there out of supply. And, with considerable bravado he stubbornly declared (as previously he had done to Wolseley): 'I have no hesitation in saying that had I the work to do over again, I should make no changes in my arrangements.' He concluded by 'trusting that the time may soon arrive when South Africa's separate Colonies will be welded into one, powerful, confederated whole'.[66]

Several points may be made here about this valedictory speech. It was not enough simply to reject the many criticisms levelled at his conduct of the campaign. His critics were not to be deflected and would continue to probe his handling of the Anglo-Zulu War and responsibility for the Isandlwana disaster once he returned home. Nor was it wise to have singled out war correspondents for their malicious reporting. Curling had reflected, with specific reference to Forbes, 'it is dangerous to be uncivil to them,'[67] and just how much so Chelmsford would discover when Forbes pursued the vendetta once back in England. And finally, Chelmsford's closing reference to the cause of South African confederation smacks of the recent conversations he had held with Frere in Cape Town when he must have been reminded that all the wars he had overseen as GOC South Africa – the Ninth Cape Frontier War; the Northern Border War; the First Anglo-Pedi War; and the Anglo-Zulu War itself – had ostensibly been waged to ease the way to confederation. The intensity of the Anglo-Zulu War had rather obscured this objective in the public mind, and Chelmsford was being true to Frere in reminding them of it. But confederation was to prove a mirage, and was soon abandoned as imperial policy when Gladstone's Liberal administration conceded the independence of the Transvaal after defeat in the disastrous Transvaal Rebellion (or First Anglo-Boer War) of 1880–1.[68] For what end, therefore, had the Anglo-Zulu War been fought and so much blood spilled?

Nevertheless, when Chelmsford sailed for Plymouth on 5 August in the Union mail-steamer *German*, he left Wolseley to tidy up after him and bring the unfortunate war to some sort of conclusion. This he did with his habitual despatch and overweening confidence, reported in what the Duke of Cambridge fulminated were 'that brute's . . . offensive' despatches, full of 'claptrap as to all *his* reductions of expenditure! Full of attacks upon Chelmsford! In short full of self-sufficiency, arrogance, impertinence! A *cad* indeed!'[69] Unaware of the unfavourable impression he was making on the Duke, Wolseley left Pietermaritzburg on 30 July and travelled overland to the Mahlabathini plain. He reached it on 10 August while Chelmsford was still at sea, and set up camp near the burnt-out oNdini. There he was joined by Clarke's Column. Between 14 and 16 August most of the senior chiefs of central and northern Zululand surrendered, and on 20 August the chiefs of south-western Zululand gave up at Rorke's Drift. Cetshwayo was finally captured on 28 August and taken aboard ship on 4 September at Port Durnford for exile at the Cape.[70]

With Cetshwayo bound for exile, the chiefs could publicly accept Wolseley's terms for a settlement with a relatively clear conscience. While it had been Frere's unswerving intention to break the military potential of the Zulu kingdom and destroy the unifying power of the monarch, it had not been part of his plan to burden Britain with the future administration of the territory. It was sufficient to ensure that the amaZulu would never again pose either a military threat to their colonial neighbours, act as a rallying-point for other African states, or generally hinder the confederation process. Wolseley had all these objectives in mind when, at an assembly on 1 September at his kwaSishwili camp close by oNdini, he imposed his settlement on the Zulu chiefs. The Zulu monarchy was suppressed, and its main prop, the military system, abolished. In line with Frere's preference for indirect rule in the style of the Indian Empire, Wolseley did not annex Zululand, but divided it up into thirteen independent territories under the nominal supervision of a British resident – precisely what Chelmsford had previously advocated. Such a settlement seemed to answer the immediate requirements of ensuring the security of Zululand's neighbours while sparing Britain any new responsibilities and financial burdens. Following considerable consultation with colonial advisors, Wolseley appointed a rag-bag of likely chiefs to rule over the thirteen fragments of the former kingdom. He cynically calculated that out of self-interest most of them could be relied upon to uphold his settlement and to ensure that there would be no resurgence of the centralised Zulu monarchy. Disregarding prescient rumbling that his railroaded settlement had consigned the Zulu people to civil war and ruin, Wolseley and his staff then left Zululand for the troubled Transvaal Territory.[71]

Meanwhile, Baker Russell's and Clarke's columns snuffed out the last, small embers of resistance in outlying north-western and southern regions of Zululand.[72] On 10 September Baker Russell's column was ordered to the Transvaal for further operations against Sekhukhune in the Second Anglo-Pedi War of 1879,[73] and Clarke's Column evacuated Zululand at the Middle Drift on 20 September. In Natal, the African auxiliaries and colonial troops were all disbanded by early October. The war was finally over.[74]

PART IV

Aftermath, 1879–1905

CHAPTER 35

The Shadow of Isandlwana, August 1879–January 1887

THE UNION MAIL-STEAMER *German* docked at Plymouth on 26 August 1879 and Chelmsford and his staff, Wood and Buller, were all received on shore with the appropriate military honours.[1] Whether they were 'worthily deserved',[2] as Chelmsford's apologists asserted, was not at all certain. Indeed, Chelmsford's reception was not unmixed in a country where until only very recently they had been singing in the music halls:

> Tho' Lord Chelmsford no doubt is a brave and honest man,
> And Sir Bartle Frere too I daresay,
> They've not led our soldiers to victory yet
> But Sir Garnet will show them the way.[3]

Of course, Chelmsford's victory at Ulundi had gainsaid this ditty, and with colonial cheers and eulogistic speeches still ringing in his ears, he arrived home with some confidence that his reputation had been restored. A cartoon in *Fun* showed Chelmsford's critics, led by Beaconsfield himself, cleaning the General's boots and removing old stains.[4] Yet Wolseley was closer to the mark when he cattily predicted of Chelmsford that 'Although in war he can never again be employed . . . I have no doubt the Horse Gds. will cover him with Honour & give him Aldershot or some other equally good place.'[5]

On his arrival back in England, Chelmsford immediately received a letter written on 11 August 1879 by Major-General Ellice, the AG at the War Office, on behalf of the Duke of Cambridge. In it, Ellis made abundantly clear the Duke's dissatisfaction with Chelmsford's responses to his enquiry of 6 March concerning Isandlwana, and spelled out the

Horse Guard's damning conclusion that Chelmsford was responsible for what had gone wrong:

> The primary cause of the misfortune, and that which led to all the others, was the underestimate of the offensive fighting power of the Zulu army . . . It would appear that your Lordship, and those with you, expected to encounter foes and a mode of warfare differing in some degree indeed, but not in kind, from that of the Caffres [amaXhosa] with whom they had lately been contending in the Cape Colony.

The consequence, Ellice concluded, was that Chelmsford had fatally adopted a poor invasion strategy that did not sufficiently concentrate his forces, had unwisely divided No. 3 Column on 22 January, had not reconnoitred sufficiently thoroughly, and had failed to provide the camp with proper defences.[6] It was fortunate for Chelmsford that this damning letter was confidential and did not add to the public disquiet over his conduct of the Zulu campaign, but it would have left Chelmsford in no doubt as to where he now stood in the estimation of the Horse Guards and of his long-time patron, the Duke.

Indeed, as Wolseley had predicted, Chelmsford's military reputation had been too badly tarnished for him ever again to be offered an active command in the field. But other forms of military employment were possible. As Wolseley had foreseen, in 1880 he was offered the command of the Western District at Devonport. Chelmsford declined the offer, citing as he had in 1877 when he turned down the post of DAG, Horse Guards, his preference for an Indian command. The determining reason, however, was the expense, far over and above his military pay, associated with this particular home command. As GOC at Devonport, Chelmsford would be expected to attend naval reviews, greet royalty and high-ranking foreign naval visitors, and generally entertain lavishly.[7] Not that Chelmsford was by any means poor, and at his death in 1905 his wealth would stand at just over £68,000, comparable in value to his father's estate. But although possessing a very comfortable fortune, Chelmsford had four surviving sons to educate at expensive public schools and university in order that they might carry on the professional and service traditions of the family by pursuing careers in the law, Army and diplomatic service. (A fifth son, Alfred Sullivan Thesiger, who was born on 5 October 1880, just over a year after Chelmsford was reunited with his wife on his return from South Africa, died to his parents' sorrow in 1889.) To afford Devonport Chelmsford had to be rich, and not simply comfortably well-off. He therefore sought an alternative posting, and on 1 January 1881 he wrote to General Whitmore, MS at the Horse Guards, enclosing a statement of his foreign, staff and active service between 1855 and 1880 with the request that the Duke of Cambridge 'be graciously pleased to take into consideration my claims for some military employment'. General Whitmore replied assuring him that his application would be considered.[8] Nothing came of it, however, despite Cambridge's willingness to offer him a new command. Gladstone's Liberal administration that came to power in April 1880 when Beaconsfield lost the general election demurred because they feared an adverse public reaction if he were, and in March 1884 Cambridge finally conceded when writing to the Queen that Chelmsford could never again be given a command.[9]

Wolseley was right again to suppose that Chelmsford's effective military unemployability would not preclude him from receiving public honours. Besides the inordinate number of VCs bestowed (twenty-one of them) and eleven Distinguished Conduct Medals, the embarrassing Anglo-Zulu War did not yield much in the way of other awards. Soldiers who served in it received a campaign medal: the silver South African Medal with the Queen's head on the obverse and a golden yellow ribbon with two thick blue bands and two thin ones. The clasp specified in which of the South African wars between 1877 and 1879 a soldier had served, and along with 1,184 others Chelmsford received the clasp for 1878–9.[10] But there were few orders distributed among the senior officers. John North Crealock, Harness, Law and Newdigate were made CBs; Buller, Henry Crealock and Newdigate received CMGs; Pearson and Baker Russell were made KCMGs; and Strickland and Wood were made KCBs. On 19 August 1879 Chelmsford alone was made Knight Grand Cross of the Bath (GCB) with its plain dark red sash carrying the badge of the Order over the left hip, its gold and silver breast star and its collar and pendant badge.[11] This high order had never before been bestowed on an officer of Chelmsford's relatively junior rank (he had reverted to his substantive rank of major-general) but, as Lord Beaconsfield informed the Queen, he 'sanctioned without hesitation the great distinction'.[12]

Yet, even though Beaconsfield had allowed the award of the GCB to Chelmsford as a necessary public gesture of his government's recognition of his services, he could not forgive him for having brought such discredit upon the ministry through his mishandling of the Zulu campaign. He therefore refused to accord Chelmsford anything but the coldest 'official' interview' at Downing Street, snubbed the Queen's request that he receive him at Hughenden, his country seat, and did not mince his words in itemising in damning detail to the Queen his reasons for cold-shouldering him. But the Queen, who was grieved and astonished at Beaconsfield's pettiness, was determined to invite Chelmsford to Balmoral. She believed it showed 'a want of generosity' to condemn him unheard, even if she suspected that he had indeed 'made mistakes'. Besides, as she pointed out, '*He* has obtained the decisive victory at Ulundi.'[13] On 2 September the Queen bestowed the insignia of the GCB on Chelmsford in a private audience at Balmoral. He in turn, as she recorded in her journal, brought her 'a Zulu shield . . . taken out of the King's Shield House, in his kraal, at Ulundi', which he presented to her in another private audience the following day, along with a map of Zululand on which he demonstrated the difficulties of the campaign. Indeed, the Queen, who found Chelmsford thin and tired looking, had a 'great deal of conversation' with him 'about many things' during which he explained to her satisfaction much about the campaign 'which was *not* understood here'. Moreover, as she reported to Beaconsfield, 'He is most amiable . . . and is most generous to others,' especially to Pearson, Wood and Buller.[14] So 'very satisfactory' was Chelmsford's visit that she asked him to extend his stay to 6 September. She also wanted a photograph of Chelmsford's wife, and one too of John Dunn, and he urgently telegraphed Adria instructing her to send them 'at once'.[15]

Not everyone at Balmoral was as charmed as the Queen, however. Major-General Sir Henry Ponsonby, Grenadier Guards, veteran of the Crimea and Private Secretary to the Sovereign since 1870, while conceding that everyone liked him and that he did not put on airs, complained to his wife that Chelmsford's by now characteristic 'incessant whining' about the difficulties of command did not mark him out as a great but maligned general.[16] Nor was Beaconsfield subsequently swayed by the Queen's renewed injunction after Chelmsford's successful visit that 'he must be generous and see poor Lord Chelmsford. . . It would do harm if he did *not*.'[17]

As it turned out, the Queen had her faith in Chelmsford's exposition defending his conduct of the campaign modified when, three days after he left, Buller and Wood arrived to stay at Balmoral on 9 September. During their visit she pinned the VC he had won at Hlobane on Buller's chest and bestowed Wood's knighthood. When pressed, the two men, while emphasising their chief's bravery and kindness, questioned his ability as a general and dwelt on his indecisiveness.[18]

Nevertheless, these strictures were not sufficient to spoil Chelmsford in the Queen's eyes. He evidently possessed the manners, dignified demeanour, temperament and familiarity with aristocratic society to make a good courtier. Lady Ely, the Queen's Lady of the Bedchamber, afterwards confirmed that he had 'made a very favourable impression here'.[19] The Queen's very public fêting of Chelmsford at Balmoral enraged Wolseley, and as he snarled in his journal with perceptive paranoia: 'Because he is my Lord, society will back him up, the court included.'[20] And certainly, besides the Queen who (as we shall see) continued conspicuously to favour him, Chelmsford enjoyed the patronage of the Prince of Wales. The Prince, who had written immediately on learning of Chelmsford's 'grand victory' to congratulate Lady Chelmsford, made a point of meeting Chelmsford on his return from South Africa, and wrote that 'It gave me such pleasure seeing you looking so well . . . after all the severe trials you have been through.'[21] The Duke of Cambridge, his old patron, was certainly disappointed in Chelmsford, but that did not stop his mother, the 82-year-old Duchess of Cambridge, summoning him straightaway to St James's Palace to congratulate him in person on his victory at Ulundi.[22] There was a further strong reason for her doing so because Chelmsford's youngest sister, the Hon. Mary Lincoln Thesiger (1840–1914), was Lady in Waiting to the rumbustious and charitable Princess Mary Adelaide of Cambridge, Duchess of Teck, the old Duchess of Cambridge's daughter and sister to the Duke of Cambridge.[23] Nor did the Thesigers' royal connections stop there. Another sister, the Hon. Julia Inglis (d. 1904), the widow of the hero of Lucknow, was the recipient of royal patronage with her appointment as Housekeeper of the State Apartments at St James's Palace. And to Chelmsford's deep gratification at the Queen's continuing favour towards him and his family, in December 1884 she appointed his fourth son, the ten-year-old Eric, as Page of Honour, a position at court he would hold until 1900.[24]

While royal patronage would prove essential for Chelmsford's status and well-being during the remainder his life, there was no disguising that his active military career had fatally stalled as a result of his controversial command in South Africa. Even if his victory at Ulundi had gone some way to restoring his honour and rehabilitating his reputation, Chelmsford knew that the disaster at Isandlwana would continue to haunt him. He therefore resolved never, if he could help it, to raise the issue. Even before landing at Plymouth, he made it known through a letter to *The Times* that he was resolved to maintain a dignified reticence about his command in South Africa.[25] A year later, he somewhat disingenuously informed the House of Lords in the debate on his conduct of the war: 'Since he had returned from South Africa he had studiously avoided in public, and almost in private, making any allusion to it [Isandlwana], not because he was afraid of inquiry for himself, but because he respected the feelings of the friends of those who were lost.'[26]

Yet the unfortunate war itself could not simply be swept away under the carpet. The government could not forget that the total net cost for the British taxpayer had come to £5,230,323, far too much for what should have been a minor, colonial campaign.[27] The casualty rate had also proved unacceptably high, and what made British and colonial casualty figures even worse in the eyes of the military hierarchy was that in colonial campaigns combat losses were never expected to exceed deaths from disease, and in Zululand they were a staggering three times higher: 58 officers (40 of them British) and 1,319 NCOs and men (804 British) killed in action or died of wounds, plus 28 officers (23 British) and 259 NCOs and men (173 British) wounded, against 14 British officers and 440 NCOs and men (289 British) who died of disease, along with another British officer and 34 NCOs and men (16 British) who died in accidents.[28] And to make matters worse, if the Zulu casualty rate had been a very high 20 per cent (at least 6,000 of the *amabutho* who took the field were killed), then that figure was only a few per cent greater than the 17 per cent of his forces Chelmsford had lost in the field, either killed in action, incapacitation through wounds, dead by accident or perished from disease.[29]

Even if Beaconsfield's embarrassed government would have preferred to let the whole miserable affair sink from sight, unfortunately for Chelmsford, there were those who were determined not to let the matter rest. Foremost among them was Archibald Forbes, the rebarbative and egotistical 'special' from the *Daily News* with whom Chelmsford had long been at odds, and who, on his return to England, embarked on a series of histrionic public lectures recounting his adventures in Zululand. Chelmsford had unwisely thrown down the gauntlet in his final speech in Cape Town when he caustically referred to the political bias of the 'specials' in Zululand. The day after Chelmsford disembarked at Plymouth, the *Daily News* ran an article by Forbes in which he witheringly declared: 'If Lord Chelmsford has indeed been misrepresented by the correspondents accompanying his army, he has been misrepresented with a strange malignity and unanimity.'[30]

If that were not enough, Forbes followed up in February 1880 with an article published in the *The Nineteenth Century*.[31] Forbes made no attempt to hide that his article was written in 'just resentment' against the 'aspersion' Chelmsford had cast against the integrity of the 'specials' reporting the war in Zululand, and that his intention was to 'punish a wanton calumny on an honourable profession'.[32] Forbes's highly effective critique incensed Major French when he came to write Chelmsford's biography, and there is indeed a certain truth when he declared that Forbes had ventured with deliberate malice:

> . . . to denounce Chelmsford in highly offensive terms, to criticise his conduct of the war generally, and with almost unbelievable effrontery to give his own views as to what Lord Chelmsford should or should not have done. This vindictive and scurrilous article was composed for the most part of misstatements, gross exaggerations, and personal abuse.[33]

Perhaps so, and Chelmsford made no public rejoinder, but Forbes's critique was incisive enough to touch a very raw nerve. It caused Chelmsford immediately to set about and to continue polishing a series of memoranda in a page-by-page, point-by-point but ultimately unpublished refutation of the criticisms Forbes levelled against him.[34] 'Mr Forbes has condemned me without that knowledge of the secret springs which so often have to guide a General in command,' he jotted down in Memorandum C.[35] It seems a finalised memorandum was privately circulated among Chelmsford's friends and patrons, including members of the royal family. Lieutenant-General Sir Dighton Probyn, Secretary to the Prince of Wales, wrote to Chelmsford referring to the 'pamphlet' answering Forbes's fallacious arguments, and informing him that he had taken notes to show the Prince, 'who has taken an interest in it'. Probyn added that he hoped the Duke of Cambridge had also seen the memorandum.[36]

Yet, for all the effort Chelmsford put into the memorandum, it was eclipsed by the article Lieutenant-Colonel Harness, who had served with him throughout much of the campaign, published in April 1880 in *Fraser's Magazine*, a Tory journal.[37] His was a measured, systematic and very effective counter-blast to Forbes's article in which 'so much personal animus is shown', wrote Harness, that it could not but 'excite a feeling of indignation in those who have served with Lord Chelmsford and know his worth'.[38]

Chelmsford might have hoped to keep his head below the parapet, but the public debate between Forbes and Harness, and the conflicting evidence the two writers presented, served to reignite critical interest in Isandlwana and the conduct of the Zulu campaign more generally. The upshot was that Chelmsford was forced to break his silence and defend himself when, on 19 August and 2 September 1880, Field Marshal Lord Strathnairn severely slated his generalship in the House of Lords. Strathnairn was none other than the former Sir Hugh Rose under whom the young Thesiger had served in India, and who had been created Baron Strathnairn of Strathnairn and of Jhansi in 1866. He had retired in 1870 after serving as CinC Ireland and had been raised to field marshal in 1877. Strathnairn was a staunch Tory and therefore no supporter of Gladstone's Liberal administration, then in power. He therefore had no party-political motive in raising the issue in the Lords, and he knew Chelmsford both professionally and socially and was said to hold him in regard. Punctiliously, in his all but indecipherable hand he invited Chelmsford to his house in Berkeley Square 'to see all I have written' on the subject and promising to send him a copy of the speech he intended to deliver in the Lords.[39] But, these courtesies aside, Strathnairn was a dedicated soldier with a powerful will. He had proven a very effective field commander and administrator and was unprepared, in the interests of the Army, to countenance military ineffectiveness. After Isandlwana, so indignant was he, that he had volunteered for service in Zululand, an offer tactfully declined on account of his seniority and age (he was then seventy-eight).[40] Now, with so much printed evidence before him, including the official correspondence in the *Blue Books*, he was not prepared to let the matter rest.

Having to defend his own conduct in public before his peers in the Lords was naturally an ordeal for Chelmsford, one that he had striven to avoid.[41] Yet, having fortuitously put his ideas into order when he composed his memoranda in reply to Forbes, he was able to respond with eloquence and at length, if not entirely convincingly. However, he laid up further troubles for himself when, in the first day of the debate, he obliquely but unmistakably referred to Colonel Durnford and squarely laid the blame for the loss of the Isandlwana camp on his impulsive disregard of orders:

> Everyone, he thought, must admit that the camp had not been lost through having an insufficient garrison, or because the position was an unfit one for the number of troops to defend, but because the strict orders for its defence which had been given had not been carried out. He regretted that he should have had to reopen so painful a matter.[42]

During the second day of the debate, the disconcertingly well-informed and acute Strathnairn resumed his attack. Referring to his own considerable experience as a commander in the field, he identified what were (in his opinion) the cardinal mistakes Chelmsford had committed. Echoing (whether by coincidence or collusion) the points Major-General Ellice had made in his damning letter of 11 August the previous year, he questioned the flawed strategy of sending in columns too widely separated for mutual support; the poor siting of the camp at Isandlwana; its lack of prepared defences; the inadequate reconnaissance that allowed the Zulu to surprise the camp; and Chelmsford's own failure to return immediately to the camp when it came under attack. Finally, he came to Durnford's defence, characterising him as an able officer who had to 'cope with almost unexampled difficulties' in taking over 'the defence of an indefensible camp against an enemy overwhelming in numbers'.[43]

Yet Chelmsford, stubborn as ever, remained unbowed before Strathnairn's assault. He replied with dignity that, 'He looked back to the campaign with mixed feelings – regret at the loss of the gallant men who fell, and for that sad day at Isandlana, but with pride at what had been accomplished.' He went on to insist that when the inhospitable 'nature of the countryside' and 'the numerous difficulties of supply and transport' were taken into account, that he 'could not but think it unreasonable to say that the undue delays had arisen in consequence of the steps which he thought it necessary to take in order to secure the completeness of the expedition'.[44] But Strathnairn remained as unconvinced by these excuses as had been the Duke of Cambridge and the Horse Guards. His were the telling (if inelegant) final words in the debate: 'Whatever might be said, there were not the necessary precautions taken to protect a camp in which most of our stores were.'[45]

The debate in the Lords garnered Chelmsford some welcome public support. Wesley Francis, the mayor of Pietermaritzburg, and two other leading citizens of Natal were invited by Wood to present Chelmsford with a piece of plate at Chatham in September 1880 to express (as Francis put it) their 'deep sense of the high service' he had done for the Colony, especially in the light of 'the attack of Lord Strathnairn'.[46] But criticism of Chelmsford's role in the Anglo-Zulu War rumbled on. Some of the critics were all too well known to Chelmsford. One was Archibald Forbes who in mid-1880 insisted that he was entitled to the South African campaign medal on account of Chelmsford having supposedly entrusted him with official despatches on his 'Ride of Death' after Ulundi. As we have seen, Forbes had carried only private telegrams from various officers including a communication from Colonel Crealock to his wife but, as Gossett minuted in red on the correspondence, Forbes had 'made capital' of the situation and 'lied freely' to obtain the medal. There were consequently months of wrangling with the War Office, and Chelmsford was drawn in. It must have given him considerable satisfaction to affirm unequivocally that Forbes had carried no despatches sufficiently official to merit the medal. Finally, Hugh Childers, who was now the Secretary for War in Gladstone's cabinet, ruled on 2 June 1881 that war correspondents, as non-combatants, were not eligible for war medals. Forbes was deeply affronted, and Chelmsford perhaps had the satisfaction of knowing he had been instrumental in denying Forbes the decoration he so craved.[47]

Forbes had finally met his match, and the lamentable shortcomings of the British forces in the Transvaal campaign of 1880–1 (the First Anglo-Boer War) seemed set to eclipse the Anglo-Zulu War in the public mind. In a 'Military Ode' to the British infantry, the satirical magazine *Punch* declared:

> Britannia needs instructors
> To teach our boys to shoot,

Fixed targets and mere red-tape drill
Have borne but bitter fruit . . .[48]

And it must have afforded Chelmsford sour satisfaction that the comprehensively unsuccessful commander in the inglorious war had been Major-General Sir George Pomeroy Pomeroy-Colley, one of Wolseley's closest acolytes who had been his Chief of Staff in Zululand and had succeeded his mentor in April 1880 as High Commissioner for South-East Africa. Colley's unrelieved string of defeats in 1881 at Laing's Nek (28 January), Ingogo (8 February) and finally at Majuba (27 February), where he perished in the humiliating rout, helped put Chelmsford's own disasters in the shade. At least he had finally retrieved the situation in Zululand at Ulundi, whereas Colley's failures culminated in the ignominious retrocession of the Transvaal on 3 August 1881.[49]

Yet, even so, Chelmsford still could not shake free from the fall-out of the Zululand campaign since a new and determined set of adversaries had emerged to challenge him. Lieutenant-Colonel Edward Durnford was Colonel Anthony Durnford's brother. He was determined to rehabilitate Anthony's reputation that had been sullied by the Isandlwana debacle and the findings of the subsequent Court of Inquiry. In April 1879 he had published his first pamphlet in his brother's defence, *Isandhlwana, 22nd January*, in which, as he declared, he had 'endeavoured to put together a true and connected account of what occurred', trusting that 'many unjust, and ungenerous remarks, written and spoken, may be refuted'.[50] In December 1879 he followed up by requesting Chelmsford to write a few words justifying his brother's actions at Isandlwana.[51] In his response, Chelmsford declared that Edward Durnford's letter had given him 'much pain'. He explained that his estimation of Anthony Durnford's military conduct could only be based on the 'evidence published to the world', and that whatever opinion he expressed was open to interpretation and 'would necessarily be challenged by one side or another'. Keeping true to his decision never to bring up the subject of the conduct of the war in public, he added that if he did so, 'I should feel the pain of having revived all the painful recriminations and distressing discussions which I trust are now not likely to be renewed.'[52]

But Edward Durnford was not to be deflected from his mission by such considerations. He was spurred on by Chelmsford's remarks made on 19 August 1880 during the debate in the Lords that (as we have seen) once more placed the blame for the Isandlwana disaster squarely on his brother's shoulders. He rapidly responded in November 1880 in his second pamphlet, *Isandhlwana*, in which he declared that: 'I comment on Lord Chelmsford's remarks, which I assert do not contain "the true history".'[53] Yet, despite pointing out the discrepancies between Chelmsford's statements in the Lords on the one hand, and the evidence presented at the Court of Inquiry and in Chelmsford's own despatches on the other, the pamphlet produced insufficient conclusive proof for the reluctant military establishment to institute any sort of formal inquiry into Chelmsford's own misjudgement or negligence. The Horse Guards had done with the unfortunate fall-out from the Zulu campaign and now had the war in the Transvaal to contend with.[54]

Chelmsford could be excused in supposing the matter would end there, but he did not have the measure of Edward Durnford. Temporarily baulked, the latter was more determined than ever to pursue his crusade to exonerate his brother, and Chelmsford would be subjected to further vexation and embarrassment. In his quest, Edward Durnford secured a fanatically determined ally. She was Frances (Fanny) Colenso, the daughter of the controversially heretical and pro-Zulu Anglican Bishop of Natal. She had fallen in love with the charming and highly principled Anthony Durnford despite his being twice her age and with a wife, although he had been separated from her since 1860. It is not known if the two were actually lovers, but Frances persisted in regarding Anthony as her wronged, chivalrous knight-at-arms.[55]

In 1880 Edward Durnford and Fanny Colenso planned and wrote together their *History of the Zulu War* that set out to show not only that the war had been unjustly brought about, but that Anthony Durnford had been wickedly traduced by those who suggested he was responsible for the defeat at Isandlwana.[56] Then, in 1882 Edward Durnford, with Fanny Colenso's contribution, brought out his brother's selectively edited correspondence in *A Soldier's Life and Works in South Africa*. The final chapters were a blow-by-blow attempt to clear his good name. Embarrassing as their latest book was, Chelmsford could afford to ignore it because it contained little new or convincing evidence.[57]

But then, Edward Durnford and Fanny Colenso launched a fresh attack from an unexpected quarter. In late 1880 word had reached Edward

Durnford from Veterinary Surgeon S. Longhurst of the King's Dragoon Guards that, on 21 May 1879 during the reconnaissance-in-force of the Isandlwana battlefield, he had observed Captain Theophilus (Offy) Shepstone remove 'a packet of letters' from Durnford's body along with two finger rings and a pocket knife. Offy Shepstone, a prominent member of colonial society and a member of the Natal Legislative Council, had commanded various units of colonial mounted troops throughout the Anglo-Zulu War, but had not been present at Isandlwana. Edward Durnford decided he must pursue Longhurst's lead, not simply because he believed such papers might contain evidence clearing his brother's name, but because (if the accusation were true) it could prove that Shepstone had suppressed them to protect Chelmsford's reputation. When Shepstone vehemently denied the allegation, Durnford decided not to pursue the matter.[58]

But Fanny Colenso was not so squeamish. Brooding on the injustice being done to her knight errant's memory, she stepped in. It is no coincidence that her father, the Zuluphile Bishop Colenso, had broken with Offy's father and old friend Sir Theophilus Shepstone over the latter's segregationist 'native policy' in Natal. Unlike Edward Durnford, she refused to accept Offy's word. For the next four years she doggedly attempted to build up a case against him, asserting that he had abstracted the papers under the specific direction of Chelmsford or a member of his staff with the deliberate intention of fastening the blame for the Isandlwana disaster on Anthony Durnford. Almost unhinged by her campaign, she came to regard all who did not agree with her as her personal enemies, and tried to bully her dearest friend, Offy's wife, into forcing her husband into confessing his alleged guilt. Anthony Durnford had been a Royal Engineer, and Fanny worked on successive commanders of the Royal Engineers in Natal to convince them that the honour of the Royal Engineers was at stake and that Offy was lying.

At length, in early 1886, Colonel Charles Luard, RE, declared himself ready to prosecute and Offy Shepstone's friends advised him to settle the question through requesting a military inquiry into the 'absolutely false' charges against him.[59] Lieutenant-General H. Torrens, the acting High Commissioner and GOC in South Africa, was determined that the scope of any inquiry should be limited to whether or not any papers had been removed, and that, in order to prevent 'distinguished names' from being dragged in, there should be no investigation of the motives behind their alleged abstraction. In restricting the investigation to this simple question, Torrens was in effect emulating Chelmsford's procedure in his own circumscribed investigation into Isandlwana, and of course the 'distinguished name' Torrens had in mind to protect was Chelmsford's.

It was only in March 1886, when Offy Shepstone wrote to him soliciting his help, that Chelmsford learned of Fanny Colenso's allegations against Shepstone.[60] The bizarre and unexpected episode caused him much vexation and embarrassment, since it raised up issues he doubtless would have preferred to have let lie. Provoked, he did his determined best to assist Offy's case by writing to deny emphatically that he had in any way been involved in the rifling of Durnford's papers. Obviously nettled, he added that until that moment he had been 'in absolute ignorance that such a disgraceful story, so void of foundation, had been concocted'.[61] When the Court of Inquiry was convened in late April 1886, the case against Shepstone collapsed for lack of evidence. Torrens wrote to a relieved Chelmsford that the 'wretched charges' against Shepstone had been dismissed.[62] Frances Colenso was devastated. She died of tuberculosis on 29 April 1887 insisting to the last that 'Durnford's last orders were on him when he fell'.[63] Edward Durnford did not give up immediately either, and continued to write to Chelmsford. He only ungraciously desisted in September 1886 when Chelmsford, who was in no doubt that the charges brought against Offy were in reality aimed at him,[64] refused to engage with him any further in the matter.[65] The weird issue was finally laid to rest when Edward Durnford reluctantly exonerated Shepstone in a letter to the newspapers on 5 January 1887.[66] Thereafter, Chelmsford could at last put Isandlwana behind him.

CHAPTER 36

The Courtier General, April 1882–April 1905

PERENNIAL FRETS ABOUT ISANDLWANA doubtless troubled Chelmsford's sleep. But, as the years passed, so the memories of his controversial command during the Anglo-Zulu War receded in the public consciousness. The Horse Guards never forgot, however. Chelmsford was only fifty-two years of age when he won the battle of Ulundi, still quite young enough to hold another active command in the field, but he was never again offered one, nor an Indian command which is what he really wanted. He nevertheless remained in the Army and, through seniority, was routinely promoted on 1 April 1882 to the substantive rank of lieutenant-general. He was extremely fortunate to retain the Queen's favour for, when the unwelcome prospect of compulsory retirement from the Army began to loom, she came to his assistance. The appointment of Lieutenant of the Tower was in the Queen's gift. Thanks to her, on 4 June 1884, Chelmsford succeeded Lieutenant-General C. L. B. Maitland, and held the position until 28 March 1889.[1] In due course, he was promoted to full general on 16 December 1888. Before the revised regulations of 1886 came into force, he would have had to retire in 1889 at the age of sixty-two, but now the retirement age of full generals was extended to sixty-seven with a pension of £1,000 to follow. Chelmsford was finally placed on the retired list on 7 June 1893.

Throughout these years and until his death, Chelmsford and his family lived at 5 Knaresborough Place, London SW5, a spacious yellow brick and white stucco terrace house newly built in Earl's Court, a district of Kensington that was being developed in the 1870s. As an address it did not have the aristocratic cachet of his father's house in Eaton Square, but with its four stories and portico with two Tuscan pillars it was a substantial and comfortable abode. Like any gentleman of the time, Chelmsford belonged to clubs where he spent much of his leisure time mingling socially with members of like background and mind. Revealingly and predictably enough, his two clubs were the United Service Club ('the Senior') in Pall Mall where membership was confined to senior officers of the Army and Navy, and the Carlton Club which was essentially a political club and the nerve-centre of the Conservative Party.[2]

Age brought with it fresh honours, for the unsatisfactory commander in Zululand had transposed into a dignified veteran, his chest covered in orders and decorations, still dapper, upright and handsome with a full head of greying hair, neat beard and sweeping moustaches. On 30 January 1889 he was appointed Honorary Colonel of the Sherwood Foresters (Derbyshire Regiment). The honour greatly gratified Chelmsford because his old regiment, the 95th Foot, in which he had served in India, was now the 2nd Battalion of the Sherwood Foresters. The Childers Reforms had introduced 'territorialisation' into the Army, whereby from 1 July 1881 the United Kingdom was divided into regimental districts, each allocated a two-battalion regiment, usually bearing a 'county' title. Regimental numbers were abolished, and the 1st to 25th Regiments of Foot which were already made up of two battalions adopted new regimental titles. The remaining, single-battalion regiments – such as the 95th Foot – were paired to become the 1st or 2nd battalions of new regiments.[3]

Then, on 27 September 1900, the 73-year-old Chelmsford exchanged the Colonelcy of the Sherwood Foresters for that of the 2nd Life Guards. The Life Guards is the senior regiment of the British Army and forms part of the Household Cavalry of the Household Division. Such a prestigious honour could not have been given without the approval of the Queen, not least because it made Chelmsford eligible for her to appoint him Gold Stick, a ceremonial office at court open to Colonels of the Life Guards. To this day Gold Stick-in-Waiting attends the sovereign at all state occasions including the State Opening of Parliament. Chelmsford did not serve Queen Victoria as Gold Stick for long, however, and only a few months after his appointment he found himself assisting at her state funeral in February 1901. He remained Gold Stick, however, for on his accession in January 1901 King Edward VII, who had known and supported Chelmsford for several decades, confirmed him in his post, and in August 1902 he took part in the new king's coronation procession. In the Birthday

Honours of November 1902 the King made him Knight Grand Cross of the Victorian Order (GCVO), and Chelmsford had another glittering breast star to affix next to that of the GCB. The Victorian Order was instituted by Queen Victoria in 1896 and remains exclusively in the gift of the sovereign. It is generally conferred for service to the royal family, such as Chelmsford had proffered over many years.[4]

Besides his honorary duties in the Army and at court, Chelmsford, who since his return from South Africa had been a church warden at his parish church, the neo-Gothic St Jude's, Collingham Gardens, not far from his house, became earnestly involved in several military-related charities that reflected his deep commitment as a practising Anglican and teetotaller. He served as the first Governor of the essentially middle-class (rather than working-class) Church Lads' Brigade formed in 1891, and was chair for twenty years of the Royal Victoria Patriotic Asylum in Wandsworth, which had been established as an orphanage for the children of troops killed in the Crimean War. In 1890 he was Chair of the Committee of the Royal Military Exhibition in aid of the establishment and maintenance of the Church of England Soldiers' Institutes that provided alcohol-free 'homes from home' for military personnel serving overseas, and also housing for ex-servicemen and their families in Britain.

A little over a year before his own death, it was Chelmsford's duty on 22 March 1904 as Gold Stick to assist in the grand, military funeral in Westminster Abbey of his old patron the Duke of Cambridge, attended by a vast company of officers, politicians and royalty with Edward VII as the chief mourner. With a certain irony, bearing in mind the years of antagonism between the competing 'rings' in the Victorian Army, among the pall-bearers were Roberts, Wolseley, Wood and Buller.[5]

Observing these four during the ceremony, Chelmsford might well have contemplated their diverse fates. Field Marshal Earl Roberts of Kandahar, Waterford and Pretoria, with whom Chelmsford had never served, had fared best of all. Roberts had taken up his appointment as CinC of the British Army in January 1901, and had recently retired in February 1904. When he did so, the recommendations of the Esher Report were implemented, and the office of CinC that had played such a determining role in Chelmsford's career was replaced with the creation of the Army Council and the appointment of a Chief of the General Staff, a position first held by General Sir Neville Lyttleton. The title of CinC of the British Armed Forces reverted to the sovereign. Roberts, a popular imperial hero with a consuming personal ambition who knew, as did Wolseley, how to manipulate the media and public opinion, weathered the crisis of the Second Anglo-Boer (South African) War of 1899–1902 with his reputation enhanced.[6] The same could not be said for Wolseley, his ancient rival and Chelmsford's bane.

Field Marshal Viscount Wolseley had gone on from strength to strength after he left South Africa. He had led successful campaigns in Egypt and the Sudan and held a series of top military administrative posts. When the 76-year-old Cambridge was finally pressured into resigning as CinC, Wolseley stepped into his shoes on 1 November 1895. Having waited so long to be in a position to implement the reform of the Army, Wolseley failed to live up to his promise and overcome the entrenched military system. His reorganisation of the War Office did not prove sufficiently effective to rise to the challenge of the Boer War, and he retired in November 1900 aged sixty-seven, a thwarted, disappointed man.[7]

Of the two others, Sir Evelyn Wood and Sir Redvers Buller, who had been key figures in Wolseley's Ashanti Ring, and who had been Chelmsford's main supports during the Anglo-Zulu War, fortune had smiled only on the former. Wood had crowned an illustrious career (during which he – like Chelmsford – had enjoyed the friendship and support of the Queen) with his appointment as AG in October 1897, and was promoted field marshal in April 1903.[8] General Buller, on the other hand, ended his career in disgrace and there was good reason for Chelmsford to regard his story with considerable empathy born of his own experiences.

If Roberts's reputation had been greatly enhanced by his time as CinC in South Africa during the Boer War, if Wood had only just been able to hang on to his in the same conflict, and if Wolseley's had been distinctly dented, then the same war utterly destroyed Buller's. Buller was the renowned veteran of numerous campaigns (he was the most dashing commander to have emerged in the Anglo-Zulu War) and the holder of a series of the top military administrative posts. He had even been the initial choice to replace Cambridge as CinC, and was frustrated when, at the last moment, a Tory administration replaced the Liberal one that favoured him, and gave the post to Wolseley instead. He was appointed CinC, South Africa in October 1899, but after a series of military disasters against the Boers was superseded by Roberts only a month later. Unlike

Chelmsford in similar circumstances, he stayed on for nearly a year in a subordinate position before requesting that he be relieved and allowed to resume his command at Aldershot. But then, goaded as Chelmsford had been by the hounds of the press, he unwisely uttered some indiscreet words in public rejecting what was being said of his command in South Africa. Roberts, seizing the opportunity and on his insistence as CinC, saw to it that Buller was dismissed in October 1901 from the Aldershot command.[9] Reflecting on Buller's ignominious fall from grace, and noting the similarity of his trajectory to his own, Chelmsford might well have perceived that he was fortunate not to have suffered a comparable fate.

Gilded with honours, Chelmsford died in London at 9.30 a.m. on 9 April 1905 in the magnificent but ponderous United Service Club. He had been felled by a sudden 'seizure' (stroke) while playing billiards there the previous evening and had been too ill to be moved to hospital. Appropriately, the club stood across the road from the Crimean War memorial with its three Guardsmen cast from the bronze of Russian guns captured at the fall of Sebastopol where Chelmsford had been present fifty years before.

Chelmsford's funeral, with full military honours, was held on 13 April 1905 at his parish church of St Jude's. His coffin, draped with the Union Flag, was drawn on a gun carriage. Men of the 2nd Life Guards and the Irish Guards formed the guard of honour and girls from the Royal Victoria Patriotic Asylum, wearing their red cloaks, walked behind the coffin. King Edward VII himself attended, as did his brother Field Marshal Prince Arthur Duke of Connaught and Strathearn, the Inspector-General of the Forces. Among other high members of the military who were present was General Sir Archibald Alison who had been the DQMG for Intelligence at the War Office during the Anglo-Zulu War and who had received dozens of confidential letters from officers serving with Chelmsford. Field Marshal Lord Roberts, who had agreed to be one of the pallbearers, was too unwell on the day to serve. Buller, whose military career had come to such an humiliating end in 1901, and who would die from gall-bladder cancer in 1908, did not make the journey from Downes, his seat near Crediton in Devonshire. Significantly, perhaps, Field Marshal Sir Evelyn Wood did not choose to be present either. Yet, even though the two officers on whom he had most relied in his South African campaigns were not there to pay their respects, it was evident to all that his royal patrons, the military establishment and the charities he had served had all rallied around to honour one of their own, his now distant misadventures in Zululand laid to rest alongside him.[10]

Chelmsford was buried in a simple granite tomb carved with a plain cross behind his father's heraldically ornate resting-place on the eastern side of the main avenue that runs through London's Brompton Cemetery. The inscription reads: *Frederic Augustus, 2nd Baron Chelmsford, G.C.B., G.C.V.O., General. Colonel of the 2nd Life Guards. May 31st 1827 – April 9th 1905.* Twenty-one years later his widow, Adria, Lady Chelmsford, joined him in his tomb surrounded by a cluster of other family members.

Chelmsford's eldest son, Frederic, succeed his father as the third Baron Chelmsford and would outshine both his father and grandfather. A first-class cricketer (he captained the Oxford University eleven in 1892), he was also an outstanding law student and was elected to a fellowship at All Souls (1892–9). He pursued a stellar public career as a proconsul of empire, being successively Governor of Queensland (1906–9) and New South Wales (1910–13), and briefly served as Governor-General of Australia (1909–10). His mother (after whom he took in looks) lived to see him consummate his father's Indian connection when he was appointed Viceroy of India between 1916 and 1921. On his retirement he was advanced in the peerage on 3 June 1921 to be the first Viscount Chelmsford. He then went on to join the first Labour government in 1924 as First Lord of the Admiralty, and until his death in 1933 remained a steadfast champion of Indian nationalist interests. Indeed, this honourable, dedicated public servant, whose achievements have usually been underrated, can claim to be one of the architects of modern India.[11] Yet, proud as his father would have been of his heir's stellar achievements in the public service, one must suppose that the gap between a conservative, courtier soldier imbued with all the values and attitudes of the Victorian era, and a Labour politician who was an advocate for Indian independence, would have situated them increasingly far apart in what had become alien worlds. The first Viscount Chelmsford had children (his elder son, Lieutenant the Hon. Frederic Thesiger, died in May 1917 from wounds received in Mesopotamia during the First World War) and the present holder of the title is the fourth Viscount Chelmsford.[12]

Since the great prominence (and occasional notoriety) of the first two barons and the first viscount, the Chelmsford line has faded from the public eye. The exception was Sir Wilfred Thesiger, KBE (1910–2003), General Lord Chelmsford's grandson, the eldest of the four sons of Captain the Hon. Wilfred Thesiger, DSO, Chelmsford's third son. Wilfred Thesiger was born in Addis Ababa where his father was then Minister Plenipotentiary. As a boy in Abyssinia (now Ethiopia), before being educated at Eton College and Magdalen College, Oxford, he developed his craving for adventure, big-game hunting and exploration. He made his name in arduous desert travel in North Africa and Arabia, and his book published in 1964 on the Marsh Arabs of southern Iraq confirmed his high reputation as a writer and photographer. In some fifty years spent travelling in remote regions he vividly documented fast-disappearing ways of life and bequeathed an invaluable record to posterity.[13] A legacy, one is tempted to suggest, of more lasting significance than the military career of the grandfather he never knew.

CONCLUSION

'Ill-Luck Always Attends upon Mismanagement'

CHELMSFORD'S VICTORY at the battle of Ulundi served somewhat to restore his military reputation, but he could never quite shake off the stigma of Isandlwana and his responsibility for the disaster. Much like Sir Redvers Buller, whose string of defeats in the Second Anglo-Boer War led to the humiliation of being superseded in his command, Chelmsford had to live with the burden of failure. But, unlike Buller, he managed to keep his head down under the barrage of criticism, and by not responding too injudiciously was able, with royal support, to rebuild his career as a courtier and garner many honours in his venerable old age, dying a veritable pillar of the establishment.

Yet 'Spy' (Leslie Ward) knew what he was about when in his caricature of Chelmsford in the satirical journal *Vanity Fair* of 3 September 1881, he cryptically captioned his portrayal of the gawky, ill-at-ease General facing down the criticisms of his peers in the House of Lords: 'Isandula'. That one word alone was enough instantly to identify his subject, forever branded in the public mind with the shame of that terrible defeat.

The unsparing commentary by 'Jehu Junior' (Thomas Gibson Bowles, *Vanity Fair's* owner-editor) that accompanied 'Spy's' caricature, owed much to Archibald Forbes's hostile critiques of Chelmsford, and scathingly insisted that at Isandlwana Chelmsford had been 'outwitted, out-manoeuvred, and beaten in strategy by ignorant savages'. Bowles condescendingly concluded: 'Lord Chelmsford is not a bad man. He is industrious and conscientious so far as his lights guide him. But Nature has refused to him the qualities of a great captain. He has suffered much and is entitled to certain commiseration.'[1]

Bowles was perceptive in writing these final sentences. Chelmsford was indeed 'not a bad man'; quite the opposite, in fact. 'A charming man; well read and posted in every detail of his profession,' proclaimed *The Times* in his obituary.[2] This appreciation of Chelmsford as a person accorded well with the opinion of the Duke of Cambridge, expressed in 1879: 'a gallant, estimable and high-principled man, generous to others, unsparing of himself, and modest withal'.[3] Charles Low, in his *Soldiers of the Victorian Age* that appeared shortly before the *Vanity Fair* caricature, summed Chelmsford up in less bilious, more even-handed, but perhaps over-sympathetic terms:

> Though public opinion in the press, in society, and in the army, was much divided as to the generalship displayed by Lord Chelmsford, everyone was agreed that he was actuated by a determination to do his best without regard to personal convenience, and that he never spared himself in the public interest ... His upright character and blameless life have acquired for him the respect and affection of his numerous friends.[4]

Certainly, as this study has shown, as a man Chelmsford was unfailingly courteous and considerate. He was happily married and took his religious faith and its obligations seriously. Nor is there any doubting his professionalism, energy, dedication to duty, his care for the men under his command, and his generous loyalty to colleagues. He was also commendably brave under fire. When he believed circumstances required it, he could be tough-minded. He did not flinch from flogging soldiers on campaign when their misdemeanours merited the punishment; and he was prepared to take the war to African civilians in the Eastern Cape and Zululand when he believed it was necessary to do so to in order to prevent their supplying their warriors in the field and to induce their surrender. Nor did he shy away from employing what were in effect underhand means when he considered the ends were justified. Such were his dealing with Sir Henry Bulwer when he was determined to pursue the 'active defence' across the Natal border into Zululand despite the Lieutenant-Governor's opposition; likewise, his final negotiations with King Cetshwayo were intended to deter the amaZulu from attacking his forces at the White Mfolozi until his own preparations were complete. The last, at least, was a subterfuge much employed in war then and now and not considered reprehensible by contemporaries.

More negatively, Chelmsford could be rash and impulsive on occasions, although unnecessarily pettifogging, indecisive and over-cautious on others. His tendency to obstinacy could lead him to hold stubbornly to his own course even if it did not serve him well, and his ingrained conservatism and reliance on conventional practice could work against him in military situations that required innovation. In other words, as Bowles wrote of him, he was 'industrious and conscientious so far as his lights guide him,' but these (as he implied) were not sufficient for the purpose. And therein lay the problem: by temperament Chelmsford lacked the attributes Bowles identified as 'the qualities of a great captain'.

The shrewd Lord Beaconsfield put his finger on it when he told Wolseley that Chelmsford's misfortunes were 'partly mismanagement & partly ill-luck, for ill-luck always attends upon mismanagement.'[5] The Latin motto on the Chelmsford the coat-of arms is '*Spes et Fortuna*', or 'Hope and Fortune'. Major Clery considered that 'Lord C. has certainly had no *luck*, as such.'[6] Certainly, in Zululand Chelmsford had no unexpected lucky breaks and was afflicted by certain strokes of ill-fortune such as the avoidable death of the impulsive Prince Imperial. But, until the Zulu campaign, Chelmsford had in fact been the darling of fortune, and when things went badly wrong in Zululand, much of the reason undeniably lay in his own 'mismanagement' rather than in extraneous circumstances over which he had no control.

Chelmsford had the inestimable good fortune to be born into the socially ambitious Thesiger family, the eldest son of the first Lord Chelmsford who thrust his way up by way of the law and political office with the Tory Party to join the lower ranks of the aristocracy. The money was therefore at hand for his heir to be educated at Eton College in order to fit him for his social standing – indeed, for him in later life to take with aplomb to the role of courtier – and for him to rise rapidly in rank in the Army through purchase; while social connections and the vital patronage of the Horse Guards facilitated exchanges into the socially prominent Grenadier Guards and then, controversially, into the 95th Regiment and with it service in India. His social standing and contacts within the military establishment rather than outstanding talent led to a series of desirable staff appointments in Ireland, the Crimea and India.

There is nevertheless no denying that Chelmsford did prove himself an able military administrator in his various staff appointments culminating in his becoming AG in India, an environment where he was at his most fulfilled and content, and where he married and began to raise a family.

Chelmsford saw active service in the siege of Sebastopol during the Crimean War, in the last stages of the Indian Mutiny where he held his first command in the field at the battle of Koondrye, and in Abyssinia where he was appointed DAG, Abyssinian Field Force. He took the profession of arms seriously and, more so than many another officer, assiduously studied the latest works on military theory and practice. Yet, despite his experiences in the Abyssinian campaign, a classic 'small war', he was curiously resistant to its lessons. In South Africa he remained wedded to conventional tactical practices more appropriate for operations such as he had taken part in during the Crimean War and Indian Mutiny than for asymmetric warfare against African warriors. Indeed, as Jeff Mathews has concluded, to a large degree Chelmsford lacked the flair and imagination to 'rise above the limitations and constraints' of the military establishment.[7] He fell in temperamentally with his patron the Duke of Cambridge and his conservative circle, rather than with the likes of Wolseley and his reformist 'ring', and by and large identified with the conventional outlook and assumptions of the majority of the officer corps in whose company he spent the whole of his adult life. That is not to say that during the course of Chelmsford's career the British Army was not steadily adapting to the new face of warfare, adopting modern weaponry and more appropriate uniforms and accoutrements, reforming its organisation and revising its tactical doctrine. But it was one thing to lay down on paper how operations should ideally be conducted in the field against conventional as well as unconventional forces; it was another for officers and commanders to apply theory in practice. It is consequently disheartening to read Chelmsford's letter to Sir Theophilus Shepstone written at the end of the Ninth Cape Frontier War during which he had reluctantly accepted the advice proffered by the colonists who were long used to the irregular style of warfare practised by the amaXhosa: 'The broad principles of tactics hold good in Africa equally as well as in Europe, and the idea of South African colonists that there is a specialité in African fighting is quite a mistake.'[8]

In order to bring the Ninth Cape Frontier War to a successful conclusion, Chelmsford had been compelled, against his natural inclinations and penchant for conventional, European-style campaigning, to conduct what amounted to grinding counter-insurgency operations against irregular Xhosa forces. However, when he planned the Zululand campaign, he anticipated that the Zulu armies would stand and fight in set-piece battles similar to those that had marked the earlier stage of the Ninth Cape Frontier War before he assumed command. Consequently, he was confident that he would be able to employ the orthodox strategy and tactics he preferred in defeating the amaZulu. This calculation would be proved catastrophically wrong on account of his initial underestimation of the marked warlike abilities of the amaZulu, a misconception shared by his staff and one that permeated the ranks of his officers.

Major Clery was in no doubt that 'The experience of the war in the old colony last year and the easy promenade that affair turned out to be, made them all go into this business with light hearts.'[9] The Horse Guards likewise concluded that his failure to appreciate the fighting qualities of the amaZulu was the root cause behind Chelmsford's strategic and tactical errors.[10] In this view, his deployment of several widely spaced invading columns meant they were too dispersed to cooperate effectively and permitted the amaZulu to concentrate their main force against the one they had targeted. For Chelmsford, however, this was not a drawback since it was his intention to tempt the amaZulu to do battle. His over-confident calculation was that, based on the precedent of the three victorious set-piece battles during the Ninth Cape Frontier War, any single one of the columns would assuredly defeat a numerically far stronger Zulu army thanks to its discipline, and to the overwhelming superiority of its firepower. However, the Horse Guards concluded that Chelmsford's overweening confidence in his secure tactical edge lulled him during the Isandlwana campaign to divide his forces in the face of the enemy and to leave his camp without prepared defences. 'It was a case,' concluded Chelmsford's obituarist in *The Times* who clearly had the more recent instances during the two Anglo-Boer Wars close to mind, 'as it has invariably been with us, of underestimating the enemy, with the result to which we have become so painfully accustomed.'[11]

Chelmsford might be said to have been 'unfortunate' in that the main Zulu army descended on No. 3 Column on 22 January instead of on No. 4 Column that, on the very same day, Colonel Wood had divided and marched out to disperse the Zulu irregulars on Zungwini Mountain. The same applied to Colonel Pearson's No. 1 Column, unsuccessfully ambushed by inferior Zulu forces while it was dangerously strung out as it crossed the Nyezane River. In both these cases, the consequences for the British, operating in the open and not ensconced behind prepared defences, would more than likely have been the same as at Isandlwana if the amaZulu had attacked them in full force, a fate Wood's near-disaster on Hlobane later in the war would confirm. Yet whether the amaZulu had crushed the British on 22 January at Isandlwana, Zungwini or Nyezane is beside the point. The issue is that in all three instances the British were operating in negligent disregard of the real menace posed by the main Zulu army. And for that Chelmsford, as GOC in charge of operations, has to bear the prime responsibility. And to make matter worse for him, he had effectively taken over command of the Centre Column from Colonel Glyn, compounding his accountability for the Isandlwana disaster. There was no denying, as Bowles charged in *Vanity Fair*, that Chelmsford had been 'outwitted, out-manoeuvred, and beaten'.

Nevertheless, it must be remembered that Chelmsford was not superseded in his South African command solely on account of the Isandlwana disaster. Further mounting problems and failures, what Beaconsfield meant by 'mismanagement', exposed his shortcomings as a commander and finally persuaded the government in London to place overall responsibility for operations in Zululand in Wolseley's hands.

In the weeks following the Isandlwana calamity Chelmsford was on the verge of a nervous collapse. As Major Elliott expressed it: 'His soul was wrung to such a degree by that sight of hundreds upon hundreds of dead men lying about him in the dimness . . . that it was feared in England for some time his mind had become unstrung.'[12] The consequence was that Chelmsford sent panic-stricken requests to London for reinforcements and very unwisely admitted to his damaged health and shaken morale. But it is to his credit that he soon recovered his nerve and equilibrium, arranged for the defence of Natal and successfully evacuated the blockaded garrison in Fort Eshowe. In the process, he demonstrated that he could learn from experience and adapt. The Eshowe Relief Column advanced taking every precaution against attack and laagering wherever it halted. At Gingindlovu on 2 April, having learned the lessons of Isandlwana and

Rorke's Drift, Chelmsford did not deploy his force in skirmishing order in the open, but fought a classic action from behind prepared defences, and secured a substantial victory.

However, his difficulties redoubled and his inadequacies were exposed once Eshowe was relieved. The reinforcements he had requested were pouring in, along with four major-generals. He had now to decide how best to deploy this embarrassment of military manpower in the renewed invasion of Zululand. Against the advice of many of his commanders, he could think of nothing better than to recapitulate the strategy he had adopted in the first invasion, and to send in several columns to converge on oNdini with the objective of defeating the Zulu army in the field and compelling Cetshwayo to submit. Once again, the great distances between the columns and the inhospitable terrain made it difficult to coordinate operations, while their dispersal added considerably to the complications of keeping them adequately supplied in the field. One indubitable advantage, however, of campaigning simultaneously in different parts of Zululand was that the widespread British presence enabled commanders to implement Chelmsford's policy of offering easy terms of surrender to local chiefs. Consequently, although the 1st Division achieved little militarily and gave the other columns no tangible support, it secured the submission of the entire Zulu coastal region.

Chelmsford was not a political soldier in the Wolseley mould. Like General Cunynghame during the Ninth Cape Frontier War, he allowed Sir Bartle Frere to take the lead in framing policy, and as GOC saw his role as being confined to carrying out the military solutions the High Commissioner required. Nevertheless, it was essential for him to cooperate closely with the civil authorities in Natal in the interests of the war effort, and his failure to do so bedevilled the vital provision of supplies and transport. To make matters worse, Chelmsford became embroiled in an increasingly personal dispute with Sir Henry Bulwer, the Lieutenant-Governor, over the deployment of the Natal border levies, a wrangle that echoed the clash General Cunynghame had had with the Cape government over the competing boundaries of civil and military authority in the Ninth Cape Frontier War. In both cases the government finally supported the primacy of military over civilian interests, but the political fallout that had led to Cunynghame's recall was likewise the final, determining factor in Chelmsford's supersession.

Besides his enervating dispute with the Natal authorities, there were many other shortcomings on Chelmsford's part that eventually forfeited the support of the Horse Guards and the government. Isandlwana was a major embarrassment for the Tory administration as well as for the Horse Guards, and both had to sustain bruising attacks in Parliament and in the press. But, as Ian Beckett has put it, 'What condemned . . . Lord Chelmsford as much as his military failure in 1879, was his inability to comprehend the requirements of public opinion.'[13] Despite repeated promptings by his patron, the Duke of Cambridge, he failed to write full and convincing despatches that satisfactorily explained what had gone wrong at Isandlwana. (Of course, his need to wriggle out from taking the blame made obfuscation inevitable.) His relations with the swarm of war correspondents who descended on Zululand after Isandlwana were lukewarm at best and positively antagonistic at worst, ensuring that the 'specials' (notably Archibald Forbes who waged an outright vendetta against him) denigrated him in their reports, irretrievably damaging his reputation in the eyes of the public. Nor were their strictures necessarily unfounded.

All 'small wars' were bedevilled by inhospitable terrain and climate, disease, distance, poor roads and communications, lack of reliable maps and intelligence, and crippling problems of transport and supply. The Zululand campaign was no exception, and its challenges should not have been unanticipated by Chelmsford after his experiences in the expedition to Abyssinia. However, when the second invasion of Zululand made slow progress, he harped on all these routine difficulties as if they were quite exceptional and all but insurmountable.

One of the root causes of Chelmsford's many problems was his reluctance to delegate, a tendency exacerbated by inadequate staff support. He consequently allowed himself to be overwhelmed by the pettifogging administrative work of managing a campaign (and his attention to detail was undeniably impressive), but his efforts would have been better employed in paying attention as GOC to the wider strategic picture and leaving the details to his subordinates. The problem, it seems, was that while as an experienced staff officer he would undoubtedly have found the routines of military administration on campaign comfortingly familiar, he was far less at home with the novel experience of an independent command in the field. One can only conclude that he would have been far more at ease and successful as a diligent chief of staff rather than as a commander.[14] Certainly, his plodding, over-methodical strategy in the Eastern Cape and Zululand, based more on the military manuals he had assiduously studied than on practical experience commanding in the field, distinctly lacked flair or dash. It must be assumed that his bouts of indecisiveness, irascibility and reluctance to take advice stemmed from his fundamental sense of inadequacy as a field commander. As he testily told Wood: 'I am the one to be hanged if anything goes wrong.'[15] His self-confidence as a general had been temporarily buoyed up by his success in the Eastern Cape – too much so, indeed – but Isandlwana dealt it a fatal blow, only ever partially deflected by his subsequent victories at Gingindlovu and Ulundi. One can only suppose that his habitual obstinacy was the recourse of the insecure.

Paradoxically for a commander so obsessed with detail, and one who understood staff work so thoroughly, Chelmsford allowed himself to be overwhelmed by logistical problems. These he could well have alleviated, even if never quite overcome, if he had established a better relationship with the Natal government, and if he had taken a more determined hand in restructuring and improving the over-burdened Commissariat and Transport Department. This was perhaps the one situation where he should not have delegated, and not abdicated the matter to the rather unenterprising Commissary-General Strickland. As it turned out, during the second invasion transport and supply nigh on collapsed under the weight of the demands made by the heavily reinforced army in the field. Chelmsford consequently found his advance initially stalled altogether, and then greatly slowed down. His resulting failure to bring the expensive and unpopular war to a speedier termination formed a vital element in the decision to supersede him.

An additional reason for Chelmsford's slow advance during the second invasion was that because of his disaster at Isandlwana – and to a lesser extend Wood's rout on Hlobane – he was no longer willing to take the slightest risk. His insistence on exhaustive forward reconnaissance (made necessary by poor maps and inadequate intelligence), and his practice of laboriously laagering while on the march and halting to construct fortified depots that needed to be filled with supplies from the rear, decidedly retarded the pace of his advance. His extreme caution forfeited the confidence of many of his officers and men, and most certainly exasperated his masters in London. He might defensively declare that 'slow and steady wins the race',[16] but no one was convinced. And then, as if to show up the fallaciousness of this maxim, the moment Chelmsford learned that General Wolseley had been sent out to supersede him and was hellbent on stealing his thunder, he suddenly found it possible to push his forces forward at a much-accelerated pace to secure his decisive victory at Ulundi.

Chelmsford naturally could only view his supersession by the popular, reformist and nakedly ambitious Wolseley as a withering personal rebuke and a signal that he had lost not only the support of the government, but that of the Horse Guards and of his disappointed patron, the Duke of Cambridge. His determination nevertheless to turn a deliberate blind eye to his supersession until he had obtained his redemptive victory once again displayed both his obduracy and his deviousness when determined to secure his objective. The less attractive side of his personality was further exposed in his petulance and self-justification when it was no longer possible after Ulundi to ignore that Wolseley was indeed his superior officer. Humiliated and resentful, he resigned his command on 9 July in a fit of pique and brought his active career to a premature end. Twenty years later, in December 1899 during the Second Anglo-Boer War, when Buller was superseded by Roberts as CinC, he nevertheless continued in his Natal command until October 1900, and thereafter resumed his command at Aldershot.[17] Chelmsford, if he had similarly swallowed his hurt pride and not resigned, might likewise have extend his career.

As it was, no longer on the active list, Chelmsford spent his declining years garnering honours, supporting charitable causes and reinventing himself as a courtier. His tranquillity was periodically troubled by fresh bouts of questioning about his responsibility for the Isandlwana disaster. Defensively, he stuck to his guns, never deviating from the line he had adopted following the report of the Court of Inquiry he had convened after the battle, obsessively maintaining that Durnford, not he, was culpable. This sustained refusal to acknowledge the fatal consequences of his own strategic and tactical shortcomings as a general displays a flaw of character that, for all his many admirable personal qualities, can only reduce him in our estimation.

As for his record as a commander, he had been appointed GOC South Africa through the patronage of the Horse Guards and, because the post was not considered a particularly demanding one; it was assumed that he would be up to the task even though he had not previously held an independent command. In the event, although he proved sufficiently competent to bring the Ninth Cape Frontier War to a successful conclusion,[18] it was otherwise with the Zululand campaign. His victory in the Eastern Cape lulled Chelmsford and his officers into fatally underestimating the fighting calibre of the amaZulu with initially catastrophic results. Chelmsford's forces, if properly deployed, did nevertheless possess distinct military advantages over the amaZulu, and after Isandlwana Chelmsford did make the required tactical adjustments. But the multifarious demands and mounting scale of the Anglo-Zulu War taxed his mediocre and conventional abilities to breaking-point, leaving him at certain moments daunted and overwhelmed, and caused him to forfeit the confidence of his superiors. His consequent supersession was a bitter humiliation, only partially redeemed by his victory at Ulundi.

Nothing, however, would erase the stigma of Isandlwana. None of his protestations to the contrary, nor those of his small cohort of defenders such as Harness or French, would ever absolve him of his responsibility for the disaster, one which was the irrefutable consequence of a failure in command, rather than of the British military system as such. As 'Spy' understood when he captioned his caricature in *Vanity Fair*, in the eyes of his contemporaries the names 'Chelmsford' and 'Isandlwana' had become synonymous, and they have remained so ever since.

Chronology

Chelmsford's personal details and appointments ***in bold italic***;
his father's appointments *in italic.*

31 May 1827	***Frederic Augustus Thesiger born***
1834–5	Sixth Cape Frontier War
20 June 1837	accession of Queen Victoria
1838–42	percussion cap smoothbore musket adopted
1839–42	First Anglo-Afghan War
1840–4	***Educated at Eton College***
Sep. 1841	Sir Robert Peel's second administration
15 Aug. 1842	Field Marshal Duke of Wellington appointed CinC
Apr. 1844	*Frederick Thesiger appointed Solicitor-General and knighted*
31 Dec. 1844	***commissioned by purchase as Second Lieutenant, Rifle Brigade***
1845	***stationed in Halifax, Nova Scotia, with the 2nd Bn, Rifle Brigade***
June 1845–July 1846	*Sir Frederick serves as Attorney General*
28 Nov. 1845	***exchanges by purchase as Ensign and Lieutenant into Grenadier Guards stationed in London***
1845–1846	First Anglo-Sikh War
July 1846	Lord John Russell's first administration
1846–1847	Seventh Cape Frontier War
1848–1849	Second Anglo-Sikh War
27 Dec. 1850	***promotion by purchase to Lieutenant and Captain, Grenadier Guards***
1850–3	Eighth Cape Frontier War
1851	percussion cap Minié rifle musket adopted

Feb. 1852	Lord Derby's first administration
Feb.–Dec. 1852	*Sir Frederick holds office as Attorney General*
Feb. 1852	***appointed ADC to Lord Lieutenant of Ireland***
Dec. 1852	Lord Aberdeen's administration
1852–1853	Second Anglo-Burmese War
28 Sep. 1852	Field Marshal Viscount Hardinge appointed CinC
8 Jan. 1853	***appointed ADC to CinC, Ireland***
1853	percussion cap Enfield rifle musket adopted
5 Oct. 1853	Ottomans declare war on Russia (Crimean War)
27 March 1854	Britain declares war on Russia (Crimean War)
Aug. 1854	***returns to regimental duties in London***
25 Sep. 1854	British and French forces invest Sebastopol
Feb. 1855	Lord Palmerston's first administration
31 May 1855	***joins 3rd Grenadier Guards before Sebastopol***
8–9 June 1855	failed British assault on Sebastopol
18 June 1855	failed British assault on Sebastopol
18 July 1855	***appointed ADC to GOC, 2nd Division, Crimea***
8 Sep. 1854	failed British assault on Sebastopol; French success
9 Sep. 1855	Russians evacuate Sebastopol
2 Nov. 1855	***promoted Brevet Major***
8 Nov. 1855–24 June 1856	***DAQMG on HQ Staff, Crimea***
27 Apr. 1856	ratification of Peace of Paris ends Crimean War
15 July 1856	HRH Prince George, Duke of Cambridge appointed CinC
July 1856	***resumes duties with Grenadier Guards in London***
Oct. 1856	outbreak of the Second Anglo-Chinese War
10 May 1857	outbreak of Indian Mutiny
30 May–17 Nov. 1857	siege of Lucknow residency by mutineers
28 Aug. 1857	***promotion by purchase to Captain and Lieutenant-Colonel, Grenadier Guards***
Feb. 1858	Lord Derby's second administration
Feb. 1858–June 1859	*Sir Frederick Thesiger serves as Lord Chancellor*
1 March 1858	*Sir Frederick Thesiger created first Baron Chelmsford*

30 Apr. 1858	*exchanges as Lieutenant-Colonel into 95th (Derbyshire) Regiment*
June 1858	termination of Second Anglo-Chinese War
Nov. 1858	*joins 95th Regiment in the Central India Field Force*
14 Nov. 1858	battle of Koondrye
May 1859	close of Central India campaign
May 1859	*stationed with 95th Regiment in Bombay Presidency*
June 1859	Lord Palmerston's second administration
1859–60	Third Anglo-Chinese War
13 July 1861–31 Dec. 1862	*DAG British Forces, Bombay Presidency*
Apr. 1861	outbreak of the American Civil War
30 Apr. 1863	*promoted Brevet Colonel*
1865	Snider-Enfield breech-loading rifle adopted
May 1865	termination of the American Civil War
Oct. 1865	Sir John Russell's second administration
1866	Austro-Prussian War
June 1866	Lord Derby's third administration
June 1866–Feb. 1868	*1st Lord Chelmsford serves as Lord Chancellor*
1867	Hale's Rocket adopted
1 Jan. 1867	*marries Adria Fanny Heath in Karachi*
19 Nov. 1867	Britain declares war on Abyssinia
21 Jan.–10 June 1868	*DAG, Abyssinian Field Force*
Feb. 1868	Disraeli's first administration
Dec. 1868–Feb. 1874	Gladstone's first administration
13 Apr. 1868	storming of Magdala
15 Aug. 1868–14 Mar. 1877	*ADC to Queen Victoria*
17 Mar. 1869–15 Mar. 1874	*AG of the Indian Army*
1870	Red River Expedition
1870	War Office Act; Army Enlistment Act
July 1870–May 1871	Franco-Prussian War
1871	Army Regulation Act, Gatling gun adopted, 9-pdr RML gun adopted

1873	Localisation Act
1873	7-pdr RML Mark IV gun adopted
Oct.–Dec. 1873	Langalibalele Rebellion in Natal
1873–4	Third Anglo-Asante War
Feb. 1874	Disraeli's (Lord Beaconsfield's) second administration
1874	Martini-Henry Mark I breech-loading rifle adopted
1 Oct. 1874–31 Dec. 1876	*Colonel on the Staff commanding Shorncliffe Camp*
Mar.–Oct. 1875	Diamond Field Revolt, Griqualand West
1876	Martini-Henry Mark II breech-loading rifle adopted
July 1876–Feb. 1877	Boer–Pedi War
1 Jan. 1877	*promoted Brigadier General commanding 1st Infantry Brigade, Aldershot*
15 Mar. 1877	*promoted Major-General*
12 Apr. 1877	British annexation of the Transvaal Territory
Aug. 1877	outbreak of the Ninth Cape Frontier War
29 Sept. 1877	battle of Ibeka
13 Jan. 1878	battle of Nyumaga
24 Jan. 1878	*appointed GOC, Her Majesty's Forces at the Cape of Good Hope, Natal and St Helena*
7 Feb. 1878	battle of Kentani
25 Feb. 1878	*takes up command in Cape Town with local rank of lieutenant-general*
Mar.–July 1878	Ninth Cape Frontier War: Operations against the amaNgqika in the Ciskei and the amaGcaleka in the Transkei
Apr. 1878	outbreak of Northern Border War in Griqualand West
1 Aug. 1878	official end of the Ninth Cape Frontier War
9 Aug. 1878	*sets up HQ in Pietermaritzburg, Natal*
31 Aug. 1878	annexes Port St John's
Sept. 1878	First Anglo-Pedi War
5 Oct. 1878	*succeeds father as 2nd Baron Chelmsford*
Nov. 1878	end of Northern Border War
Nov. 1878	outbreak of the Second Anglo-Afghan War
11 Dec. 1878	British deliver ultimatum to Zulu king
11 Jan. 1879	British invasion of Zulu kingdom

12 Jan. 1879	skirmish at kwaSogekle
22 Jan. 1879	battle of Isandlwana; battle of Nyezane
22–3 Jan. 1879	defence of Rorke's Drift
23 Jan. 1879	Pearson begins fortifying mission station at Fort Eshowe
24 Jan. 1879	***returns to Pietermaritzburg to organise defence of Natal***
27–9 Jan. 1879	***orders Court of Inquiry into Isandlwana***
23 Jan. 1879	Pearson takes up position in Fort Eshowe
31 Jan. 1879	Wood forms fortified camp at Khambula
12 Mar. 1879	battle of Ntombe
11 Mar. 1879	Pinetown meeting between Chelmsford and Buller over deployment of colonial levies
28 Mar. 1879	battle of Hlobane
29 Mar. 1879	battle of Khambula
29 Mar. 1879	advance of Eshowe Relief Column begins
2 Apr. 1879	battle of Gingindlovu
2–3 Apr. 1879	trans-border raids at Middle Drift
4–7 Apr. 1879	evacuation of Eshowe garrison
2 May 1879	2nd Division masses at Landman's Drift
5 May 1879	Flying Column begins march from Khambula to join up with 2nd Division
20 May 1879	trans-border raid at Middle Drift
21 May 1879	partial burial of the British dead at Isandlwana
26 May 1879	***Superseded in command by General Wolseley***
31 May 1879	2nd Division crosses the Ncome into Zululand
1 June 1879	Prince Imperial of France killed in Zulu ambush
3 June 1879	2nd Division and Wood's Flying Column join together
5 June 1879	skirmish at Zungeni Mountain
16 June 1879	***ignores telegram informing him of supersession***
20 June	1st Division concentrates at Fort Chelmsford
27 June 1879	combined column laagers on Mthonjaneni heights
28 June	Wolseley lands at Durban
1 July	1st Division encamps at Port Durnford
1 July	Combined column forms joint laager at White Mfolozi River

2 July 1879	*ignores Wolseley's orders to fall back*
2–4 July	Wolseley unable to land at Port Durnford
3 July 1879	reconnaissance in force across the White Mfolozi
4 July 1879	battle of Ulundi
4 July 1879	1st Division burns emaNgweni *ikhanda*
5 July 1879	*receives official letter of supersession*
6 July 1879	*requests permission to resign*
6 July 1879	1st Division burns old oNdini *ikhanda*
8 July 1879	*receives Wolseley's General Order confirming supersession*
9 July 1879	*resigns command in South Africa*
9 July 1879	combined column broken up and withdraws from Mthonjaneni
15 July 1879	*meets Wolseley at St Paul's*
16 July 1879	*reverts in rank to Major-General*
5 Aug. 1879	*sails from Cape Town for England*
1 Sept. 1879	Zulu chiefs accept Wolseley's settlement of Zululand
Nov.–Dec. 1879	Second Anglo–Pedi War
Apr. 1880	Gladstone's second administration
19 Aug., 2 Sept. 1880	*defends his record in the House of Lords*
Sept. 1880	termination of the Second Anglo-Afghan War
Dec. 1880–Aug. 1881	First Anglo-Boer War (Transvaal Rebellion)
July 1881	Childers Reforms
1 Apr. 1882	*promoted lieutenant-general*
4 June 1884–28 Mar. 1889	*Lieutenant of the Tower of London*
June 1885	Lord Salisbury's first administration
Feb. 1886	Gladstones' third administration
Aug. 1886	Lord Salisbury's second administration
1888	Lee-Metford Mark I bolt action magazine rifle adopted
16 Dec. 1888	*promoted General*
30 Jan. 1889	*appointed Hon. Colonel of the Sherwood Foresters (Derbyshire Regiment)*
7 June 1893	*placed on retired list*
1 Nov. 1895	Field Marshal Viscount Wolseley appointed CinC
1899–1902	Second Anglo-Boer (South African) War

27 Sept. 1900	***exchanges Hon. Colonelcy of Sherwood Foresters for 2nd Life Guards; appointed Gold Stick-in-Waiting***
3 Jan. 1901	Field Marshal Earl Roberts appointed CinC
22 Jan. 1901	accession of King Edward VII
May 1902	end of Second Anglo-Boer (South African) War
12 Feb. 1904	office of CinC abolished
9 Apr. 1905	***dies in United Service Club, London***
13 Apr. 1905	***funeral at St Jude's Church, London; buried in Brompton Cemetery***

Orders:	CB (1868); KCB (1878); GCB (1879); GCVO (1902)
Medals:	British Crimea Medal with clasp for Sebastopol (1856); Indian Mutiny Medal with clasp for Central India (1861); Abyssinian War Medal (1869); South Africa Medal with clasp for 1878–9 (1879)
Foreign decorations:	Turkish Order of the Medjidie 5th Class; Sardinian Crimea Medal; Turkish Crimea Medal (1856)

Notes

PREFACE: A Case of Incompetency?

1. *The Times*, 6 June 1910: Jenkins's obituary. See the caricature by 'Spy' in *Vanity Fair*, August 1878.
2. *The Times*, 10 May 1895: Peel's obituary.
3. *Hansard*, 3rd series, Vol. 244, c. 2019: House of Commons, 28 March 1879: Sir R. Peel.
4. See War Office, *Field Operations*, pp. 156–7, for the official death toll at Isandlwana. For Inkerman, see the official toll quoted in Cadogan and Calthorpe, *Cadogan's Crimea*, p. 110. Of course, many of the 103 officers wounded at Inkerman would not have survived.
5. *Hansard*: 3rd series, Vol. 244 cc. 910–911, 914: House of Commons, 14 March 1879: E. Jenkins.
6. CP 26/36: General M. W. E. Gossett to Lady Chelmsford, 7 June 1906.
7. French, *Chelmsford*, p. x.
8. Morris, *Washing of the Spears*, p. 620.
9. Manning, *Britain against the Xhosa and Zulu*, p. xv.
10. *Hansard*: 3rd series, Vol. 244 c. 2077: House of Commons, 28 March 1879: Col. Stanley.
11. Haythornthwaite, *Colonial Wars*, pp. 59–60.
12. Presumably, it was because of the notoriety of Isandlwana that Chelmsford was included among leading commanders such as Wolseley and Roberts in Corvi and Beckett (eds), *Victoria's Generals*, but escaped inclusion in a recent, similar collection edited by Chris Brice with the rather demeaning title of *Forgotten Victorian Generals*.

CHAPTER 1: The Thesigers: A Family on the Rise

1. For biographical information concerning the first Baron Chelmsford, see Hamilton, 'Thesiger, Frederick, first Baron Chelmsford'. For basic biographical information throughout this book relating to the second Lord Chelmsford, see enc. in CP 18/34: Statement of foreign, staff and active service of Major-General Lord Chelmsford, 1 January 1881; *The Times*, 10 April 1905: Lord Chelmsford's obituary; Low, *Soldiers of the Victorian Age*, Vol. II, pp. 80–108; Lloyd, 'Thesiger, Frederic Augustus, second Baron Chelmsford'; Laband 'Thesiger, Frederic Augustus, second Baron Chelmsford'; and Greaves and Knight, *Who's Who*, Vol. 1, pp. 54–60. See also Burke, *Peerage* (1894), pp. 273–4; *Debrett's Peerage*

(1896), pp. 162–3 and (1904), pp. 178–9; *Cracroft's Peerage*: Chelmsford; and Lundy, *The Peerage*: Thesiger.

2. Legacies of British Slave-Ownership Database, 'Charles Thesiger'. For the economy of a typical sugar plantation and the nature of slave labour in the British West Indies, see Hall, 'Slaves and Slavery'.
3. Carlyle, 'Thesiger, Sir Frederick'.
4. La Soufrière last erupted in April 2021 forcing a mass evacuation of the island.
5. There are various ways of computing the relative value today of the pound sterling in the past, such as consulting the Bank of England's Inflation Rate Calculator, employing the GDP deflator, or taking into account average earnings or per capita GDP. See http://www.MeasuringWorth.com. Using the retail price index (rpi) gives the lowest relative value, but is useful in suggesting contemporary buying power. Throughout the second half of the nineteenth century the value of the pound remained steady (unlike the case today). Taking all this into account, pounds then had approximately one hundred times the value of those today.
6. The Chelmsford coat of arms is described heraldically as 'Arms, – Gules: a Griffin, segreant, or, within an orle of roses argent, barbed and seeded proper. Crest. – A cornucopia fesswise, the horns or, the fruit proper, thereupon a dove holding in the beak a sprig of laurel also proper. Supporters, – On either side a griffin or, winged vaire.' The motto: 'Spes et Fortuna', or 'Hope and Faith'. See *Debrett's Peerage* (1904), p. 178.
7. Queen Victoria's Journal, 29 February 1868, in Longford, *Victoria R.I.*, p. 156; Atlay, *Victorian Chancellors*, Vol. II, pp. 120–5.
8. Cannadine, *British Aristocracy*, pp. 250–1.
9. Alfred and his elder brother Charles married sisters, the two elder daughters of the fifth son of the second Baron Castlemaine.
10. Spiers, *Army and Society*, pp. 8–9; Spiers, *Late Victorian Army*, pp. 94–5; Clayton, *British Officer*, p. 107; Razzell, 'Officers', p. 258.

CHAPTER 2: The Making of an Officer

1. Harries-Jenkins, 'Victorian Army', pp. 480–2, 486; Braudy, *Chivalry to Terrorism*, pp. 339–44; Dominy, *Last Outpost*, pp. 13–14.
2. Clayton, *British Officer*, p. 2.
3. Harries-Jenkins, 'Victorian Army', pp. 473, 479–80, 486; Beckett, *Politics of Command*, p. 4; Clayton, *British Officer*, pp. 7–8, 109; Laband, 'British Way of War', pp. 14–15.
4. Spiers, *Late Victorian Army*, pp. 96–7.
5. Lejeune and Lewis, *Gentlemen's Clubs*, pp. 26–31, 128–33, 161–7, 276–83.
6. Beckett, *Politics of Command*, pp. 4, 14, 21; Harries-Jenkins, 'Victorian Army', p. 487.
7. Harries -Jenkins, *Army*, pp. 98–9.
8. Spiers, *Army and Society*, pp. 7–11, 296–8; Spiers, *Late Victorian Army*, pp. 94, 97–8; Razzell, 'Officers', pp. 253–5, 258.
9. Spiers, *Army and Society*, pp. 2–6; Beckett, *Politics of Command*, pp. 20–1.
10. Harries-Jenkins, 'Victorian Army', pp. 477–8.
11. Woodward, *Age of Reform*, pp. 662–3.

12. For Wellington as Commander-in-Chief, see Muir, *Wellington*, pp. 545–8.
13. Beckett, *Politics of Command*, p. 63.
14. The Duke of Wellington to Lord Lyndhurst, 22 July 1843, quoted in French, *Chelmsford*, p. 1.
15. Muir, *Wellington*, p. 587; Beckett, *Politics of Command*, p. 65.
16. In the early decades of the nineteenth century a black market had existed in the purchase of commissions that had sometimes driven the price up to twice that laid down in the regulations.
17. Spiers, *Army and Society*, pp. 11, 17: Table 1.6: Regulation of prices of commissions established by the Royal Warrant of 1821; Spiers, *Late Victorian Army*, p. 104; Clayton, *Officer*, pp. 82–3, 112–13; Knight, *British Soldier*, pp. 22–3.
18. CP 18/35: Chelmsford to General Whitmore: draft of a letter sent on 2 January 1881 for the consideration of the Duke of Cambridge.
19. In 1861 the 14th Light Dragoons were renamed the 14th Hussars, and in 1896 Lt.-Gen. the Hon. Charles Thesiger was appointed their Colonel.
20. Luscombe, 'Lieut-General Charles Thesiger'; Beckett, *Politics of Command*, p. 43. Clayton, *British Officer*, pp. 84–5; Razzell, 'Officers', p. 251.
21. Beckett, *Politics of Command*, pp. 4–5.

CHAPTER 3: **With the Rifle Brigade in Halifax, Nova Scotia, 1845**

1. 'Annual Returns of British Regiments Stationed in Nova Scotia'. The Rifle Brigade would leave Halifax in 1846 for active service in the Cape Colony during the Seventh Cape Frontier War (1846–7).
2. Burroughs, 'Defence and Imperial Disunity', pp. 324–5. For a list of home stations and stations overseas in 1842, see Haythornthwaite, *Colonial Wars*, pp. 12–13.
3. Knight, *British Soldier*, pp. 247–8.
4. Laband, *Land Wars*, p. 139; Knight, *British Soldier*, p. 15.
5. Conrad and Finkel, *Canadian Peoples*, Vol. 1, pp. 109–10, 150–8. See Anderson, *Crucible of War*, for a superb account of Anglo-French wars in North America.
6. For the Canadian colonies and military threats to them between the American Revolutionary War and the Rebellions of the 1830s in British Canada, see Conrad and Finkel, *Canadian Peoples*, Vol. 1, pp. 172–8, 193–9, 283–93.
7. Dominy, *Last Outpost*, pp. 4–9; Beveridge, *Halifax Citadel*, pp. 6–21, 60–4.
8. Richards, *Her Majesty's Army*, pp. 53–9. The Rifle Brigade's former number was reassigned in 1824 to a newly formed county regiment, the 95th (Derbyshire).
9. Laband, 'British Way of War', p. 13.
10. Knight, *British Soldier*, pp. 127–30, 132–3, 160–1; Laband, *Land Wars*, p. 205.
11. Rogers, *Weapons*, p. 225.
12. Rogers, *Weapons*, pp. 147–52, 172–4; Holmes, *Redcoat*, pp. 200–1; Knight, *British Soldier*, pp. 155–6, 160; Haythornthwaite, *Colonial Wars*, pp. 35–7; Laband, *Land Wars*, pp. 205–6.
13. Unless otherwise specified, this section on the British infantry is drawn from Clayton, *British Officer*, pp. 3, 6, 75, 87–88; Dominy, *Last Outpost*, pp. 16–22; Haythornthwaite, *Colonial Wars*, pp. 18–20, 29–35; Knight, *British Soldier*, pp. 15–21, 24; and Laband, *Land Wars*, pp. 138–9.
14. Mansel, *Pillars of Monarchy*, p. 162.

15. For barrack life in this period, see Burroughs, 'Unreformed Army', pp. 172–3.
16. Laband, *Land Wars*, p. 248.
17. Low, *Soldiers of the Victorian Age*, Vol. II, p. 108.
18. Spiers, *Late Victorian Army*, pp. 107–8.
19. Harries-Jenkins, 'Victorian Army', p. 480.
20. Beveridge, *Halifax Citadel*, pp. 38–46.
21. Thesiger, *Practically True*, pp. 15, 84.

CHAPTER 4: Grenadier Guards, London and Dublin, 1845–1855

1. Colley, 'Army', p. 573.
2. Lloyd, revised by Sweetman, 'Somerset'.
3. Clayton, *British Officer*, p. 86.
4. Mansel, *Pillars of Monarchy*, p. 45; Simkin and Gibbs, *The Guards*, pp. 6–7. For the service history of the Grenadier Guards up to the Crimean War, see Richards, *Her Majesty's Army*, pp. 140–50.
5. Mansel, *Pillars of Monarchy*, p. 78: Table I; Harries-Jenkins, *Army*, pp. 24–5.
6. See Spiers, *Army and Society*, pp. 11, 17: Table 1.6: Regulation of prices of commissions established by the Royal Warrant of 1821; Spiers, *Late Victorian Army*, p. 104.
7. See CP 26/1 for Henry Poole & Co.'s bill of October 1878 for making suits, pantaloons and trousers for General Thesiger.
8. Simkin and Gibbs, *The Guards*, p. 7.
9. Mansel, *Pillars of Monarchy*, pp. 159, 169.
10. Harrison, *Recollections*, p. 28.
11. Pearsall, *Worm in the Bud*, pp. 245–74.
12. Mansel, *Pillars of Monarchy*, pp. 147, 151; Clayton, *British Officer*, pp. 86, 105–6.
13. Low, *Soldiers of the Victorian Age*, Vol. II, pp. 82, 84.
14. Harrison, *Recollections*, p. 28.
15. Lugubu Mbata, in Thompson, *Black Soldiers*, p. 34; Montague, *Campaigning*, p. 133.
16. Spiers, *Late Victorian Army*, pp. 105–6; Clayton, *British Officer*, pp. 101, 109; Beckett, *Politics of Command*, pp. 19–20.
17. Spiers, *Army and Society*, p. 17: Table 1.6; p. 19.
18. Beckett, *Politics of Command*, pp. 30, 63–5; Spiers, *Army and Society*, p. 18; Harries-Jenkins, 'Victorian Army', pp. 481–2.
19. Fitzpatrick, 'Ireland', pp. 494–6.
20. Millar, 'Montgomerie'.
21. Woodward, *Age of Reform*, pp. 329, 352–9.
22. Fitzpatrick, 'Ireland', pp. 498, 500, 504.
23. Hardinge would be raised to field marshal in October 1855.
24. Pine (ed.), *Burke's Peerage*, p. 1058; Howlett, 'Hardinge'; Haythornthwaite, *Colonial Wars*, pp. 309–10.
25. Fred Thesiger to Jack Inglis, 5 August 1855, in French, *Chelmsford*, p. 3.
26. Boase, revised by Sweetman, 'Blakeney'. Blakeney was CinC in Ireland between 1836 and 1855. On his retirement, he was appointed Governor of Chelsea Hospital and died in 1865 a field marshal and Colonel-in-Chief of the Rifle Brigade.

27. Clayton, *British Officer*, pp. 109–10.
28. Mansel, *Pillars of Monarchy*, p. 155.

CHAPTER 5: In the Crimea, 1855–1856

1. For a stimulating and convincing analysis of the origins of the Crimean War, see Figes, *Crimean War*, pp. 1–164. For his own summary, see Figes, *Story of Russia*, pp. 149–52. For a succinct account of the conflict, see Holmes, 'Crimean War'.
2. Simkin and Gibbs, *The Guards*, p. 7.
3. For the Duke of Cambridge, see Spiers, 'George, Prince'.
4. Rogers, *Weapons*, pp. 182–3; Haythornthwaite, *Colonial Wars*, pp. 36–7.
5. Knight, *British Soldier*, pp. 133, 172–81; Haythornthwaite, *Colonial Wars*, pp. 51, 55–6, 37–8, 57.
6. For the fighting from the Alma to Inkerman, see Figes, *Crimea*, pp. 200–77.
7. For the deplorable conditions in the British camp before Sebastopol during the winter of 1854–5, and the inadequate medical services, see Figes, *Crimea*, pp. 278–306.
8. Sweetman, 'Airey'.
9. Knight, *British Soldier*, p. 195.
10. Knight, *British Soldier*, p. 194.
11. Knight, *British Soldier*, pp. 135–6.
12. Portlock and Nugent, 'Fortification', pp. 433–4, 436–7.
13. Tyrrell, *War with Russia*, Vol. III, pp. 159–64; Cadogan and Calthorpe, *Cadogan's Crimea*, pp. 186–99. Lt.-Col. Somerset J. Gough Calthorpe, was Raglan's nephew and ADC. He published his informed impressions in book form as *Letters from Headquarters by a Staff Officer*. London: John Murray, 1856.
14. Tyrrell, *War with Russia*, Vol. III, pp. 164–74; Cadogan and Calthorpe, *Cadogan's Crimea*, pp. 200–18.
15. For Raglan's death, obsequies and conveyance back to Britain, see Cadogan and Calthorpe, *Cadogan's Crimea*, pp. 218–25.
16. Tyrrell, *War with Russia*, Vol. IV, p. 326; Lloyd, revised by Falkner, 'Simpson'.
17. Obituary of Sir Edwin Markham, *The Times*, 2 April 1918.
18. Chichester, revised by May, 'Inglis'.
19. Thesiger to Inglis, 5 August 1855, in French, *Chelmsford*, pp. 2–4.
20. Cadogan and Calthorpe, *Cadogan's Crimea*, pp. 225, 227.
21. Figes, *Crimea*, pp. 381–5.
22. Tyrrell, *War with Russia*, Vol. IV, pp. 231–47; Cadogan and Calthorpe, *Cadogan's Crimea*, pp. 230–8, 240–2.
23. Portlock and Nugent, 'Fortification', pp. 422–3.
24. Tyrrell, *War with Russia*, Vol. IV, pp. 249–51.
25. See Cadogan and Calthorpe, *Cadogan's Crimea*, pp. 274–5: Appendix C.
26. Tyrrell, *War with Russia*, Vol. IV, pp. 327–8; Sweetman, 'Codrington'.
27. For the battle of the Redan, see Tyrrell, *War with Russia*, Vol. IV, pp. 251–9; Cadogan and Calthorpe, *Cadogan's Crimea*, pp. 243, 246–7, 250–1, 254–5, 258–9, 262; Figes, *Crimea*, pp. 386–92.
28. For Thesiger's personal account of the battle, see Thesiger to Inglis, 20 September 1855, in French, *Chelmsford*, pp. 4–6.

29. Figes, *Crimea*, pp. 392–5.
30. Colley, 'Army', p. 576.
31. Tyrrell, *War with Russia*, Vol. IV, pp. 326–7.
32. Colley, 'Army', pp. 575, 577.
33. Figes, *Crimea*, pp. 396, 409.
34. Cadogan and Calthorpe, *Cadogan's Crimea*, p. 267.
35. As an Order, the Medjidie was worn after British campaign medals but before other foreign medals.

CHAPTER 6: Exchanging into the 95th Regiment, 1856–1858

1. This conflict, known variously as the Indian Mutiny, the Indian Rebellion, the First War of Indian Independence, or the Sepoy War, depending on the historian's perspective, has generated an enormous literature. For an authoritative recent analysis, see Peers, 'Indian Rebellion', pp. 8–39. Hibbert, *Great Mutiny*, *passim*, remains the best modern narrative treatment, but see James, *Raj*, pp. 233–98, for a fine, succinct account.
2. For the siege of the residency at Lucknow, see Hibbert, *Great Mutiny*, pp. 216–66, 327–48.
3. Chichester, revised May, 'Inglis'. The legislature of his native Nova Scotia presented Inglis with a sword of honour and to this day Inglis Street in Halifax connects with Lucknow Street. In 1860 Inglis left India to take command of the troops in the Ionian Islands. He died in 1862 and is buried in St Paul's Cathedral in London.
4. See Holmes, *Sahib*, pp. 146–77, 231–2; Spiers, *Late Victorian Army*, p. 105.
5. Spiers, *Army and Society*, p. 17: Table 1.6, p. 18.
6. Raines, *95th Regiment*, pp. 8, 59, 67–8.
7. Preston (ed.), *Wolseley's Journal*, p. 197: 28 December 1879.
8. Low, *Soldiers of the Victorian Age*, Vol. 11, p. 82.
9. Yorke retired from active service in 1860, and ended his career as a field marshal and Constable of the Tower. See Lloyd, revised by Matthew, 'Yorke'.
10. Howlett, 'Hardinge'.
11. St Aubyn, *Royal George*, pp. 87–101; Spiers, 'Cambridge'.
12. Colley, 'Army', pp. 572–3; Bond, 'Introduction', p. 13; Beckett, *Politics of Command*, pp. 109.
13. See Spiers, 'Cambridge'; St Aubyn, *Royal George*, pp. 360–99, 352–67.
14. *See* Chapter 14 for a discussion of the 'rings' of reformist officers and their agendas.
15. Quoted in St Aubyn, *Royal George*, p. 359.

CHAPTER 7: The Indian Mutiny: Central India Campaign, 1858–1859

1. For the 95th Regiment's campaign in Central India, see Raines, *95th Regiment*, pp. 7–65; Richards, *Her Majesty's Army*, Vol. 1, pp. 206–8. The regiment remained in India until October 1870 when it sailed for Britain.
2. Peers, 'Indian Rebellion', pp. 17–18, 21–2; Hibbert, *Great Mutiny*, pp. 178–9, 384, 387. For a vivid account of the Rani of Jhansi's career, see Fraser, *Warrior Queens*, pp. 301–30.

3. Hibbert, *Great Mutiny*, pp. 377–85; Robson, 'Rose'; Brice, 'Napier', p. 92. For the role of the 95th in these operations, see Raines, *95th Regiment*, pp. 7–56.
4. Hibbert, *Great Mutiny*, pp. 385–6; Raines, *95th Regiment*, pp. 59–64.
5. Raines, *95th Regiment*, pp. 1–4; Kincaid, *British Social Life in India*, pp. 139–43; Holmes, *Sahib*, pp. 91–3, 100. It was not until the 1870s that big steam-driven, custom-built troopships with decks below for the rank-and-file would come into operation between the Suez Canal and Bombay.
6. Knight, *British Soldier*, pp. 136–8.
7. Wilkinson and Wilkinson, *Memoirs*, p. 256.
8. Rikhye, 'Raja Man Singh'; Brice, 'Napier', pp. 92–3.
9. This account of the operations of 13–14 November 1858 and the engagement at Kundraye is based on *Supplement to the London Gazette*, 24 March 1859, pp. 1267–9, no. 44: Brigadier Smith to the Assistant Adjutant-General Malwa Division, 20 November 1858; Raines, *95th Regiment*, pp. 57–9; Duberly, *Campaigning Experiences*, pp. 227–32.
10. *Supplement to the London Gazette*, 24 March 1859, p. 1267, no. 43: Maj.-Gen. J. Michel, Commanding Malwa Division to Lt.-Col. W. Mayhew, AG of the Army, 4 December 1858.
11. Haythornthwaite, *Colonial Wars*, p. 51.
12. De Salis, the son of the fourth Count de Salis-Soglio, an old Etonian and veteran of the Crimean War, was a truer aristocrat than Thesiger. His was a noble family from the Grisons in Switzerland dating back to the thirteenth century that had been naturalised British in 1731 and created Counts of the Holy Roman Empire in 1748. Wikiwand.com, 'De Salis' (accessed 17 August 2022).
13. Duberly, *Campaigning Experiences*, pp. 231–2.
14. *Supplement to the London Gazette*, 24 March 1859, p. 1268, no. 44: Smith to the AAG Malwa Division, 20 November 1858.
15. Raines, *95th Regiment*, pp. 59–64; Hibbert, *Great Mutiny*, p. 386; Brice, 'Napier', p. 93; Peers, 'Indian Rebellion', p. 30. Rao Saheb managed to elude capture until 1862, when he too was hanged.
16. Raines, *95th Regiment*, pp. 60–1.
17. Duberly, *Campaigning Experiences*, p. 236.
18. Raines, *95th Regiment*, p. 65; Duberly, *Campaigning Experiences*, p. 235.
19. Raines, *95th Regiment*, pp. 65–6.

CHAPTER 8: The Bombay Presidency, 1859–1867

1. Enc. in CP 18/34: Statement of foreign, staff and active service of Major-General Lord Chelmsford, 1 January 1881.
2. This arrangement lasted until 1 April 1895 when the Presidency armies were abolished and the Army of India was divided into four commands.
3. The three regiments of Company European infantry in the Bombay Presidency were all absorbed into the British Army as regiments of the line.
4. In the Bombay Presidency three regiments of the Bombay Native Infantry were disbanded, and replaced by three new regiments recruited from among the Baluchi people of Sindh, who were considered a 'martial race' and more reliable.

5. Confusingly, members of the Indian Staff Corps were not to be confused with officers holding staff appointments.
6. Moore, 'Imperial India', pp. 422, 423–9; Peers, 'Indian Rebellion', pp. 37–8; Holmes, *Sahib*, pp. 80–1, 216, 182–4, 254–5; Haythornthwaite, *Colonial Wars*, pp. 107–9.
7. Duberly, *Campaigning Experiences*, p. 16; Kincaid, *British Social Life in India*, pp. 139, 143, 267; Holmes, *Sahib*, pp. 118–20, 444.
8. Holmes, *Sahib*, pp. 186, 189, 192; Beckett, *Politics of Command*, p. 85.
9. Robson, 'Rose'.
10. Moreman, 'Mansfield'. Mansfield was created Baron Sandhurst in 1871.
11. Holmes, *Sahib*, p. 328.
12. Laband, 'Crealock, John North'.
13. Benyon, 'Frere'.
14. Brice, 'Napier', pp. 71–100; Moreman, 'Napier'.
15. Rogers, *Weapons*, pp. 238–41; Haythornthwaite, *Colonial Wars*, pp. 51–2; Knight, *British Soldier*, pp. 156–8; Holmes, *Sahib*, p. 217; Clayton, *British Officer*, pp. 99–100; Beckett, *Politics of Command*, p. 233.
16. The airpipe helmet was made of calico over a rattan wicker-work frame. It had two layers with a chamber between them cooled by an airhole in the tall comb over the dome of the helmet.
17. Knight, *British Soldier*, pp. 138–9.
18. See Hyam, *Empire and Sexuality*, 121–7; Hyam, 'Empire and Sexual Opportunity', pp. 384–9.
19. Holmes, *Sahib*, pp. 97, 138–45, 171, 402, 415–25, 433–4, 468–73, 480–1.
20. Low, *Soldiers of the Victorian Age*, Vol. II, p. 84; Wilkinson and Wilkinson, *Memoirs*, p. 84; Burroughs, 'Unreformed Army', p. 187.
21. Enc. in CP 18/34: Statement of foreign, staff and active service of Major-General Lord Chelmsford, 1 January 1881; Wilkinson and Wilkinson, *Memoirs*, pp. 256–7; Holmes, *Sahib*, p. 175.
22. Low, *Soldiers of the Victorian Age*, Vol. II, p. 108.
23. Laband, 'Lord Chelmsford', pp. 98–9.
24. Spiers, *Late Victorian Army*, p. 74.
25. *BPP* (C. 2719): Report of the Committee of General and Other Officers of the Army on Army Reorganisation, Q. 4699.
26. Orman, 'British Military Law', pp. 96–7.
27. Lt.-Col. J. N. Crealock to Gen. Sir A. Alison, 14 January 1879, in Clarke, *Zululand at War*, p. 74.
28. Harrison, *Recollections*, p. 28; Low, *Soldiers of the Victorian Age*, Vol. II, p. 83.
29. Holmes, *Sahib*, pp. 146–75, 266–70; Kinkaid, *British Social Life in India*, pp. 139–69.
30. For a list of the minimum number of servants required by a married officer, see Duberly, *Campaigning Experiences*, pp. 17–18.
31. Laband, 'British Way of War', pp. 12–14.
32. Mason, *Indian Army*, pp. 367–8; Holmes, *Sahib*, pp. 444–6, 485–98; Hyam, *Empire and Sexuality*, pp. 118–20; Beckett, *Politics of Command*, pp. 131–2, 135–40; Clayton, *British Officer*, p. 107.

33. Low, *Soldiers of the Victorian Age*, Vol. II, p. 83
34. Lt.-Gen. Sir R. Napier to the Secretary of State for India, 1 June 1868, in Holland and Hozier, *Expedition to Abyssinia*, Vol. II, p. 478.
35. Robb, 'Viscount Chelmsford'.

CHAPTER 9: The Expedition to Abyssinia, 1867–1868

1. Lt.-Gen. Sir R. Napier to the Secretary of State for India, 1 June 1868 in Holland and Hozier, *Expedition to Abyssinia*, Vol. II, p. 478. This despatch (with Napier's praise of Thesiger) was made public when printed in the *London Gazette* of 30 June 1868.
2. O'Connor, 'Transport Corps in Abyssinia', p. 75.
3. Callwell, 'Lessons to be Learned'.
4. Established as a leading military theorist, Callwell rose to the rank of major-general and was appointed Director of Military Operations and Intelligence at the War Office (1914–16). He was created KCB in 1917. See Moreman, 'Callwell'.
5. Callwell, *Small Wars*, pp. 4, 21–3; Harries-Jenkins, 'Victorian Army', p. 485; Whitehouse, *Battle in Africa*, p. 7.
6. Callwell, *Small Wars*, pp. 27–8.
7. Markham, *Abyssinian Expedition*, p. 389. Brice, 'Expedition to Abyssinia', pp. 62–9; Laband 'Ethiopian Military Culture', p. 347; Curtin, *Disease and Empire*, pp. 30, 32, 35–7.
8. Bond, 'Editor's Introduction', p. 22.
9. Moreman, 'Napier'.
10. MacLeod, 'Bombay Native Army', p. 375; Brice, 'Expedition to Abyssinia', p. 71.
11. War Office, *Field Operations*, pp. 145–51, 168–70; Laband and Thompson, *Anglo-Zulu War*, pp. 36–9.
12. Harries-Jenkins, 'Victorian Army', p. 484; Bond, 'Editor's Introduction', p. 21; Brice, 'Expedition to Abyssinia', p. 72.
13. *The Times*, 1 May 1868.
14. Curtin, *Disease and Empire*, pp. 47–8.
15. Brice, 'Napier', pp. 101–2.
16. Brice, 'Expedition to Abyssinia', pp. 70, 73–4; O'Connor, 'Transport Corps in Abyssinia', p. 75; Laband 'Ethiopian Military Culture', pp. 345–7; Curtin, *Disease and Empire*, pp. 35–7, 39–40.
17. O'Connor, 'Transport Corps in Abyssinia', pp. 72–4; Brice, 'Expedition to Abyssinia', pp. 72, 78. At the conclusion of the campaign, 13,000 animals were sold or given away to Ethiopians, and 15,000 embarked.
18. War Office, *Field Operations*, p. 172; War Office, *Précis of Information*, p. 58. There were number 36,094 draught animals employed in Abyssinia, as opposed to 32,256 in Zululand.
19. Bond, 'Editor's Introduction', p. 21.
20. Charcoal pocket filters were used to improve the smell of water and strain out impurities, but these would have had no effect on its potentially harmful bacterial content.
21. Staff officer, *Sheffield Daily Telegraph*, 8 May 1868, in Emery, *Marching over Africa*, p. 41. For the British baggage train, see O'Connor, 'Transport Corps in

Abyssinia', p. 75; Whitehouse, *Battle in Africa*, pp. 12–13; Curtin, *Disease and Empire*, pp. 41–2; Brice, 'Expedition to Abyssinia', p. 79.
22. Holland and Hozier, *Expedition to Abyssinia*, Vol. 1, p. 331.
23. Knight, *British Soldier*, p. 140.
24. Unnamed officer, *Sheffield Daily Telegraph*, 30 April 1868, in Emery, *Marching over Africa*, p. 40.
25. Brice, 'Expedition to Abyssinia', p. 75; O'Connor, 'Transport Corps in Abyssinia', p. 75
26. Low, *Soldiers of the Victorian Age*, Vol. 11, p. 83.
27. Napier to Cambridge, 3 April 1874, in Beckett, *Profession of Arms*, p. 202.
28. Bates, *Abyssinian Difficulty*, p. 162; Brice, 'Napier', p. 104; Chandler, 'Expedition to Abyssinia', pp 134–5.
29. Lt.-Gen. Sir R. Napier to the Secretary of State for India, 1 June 1868, in Holland and Hozier, *Expedition to Abyssinia*, Vol. 11, p. 478
30. Curtin, *Disease and Empire*, p. 40.
31. For the members of the Headquarters Staff, see Holland and Hozier, *Expedition to Abyssinia*, Vol. I, p. 181. For Napier's mention of the services of individual officers, see Lt.-Gen. Sir R. Napier to the Secretary of State for India, 1 June 1868, in Holland and Hozier, *Expedition to Abyssinia*, Vol. 11, p. 475–80.
32. For a vivid, first-hand account of the engagement, see the diary entry for 10 April 1868 by Lt Edward Woodgate, in Emery, *Marching over Africa*, pp. 33, 35–6.
33. Brice, 'Expedition to Abyssinia', pp. 75–8; Brice, 'Napier', pp. 104–6.
34. Brice, 'Expedition to Abyssinia', pp. 73, 78; Laband, 'Ethiopian Military Culture', pp. 347–8.
35. Cholera, the great killer in India, was largely absent in Ethiopia, as was malaria. No proper records were kept, though of the number of followers who died of illness or privation, perhaps as many as 40 per cent of their original number.
36. Curtin, *Disease and Empire*, pp. 40–8; Brice, 'Expedition to Abyssinia', pp. 80–1.
37. *The Times*, 1 May 1868.

CHAPTER 10: **Adjutant-General in India, 1868–1874**

1. Beckett, *Politics of Command*, pp. 7, 30–1, 33, 37; Clayton, *British Officer*, p. 87; Holmes, *Sahib*, pp. 323, 325–7.
2. Moreman, 'Napier'.
3. See Patterson, 'Third Anglo-Asante War', pp. 106–25.
4. Beckett (ed.), *Wolseley and Ashanti*, pp. 374–6.
5. Duckers, *British Orders*, pp. 21–4.
6. Colley. 'Army', p. 425.
7. After leaving India in 1876 after forty-eight years' service there, Napier was made field marshal in 1883 and Constable of the Tower in 1887.
8. Brice, 'Napier', pp. 106–7; Moreman, 'Napier'. At the Duke of Cambridge's request, Napier extended his term as CinC for another year.
9. French, *Chelmsford*, p. 7.
10. Fido, *Kipling*. pp. 50 –1. The viceroys during Thesiger's posting as AG were the Earl of Mayo (1869–72) and Lord Northbook (1872–6)
11. Kincaid, *British Social Life in India*, 241, 245–50.

12. Allen (ed.), *Plain Tales from the Raj*, pp. 21–33.
13. Low, *Soldiers of the Victorian Age*, Vol. II, pp. 83–4.
14. Brice, 'Napier', p. 107.
15. Bates, *Abyssinian Difficulty*, pp. 85–92.
16. *Hansard*: 3rd series, Vol. 249, c.1574: House of Commons, 5 August 1879: Chancellor of the Exchequer (R. Lowe).
17. Spiers, *Late Victorian Army*, p. 276; Beckett (ed.), *Wolseley and Ashanti*, p. 372.
18. War Office, *Field Operations*, p. 174.
19. Napier, *Napier of Magdala*, p. 265.
20. Brice, 'Napier', p. 107; Moreman, 'Napier'.
21. Enc. in CP 18/34: Statement of foreign, staff and active service of Major-General Lord Chelmsford, 1 January 1881.
22. Thesiger, 'Radical Change'.
23. Adams, 'Military View of Empire', pp. 60–2.
24. Preston, 'British Military Thought', pp. 68–9. See especially Hamley, *Operations of War*, pp. 39–45: 'Differences between offensive and defensive war'; and pp. 301–17: 'Changes that have led to the modern system of tactics.'
25. Preston, 'British Military Thought', pp. 72–3. Home's work was a compilation of extracts from seventy-six Continental and British books and military journals.
26. Thesiger, 'Radical Change', pp. 421–3.
27. Enc. in CP 18/34: Statement of foreign, staff and active service of Major-General Lord Chelmsford, 1 January 1881.
28. Holmes, *Sahib*, p. 501.

CHAPTER II: Home Commands and the Cardwell Reforms, 1874–1878

1. Beckett, *Politics of Command*, pp. 47, 127; Chichester revised by May, 'Horsford'.
2. Spiers, *Late Victorian Army*, pp. 139, 141; Bond, 'Cardwell Reforms', p. 522; Lloyd revised by Lunt, 'Steele'.
3. Beckett, *Politics of Command*, p. 42–3; Holmes, *Sahib*, pp. 227–8.
4. Beckett, *Politics of Command*, p. 142.
5. Spiers, *Army and Society*, pp. 194–5; Spiers, *Late Victorian Army*, pp. 91–2.
6. CP 18/34: Chelmsford to General Whitmore: draft of a letter sent on 2 January 1881 for the consideration of the Duke of Cambridge; enc. in CP 18/34: statement of foreign, staff and active service of Major-General Lord Chelmsford, 1 January 1881; Beckett, *Politics of Command*, pp. 48, 127; Bond, 'Cardwell', p. 523; St Aubyn, *Royal George*, p. 155.
7. Colley, 'Army', pp. 572–3; Bond, 'Introduction', p. 13; Bond, 'Cardwell'; St Aubyn, *Royal George*, pp. 148, 151–2; Beckett, *Politics of Command*, pp. 109–10, 159; Clayton, *British Officer*, p. 98. For the best comprehensive accounts of the Cardwell reforms in all their aspects, see Spiers, *Army and Society*, pp. 177–205 and *Late Victorian Army*, pp. 2–28.
8. 'Statesmen, No. 47. His Royal Highness the Duke of Cambridge', *Vanity Fair*, 23 April 1870.
9. For late Victorian officers, see Spiers, *Army and Society*, pp. 1–34; Spiers, *Late Victorian Army*, pp. 89–117.

10. Bond, 'Cardwell'; Erickson, 'Abolition of Purchase', p. 75; Spiers, *Army and Society*, p. 16, 194–5; *Late Victorian Army*, pp. 90–3; Clayton, *British Officer*, pp. 98–9, 101; St Aubyn, *Royal George*, pp. 148–9, 163–4; Beckett, *Politics of Command*, pp. 6, 39, 41.
11. St Aubyn, *Royal George*, p. 361.
12. See Spiers, *Army and Society*, pp. 35–71; Spiers, *Late Victorian Army*, pp. 118–51.
13. Emery, *Marching over Africa*, pp. 14, 18.
14. Bond, 'Cardwell Reforms', pp. 515–16, 521–4; Spiers, *Late Victorian Army*, p. 73; Beckett, *Politics of Command*, p. 74.
15. Burroughs, 'Defence and Imperial Disunity, pp. 326–8.
16. Bond, 'Cardwell'; Bond, 'Cardwell Reforms', pp. 516–20; Clayton, *British Officer*, pp. 98–9, 102.

CHAPTER 12: The Nature of the South African Command, 1873–1875

1. Gon, *Road to Isandlwana*, pp. 42–3.
2. Laband, 'Cunynghame', pp. 154–5, 160–4, 197.
3. Cunynghame, *My Command*, p. 371; Beckett, 'High Command', pp. 64–5. For Wolseley's reception in Britain after the Third Anglo-Asante War, see Beckett (ed.), *Wolseley and Ashanti*, pp. 375–7.
4. Cunynghame, *My Command*, pp. 2–6; Laband, *Zulu Warrior*, pp. 15–16, 20–6.
5. Laband, *Zulu Warriors*, pp. 18–21, 26.
6. Cunynghame, *My Command*, p. 4
7. See Benyon, *Proconsul and Paramountcy*, p. 353: Appendix A (1): Sir Henry Pottinger's High Commission of 10 October, 1846
8. Harlow, 'Cape Colony', pp. 206–8; Benyon, *Proconsul*, pp. 7–11, 69–70, 212–13, 353–5: Appendix A (1–4): commissions illustrating the growth and closer definition of powers, 1846–1877; 358–9: Appendix B: diagram of the structure of imperial government.
9. Beckett, 'Command in South Africa', pp. 95–6.
10. De Kiewiet, 'Responsible Government', pp. 452, 455, 458.
11. WO 32/7680: Memorandum, Col. W. Bellairs to Sir Bartle Frere, 20 January 1878.
12. Beckett, 'High Command', p.60; Spiers, 'British Army in South Africa', p. 72.
13. For the Natal garrison, see Dominy, 'Fort Napier', pp. 102–9. For a comprehensive account of the imperial garrison at Fort Napier from 1843 until its withdrawal in 1914, see Dominy, *Last Outpost*, *passim*.
14. Gon, *Road to Isandlwana*, pp. 22 –3, 27; Greaves and Knight, *Who's Who*, Vol. 1, pp. 104–5.
15. For British military organisation, see Laband, *Historical Dictionary*, p. 163.
16. See Bou, 'Modern Cavalry', pp. 99–105; O'Connor, 'Dragoons and Commandos', pp. 92–3.
17. Knight, *Companion*, p. 145.
18. For uniforms and equipment, see Knight, *British Soldier*, pp. 140–8.
19. See WO 33/39: Report of the Colour Committee, 1883. The last time scarlet was worn on campaign was in Zululand in 1888. See Laband, *Later Zulu Wars*, p. 16.

20. Butterfield (ed.), *War and Peace in South Africa*, p. 67: Lt.-Col. Anstruther to his wife, Zaida, 20 October 1878; p. 134: Anstruther to Zaida, 14 November, 1880.
21. Rogers, *Weapons*, pp. 241–6; Knight, *British Soldier*, pp. 158–9; Laband, *Historical Dictionary*, p. 151. Although a Martini-Henry Mark III was accepted into service in August 1879, it was designed for the British Volunteers, Militia, and the troops of dominion governments rather than for British regulars.
22. Some experts nevertheless preferred the older Snider-Enfield rifle for bush fighting because its bullet penetrated a body less cleanly than a Martini-Henry's, making an appalling exit wound that had even greater stopping-power. See Molyneux, *Campaigning*, pp. 69–70.
23. Knight, *British Soldier*, p. 160; Laband, *Historical Dictionary*, pp. 12–13. Infantry sergeants carried the 1871-pattern sword bayonet.
24. Knight, *British Soldier*, p. 161; Laband, *Historical Dictionary*, p. 278.
25. Knight, *British Soldier*, pp. 161–2; Laband, *Historical Dictionary*, p. 237.
26. Hall, 'Field Artillery'; Hall, 'Artillery in the Zulu War', pp. 156–7; Knight, *British Soldier*, pp. 165–6; Laband, *Historical Dictionary*, pp. 8–9.
27. Cunynghame, *My Command*, pp. 49–52, 112, 306–10; Laband, *Zulu Warriors*, pp. 114–15.
28. Laband and Thompson, *Anglo-Zulu War*, pp. 23, 36; Laband, *Historical Dictionary*, p. 176.
29. Laband and Thompson, *Anglo-Zulu War*, pp. 23, 36; Laband, *Historical Dictionary*, pp. 177, 182. The Corps' organisation and regulations were defined by the Volunteer Ordnance of 1872.
30. Cunynghame, *My Command*, p. 309; Laband and Thompson, *Anglo-Zulu War*, pp. 23; Laband, *Historical Dictionary*, pp. 52–3; Laband, *Zulu Warriors*, p. 115.
31. Laband and Thompson, 'African Levies', pp. 49–50.
32. British troops had learned to be effective in irregular 'bush fighting' during the Seven Years War in North America, but since the mid-eighteenth century the art had been largely lost and conventional tactics prevailed. See Anderson, *Crucible of War*, pp. 410–11.
33. Stapleton, 'The Fingo (or Mfengu)', p. 15–36, 46–7; Laband, *Zulu Warriors*, pp. 99–103, 118.
34. See Laband, *Historical Dictionary*, pp. 7, 8, 53, 111, 210.

CHAPTER 13: The Ninth Cape Frontier War, 1875–1878

1. Cunynghame, *My Command*, pp. 100–7.
2. For a brief but recent discussion of the mainsprings of the confederation policy, see Laband, *Zulu Warriors*, pp. 68–70.
3. Saunders and Smith, 'Southern Africa', p. 606.
4. Lewsen (ed.), *Merriman Correspondence*, p. 26; Gon, *Road to Isandlwana*, p. 107.
5. Cunynghame, *My Command*, pp. 171–93, 204–5; Gon, *Road to Isandlwana*, pp. 31–42, 45–9, 59–61; Laband, *Zulu Warriors*, pp. 155, 162–3.
6. Guest, 'Colonists', pp. 157–62. The Natal Constitution Amendment Law came into effect on 24 December 1875.
7. *BPP* (C. 1748), enc. in no. 191: Cunynghame to the Secretary of State for War, 26 November 1876.

8. For the Boer–Pedi War of 1876, see Laband, *Zulu Warriors*, pp. 63–8.
9. Laband, *Transvaal Rebellion*, pp. 18–19.
10. Preston (ed.), *Wolseley's Journal*, p. 39: 21 June 1879.
11. Molyneux, *Campaigning*, p. 32.
12. Benyon, 'Frere'; Emery, 'Geography and Imperialism', pp. 342–50.
13. Laband, *Transvaal Rebellion*, p. 19.
14. Gon, *Road to Isandlwana*, pp. 83–4.
15. *BPP* (C. 1776), enc. 1 in no. 92: Cunynghame to Sir Henry Bulwer, 28 February 1877; no. 88: Sir Henry Barkly to Lord Carnarvon, 23 March 1877.
16. Laband, *Zulu Warriors*, p. 113.
17. *BPP* (C. 1776), enc. 1 in no. 109: Cunynghame to Sir Bartle Frere, 10 April 1877; no. 107: Major-General F. A. Campbell, Director of Artillery and Stores, to the Under Secretary of State, Colonial Office, 10 May 1877.
18. Cunynghame, *My Command*, pp. 238–95.
19. For Fort Amiel, see Laband, Thompson with Henderson, *Buffalo Border*, pp. 88–9.
20. Cunynghame, *My Command*, p. 374.
21. *BPP* (C. 2144), enc. in no. 102: memorandum by Cunynghame, 4 April 1878.
22. Gon, *Road to Isandlwana*, pp. 43, 76.
23. Peires, *House of Phalo*, pp. 1–2.
24. Laband, *Land Wars*, pp. 89–90.
25. For traditional Xhosa warfare, see Peires, *House of Phalo*, pp. 135–9; Soga, *Ama-Xhosa*, pp. 65–81, 312–13.
26. Storey, *Guns*, pp. 55, 67–70, 72–3.
27. Stapleton, *Military History*, p. 20.
28. Laband, *Land Wars*, 265–7.
29. Storey, *Guns*, pp. 199–200, 210, 227.
30. *BPP* (C. 1961), enc. in no. 83: Col. John Eustace to Charles Brownlee, 18 August 1877.
31. Benyon, *Proconsul and Paramountcy*, p. 149.
32. Quoted in Switzer, *Ciskei Xhosa*, p. 73.
33. See Lewsen, *John X. Merriman*, pp. 65–8.
34. *BPP* (C. 1961), enc. in no. 61, Commandant C. Griffith to Military Secretary, 17 October 1877; Smith, *Wedding Feast War*, pp. 121–4.
35. *BPP* (C. 1961), enc. 3 in no. 102: Proclamation by Sir Bartle Frere, 21 November 1877.
36. *BPP* (C. 2000), enc. 1 in no. 22: Inspector J. H. W. Bourne's report, 3 December 1878.
37. Laband, 'Cunynghame', p. 186.
38. *BPP* (C. 2000), enc. in no. 27: Cunynghame to Secretary of State for War, 12 December 1877.
39. Cunynghame, *My Command*, pp. 327–8, 340–1; Laband, *Historical Dictionary*, pp. 71–2, 102, 118, 241. The Naval Brigade left its six 12-pounder guns on board HMS *Active*.
40. For lurid memories of trying to discipline these roughs, see Hamilton-Browne, *Lost Legionary*, pp. 36–42.

41. Laband, *Historical Dictionary*, p. 100. The FLH was finally disbanded in December 1879 after service against the amaZulu and Bapedi as well as the amaXhosa.
42. Smith, *Wedding Feast War*, pp. 148–55.
43. Cunynghame, *My Command*, pp. 341–2.
44. Cunynghame, *My Command*, pp. 343, 355–7, 359–61; Smith, *Wedding Feast War*, pp. 196–201.
45. Laband, 'Cunynghame', p. 189.
46. Cartoon by 'Ape', *Vanity Fair*, 22 August 1874. Scagliola is a type of imitation marble.
47. Pugh, 'Hicks Beach'.
48. *BPP* (C. 2079), no. 86: Frere to Hicks Beach 21 May 1878.
49. Laband, 'Cunynghame', pp. 189–90.
50. For the engagement at Nyumaga, see Cunynghame, *My Command*, pp. 351–5; Smith, *Wedding Feast War*, pp. 201–4.
51. See Molyneux, *Campaigning*, p. 207.
52. War Office, *Field Exercise*, pp. 53–4, 93–4, 96–9, 210–41.
53. Laband, 'Cunynghame', pp. 192–3.
54. For the battle of Kentani, see WO 32/7681: Cunynghame to Secretary of State for War, 15 February 1878; *BPP* (C. 2079), no. 81, enc. 1 with official despatches and reports of the engagement; Smith, *Wedding Feast War*, pp. 207–13.
55. Report by 'Gaika warrior' quoted in Hallam Parr, *Kafir and Zulu Wars*, p. 86.
56. Milton, *Edges of War*, pp. 267–9.
57. Smithers, *Kaffir Wars*, p. 271.
58. *BPP* (C. 2144), enc 1 in no. 102: Memorandum by Cunynghame, HMS *Himalaya*, at sea, 4 April 1878.
59. Carnarvon resigned over the Eastern Question. By advocating neutrality, he crossed the Prime Minister, Lord Beaconsfield, who was contemplating war against Russia to maintain Ottoman control over the Dardanelles and so keep the Russian Black Sea Fleet out of the Mediterranean where it might threaten the British route to India. See Gordon, 'Carnarvon'.
60. Goodfellow, *Confederation*, p. 155.
61. Cunynghame Papers 7805-42: Memorandum by Cunynghame, Queen Anne's Mansions, Westminster, 6 May 1878.
62. Cambridge to Gathorne Hardy, 30 January 1878, in Goodfellow, *Confederation*, p. 155.
63. Cunynghame Papers 7805-42: Memorandum by Cunynghame, 6 May 1878.

CHAPTER 14: General Officer Commanding South Africa, 1878

1. Beckett, *Politics of Command*, pp. 56–62, 65, 74–6, 98–102, 141–2, 144.
2. Preston (ed.), *Wolseley's Journal*, p. 304, Appendix C: Wolseley, Memoir, 27 May 1881.
3. Beckett (ed.), *Wolseley and Ashanti*, pp. 38–44.
4. Farwell, *Victorian Soldiers*, p. 177; Beckett, *Politics of Command*, pp. 87–8.
5. Beckett, 'High Command', pp. 60–3.
6. Beckett, *Politics of Command*, p. 201; Laband, *Land Wars*, pp. 182–3, 218–19.

7. Beckett, 'Colley', pp. 74–9.
8. Preston, 'British Military Thought', pp. 64–5, 71.
9. Greaves and Knight, *Who's Who,* Vol. 1, p. 62; Laband, 'Chelmsford', p. 114.
10. Beckett, *Politics of Command*, p. 202.
11. Molyneux, *Campaigning*, p. 17; Laband, 'Chelmsford', p. 97.
12. Quoted in Beckett, *Politics of Command*, p. 85.
13. Beckett, *Politics of Command*, p. 37.
14. Chichester, revised by Stearn, 'Michel'.
15. See Laband, *Land Wars*, pp. 215, 248–9.
16. CP 2/13: Michel to Thesiger, 28 January 1878; French, *Chelmsford*, pp. 7–12.
17. CP 2/13: Michel to Thesiger, 28 January 1878.
18. Beckett, *Politics of Command*, pp. 79–81, 84–7, 101.
19. Clayton, *British Officer*, pp. 109–11. It would not be until the 1890s that the Staff College gained real credibility. See Spiers, *Late Victorian Army*, pp. 109–12.
20. French, *Chelmsford*, pp. 14–15.
21. Laband, 'Crealock'; Laband (ed.), *Chelmsford's Zululand Campaign*, pp. 275, 277, 279.
22. Laband, *Companion to Narrative of Field Operations*, pp. 6–8.
23. Thesiger to Sir Archibald Alison, 19 December 1878, in Clarke, *Zululand at War*, p. 52.
24. Laband, *Companion to Narrative of Field Operations*, pp. 9–10.
25. Gossett was subsequently AAG and AQMG to the 2nd Division during the second invasion of Zululand and was present at the battle of Ulundi.
26. CP 26/36: General M. W. E. Gossett to Lady Chelmsford, 7 June 1906.
27. J. N. Crealock to Sir A. Alison, 21 July 1879, in Clarke, *Zululand at War*, p. 26.

CHAPTER 15: Finishing the Ninth Cape Frontier War, 1878

1. *BPP* (C. 2100), no. 56: General Order by Col. Bellairs, 11 March 1878; *Illustrated London News*, 6 April 1878.
2. WO 32/7684: Cunynghame to Gathorne Hardy, 27 February 1878.
3. Hummel (ed.), *Crealock*, p. 22: 4 March 1878.
4. Thesiger to Cambridge, 11 March 1878, in French, *Chelmsford*, p. 24.
5. See French, *Chelmsford*, pp. 18–22, for these letters.
6. *BPP* (C. 2100), enc. in no. 43: Thesiger to Gathorne Hardy, 12 March 1878.
7. Spiers, *Late Victorian Army*, p. 272.
8. Molyneux, *Campaigning*, p. 19.
9. Thesiger to Griffith, 5 March 1878, in French, *Chelmsford*, pp. 19–20.
10. Laband, *Land Wars*, p. 265; Gon, *Road to Isandlwana*, pp. 150–1.
11. Smithers, *Kaffir Wars*, p. 271; CP 2/13: Thesiger to Gathorne Hardy, 12 March 1878.
12. Smith, *Wedding Feast War*, p. 217.
13. Molyneux, *Campaigning*, p. 43.
14. Milton, *Edges of War*, pp. 271–2; Gon, *Road to Isandlwana*, p. 151; Mostert, *Frontiers*, p. 1252; Stapleton, *Military History*, p. 62
15. Hallam Parr, *Kafir and Zulu Wars*, pp. 87–8.

16. CP 2-12: Thesiger to Gathorne Hardy, 12 March 1878.
17. Anon., *24th Regiment*, p. 2.
18. Smithers, *Kaffir Wars*, p. 271; Manning, 'Evelyn Wood', p. 39.
19. Manning, 'Evelyn Wood', pp. 28–37; Greaves and Knight, *Who's Who*, Vol. 1, pp. 184–6.
20. See Hummel (ed.), *Crealock*, pp. 19–105.
21. Low, *Soldiers of the Victorian Age*, Vol. 2, p. 85.
22. Hummel (ed.), *Crealock*, p. 26: 14 March 1878.
23. See *BPP* (C. 2144), enc. in no. 20: Thesiger's diary of operations, 12 to 22 March 1878.
24. CP 2/12: Thesiger to Gathorne Hardy, 25 March 1878.
25. Anon., *24th Regiment*, pp. 6–7, 9.
26. Mathews, 'Chelmsford', pp. 43–4; Gon, *Road to Isandlwana*, pp. 153 –5; Gon, 'Last Frontier War'; Milton, *Edges of War*, pp. 274–5; Smith, *Wedding Feast War*, pp. 218–25; Stapleton, 'Fingo', p. 41.
27. WO 32/7688: Thesiger to Gathorne Hardy, 25 March 1878.
28. Hummel (ed.), *Crealock*, pp. 37–8: 18 March 1878; p. 47: 22 March 1878.
29. CP 26/12: Bellairs, *Regulations for the Colonial Forces*.
30. For this offensive, see *BPP* C. 2144, enc. in no. 29: Thesiger to Secretary of State for War, 10 April 1878.
31. Private George Morris to his father, March 1878, in Emery, *Marching over Africa*, pp. 54–5.
32. Mathews, 'Chelmsford', pp. 44, 46.
33. CP 2/12: Thesiger to Gathorne Hardy, 10 April 1878; Gon, *Road to Isandlwana*, p. 156; Stapleton, *Military History*, p. 62.
34. Hummel (ed.), *Crealock*, p. 57: 5 April 1878; p. 65: 6 April 1878.
35. The Dutch rulers of the Cape first used the desolate Robben Island in Table Bay to incarcerate political prisoners in the seventeenth century, and the British followed suit, imprisoning many defeated Xhosa leaders there during the course of the Cape Frontier Wars.
36. Milton, *Edges of War*, p. 275; Smith, *Wedding Feast War*, pp. 189–92.
37. See *BPP* (C. 2144), enc. in no. 11: Thesiger's diary of operations, 10 to 17 April 1878; enc. in no. 31: Thesiger to Secretary of State for War, 24 April 1878.
38. CP 2/12: Thesiger to Gathorne Hardy, 10 April, 1878; Stapleton, 'Fingo', pp. 41–2; Milton, *Edges of War*, p. 275; Gon, *Road to Isandlwana*, p. 158; Smith, *Wedding Feast War*, pp. 226–8.
39. WO 32/7690: Thesiger to Stanley, 24 April 1878.
40. For these operations, see *BPP* (C. 2144), enc. in no. 46: Thesiger to Stanley, 5 May 1878; enc. in no. 47: diary of Quartermaster-General's Department, 8 May 1878; enc. in no. 55: Thesiger to Stanley, 15 May 1878.
41. Molyneux, *Campaigning*, p. 81.
42. Anon., *24th Regiment*, pp. 12–13; Smithers, *Kaffir Wars*, p. 272; Milton, *Edges of War*, p. 276; Stapleton, *Military History*, p. 62; Smith, *Wedding Feast War*, pp. 226–32.
43. CP 2/12: Thesiger to Stanley, 15 May 1878; Anon., *24th Regiment*, pp. 15–17; Milton, *Edges of War*, p. 276; Smith, *Wedding Feast War*, pp. 232–6.

44. Hummel (ed.), *Crealock*, p. 81: 3 May 1878.
45. Gon, *Road to Isandlwana*, p. 163.
46. *Cape Mercury*, 12 June 1878.
47. Gon, *Road to Isandlwana*, p. 163; Mathews, 'Chelmsford', p. 49; Stapleton, *Military History*, p. 62; Laband, *Land Wars*, p. 250.
48. *BPP* (C. 2144), no. 11: Captain H. Spalding to Frere, 17 April 1878.
49. *BPP* (C. 2144), enc. in no. 55: Thesiger to Stanley, 15 May 1878; enc. in no. 56: diary of Quartermaster-General's Department, 15 May 1878; encs 1, 2 and 3 in no. 77: Thesiger's reports to Frere, 22 May, 29 May, 2 June 1878; encs 1 and 2 in no. 91: operations from 29 May to 5 June 1878.
50. *BPP* (C. 2144), no. 32: Frere to Sir Michael Hicks Beach, 30 April 1878.
51. Hallam Parr, *Wars*, p. 94; Mathews, 'Chelmsford', p. 48; Milton, *Edges of War*, pp. 274, 276–8; Smith, *Wedding Feast War*, pp. 236–7; Stapleton, *Military History*, pp. 60–1.
52. For Thesiger's tour of the Transkei, see Hummel (ed.), *Crealock*, pp. 91–105: 23 May–6 June 1878.
53. *The Eastern Star*, 14 June 1878, in Crwys-Williams (ed.), *South African Despatches*, pp. 35–9; Hummel (ed.), *Crealock*, pp. 163–7: Appendix A: The Controversy and Legends Surrounding Sandile; Mostert, *Frontiers*, p. 1252; Milton, *Edges of War*, pp. 278–9; Smith, *Wedding Feast War*, pp. 237–9.
54. For Thesiger's detailed report on his conduct of operations from March 1878, see *BPP* (C. 2144), enc.1 in no. 126: Thesiger to Stanley, 26 June 1878.
55. Thesiger to Frere, 21 June 1878, in French, *Chelmsford*, p. 26.
56. Milton, *Edges of War*, pp. 280–1; Gon, *Road to Isandlwana*, p. 166; Gon, 'Frontier War'; Stapleton, 'Fingo', pp. 42–3; Smith, *Wedding Feast War*, p. 245.
57. Soga, *Ama-Xhosa*, pp. 118–23; Mostert, *Frontiers*, p. 1254; Smith, *Wedding Feast War*, pp. 239–40.
58. Low, *Soldiers of the Victorian Age*, Vol. 2, p. 85.
59. *BPP* (C. 2144), enc. 3 in no. 110: DAG to Military Secretary, 21 June 1878; Milton, *Edges of War*, p. 274; Mostert, *Frontiers*, pp. 1254, 1281; Switzer, *Ciskei Xhosa*, p. 74.
60. Switzer, *Ciskei Xhosa*, pp. 74–5; Milton, *Edges of War*, p. 282; Mostert, *Frontiers*, pp. 1252–3; Smith, *Wedding Feast War*, pp. 241–4. About half the amaNgqika succeeded in avoiding expulsion by seeking work as wage-earning labourers on white-owned farms in the Ciskei, or by agreeing to be transported to the distant Cape peninsula as indentured labourers.
61. Laband, *Land Wars*, p. 286.
62. Milton, *Edges of War*, p. 281; Storey, *Guns*, pp. 240–2.
63. Storey, *Guns*, pp. 246–52.
64. *BPP* (C. 2144), no. 131: Frere to Hicks Beach, 9 July 1878.
65. Thesiger to Cambridge, 1 July 1878, in French, *Chelmsford*, pp. 26–7.
66. The neck badge was a gold Maltese cross with eight points enamelled in white and suspended on a scarlet ribbon. See Duckers, *British Orders*, pp. 21–4.

CHAPTER 16: Establishing Headquarters in Pietermaritzburg

1. TS 31: Thesiger to Shepstone, 21 July 1878.
2. H. S., 'Kaffir War', p. 258.

3. Hallam Parr, *Kafir and Zulu Wars*, pp. 101–2.
4. *BPP* (C. 2252), enc. in no. 3: minute by Chelmsford, 25 November 1878.
5. For the Northern War, see Laband, *Zulu Warriors*, pp. 153–82.
6. *BPP* (C. 2222), enc. in no. 36: O. Lanyon to Frere, 19 November 1878.
7. Norris-Newman, *With the Boers*, p. 81.
8. Delius, *Pedi Polity*, p. 227; Laband, *Transvaal Rebellion*, p. 20.
9. Theophilus Shepstone to Frere, 30 April 1878, in Martineau, *Bartle Frere*, Vol. II, p 235; Delius, *Pedi Polity*, p. 225.
10. *BPP* (C. 2100), enc. 1 in no. 39: A. Nachtigahl to G. A. Roth, Landdrost of Lydenburg, 14 January 1878. See Monteith, 'Cetshwayo and Sekhukhune', pp. 170–6.
11. *BPP* (C. 2222), no. 5: Frere to Sir Michael Hicks Beach, 10 December 1878. For Shepstone's identical thoughts about the 'black conspiracy 'and the Zulu as the 'root of all evil', see Laband, *Zulu Nation*, p. 190.
12. *BPP* (C. 2222), enc. 2 in no. 38: memorandum by C. Brownlee, 12 November 1878.
13. Laband, *Historical Dictionary*, pp. 64–5.
14. Laband, *Zulu Nation*, pp. 150, 158–60, 183, 190; Cope, *Ploughshare of War*, p. 161.
15. *BPP* (C. 2242), appendix III, no. 1: Shepstone to Carnarvon, 1 December 1877. See Cope, *Ploughshare of War*, pp. 162–6, for an analysis of the meeting. For the contemporary Zulu perspective, see Webb and Wright (eds), *Zulu King Speaks*, pp. 23–4, 48–50.
16. Shepstone to Carnarvon, 11 December 1877, in Delius, *Pedi Polity*, p. 232.
17. For the most comprehensive account of the political build-up to the Anglo-Zulu War, see Cope, *Ploughshare of War*, chapters 7–9.
18. Cope, *Ploughshare of War*, pp. 217–18; Storey, *Guns*, p. 240.
19. Thesiger to Cambridge, 1 July 1878, in French, *Chelmsford*, p. 27
20. CP 29: Thesiger to Shepstone, 2 June 1878; Greaves and Knight, *Who's Who*, Vol. 1, pp. 149–50, 161–2.
21. CP 29: Thesiger to Colonel Rowlands, 20 July 1878.
22. TS 31: Thesiger to Shepstone, 21 July 1878.
23. Laband and Thompson, *Anglo-Zulu War*, pp. 186–7.
24. CP 29: Thesiger to Frere, 13 August 1878.
25. Frost, 'Government House', in Laband and Haswell (eds), *Pietermaritzburg*, p. 88.
26. CP 10/6: Thesiger to Frere, 11 September 1878.
27. Preston (ed.), *Wolseley's Journal*, p. 48: 30 June 1879.
28. CP 29: Thesiger to Frere, 11 August 1878.
29. Major Cornelius Clery to Alison, 22 October 1878, in Clarke, *Zululand at War*, p. 59.
30. Sir H. Bulwer to Edward Bulwer, 8 December 1878, in Clarke, *Invasion of Zululand*, p. 213–14.
31. Preston (ed.), *Wolseley's Journal*, p. 48: 30 June 1879.
32. Preston (ed.), *Wolseley's Journal*, p. 48: 30 June 1879.
33. TS 32: Thesiger to Shepstone, 10 August 1878.
34. See Crealock's unflattering watercolour drawing of Bulwer in Brown (ed.), *Road to Ulundi*, no. 2.

35. Clery to Alison, 22 October 1878 (very confidential), in Clarke, *Zululand at War*, p. 59.
36. CP 29: Thesiger to Frere, 13 August 1878.
37. Chelmsford to Cambridge, 11 April 1879, in French, *Chelmsford*, p. 141.
38. See Laband, 'Divided Command', pp. 340–3.
39. Thesiger to Frere, 21 June 1878, in French, *Chelmsford*, p. 31.
40. TS 32: Thesiger to Shepstone, 14 and 16 August 1878.
41. *BPP* (C. 2220), enc. 1 in no. 72: Thesiger to Frere, 2 September 1878.

CHAPTER 17: **Readying the Invasion Force, August 1878–January 1879**

1. See CP 10/5: Memorandum by Thesiger to Bulwer, 24 August 1878.
2. The standard language of the telegraph was Morse's code using sounding keys. Duplex and quadruplex systems allowed the simultaneous transmission of several messages in both directions, and the galvanometer made possible the transmission of messages over a long distance with a low voltage and current.
3. Webb, 'Lines of Power', p. 31; Thompson, 'Great Britain and the Afrikaner Republics', pp. 289–90.
4. WP 26/11: Chelmsford to Wood, 7 November 1878.
5. See War Office, *Field Operations*, pp. 5, 8, 12–13. Chelmsford's correspondence in the month leading up to the invasion of Zululand was heavily larded with details of proposed or actual troop movements.
6. WO 32/7704: Chelmsford to Stanley, 25 November 1878.
7. Miller, 'Buller', pp. 51–4; Beckett, 'Buller'.
8. WO 32/7702: Thesiger to Col. F. A. Stanley, 14 September 1878; WO 32/7699: Thesiger to Stanley, 28 September 1878.
9. *Hansard:* 3rd series, Vol. 244 c. 2070: House of Commons, 28 March 1879: Colonel Stanley.
10. CO 879/14 (African), no. 164: Memorandum on the Zulu Question, p. 54: Hicks Beach to Frere, 21 November 1878.
11. War Office, *Field Operations*, pp. 14, 18–19.
12. War Office, *Field Operations*, pp. 14, 19.
13. Laband, 'Durnford'; Laband, *Zulu Warriors*, pp. 15–16, 22–5; Greaves and Knight, *Who's Who*, Vol. 1, pp. 81–3.
14. CP 26/11: Bellairs, *Management of Natives*.
15. The fullest and most reliable treatment of the enrolment and organization of the NNC and NNPC is to be found in Thompson, *Black Soldiers*, pp. 5–36. See also Laband and Thompson, 'African Levies', pp. 53–5; Laband, *Historical Dictionary*, pp. 178–82; Castle, *Zulu War*, pp. 4–10.
16. WO 32/7704: Chelmsford to Stanley, 25 November 1878.
17. Laband, *Historical Dictionary*, pp. 71,163. A squadron of Mounted Infantry nominally consisted of three officers and 110 men.
18. O'Connor, 'Dragoons and Commandos', pp. 92–3; Laband, *Historical Dictionary*, p. 166.
19. Laband, *Historical Dictionary*, p. 182; Castle, *Zulu War*, pp. 16–24, 33.
20. Castle, *Zulu War*, pp. 33–42.
21. Laband, *Historical Dictionary*, p. 181; Castle, *Zulu War*, pp. 11–12.

22. It was not understood that horse sickness was caused by the bite of the tsetse fly, and many other causes were falsely adduced.
23. For the First Anglo-Pedi War, see War Office, *Field Operations*, pp. 5–10; Laband, *Zulu Warriors*, pp. 185–94.
24. TS 33: Chelmsford to Shepstone, 21 October 1878.
25. *BPP* C. 2222, enc. 1 in no. 12: Gen. Thesiger to the Secretary of State for War, 11 November 1878.
26. Quoted in Monteith, 'Cetshwayo and Sekhukhune', p. 166.
27. TS 35: Chelmsford to Shepstone, 7 December 1878.
28. War Office, *Field Operations*, p. 146.
29. See Crealock's watercolour drawing in Brown, *Road to Ulundi*, no. 25.
30. See War Office, *Field Operations*, pp. 171–2: 'Transport in South Africa'; War Office, *Précis of Information*, p. 58; Bennett, *Eyewitness*, pp. 43–5, 49–54; Callwell, *Small Wars*, pp. 57–9, 64, 66; Mathews, 'Problems of Transport', pp. 1–9, 42–3; Mathews, 'Chelmsford', pp. 71–84, 111–12, 243–4; Spiers, *Late Victorian Army*, pp. 76–8; Laband and Thompson, *Anglo-Zulu War*, pp. 28–30.
31. CP 27: Chelmsford to Strickland, 30 December 1878.
32. For an example of Chelmsford's abortive attempts to improve supply and transport, see CP 5/20: Memorandum by Chelmsford for District Commissary-General E. Strickland, undated [probably 7 November 1878]. For his ongoing concern that 'a proper system' be established, see CP 27: Chelmsford to Strickland, 30 December 1878.
33. WP 26/11: Chelmsford to Wood, 7 November 1878.
34. CP 27: Chelmsford to War Office, 19 January 1879.

CHAPTER 18: Planning the Invasion, August 1878–January 1879

1. Callwell, *Small Wars*, pp. 10–12.
2. Mathews, 'Chelmsford', pp. 43–4. See CP 24/5: Memorandum by Chelmsford, [?] February 1880.
3. TS 35: Chelmsford to Shepstone, 28 November 1878.
4. Harness, 'Zulu Campaign', pp. 478–9. See Callwell, *Small Wars*, pp. 37–9, 90–1, 93, 103–4, 106.
5. For the successful deployment in 1838 of Boer laagers against the amaZulu in the battles of Veglaer (emaGebeni) and Blood River (Ncome) and defeats when fighting in the open at eThaleni, the Thukela (Dlokweni) and the White Mfolozi (oPathe), see Laband, *Zulu Kingdom and Boer Invasion*, pp. 163–85, 189–210.
6. See Anon., *Regulations for Field Forces*, p. 3: item 19.
7. Hallam Parr, *Kafir and Zulu Wars*, pp. 166–8; Laband and Thompson, *Umvoti*, pp. 15–17; Laband and Thompson, *Buffalo Border*, pp. 19–20.
8. Laband and Thompson, *Anglo-Zulu War*, pp. 68–9.
9. CP 10/17: Chelmsford to Frere, 26 October 1878.
10. CP 10/13: Memorandum by Chelmsford on the military requirements of the Natal Colony with regard to its N Eastern Border should offensive or defensive measures against Zululand be considered necessary, 23 October 1878; Laband, 'Border Levies', pp. 150–3; Laband and Thompson, *Anglo-Zulu War*, pp. 35–9, 68–9.

11. H. Bulwer to E. Bulwer, 19 January 1879, in Clarke (ed.), *Invasion of Zululand*, p. 215.
12. TS 35: Chelmsford to Shepstone, 7 December 1878.
13. CP 10/13: Memorandum by Chelmsford, 23 October 1878; Crealock to Alison, 23 October 1878, in Clark *Zululand at War*, p. 56.
14. De Watteville, 'Clery'.
15. Maj. C. F. Clery to Colonel G. B. Harman, 17 February [1879], in Clark, *Zululand at War*, p. 82.
16. War Office, *Field Operations*, p. 141; Laband, *Chelmsford's Zululand Campaign*, pp. 273, 279.
17. Crealock to Alison, 26 August 1878, in Clarke, *Zululand at War*, p. 53.
18. Clery to Alison, 6 December 1878, in Clarke, *Zululand at War*, p. 52.
19. Clery to Alison, 1 February and 18 March 1879, in Clarke, *Zululand at War*, pp. 61, 124.
20. Mathews, 'Chelmsford', pp. 26–7, 39–41, 341–2.
21. Crealock to Alison, 11 April 1879, in Clarke, *Zululand at War*, p. 205.
22. Spiers, 'Late Victorian Army', p. 194.
23. Laband and Thompson, *Buffalo Border*, pp. 16, 41–2.
24. Tabler, *Pioneers of South Africa*, pp. 31–2; Greaves and Knight, *Who's Who*, Vol. 1, pp. 75–6; *Illustrated London News*, 31 May 1879.
25. Longcast went on to serve under Wolseley in Zululand, and accompanied the captive King Cetshwayo to Cape Town as his interpreter. In later years this transfrontiersman became an outcast when Zululand finally fell under British rule, and he died indigent in 1909, his services to the British forces in 1879 forgotten and unrewarded, except for the campaign medal. See Laband, 'Longcast'.
26. See CP 10/5: Memorandum by Thesiger to Bulwer, 24 August 1878; WO 32/7702: Thesiger to Stanley, 14 September 1878.
27. Laband, *Kingdom in Crisis*, pp.122–4. See WP 26/2: Thesiger to Wood, 1 October 1878; WP 26/6: Thesiger to Wood, 26 October 1878.
28. TS 33: Thesiger to Shepstone, 21 October 1878.
29. War Office, *Field Operations*, pp. 18–19, 141–6.
30. CP 25/6: Sketch of Zululand &c. by A. W. Durnford, Natal, September 1878; CP 20/3: Horse Guards to Chelmsford, 9 October 1878. Durnford's lithographed map would be titled *Sketch of Zululand &c. Compiled from Original Sources and from Personal Observation & Information* (September 1878). While an improvement over Durnford's map, even the Intelligence Branch of the Quartermaster-General's Department of the War Office's *Military Map of Zulu Land Compiled from Most Recent Information*, published in March 1879, was still far from accurate.
31. War Office, *Précis of Information*, pp. 3–18, 21–6.
32. CP 28: Chelmsford to Stanley, 10 June 1879.
33. Ashe and Wyatt-Edgell, *Zulu Campaign*, p. 189.
34. See Bonner, *Swazi State*, pp. 109–44, 155–7; Maylam, *African People*, pp. 92–5
35. Laband, *Kingdom in Crisis*, pp. 59–60. See WC II/2/2: Chelmsford to Wood, 23 November 1878; Chelmsford to Wood, 4 December 1878.

36. The heliograph was a simple apparatus. It sent its Morse code signals by reflecting sunlight with a mirror mounted on a tripod, the beam being keyed on and off with a shutter or tilting mirror at the rate of up to twelve words a minute, depending on the skill of the operator.
37. CP 10/30: Memorandum by Chelmsford, 5 November 1878; WC II/2/2: Chelmsford to Col. Glyn, 17 December 1878 (copy).
38. WC II/2/2: Chelmsford to Wood, 4 January 1879. Realistically, a horse could not go further than thirty miles a day over the difficult terrain.
39. PP 3: Chelmsford to Pearson, 31 December 1878.
40. See CP 10/30: Memorandum by Chelmsford, 5 November 1878; PP: Chelmsford to Pearson, 15 December 1878; WC II/2/2: Chelmsford to Wood, 16 December 1878; WC II/2/2: Chelmsford to Glyn, 17 December 1878; PP 3: Chelmsford to Pearson, 31 December 1878.
41. WC II/2/2: Chelmsford to Wood, 4 January 1879.
42. H. Bulwer to E. Bulwer, 8 December 1878, in Clarke, *Invasion of Zululand*, p. 213.
43. Crealock to Alison, 9 December 1878, in Clark, *Zululand at War*, p. 66.
44. TS 35: Chelmsford to Shepstone, 13 December 1879.
45. Frere to Hicks Beach, 30 September 1878, in Martineau, *Frere*, Vol. II, p. 238.
46. TS 34: Frere to Shepstone, 30 November 1878.
47. Frere to Hicks Beach, 8 December 1878, in Martineau, *Frere*, Vol. II, p. 253.
48. For a résumé of this correspondence, see O'Connor, *Frere*, pp. 149–51.
49. O'Connor, 'Causes of the Anglo-Zulu War', pp. 31–5; Atwood, 'Second Afghan War', pp. 126–45.
50. Frere to Hicks Beach, 28 October 1878, in Martineau, *Frere*, Vol. II, pp. 259–60; *BPP* C. 2222, no. 54: Frere to Hicks Beach, 14 December 1878.
51. SNA 1/6/3: Original draft of the ultimatum, sighed by Bulwer, 4 December 1878.
52. TS 35: Chelmsford to Shepstone, 13 December 1878.
53. CP 27: Chelmsford to Frere, 1 January 1879.
54. CP 27: Chelmsford to Frere, 1 January 1879.

CHAPTER 19: Opening Moves of the Zulu Campaign, January 1879

1. Throughout the rest of this book, the details of field operations while Chelmsford was in command are based on War Office, *Field Operations*, pp. 22–125. The officer responsible for compiling *Field Operations* was Major John Rothwell RA, a DAQMG at the Intelligence Branch of the War Office. He based his narrative on official despatches, reports, and memoranda forwarded to the Intelligence Branch, and on the journals and diaries of operations of the various columns or divisions operating in Zululand. These papers are to be found in the National Archives, Kew, and are known as the War Office Papers relating to the Anglo-Zulu War, numbered WO 32/7698 to WO 32/7785, 1878–1879. (See Laband, *Companion to Narrative of Field Operations*, pp. 5, 10–13.) For a condensed account of operations and four detailed maps, see Laband and Thompson, *Anglo-Zulu War*, pp. 48–62.
2. *BPP* (C. 2242), enc. 6 in no. 20: Chelmsford to Stanley, 14 January 1879; Biggarsberg Correspondent, 11 January 1879 and Special War Correspondent,

13 January 1879, in Lock and Quantrill (comps), *Red Book*, pp. 23–4, 25–6; War Office, *Field Operations*, p. 26; Norris-Newman, *In Zululand*, pp. 35–7.

3. Biggarsberg Correspondent, 11 January 1879, in Lock and Quantrill (comps), *Red Book*, p. 24.
4. Clery to Alison, 28 April 1878, in Clarke, *Zululand at War*, p. 128, 129; Mathews, 'Chelmsford', pp. 132–3.
5. War Office, *Field Operations*, p. 22. For Fort Pearson, see Laband and Thompson, *Anglo-Zulu War*, p. 77.
6. Crealock to Alison, 14 February 1879, in Clarke, *Zululand at War*, p. 140.
7. WP 26/2: Thesiger to Wood, 1 October 1878.
8. WP 26/6: Thesiger to Wood, 26 October 1879.
9. Laband, *Historical Dictionary*, p. 129.
10. For descriptions and diagrams of these fortifications, see Laband and Thompson, *Anglo-Zulu War*, pp. 133–4.
11. Many of these levies were of Swazi origin and were armed and accoutred in Swazi, rather than Zulu, style. See Laband, *Historical Dictionary*, pp. 309–10.
12. *BPP* (C. 2242), enc. 8 in no. 20: Chelmsford to Stanley, 14 January 1879; War Office, *Field Operations*, pp. 26, 50; Norris-Newman, *In Zululand*, p. 37; Wood, *Midshipman to Field Marshal*, Vol. II, p. 19.
13. Laband, *Historical Dictionary*, pp. 135, 144, 153, 224–5. For a succinct description of the local inhabitants and political developments before the Anglo-Zulu War, see Laband, 'Phongolo River Frontier', pp. 181–93. For a minutely detailed account, see Jones, *The Boiling Cauldron*, pp. 1–191.
14. For Wood's opening operations, see Laband, *Kingdom in Crisis*, pp. 124–8; *Narrative*, pp. 50–2.
15. War Office, *Field Operations*, pp. 26–7; *BPP* (C. 2242), enc. 5 in no. 20: reports by Lt.-Col. Crealock, 12 and 15 January 1879; enc. 8 in no. 20: Chelmsford to Stanley, 14 January 1879; Special War Correspondent, 13 January 1879, in Lock and Quantrill (comps), *Red Book*, pp. 26–7; Anon., *24th Regiment*: 'Zulu War', p. 6; Thompson, *Black Soldiers*, pp. 37–40.
16. Child (ed.), *Harford*, pp. 18–21.
17. Clery to Alison, 13 April 1879, in Clarke, *Zululand at War*, pp. 125, 126.
18. CP 27: Chelmsford to Frere, 12 January 1879.
19. Laband and Mathews, *Isandlwana*, p. 19.
20. Clery to Alison, 18 March 1879, in Clarke, *Zululand at War*, p. 122.
21. Anon., *Regulations for Field Forces*, pp. 1–65.
22. See Anon., *Regulations for Field Forces*, p. 3: items 18 and 19 under 'Encampments'.
23. Durnford, *Lord Chelmsford's Statements*, pp. 11–12.
24. Clery to Alison, 18 March 1879, in Clarke, *Zululand at War*, p. 122.
25. CP 8/31: Notes by Chelmsford on the findings of the Court of Enquiry, n.d.
26. Durnford, *Lord Chelmsford's Statements*, p. 12.
27. Forbes, 'Lord Chelmsford', p. 221.
28. CP 27: Chelmsford to Wood, 16 January 1879; CP 24/ 5: Memorandum 'B', n.d. This memorandum, and three others, 'A', 'C' and 'D', are all drafts, written by Chelmsford in early 1880 but never submitted, in attempted rebuttal of the points raised by Archibald Forbes. See also Harness. 'Zulu Campaign', pp. 479–80.

29. For the layout of the camp, see Anon., *24th Regiment*: 'Zulu War', pp. 8–9; Beckett. *Isandlwana*, pp. 36–8.
30. See Mathews, 'Chelmsford', pp. 131–2, for the various expressions of misgiving about the camp.
31. Anon., *24th Regiment*, p. 9.
32. Clery to Alison, 13 April 1879, in Clarke, *Zululand at War*, p. 126.
33. WC II/2/2: Chelmsford to Wood, 18 January 1879; CP 27: Chelmsford to Frere, 21 January 1879; CP 13/44: Memorandum by Chelmsford, 8 June 1879.
34. CP 27: Chelmsford to Frere, 16 January 1879.
35. TS 34: Thesiger to Shepstone, 2 November 1878; CP 27: Chelmsford to Wood, 11 January 1879; Chelmsford to Frere, 16 January 1879; WC II/2/2: Chelmsford to Wood, 16 January 1879; TS 36: Frere to Shepstone, 21 January 1879. See Ashe and Wyatt-Edgell, *Zulu Campaign*, pp. 306–7, Harness, 'Zulu Campaign', p. 478; Callwell, *Small Wars*, pp. 40–1, 146, 245–8, 403.
36. GH 601, no. 12A/79: Notification by his Excellency the High Commissioner, 4 January 1879.
37. CP 27: Chelmsford to Colonel W. Bellairs, 31 December 1878.
38. Special War Correspondent, 13 January 1879, in Lock and Quantrill (comps.), *Red Soldier*, p. 25; Thompson, *Black Soldiers*, p. 33.
39. A574: Lord Chelmsford to Biggs Andrews, 15 May 1878.
40. See Laband, 'Zulu Civilians', pp. 64–76.
41. TS 35: Frere to Shepstone, 4 December 1878.
42. TS 35: Chelmsford to Shepstone, 21 November 1878.
43. *BPP* (C. 2252), no. 20: Lord Chelmsford's order of 17 January 1879.
44. CP 13/1: Memorandum by Chelmsford, 30 October 1878; WC II/2/2: Chelmsford to Wood, 11 and 16 December 1878; CP 27: Chelmsford to Frere, 13 January 1879; Laband, 'Cohesion of Zulu Polity', pp. 3–7.
45. WC II/2/2: Chelmsford to Wood, 16 December 1878.
46. Fynney, *Zulu Army*, *passim*. See Laband, 'Zulu Army', pp. 36–7.
47. Callwell, *Small Wars*, pp. 32–3, 47.
48. Regan, *Military Incompetence*, pp. 22–6.
49. Clery to Alison, 13 April 1879, in Clarke, *Zululand at War*, p. 126.
50. Clery to Alison, 18 March 1879, in Clarke, *Zululand at War*, p. 122.

CHAPTER 20: Zulu Preparations to Resist, January 1879

1. See Laband, *Zulu Kings*, pp. 11–241.
2. See Fynney, *Zulu Army*, 'Distinguishing Regimental Marks'.
3. For detailed descriptions of the Zulu military system, see Knight, *Zulu Army*, pp. 46–90; and Laband and Thompson, *Anglo-Zulu War*, pp. 9–19.
4. The following discussion is based on Laband, 'War-Readiness', pp. 37–41.
5. Iliffe, *Honour*, p. 142.
6. See Fynney, *Zulu Army*, 'The Zulu Army in Attack Formation'.
7. For a discussion on Zulu battle tactics, see Laband, *Zulu Nation*, pp. 39–41; Knight, *Zulu Army*, pp. 192–223.
8. The ensuing discussion on the Zulu import of firearms in the 1870s is based on Guy in 'Firearms', pp. 559–60.

9. In February 1878 the British pressured the Portuguese to halt the sale of guns and ammunition to Africans through Delagoa Bay, although it took until August that year to make the ban effective.
10. Ballard, *John Dunn*, pp. 112–22.
11. See Guy, 'Firearms', p. 560; Storey, *Guns*, pp. 270–2; Knight, *Zulu Army*, pp. 167–9.
12. For the Zulu adoption of firearms and their military culture, see Laband, 'Firearms and the Zulu Kingdom', pp. 229–43.
13. Webb and Wright (eds), *James Stuart Archive*, Vol. 2, p. 144: Mahungane and Nkomuza, 20 November 1900.
14. C. Peers, *African Wars*, pp. 10–13; Laband and Thompson, *Anglo-Zulu War*, pp. 14–15; Laband, *Historical Dictionary*, p. 86.
15. CP 8/40: Report by Bishop Schreuder on conversation with the *induna* Ulankana son of Undikile, 10 February 1879
16. Vijn, *Cetshwayo's Dutchman*, p. 39.
17. Nzuzi, 'Supplement', *Natal Mercury*, 22 January 1929.
18. Webb and Wright (eds), *Zulu King*, p. 30.
19. Laband, *Kingdom in Crisis*, p. 54.
20. Laband, 'Zulu Strategic and Tactical Options', pp. 5–7.
21. The amaMpondo would be annexed by the Cape in 1884.
22. Monteith, 'Cetshwayo and Sekhukhune', pp. 173–6; Delius, *Pedi Polity*, pp. 236, 238.
23. Webb and Wright (eds), *Zulu King Speaks*, pp. 29–31; Vijn, *Cetshwayo's Dutchman*, pp. 31, 96–7.
24. Webb and Wright (eds), *Zulu King Speaks*, pp. 30–1.
25. Vijn, *Cetshwayo's Dutchman*, p. 31.
26. See Fynney, *Zulu Army*, for the number of men he assigns each 'Corps or Regiment'.
27. Laband, 'Zulu Civilians', p. 65; Laband, 'Zulu Strategic and Tactical Options', p. 5.
28. For Cetshwayo's strategic calculations, see Webb and Wright (eds), *Zulu King Speaks*, pp. 30–2, 55.
29. Norbury, *Naval Brigade*, p. 219.
30. Laband, *Kingdom in Crisis*, pp. 59–60.
31. Laband, 'Zulu Strategic and Tactical Options', p. 8.
32. See Laband, 'Zulu War Rituals', pp. 1824–5.
33. Laband, 'Zulu Civilians' p. 64.
34. Knight, *Zulu Rising*, p. 431.
35. Nzuzi, 'Supplement', *Natal Mercury*, 22 January 1929.
36. Greaves and Knight, *Who's Who*, Vol. 2, pp. 143–5, 165–6, 199–201; Laband, *Historical Dictionary*, p. 105, 152–3, 204–5.

CHAPTER 21: **Isandlwana: The Division of Forces**

1. There is an excellent discussion of the Isandlwana campaign in Beckett, *Isandlwana 1879*, pp. 47–91, and a short but authoritative account in Beckett, *Rorke's Drift*, pp. 40–61, but the best full description is in Knight, *Zulu Rising*,

pp. 233–473. See Laband and Thompson, *Anglo-Zulu War*, pp. 99–108, for a succinct account.

2. CP 27: Chelmsford to Durnford, 19 January 1879.
3. Mathews, 'Chelmsford', pp. 135–6.
4. Greaves and Knight, *Who's Who*, Vol. 2, pp. 57–8.
5. Laband, *Kingdom in Crisis*, p. 78.
6. Thompson, *Black Soldiers*, pp. 42–3.
7. Laband, *Kingdom in Crisis*, pp. 75–9; Greaves and Knight, *Who's Who*, Vol. 2, pp. 172–5; Laband, *Historical Dictionary*, pp. 157–8.
8. Norris-Newman, *In Zululand*, p. 52; Thompson, *Black Soldiers*, p. 43; Knight, *Zulu Rising*, pp. 278–84.
9. *BPP* (C. 2260), enc. 2 in no. 13: Glyn's evidence to the Court of Inquiry, 27 January 1879.
10. Clery to Colonel Harman, 17 February [1879], in Clarke, *Zululand at War*, p. 83.
11. Knight, *Zulu Rising*, pp. 287–9.
12. Anon, *24th Regiment*, 'Zulu War', pp. 11–12.
13. Mathews, 'Isandlwana', p. 118.
14. Droogleever, *Road to Isandlwana*, p. 224.
15. CP 27: Chelmsford to Durnford, 14 January 1879.
16. Mathews, 'Chelmsford', pp. 123–4.
17. CP 27: Chelmsford to Durnford, 19 January 1879.
18. Clery to Colonel Harman, 17 February [1879], in Clarke, *Zululand at War*, p. 83.
19. Clarke, *Invasion of Zululand*, pp. 65, 67, 77–8, n. 27.
20. *BPP* (C. 2260), enc. 2 in no. 12: Statement of Lieutenant-Colonel J. Crealock, n.d. (Henceforth, Crealock's Statement.)
21. Clery to Alison, 28 April 1879, in Clarke, *Zululand at War*, p. 128.
22. Clery to Alison, 28 April 1879, in Clarke, *Zululand at War*, pp. 128–9.
23. Snook, *How Can Man Die Better*, pp. 90–1.
24. *BPP* (C. 2260), enc. 2 in no. 13: Clery's evidence to the Court of Inquiry, 27 January 1879. When writing to Colonel Harman on 17 February 1879, however, Clery put forward another version of his evidence, claiming that he had added at the end of the note: 'Act strictly on the defensive. Colonel Durnford has been ordered up from Rorke's Drift to reinforce the camp.'
25. Crealock's Statement.
26. *BPP* (C. 2454), sub-enc, Appendix: Report on Proceedings of 21st, 22nd, 23rd and 24th January 1879 by Lieutenant A.B. Milne, n.d. (Henceforth Milne's Report.)
27. Snook, *How Can Man Die Better*, pp. 90–1.
28. Clery to Alison, 28 April 1879, cited in Clarke, *Zululand at War*, p. 129.
29. *BPP* (C. 2252), enc. 2 in no. 22: Chelmsford to Stanley, 27 January 1879.
30. Harness, 'Zulu Campaign', p. 480.
31. Crealock's Statement.
32. Clery to Harman, 17 February [1879], in Clarke, *Zululand at War*, p. 84. See also Clery to Alison, 28 April 1879, in Clarke, *Zululand at War*, p. 129, for a reiteration of this statement.
33. Child (ed.), *Harford*, p. 23.

34. Henry Curling to Mother, 2 February 1879, in Greaves and Best (eds), *Curling Letters*, pp. 91–2.
35. For the official chronology of events outside the camp on 22 January, see War Office, *Field Operations*, pp. 38–44.
36. Norris-Newman, *In Zululand*, p. 54.
37. Thompson, *Black Soldiers*, pp. 43–4.
38. For a facsimile of the message, see Laband and Mathews, *Isandlwana*, opposite p. 1. The original is in the Royal Welsh Regimental Museum, Brecon.
39. Clery to Harman, 17 February [1879], in Clarke, *Zululand at War*, p. 84.
40. Milne's Report.
41. War Office, *Field Operations*, p. 40.
42. *BPP* (C. 2260). Enc. In no. 13: Court of Inquiry, 27 January 1879: Captain Gardner's evidence; *BPP* (C.2260), enc. 2 in no. 12: Gardner's statement, 26 January 1879.
43. Hamilton-Browne, *Lost Legionary*, p. 127.
44. Crealock's Statement.
45. Hamilton-Browne, *Lost Legionary*, p. 132.
46. Thompson, *Black Soldiers*, p. 45.
47. Hamilton-Browne, *Lost Legionary*, pp. 126–33.
48. For Harness's account of events, see Harness to Co., 25 January and 4 June 1879; in Clarke, *Invasion of Zululand*, pp. 70, 135.
49. Durnford, 'Isandhlwana', p. 14.
50. Anonymous letter in the *Daily News*, in Clarke, *Invasion of Zululand*, p. 68.
51. Milne's Report.
52. Harness to Co., 25 January 1879, in Clarke, *Invasion of Zululand*, p. 70.
53. Durnford, 'Lord Chelmsford's Statements', pp. 13–14.
54. Norris-Newman, *In Zululand*, p. 57.
55. Clery to Alison, 18 March 1879, in Clarke, *Zululand at War*, p. 122.
56. Crealock's Statement.
57. Crealock's Statement.
58. Milne's Report.
59. Norris-Newman, *In Zululand*, p. 58.
60. Ashe and Wyatt-Edgell, *Zulu Campaign*, pp. 57–8. Maj. Waller Ashe was in fact the sole author, or rather the coordinator of the book, and his main informant was Capt. the Hon. Edmund Wyatt-Edgell of the 17th Lancers who was killed in the battle of Ulundi.
61. Child (ed.), *Harford*, p. 30.
62. CP 8/15: Chelmsford to Frere, 23 January 1879.
63. Hamilton-Browne, *Lost Legionary*, p. 134.
64. Hamilton-Browne, *Lost Legionary*, pp. 134–5.
65. Crealock's Statement; Hamilton-Browne, *Lost Legionary*, p. 135; Norris-Newman, *In Zululand*, p. 59; Child (ed.), *Harford*, pp. 30–1.
66. Captain Matthew Gossett, in Knight, *Zulu Rising*, p. 111.
67. Milne's Report.
68. Clery to Harman, 17 February [1879], in Clarke, *Zululand at War*, p. 85.

69. 'Letter from an Abergavenny Man,' *Abergavenny Chronicle*, 29 March 1879, in Spiers, *Victorian Soldier*, p. 42.

CHAPTER 22: Isandlwana: Return to the Camp and Rorke's Drift

1. Crealock's Statement.
2. Coghlan, *Anglo-Zulu War Diaries*, p. 17.
3. Hallam Parr, *Kafir and Zulu Wars*, p. 194.
4. Crealock's Statemen; Milne's Report.
5. Hallam Parr, *Kafir and Zulu Wars*, p. 196.
6. Clery to Harman, 17 February [1879], in Clarke, *Zululand at War*, p. 85.
7. Milne's Report.
8. See War Office, *Field Exercise*, pp. 224–6: 'Advance by a Battalion in Fighting Formation'; Thompson, *Black Soldiers*, p. 68.
9. Crealock's Statement.
10. Arthur Harness to Co., 25 January 1879, in Clarke, *Invasion of Zululand*, pp. 70–1.
11. The eclipse was most complete at 2.29 p.m.
12. Clery to Harman, 17 February [1879], in Clark, *Zululand at War*, p. 86.
13. CP 8/15: Chelmsford to Frere, 23 January 1879.
14. Elliott, *Victoria Cross in Zululand*, p. 83.
15. *BPP* (C. 2454), sub-enc, Appendix: Notes on the Report on Proceedings, n.d.
16. Sergeant W. E. Warren, RA, *The Bristol Observer*, 29 March 1879, in Emery, *Red Soldier*, p. 94.
17. Child (ed.), *Harford*, pp. 34–5.
18. Hamilton-Browne, *Lost Legionary*, pp. 138.
19. Milne's Report.
20. Thompson, *Black Soldiers*, p. 69.
21. Child (ed.), *Harford*, p. 33.
22. Clery to Harman, 17 February [1879], in Clarke, *Invasion of Zululand*, p. 88.
23. Milne's Report.
24. Quoted in Knight, *Zulu Rising*, p. 518.
25. Hamilton-Browne, *Lost Legionary*, pp. 141–2.
26. Sergeant W. E. Warren, RA, *The Bristol Observer*, 29 March 1879, in Emery, *Red Soldier*, p. 94.
27. Laband, *Kingdom in Crisis*, pp. 88, 109.
28. Laband, 'Zulu War Rituals', p. 1825.
29. WO 33/34: Chelmsford to Secretary of State for War, 27 January 1879; Child (ed.), *Harford*, pp. 35–6; Thompson, *Black Soldiers*, p. 69; Knight, *Zulu Rising*, pp. 519–20.
30. Norris-Newman, *In Zululand*, p. 65.
31. Milne, Report.
32. Coghlan, *Anglo-Zulu War Diaries*, pp. 21–2.
33. Knight, *Rorke's Drift*, p. 112.
34. Quoted in Knight, *Zulu Rising*, p. 526.
35. Webb and Wright (eds), *Zulu King Speaks*, pp. 30–1.
36. There is a considerable literature on the battle of Rorke's Drift. For a concise account, see Laband and Thompson, *Anglo-Zulu War*, pp. 109–13. The Zulu

perspective is explored in Laband, *Kingdom in Crisis*, pp. 96–113. An excellent analysis is given in Yorke, *Rorke's Drift*, pp. 77–138, and exhaustive accounts are to be found in Knight, *Rorke's Drift*, pp. 34–116, in Knight, *Zulu Rising*, pp. 424–532, and in Snook, *Like Wolves on the Fold*, pp. 1–126. See also Greaves, *Rorke's Drift*, 98–135.

37. CP 8/15: Chelmsford to Frere, 23 January 1879.
38. Laband and Thompson, *Buffalo Border*, pp. 44–5, 110.
39. WC II/2/2: Chelmsford to Wood, 28 January 1879.
40. Milne's Report; War Office, *Field Operations*, p. 59; Laband and Thompson, *Buffalo Border*, pp. 45, 100; Thompson, *Black Soldiers*, pp. 74–5.
41. War Office, *Field Operations*, pp. 59–60; Laband and Thompson, *Buffalo Border*, pp. 97–8, 110.

CHAPTER 23: Panic in Natal and the Despatch of Reinforcements

1. CP 8/29: telegram, Chelmsford to Stanley, 27 January 1879.
2. CP 28: Chelmsford to Cambridge, 10 February 1879.
3. Laband and Thompson, *Field Guide*, pp. 184–7.
4. Thompson, 'Defence of Pietermaritzburg', p. 284.
5. Laband and Thompson, *Anglo-Zulu War*, pp. 188–90; Thompson, 'Defence of Durban', pp. 307, 309.
6. Robinson, *Life Time in South Africa*, pp. 133–4.
7. Figes, *Crimea*, p. 372.
8. RA VIC/ADD/E/1/8513: Chelmsford to Cambridge, 27 January, 1879.
9. James Sivewright to Mrs Merriman, 8 February 1879, in Mathews, 'Chelmsford', p. 225.
10. RA VIC/ADD/E/1/8534: Chelmsford to Cambridge, 10 February 1879.
11. WC II/2/2: Chelmsford to Wood 28 January 1879.
12. CP 8/48: Chelmsford to Stanley, 8 February 1879.
13. WC II/2/2: Chelmsford to Wood, 3 February 1879.
14. Laband and Thompson, *Field Guide*, tables on pp. 31–3; Thompson, 'Town and Country', pp. 226–44.
15. CP 8/29: telegram: Chelmsford to Stanley, 27 January 1879.
16. CP 28: Chelmsford to Cambridge, 1 February 1879.
17. RA VIC/ADD/E/1/8535: Stanley to Cambridge 11 February 1879.
18. Beckett, *Politics of Command*, pp. 208–9.
19. RA VIC/ADD/E/1/85343: Chelmsford to Cambridge, 10 February 1879.
20. Cambridge to Frere, Private, 13 February 1879, in Clark, *Zululand at War*, pp. 109–10.
21. War Office, *Field Operations*, Appendix B: 'The Zulu War – Despatch of Troops to Natal after the Receipt of Intelligence of the Affair at Isandhlwana'.
22. War Office, *Field Operations*, pp. 83–4. For a full account of the wreck of the *Clyde*, see *Supplement to the London Gazette*, 7 May 1879, pp. 3251–4.
23. CP 8/48: Chelmsford to Stanley, 8 February 1879.
24. Cambridge to Frere, 22 May 1879, in Clark, *Zululand at War*, p. 114.
25. Quoted in St Aubyn, *Royal George*, pp. 191–2.
26. Cambridge to Frere, Private, 13 February 1879, in Clark, *Zululand at War*, p. 110.

27. CP 28: Chelmsford to Cambridge, 1 February 1879.
28. Laband and Thompson, *Buffalo Border*, pp. 46–7; Beckett, 'Chelmsford's Major-Generals', pp. 122–3.
29. Beckett, 'Chelmsford's Major-Generals', pp. 123–6; Beckett, *Politics of Command*, pp. 209–11; Laband (ed.), *Chelmsford's Zululand Campaign*, pp. 274, 275, 279–80.
30. Cambridge to Frere, 27 February 1879, in Clark, *Zululand at War*, p. 110.
31. Crealock to Alison, 2 and 9 February 1879, in Clarke, *Zululand at War*, p. 93.
32. WO 32/7709: Chelmsford to Stanley, 9 February 1879.
33. *Hansard*, 3rd series, Vol. 244, c. 1497: Duke of Cambridge, House of Lords, 24 March 1879.
34. Chelmsford to Maj.-Gen. Martin Dillon, 14 May 1879, in Clark, *Zululand at War*, p. 94.
35. CP 28: Chelmsford to Cambridge, 1 February 1879.
36. WC II/2/2: Chelmsford to Wood, 16 February 1879.
37. WC II/2/2: Chelmsford to Wood, 3 March 1879.
38. WC II/2/2: Chelmsford to Wood, 24 March 1879.

CHAPTER 24: **Regrouping, January–April 1879**

1. Crealock to Alison, 9 February 1879, in Clarke, *Zululand at War*, p. 93.
2. WW II/2/2: Chelmsford to Wood, Private, 3 February 1879.
3. CP 28: Chelmsford to Cambridge, 1 February 1879.
4. The FLH, Kaffrarian Rifles and the Transvaal Burgher Force were already with No. 4 Column; while Raaff's Transvaal Rangers and Weatherley's Border Horse were with No. 5 Column. The only new mounted troops to join Wood would be Baker's Horse raised in the Eastern Cape; and the Natal Native Horse, reconstituted from the Edendale Horse and Hlubi's Troop that had fought at Isandlwana. See Laband, *Historical Dictionary*, pp. 10, 100, 129, 180–1, 226–7, 288–9, 303.
5. CP 26/23: Memorandum by Chelmsford, 20 February 1879.
6. WC II/2/2: Chelmsford to Wood, 6 March 1879.
7. CP 9/102: Wood to Chelmsford, 16 February 1879); WC II 2/2/: Chelmsford to Wood, 23 February 1879.
8. For the operations of the Left Column from 22 January to 12 March 1879, see War Office, *Field Operations*, pp. 51–2, 67–72; Jones, *Boiling Cauldron*, pp. 213–50.
9. WC II/2/2: Chelmsford to Wood, 28 January 1879.
10. Laband, 'Phongolo River Frontier', pp. 193–8.
11. WC II/2/2: Chelmsford to Wood, 29 January 1879.
12. WC II/2/2: Chelmsford to Wood, 13 February 1879.
13. Laband, *Transvaal Rebellion*, p. 21.
14. Laband, 'Phongolo River Frontier', pp. 198–9; Laband and Thompson, *Zulu War*, pp. 138–41.
15. RA VIC/ADD/E/1/8630: Cambridge to Chelmsford, 16 April 1879.
16. For the operations of Pearson's No. 1 Column between mid-January and mid-March 1879, see *BPP* (C. 2367), enc. (A) in no. 19: Pearson to Military Secretary, 9 April 1879; War Office, *Field Operations*, pp. 53–8, 60–1; Castle and Knight, *Fearful Hard Times*, pp. 36–142.

17. Laband and Thompson, *Anglo-Zulu War*, pp. 82–5.
18. CP 28: Chelmsford to Cambridge, 1 February 1879.
19. Laband, 'British Fieldworks', pp. 70–7.
20. *BPP* (C. 2260), enc. A in no. 3: telegram: Chelmsford to Pearson, 27 January 1879.
21. PP 3: Chelmsford to Pearson, 2 February 1879.
22. CP 7/13: Pearson to Chelmsford, 2 February 1879.
23. *BPP* (C. 2260), enc. A in no. 3: telegram: Lieutenant Kingscote to Bellairs, 29 January 1879.
24. Laband, *Kingdom in Crisis*, pp. 137–8.
25. CP 28: Chelmsford to Cambridge, 1 February 1879.
26. WC II/2/2: Chelmsford to Wood, 3 February 1879; PP 3: Chelmsford to Pearson, 2 February 1879; CP 28: Chelmsford to Pearson, 8 February 1879; CP 28: Chelmsford to Cambridge, 10 February 1879.
27. Mathews, 'Chelmsford', p. 231.
28. WC II/2/2/: Chelmsford to Wood, 7 February 1879.
29. WC II/2/2: Chelmsford to Wood, 16 February 1879.
30. CP 26/23: memorandum by Chelmsford, 20 February 1879.
31. CP 7/24: Major Barrow to Crealock, 25 February 1879.
32. War Office, *Field Operations*, note to p. 57.
33. WO 32/7718: Chelmsford to Stanley, [17] March 1879.
34. CP 28: Chelmsford to Cambridge, 1 February 1879.
35. War Office, *Field Operations*, p. 170; Thompson, *Black Soldiers*, pp. 85–9.
36. *BPP* (C. 2318), no. 4: Bulwer to Frere, 29 January 1879.
37. WC II/2/2: Chelmsford to Wood, 23 February 1879.
38. *BPP* (C. 2318): no. 6: Chelmsford to Frere, 31 January 1879.
39. *BPP* (C. 2318), no. 14: memorandum by Chelmsford, 4 March 1879. In April 1879, 600 members of the disbanded 3rd NNC were reassembled to make up the Weenen Contingent deployed in Defensive District II. It was mustered in traditional African fashion and not along British military lines, but its morale remained poor, thus undercutting Bulwer's argument. See Laband, *Historical Dictionary*, p. 303.
40. *BPP* (C. 2318): no. 8: Frere to Bellairs, 11 February 1879.
41. *BPP* (C. 2318), no. 14: Frere to Bulwer, 5 March 1879.
42. *BPP* (C. 2318), no. 21: Bulwer to Frere, 7 March 1879; *BPP* (C. 2318), no. 22: memorandum by Frere, 11 March 1879.
43. *BPP* (C. 2316), no. 18: Frere to Hicks Beach, 20 March 1879.
44. AGO 1/16/1, p. 405: memorandum by M. H. Gallway, 14 March 1879.
45. See Laband, 'Divided Command', pp. 342–5 and Laband, 'Border Levies', pp. 154–7 for a discussion about the dispute over the use of the border levies.
46. Laband and Thompson, *Anglo-Zulu War*, p. 38.
47. GH 1325, no. 6/79: Chelmsford to Bulwer, 13 January 1879.
48. GH 1325, no.1356/79: Bulwer to Chelmsford, 28 February 1879.
49. *BPP* (C. 2318) enc. 10 in no. 1: minute by Frere, 11 February 1879.
50. CP 12/16: Frere to Chelmsford, 18 February 1879.
51. See *BPP* (C. 2318), no. 19: Extracts from Minutes of the Proceedings of the Executive Council, 1 March 1879. The Natal government was proved right when

cross-border raids did indeed provoke Zulu retaliation at Middle Drift on 25 June, setting off a renewed invasion panic in Natal. See Laband and Thompson, *Anglo-Zulu War*, pp. 128–31; Laband and Thompson, *Umvoti*, pp. 56–62.

52. WC II/2/2: Chelmsford to Wood, 3 March 1879.
53. WC II/2/2: Chelmsford to Wood, 17 March 1879
54. GH 1326, no. 32/79: Bulwer to Frere, 9 April 1879; *BPP* (C. 2318), enc. I in no. 13: Bulwer to Chelmsford, 9 April 1879.
55. Laband and Thompson, *Umvoti*, pp. 47–9.
56. CP 28: Chelmsford to Cambridge, 1 February 1879; CP 8/48: Chelmsford to Stanley, 8 February 1879.
57. Webb and Wright (eds), *Zulu King Speaks*, pp. 29, 56–7.
58. CP 13/5: minute by Frere, 4 April 1879. For the government's identical position regarding the terms of the rejected ultimatum, see *Hansard*: 3rd Series, Vol. 244, c. 1626: House of Lords, 25 March 1879: Viscount Cranbrook.
59. For Zulu negotiations during March 1879, see Laband, 'Humbugging the General?', pp. 49–54.
60. *BPP* (C. 2318), enc. 2 in no. 9: J. E. Fannin to Colonial Secretary, 2 March 1879.
61. CP 13/50: General Clifford to Chelmsford, 13 June 1879.
62. *BPP* (C. 2318), enc. 2 in no. 9: Frere to Chelmsford, 3 March 1879.
63. FC 2/4: Fannin to his wife, 10 March 1879.
64. Crealock to Alison, 2 March 1879, in Clark, *Zululand at War*, p. 155.
65. WC II/2/2/: Chelmsford to Wood, 3 March 1879.
66. *BPP* (C. 2316), no. 14 (and seven encs): Frere to Hicks Beach, 14 March 1879; *BPP* (C. 2318), no. 2: Wood to Hallam Parr, 16 March 1879; Laband, *Kingdom in Crisis*, pp. 140–2, 148–9.
67. *BPP* (C. 2318), enc. 1 in no. 10: telegram, Col. Horston to F. S. Haden, n.d. The three messengers were sent off on 15 April to find Chelmsford, fruitlessly going first to Pietermaritzburg, and then pursuing him into the field in Zululand. See Laband, 'Humbugging the General?', pp. 52–3.

CHAPTER 25: Failing to Shift the Blame, January–April 1879

1. CP 8/29: telegram, Chelmsford to Stanley, 27 January 1879. For Chelmsford's full despatch concerning the battle of Isandlwana, see *BPP* (C. 2252): enc. 2 in no. 22: Chelmsford to Stanley, 27 January 1879.
2. *BPP* (C. 2260), enc. 2 in no. 13: Proceeding of Court of Inquiry, 27 January 1879.
3. CP 8/44: Bellairs to Chelmsford, 5 February 1879. Ino fact, besides the eight whose testimony was recorded, that of many other witnesses was taken but, as Harness explained, 'was not considered sufficiently reliable to be placed on record'. (Harness, 'Zulu Campaign', p. 480.)
4. *BPP* (C. 2260), enc. 2 in no. 13: Colonel F. C. Hassard, Helpmekaar, 29 January 1879. As Harness wrote to his sister on 7 February 1879, 'We merely took evidence and did not give any opinion.' (Clarke, *Invasion of Zululand*, p. 93.)
5. Forbes, 'Lord Chelmsford', p. 223.
6. Harness, 'Zulu Campaign', pp. 481–2.
7. Evidence printed in WO 33/34: *Zulu War, Miscellaneous, 1878–9*, pp. 234–42. It is conveniently reprinted in Beckett, *Isandlwana*, pp. 105–21.

8. *BPP* (C. 2260), enc. 2 in no. 13: Chelmsford to Stanley, Durban, 8 February 1879.
9. RA VIC/ADD/E/1/8578: Chelmsford to Cambridge, 7 March 1879.
10. See Lock and Quantrill, *Zulu Victory*, pp. 236–46, 251–7 for their careful assessment of the evidence.
11. Clarke, *Zululand at War*, pp. 26–9.
12. War Office, *Field Operations*, pp. 31–49 and the map, 'Military Survey of the Battle-Field of Isandhlwana'.
13. Laband, 'Durnford'.
14. CP 8/31: Chelmsford's notes on the findings of the Court of Inquiry, n.d.
15. War Office, *Field Exercise*, pp. 53–4, 97–9.
16. CP 8/44: Bellairs to Chelmsford, 5 February 1879
17. RA VIC/ADD/E/1/8513: Chelmsford to Cambridge, 27 January 1879.
18. *BPP* (C. 2252), no. 21: Frere to Hicks Beach, 27 January 1879 (received 1 March 1879).
19. Droogleever, *Road to Isandhlwana*, pp. 181–2; Beckett, *Isandlwana*, p. 75.
20. WC II/2/2: Chelmsford to Wood, 16 February 1879.
21. Bell, 'Offensive Defensive', pp. 157, 159.
22. Laband and Mathews, *Isandlwana*, p. 50; Beckett, *Rorke's Drift*, pp. 55–7.
23. CP 8/31: Chelmsford's notes on the findings of the Court of Inquiry, n.d.
24. Thompson, *Black Soldiers*, pp. 48–57.
25. War Office, *Field Operations*, p. 36.
26. For the report on the action at Rorke's Drift, see WO 32/7737: Chard to Glyn, 25 January 1879.
27. CP 8/40: Chelmsford to Stanley, 8 February 1879.
28. *The Times*, 12 February 1879.
29. Beckett, *Isandlwana*, pp. 94–5; Beckett, *Politics of Command*, p. 306; Yorke, *Rorke's Drift*, p. 141.
30. RA VIC/ADD/E/1/8534: Chelmsford to Cambridge, 10 February 1879.
31. WO 30/129: Ellice to Chelmsford, 6 March 1879.
32. Cambridge to Frere, 6 March 1879, in Clarke, *Zululand at War*, p. 112. Cambridge returned to the attack on 20 March, writing to Frere: 'I do entreat you to impress upon Chelmsford the absolute necessity of sending us home all the information he can possibly give us . . . Forgive me for making this remark but it is necessary in Chelmsford's interest that I should do so.' (Clarke, *Zululand at War*, p. 114.)
33. See WO 33/34: *Zulu War, Miscellaneous, 1878–9*, pp. 281–304, for the correspondence concerning this affair.
34. Crealock to Alison, 24 February 1879, in Clark, *Zululand at War*, p. 99.
35. Forbes, 'Lord Chelmsford', p. 223.
36. RA VIC/ADD/E/1/8629: Chelmsford to Cambridge, 27 March 1879.
37. Clery to Alison, 11 March 1879, in Clarke, *Zululand at War*, pp. 100, 102.
38. Captain J. F. Maurice to Alison, 23 June 1879, in Clarke, *Invasion of Zululand*, p. 272.
39. Buckle, *Letters of Queen Victoria*, p. 10: Journal, 11 February 1879; pp. 10–11 and n. 1 on p. 11: Colonel Ponsonby to Colonel Stanley, 11 February 1879. Beaconsfield was sceptical and wrote acerbically to the Queen on the same day: 'It is to be hoped that [Lord Chelmsford] may be equal to the occasion.'

40. RA VIC/ADD/E/1/8578: Chelmsford to Cambridge, 7 March 1879.
41. Yorke, *Rorke's Drift*, pp. 142–3.
42. Prince of Wales to Lady Frere, 27 March, in Clarke, *Zululand at War*, p. 116.
43. Beaconsfield to Queen Victoria, 12 March 1879, in Yorke, *Isandlwana*, p. 142.
44. Blake, *Disraeli*, p. 674.
45. *BPP* (C. 2260), no. 15: Hicks Beach to Frere, 19 March 1879.
46. *Hansard*, 3rd Series, Vol. 244, cc. 908, 922: House of Commons, 14 March 1879: E. Jenkins.
47. Beckett, *Rorke's Drift*, pp. 92–4, 96–7.
48. See Emery, *Red Soldier*, for the classic collection of soldiers' letters from the Anglo-Zulu War.
49. Beckett, *Rorke's Drift*, pp. 90–1.
50. *Hansard*, 3rd Series, Vol. 244, cc. 1606, 1695: House of Lords, 25 March 1879.
51. *Hansard*, 3rd Series, Vol. 244, c. 1865: House of Commons, 27 March 1879: Sir Charles Dilke.
52. *Hansard*, 3rd Series, Vol. 244, c. 1909: House of Commons, 27 March 1879: J. Chamberlain [*sic*].
53. *Hansard*, 3rd Series, Vol. 244, cc. 2011–12, 2020, 2021: House of Commons, 28 March 1879: Sir Robert Peel.
54. *Hansard*, 3rd Series, Vol. 244, cc. 2023–28: House of Commons, 28 March 1879: Sir Charles Russell.
55. *Hansard*, 3rd Series, Vol. 244, cc. 2032–33: House of Commons, 28 March 1879: Evelyn Ashley.
56. *Hansard*, 3rd Series, Vol. 244, cc. 2070, 2077: House of Commons, 28 March 1879: Colonel Stanley.
57. *Hansard*, 3rd Series, Vol. 245, c. 123: House of Commons, 30 March 1879.
58. Prince of Wales to Frere, 4 April March, in Clarke, *Zululand at War*, p. 116

CHAPTER 26: The Eshowe Relief Column, March–April 1879

1. War Office, *Field Operations*, p. 57.
2. WO 32/7718: Chelmsford to Stanley, [17] March 1879.
3. War Office, *Field Operations*, pp. 63, 162–3.
4. WC II/2/2: Chelmsford to Wood, 27 February and 14 March 1879.
5. *BPP* (C. 2316), enc. 1 in no. 17: Chelmsford to Stanley, 17 March 1879.
6. WC II/2/2: Chelmsford to Wood, 26 March 1879.
7. CP 36: telegram, Chelmsford to Hicks Beach, 25 March 1879.
8. WO 32/7722: Chelmsford to Stanley, 25 March 1879.
9. WC II/2/2: Chelmsford to Wood, 26 March 1879.
10. CP 26/9.
11. CP 26/9: Chelmsford, *Special Instructions*, p. 3.
12. CP 7/37: Memorandum by Chelmsford, n.d. [*c.* 26 March 1879].
13. For Dunn's career up to this point, see Ballard, *John Dunn*, pp. 15–135.
14. Molyneux, *Campaigning*, p. 125.
15. Moodie (ed.), *John Dunn*, p. 101.
16. Moodie (ed.), *John Dunn*, pp. 98–101, 105.
17. Mathews, 'Chelmsford', p. 247.

18. WO 32/7727: Chelmsford to Stanley, 10 April 1879.
19. Norris-Newman, *In Zululand*, pp. 129–30.
20. Laband and Knight, *War Correspondents*, pp. v–vi, viii–ix, xi; Laband, 'British Way of War', p. 18.
21. Laband and Thompson, *Umvoti*, pp. 47–9; Thompson, 'Captain Lucas', pp. 172, 174.
22. CP 7/38: Drummond to Chelmsford, 27 March 1879: report of spy Magumbi; Laband, *Kingdom in Crisis*, pp. 170–1.
23. For the advance of the Eshowe Relief Column, see WO 32/7727: Chelmsford to Stanley, 10 April 1879; War Office, *Field Operations*, pp. 63–4; Norris-Newman, *In Zululand*, pp. 130–6; Molyneux, *Campaigning*, pp. 121–30; Mathews, 'Chelmsford', pp. 248–51; Castle and Knight, *Fearful Hard Times*, pp. 182–6.
24. Moodie (ed.), *John Dunn*, p. 102.
25. Moodie (ed.), *John Dunn*, p. 105.

CHAPTER 27: The Battle of Gingindlovu, 2 April 1879

1. Molyneux, *Campaigning*, p. 130.
2. Laband, *Kingdom in Crisis*, pp. 172–3.
3. Ashe and Wyatt-Edgell, *Zululand Campaign*, p. 165.
4. For the battle of Gingindlovu, see WO 32/7727: Chelmsford to Stanley, 10 April 1879; *Supplement to the London Gazette*, 7 May 1879, pp. 3247–50; Norris-Newman, *In Zululand*, pp. 136–42; Molyneux, *Campaigning*, pp. 131–8; Moodie, *Moodie's Zulu War*, pp. 135–44; Mathews, 'Chelmsford', pp. 251–9; Laband, *Kingdom in Crisis*, pp. 173–8; Castle and Knight, *Fearful Hard Times*, pp. 189–214; Laband and Thompson, *Anglo-Zulu War*, pp. 86–9; Thompson, *Black Soldiers*, pp. 93–5.
5. Capt. Alan Hart, in Knight, *Zulu War*, p. 203.
6. Fynney, *Zulu Army*.
7. For these units of irregular horse, see Laband, *Historical Dictionary*, pp. 128–9, 146, 174–5, 182–3; Thompson, *Black Soldiers*, pp. 91–2.
8. Molyneux, *Campaigning*, p. 131.
9. Ashe and Wyatt-Edgell, p. 167.
10. *Natal Mercury*, Zulu War Supplement, April 1879: 'From our own Correspondent', dated 11 April 1879; Norris-Newman, *In Zululand*, p. 138; Mackinnon and Shadbolt, *South African Campaign*, pp. 247–8; Castle and Knight, *Fearful Hard Times*, p. 205.
11. Mynors, *Letters*, p. 30: 2 April 1879. Mynors was destined to die ingloriously of dysentery at Fort Pearson on 25 April 1879 See Mackinnon and Shadbolt, *South African Campaign*, pp. 221–2. His affecting last moments were described by Lieutenant Edward Hutton to his father, M. Baskerville Mynors, in a letter of 8 May 1879 (Mynors, *Letters*, pp. 49–50).
12. Castle and Knight, *Fearful Hard Times*, p. 168.
13. Mackinnon and Shadbolt, *South African Campaign*, pp. 213–4.
14. Hamilton-Browne, *Lost Legionary*, p. 208.
15. Castle and Knight, *Fearful Hard Times*, pp 199–200.
16. Hamilton-Browne, *Lost Legionary*, p. 213.
17. Norris-Newman, *In Zululand*, p. 140.

18. Moodie (ed.), *John Dunn*, pp. 102–3.
19. Molyneux, *Campaigning*, p. 135.
20. Molyneux, *Campaigning*, pp. 133–4.
21. Lt Julius Backhouse, in Knight, *Zulu War*, p. 208.
22. Ashe and Wyatt-Edgell, *Zululand Campaign*, pp. 175–6.
23. Molyneux, *Campaigning*, p. 140.
24. Molyneux, *Campaigning*, p. 141.
25. Ashe and Wyatt-Edgell, *Zulu Campaign*, pp. 180–2; Molyneux, *Campaigning*, pp. 141–3.
26. Castle and Knight, *Fearful Hard Times*, p. 247.
27. CP 28: Chelmsford to Cambridge, 11 April 1879.
28. For this night alarm, see War Office, *Field Operations*, pp. 82–3; Molyneux, *Campaigning*, pp. 143–5.
29. WO 32/7727: Chelmsford to Stanley, 10 April 1879.
30. Castle and Knight, *Fearful Hard Times*, pp. 246–7; *Supplement to the London Gazette*, 7 May 1879, p. 3250.
31. Moodie (ed.), *John Dunn*, p. 104.
32. Molyneux, *Campaigning*, p. 146.
33. CP 28: Chelmsford to Cambridge, 11 April 1879.

CHAPTER 28: Preparing for the Second Invasion, April–May 1879

1. CP 23/28: Wood to Chelmsford, 10 April 1879.
2. Jones, *Boiling Cauldron*, pp. 252–82; Laband and Thompson, *Anglo-Zulu War*, pp. 176–9
3. See Laband, *Kingdom in Crisis*, pp. 147–66; Laband and Thompson, *Anglo-Zulu War*, pp. 180–3. For Wood's two official reports of 30 March 1879 on the battles of Hlobane and Khambula, see *Supplement to the London Gazette*, 7 May 1879, pp. 3243–6.
4. *Natal Colonist*, 25 September 1879: Cetshwayo's comments taken from the *Cape Times*.
5. WC II/2/2: Chelmsford to Wood, [*c.* 15] April 1879.
6. Crealock to Alison, 11 April 1879 in Clarke, *Zululand at War*, p. 169.
7. WC II/2/2: Chelmsford to Wood, 22 April 1879.
8. Crealock to Alison, 19 March 1879, in Clarke, *Zululand at War*, p. 151.
9. CP 19/9: Chelmsford to Stanley, 20 April 1879.
10. Crealock to Alison, 14 April 1879 in Clarke, *Zululand at War*, pp. 170–1.
11. War Office, *Field Operations*, p. 92.
12. RA VIC/ADD/E/1/8678: Cambridge to Chelmsford, 22 May 1879.
13. RA VIC/ADD/E/1/8681: Cambridge to Chelmsford, 23 May 1879.
14. Clery to Alison, n.d. [May 1879], in Clarke, *Zululand at War*, p. 181.
15. See the collection of tradesmen's invoices for March–April 1879 in CP 26/1 and CP 26/2.
16. See CP 28: Chelmsford to Cambridge, 11 April 1879; and WC II/2/2: Chelmsford to Wood, 25 April 1879; Mathews, 'Chelmsford', p. 264.
17. CP 15/36: Chelmsford to H. Crealock, 12 April 1879.
18. CP 24/5: Memorandum 'C' by Chelmsford, [?] February 1880.

19. Major F. S. Russell to Alison, 31 July 1879, in Clarke, *Invasion of Zululand*, p. 267.
20. WO 32/7732: Chelmsford to Stanley, 20 April 1879; WC II/2/2: Chelmsford to Wood, 22 and 25 April 1879.
21. Laband and Thompson, *Umvoti*, 50–1; Laband and Thompson, *Buffalo Border*, pp. 63–5; Thompson, 'Captain Lucas', pp. 172, 4; Thompson, 'Active Defence', p. 145.
22. For a detailed analysis of the 2nd Division's logistical problems, see Mathews, 'Transport and Supply', pp. 111–48 and 'Chelmsford', pp. 71–4, 267–9, 272–7; and French, *Chelmsford*, pp. 169–74.
23. WC II/2/2: Chelmsford to Wood, 22 April 1879.
24. RA VIC/ADD/E/1/8630: Cambridge to Chelmsford, 16 April 1879.
25. CP 28: Chelmsford to Cambridge, 11 April 1879.
26. WO 32/7732: Chelmsford to Stanley, 20 April 1879.
27. CO 879/15, African no. 198: Clifford to Bulwer, 24 May 1879.
28. CP 17/9: Clifford to Chelmsford 4 May 1879.
29. CP 17/13: Clifford to Chelmsford, 13 May 1879
30. WO 32/7736: Chelmsford to Stanley, 1 May 1879.
31. CP 16/15: Chelmsford to Stanley, 14 May 1879.
32. RA VIC/ADD/E/1/8681: Chelmsford to Cambridge, 23 May 1879.
33. CP 28: Chelmsford to Cambridge, 14 May 1879.
34. WO32/7732: Chelmsford to Stanley, 20 April 1879.
35. WO 32/7736: Strickland to Chelmsford, 26 April 1879. See also CP 17/8: Strickland to Clifford, 30 April 1879.
36. WO 32/7736: Chelmsford to Stanley, 1 May 1879.
37. CP 19/9: Chelmsford to Stanley, 20 April 1879.
38. CO 879/15, African, no. 198: Clifford to Bulwer, 3 May 1879.
39. *BPP* (C. 2367), no. 53: Frere to Hicks Beach, 5 May 1879.
40. French, *Chelmsford*, p. 174.
41. The *Natal Colonist*, 12 July 1879.

CHAPTER 29: Launching the Second Invasion, May–June 1879

1. Laband and Thompson, *Anglo-Zulu War*, pp. 74, 80, 81. The remains of Fort Crealock still exist, but those of Fort Chelmsford no longer do.
2. WO 32/7739: Chelmsford to Stanley, 14 May 1879.
3. WO 32/7752: Chelmsford to Stanley, 16 June 1879.
4. For the 2nd Division's advance up to 16 June 1879, see War Office, *Field Operations*, pp. 86–8; Mathews, 'Chelmsford', pp. 292–4, 297–8, 300–2, 307–8.
5. For the Prince Imperial's life up to the Anglo-Zulu War, see Knight, *Face to the Foe*, pp. 58–91.
6. Knight, *Face to the Foe*, pp. 106–10.
7. Queen Victoria's Journal, 24 February 1879, in Buckle (ed.), *Letters of Queen Victoria*, Vol. 3, pp. 11–12.
8. Queen Victoria to Cambridge, 24 February 1879, in Clarke, *Zululand at War*, p. 198, n. 3.
9. Cambridge to Frere, private, 25 February 1879 in Clarke, *Zululand at War*, p. 187.
10. RA VIC/ADD/E/1/8559: Cambridge to Chelmsford, 25 February 1879.

11. CP 28: Chelmsford to Cambridge, 11 April 1879.
12. Deléage, *End of a Dynasty*, p. 102.
13. Deléage, *End of a Dynasty*, p. 64.
14. WC II/2/2: Chelmsford to Wood, 1 May 1879.
15. Laband and Thompson, *Buffalo Border*, p. 67
16. Laband and Thompson, *Buffalo Border*, pp. 67–8 and *Anglo-Zulu War*, p. 94.
17. *BPP* (C. 2454), enc. 2 in no. 21: W. D. Wheelwright to Colonial Secretary, Natal, 21 May 1879.
18. Laband and Thompson, *Buffalo Border*, pp. 69–70; Laband and Thompson, *Umvoti*, pp. 56–67; Laband, *Kingdom in Crisis*, pp. 184–5; Thompson, 'Captain Lucas', p. 175.
19. For a discussion on the effect of the Anglo-Zulu War on Zulu civilians, see Laband, 'Kid Gloves', pp. 179–96 and 'Zulu Civilians', pp. 64–77.
20. WC II/2/2: Chelmsford to Wood, 25 April 1879.
21. WO 32/7772: Crealock to Wolseley: Memorandum on Operations of the First Division, 18 April to 7 July 1879.
22. Crealock to Alison, 28 June 1879, in Clarke, *Zululand at War*, p. 229.
23. Vandervort, *Wars of Imperial Conquest*, pp. 209–10.
24. Norris-Newman, *In Zululand*, p. 47.
25. *Natal Witness*, 23 August 1879: Ulundi correspondent.
26. Ashe and Wyatt-Edgell, *Zulu Campaign*, p. 305.
27. Lieven, 'Total War', p. 616. For further specific reference to 'total war' and/or 'genocide', see pp. 624, 618, 630, 631, 632.
28. Roberts and Guelff, *Documents on the Laws of War*, p. 181.
29. Laband. 'Zulu Civilians', pp. 72–5.
30. WC II/2/2: Chelmsford to Wood, 19 May 1879.
31. WC II/2/2: Chelmsford to Wood, 16 May 1879.
32. Deléage, *End of a Dynasty*, pp. 131–2.
33. CP 13/19: Chelmsford to Stanley, 25 May 1879.
34. Laband and Thompson, *Buffalo Border*, pp. 71–3.
35. CP 13/19: Chelmsford to Stanley, 25 May 1879; WC II/2/2: Chelmsford to Wood, 30 May 1879.
36. Clery to Alison, 27 May, in Clarke, *Zululand at Ward*, p. 183; Forbes, 'Lord Chelmsford', pp. 227–8; Laband and Thompson, *Anglo-Zulu War*, p. 95.
37. Mathews, 'Lord Chelmsford', p. 280.
38. WC II/2/2: Chelmsford to Wood, 19 May 1879. Chelmsford quoted the proverb in Italian: '*Chi va piano, va sano e va lontano*.'
39. WC II/3/1: Chelmsford to Wood, n.d. [May 1879].
40. RA VIC/ADD/E/1/8681: Chelmsford to Cambridge, 23 May 1879.
41. Montague, *Campaigning*, pp. 132–3.
42. Montague, *Campaigning*, p. 170.
43. WC II/2/2: Chelmsford to Wood, 27 May 1879.
44. Molyneux. 'Hasty Defences', pp. 811–13; Plé, *Laagers*, pp. 11–16 and plates I and II; Molyneux, *Campaigning*, p. 156; Montague, *Campaigning*, 160.
45. Deléage, *End of a Dynasty*, p. 145.
46. WO 32/7752: Memorandum by Chelmsford, 15 June 1879.

47. WO 32/7744: Chelmsford to Stanley 31 May 1879.
48. Deléage, *End of a Dynasty*, pp. 145, 146.
49. Lord St Vincent's diary, *c.* 25 May 1879, in Clarke, *Invasion of Zululand*, p. 201.
50. CP 22: Chelmsford to H. Crealock, 31 May 1879.
51. CP 15/36: Chelmsford to H. Crealock, 12 April 1879.
52. Laband, 'Phongolo River Frontier', pp. 202–3.
53. For the operations of the Flying Column from 21 April to 17 June, see War Office, *Field Operations*, pp. 100–3.
54. Laband and Thompson, *Anglo-Zulu War*, pp. 158–60; Mackinnon and Shadbolt, *South African Campaign*, pp. 52–4.
55. Preston (ed.), *Wolseley's Journal*, p. 64: 27 July 1879.
56. WO 32/7752: Chelmsford to Stanley, 16 June 1879.
57. Preston (ed.), *Wolseley's Journal*, pp. 57, 64: 18 and 27 July 1879.
58. For a description of the confusion, see Bandsman M. M. Tuck, in Knight, *Zulu War*, p. 242.
59. For accounts of this false alarm, see Molyneux, *Campaigning*, pp. 169–70; *Mathews*, 'Chelmsford', pp. 300–1.
60. Clery to Alison, 17 June 1879, in Clarke, *Zululand at War*, p. 206.
61. Wood, *Midshipman to Field Marshal*, Vol. II, p. 76.
62. *BPP* (C. 2454), enc. 1 in no. 51: Buller to Chelmsford, 16 June 1879.
63. Fripp, 'Zulu War', p. 554.
64. WO 32/7752: Chelmsford to Stanley 16 June 1879; Molyneux, 'Hasty Defences', p. 807; Plé, *Laagers*, pp. 8–11; Laband and Thompson, *Anglo-Zulu War*, pp. 147–8.
65. Laband, *Kingdom in Crisis*, p. 192.
66. CP 13/5: minute by Frere, 4 April 1879.
67. Crealock to Alison, 31 May 1879, in Clarke, *Zululand at War*, p. 220.
68. WC 11/2/2: Chelmsford to Wood, 16 May 1879.
69. WO 32/7740: telegram, Crealock to Chelmsford, 16 May 1879.
70. CP 13/18: Crealock to Colonial Secretary, 21 May 1879.
71. *BPP* (C. 2374), enc. 10 in no. 32: telegram: Frere to Chelmsford, recd. 30 May 1879.
72. Laband, 'Humbugging the General', pp. 54–5.
73. *BPP* (C. 2454), D in enc. In no. 33: Report by W. Drummond, 6 June 1879.
74. Harness to Co, 4 June 1879, in Clarke, *Invasion of Zululand*, p. 133.
75. WO 32/7745: Chelmsford to Stanley, 2 June 1879.
76. CP 13/37: Chelmsford's message to the Zulu king, 4 June 1879, with the amendment of 5 June 1879; CP 13/39: notes by Crealock on the conversation between Chelmsford and the Zulu messengers, 5 June 1879.
77. CP 15/44: Crealock to Chelmsford, 11 June 1879.
78. *BPP* (C. 2454), C in enc. 7 in no. 51: Message from Chelmsford to the Zulu Chiefs, 16 June 1879.
79. WO 32/7752: Chelmsford to Drummond, 16 June 1879.

CHAPTER 30: **Misfortunes and Disputes, June 1879**

1. CP 11/8: Chelmsford to Stanley, 2 June 1879.

2. Harrison, *Notes on My Life*, p. 41.
3. Chelmsford to Cambridge, 2 June 1879, in Mathews, 'Chelmsford', p. 295.
4. For the death of the Prince Imperial and the conveyance of his remains to Britain, see CO 879/15, African, no. 196: Death of the Prince Imperial, 9 July 1879; War Office, *Field Operations*, pp. 93–5; Deléage, *End of a Dynasty*, pp. 172–6. For the best modern account, see Knight, *Face to the Foe*, pp. 194–221, 223–8. For Zulu accounts of his death, see Laband, 'Fought like a Lion', pp. 198–201.
5. Lt. Fred Slade to his mother, 2 June 1879, in Mathews, 'Chelmsford', p. 296; Montague, *Campaigning*, p. 160.
6. Maj. F. W. Grenfell, in Knight, *Face to the Foe*, p. 211.
7. WO 32/7754: 2nd Division, S.A. Army: Maj.-Gen. Newdigate's diary for the week ending 8 June 1879: 2 June 1879.
8. H. Scrivener to Mrs Bousfield, 22 December 1879, in Mathews, 'Chelmsford', p. 296.
9. Lt. James MacSwinney, in Knight, *Zulu War*, p. 203.
10. Deléage, *End of a Dynasty*, p. 176.
11. *Supplement to the London Gazette*, 21 June 1879.
12. Maj. Philip Anstruther to his wife Zaida, 11 and 13 June 1879, in Butterfield, *War and Peace in South Africa*, pp. 32–3.
13. WO 91/48: proceedings of a general court martial, 12 June 1879. See too WO 71/343: Chelmsford to Cambridge, 19 June 1879: Minutes of the Court Martial of Lt Carey for the death of the Prince Imperial.
14. WO 91/48: memorandum by Chelmsford, 19 June 1879.
15. Norris-Newman, *In Zululand*, p. 128.
16. Laband and Knight, *War Correspondents*, pp. 126.
17. See *Hansard*, 3rd Series, Vol. 247 cc. 401–3, 686–9: House of Commons: Questions, 19 and 26 June 1879.
18. RA VIC/ADD/E/1/8759: Cambridge to Chelmsford, 26 June 1879.
19. For Carey's court martial and reception in England, see Knight, *Face to the Foe*, pp. 238–47, 256–64.
20. WO 91/48: J. C. O'Dowd to Cambridge, 16 August 1879. Captain Carey (his promotion had been approved before the fatal patrol had taken place) returned to his regiment with his reputation in ruins, and died of peritonitis in 1883 while on duty in India.
21. Ellice to Wolseley, 16 August 1879, in Norris-Newman, *In Zululand*, pp. 313–15.
22. Queen Victoria to Frere, 21 August 1879, in Clarke, *Zululand at War*, p. 197.
23. CP 11/7: Ellice to Chelmsford, 10 October 1879.
24. Clery to Alison, 11 May [*should read* June] 1879, in Clarke, *Zululand at War*, p. 207.
25. Captain J. McSwiney to his mother, n.d., in Mathews, 'Chelmsford', p. 306.
26. Gunner of N Battery, 6th Brigade, RA, 6 June 1879, letter in *Aberystwyth Observer*, 26 July 1879, in Emery, *Red Soldier*, pp. 223–4.
27. Deléage, *End of a Dynasty*, pp. 163–4.
28. Preston (ed.), *Wolseley's Journal*, p. 68: 31 July 1879.
29. Crealock to Alison, 11 May [*should read* June] 1879, in Clarke, *Zululand at War*, p. 204.
30. Deléage, *End of a Dynasty*, p. 144.

31. WC II/2/2: Chelmsford to Wood, [?15 April 1879]
32. For Chelmsford's querulous comments about hostile war correspondents, see CP 28: Chelmsford to Stanley, 10 June 1879.
33. For the growing dissent between Clifford and Chelmsford, see French, *Chelmsford*, pp. 173–82; Beckett, *Politics of Command*, pp. 212–13.
34. CP 17/1: Gossett's memorandum on Clifford, n.d.
35. RA VIC/ADD/E/1/8852: Cambridge to Clifford, 12 August 1879.
36. Preston (ed.), *Wolseley's Journal*, p. 49: 30 June 1879.
37. See CP 17/34: memorandum by Chelmsford, 2 July 1879; Beckett, 'Chelmsford's Major-Generals', pp. 123, 125–7.
38. *See* Chapter 29.
39. CP 17/27: Clifford to Chelmsford, 19 June 1879.
40. CP 17/34: memorandum by Chelmsford, 2 July 1879.
41. RA VIC/ADD/E/1/8636: Clifford to Cambridge, 21 April 1879.
42. See Laband, 'Divided Command', pp. 345–7; Laband, 'Border Levies', pp. 157–61.
43. CP 28: Chelmsford to Cambridge, 11 April 1879.
44. *BPP* (C. 2318), enc. 2 in no. 13: Chelmsford to Bulwer, 12 April 1879.
45. GH 1326, no. 40/79: Bulwer to Chelmsford, 15 April 1879.
46. *BPP* (C. 2318), no. 18: Chelmsford to Bulwer, 18 April 1879.
47. GH 1221, no. 67/79: Bulwer to Hicks Beach, 16 April 1879; see *BPP* (C. 2318), no. 13 and seven encs: Bulwer to Hicks Beach, 16 April 1879 [recd 22 May].
48. WC II/2/2: Chelmsford to Wood, 25 April 1879.
49. GH 500, no. 2576/79: Chelmsford to Bulwer, 7 May 1879.
50. Laband and Thompson, *Anglo-Zulu War*, pp. 128–31.
51. *BPP* (C. 2482), no. 37: Wolseley to Hicks Beach, 27 July 1879.
52. Preston (ed.), Wolseley's Journal, p. 47: 28 June 1879.
53. *BPP* (C. 2318), no. 11: telegraphic, Hicks Beach to Bulwer, 19 May 1879.
54. See CO 879/15, African, no. 181a: Correspondence Relating to Native Levies for Raids into Zululand, 9 June 1879, pp. 2–10.

CHAPTER 31: **Supersession, May–June 1879**

1. WO 30/129: Ellice to Chelmsford, 6 March 1879. See Lock and Quantrill, *Zulu Victory*, pp. 265–80, for an analysis of Ellice's questions and Chelmsford's responses.
2. CP 28: Chelmsford to Cambridge,11 April 1879. See CP 8/56: Adjutant-General to Chelmsford, 6 March 1879, with Chelmsford's draft answers.
3. Chelmsford to Cambridge, 19 March 1879, in Duckers, 'War Letter from Lord Chelmsford'. This letter is from the collection of the late Peter Metcalf and is reproduced with permission of its current owner.
4. RA VIC/ADD/E/1/8646: Cambridge to Chelmsford, 1 May 1879.
5. Cambridge to Frere, 22 May 1879, in Clarke, *Zululand at War*, p. 114.
6. War Office, *Field Operations*, p. 174.
7. Stanley's private letter to Chelmsford does not appear to have been preserved with the Chelmsford Papers, but Cambridge's is in the Royal Archives. See RA VIC/ADD/E/1/ 8658: Cambridge to Chelmsford, 8 May 1879. See also Mathews, 'Chelmsford', pp. 302–3.

8. CP 28: Chelmsford to Stanley, 10 June 1879.
9. RA VIC/ADD/E/1/8715: Chelmsford to Cambridge, 10 June 1879.
10. Laband, *Transvaal Rebellion*, pp. 21–2.
11. Monypenny and Buckle, *Beaconsfield*, Vol. 2, pp. 1300–1.
12. Preston (ed.), *Wolseley's Journal*, pp. 25–7: 8 June 1879.
13. Beaconsfield to Queen Victoria, 30 May 1879, in Beckett, *Politics of Command*, p. 216. Beaconsfield noted that this batch of despatches on the trans-border raids and the Eshowe relief expedition was received on 21 May but they actually arrived on the 22nd, see *BPP* (C. 2318), nos. 13–17.
14. CP 19/13: Stanley to Chelmsford, 29 May 1879. On the same day, Chelmsford's old commander from Indian Mutiny days, now General Sir Alfred Horsford, the MS at the Horse Guards since 1874, wrote him a brief note warning him that Cambridge had ordered him to pen an official reprimand that 'may sound somewhat stiff'. However, in the light of their old camaraderie, Horsford added 'privately' that Chelmsford could 'depend' on his giving him 'every aid in my powers'. (CP 23/16: Horsford to Chelmsford, 29 May 1879).
15. Salisbury to Wolseley, 7 March 1879, in Preston (ed.), *Wolseley's Journal*, p. 310, n. 26.12.
16. Preston (ed.), *Wolseley's Journal*, p. 9.
17. Preston (ed.), *Wolseley's Journal*, p. 31: 25 May 1879.
18. *Hansard*: 3rd series, Vol. 246 c. 1250: House of Commons, 26 May 1879: Colonel Stanley.
19. Monypenny and Buckle, *Beaconsfield*, Vol. 2, p. 1297.
20. Monypenny and Buckle, *Beaconsfield*, Vol. 2, pp. 1301–6; Preston (ed.), *Wolseley's Journal*, pp. 6–7.
21. Buckle, *Letters of Queen Victoria*, pp. 22, 24: Journal, 18 and 26 May 1879.
22. Lord Beaconsfield to Queen Victoria, 27 May 1879, in Monypenny and Buckle, *Beaconsfield*, Vol. 2, p. 1304.
23. Queen Victoria to Beaconsfield, 23 and 26 May 1879, in Yorke, *Rorke's Drift*, p. 145.
24. Preston (ed.), *Wolseley's Journal*, p. 28: 23 May 1879.
25. St Aubyn, *Royal George*, p. 193.
26. WC II/2/2: Lady Wolseley to Wood, 21 June 1879.
27. Preston (ed.), *Wolseley's Journal*, p. 32: 23 May 1879.
28. *Hansard*: 3rd series, Vol. 246 c. 1242: House of Commons, 26 May 1879: Sir Robert Peel.
29. *Hansard*: 3rd series, Vol. 246 c. 1246: House of Commons, 26 May 1879: Sir Henry Havelock.
30. *Hansard*: 3rd series, Vol. 246 cc. 1250–1: House of Commons, 26 May 1879: Colonel Stanley.
31. *BPP* (C. 2318), no. 19, Appendix: Commissions issued to Lieutenant-General Sir Garnet Wolseley by Her Majesty's command, 28 May 1879.
32. Preston (ed.), *Wolseley's Journal*, pp. 33–4: 29 May 1879.
33. *BPP* (C. 2318), no. 21: Hicks Beach to Frere, 28 May 1879; no. 19: Hicks Beach to Bulwer, 28 May 1878; no. 22: Stanley to Chelmsford, 28 May 1879.
34. CP 17/24: Frere to Clifford, 15 June 1879.

35. *BPP* (C. 2482), enc. 1 in no. 12: Clifford to Bulwer, 16 June 1879.
36. War Office, *Field Operations*, p. 98.
37. CP 19/12: telegram, Stanley to Chelmsford, 28 May 1879.
38. Crealock to Alison, 16 June 1879, in Clark, *Zululand at War*, p. 209.
39. CP 11/23: Frere to Chelmsford, 18 June 1879.
40. F. Russell to Alison, 15 June 1879, in Clarke, *Zululand at War*, p. 210.
41. Crealock to Alison, 9 July 1879, in Clark, *Zululand at War*, p. 245.
42. Crealock to Alison, 16 June 1879, in Clark, *Zululand at War*, p. 209.
43. CP 17/25: Clifford to Chelmsford, 15 June. Despite all the bad blood between them, Clifford would write to Chelmsford regretting it had been so, and insisting (against the evidence) that he had served him loyally. (CP 17/33: Clifford to Chelmsford, 30 June 1879).
44. CP 11/23: Frere to Chelmsford, 18 June 1879.
45. WP 27/17: Adria Lady Chelmsford to Wood, Bath, 3 June 1879.
46. WC II/2/2: Chelmsford to DAG, 16 June 1879.
47. WO 32/7752: Chelmsford to Stanley, 16 June.
48. Crealock to Alison, 17 June 1879, in Clarke, *Zululand at War*, pp. 206–7.

CHAPTER 32: The Advance to the White Mfolozi, June–July 1879

1. For diagrams of the two forts, see Laband and Thompson, *Anglo-Zulu War*, pp. 148–9.
2. CP 16/42: Chelmsford to Stanley, 20 June; Laband and Thompson, *Anglo-Zulu War*, p. 149.
3. War Office, *Field Operations*, pp. 109–10; Laband, *Kingdom in Crisis*, p. 189.
4. *BPP* (C. 2482), enc. 1 in no. 23: Wood to DAG, 27 June 1879.
5. Ashe and Wyatt-Edgell, *Zulu Campaign*, p. 329.
6. Laband, *Kingdom in Crisis*, p. 208.
7. CP 16/51: Chelmsford to Stanley, 28 June 1879.
8. Ashe and Wyatt-Edgell, *Zulu Campaign*, p. 330 –2.
9. Crealock to Alison, 28 June 1879, in Clark, *Zululand at War*, pp. 229–30.
10. For a full account of the peace negotiations, see Laband, 'Humbugging the General?', pp. 57–9.
11. Vijn, *Cetshwayo's Dutchman*, pp. 42–9.
12. Vijn, *Cetshwayo's Dutchman*, pp. 134–5: Bishop Colenso's notes.
13. Vijn, *Cetshwayo's Dutchman*, pp. 49–50.
14. War Office, *Field Operations*, p. 110; *Illustrated London News*, 23 August 1879.
15. *BPP* (C. 2318), no. 22: Stanley to Chelmsford, 29 May 1879.
16. CP 13/54: message from Cetywayo to Chelmsford, 26 June 1879; *BPP* (C. 2482), no. 47: Chelmsford to Stanley, 28 June 1879: message to Ketshwayo from Chelmsford, 27 June 1879.
17. WO 32/7761: Gen. Newdigate's diary for the week ending 29 June 1879: 28 June 1879.
18. Crealock to Alison, 28 June 1879, in Clarke, *Zululand at War*, p. 229.
19. Preston (ed.), *Wolseley's Journal*, p. 40: 21 June 1879.

20. For Wolseley's movements between 23 June and 6 July, see *BPP* (C. 2482), no. 47: Wolseley to Hicks Beach, 30 June 1879 and 10 July 1879; Preston (ed.), *Wolseley's Journal*, pp. 42–52: 23 June to 6 July 1879.
21. For the content of these telegrams, see CP 16/46 and 17/31: Clifford to Major Degacher for forwarding on Wolseley's behalf, 26 June 1879. For Wolseley's unequivocal statement of the scope of his powers, see CP 16/53: telegram, Wolseley to Maj.-Gen. Marshall, 29 June 1879: 'I am not only full General and Commander in Chief of all troops in South Africa but High Commissioner with power to make peace without reference home.'
22. Preston (ed.), *Wolseley's Journal*, p. 45: 26 June 1879.
23. *BPP* (C. 2482), no. 47: Wolseley to Hicks Beach, 30 June.
24. CP 19/29: telegram, Clifford to Chelmsford. 24 June. Chelmsford only received this telegram on 2 July, and it elicited a furious memorandum: 'What he means by saying "his communication is cut off" I am at a loss to understand. Our communications have never been cut off for a day since I left Landman's Drift.' (CP 17/34: Chelmsford to Clifford, 2 July 1879.)
25. Preston (ed.), *Wolseley's Journal*, pp. 47, 48–9: 28 and 30 June 1879.
26. CP 21/1: telegram, Wolseley to Chelmsford, 28 June 1879.
27. Crealock to Alison, 2 July 1879, in Clarke, *Zululand at War*, p. 230.
28. *BPP* (C. 2454), enc. 1 in no. 42: telegram, Wolseley to Frere, Pietermaritzburg, 30 June 1879; *BPP* (C. 2482), no. 47: Wolseley to Hicks Beach, 30 June 1879.
29. *BPP* (C. 2482), no. 47: Wolseley to Hicks Beach, 30 June 1879.
30. WO 32/7757: Wolseley to Stanley, 30 June 1879.
31. Crealock to Alison, 29 June 1879, in Clarke, *Zululand at War*, p. 230.
32. CP 16/51: Chelmsford to Stanley, 28 June 1879.
33. WO 32/7771: Chelmsford to Wolseley, 28 June 1879. See too, CP 16/50: Chelmsford's memorandum to Wolseley, 28 June 1879.
34. *BPP* (C. 2482), no. 47: Wolseley to Hicks Beach, 30 June 1879.
35. Preston (ed.), *Wolseley's Journal*, p. 49: 1 July 1879.
36. CP 21/1: telegram, Wolseley to Chelmsford, 1 July 1879. See War Office, *Field Operations*, p. 114.
37. For the progress of the 1st Division between 20 June and 6 July, see War Office, *Field Operation*, pp. 104–107; and Mathews, 'Chelmsford', pp. 318–21. For Zulu submissions, see Laband, *Kingdom in Crisis*, pp. 191–2, 199–200 and 'Cohesion of the Zulu Polity', pp. 12–14.
38. Preston (ed.), *Wolseley's Journal*, p. 52: 5 and 6 July 1879; War Office, *Field Operations*, pp. 117–18.
39. WO 32/7771: Chelmsford to Wolseley, 28 June 1879; CP 16/51: Chelmsford to Stanley, 28 June 1879.
40. For Chelmsford's advance down to the White Mfolzoi up to 3 July, see Laband, *Ulundi*, pp. 10–15; War Office, *Field Operations*, 111–13.
41. *BPP* (C. 2482), enc. in no. 32: Chelmsford to Stanley, 6 July 1879.
42. *BPP* (C. 2482), Aa in enc. in no. 32: message from the Zulu king to Chelmsford, 30 June 1879.
43. *BPP* (C. 2482), A in enc. in no. 32: message from Chelmsford to Ketshwayo, 30 June 1879.

44. Crealock to Alison, 2 July 1879, in Clarke, *Zululand at War*, p. 231.
45. Robinson to Maude Lefroy, 6 July 1879, in Clarke, *Zululand at War*, p. 235.
46. Laband, 'Humbugging the General?', p. 58.
47. Molyneux, *Campaigning*, pp. 181–2.
48. Vijn, *Cetshwayo's Dutchman*, pp. 50–1; p. 144: Bishop Colenso's notes; Webb and Wright (eds), *Zulu King Speaks*, p. 58; Laband, *Kingdom in Crisis*, p. 211.
49. *BPP* (C. 2454), enc. 2 in no. 55: telegram no. 2: Chelmsford to Officer Commanding Landman's Drift, 2 July 1879.
50. Crealock to Alison, 2 July1879, in Clarke, *Zululand at War*, p. 231.
51. *BPP* (C. 2584), enc. B in no. 55: Wolseley to Chelmsford, telegram, 1 July 1879.
52. Molyneux, *Campaigning*, pp. 179.
53. *BPP* (C. 2454), enc. 3 in no. 55: telegram no. 3, Chelmsford to Clifford 3 July 1879.

CHAPTER 33: **The Battle of Ulundi, July 1879**

1. Molyneux, *Campaigning*, p. 186. 'Ant-bears' (or aardvarks) was a reference to earthworks because these long-snouted animals burrow into termite nests.
2. Mathews, 'Chelmsford', p. 323.
3. For Buller's reconnaissance, see WO 32/7764: Wood to DAG, 5 July 1879; WO 32/7763: Chelmsford to Stanley, 6 July 1879; War Office, *Field Operations*, p. 113; Ashe and Wyatt-Edgell, *Zulu Campaign*, pp. 337–41; Molyneux, *Campaigning*, pp. 183–4; Laband, *Ulundi*, pp. 16–19; Laband, *Kingdom in Crisis*, pp. 212–13; Laband and Thompson, *Anglo-Zulu War*, pp. 161–4.
4. Major Robinson to Maude Lefroy, 6 June 1879, in Clarke, *Zululand at War*, p. 237; Lord St Vincent's diary, 3 July 1879, in Clarke *Invasion of Zululand*, p. 193; Laband, *Ulundi*, p. 19–20
5. The account of the battle of Ulundi is based on the following sources: WO 32/7763: Chelmsford to Stanley, 6 July; *BPP* (C. 2482), no. 32: War Office to Colonial Office, 22 August 1879: Chelmsford to Stanley, 6 July 1879 and enclosures A to I; Chelmsford to Stanley, 7 July 1879 and enclosures; War Office, *Field Operations*, pp. 114–17, 164–6; Major Robinson to Maude Lefroy, 6 July 1879, in Clarke, *Zululand at War*, pp. 235, 237–9; Norris-Newman, *In Zululand*, pp. 316–27: Appendix I; Fripp, 'Zulu War', pp. 555–62; Molyneux, *Campaigning*, pp. 185–90; Ashe and Wyatt-Edgell, *Zulu Campaign*, pp. 341–51; Dawnay, *Campaigns*, pp. 65–71; Moodie, *Moodie's Zulu War*, pp. 194–213, for a selection of newspaper accounts; Emery, *Red Soldier*, pp. 226–38, for soldiers' letters describing the battle; French, *Chelmsford*, pp. 223–7; Mathews, 'Chelmsford', pp. 324–36; Laband, *Ulundi*, pp. 21–45; Laband, *Kingdom in Crisis*, pp. 213–31; Laband and Thompson, *Anglo-Zulu War*, pp. 165–9; Thompson, *Black Soldiers*, pp. 148–52.
6. For the employment of infantry squares in colonial warfare, see Callwell, *Small Wars*, pp. 256–76.
7. Ashe and Wyatt-Edgell, *Zulu Campaign*, p. 344.
8. Ashe and Wyatt-Edgell, *Zulu Campaign*, p. 346.
9. Laband, *Kingdom in Crisis*, p. 207.
10. Wood, *Midshipman*, Vol. II, p. 81.
11. See Guy, *Zulu Kingdom*, pp. 58–9; Belich, *New Zealand Wars*, p. 322.
12. Colenso, *Zulu War*, p. 447; Callwell, *Small Wars*, p. 439.

13. Laband, *Kingdom in Crisis*, p. 176.
14. RA VIC/ADD/E/1/8777: Chelmsford to Cambridge, 6 July 1879.
15. NCO of the 17th Lancers, *North Devon Herald*, 18 September 1879, in Emery, *Red Soldier*, p. 233.
16. Molyneux, *Campaigning*, p. 186.
17. Dawnay, pp. 70–1.
18. Fripp, 'Zulu War', p. 560.
19. Forbes, *Daily News*, despatch dated 5 July 1879, in Moodie, *Moodie's Zulu War*, p. 202.
20. Melton Prior in the *Times of Natal*, in Moodie, *Moodie's Zulu War*, p. 197.
21. Lord St Vincent's diary, 4 July 1879, in Clarke, *Invasion of Zululand*, p. 195.
22. Ashe and Wyatt-Edgell, *Zulu Campaign*, p. 348.
23. Molyneux, *Campaigning*, pp. 189.
24. Dawnay, *Campaigns*, p. 70.
25. Rumour in colonial circles had it that Drummond was drunk when he rode into oNdini. See Tabler, *Pioneers of Natal*, p. 32.
26. WO 32/7763: Chelmsford to Stanley, 6 July 1879.
27. Frank Russell to Alison, 6 July 1879, in Clarke, *Zululand at War*, pp. 233–4.
28. Robinson to Maud Lefroy, 6 July 1879, in Clarke, *Zululand at War*, p. 239.
29. Harness to his sister Co., 6 July 1879, in Clarke, *Invasion of Zululand*, p. 150.
30. Robinson to Maud Lefroy, 6 July 1879, in Clarke, *Zululand at War*, p. 239.

CHAPTER 34: **Resignation, July–August 1879**

1. Molyneux, *Campaigning*, p. 190.
2. Greaves and Best (eds), *Curling Letters*, p. 135: Curling to Mama, 5 July 1879.
3. Preston (ed.), *Wolseley's Journal*, p. 54: 11 July 1879.
4. See the *Illustrated London News*, 9 August 1879, for the eulogising of Forbes's ride.
5. Laband and Knight, *War Correspondents*, pp. xii–xiv, 143–5.
6. See WO 32/7763: Chelmsford to Stanley, 6 July 1879: *BPP* (C. 2482), enc. in no. 32: Chelmsford to Stanley, 7 July 1879.
7. Dawnay, *Campaigns*, pp. 72–3.
8. *BPP* (C. 2454), enc. 1 in no. 55: Military Secretary to Captain Parr, 6 July 1879.
9. *BPP* (C. 2454) no. 45: telegram, Frere to Hicks Beach, 8 July 1879.
10. *BPP* (C. 2454) no. 49: Hicks Beach to Frere, 24 July 1879.
11. *BPP* (C. 2454) no. 49: Hicks Beach to Wolseley, 24 July 1879.
12. CP 16/61: Prince of Wales to Lady Chelmsford, 24 July 1879.
13. CP 16/61: Stanley to Lady Chelmsford, 28 July 1879.
14. CP 16/61: Alfred Thesiger to Lady Chelmsford, 23 July 1879.
15. CP 16/61: Lady Frere to Lady Chelmsford, telegram delivered on 24 July 1879.
16. War Office, *Field Operations*, pp. 107–8, 119–21; Mathews, 'Chelmsford', pp. 318–21; Laband, *Kingdom in Crisis*, pp. 201–2.
17. For the movements of the 2nd Division and the Flying Column between 4 and 19 July, see War Office, *Field Operations*, pp. 116–18; 122–3, 124.
18. CP 21/1: telegram: Wolseley to Chelmsford, 1 July 1879.
19. CP 19/13: Stanley to Chelmsford, 29 May 1879.
20. CP 28/1: Chelmsford to Stanley, n.d. [5 July 1879].

21. WO 32/7763: Chelmsford to Stanley, 6 July 1879. This despatch was omitted when the *British Parliamentary Papers* for the period were published.
22. RA VIC/ADD/E/1/8777: Chelmsford to Cambridge, 6 July 1879.
23. See Crealock to Alison, 9 July 1879, in Clarke, *Invasion of Zululand*, p. 245.
24. *BPP* (C. 2482), no. 58: War Office to Colonial Office: Lord Chelmsford's General Order No. 124, 6 July 1879.
25. CP 21/1: telegram, Chelmsford to Wolseley, 6 July 1879.
26. Molyneux, *Campaigning*, pp. 191.
27. WO 32/7771: Chelmsford to Wolseley, 7 July 1879.
28. Orders, No. 62, in Clarke, *Zululand at War*, p. 263, n. 3.
29. Crealock to Alison, 9 July 1879, in Clarke, *Invasion of Zululand*, p. 245.
30. WO 32 /7770: telegram, Chelmsford to Wolseley, n.d. [9 July 1879].
31. WO 32/7770: Chelmsford to Stanley, 9 July 1879. For the original draft of this despatch, see CP 21/7.
32. RA VIC/ADD/E/1/8782: Chelmsford to Cambridge, 10 July 1879.
33. Cambridge to Frere, 26 August 1878, in Clarke, *Zululand at War*, 275.
34. Ashe and Wyatt-Edgell, *Zulu Campaign*, pp. 354–5.
35. WO 32/7771: Chelmsford to Wolseley, telegram, 9 July 1879. See also CP 21/7.
36. WO 32/7767: Precis of Diaries of Officers Commanding Posts on Frontiers and Lines of Communication: Fort Newdigate, 6–9 July; Fort Evelyn [?] July; Conference Hill, 7–9 July 1879.
37. CP 21/5: telegram: Wolseley to Chelmsford, 9 July 1879.
38. Preston (ed.), *Wolseley's Journal*, pp. 53–4: 9 July 1879.
39. *BPP* (C. 2482), enc. in no. 47: Wolseley to Stanley, 10 July 1879. For Wolseley's despatch to Hicks Beach along similar lines, see *BPP* (C. 2454), no. 62: Wolseley to Hicks Beach, 10 July 1879.
40. Laband and Thompson, *Anglo-Zulu War*, p. 153.
41. CP 21/4: Lt.-Col. H. Brackenbury to Chelmsford, 8 July 1879.
42. *BPP* (C. 2584), enc. E in no. 55: Chelmsford to Wolseley, 11 July 1879.
43. *BPP* (C. 2482), no. 36: Wolseley to Hicks Beach, 27 July 1879.
44. Bulwer to Edward Bulwer, 26 July 187, in Clarke, *Invasion of Zululand*, p. 220.
45. CP 21/10: Chelmsford to Stanley, 20 February 1879 with annexures A to E.
46. *BPP* (C. 2584): enc. in no. 55: Chelmsford to Stanley, February 20 1879.
47. Preston (ed.), *Wolseley's Journal*, pp. 54–5: 12 July 1879.
48. CP 21/9: Wolseley to Chelmsford, 12 July 1879.
49. CP 28/1: Chelmsford to Wolseley, 14 July 1879.
50. Molyneux, *Campaigning*, pp. 193.
51. Clery to Alison, 12 July 1879, cited in Clarke, *Zululand at War*, pp. 248.
52. Preston (ed.), *Wolseley's Journal*, p. 56: 15 July 1879; p. 57: 16 July 1879; *BPP* (C. 2482), enc. in no. 47: Wolseley to Stanley, 18 July 1879; Molyneux, *Campaigning*, p. 194.
53. Preston (ed.), *Wolseley's Journal*, p. 57: 16 July.
54. *BPP* (C. 2482), enc. in no. 47: Wolseley to Stanley, 18 July 1879.
55. War Office, *Field Operations*, pp. 120–8.
56. Preston (ed.), *Wolseley's Journal*, p. 61: 20 July 1879.
57. Molyneux, *Campaigning*, pp. 201.

58. *Natal Mercury*, 21, 25 July.
59. Preston (ed.), *Wolseley's Journal*, p. 62: 22 July 1879.
60. Crealock to Alison, 21 July 1879, in Clarke, *Zululand at War*, p. 249.
61. *Natal Mercury*, 28 July 1879.
62. Preston (ed.), *Wolseley's Journal*, p. 63: 24 July 1879.
63. Bulwer to Edward Bulwer, 26 July 1879, in Clarke, *Invasion of Zululand*, pp. 220–1.
64. Molyneux, *Campaigning*, pp. 202; Ashe and Wyatt-Edgell, *Zulu Campaign*, pp. 371–2.
65. *Natal Mercury*, 29 July 1879.
66. CP 24/1: text of Chelmsford's speech in Cape Town written on Government House paper, n.d.; Molyneux, *Campaigning*, pp. 203–4.
67. Greaves and Best (eds), *Curling Letters*, p. 135: Curling to Mama, 5 July 1879.
68. For a succinct account of the Transvaal Rebellion, see Laband, 'First Anglo-Boer War', pp. 167–86.
69. Quoted in St Aubyn, *Royal George*, p. 194.
70. War Office, *Field Operations*, pp. 128, 132–6; Guy, *Destruction of the Zulu Kingdom*, pp. 60–4.
71. War Office, *Field Operations*, pp. 136–8; Guy, *Destruction of the Zulu Kingdom*, pp. 69–78; Laband and Thompson, 'Reduction of Zululand', pp. 201–7; Laband, *Later Zulu Wars*, pp. 32–5.
72. For a map of the operations of Baker Russell's and Clarke's Columns, see Laband and Thompson, *Anglo-Zulu War*, p. 63.
73. For the Second Anglo-Pedi War, see Laband, *Zulu Warriors*, pp. 265–77.
74. War Office, *Field Operations*, pp. 129–31; Laband, *Zulu Nation*, pp. 330–2; Thompson, *Black Soldiers*, 166–72.

CHAPTER 35: The Shadow of Isandlwana, August 1879–January 1887 421

1. Molyneux, *Campaigning*, p. 206.
2. Ashe and Wyatt-Edgell, *Zulu Campaign*, p. 371.
3. Russell, 'We Carved Our Way to Glory', p. 58.
4. Laband and Knight, *War Correspondents*, p. 150.
5. Preston (ed.), *Wolseley's Journal*, p. 61: 20 July 1879.
6. WO 30/129: Ellice to Chelmsford, 11 August 1879. See Lock and Quantrill, *Zulu Victory*, pp. 280–3.
7. Beckett, *Politics of Command*, p. 127.
8. CP 18/34: Chelmsford to Military Secretary, Horse Guards, 1 January 1881 and enclosure; CP 18/35: General Whitmore to Chelmsford, 10 January 1881.
9. Beckett, *Rorke's Drift*, p. 90.
10. Best, 'Victoria Cross Holders'; Michell, 'Medals of the Zulu War'.
11. The robes of the GCB are of crimson satin lined with white taffeta with the star of the order embroidered on the left shoulder. The high-crowned hat is of black velvet with a plume of white ostrich feathers. See Duckers, *British Orders*, pp. 22–4.
12. Beaconsfield to Queen Victoria, 4 September 1879, in French, *Chelmsford*, p. 272. Wolseley was later also made GCB at the termination of the Zulu campaign.

13. Beaconsfield to Queen Victoria, 30 August 1879; Queen Victoria to Beaconsfield, 1 September 1879, in Monypenny and Buckle, *Beaconsfield*, Vol. 2, pp. 1331–2. See also Blake, *Disraeli*, pp. 673–4.
14. Buckle, *Letters of Queen Victoria*, p. 40: Journal, 3 September 1879; p. 42: Queen Victoria to Beaconsfield, 6 September 1879.
15. CP 16/61: telegram, Chelmsford to Lady Chelmsford, 4 September 1879.
16. Preston (ed.), *Wolseley's Journal*, p. 320, n, 61.2; David, *Zulu*, pp. 379–80.
17. Buckle (ed.), *Letters of Queen Victoria*, p. 44: Queen Victoria to Beaconsfield, 11 September 1879.
18. Manning, *Britain against the Xhosa and Zulu*, pp. 197–8; Manning, *Evelyn Wood*, pp. 137–8.
19. Quoted in French, *Chelmsford*, p. 240.
20. Preston, ed., *Wolseley's Journal*, p. 107: 4 September 1879.
21. Quoted in French, *Chelmsford*, pp. 241, 242.
22. Quoted in French, *Chelmsford*, p. 242.
23. Prochaska, 'Duchess of Teck'. In 1893 Mary Adelaide of Teck's daughter Victoria Mary married the future King George V.
24. French, *Chelmsford*, p. 300. Lt.-Col. the Hon. Sir Eric Thesiger, DSO, would live until 1961.
25. *The Times*, 25 August 1879: Chelmsford's letter to the editor.
26. *Hansard*: 3rd series, Vol. 255 c. 1561: House of Lords, 19 August 1880: Lord Chelmsford.
27. *BPP* (Printed Paper no.148 of 1880): *Copy of Reports into Recent Expenditure in South Africa, 18 March 1880*: Report 1: Zulu War, p. 12.
28. *BPP* (Printed Paper no. 150 of 1880): *Casualties among the Troops, British and Native, engaged in the Transkei and Zulu Campaigns, 15 February 1880*, pp. 3–5; Spiers, *Victorian Army*, p. 296.
29. For a discussion on relative Zulu and British casualty rates, see Laband, 'Kid Gloves', pp. 185–7.
30. Laband and Knight, *War Correspondents*, p. xiv.
31. Forbes, 'Lord Chelmsford, pp. 216–34.
32. Forbes, 'Lord Chelmsford', p. 216.
33. French, *Chelmsford*, p. 259.
34. CP 24/5: Memoranda A and B are the initial, pencilled drafts of memorandum C (February 1880) that attempts to rebut Forbes page by page from p. 216 to p. 230 of his article; while Memorandum D engages with pp. 231–4 of the article which mainly cover the landing of stores at Port Durnford and the withdrawal from Ulundi. The detailed and extremely lengthy notes in memorandum D attempt to refute Forbes point by point.
35. CP 24/5: Memorandum C by Lord Chelmsford, February 1879.
36. CP 22/15: Sir Deighton Probyn to Chelmsford, 15 March 1880.
37. Harness, 'Zulu Campaign', pp. 806–14.
38. Harness, 'Zulu Campaign', p. 483.
39. CP 22/30: Lord Strathnairn to Chelmsford, 16, 17 August 1880; CP 24/2: Strathnairn to Chelmsford, 17 August 1880.
40. Robson, 'Rose'.

41. For the full debates, see *Hansard:* 3rd Series, Vol. 255 cc. 1543–67; and Vol. 256 cc. 1025–35: House of Lords: Motion: 19 August and 2 September 1880.
42. *Hansard*: 3rd series, Vol. 255 c. 1561: House of Lords, 19 August 1880: Lord Chelmsford.
43. *Hansard*: 3rd series, Vol. 256 cc. 1026–8: House of Lords, 2 September 1879: Lord Strathnairn.
44. *Hansard*: 3rd series, Vol. 256 c. 1035: House of Lords, 2 September 1880: Lord Chelmsford.
45. *Hansard*: 3rd series, Vol. 256 c. 1035: House of Lords, 2 September 1880: Lord Strathnairn.
46. CP 22/21: Wesley Francis to Chelmsford, 2 September 1880.
47. CP 20/l: claims by Forbes, 10 May, 2 and 4 June 1881; CP 20/7: Horse Guards to Chelmsford, 10 May 1881; Ralph Thompson, Horse Guards to Forbes, 2 June 1881; Laband and Knight, *War Correspondents*, p. 145.
48. *Punch*, 7 May 1881.
49. For Colley's career, see Beckett, 'Colley', pp. 74–81; for Colley's defeats, see Laband, *Majuba*, pp. 76–90; 103–22; Laband, 'First Anglo-Boer War', pp. 176–83.
50. E. Durnford, *Isandhlwana, 22nd January*, p. 24.
51. CP 22/5: E Durnford to Chelmsford, 2 December 1879.
52. CP 22/6: Chelmsford to E. Durnford, [?] December 1879.
53. E. Durnford, *Lord Chelmsford's Statements*, p. 3.
54. Droogleever, *Road to Isandhlwana*, pp. 243–4.
55. Guy, *View across the River*, pp. 46–7; Laband, 'Durnford'.
56. Frances Colenso assisted by Edward Durnford, *Zulu War.*
57. Edward Durnford (ed.), *Soldier's Life*. See Droogleever, *Road to Isandhlwana*, pp. 244–5; Guy, *View across the River*, pp. 56–7.
58. For the affair over the papers supposedly taken from Anthony Durnford's body, see French, *Chelmsford*, pp. 248–54; Droogleever, *Road to Isandhlwana*, pp. 245–6; Guy, *View across the River*, pp 77, 120–2, 149; and Beckett, *Isandlwana*, pp. 76–7.
59. CP 22/38: T. Shepstone to Colonel Curtis, 11 March 1886.
60. CP 22/39: Theophilus Shepstone Jnr to Chelmsford, 15 March 1886.
61. CP 22/41: Chelmsford to T. Shepstone, 14 April 1886.
62. CP 22/45: General H. Torrens to Chelmsford, n.d.
63. *Times of Natal*, 10 December 1886: Frances Colenso to the editor.
64. CP 22/44: Chelmsford to Colonel Harman, 8 July 1886.
65. CP 22/52, Chelmsford to E. Durnford, 6 September 1886; CP 22/53: E. Durnford to Chelmsford, 10 September 1886.
66. *Times of Natal*, 5 January 1887: E. Durnford to the editor.

CHAPTER 36: **The Courtier General, April 1882–April 1905**

1. See French, *Chelmsford*, pp. 298–9.
2. *Debrett's Peerage*, 1904, p. 178; Lejeune and Lewis, *Gentlemen's Clubs*, pp. 85–7, 277–81. The original home of the Carlton Club in Pall Mall, which Chelmsford frequented, was destroyed by German bombs in October 1940. The United Service Club closed its doors in 1976.

3. Spiers, *Late Victorian Army*, pp. 126–7.
4. Duckers, *British Orders*, pp. 38–9.
5. St. Aubyn, *Royal George*, pp. 350–1.
6. Wessels, 'Roberts', pp. 167–89.
7. Corvi, 'Wolseley', pp. 17–25.
8. Manning, 'Evelyn Wood', pp. 37–42.
9. Miller, 'Buller', pp. 58–70.
10. See Manning, *Britain against the Xhosa and Zulu*, p. 202.
11. Robb, 'Viscount Chelmsford'.
12. 'Chelmsford, Viscount', *Cracroft's Peerage*.
13. Maitland, 'Thesiger, Sir Wilfred'. Mention might also be made of Wilfred Thesiger's first cousin once removed, Ernest Thesiger, CBE (1879–1961), the son of Sir Edward Thesiger, General Lord Chelmsford's youngest brother. Ernest was a successful stage and screen actor with a career spanning five decades. He had a lifelong interest in embroidery and needlework. See Anderson, 'Thesiger, Ernest'.

CONCLUSION: 'Ill-Luck Always Attends upon Mismanagement'

1. 'Jehu Junior', 'Statesmen. – No. CCCLXX. General Lord Chelmsford, G.C.B.', *Vanity Fair*, 3 September 1881, pp. 137–8. See Clarke, *'Vanity Fair'*, pp. 72–3.
2. *The Times*, 10 April 1905.
3. Verner and Parker, *Duke of Cambridge*, Vol. II, p. 165.
4. Low, *Soldiers of the Victorian Age*, Vol. II, p. 108.
5. Preston (ed.), *Wolseley's Journal*, pp. 25–7: 8 June 1879.
6. Clery to Alison, 11 May [*should read*] June 1879, in Clarke, *Zululand at War*, p. 207.
7. Mathews, 'Chelmsford', p. 350.
8. TS 32: Thesiger to T. Shepstone, 13 August 1878.
9. Clery to Alison, 13 April 1879, in Clarke, *Zululand at War*, p. 126.
10. WO 30/129: Ellice to Chelmsford, 11 August 1879.
11. *The Times*, 10 April 1905.
12. Elliott, *Victoria Cross in Zululand*, p. 84.
13. Beckett, 'Command in South Africa', p. 96.
14. Soon thereafter that would prove the case with Maj.-Gen. Sir George Pomeroy-Colley, Wolseley's Chief of Staff in Zululand. Although an academically brilliant soldier, his conduct of the First Anglo-Boer War proved disastrous, and culminated with his death during his defeat on Majuba in 1881.
15. WC II/3/1: Chelmsford to Wood, n.d. [May 1879].
16. WC II/2/2: Chelmsford to Wood, 19 May 1879.
17. Miller, 'Buller', pp. 65–70.
18. The distant Northern Border War and the First Anglo-Pedi War were conducted by the commanders on the spot, the first successfully, the second not.

Bibliography

Note: these sources are confined to those directly referred to in the text or footnotes.

Manuscript Sources

Campbell Collections, University of KwaZulu-Natal, Durban

KCM 89/9: Papers of Field Marshal Sir Henry Evelyn Wood:
- WP 26: Correspondence, 1878.
- WP 27: Correspondence, 1879.

The National Archives, Kew

- WO 30/129: Correspondence between the Adjutant-General and General Office Commanding, Cape of Good Hope, 1879.
- WO 32/7680: Reports on operations in Cape Colony and relations with civil government.
- WO 32/7681: Report on battle of Quintana.
- WO 32/7684: Report by General Cunynghame.
- WO 32/6690: Report by General Thesiger on military situation in Cape Colony.
- WO 32/7702: Requirements for invasion of Zululand.
- WO 32/7704: Organisation of forces.
- WO 32/7709: Chelmsford's request for relief.
- WO 32/7718: Report on disposition of forces.
- WO 32/7722: Report on preparations for relief of Eshowe.
- WO 32/7727: Report on relief of Eshowe.
- WO 32/7732: Report on disposition and condition of forces.
- WO 32/7736: Organisation of transport.
- WO 32/7737: Report on defence of Rorke's Drift.
- WO 32/7739: Report on delays in advance of burying of dead at Isandlwana.
- WO 32/7740: King Cetshwayo sues for peace.
- WO 32/7744: Disposition of cavalry regiments.
- WO 32/7745: Peace overtures by King Cetshwayo.
- WO 32/7752: Report on Organisation of forces.
- WO 32/7754: Diaries and Journals of Operations, May–June 1879.
- WO 32/7757: Dispatch on advance into Zululand.
- WO 32/7761: Dairy of Operations, June 1879.
- WO 32/7763: Report on battle at Ulundi.

WO 32/7764: Report on battle at Ulundi.
WO 32/7767: Diaries of Operations, June–July 1879.
WO 32/7770: Correspondence concerning resignation of Lord Chelmsford.
WO 32/7771: Wolseley's instructions to Lord Chelmsford.
WO 32/7772: Report of operations, April–July 1879.
WO 33/34: *War Office, Zulu War, Miscellaneous, 1878–9.*
WO 33/39: *War Office, Report of the Colour Committee, 1883.*

National Army Museum, Chelsea

6807–386: Papers of General Lord Chelmsford:
CP 2: Ninth Cape Frontier War.
CP 5: Commissariat and preparations for advance into Zululand.
CP 7: No. 1 Column, Lower Thukela.
CP 8: No. 3 Column, Isandlwana.
CP 9: No. 4 Column.
CP 10: Defence of Natal.
CP 11: Death of Prince Imperial.
CP 12: Correspondence with Sir Bartle Frere.
CP 13: Zulu peace proposals.
CP 15: No. 1 Division.
CP 16: No. 2 Division and Ulundi.
CP 17: Correspondence with Major-General Clifford.
CP 18: Appointments.
CP 19: Correspondence with Secretary of State for War.
CP 20: Miscellaneous correspondence.
CP 21: Correspondence with General Wolseley.
CP 22: Correspondence received after the Anglo-Zulu War.
CP 23: Correspondence with Major-General Crealock.
CP 24: Drafts of speeches.
CP 25: Maps.
CP 26: Miscellaneous documents and printed papers.
CP 27: Letter book, 29 December 1878–21 January 1879.
CP 28: Letter book, 29 January–14 July 1879.
CP 29: Confidential letter book, 15 February–15 August 1878.
CP 36: Telegrams, 25 March–8 July 1879.

6810-38: Collection of Correspondence between Lord Chelmsford and Colonel Pearson:
PP 3: Letters, 1878

7805-42: Papers of General Sir Arthur Cunynghame.

Pietermaritzburg Archives Repository, KwaZulu-Natal

Attorney-General's Office, Natal:
AGO 1/16/1: Depositions, Native High Court, 1876–83.

A574: Chelmsford letter, 15 May 1879.

A863: Fannin Collection:
2/4: Letters despatched, 1878–1879.

Government House, Natal:
GH 500: General Officer Commanding, South Africa: Despatches, 1878–9.
GH 601: Despatches from High Commissioner, 1879.
GH 1221: Secretary of State for Colonies, despatches, 1879.
GH 1325–6: High Commissioner: copies of despatches, 1878–9.
A96: Sir Theophilus Shepstone Papers:
TS 31–35: Letters received, 1878.
TS 36: Letters received, 1879.
Secretary for Native Affairs, Natal:
SNA 1/6/3: Papers relating to Cetshwayo.
A598: Sir Evelyn Wood Collection:
WC II/2/2: Incoming letters, 1878–9.
WC II/3/1: Outgoing letters, 1878–9.

Royal Archives, Windsor Castle

VIC/ADD/E/1: Papers of Field Marshal HRH Prince George Duke of Cambridge.

Official Printed Sources

'Annual Returns of British Regiments Stationed in Nova Scotia 1807–1865', https://sites.rootsworks.com [accessed 11 June 2021].

Anon., *Regulations for Field Forces in South Africa 1878*. Pietermaritzburg: November 1878.

Bellairs, W., DAG. By Command of Lord Chelmsford, *Regulations for the Colonial Forces Now in the Field 1878*. King William's Town: S.E. Rowles, 1878.

——, *General Instructions for Management of Natives for the Guidance of Officers appointed to the Natal Native Contingent*, Pietermaritzburg, November 1878.

British Parliamentary Papers:
LX of 1877 (C. 1748). Transvaal Native Affairs, 1875–6.
LX of 1877 (C. 1776). Papers *re* Annexation of Transvaal, 1876–7.
LV of 1878 (C. 1961), (C. 2000). S.A. Correspondence, 1877–8.
LVI of 1878 (C. 2079), (C. 2100), (C. 2144). S.A. Further correspondence, 1877–8.
LII of 1878–9 (C. 2220), (C. 2222), (C. 2242). S.A. Correspondence, 1878–9.
LIII of 1878–9 (C. 2252), (C. 2260), (C. 2316), (C. 2318), (C. 2367). S.A. Correspondence, appointment of Wolseley, 1878–9.
LIV of 1878–9 (C. 2374). S.A. Correspondence, 1878–9.
LIV of 1878–9 (C. 2454). S.A. Correspondence, Ulundi, 1878–9.
L of 1880 (C. 2482). S.A. War, Correspondence, 1879 –80.
LI of 1880 (148). Reports on recent expenditure in S.A.
XLII of 1880 (150). Returns of casualties in Transkei and Zulu campaigns.
LI of 1880 (C. 2584). S.A. Correspondence, 1879–80.
LVIII of 1881 (412). Returns *re* casualties and costs in S.A. Wars, 1875–80.
Printed Paper no.148 of 1880: *Copy of Reports of the Officers commissioned by the Treasury to inquire into Recent Expenditure in South Africa, 18 March 1880.*

XLII of 1880 (150). 150 of 1880: *Separate Returns per Regiment, Troop, or Battery, of the Numbers Killed, Died of Disease, or other Casualties among the Troops, British and Native, engaged in the Transkei and Zulu Campaigns in South Africa up to the present Day, War Office, 15 February 1880.*

Callwell, Col. Charles E., *Small Wars: Their Principles and Practice*, 3rd edn, London: His Majesty's Stationery Office, 1906.

Colonial Office Confidential Print:

CO 879/14. African, no. 164: Memorandum on the Zulu Question, 20 March 1879.

CO 879/15. African, no. 181a: Correspondence relating to Native Levies for raids into Zululand, 9 June 1879.

CO 879/15. African no. 196: Death of the Prince Imperial, June 1879.

CO 879/15. African no. 198: Transport of Troops in Colony, Correspondence April–June 1879.

Fynney, Francis., *The Zulu Army and Zulu Headmen. Compiled from Information Obtained from the Most Reliable Sources, and Published by Direction of the Lieut.-General Commanding for the Information of Those under His Command*, 2nd edn, revised. Pietermaritzburg: 1879.

Hansard's Parliamentary Debates (3rd Series): Vol. 244 (1879); Vol. 245 (1879); Vol. 246 (1879); Vol. 247 (1879); Vol. 249 (1879); Vol. 255 (1880); Vol. 256 (1880).

Holland, Maj. Trevenen J. and Capt. Henry M. Hozier, *Record of the Expedition to Abyssinia Compiled by Order of the Secretary of State for War*, 2 vols. London: Her Majesty's Stationery Office, 1870.

Home, Col. Robert, *Précis of Modern Tactics Compiled from the Works of Recent Continental Writers at the Topographical and Stationery Office of the War Office*. London: Her Majesty's Stationery Office, 1873.

Lieutenant-General Commanding, *Special Instructions Regarding the Management of Ox Transport on the Line of March, and for Conducting the Line of March when Troops March with Ox Wagon Transport, and for Forming Wagon Laagers*. Durban: 'Mercury' Press, n.d.

London Gazette, 1859, 1868, 1879.

War Office, *Field Exercise and Evolutions of Infantry*, pocket edn. London: Her Majesty's Stationery Office, 1877.

——, Intelligence Department, *Précis of Information concerning South Africa: The Transvaal Territory*. London: Her Majesty's Stationery Office, 1878.

——, Intelligence Division, *Narrative of the Field Operations Connected with the Zulu War of 1879*. London: Her Majesty's Stationery Office, 1881. (Reprinted London: Greenhill Books; California: Presidio Press, 1989.)

BIBLIOGRAPHY

Primary Printed Sources

Anon., *Historical Records of the 2nd Battalion, 24th Regiment for the Campaign in South Africa, 1877–78–79: Embracing the Kaffir & Zulu Wars*. Secunderabad, Deccan: 2nd Battalion, 'The South Wales Borders', January 1882.

Ashe, Maj. Waller and Capt. the Hon. Edmund V. Wyatt-Edgell, *The Story of the Zulu Campaign*. London: Sampson Low, Marston, Searle, & Rivington, 1880. (Reprinted Cape Town: N & S Press, 1989.)

Bell, Col. T. Lynden, 'The Offensive Defensive by Infantry in Extended Order', *Royal United Services Institution Journal*, 25, 109 (1881), pp. 157–69.

Bennett, Lt.-Col. I. H. W., *Eyewitness in Zululand: The Campaign Reminiscences of Colonel W. W. Dunne, CB, South Africa, 1877–1881*. London: Greenhill Books, 1989.

Brown, R. A. (ed.), *The Road to Ulundi: The Water Colour Drawings of John North Crealock (the Zulu War of 1879)*. Pietermaritzburg: University of Natal Press, 1969.

Buckle, George Earle (ed.), *The Letters of Queen Victoria: Second Series [Third Volume] 1879–1885*. London: John Murray, 1928.

Butterfield, Paul H., *War and Peace in South Africa 1879–1881: The Writings of Philip Anstruther and Edward Essex*. Melville, South Africa: Scripta Africana, 1987.

Cadogan, Gen. the Hon. Sir George and Lt.-Col. J. Gough Calthorpe, *Cadogan's Crimea*. London: Hamish Hamilton, 1979.

Callwell, Capt. Charles E., RA, 'Lessons to be Learned from the Campaigns in which British Forces Have Been Employed since the Year 1865', *Royal United Services Institution Journal*, 31, 139 (1887), pp. 357–412.

Cape Mercury, 1878.

Child, Daphne (ed.), *The Zulu War Journal of Colonel Henry Harford, C.B.* Pietermaritzburg: Shuter & Shooter, 1978.

Clarke, Sonia, *Invasion of Zululand 1879: Anglo-Zulu War Experiences of Arthur Harness; John Jervis, 4th Viscount St Vincent; and Sir Henry Bulwer*. Houghton: The Brenthurst Press, 1979.

——, *'Vanity Fair' in Southern Africa 1869 to 1914*. Houghton: The Brenthurst Press, 1979.

——, *Zululand at War 1879: The Conduct of the Anglo-Zulu War*. Houghton: The Brenthurst Press, 1984.

Coghlan, Mark, *Anglo-Zulu War Diaries: Trooper Fred Symons, Natal Carbineers, Enthusiasm and Misgiving, 1879*. Pietermaritzburg: KwaZulu-Natal Provincial Museum Service, n.d.

Colenso, Frances E., assisted by Lt.-Col. Edward Durnford, *History of the Zulu War and its Origins*. London: Chapman and Hall, 1880.

Colley, Col. Sir G. Pomeroy, 'Army', *Encyclopaedia Britannica*, 9th edn. Edinburgh: Adam and Charles Black; Little Brown, 1875.

Crwys-Williams, Jennifer (ed.), *South African Despatches: Two Centuries of the Best in South African Journalism*. Johannesburg: Ashanti, 1989.

Cunynghame, Arthur T., *My Command in South Africa, 1874–1878*. London: Macmillan, 1879.

Dawnay, Guy C., *Campaigns: Zulu 1879, Egypt 1882, Suakim 1885*. Privately printed, *c.*1886. (Reprinted Cambridge: Ken Trotman, 1989.)

Deléage, Paul, Fleur Webb (tr.) and Bill Guest (ed.), *End of a Dynasty: The Last Days of the Prince Imperial, Zululand 1879*. Pietermaritzburg: University of KwaZulu-Natal Press, 2008.

Duberly, Mrs Henry, *Campaigning Experiences of Rajpootana and Central India, during the Suppression of the Mutiny, 1857–1858*. London: Smith Elder, 1859. (Reprinted Cambridge: Cambridge University Press, 2012.)

Durnford, Lt.-Col. Edward C. L., *Isandhlwana, 22nd January, 1879. A Narrative, Compiled from Official and Reliable Sources*. London: P. S. King, 1879.

——, *Isandhlwana. Lord Chelmsford's Statements compared with the Evidence*. London: P. S. King, 1880.

—— (ed.), *A Soldier's Life and Works in South Africa, 1872–1879: A Memory of the Late Colonel A. W. Durnford, Royal Engineers*. London: Sampson Lowe, Marston, Searle & Rivington, 1882.

Elliott, Maj. W. J., *The Victoria Cross in Zululand and South Africa: Isandhlwana and Rorke's Drift*, Vol. I. London: Dean & Son, 1882.

Emery, Frank, *The Red Soldier: Letters from the Zulu War, 1879*. London: Hodder and Stoughton, 1977.

——, *Marching over Africa: Letters from Victorian Soldiers*. London, Hodder and Stoughton, 1986.

Forbes, Archibald, 'Lord Chelmsford and the Zulu War', *The Nineteenth Century*, 7 (February 1880), pp. 216–34.

Fripp, Charles E., 'Reminiscences of the Zulu War, 1879', *Pall Mall Magazine*, 20 (1900), pp. 547–62.

Greaves, Adrian and Brian Best (eds), *The Curling Letters of the Zulu War: 'There Was Awful Slaughter'*. Barnsley: Leo Cooper, 2001.

Hallam Parr, Capt. Henry, *A Sketch of the Kafir and Zulu Wars: Guadana to Isandhlwana*. London: C. Kegan Paul, 1880.

Hamilton-Browne, Col. G., *A Lost Legionary in South Africa*. London: T. Werner Laurie, 1912. (Reprinted Uckfield: The Naval & Military Press; London: The National Army Museum, 2010.)

Hamley, Col. Edward, *Operations of War Explained and Illustrated*. London and Edinburgh: William Blackwood and Sons, 1866.

Harness, Lt.-Col. Arthur, 'The Zulu Campaign from a Military Point of View', *Fraser's Magazine*, new series, 21 (April 1880), pp. 477–88.

Harrison, Gen. Sir Richard, *Notes on My Life for My Children*. Exeter: 1905.

——, *Recollections of a Life in the British Army during the Latter Half of the Nineteenth Century*. London: Smith, Elder, 1908.

H. S., 'The Kaffir War. By an English Officer in South Africa', *Fraser's Magazine*, new series, 18 (February 1878), pp. 250–8.

Hummel, Chris (ed.), *The Frontier War Journal of Major John Crealock 1878: A Narrative of the Ninth Frontier War by the Assistant Military Secretary to Lieutenant-General Thesiger*. Cape Town: Van Riebeeck Society, Second Series No. 19, 1989.

Illustrated London News, 1878, 1879.

Knight, Ian, *The National Army Museum Book of the Zulu War*. London: Sidgwick & Jackson in association with the National Army Museum, 2003.

Laband, John (ed.), *Lord Chelmsford's Zululand Campaign 1878–1879*. Stroud: Alan Sutton Publishing for the Army Records Society, 1994.

—— and Ian Knight, *The War Correspondents: The Anglo-Zulu War*. Stroud: Sutton Publishing, 1996.

—— (series ed.) and Ian Knight (volume ed.), *Archives of Zululand: The Anglo-Zulu War 1879*, 6 vols. London: Archival Publications International, 2000.

Lewsen, Phyllis (ed.), *Selections from the Correspondence of J. X. Merriman 1870–1890*. Cape Town: Van Riebeeck Society, 1960.

Lock, Ron and Peter Quantrill (compilers), *The Red Book: Natal Press Reports, Anglo-Zulu War 1879*. Durban: privately printed, n.d.

Ludlow, Capt. W.R., *Zululand and Cetywayo*. London: Simpkin, Marshall, 1882.

Mackinnon, J. P. and S. H. Shadbolt, *The South African Campaign of 1879*. London: Sampson Low, Marston, Searle, and Rivington, 1880.

MacLeod, Maj. Gen. W. E., 'The History of the Bombay Native Army from 1837 to 1887', *Royal United Services Institution Journal*, 32, 144 (1888), pp. 365–85.

Markham, Sir Clements R., *A History of the Abyssinian Expedition*. London: Prideux, 1869.

Martineau, J., *The Life and Correspondence of the Right Hon. Sir Bartle Frere*, Vol. II. London: John Murray, 1895.

Molyneux, Maj. W. C. F., 'Notes on Hasty Defences as Practised in South Africa', *Royal United Services Institution Journal*, 24 (1881), pp. 806–14.

——, *Campaigning in South Africa and Egypt*. London: Macmillan, 1896.

Montague, William Edward, *Campaigning in South Africa: Reminiscences of an Officer in 1879*. Edinburgh: Blackwood, 1880.

Moodie, Duncan C. F. (ed.), *John Dunn, Cetywayo, and the Three Generals*. Pietermaritzburg: Natal Printing and Publishing Company, 1886.

——, *Moodie's Zulu War*. Cape Town: N & S Press, 1988. (Reprinted selection from D. C. F. Moodie, *History of the Battles and Adventures of the British, the Boers, and the Zulus*. Adelaide: George Robertson, 1879.)

Mynors, Arthur C.B., *Letters and Diary of the Late Arthur C.B. Mynors, Lieut. 3rd Batt., 60th Rifles*. Margate: H. Keble, 1879.

Napier, H. D., *Field-Marshal Lord Napier of Magdala: A Memoir by His Son*. London: Arnold,1927.

Natal Colonist, 1879.

Natal Mercury, 1879, 1920.

Natal Witness. 1879.

Norbury, Fleet Surgeon Henry F., *The Naval Brigade in South Africa during the Years 1877–78–79*. London: Sampson Low, Marston, Searle & Rivington, 1880.

Norris-Newman, Charles L., *In Zululand with the British throughout the War of 1879*. London: W. H. Allen, 1880. (Reprinted London: Greenhill Books; California: Presidio Press, 1990.)

——, *With the Boers in the Transvaal and Orange Free State in 1880–1*. London: W. H. Allen, 1882.

Plé, James, *Les Laagers dans la Guerre des Zoulous*. Paris: Libraire Militaire de J. Dumanine, L. Baudoin, 1882.

Portlock , Maj. Gen. J. E. and Col. Sir Charles Nugent, 'Fortification', *Encyclopaedia Britannica*, 9th edn. Edinburgh: Adam and Charles Black; Little Brown, 1879.

Preston, Adrian W. (ed.), *The South African Journal of Sir Garnet Wolseley 1879–1880*. Cape Town: A. A. Balkema, 1973.

Punch, 1881.

Raines, Gen. Sir Julius, *The 95th (The Derbyshire) Regiment in Central India*. Uckfield: The Naval & Military Press in association with the Royal Artillery Museum, facsimile reprint, n.d.

Richards, Walter, *Her Majesty's Army: A Descriptive Account of Various Regiments Now Comprising the Queen's Forces, from Their First Establishment*, 3 vols. London: H. Virtue, n.d. [*c.* 1880].

Roberts, Adam and Richard Guelff, *Documents on the Laws of War*, 3rd edn. Oxford: Oxford University Press, 2005.

Robinson, John, *A Life Time South Africa*. London: Smith Elder, 1900.

Spiers, Edward M., *The Victorian Soldier in Africa*. Manchester: Manchester University Press, 2004.

Thesiger, Ernest, *Practically True*. London: Heinemann, 1927.

Thesiger, Lt.-Col. and Brevet-Col. the Hon. Frederic., 'Is a Radical Change in the Tactical Formation of our Infantry Really Necessary?', *Royal United Services Institution Journal*, 17, 73 (1873): 411–23.

The Times, 1868, 1879, 1895, 1905, 1910, 1918.

Times of Natal, 1879, 1886, 1887.

Tyrrell, Henry, *The History of the War with Russia Giving Full Details of the Operations of the Allied Armies*, 6 vols. London and New York: The London Publishing and Printing Company, n.d. [*c.* 1857].

Vanity Fair, 1870, 1878, 1881.

Vijn, Cornelius, Bishop J. W. Colenso (ed.), *Cetshwayo's Dutchman: Being the Private Journal of a White Trader in Zululand during the British Invasion*. London, Longmans, Green, 1880. (Reprinted London: Greenhill Books; California: Presidio Press, 1988.)

Webb, Colin de B. and John Wright (eds), *The James Stuart Archive of Recorded Oral Evidence Relating to the History of the Zulu and Neighbouring Peoples, Vol. 2*. Pietermaritzburg: University of Natal Press; Durban: Killie Campbell Africana Library, 1979.

——, *A Zulu King Speaks: Statements Made by Cetshwayo kaMpande on the History and Customs of His People*. Pietermaritzburg: University of Natal Press; Durban: Killie Campbell Africana Library, 1978.

Wilkinson, Osborn and Johnson Wilkinson, *Memoirs of the Gemini Generals*. London: A. D. Innes, 1896.

Wood, Field Marshal Sir Evelyn, *From Midshipman to Field Marshal, Vol. II*. London: Methuen, 1906.

Secondary Printed Sources

Adams, Paul, 'The Military View of Empire 1870–1899: As seen through the Journal of the Royal United Services Institution', *Royal United Services Institution Journal*, 143, 3 (1998), pp. 58–64.

Allen, Charles (ed.), *Plain Tales from the Raj: Images of British India in the Twentieth Century*. London: Andre Deutsch, 1975.

Anderson, Fred, *Crucible of War: The Seven Years' War and the Fate of the British Empire in North America, 1754–1766*. London: Faber & Faber, 2000.

Anderson, Michael, 'Thesiger, Ernest Frederic Graham (1879–1961)', *Oxford Dictionary of National Biography*. Oxford: Oxford University Press, online edn, 2008, https://doi-org.libproxy.wlu.ca/10.1093/ref.odnb/67820 [accessed 14 December 2022].

Atlay, James B., *The Victorian Chancellors*, Vol. II. London: Smith, Elder, 1908.

Atwood, Rodney, 'The Second Afghan War, 1878–1880', in Stephen M. Miller (ed.), *Queen Victoria's Wars: British Military Campaigns 1857–1902*. Cambridge: Cambridge University Press, 2021.

Ballard, Charles, *John Dunn: The White Chief of Zululand*. Craighall: Ad. Donker, 1985.

Bates, Darrell, *The Abyssinian Difficulty*. Oxford: Oxford University Press, 1979.

Beckett, Ian F. W., 'Military High Command in South Africa, 1854–1914', in Peter B. Boyden, Alan J. Guy and Marion Harding (eds), *'Ashes and Blood': The British Army in South Africa 1795–1914*. London: National Army Museum, 1999.

——, *Battles in Focus: Isandlwana 1879*. London: Brassey's, 2003.

——, 'Chelmsford's Major-Generals', in Ian F. W. Beckett, F. W., *The Victorians at War*. London and New York: Hambledon and London, 2003.

——, 'Command in South Africa', in Ian F. W. Beckett, *The Victorians at War*. London and New York: Hambledon and London, 2003.

——, 'Buller, Sir Redvers Henry (1839–1908)', *Oxford Dictionary of National Biography*. Oxford: Oxford University Press, online edn, 2008, https://doi-org.libproxy.wlu.ca/10.1093/ref.odnb/32165 [accessed 11 June 2021].

——, 'Wolseley, Garnet Joseph, first Viscount Wolseley (1833–1913)', *Oxford Dictionary of National Biography*. Oxford: Oxford University Press, online edn, 2008, https://doi-org.libproxy.wlu.ca/10.1093/ref.odnb/36995 [accessed 11 June 2021].

——, 'George Colley', in Steven J. Corvi and Ian F. W. Beckett (eds), *Victoria's Generals*. Barnsley: Pen & Sword Military, 2009.

—— (ed.), *Wolseley and Ashanti: The Asante War Journal and Correspondence of Major-General Sir Garnet Wolseley 1873–1874*. Stroud: The History Press for the Army Records Society, 2009.

——, *A British Profession of Arms: The Politics of Command in the Late Victorian Army*. Norman: University of Oklahoma Press, 2018.

——, *Rorke's Drift and Isandlwana*. Oxford: Oxford University Press, 2019.

Belich, James, *The New Zealand Wars and the Victorian Interpretation of Racial Conflict*. Auckland: Auckland University Press, 1986.

Benyon, John, *Proconsul and Paramountcy in South Africa: The High Commission, British Supremacy and the Sub-Continent 1806–1910*. Pietermaritzburg: University of Natal Press, 1980.

——, 'Frere, Sir (Henry) Bartle Edward, first baronet (1815–1884)', *Oxford Dictionary of National Biography*. Oxford: Oxford University Press, online edn, 2008, https://doi-org.libproxy.wlu.ca/10.1093/ref.odnb/10171 [accessed 11 June 2021].

Best, Brian, 'Zulu War Victoria Cross Holders', *Journal of the Anglo Zulu War Historical Society*, 1 (June 1992), https://www.anglozuluwar.com/journal [accessed 13 August 2018].

——, 'Zulu War Medals', *Journal of the Anglo Zulu War Historical Society*, 3 (June 1998), pp. 35–8.

Beveridge, Julian, *The Halifax Citadel*. Halifax: Formac Publishing, 2001.

Blake, Robert, *Disraeli*. London: Eyre and Spottiswood, 1966.

Boase, G. C., revised by John Sweetman, 'Blakeney, Sir Edward (1778–1868)', *Oxford Dictionary of National Biography*. Oxford: Oxford University Press, online edn, 2004, https://doi-org.libproxy.wlu.ca/10.1093/ref.odnb/136995 [accessed 24 May 2021].

Bond, Brian, 'Editor's Introduction', in Brian Bond (ed.), *Victorian Military Campaigns*. London: Hutchinson, 1967.

——, 'Cardwell, Edward, first Viscount Cardwell (1813–1886)', in *Oxford Dictionary of National Biography*. Oxford: Oxford University Press, online edn, 2009, https://doi-org.libproxy.wlu.ca/10.1093/ref.odnb/4620 [accessed 24 May 2021].

——, 'The Effect of the Cardwell Reforms in Army Organization, 1874–1904', *Royal United Services Institution Journal*, 105, 620 (1960), pp. 515–24.

Bonner, Philip, *Kings, Commoners and Concessionaires: The Evolution and Dissolution of the Nineteenth- Century Swazi State*. Johannesburg: Ravan Press, 1983.

Bou, Jean, 'Modern Cavalry: Mounted Rifles, the Boer War, and the Doctrinal Debates', in Peter Dennis and Jeffrey Grey (eds), *The Boer War: Army, Nation and Empire*. Canberra: Army History Unit, Australian Department of Defence, 2000.

Braudy, Leo, *From Chivalry to Terrorism: War and the Changing Nature of Masculinity*. New York: Alfred J. Knopf, 2003.

Brice, Christopher, *The British Campaign in Abyssinia 1867–1868*. Warwick: Helion, 2020.

——, 'The Expedition to Abyssinia, 1867–1868', in Stephen M. Miller (ed.), *Queen Victoria's Wars: British Military Campaigns 1857–1902*. Cambridge: Cambridge University Press, 2021.

——, 'Field Marshal Sir Robert Cornelis Napier, 1st Baron Napier of Magdala (1810–90)', in Christopher Brice (ed.), *Forgotten Victorian Generals: Studies in the Exercise of Command and Control in the British Army 1837–1901*. Warwick: Helion, 2021.

Burke, Sir Bernard, *The Peerage and Baronetage*. London: Harrison & Sons, 1894.

Burroughs, Peter, 'An Unreformed Army? 1815–1868', in David Chandler and Ian Beckett (eds), *The Oxford Illustrated History of the British Army*. Oxford and New York: Oxford University Press, 1994.

——, Defence and Imperial Disunity', in Andrew Porter (ed.), *The Oxford History of the British Empire*, Volume III: *The Nineteenth Century*, Oxford and New York: Oxford University Press, 1999.

Cannadine, David, *The Decline and Fall of the British Aristocracy*. New York: Vintage Books, 1999.

Carlyle, E. I., revised by Richard H. Warner, 'Thesiger, Sir Frederick (d. 1805)', *Oxford Dictionary of National Biography*. Oxford: Oxford University Press, online edn, 2007, https://doi-org.libproxy.wlu.ca/10.1093/ref.odnb/27175 [accessed 26 April 2021].

Castle, Ian, *Zulu War: Volunteers, Irregulars & Auxiliaries*. Oxford: Osprey, 2003.

—— and Ian Knight, *Fearful Hard Times: The Siege and Relief of Eshowe, 1879*. London: Greenhill Books, 1994.

Chandler, David G., 'The Expedition to Abyssinia 1867–8', in Brian Bond (ed.), *Victorian Military Campaigns*. London: Hutchinson, 1967.

Chichester, H. M., revised by Alex May, 'Horsford, Sir Alfred Hastings', *Oxford Dictionary of National Biography*. Oxford: Oxford University Press, online edn, 2004, https://doi-org.libproxy.wlu.ca/10.1093/ref.odnb/13816 [accessed 11 June 2021].

——, revised by Alex May, 'Inglis, Sir Eardley Wilmot', *Oxford Dictionary of National Biography*. Oxford: Oxford University Press, online edn, 2004, https://doi-org.libproxy.wlu.ca/10.1093/ref.odnb/14404 [accessed 11 June 2021].

——, revised by Roger T. Stearn, 'Michel, Sir John', *Oxford Dictionary of National Biography*. Oxford: Oxford University Press, online edn, 2004, https://doi-org.libproxy.wlu.ca/10.1093/ref.odnb/18649 [accessed 18 September 2021].

Clayton, Anthony, *The British Officer: Leading the Army from 1660 to the Present*. Harlow: Pearson Longman, 2006.

Clements, W. H., *The Glamour and Tragedy of the Zulu War*, London: John Lane the Bodley Head, 1936.

Conrad, Margaret and Alvin Finkel, *History of the Canadian Peoples*, 5th edn. Toronto: Pearson Longman, 2009.

Cope, Richard, *Ploughshare of War: The Origins of the Anglo-Zulu War of* 1879. Pietermaritzburg: University of Natal Press, 1999.

Corvi, Steven J., 'Garnet Wolseley', in Steven J. Corvi and Ian F. W. Beckett (eds)., *Victoria's Generals*. Barnsley: Pen & Sword Military, 2009.

Cracroft's Peerage. Heraldic Media Ltd., 2013, cracroftspeerage.co.uk/Chelmsford1858.htm and Chelmsford1921.htm [accessed 10 July 2021].

Curtin, Philip D., *Disease and Empire: The Health of European Troops in the Conquest of Africa*. Cambridge: Cambridge University Press, 1998.

David, Saul, *Zulu: The Heroism and Tragedy of the Zulu War of 1879*. London: Viking, 2004.

Debrett's Peerage, Baronetage, Knightage, and Companionage. London: Dean & Son, 1896, 1904.

De Kiewiet, C. W., 'The Establishment of Responsible Government in Cape Colony, 1870–1872', in Eric A. Walker (ed.), *Cambridge History of the British Empire, Vol. VIII: South Africa, Rhodesia and the High Commission Territories*. Cambridge: Cambridge University Press, 1963.

Delius, Peter, *The Land Belongs to Us: The Pedi Polity, the Boers and the British in the Nineteenth-Century Transvaal*. Berkeley: University of California Press, 1984.

De Watteville, H., revised by M. G. M. Jones, 'Clery, Sir Cornelius Francis (1838–1926)', *Oxford Dictionary of National Biography*. Oxford: Oxford University Press, online edn, 2006, https://doi-org.libproxy.wlu.ca/10.1093/ref.odnb/32446 [accessed 28 October 2021].

Dominy, Graham, 'Fort Napier: The Imperial Base that Shaped the City', in John Laband and Rob Haswell (eds), *Pietermaritzburg 1838–1988: A New Portrait of an African City*. Pietermaritzburg: University of Natal Press and Shuter & Shooter, 1988.

——, *Last Outpost on the Zulu Frontiers: Fort Napier and the British Imperial Garrison*. Urbana, Chicago and Springfield: University of Illinois Press, 2016.

Droogleever, R.W.F., *The Road to Isandhlwana: Colonel Anthony Durnford in Natal and Zululand*. London: Greenhill Books, 1992.

Duckers, Peter, *British Orders and Decorations*. Oxford: Shire Publications, 1988.

——, 'An Early Zulu War Letter from Lord Chelmsford', *Journal of the Anglo Zulu War Historical Society*, 52 (December 2022), https://www.anglozuluwar.com/journal [accessed 5 December 2022].

Emery, Frank, 'Geography and Imperialism: The Role of Sir Bartle Frere 1815–84', *Geographical Journal*, 150, 3 (November 1984), pp. 342–50.

Erickson, Arvel B., 'Abolition of Purchase in the British Army', *Military Affairs*, 23, 2 (Summer, 1959), pp. 65–76.

Farwell, Byron, *Eminent Victorian Soldiers: Seekers of Glory*. New York and London: W. W. Norton, 1985.

Fido, Martin. *Rudyard Kipling*. London: Hamlyn, 1975.

Figes, Orlando, *Crimea: The Last Crusade*. London: Penguin Books, 2011.

——, *The Story of Russia*. London: Bloomsbury Publishing, 2022.

Fitzpatrick, David, 'Ireland and the Empire', in Andrew Porter (ed.), *The Oxford History of the British Empire*, Volume III: *The Nineteenth century* (Oxford and New York: Oxford University Press, 1999).

Fraser, Antonia, *The Warrior Queens: Boadicea's Chariot*. London: Phoenix Press, 1988.

French, Major the Hon. Gerald, *Lord Chelmsford and the Zulu War*, Great Britain: John Lane the Bodley Head, 1939. (Reprinted Barnsley: Pen & Sword Military, 2014.)

Frost, T. B. (Jack), 'Government House', in John Laband and Rob Haswell (eds), *Pietermaritzburg 1838–1988: A New Portrait of an African City*. Pietermaritzburg: University of Natal Press and Shuter & Shooter, 1988.

Gon, Philip, 'The Last Frontier War', *Military History Journal*, 5, 6 (December 1982), http://samilitaryhistory.org/vol056pg.html [accessed 10 March 2013]

——, *The Road to Isandlwana: The Years of an Imperial Battalion*. Johannesburg: Ad. Donker, 1979.

Goodfellow, C. F., *Great Britain and South African Confederation (1870–1881)*. Cape Town: Oxford University Press, 1966.

Gordon, Peter, 'Herbert, Henry Howard Molyneux, fourth earl of Carnarvon (1831–1890)', *Oxford Dictionary of National Biography*. Oxford: Oxford University Press, online edn, 2008, https://doi-org.libproxy.wlu.ca/10.1093/ref.odnb/13035 [accessed 1 June 2021].

Greaves, Adrian, *Rorke's Drift*. London: Cassell, 2002.

—— and Ian Knight, *Who's Who in the Zulu War*. Vol. 1: *The British*; Vol. 2: *Colonials and Zulus*. Barnsley: Pen & Sword Military, 2006, 2007.

Guest, Bill, 'Colonists, Confederation and Constitutional Change', in Andrew Duminy and Bill Guest (eds), *Natal and Zululand from Earliest Times to 1910: A New History*. Pietermaritzburg: University of Natal Press and Shuter & Shooter, 1989.

Guy, Jeff, 'A Note on Firearms in the Zulu Kingdom with Special Reference to the Anglo-Zulu War, 1879', *Journal of African History*, 12, 4 (1971), pp. 557–70.

——, *The Destruction of the Zulu Kingdom: The Civil War in Zululand, 1879–1884*. London: Longman, 1979.

——, *The View across the River: Harriette Colenso and the Zulu Struggle against Imperialism*. Charlottesville: University Press of Virginia, 2002.

Hall, Maj. Darrell, 'Artillery in the Zulu War – 1879', *Military History Journal*, 4, 4 (January 1879), pp. 152–61.

——, 'Field Artillery of the British Army 1860–1960', *Military History Journal*, 5:1 (December 1980), samilitaryhistory.org/journal.html [accessed 25 August 2015].

Hall, Douglas, 'Slaves and Slavery in the British West Indies', *Social and Economic Studies*, 11, 4 (1962), pp. 305–18.

Hamilton, J. A., revised by Sinéad Agnew, 'Thesiger, Frederick, first Baron Chelmsford (1794–1878)', *Oxford Dictionary of National Biography*. Oxford: Oxford University Press, online edn, 2008, https://doi-org.libproxy.wlu.ca/10.1093/ref.odnb/27176 [accessed 11 June 2021].

Harlow, V. T., 'Cape Colony, 1806–1822', in Eric Walker (ed), *The Cambridge History of the British Empire, Volume VIII: South Africa, Rhodesia and the High Commission Territories*. Cambridge: Cambridge University Press, 1963.

Harries-Jenkins, Gwyn, 'The Development of Professionalism in the Victorian Army', *Armed Forces and Society*, 1, 4 (August 1975), pp. 472–89.

——, *The Army in Victorian Society*. London: Routledge and Kegan Paul, 1977.

Haythornthwaite, Philip J., *The Colonial Wars Source Book*. London: Caxton Editions, 2000.

Hibbert, Christopher, *The Great Mutiny: India 1857*. Harmondsworth: Penguin, 1980.

Holmes, Richard, *Redcoat: The British Soldier in the Age of Horse and Musket*. London: HarperCollins, 2001.

——, 'Crimean War', in Richard Holmes (ed.), *The Oxford Companion to Military History*. Oxford: Oxford University Press, 2001.

——, *Sahib: The British Soldier in India 1750–1914*. London: HarperCollins, 2005.

Howlett, David J., 'Hardinge, Henry, first Viscount Harding of Lahore (1785–1856)', *Oxford Dictionary of National Biography*. Oxford: Oxford University Press, online edn, 2013, https://doi-org.libproxy.wlu.ca/10.1093/ref.odnb/12271 [accessed 11 June 2021].

Hyam, Ronald, *Empire and Sexuality: The British Experience*. Manchester and New York: Manchester University Press, 1991

——, 'Empire and Sexual Opportunity', in Ronald Hyam, *Understanding the British Empire*. Cambridge: Cambridge University Press, 2010.

Iliffe, John, *Honour in African History*. Cambridge: Cambridge University Press, 2005.

James, Lawrence, *Raj: The Making and Unmaking of British India*. London: Abacus, 2001.

Jones, Huw M., *The Boiling Cauldron: Utrecht District and the Anglo-Zulu War, 1879*. Bisley: The Shermershill Press, 2006.

Kincaid, Dennis, *British Social Life in India, 1608–1937*, 2nd edn. London: Routledge & Kegan Paul, 1973.

Knight, Ian, *Nothing Remains but to Fight: The Defence of Rorke's Drift, 1879*. London: Greenhill Books, 1993.

——, *The Anatomy of the Zulu Army from Shaka to Cetshwayo 1818–1879*. London: Greenhill Books, 1995.

——, *Go to Your God like a Soldier: The British Soldier Fighting for Empire, 1837–1902*. London: Greenhill Books, 1996.

——, *Rorke's Drift: 'Pinned Like Rates in a Hole'*. London: Osprey Military, 1996.

——, *With His Face to the Foe: The Life and Death of Louis Napoleon, the Prince Imperial*. Staplehurst: Spellmount, 2001.

——, *A Companion to the Anglo-Zulu War*. Barnsley: Pen & Sword Military, 2008.

——, *Zulu Rising: The Epic Story of Isandlwana and Rorke's Drift*. London: Macmillan, 2010.

Laband, John, *The Battle of Ulundi*. Pietermaritzburg: Shuter & Shooter; Ulundi: KwaZulu Monuments Council, 1988.

——, *Companion to Narrative of the Field Operations Connected with the Zulu War of 1879*. Constantia: N & S Press, 1989.

——, 'British Fieldworks of the Zulu Campaign of 1879 with Special Reference to Fort Eshowe', in John Laband and Paul Thompson, *Kingdom and Colony at War: Sixteen Studies on the Anglo-Zulu War of 1879*. Pietermaritzburg: University of Natal Press; Cape Town: N & S Press, 1990.

——, 'Bulwer, Chelmsford and the Border Levies: The Dispute over the Defence of Natal, 1879', in John Laband and Paul Thompson, *Kingdom and Colony at War: Sixteen Studies on the Anglo-Zulu War of 1879*. Pietermaritzburg: University of Natal Press; Cape Town: N & S Press, 1990.

——, 'The Cohesion of the Zulu Polity under the Impact of the Anglo-Zulu War: A Reassessment', in John Laband and Paul Thompson, *Kingdom and Colony at War: Sixteen Studies on the Anglo-Zulu War of 1879*. Pietermaritzburg: University of Natal Press; Cape Town: N & S Press, 1990.

——, 'Humbugging the General? Cetshwayo's Peace Overtures during the Anglo-Zulu War', in John Laband and Paul Thompson, *Kingdom and Colony at War: Sixteen Studies on the Anglo-Zulu War of 1879*. Pietermaritzburg: University of Natal Press; Cape Town: N & S Press, 1990.

——, 'Mbilini, Manyonyoba and the Phongolo River Frontier: A Neglected Sector of the Anglo-Zulu War of 1879', in John Laband and Paul Thompson, *Kingdom and Colony at War: Sixteen Studies on the Anglo-Zulu War of 1879*. Pietermaritzburg: University of Natal Press; Cape Town: N & S Press, 1990.

——, 'The Zulu Army in the War of 1879', in John Laband and Paul Thompson, *Kingdom and Colony at War: Sixteen Studies on the Anglo-Zulu War of 1879*. Pietermaritzburg: University of Natal Press; Cape Town: N & S Press, 1990.

——, 'Longcast in Zululand: The Paradoxical Life of a Transfrontiersman, 1850–1909', *Journal of Natal and Zulu History*, XV (1994/5), pp. 17–39.

——, *The Rise and Fall of the Zulu Nation*. London: Arms and Armour, 1997. (First published as *Rope of Sand: The Rise and Fall of the Zulu Kingdom*. Johannesburg: Jonathan Ball, 1995.)

——, '"He Fought like a Lion": An Assessment of Zulu Accounts of the Death of the Prince Imperial of France during the Anglo-Zulu War of 1879', *Journal of the Society for Army Historical Research*, 76, 307 (Autumn 1998), pp. 194–201.

——, 'Zulu Strategic and Tactical Options in the Face of the British Invasion of January 1879', *Scientia Militaria: South African Journal of Military Studies*, 28, 1 (1998), pp. 1–15.

——, '"War Can't Be Made with Kid Gloves": The Impact of the Anglo-Zulu War of 1879 on the Fabric of Zulu Society', *South African Historical Journal*, 43 (November 2000), pp. 179–96.

——, *The Atlas of the Later Zulu Wars 1883–1888*. Pietermaritzburg: University of Natal Press, 2001.

——, '"The Danger of Divided Command": British Civil and Military Disputes over the Conduct of the Zululand Campaigns of 1879 and 1888', *Journal of the Society for Army Historical Research*, 81, 328 (Winter 2003), pp. 339–55.

——, 'Durnford, Anthony William (1830–1879)', *Oxford Dictionary of National Biography*. Oxford: Oxford University Press, online edn, 2004, https://doi-org.libproxy.wlu.ca/10.1093/ref.odnb/8325 [accessed 11 June 2021].

——, 'Crealock, John North (1836–1895)', *Oxford Dictionary of National Biography*. Oxford: Oxford University Press, online edn, 2005, http://www.doi-org.libproxy.wlu.ca/10.1093/ref:odnb/50002 [accessed 11 June 2021].

——, *The Transvaal Rebellion: The First Boer War 1880–1881*. London: Pearson Longman, 2005.

——, '*Zulu* (amaZulu) War Rituals', in Bron R. Taylor and Jeffrey Kaplan (eds), *The Encyclopedia of Religion and Nature*. London and New York: Thoemmes Continuum, 2005.

——, 'The British Way of War in South Africa: 1837–1902: New Approaches', in Ian F. W. Beckett (ed.), *Victorians at War: New Perspectives*. The Society for Army Historical Research: Special Publication No. 16, 2007.

——, *Kingdom in Crisis: The Zulu Response to the British Invasion of 1879*. Barnsley: Pen & Sword, 2007. (First published Manchester: Manchester University Press, 1992.)

——, 'Zulu Civilians during the Rise and Fall of the Zulu Kingdom, *c.*1817–1879', in John Laband (ed.), *Daily Lives of Civilians in Wartime Africa from Slavery days to Rwandan Genocide* (Westport: Greenwood Press, 2007.

——, 'Thesiger, Frederic Augustus, second Baron Chelmsford (1827–1905)', *Oxford Dictionary of National Biography*. Oxford: Oxford University Press, online edn, 2008, https://doi-org.libproxy.wlu.ca/10.1093/ref.odnb/36464 [accessed 11 June 2021].

——, *Historical Dictionary of the Zulu Wars*. Lanham: The Scarecrow Press, 2009.

——, 'Lord Chelmsford', in Steven J. Corvi and Ian F. W. Beckett (eds), *Victoria's Generals*. Barnsley: Pen & Sword Military, 2009.

——, 'The War-Readiness and Military Effectiveness of the Zulu Forces in the 1879 Anglo-Zulu War', *Natalia*, 39 (December 2009), pp. 37–46.

——, 'Zulu Wars', in Dennis Showalter (ed.), *Oxford Bibliographies Online: Military History*. New York: Oxford University Press, 2012.

——, 'Ethiopian Military Culture (Fifth Century CE–1941)', in Daniel Coetzee and Lee W. Eysturlid (eds), *Philosophers of War: The Evolution of History's Greatest Military Thinkers*, Vol. 1: *The Ancient to the Premodern World, 3000 BCE–1815 CE*. Santa Barbara, Denver and Oxford: Praeger, 2013.

——, '"Fighting Stick of Thunder": Firearms and the Zulu Kingdom: The Cultural Ambiguities of Transferring Weapons Technology', *War & Society*, 33, 4 (October 2014), pp. 229–43.

——, *Zulu Warriors: The Battle for the South African Frontier*. New Haven and London: Yale University Press, 2014.

——, *The Battle of Majuba: The Transvaal Campaign, 1880–1881*. Solihull: Helion, 2017.

——, *The Eight Zulu Kings*. Johannesburg and Cape Town: Jonathan Ball, 2018.

——, *The Land Wars: The Dispossession of the Khoisan and AmaXhosa in the Cape Colony*. Cape Town: Penguin Books, 2020.

——, 'The First Anglo-Boer War, 1880–1881', in Stephen M. Miller (ed.), *Queen Victoria's Wars: British Military Campaigns 1857–1902*. Cambridge: Cambridge University Press, 2021.

——, 'Sir Arthur Cunynghame, General Officer Commanding Her Majesty's Forces at the Cape of Good Hope (1873–78)', in Christopher Brice (ed.), *Forgotten Victorian Generals: Studies in the Exercise of Command and Control in the British Army 1837–1901*. Warwick: Helion, 2021.

——, *The Zulu Kingdom and the Boer Invasion of 1837–40*. Warwick: Helion, 2022.

—— and Rob Haswell (eds), *Pietermaritzburg 1838–1988: A New Portrait of an African City*. Pietermaritzburg: University of Natal Press and Shuter & Shooter, 1988.

—— and Jeff Mathews, *Isandlwana*. Pietermaritzburg: Centaur Publications and KwaZulu Monuments Council, 1992.

—— and Paul Thompson, *War Comes to Umvoti: The Natal-Zululand Border 1878–79*. Durban: Department of History, University of Natal, Research Monograph No. 5, 1980.

—— and Paul Thompson with Sheila Henderson, *The Buffalo Border 1879: The Anglo-Zulu War in Northern Natal*. Durban: Department of History, University of Natal, Research Monograph No. 6, 1983.

——, and Paul Thompson, *Field Guide to the War in Zululand and the Defence of Natal 1879*, 2nd revised edn. Pietermaritzburg: University of Natal Press, 1987.

—— and Paul Thompson, 'The Reduction of Zululand, 1878–1904', in Andrew Duminy and Bill Guest (eds), *Natal and Zululand from Earliest Times to 1910: A New History*. Pietermaritzburg: University of Natal Press and Shuter & Shooter, 1989.

—— and Paul Thompson, *Kingdom and Colony at War: Sixteen Studies on the Anglo-Zulu War of 1879*. Pietermaritzburg: University of Natal Press; Cape Town: N & S Press, 1990.

—— and Paul Thompson, *The Illustrated Guide to the Anglo-Zulu War*. Pietermaritzburg: University of Natal Press, 2000.

—— and Paul Thompson, 'African Levies in Natal and Zululand, 1838–1906', in Stephen M. Miller (ed.), *Soldiers and Settlers in Africa, 1850–1918*. Leiden and Boston: Brill, 2009.

Legacies of British Slave-Ownership Database, 'Charles Thesiger', http://www.depts-live.ucl.ac.uk/lbs/person/view/2146649111 [accessed 2 May 2021].

Lejeune, Anthony and Malcom Lewis, *The Gentlemen's Clubs of London*. London: Bracken Books, 1984.

Lewsen, Phyllis, *John X. Merriman: Paradoxical South African Statesman*. New Haven and London: Yale University Press, 1982.

Lieven, Michael, '"Butchering the Brutes All Over the Place": Total War and Massacre in Zululand, 1879', *History*, 84, 276 (October 1999), pp. 614–32.

Lloyd, Ernest March, 'Thesiger, Frederic Augustus, Second Baron Chelmsford', in Sidney Lee (ed.), *Dictionary of National Biography, Supplement to Vol. 3*. London: Smith, Elder, 1912.

——, revised by James Lunt, 'Steele, Sir Thomas Montague (1820–1890)', *Oxford Dictionary of National Biography*. Oxford: Oxford University Press, online edn, 2004, https://doi-org.libproxy.wlu.ca/10.1093/ref.odnb/26349 [accessed 5 June 2021].

——, revised by H. C. G. Matthew, 'Yorke, Sir Charles (1790–1880)', *Oxford Dictionary of National Biography*. Oxford: Oxford University Press, online edn, 2004, https://doi-org.libproxy.wlu.ca/10.1093/ref.odnb/30238 [accessed 5 June 2021].

——, revised by James Falkner, 'Simpson, Sir James (1792–1868)', *Oxford Dictionary of National Biography*. Oxford: Oxford University Press, online edn, 2014, http://www.doi-org.libproxy.wlu.ca/10.1093/ref:odnb/25583 [accessed 5 June 2021].

——, revised by John Sweetman, 'Somerset, Fitzroy James Henry [*known as* Lord Fitzroy Somerset], First Baron Raglan (1788–1855)', *Oxford Dictionary of National Biography*. Oxford, Oxford University Press, online edn, 2014, https://doi-org.libproxy.wlu.ca/10.1093/ref.odnb/26007 [accessed 5 June 2021].

Lock, Ron and Peter Quantrill, *Zulu Victory: The Epic of Isandlwana and the Cover-Up*. London: Greenhill Books, 2002.

Longford, Elizabeth, *Victoria R.I.* London: Weidenfeld and Nicolson, 1964.

Low, Charles Rathbone, *Soldiers of the Victorian Age*, 2 vols. London: Chapman and Hall, 1880.

Lundy, Darryl, *The Peerage*. Wellington, New Zealand, 2021, https://www.thepeerage.com [accessed 5 August 2021].

Luscombe, Stephen, 'Lieut–General Hon. Charles Wemyss Thesiger', http://www.britishempire.co.uk/forces/armyunits/britishcavalry/14thhussarcharlesthesiger.htm [accessed 5 May 2021].

Maitland, Alexander. 'Thesiger, Sir Wilfred Patrick (1910–2003)', *Oxford Dictionary of National Biography*. Oxford: Oxford University Press, online edn, 2011, https://doi-org.libproxy.wlu.ca/10.1093/ref.odnb/92678 [accessed 23 June 2022].

Manning, Stephen, *Evelyn Wood VC: Pillar of Empire*. Barnsley: Pen & Sword Military, 2007.

——, 'Evelyn Wood', in Steven J. Corvi and Ian F. W. Beckett (eds), *Victoria's Generals*. Barnsley: Pen & Sword Military, 2009.

——, *Britain against the Xhosa and Zulu Peoples: Lord Chelmsford's South African Campaigns*. Barnsley: Pen & Sword Military, 2022.

Mansel, Philip, *Pillars of Monarchy: An Outline of the Political and Social History of Royal Guards 1400–1984*. London: Quartet Books, 1984.

Mason, Philip, *A Matter of Honour: An Account of the Indian Army, Its Officers and Men*. London: Jonathan Cape, 1974.

Mathews, Jeffrey, 'Lord Chelmsford and Problems of Transport and Supply during the Anglo-Zulu War of 1879'. Unpublished MA thesis, University of Natal, 1979.

——, 'Lord Chelmsford: British General in Southern Africa'. Unpublished D. Litt. et Phil. thesis, University of South Africa, 1986.

Maylam, Paul, *A History of the Africa People of South Africa: From the early Iron Age to the 1870s*. (London: Croom Helm, 1986.

Michell, Capt. F. K., 'The Medals of the Zulu War, 11th January to 1st September, 1879', *Military History Journal*, 4, 4 (December 1978), samilitaryhistory.org/journal.html [accessed 13 August 2018].

Millar, Mary S., 'Montgomerie, Archibald William, thirteenth earl of Eglinton and first earl of Winton (1812–1861)', *Oxford Dictionary of National Biography*. Oxford: Oxford University Press, online edn, 2004, https://doi-org.libproxy.wlu.ca/10.1093/ref.odnb/19057 [accessed 24 May 2021].

Miller, Stephen M., 'Redvers Buller', in Steven J. Corvi and Ian F. W. Beckett (eds), *Victoria's Generals*. Barnsley: Pen & Sword Military, 2009.

Milton, John, *The Edges of War: A History of the Frontier Wars, 1702–1878*. Cape Town, Juta, 1983.

Monteith, Mary, 'Cetshwayo and Sekhukhune 1875–1879'. Unpublished MA thesis, University of the Witwatersrand, 1978.

Monypenny William F. and George E. Buckle, *The Life of Benjamin Disraeli Earl of Beaconsfield*, new and revised edition. New York: Macmillan, 1929.

Moore, Robert J., 'Imperial India, 1858–1914', in Porter, Andrew (ed.), *The Oxford History of the British Empire*, Volume III: *The Nineteenth Century* (Oxford and New York: Oxford University Press, 1999).

Moreman, T. R., 'Callwell, Sir Charles Edward (1859–1928)', *Oxford Dictionary of National Biography*. Oxford: Oxford University Press, online edn, 2008, https://doi-org.libproxy.wlu.ca/10.1093/ref.odnb/32251 [accessed 24 May 2021].

——, 'Mansfield, William Rose, first Baron Sandhurst (1819–1876)', *Oxford Dictionary of National Biography*. Oxford: Oxford University Press, online edn, 2006, https://doi-org.libproxy.wlu.ca/10.1093/ref.odnb/17996 [accessed 11 June 2021].

——, 'Napier, Robert Cornelis, first Baron Napier of Magdala (1810–1890)', *Oxford Dictionary of National Biography*. Oxford: Oxford University Press, online edn, 2008, https://doi-org.libproxy.wlu.ca/10.1093/ref.odnb/19770 [accessed 11 June 2021].

Morris, Donald R., *The Washing of the Spears: A History of the Rise and Fall of the Zulu Nation under Shaka and Its Fall in the Zulu War of 1879*. London: Jonathan Cape, 1966.

Mostert, Noël. *Frontiers: The Epic of South Africa's Creation and the Tragedy of the Xhosa People*. London: Pimlico, 1993.

Muir, Rory, *Wellington: Waterloo and the Fortunes of Peace, 1814–1852*. New Haven and London: Yale University Press, 2015.

O'Connor, Damian P., *The Zulu and the Raj: The Life of Sir Bartle Frere*. Knebworth: Able Publishing, 2002.

——, 'In Praise of the Tail: The Transport Corps in Abyssinia 1867–68', *Royal United Services Institute Journal*, 151, 1 (2006), pp. 72–5.

——, 'Dragoons and Commandos: The Development of Mounted Infantry in Southern Africa 1654–1899', *Royal United Services Institute Journal* 153, 1 (2008), pp. 90–4.

——, 'The Causes of the Anglo-Zulu War of 1879', *Natalia*, 39 (December 2009), pp. 28–36.

Orman, Gerard, '"The Administration of Discipline by the English is Very Rigid." British Military Law and the Death Penalty', *Crime, History and Societies*, 5, 1 (2001), pp. 93–110.

Patterson, Ryan, 'The Third Anglo-Asante War, 1873–1874, in Stephen M. Miller, *Queen Victoria's Wars. British Military Campaigns 1857–1902* (Cambridge: Cambridge University Press, 2021.

Pearsall, Ronald, *The Worm in the Bud: The World of Victorian Sexuality*. Toronto: Macmillan, 1969.

Peers, Chris, *The African Wars: Warriors and Soldiers of the Colonial Campaigns*. Barnsley: Pen & Sword Military, 2010.

——, *Rorke's Drift and Isandlwana 22nd January 1879: Minute by Minute*. Barnsley: Greenhill Books, 2021.

Peers, Douglas M., 'The Indian Rebellion, 1857–1858', in Stephen M. Miller (ed.), *Queen Victoria's Wars. British Military Campaigns 1857–1902*. Cambridge: Cambridge University Press, 2021.

Peires, J. B., *The House of Phalo: A History of the Xhosa People in the Days of their Independence*. Johannesburg: Ravan Press, 1981.

Pine, L. G. (ed), *Burke's Peerage, Baronetage & Knightage*, 102nd edn. London: Burke's Peerage, 1959.

Preston, Adrian W., 'British Military Thought, 1865–90', *Army Quarterly and Defence Journal*, 89 (1964), pp. 57–74.

Prochaska, Frank, 'Mary Adelaide, Princess [Princess Mary Adelaide of Cambridge], duchess of Teck', *Oxford Dictionary of National Biography*. Oxford: Oxford University Press, online edn, 2004, https://doi-org.libproxy.wlu.ca/10.1093/ref.odnb/40730 [accessed 11 June 2021].

Pugh, Martin, 'Michael Edward Hicks Beach, first Earl St Aldwyn (1837–1916)' *Oxford Dictionary of National Biography*. Oxford: Oxford University Press, online edn, 2010, https://doi-org.libproxy.wlu.ca/10.1093/ref.odnb/33859 [accessed 24 May 2021].

Razzell, P. E., 'Social Origins of the Officers in the British and Indian Home Armies, 1758–1962', *British Journal of Sociology*, 14, 3 (September 1963), pp. 248–61.

Regan, Geoffrey, *Someone Had Blundered: A Historical Survey of Military Incompetence*. London: Batsford, 1987.

Rikhye, Ravi, 'Revolt of Raja Man Singh of Narwar against the British, August 1858', V.1.0 September 21, 2005, https://Yumpu.com/en/document/view/24975969 [accessed 6 August 2021].

Robb, P. G., 'Thesiger, Frederick John Napier, first Viscount Chelmsford', *Oxford Dictionary of National Biography*. Oxford: Oxford University Press, online edn, 2008, https://doi-org.libproxy.wlu.ca/10.1093/ref.odnb/36465 [accessed 10 August 2021].

Robson, Brian, 'Rose, Hugh Henry, Baron Strathnairn', *Oxford Dictionary of National Biography*. Oxford: Oxford University Press, online edn, 2008, https://doi-org.libproxy.wlu.ca/10.1093/ref.odnb/24093 [accessed 11 June 2021.

Rogers, Col. H. C. B., *Weapons of the British Soldier*. London: Sphere Books, 1972.

Russell, D., '"We Carved Our Way to Glory": The British Soldier in Music Hall Song and Sketch, *c.* 1880–1914', in John M. MacKenzie (ed.), *Popular Imperialism and the Military, 1850–1950*. Manchester: Manchester University Press, 1992.

Saint Aubyn, Giles, *The Royal George 1819–1904: The Life of HRH Prince George Duke of Cambridge*. New York: Alfred A. Knopf, 1964.

Saunders, Christopher and Iain R. Smith, 'Southern Africa, 1795–1910', in Andrew Porter (ed), *The Oxford History of the British Empire, Volume 2: The Nineteenth Century*. Oxford: Oxford University Press, 2001.

Simkin, Peter and Barry Gibbs, *The Guards*. London: Pitkin Pictorials, 1972.

Smith, Keith, *The Wedding Feast War: The Final Tragedy of the Xhosa People*. London: Frontline Books, 2012.

Smithers, A. J., *The Kaffir Wars 1779–1877*. London: Leo Cooper, 1973.

Snook, Lt.-Col. Mike, *Like Wolves on the Fold: The Defence of Rorke's Drift*, revised edn. Barnsley: Frontline Books, 2010.

——, *How Can Man Die Better: The Secrets of Isandlwana Revealed*, revised edn. Barnsley: Frontline Books, 2018.

Soga, John Henderson, *The Ama-Xhosa: Life and Custom*. Lovedale: Lovedale Press; London: Kegan Paul, Trench, Trubner, *c.*1932.

Spiers, Edward M., *The Army and Society 1815–1914*. London and New York: Longman, 1980.

——, *The Late Victorian Army 1868–1902*. Manchester: Manchester University Press, 1992.

——, 'The Late Victorian Army 1868–1914', in David Chandler and Ian Beckett (eds), *The Oxford Illustrated History of the British Army*. Oxford and New York: Oxford University Press, 1994.

——, 'The British Army in South Africa: Military Government and Occupation, 1877–1914', in Peter B. Boyden, Alan J. Guy and Marion Harding (eds), *'Ashes and Blood': The British Army in South Africa 1795–1914*. London: National Army Museum, 1999.

——, 'George, Prince, second duke of Cambridge (1819–1904)', *Oxford Dictionary of National Biography*. Oxford: Oxford University Press, online edn, 2009, https://doi-org.libproxy.wlu.ca/10.1093/ref.odnb/33372 [accessed 11 June 2021].

Stapleton, Timothy J., '"Valuable, Gallant and Faithful Assistants": The Fingo (or Mfengu) as Colonial Military Allies during the Cape-Xhosa Wars, 1835–1881', in Stephen M. Miller (ed.), *Soldiers and Settlers in Africa, 1850–1918*. Leiden and Boston: Brill, 2009.

——, *A Military History of South Africa from the Dutch–Khoi Wars to the End of Apartheid*. Santa Barbara: Praeger, 2010.

Storey, William Kelleher, *Guns, Race and Power in Colonial South Africa*. Cambridge: Cambridge University Press, 2008.

Sweetman, John, 'Airey, Richard, Baron Airey (1803–1881)', *Oxford Dictionary of National Biography*. Oxford: Oxford University Press, online edn, 2004, https://doi-org.libproxy.wlu.ca/10.1093/ref.odnb/250 [accessed 11 June 2021].

——, 'Codrington, Sir William John (1804–1884)', *Oxford Dictionary of National Biography*. Oxford: Oxford University Press, online edn, 2004, https://doi-org.libproxy.wlu.ca/10.1093/ref.odnb/5800 [accessed 11 June 2021].

Switzer, Leo, *Power and Resistance in an African Society: The Ciskei Xhosa and the Making of South Africa*. Madison: University of Wisconsin Press, 1993.

Tabler, Edward C., *Pioneers of Natal and Southeastern Africa 1552–1878*. Cape Town and Rotterdam: A. A. Balkema, 1977.

Thompson, Leonard, 'Great Britain and the Afrikaner Republics, 1879–1899', in Monica Wilson and Leonard Thompson (eds), *Oxford History of the British Empire*, Vol. II: *South Africa 1870–1966*. Oxford: Oxford University Press, 1971.

Thompson, Paul S., 'The Active Defence after Isandlwana: British Raids across the Buffalo, March–May 1879', in John Laband and Paul Thompson, *Kingdom and Colony at War: Sixteen Studies on the Anglo-Zulu War of 1879*. Pietermaritzburg: University of Natal Press; Cape Town: N & S Press, 1990.

——, 'Captain Lucas and the Border Guard: The War on the Lower Thukela, 1879', in John Laband and Paul Thompson, *Kingdom and Colony at War: Sixteen Studies on the Anglo-Zulu War of 1879*. Pietermaritzburg: University of Natal Press; Cape Town: N & S Press, 1990.

——, 'The Defence of Durban', in John Laband and Paul Thompson, *Kingdom and Colony at War: Sixteen Studies on the Anglo-Zulu War of 1879*. Pietermaritzburg: University of Natal Press; Cape Town: N & S Press, 1990.

——, 'Town and Country and the Zulu Threat, 1878–9: The Natal Government's Arrangements for the Protection of Settlers', in John Laband and Paul Thompson, *Kingdom and Colony at War: Sixteen Studies on the Anglo-Zulu War of 1879*. Pietermaritzburg: University of Natal Press; Cape Town: N & S Press, 1990.

——, '"The Zulus Are Coming!" The Defence of Pietermaritzburg, 1879', in John Laband and Paul Thompson, *Kingdom and Colony at War: Sixteen Studies on the Anglo-Zulu War of 1879*. Pietermaritzburg: University of Natal Press; Cape Town: N & S Press, 1990.

——, *Black Soldiers of the Queen: The Natal Native Contingent in the Anglo-Zulu War*. Tuscaloosa: University of Alabama Press, 2006.

Vandervort, Bruce, *Wars of Imperial Conquest in Africa 1830–1914*. London: UCL Press, 1998.

Verner, William W. C. and Erasmus D. Parker, *The Military Life of H.R.H. George, Duke of Cambridge*, 2 vols. London: John Murray, 1905.

Webb, Colin de B., 'Lines of Power: The High Commissioner, the Telegraph and the War of 1879', *Natalia*, 8 (December 1978), pp. 31–7.

Wessels, André, 'Frederick Roberts', in in Steven J. Corvi and Ian F. W. Beckett (eds), *Victoria's Generals*. Barnsley: Pen & Sword Military, 2009.

Whitehouse, Howard, *Battle in Africa 1879–1914*. Mansfield: Fieldbooks, 1987.

Woodward, Sir Llewellyn, *The Age of Reform 1815–1870*.Oxford: Clarendon Press, 1962.

Yorke, Edmund, *Rorke's Drift 1879: Anatomy of an Epic Zulu War Siege*. Stroud: Tempus, 2001.

Acknowledgements

I WISH TO ACKNOWLEDGE the gracious permission of His Majesty King Charles III to quote from papers held in the Royal Archives, Windsor Castle. I must also express my appreciation for the willing and expert assistance I received from Julie Crocker, Senior Archivist, Royal Archives, and her staff. Likewise, I received cheerful assistance from Bethany Slater, Librarian, National Army Museum, Chelsea, and from her staff in the Templer Study Centre. I am most grateful for the financial assistance provided through Faculty Research Funding, Stellenbosch University, South Africa, that made my research trip to Britain in 2022 possible.

Much of the research towards this book was conducted during the COVID-19 pandemic when travel was circumscribed. I am fortunate that in previous years I had accumulated research notes in South Africa from the Pietermaritzburg Archives Repository and from the Killie Campbell Africana Library, University of KwaZulu-Natal, Durban; that I had access to the microfilm of the Chelmsford Papers held in the National Army Museum, and possessed microfilms and microfiches of the relevant War Office Papers held in the National Archives, Kew.

Senzosenkosi Mkhize, Head of the Campbell Collections, University of KwaZulu-Natal, Durban, and Mbalenhle Zulu, the Senior Librarian there, along with Kenneth Hlungwane, Research Officer, MuseumAfrica, Johannesburg, lent me efficient assistance in acquiring some of the illustrations reproduced in this book. I also owe a debt of gratitude to Ian Knight who supplied me with many images from his collection and who facilitated the provision of yet others from private collections.

I should never have attempted this book had not Michael Leventhal, the publisher of Greenhill Books, suggested that I write a new biography of General Lord Chelmsford. Once I took on the challenge, he enthusiastically and generously supported me every step of the way. As once before, Peter Wilkinson has exercised his considerable cartographic skill (and patience) in turning my scruffy sketches into clear and elegant maps. Likewise, Donald Sommerville has again been the meticulous editor of a book of mine and with great forbearance has purged the text of its infelicities and other errors. Fenella, as always, has patiently sustained me throughout the writing of this long book.

This biography is the culmination of forty-five years of working in the field of British colonial wars in southern Africa, with a particular emphasis on the Anglo-Zulu War. Many fine scholars, both still living or now dead, have laboured alongside me, and without the benefit of their dedication and expertise I would never have undertaken this work. They cannot be held accountable, however, for any gaffes I may have committed, or any misjudgements I may have arrived at. I wish to dedicate this volume to two of them, both regrettably deceased, who knew the subject matter of this biography every bit as well as or better than I. Friends, colleagues, companions in the field and co-authors of mine, they are Professor Paul Thompson and Dr Jeff Mathews.

Index

Words from Nguni languages are entered under the root rather than under the prefix.

INDEX

INDEX